CULTURAL ECONOMICS

Without question, quantification, quali-
fication and/or equivocation, but with
affection and devotion growing expo-
tentially, this book is dedicated to

June Eileen

Cultural Economics

Richard L. Brinkman

HERITAGE

HERITAGE PUBLISHERS

NEW DELHI 1991

Reissued 1991
PRICE : Rs. 250

Library of Congress Number 79-93042
ISBN 0-913244-15-5

Heritage Publishers
Madan Mohan Street
4C Ansari Road
Daryaganj
New Delhl 11C002
India

Printed at
Kay Kay Printers
150 D Kamla Nagar
Delhi 110007

CONTENTS

Introduction

Cultural economics is directed toward the advance and formulation of a general theory of economic development in the conceptual framework of culture evolution. Such a theory would be predicated upon the conceptual clarification of the process of economic growth and development. The continuous and ongoing development of concept and theory serves as a necessary condition for the evolution of science. In advancing concepts we advance the base for theory which in turn provides for a further clarification of concept and, on and on, the wheel of science spins in the framework of circular and cumulative causation. Gunnar Myrdal's circular and cumulative causation concerns not simply economic evolution but the evolution of knowledge and science, itself, from which as this study will try to explain, the economic process is derivative.

Culture constitutes a key concept to be understood in analyzing and explaining the economic process. Substantively, what experiences growth and development in the dynamics of economic evolution is culture. In this study culture is conceptualized in the tradition of Edward B. Tylor's basic formulation and entails the complex whole, the totality of the material and nonmaterial in the sense as contained in an organic whole of man's social heritage. Culture so conceptualized provides the basis for an interdisciplinary or holistic approach to analyze and explain the economic process.

Culture, however, does not stand still but evolves and is transformed over time. Evolution, in turn, entails a process of both growth, as quantitative replication and reproduction, as well as development which involves the qualitative as structural transformation and mutation. This study, directed toward an analysis and explanation of economic evolution, consequently, concerns economic growth as well as economic development.

And while the two terms growth and development are interrelated, as this study will try to show, they are not synonymous. Broadly speaking, then, the study represents an attempt to conceptualize and explain economic phenomena in the context of general culture evolution and we call the methodology and associated theory: *cultural economics*.

It has been suggested in the literature that if Adam Smith were alive today he might have difficulty securing academic tenure given the current direction and methodology of mainstream economics.[1] Normal science in economics has become so mathematical and abstract in its methodology and theory that it is essentially devoid of the cultural and the social. The quest for most economists is apparently beyond mere applause; probability dictates that the road to fame and fortune, status and recognition, is usually not to be found in the field of economic development. Rather, the hierarchy of the pecking order in economics reveals pride of place for microeconomics, macroeconomics, and econometrics. Those economists who delve in economic development in the sense of the dynamic and who introduce the forces of technological change, not as shifting production functions but in the framework of social and cultural transformation, are therefore required to dip into areas outside the confines delineated by mainstream methodology and theory. Consequently, economists who swim "against the stream" and engage the "noneconomic" are frequently classified as noneconomists.[2] Normal science in economics today is essentially directed toward the processes of economic growth in a static theoretical framework. All this is not to infer that the neoclassical synthesis is necessarily wrong, in so far as it goes, but that it does not go far to include the dynamics of technological change in a social and cultural matrix. To our view, however, a correct understanding and analysis of economic phenomena requires a general theory of economic development and, further, that such a theory can be originated in the context of the framework of culture and its evolution.

Consequently, the neoclassical synthesis, given its static analysis of parts outside the framework of the evolving whole, tends to obfuscate and obscure, rather than to correctly delineate, the true nature of our current problems. "THE ULTIMATE TEST of a set of economic ideas—a system, if the word be allowed—is whether it illuminates the anxieties of the time."[3] Science not only serves to solve given problems but science also functions to correctly identify the problems to be resolved. A correct formulation of a problem as a scientific question serves as a prerequisite to its resolution. It is frequently argued that the major economic problems of the current period concern not merely the manipulation of quantitative economic variables, as inferred by mainstream economic theory, but also concern qualitative changes in structure in both social and material culture. Consequently, if the current anomalies of our economy are in actuality at root social in nature, a theoretical framework which denies the social will also deny the solution.

In the field of economic development it is becoming increasingly more evident that orthodox economic theory exhibits serious shortcomings in its relevancy and applicability to the problems facing the LDC world.[4] We are carrying this position further and argue that the basic problems confronting the advanced countries are also primarily developmental in nature and therefore, require a more complete and relevant framework of theory. In this study, it will be argued that sustained exponential economic growth requires continuous structural change wrought by the processes of economic development. The "principle of similitude" dictates that sustained growth on a continuum requires structural change as a necessary condition.[5] We do not grow simply by growing; sustained economic growth requires continuous structural change viewed as the process of technological advance and economic development. Consequently, theories of economic growth, alone and by themselves, will not suffice to explain, analyze and resolve problems of economic growth. Such theories must be supplemented by and integrated into theories of economic development.

And again, the emphasis is not that neoclassical theory be supplanted but rather that it be supplemented by a theoretical framework relevant to the processes of economic development as the technological embedded in a social and cultural matrix. In that normal science in economics is essentially oriented toward processes of economic growth and avoids the dynamics of the processes of economic development, the current problems are not correctly identified as to their fundamental nature and causation. Consequently, the anomalies and crises appear as ongoing and beyond resolution. "The problems of the present indicate the path to the future. A reconstruction of economics—a new synthesis and a new paradigm. . . " apparently is in order.[6]

It is our position that the correct formulation of the problems, as questions to be answered through the science of economics, will be predicated upon the further advance and evolution of a general theory of economic development. Problems associated with the processes of economic development are not just applicable and relevant to the LDC world but are equally relevant to advanced countries as well. The process of economic development has not been arrested through the achievement of mature industrial capitalism; the process of economic development is ongoing and unending. Resolution of the basic problems will take on the form of economic policy advanced by the application of science. In the science of economics, theory and policy cannot be divorced; each disciplinary matrix has its concomitant policy as prescribed social organization. All the major schools of thought in economics have concomitant types of social organization: be it the classical and neoclassical school and laissez faire; the Keynesians and deficit spending and the mixed economy; the institutionalists and democratic economic planning; and the Marxists and totalitarian economic planning. The monetarist science of Milton Friedman could no more have economic planning as a concomitant form of social organization than the science of canal building could be used to explain and perfect air travel.

One of the great mysteries of our time concerns the unravelling of the logic employed by mainstream economists who while on the one hand seek to perfect the social organization to serve as a concomitant to economic production and, yet, on the other hand ignore and remove the social and the cultural from their theory and analytical purview. Certainly, Adam Smith in performing his role as an economist did not seek, in the application of his science, the perfection of bridges, buildings, roads and machinery of material culture but rather directed his attention and efforts toward the perfection of the social structure in the form of markets and the price mechanism. Explicit in our study is the assumption that economics is a science of social organization. A central thrust and underlying theme of our analysis is contained in the idea that social organization can be further perfected via the advance and application of the science of economics. In order to do so, the science of economics must take the dynamics as well as the statics of social organization, explicitly, into account. What we are saying, therefore, is not simply that the field of economic development be further perfected but, in addition, that main-stream economics become permeable to the concepts, variables and processes of economic development. " . . . it is clear that as the accumulating interdisciplinary knowledge is synthesized, economic development is likely to become not just a special branch but a very much needed restatement of economics."[7]

Even assuming that such a view be warranted and correct, a problem still presents itself; it is frequently claimed in the literature that a general theory of economic development is nonexistent.[8] It is our view, however, that such a theory, though perhaps rudimentary, is already at hand; we speak here of the Veblen-Ayres matrix as mainstream institutional economics.[9]

> "Such a unified theory exists in embryo at least. Although it is not generally identified as institutionalism and may never be, its germ has been present in the theory that was implicit in Veblen's work and has likewise been implicit in the dedicated empiricism of later institutionalists and even of the profession generally. That germ is the later nineteenth-century concept of culture which Veblen absorbed during his formative years and which has become the foundation concept of all twentieth-century social thinking."[10]

And while the general theory of economic development embodied in mainstream institutional economics is in the embryo stage and, consequently, on the surface might appear simple, an actual understanding of the complexities of the underlying subject matter is not that easy. Veblen and Ayres have taken some of the most difficult and intractable concepts in the social sciences, into their calculus of the economic process, and made them comprehensible and understandable. In explaining the process of culture evolution the theory has as its foundation the basic dichotomy whereby the dynamics of technological advance are juxtaposed to the statics of institutional change. While the Veblen-Ayres dichotomy, by itself, might appear as overly simplistic theory, it represents the tip of the iceberg. The underlying bulk of the iceberg concerns not mere description but rather represents a large and complex corpus of a theory of economic development dealing with a synthesis of the open-ended concepts of technology, culture, evolution, institutions, value and so on.

Before we get lost in the trees of our eclectic analysis, it should, consequently, be asserted that an overview of the forest of our study is contained in a continuity of mainstream institutional economics. Our study represents an attempt at modification and advance of that theory of economic development which has as its cornerstone, culture and its evolution.[11] However, in order to emphasize an interdisciplinary or holistic methodology references used in this study will be primarily eclectic and from the many contributors to the social sciences at large, rather than from the specific literature of mainstream institutional economics and/or the neoinstitutional economics of the current period. And from that overall literature three social scientists will receive primary attention. The general theory of Veblen and Ayres will be drawn and pulled by an intellectual troika: Simon Kuznets, economics; William F. Ogburn, sociology; and Leslie A White, anthropology. Overall, however, even though the approach is eclectic, and while suggesting certain modifications, cultural economics basically and at root represents a continuity of mainstream institutional economics, as the Veblen-Ayres tradition. The problem facing us in this study is, consequently, not one of originating a general theory of economic development; the problem is more one of advancing that which is already at hand.

The general theory provided by Veblen and Ayres was not to serve as a way station, as goal or end in itself, but as science was to serve in transit as a means for problem solving. Veblen and Ayres used their theory of development as an analytical tool for a critique, and perfection of a given structure of social organization, i.e., industrial capitalism. It can be argued that currently the material technology and energy potential necessary to provide for a decent standard of living for all of mankind, already exists. The problem resides, therefore, not in the sector of material technology but rather in the choice of the social technology, as the correct and appropriate institutional structure, to make such a condition possible.[12] A fundamental theme of this study is that in order to maintain the economic process, as an ongoing function, there is a need for continuous change in structure, both material and social. A basic question raised by institutional economists concerns which social structure best serves the instrumental function, in the context of ongoing exponential economic growth and development, to advance the human life process? Institutional economics, therefore, not only focuses on a general theory of economic development, per se, but interwoven into such a theory is a theory of value. Whereas to Veblen value was implicit, Ayres made the issue explicit: "Economics is nothing if it is not a science of value."[13] In terms of function, the economic process is ongoing and appears as the exponential; the underlying structure, as forms of economic production and social organization, requires continuous change and transformation and is manifest in a paradigm of logistic surges. Which new or modified institutional structure, among the possible alternatives, best serves the instrumental function in promoting the human life process? By posing such a question institutional economists not only integrate value judgments into the corpus of their overall theory but in addition argue that the issue of value can be addressed and resolved scientifically. A relevant question for science then becomes: "Which direction is forward?"[14]

Institutional economics does not offer or provide precise details of future institutional structures but is concerned more with the process through which such new structures are originated and innovated. In a general sense, however, the concomitant policy usually associated with institutional economics, and to be innovated in the future, appears as some form of economic planning nurtured in the political milieu of a participatory democracy..[15] In that institutional economists tend to look upon theory as a problem solving vehicle, unresolved problems indicate the need for a new vehicle. Mainstream economic theory of the current period and its concomitant policy appear incapable to adjust and setright the malfunctioning economy. The continued pressure generated by unresolved anomalies will, in turn, necessitate the innovation of a new policy direction for overall social organization.

This is not to infer that institutional economists will, themselves, innovate the new policy direction of economic planning but, rather, that the unresolved anomalies of the current period will be resolved through practical politics manifest in economic planning. In this context it might be said that Keynesian economics was not innovated in the United States by economists but rather evolved to the lofty position of normal science in that Keynesian economics served as the primary policy explicator of the new structure of social organization inherent in Franklin Delano Roosevelt's New Deal and deficit spending. Therefore, if a participatory democracy nurtures the innovation of voluntary economic planning it will also direct the evolution of the science of economics toward the innovation of a matrix of theory associated with the policy of economic planning. And the theory, concomitant to the policy of democratic economic planning, we submit, does not reside in classical, neoclassical, monetarist, Keynesian or Marxian schools of economics, but rather resides in institutional economics. With Fabian patience, institutional economists mark time; the disciplinary matrix is not extinct, but, rather, embodies the correct forward direction for the future evolution of normal science in economics.

Institutional economics, therefore, weaves into its matrix of theory, three major and interrelated concerns: (1) a general theory of economic development; (2) a theory of value; and (3) a policy direction toward economic planning in the context of a participatory democracy. Though recognizing the importance and interrelation between the three areas, cultural economics as presented in this study focuses primarily on a general theory of economic development and, consequently, assigns value and economic planning peripheral treatment. Underlying our study, however, is the assumption that the advance of a general theory of economic development will also serve to advance a theory of value and aid in the promotion and perfection of a policy of democratic economic planning.

We will now present a brief summary of the eleven chapters of our study which, as an organic whole, is directed toward the overriding objective of a general theory of economic development. If the goal is to advance a theory of economic development and to offer a conceptual clarification of the process, logic would have it to first clarify and delineate the substance which actually experiences the process of growth and development. A theory of economic development should explain the economic process in terms of its own substance.[16] This issue is dealt with in Chapter I, "The Crucible and Clay of Economic Development." The crucible experiences conceptual discontinuity as one institutional structure, the tribe, the city, the nation, gives rise to the next in its function as the container of culture. The clay has had conceptual continuity in the form of culture. It is culture in its scientific conceptualization as an organic whole that comprises the material and nonmaterial ingredients of the clay which is transformed and accumulated in the process of growth and development.

Granting that culture in its material and nonmaterial composition constitutes the substance, if a culture grows and accumulates will it also develop in the process? Chapter II, "Normal Science and the Conceptualization of Economic Growth and Development" is addressed to the treatment of the concepts of economic growth and development by economists of mainstream predilections. A review of the general literature, encyclopedias, dictionaries and on, reveals that practitioners of normal science in economics tend to treat the concepts of growth and development as conceptual equivalents; the two terms are assumed to be synonymous. This conceptual treatment, equating growth and development, is a by-product of the fact that the theory used by the mainstream economist is essentially a static theory of economic growth. When called upon to explain economic development, in that the mainstream economist lacks such a theory, the economist uses the next best alternative and interjects his theory of economic growth. In order to make such growth theory relevant to development, however, it must be assumed that growth and development are conceptual equivalents. But in actuality, if a culture, demarcated by tribal, national or regional boundaries, grows will it also be developing as assumed and inferred by normal science in economics?

Chapter III, "Economic Growth and No Development," focuses on the issue of empirical evidence and offers as a primary case in point, the antebellum South to provide an example of a real-world case exemplifying growth and no development. If empirical evidence supports the contention that growth is not the conceptual equivalent of development, then theories of growth lack relevancy in that they cannot be used as complete explanations of the process of economic development. This conclusion becomes of even greater significance when it is further noted that the processes of economic development concern not just the LDC but are relevant to cultures in the advanced stages of modern economic growth as well.

Rather than mere growth as replication and duplication economic development entails qualitative changes manifest in the process of transformation and evolution. To concede that the process of economic development is evolutionary and entails the transformation of one structure to the next is to concede the validity of a stages' methodology. A stages' methodology constitutes an integral part of any theory purporting to be a general theory of economic development. In order to overcome the unilinear fallacy associated with the stages' approach, Chapter IV, "A Process of Transformation and Evolution," introduces the very important distinction noted in the literature, between specific and general culture evolution.[17] A stages' methodology basically confronts two major issues: (1) *taxonomy*, as description and quantification, and (2) *theory*, as explanation of the process of transformation from one stage to the next.

Chapter V, "Energy Transformation as an Indicator of the Process of Economic Development," serves to provide a basis for the quantification of the stages delineated and described in Chapter IV. Nothing moves in the cosmos without energy transformation, the economic process included. If energy, defined as "the capacity to do work" is not relevant to the economic process then nothing is. Consequently, data on energy control and consumption serve to indicate the process of development because the process of energy transformation is so intimately interwoven with the process of economic development. It is through culture evolution that mankind gains control of greater and greater amounts of free energy and, thereby, countermands the long-term tendency toward entropic degradation inherent in the Entropy Law. Statistics on energy control and consumption reveal the exponential and the underlying paradigm of logistic surges as one energy gestalt gives rise to the next. Given the classification of the stages of economic development, based upon energy utilization, the data on energy provide a measure used in the quantification of the stages of economic development.

Chapter VI, "The Dichotomy of Useful Knowledge," marks the start of an attempt at a systematic explanation of the process of economic transformation and evolution. The essence of the process of economic development resides in the advance of useful knowledge; the advance of useful knowledge provides the fountainhead for the dynamics of culture evolution."[18] Knowledge appears in many forms; it is a protean concept. Knowledge in its *application*, as technics of economic production and social organization, appears on the one hand as technology and on the other, in its *store*, as culture. Consequently, to advance technology is also in the process to advance and transform culture. The tautological relation between technology and culture provides the basis for an explanation of the process of culture evolution in terms of its own substance. Technology, as concreted knowledge, therefore, appears in both material and nonmaterial forms. Consequently, social technology, as institutions of social organization, in addition to material technology, can also serve an instrumental function and provide for the dynamics of the process of economic evolution.

If useful knowledge represents the essence and dynamics of the process, how does it originate and advance? Chapter VII, "The Wheel of Economic Development," represents an attempt to explain the advance of useful knowledge in the framework of Myrdal's circular and cumulative causation. Origination, as well as permeability and innovation, are all related to an environment comprised not only of culture but the physical resource base as well. But the wheel does not always spin freely and advance without friction. Are the concomitant parts of material and social technology synchronized? Chapter VIII, "The Theory of Cultural Lag," is addressed to the lopsided nature of culture evolution in which some parts accelerate faster than others and, thereby, generate cultural lags. A frictionless wheel of economic development might be derived in the future through the further advance and application of the social sciences (economics) to the structure of social organization.

Such a process, in an attempt at synchronization, will probably be manifest in the policy direction of economic planning.

In addition to the processes of origination and innovation of new technics, the study is also directed toward an analysis of the form or structure, and the rate of accumulation, resulting and derived from general culture evolution. Chapter IX, "Exponential Culture Evolution and the Paradigm of Logistic Surges," as indicated in the title, focuses on an explanation and analysis of the structure in the form of the overall exponential plus the underlying paradigm in the form of logistic surges. The structure of culture evolution is a manifestation of the "principle of similitude" in that ongoing exponential growth has been made possible through continuous changes in structure wrought by technological advance. In this context it can be said that ongoing economic growth is a function of the process of economic development.

Consequently, consistent with a theory of economic development and supported by empirical evidence, the path of general culture evolution has been exponential. But can it all continue into the proximate future? Whereas in the framework of cultural economics, exponential cultural evolution is viewed as a necessary condition for the past and future progress of mankind, others interpret the exponential as a lead into a doomsday denouement. Chapter X, "Mankind at the Starting Point," is addressed to this issue and to the future. A conclusion is reached, and with optimism, that given the assumption of an ultimate ZPG (zero population growth) that there are no compelling reasons to assume a limit to culture evolution. The exponential need not give way to the logistic.

Chapter XI, "Cultural Economics," serves as an integrative and summary statement of the general theory of economic development presented in the study. Also certain issues, such as value theory and the *sui generis* of Leslie A. White are given more direct attention and related to the overall study. Implied in cultural economics is the basic policy conclusion that it is not enough for mankind to simply understand the processes of culture evolution and economic development but, in addition, to use that understanding in the future control and planning of culture evolution. Not as an end in itself but to provide for, as a necessary condition, the basic value inherent in the further advance of the process of human evolution and development. Consequently, as we press forward the advance of the science of economics, as a theory of economic development, we will enhance our capacity and "power to determine the future and not simply to predict it" through a further extension and perfection of the process started during the epoch of modern economic growth; we speak here of the application of science to social organization.[19] Consequently, when the science of economics comes of age it will in all probability be in the form of a science of economic planning. The desire is to provide humanity with a greater control of its destiny via a direct control of culture evolution.

REFERENCES

[1]David A. Reisman, *Adam Smith's Sociological Economics* (New York: Harper and Row, 1976), p. 12.

[2]"I am even referred to as a sociologist. And by that, economists usually do not mean anything flattering. Another . . . like minded rebel, Galbraith . . . is often handled even more rudely by sometimes being classified by his colleagues as a journalist. But we insist on remaining economists." Gunnar Myrdal, *Against the Stream* (New York: Random House, 1972), pp. 14-15. On the pecking order and hierarchy, note Benjamin Ward, *What's Wrong with Economics?* (New York: Basic Books, 1972), p. 10.

[3]John Kenneth Galbraith, *Economics and the Public Purpose* (Boston: Houghton Mifflin Company, 1973), p. 198.

[4]Many references could be cited in support of this contention, cf., Michael P. Todaro, *Economic Development in the Third World* (New York: Longman, 1977), pp. 10-14.

[5]On the "principle of similitude" or "structural differentiation" note: Daniel Bell, "The Measurement of Knowledge and Technology," in *Indicators of Social Change* (New York: Russell Safe Foundation, 1968), ed., E. B. Sheldon and W.E. Moore, pp. 149-152, and *The Coming Post-Industrial Society* (New York: Basic Books, 1973), pp. 172-174.

[6]Daniel R. Fusfeld, "Post-Post-Keynes: A Shattered Synthesis," *Saturday Review* 55 (January 22, 1972), pp. 36-39; "If intellectual history is a reliable guide, we appear to be at one of those large turning points in the development of ideas in which a new view of the world and human behavior and new ways of explaining things are appearing." "The Conceptual Framework of Modern Economics," *Journal of Economic Issues* 14 (March 1980), pp. 1-52.

[7]Joseph A. Raffaele, *The Economic Development of Nations* (New York: Random House, 1971), p. 38.

[8]"Nevertheless, no integrated, explicit, and unique theory of development exists as of today. The nature of the subject may preclude any such abstract and complete analysis." Stephen Enke, "Economists and Development: Rediscovering Old Truths," *Journal of Economic Literature* 7 (December 1969), pp. 1125-1139, 1127.

[9]". . . a general theory which is already at hand. Veblen left to institutionalism a general theory . . ." p. 65, 69, and, "Institutional economics is a problem solving method . . . it does have a general theory, and its usefulness today is reduced appreciably by the reluctance of many institutionalists to make a forthright use of that theory." p. 70, David Hamilton, "Institutionalism: Present Status and Future Prospects," *Social Science Journal* 15 (January 1978), pp. 63-70.

[10]Clarence E. Ayres, "Institutionalism and Economic Development," *Social Science Quarterly* 41 (March 1970), pp. 1036-1054, p. 1051. "What is true of Veblen's work in this respect is true of institutional economics in general—the fact that there is more often than not a general recognition of culture as the master principle of social analysis." Louis J. Yunker, "Theoretical Foundations of Neo-Institutionalism," *The American Journal of Economics and Sociology* 27 (April 1968), pp. 197-213, p. 201 and, "Genuine or Spurious Institutionalism," *American Journal of Economics and Sociology* 38 (April 1979), pp. 206-223, p. 214. And Morris A. Copeland, ". . . the obvious analogue . . . of the evolution of species in the field of social science is cultural evolution, and Veblen thought economists should be extensively concerned with this analogue." *Thorstein Veblen: A Critical Reappraisal* (Ithaca: Cornell University Press, 1958), ed., Douglas F. Dowd, p. 67.

[11]Modifications and new concepts, such as: the dichotomy of useful knowledge; a gestalt conceptualization of technology; an inclusion of the Entropy Law; the principle of similitude and logistic surges; the wheel of economic development; a three dimensional view of the process of culture evolution; a quantification of the stages of economic development; a cross-sectional analysis of culture evolution to incorporate the static and the dynamic; and on. Our study will focus on a general theory, as such, rather than a comparison between the Veblen-Ayres matrix and cultural economics.

[12]Wendell Gordon, *Economics from an Institutional Viewpoint* (Austin: University Stores, 1973), p. 3.

[13]Clarence E. Ayes, *The Theory of Economic Progress* (Kalamazoo: New Issues Press, 1978), p. 208. "for whether or not it continues to be a science of price, economics must be a science of value." pp. 84-85.

[14]Marc R. Tool, *The Discretionary Economy: A Normative Theory of Political Economy* (Santa Monica: Goodyear Publishing Company, 1979), p. 85; "A Social Value Theory in Neoinstitutional Economics" *Journal of Economic Issues* 11 (December 1977), pp. 820-843; and, "The Social Value Theory of Orthodoxy," *Journal of Economic Issues* 14 (June 1980), pp. 309-326.

[15]Allan G. Gruchy has not only served as the leading historiographer of institutional economics, *Modern Economic Thought* (New York:

Prentice-Hall, 1974); and *Contemporary Economic Thought* (Clifton: Augustus M. Kelley, 1972) but in addition has made substantive contributions to neoinstitutional economics as well. Note: *Institutional Economics: Essays in Honor of Allan G. Gruchy* (Boston: Martinus Nijhoff, 1980), ed., John Adams, for the "Futuristic Economics of Allan G. Gruchy" and the focus on a "democratically planned economic system." pp. 3-18.

[16]And the frequently cited passage from Thorstein Veblen, *The Place of Science in Modern Civilization* (New York: Russell & Russell, 1961), ". . . it appears that an evolutionary economics must be the theory of a process of cultural growth as determined by the economic interest, a theory of a cumulative sequence of economic institutions stated in terms of the process itself." p. 77.

[17]Note pp. viii-ix, and "Evolution: Specific and General," pp. 12-44 in Marshall D. Sahlins and Elman R. Service, *Evolution and Culture* (Ann Arbor: University of Michigan Press, 1960).

[18]The advance of knowledge in its various forms provided the foundation for Veblen's famous dichotomy and his explanation of culture evolution, note *Place of Science*, pp. 1-31, especially pp. 2-4, 8-9, footnote 5 and pp. 29-31.

[19]p.8, Gerald Feinberg, *Consequences of Growth: The Prospects for a Limitless Future* (New York: Seabury Press, 1977); Karl W. Deutsch, John Platt, and Dieter Senghaas, "Conditions Favoring Major Advances in Social Science," 171 *Science* (5 February 1971) pp. 450-459, "The radical increase in natural science knowledge and in its application has produced a radical increase in the problems of coordination in all industrialized societies. To cope with this radical increase in urgent problems it seems essential to produce an early and large increase in social science knowledge and its constructive application. The evidence here suggests that the intellectual and organizational means for such an increase are at hand if we care to use them." p. 459; Richard A. Easterlin, "Economic Growth: Overview," *International Encyclopedia of the Social Sciences* (New York: The Macmillan Company and the Free Press, 1968) David L. Sills, ed., Vol. 4, pp. 395-408, "The capacity to cope with these problems has been limited by man's inadequate grasp of social phenomena. . . . If, therefore, one turns from the question of the originas of modern economic development, which lie in the growth of natural science, to that of the future outlook, much would seem to turn on the prospect for comparable progress in social science." p. 407.

[illegible] 1954," and "Long-range Economic Projection," [illegible] Mason, [illegible] in the [illegible] of [illegible] Economic History of [illegible] John [illegible] for the [illegible] of [illegible] the [illegible] democratically planned economy," pp. 216.

[illegible] clearly stage from Thorstein Veblen, The Place of Science in Modern Civilization (New York: Russell & Russell, 1961): "It appears that an evolutionary economics must be the theory of a process of cultural growth as determined by the economic interest, a theory of a cumulative sequence of economic institutions stated in terms of the process itself," p. 77.

[illegible] Work, and Mechanism, Specific and General," pp. 1–24 in Marshall D. Sahlins and Elman R. Service, *Evolution and Culture* (Ann Arbor: University of Michigan Press, 1960).

[illegible] The advance of knowledge in its various forms provided the basis for Veblen's famous dichotomy and his explanation of culture [illegible], *Place of Science*, pp. 1–31, especially pp. 4, 8–9, 1[illegible] and pp. 16–31.

[illegible] p. 8. Gerald Feinberg, *Consequences of Growth: The Prospects for a Limitless Future* (New York: Seabury Press, 1977); Karl W. Deutsch, [illegible] Platt, and Dieter Senghaas, "Conditions Favoring Major Advances in Social Science," 171 *Science* (5 February 1971) pp. 450–459: "The radical increase in natural science knowledge and in its application has produced a radical increase in the problems of [illegible] for all [illegible] societies. To cope with this radical increase in [illegible] problems it seems essential to produce an early and large increase in social science knowledge and its constructive application. The evidence [illegible] suggests that the intellectual and organizational means for such an increase are at hand if we care to use them," p. 459. [illegible] Kuznets, "Economic Growth: Overview," *International Encyclopedia of the Social Sciences* (New York: The Macmillan Company and the Free Press, 1968) David L. Sills, ed., Vol. 4, pp. 395–408: "The capacity to cope with these problems has been limited by various inadequate [illegible] of social phenomena. . . . If, therefore, one turns from the question of the [illegible] of modern economic development, which lie in [illegible] of natural science, to that of the future outlook, much would seem to turn on the prospect for comparable progress in social science," p. 407.

CHAPTER I

The Crucible and Clay of Economic Development

The focus of our study concerns the advance of a general theory of economic development. However, in order to advance theory we must also in the process advance and clarify concept Concept and theory advance together in the framework of circular and cumulative causation, to advance one aids in the advance of the other. Unfortunately, our starting point is enmeshed in a briar-patch of conceptual confusion for we find no agreed upon or clear-cut conceptualization of the process of economic development.[1] A problem presents itself in that a multiplicity of concepts breeds and is manifest in a multiplicity of theories of economic development. An improved upon conceptualization of economic development would consequently serve as a concomitant to an advance and improvement in theory.

Consequently, in view of the close interrelationship between theory and concept and in line with our basic objective to achieve an advance of theory our study is also directed toward a conceptual clarification of economic development and the associated concept of economic growth.[2] A conceptual clarification is a root problem; logic would have such a conceptual clarification as a necessary condition for scientific analysis and explanation. A more correct conceptualization of economic development serves as a necessary condition for the further advance of theory. Advances in theory, in turn, add to improvements in conceptualization. Not clarifying the conceptual framework of economic development in a theoretical analysis of economic development would be tantamount to a brave leader commanding his legions to charge without first delineating the general direction of the enemy.

It should be noted, however, that we do not speak of concept and theory in any finite sense but rather view the process as one of continuous advance and improvement. The path of science progresses along an unending exponential continuum; consequently, a goal of finite knowledge is unattainable in that our destination is infinity. We therefore do not view the process of science as one which achieves finite concepts and theories but rather that we achieve cumulative advances in the long-term evolutionary advance of scientific inquiry.

But before attempting to fulfill our objectives of conceptual clarity and theoretical explanation we must first identify the substance which actually experiences economic growth and development in its cumulation and transformation. How can we conceptualize and explain a process without first identifying the nature of the substance which actually experiences the process? When we speak of economic development, what is the substance of that development? In this chapter we will try to draw the distinction between the crucible (as the basic unit of observation) and the clay (as the substance) of that development.

As an aid in clarification let us draw an analogy to the biological sciences. Our understanding and explanation of biological evolution and development would be less than complete if we focused on *man* alone and if we excluded from our purview the many other previous forms through which life has evolved. In the biological sphere the various forms of life have appeared as different structures in the process of evolution. It has been protoplasm and DNA, as the code of biological life, which have provided physical substance of evolution exhibiting an historical thread of continuity. Though the units of observation have been altered over time and appear as different structures in a myriad of forms, as plants, fishes, reptiles, mammals, and so on, it is DNA and protoplasm which have provided the substance which exhibits conceptual continuity. Similarly in our explanation of economic evolution (development) our quest will be for a social DNA, which will manifest itself in various forms known as the tribe, the city, the empire, the nation-state, the region and beyond. Such a variety of social aggregates would serve as a prerequisite for a general theory of economic development amenable to long-term historical and evolutionary analysis.

Our objective is a universal conceptualization and theory of economic development for all times and all places. Just as the study of homo sapiens alone would be insufficient for a general theory of biological evolution so do we argue that the study of the nation, alone, as the basic unit of observation also precludes a long-term evolutionary analysis in the social sphere. The nation state is of limited historical relevance in terms of man's long-term processes of economic development. We submit, and a point which will be developed in the course of our analysis, that man's social DNA is culture. It is culture, as a code of man's social life which programs man's behavior patterns in general, as well as those particular patterns which serve as concomitants to economic processes. It is culture which provides the substantive and historical continuity necessary for a general theory of economic development. Analogous to biological evolution it is culture which constitutes the substance or clay of development and the social aggregate, called the nation, serves as its current crucible for analysis.

While there is a distinction in that conceivably a nation might exist without having advanced to the sovereign status of a nation state, for the purposes of our study we will basically treat the concepts interchangeably. In general and unless noted otherwise we will refer to both the nation and the nation state as simply the nation.[3] In the current stage of economic development characterized by modern economic growth, the unit of observation most frequently used by economists in theory and in the economic accounting of growth and development is the social aggregate known as the nation.[4] And there are many good reasons as to why this is so. In the first place theoretical constructs explaining growth and development emanate primarily from mature industrial countries. Such industrial countries are in a stage of economic development characterized by the basic social aggregate known as the nation. Statistics and theory of mainstream economics originate in nations engaged in the processes of modern economic growth. In such a context the nation is considered to be the relevant unit of observation for theory, quantification and analysis.

For empirical analysis we need some unit for statistical collection and organization and the nation currently performs this function.[5] In addition the nation has become important in the formulation and direction of economic policy which in turn alters the path of growth and development.[6] Mainstream economics currently dominated by Keynesian economics, interpreted as the neoclassical synthesis, would logically then use the nation as the basic unit of economic accounting and observation. Simon Kuznets and others have added the empirical world to the theoretical world of Keynes with the development of national income accounting and the concept of GNP.

From the statistical and theoretical emphasis on the nation and national income the tendency is to infer that it is the conceptual entity known as the nation which embodies economic growth and development. This is a misconception and presents somewhat of a mental fixation (predilection) in that it assumes that the form or container of the development process is also the substance. The use of the nation by mainstream economists tends to divert attention away from the real substantive nature of the process which is contained in overall culture. The focal point of this chapter is directed toward the position that it is culture, rather than the nation, which serves as the relevant scientific concept for an analysis and general theory of economic growth and development. A conceptual framework of the processes of long-term economic development based upon the nation constitutes a misconception and is in error. The attention given to the nation and its role in economic growth and development obscures the fact that the nation is a unit of observation rather than the basic or overall substance of that development. Consequently, in any general or universal theory of economic development, the conceptual framework, analysis and theory should be of culture evolution rather than nation evolution. It is conceptually culture which is transformed, grows and develops over time and not the nation, per se, as it is currently conceptualized in the literature. But how, then, is the nation as such dealt with in the literature?

The concepts of nationality, the nation and nationalism are among the more important concepts dealt with in the whole of the social sciences.[7] Specifically, as a part of the overall literature, mainstream economic theory treats the nation as a container or territorial "bundle" of economic factor inputs.[8] The concepts of GNP and NNP are expressions of aggregate factor inputs on a national basis of given territorial dimensions. For example, the concept of national income viewed as the lower loop of the circular flow of income is really an aggregation of payments to factor inputs plus the residual of profits. In the form of a tautology, the Keynesian matrix presents the position that a growth in production is also a growth in factor inputs. In this way the growth of national factor inputs of economic production becomes conceptualized and theoretically explained as the process of economic growth and indicated, for example, by sustained percentage increases in GNP/capita. Economic growth, as the growth of national factor inputs, is then conceptually treated as being synonymous with the process of economic development.

The nation as a social institution or cultural entity is fixed and given as a parameter and, by comparison, the variables of the process of growth concern national economic factor inputs. Such an analysis is obviously consistent with mainstream economic theory which in its methodology excludes the "non-economic" from economic analysis. Orthodox theory has historically divorced economic processes from the cultural matrix and the treatment of the nation by the economist is in keeping with this long-term tradition. The end result is that economists tend to focus on the quantitative growth of economic factor inputs. Such a conceptual framework tends to divert attention away from the cultural nature of the process of economic development and reinforces and molds the view that economic development is essentially a quantitative growth process of economic factor inputs. And while all this is acceptable as a part of the process of growth and development in so far as it goes, it does not go far enough to incorporate the whole or totality of that process.

To some, to define economic development as the "... upward movement of the entire social system ..." constitutes a more accurate and meaningful conceptual framework to be explained and analyzed in the context of theory. Such an alternative conceptual framework includes more than just autonomous economic factor inputs but comprises the social structure as well. If it is correct to assume that the economic factors of production are embedded in a cultural matrix, a conceptual framework dealing with the process of economic development cannot be restricted, simply, to economic factor inputs. Such a framework must include the social and the cultural as endogenous variables of the theoretical framework. Consequently, and again, we note that it is impossible to divorce the conceptualization of the process from the theory of the process.

The mainstream economist, to our view, incorrectly uses the nation in two fundamental areas. In the first place, the nation as a social institution is relegated to the "noneconomic" and consequently is treated as a parameter but not a variable. In reality the nation, as a social institution and as a part but not the whole of culture, serves as an integral part of the overall process. The nation as a social institution is not "non-economic" but, rather, serves very important economic functions. Yet historically orthodox economics has been devoid of institutional analysis. The very existence of a nation as well as its stage of development has a very important bearing on the overall process of economic development. And secondly, when the economist does in fact use the nation he uses it in a restricted sense as a container, as a unit of observation, of simple economic factor inputs. What is contained inside a nation, however, is that complex concept called culture.

In the overall literature, social scientists tend to treat the nation in cultural terms and tend to analyze the nation and the associated terms of nationality and nationalism in an interdisciplinary methodology.[9] To begin with, the nation is viewed by social scientists in general, as opposed to economists in particular, as a social institution which constitutes an integral part of overall culture, and not simply as a bundle of factor inputs. Also, the nation is hardly assumed to serve as a fixed parameter. In fact a basic difficulty, noted in the literature conceptualizing the nation and nationalism, is that the phenomena evolve and are transformed over time and hardly, if ever, appear as constants or invariant.[10] As a case in point, the nation and nationalism existing in the United States during the period of the American Revolution are in marked contrast to the nation and the nationalism of the 1960's and 1970's and the Vietnam War. Nationality, the nation and nationalism, have been transformed and have evolved historically in the context of general culture evolution. It is culture, as the overall whole, which constitutes the general framework of analysis and the nation is but a part of that overall whole. In order to understand the part we must have a conceptual framework of the whole.

While precise and agreed upon definitions and conceptualizations of the nation, nationality and nationalism are not apparent in the literature there are still, nonetheless, certain salient features and characteristics of the phenomena which are relevant and useful for our purposes.[11] The origins of the nation state are dated during the Commercial Revolution and in this context comprised an integration of the basic ingredients of nationality, the nation and the state.[12] The nation might be viewed as the collectivity of nationality and when the nation achieved and was manifest in the political sovereignty of the state we note the genesis of the nation state. The power and sovereignty of the nation state was then used to promote the interests and well-being of a given nationality. The intensification of this relationship, as the nationality became increasingly loyal and duty-bound and identified its interests with that of the nation state, is what constitutes the phenomenon of modern nationalism.

In the earlier phase of its development the nation state and its well-being was symbolized by the monarch. In the literature the view is presented that the intense loyalty and identification of a nationality toward the nation state, characteristic of modern nationalism, did not take place until the eighteenth century with the advent of republicanism. The strong identification and loyalty of a nationality toward a nation state was achieved when "we, the people" came to be symbolic of the interests and well-being of the nation state rather than the monarch. A nation state was, therefore, of the people, by the people, and for the people. The people, of a given nationality, became in the process intensely loyal and duty-bound to the nation in that the nation state had come to be a manifestation and symbol of themselves. Consequently, the development and well-being of the nation-state marked the well-being and development of themselves, as the nationality, rather than the monarch. This transition marked the genesis of modern nationalism and had its origins in the American and French Revolutions.[13] The evolution of man's basic social aggregate into the form of the nation state was of great significance in relation to economic development. The transformation from the political fragmentation characteristic of feudalism to the political integration of the nation-state was a necessary pre-condition for the evolution into industrialism and was interrelated with the development of republicanism. The phenomena conceptually identified as nationalism, industrialism and republicanism were primary forces of culture evolution and economic development and marked their appearance as an integrated whole during the eighteenth century.[14] Discussions of the nation state as the basic unit of observation are consequently only relevant to the processes of economic development taking place chronologically during and after the Commercial Revolution.

In that our goal is a universal and general theory of economic development we note that the usage of the nation as the basic social aggregate is of limited historical relevance. Whereas the processes of growth and development are universal and relevant to all stages of economic development the usage of the nation restricts analysis basically to the growth and development taking place during the modern period of industrialism.

In this regard Lane questions the vogue of viewing growth and development through the limited portholes of the nation state rather than through alternative apertures of greater historical perspective.[15] The nation state represents a limited segment of man's social heritage; it marks a very brief period of man's chronological record viewed from the perspective of long-term culture evolution. Our study is directed towards a general theory and this requires a conceptualization of the process in a universal sense relevent to all epochs or stages of man's economic development. The sole use of the nation, as the basic social aggregate, tends to negate and obscure the evolutionary nature of the process of economic development. The use of the nation as the unit of observation tends to restrict analysis and theory to an industrial system characterized by modern economic growth.

A general theory of economic development, however, should also be an evolutionary theory. By concentrating on the nation we tend to obscure the evolutionary nature of the process of economic development. Evolution constitutes a process of transforming a given structure or form to a higher level of complexity and development. Consequently a general theory, incorporating an evolutionary framework, needs a variety of social aggregates to choose from and which could conceivably serve as the basic unit of observation. We speak here of such alternative forms and structures such as the tribe, the village, the town-economy, the city-state, the empire, the nation, the MNC and the region, among others.[16] Such a variety of social aggregates serves to provide a base for a comparative anatomy of social aggregates. By focusing on the nation we tend to reinforce the view that the social aggregate relevent for economic analysis is fixed when in actuality it evolves and varies over time. The social aggregate is transformed and grows in size and complexity and, in that a tribe is different and not synonymous with a nation, the social structure also exhibits conceptual discontinuity.[17] Also, it should be noted, again, that not only does the nation serve as a unit of observation but that the nation, as a social institution, is embedded in the cultural matrix and consequently, also functions as an endogenous variable and as an integral and substantive part of the development process itself. The birth of the "new nation", as the United States, was of great significance in the further growth and development of the American economy.[18]

All this is not to infer that the use of the nation as the basic unit of observation is incorrect, per se, but rather that it restricts our analytical purview and does not go far enough if the overall objective is a general theory of economic development. The social aggregate chosen from among various alternatives is the one considered to be most relevant to the particular stage of economic development being submitted to analysis. Conceptually, the unit of observation, as the container or crucible, changes in the process of economic development and evolution. Such concepts known as the nation, the city, and the region are not synonymous and conceptually exhibit discontinuity. However, the substance contained within a given alternative social aggregate is conceptually covered best by the concept of culture and as such constitutes conceptual continuity. The concept of culture is universal and relevant to all social aggregates for all times and places and from the paleolithic on to modern industrialism.

But even granting that our analysis be of the current stage of economic development, as innovated through the Industrial

Revolution, there are still certain shortcomings; in terms of the use of the nation state as the basic unit of observation. One of the biggest shortcomings, and certainly this point is emphasized by Kuznets, is found in the transnational character of technology.[19] Technology is conceptually relevant to culture rather than to the nation, technology is an integral and substantive part of culture as it is currently conceptualized. For example, in the case of the United States, would our current level of advanced technology and the resulting high levels of growth and productivity be best explained by the nation, per se, as it is currently conceptualized? Or rather by the fact that the American economy, as an appendage of European culture, absorbed European technology and modern industrialism characteristic of European culture. Are the differences of growth and development characteristic of the United States, Canada and Mexico due to the nations, as such, or rather their respective cultures.[20] Is the advanced growth and development of Canada compared to Mexico due to the Canadian nation, as such, or due to the fact that the political borders of Canada have proved permeable to the culture and technology of the United States? Is the fact that the European nations stand so high in the world-wide growth and development scale due to the nations of Europe or to the industrial culture of Europe? Should not our theoretical analysis of economic development be most concerned with the primary elements and substance of the process? And what is more intimately associated with the process of economic development than technology and is not that transnational stock of knowledge best covered by the concept of culture?

That the nation state system is proving increasingly anachronistic to the needs of a modern industrial society is precisely because it serves as an inadequate container and producer of modern technology. The current period reveals a trend, especially in the context of mature industrial countries of relatively small market size, toward regional integration. For the region of Western Europe, the nation is viewed as being anachronistic to the needs of a modern industrial society and supranationalism appears as a guiding force in the long-term movement toward European integration. A new basis of loyalty, not nationality, but the requirements of a modern industrial society are viewed as compelling forces for the emerging new

Europe. Territorial areas of the future will be marked off by culture-bearing social aggregates directed toward the needs of modern technology rather than a restricted base of nationality.[21] Conceivably, the social aggregate of the proximate future for many of our current political units in the world labelled as nations will be in the form of a regional bloc. In the process, the melting of national units into one large unit as a regional bloc would produce an integrated social aggregate more adaptable and capable of dealing with the growing political, economic and military requirements of the twentieth century.[22]

During the current period, and for the more mature industrial countries, another powerful and dynamic force eroding the nation-state would be contained in the social aggregate known as the multinational corporation. Again, we find the transnational force of technological diffusion but in the case of the MNC it appears in the agency of direct private foreign investment. In 1970 only twenty-two nations surpassed General Motors as a basic unit of economic production and advance. Of the top one hundred units of production fifty-nine are nations and forty-one are corporations.[23] Consequently, can we discount the MNC as a relevant social aggregate and as a unit of observation in any conceptualization, explanation and analysis of economic growth and development?[24]

Starting with Adam Smith and *The Wealth of "Nations"* and on to Keynes, mainstream economic analysis has focused on the nation as the basic social aggregate. Nations and nation states, however, have not always existed but, as we have noted, in their origins marked the transition of the feudal and agrarian cultures of the past into modern industrialism. But it should be noted that during much of the period of modern economic growth we find that the social structure of the less developed countries (LDC's) had yet to achieve the status of nationhood. In this regard the relevance and transference of orthodox economic analysis, based upon the nation, to an analysis of the problems of the LDC's would be less than perfect, if the particular LDC had yet to emerge as a nation. Can the nation state serve as crucible or unit of observation for something (economic development) which was taking place prior to the existence of the nation state? For many peoples and regions of the world during the period of modern economic growth, and especially prior to WW II, the nation and nationalism were nonexistent.[25] It is only recently that many less developed countries could in actuality be called less developed nations. "In 1939 there were 71 states, not all national, in 1975 over 140, that depending on definition were national. The Africa of 1950 had only 4 so-called independent states, in 1976 over 40 called themselves nation states."[26] Consequently, for the time span when orthodox or mainstream economic theory was applied to the LDC's, many of the LDC's did not contain the prerequisite social institution known as the nation state.

In the long-term course of economic development it appears that, currently, the nation state is becoming less relevant to the DC's as the basic social aggregate for analysis and at the same time more relevant to the LDC's. A basic function of the nation state, historically, has been to promote the political, social and economic integration of a region and its inhabitants in the transition from that of an agrarian society to that of modern science and industrialism. Consequently for much of the world and in the proximate future the forces and power associated with the nation state and nationalism will in all probability grow in intensity and importance.[27] During the current period the rise of the nation state and nationalism as the basic social structure for the majority of mankind is predictable. But it is also our view, and one which we will try to support in the course of this study, given the assumption of continued economic development, that the ultimate demise of the nation state is a predictable cultural phenomenon of long-term exponential culture evolution.[28] Advanced economic development of the future will mark the denouncement of the nation state; ultimately the nation state will recede into the dim record of the past as the fossil remains of an antiquated social structure.

Briefly then, the nation state came into being during the stage of economic development known as the Commercial Revolution. It served as one of the basic pre-conditions established during the period of transition between feudalism and capitalism and is the characteristic political unit of the modern period. The political structure of the nation state in its evolution provided the unification and centralization necessary for the greater levels of economic production associated with the Industrial Revolution. Modern nationalism did not evolve in isolation but emerged during the eighteenth century interrelated with the associated developments known as industrialism and republicanism. The nation state, as a social institution is but one, albeit a very important one, cultural ingredient of modern economic growth and development. But the roots of economic development, as the processes of accumulating technology and useful knowledge, go way back and did not just start with the industrialism and the associated rise of the nation state. If the process of development has had historical continuity, if it has been cumulative over time in its evolution, so then should the substance of development which we submit to theoretical analysis and explanation. The concept of culture fulfills that analytical and theoretical need. In fact, if one is correct in assuming that the process of economic development started with the development of culture, the nation, as such, was of course nowhere near in sight. Consequently, our next question: what then is culture?

While the specific definitions of culture are quite numerous, the overall conceptualization tends to have had a general acceptance and focuses on that originally offered by Tylor in 1871.[29] In the Kroeber and Kluckhohn study of the concept some one hundred and sixty-four definitions of culture are cited.[30] Culture, in our analysis, will be viewed in the broad "holistic" sense as formulated by Tylor and still followed today though in modified and refined forms, through the emphasis on "that complex whole" as a totality.[31] And also from such a broadly based conceptualization that culture is the equivalent of man's social heritage, the superorganic and as an extrasomatic residue of man's accumulated knowledge.

A specific definition of the Tylor conceptualization might be: "The sum total of the social and political rules, technological inventions, and economic institutions, the arts shared beliefs and practices—that is the culture. . . ."[32] Such a definition embraces the entirety of the many variables associated with the process of economic development and consequently represents the substantive whole. In addition, overall culture is also viewed as a basic dichotomy comprising material and nonmaterial culture. In material culture we have the basic grist for the mill of mainstream economic analysis. We speak here of the basic elements of capital goods, machinery, building and also consumer goods as the basic economic tools and material artifacts of culture. Such elements of material culture do not operate *sui generis* but rather require the elements of nonmaterial culture as the institutional webbing holding it all together. Nonmaterial culture makes material culture operable through the institutional structuring of human behavior. While there are many parts of culture, culture overall operates as an organic totality, as a gestalt, in which the whole is greater than the sum of its parts. Analyzing only factor inputs of material culture, as economists normally tend to do, is really only telling one-half of the story and perhaps the least significant at that. Man's economic production might be looked upon as a physical residue of his learned behavior patterns. Without man's learned behavior patterns, essentially stored in nonmaterial culture, there would be no concretion of man's accumulated knowledge in the form of physical production.

We also note a basic distinction between a cultural and culture analysis and why in our study we speak of culture evolution rather than cultural. There are many parts which, as cultural variables, go to make up the whole known as culture. Cultural refers to a part whereas culture refers to the composite whole of culture viewed as a gestalt. Capital goods, machinery, buildings, consumer goods, energy control, private property, the Protestant ethic, values, government, laissez-faire, the nation state, are all cultural variables of the composite whole known as culture. In a basic dichotomy of culture, some cultural parts are related to material culture and others form nonmaterial culture; cultural traits as the many parts of material and nonmaterial culture viewed as an integrated whole form the gestalt of culture. Our analysis will be primarily of culture which is the scientific concept capable of bringing the social sciences together as a unified, interdisciplinary whole. If the analysis is to be inter-disciplinary and include many cultural variables, as the "noneconomic", the relevant scientific concept is that of culture. And while there have been many theories which might be classified as cultural there have not been that many, by comparison, which have focused on Tylor's omnibus conceptualization of culture as the basis for their theoretical framework.[33]

Culture may be conceptualized in a variety of ways and

related to basic functions performed by culture. Such interpretations and the myriad of definitions derived therefrom need not necessarily be inconsistent with Tylor's omnibus view as "that complex whole." In our analysis, focusing on economic development, a relevant view would be that culture serves in a basic function to store knowledge. Over time man accumulates, advances and transforms his useful knowledge which is really stored by culture. As man interacts with culture and applies the knowledge stored by culture he originates new forms of technology. Technology as problem solving, both social and material, is becoming increasingly central in discussions of economic growth and development. Technology cannot, to our view, be correctly conceptualized and analyzed outside the culture matrix. As we will try to show, technology and culture are really opposite sides of the same coin, the coin of useful knowledge.

Consequently, in that the basic cultural elements of economic development are substantively contained in the concept of the whole known as culture we support the logic of trying to understand the parts through an analysis and conceptualization of the whole. Substantively, what man accumulates, and transforms in the process of economic development is in reality, then, his culture. And consequently, we argue that it is culture which should receive the primary focus in any explanation of the process of economic development and growth. The basic elements of economic development are cultural and are the elements which comprise the whole of culture. The nation as a specific social institution is but a cultural part of the whole of culture and is of limited historical relevance.

Another basic premise underlying the importance of culture and why culture should be the focal point of any theory of economic development is that human behavior, overall, is generally conceded to be a function of culture. Such a conception of human behavior does not completely exclude the innate or biological explanation but rather places primary emphasis on the cultural setting as the dominant force in any general explanation of human behavior.[34] In that man's economic behavior patterns are a part of the whole of his overall behavior it is incorrect to explain and analyze economic behavior exclusively outside the framework of culture.

Certain empirical realities stand out, in the first place we know that man's overall behavior, including the specifics of economic behavior, has changed drastically and increased in complexity as man has made the transition from that of a hunting and gathering culture of the past to that of the advanced industrialism of the present. Secondly, we also know that man has changed very little biologically over the last several thousand years. Therefore while on the one hand the biological nature of man has remained relatively constant during a given time span his social and cultural activities and his learned behavior patterns have increased enormously in scope and complexity. Consequently such behavior changes cannot be explained via a constant, as the biological, but rather must be explained in terms of a variable such as an evolving culture.[35] Man interacting with culture brings about a transformation and accumulation of culture through technological advances, and in the process of transforming culture, man thereby also transforms himself. Through the processes of economic development man promotes the evolution of culture which in turn promotes the further evolution of man's behavior, overall, and his economic behavior in particular. That human behavior is essentially a function of culture is but another argument for the use of a culture framework in any conceptual and theoretical explanation of the process of economic development. Culture, then, as the basic substance of the process of economic development assumes a central conceptual position in any general theory of the process of economic development.

> "Of all the theories or explanations of the course of growth. . .that which runs in terms of culture (broadly defined) . . .is logically the most adequate albeit the most difficult to formulate effectively."[36]
>
> "What is needed, therefore, is not merely a theory of economic growth in purely economic terms but a theory relating economic development to cultural change."[37]

In summary, in this chapter we have argued the need for a new conceptual framework in order to advance a general theory of the process of economic growth and development. The tendency is for mainstream economics to treat the process of growth and development in the conceptual framework of the nation. We have argued, and for a variety of reasons, that the relevant and correct conceptual framework for the process of development resides in the concept of culture rather than that of the nation. In that mainstream economics treats the "non-economic" as fixed or given, the nation as a social institution is also treated as being invariant. The social aggregate called the nation serves as a unit of observation, as a crucible, containing the basic economic factors of production which function as the variables explaining economic growth. Such economic growth is then treated as being synonymous with development.

However, even granting that, currently, the nation is the most relevant unit of observation, at least up to the present, and for the stage of development characterized by modern economic growth, its current usage by economists is somewhat insufficient. Perhaps the nation can correctly be viewed in static terms and also simply as a container of factor inputs if the focus and objective of analysis is that of simple economic growth, But such a conceptual framework while correct in so far as it goes, does not go far enough. It constitutes a theory of economic growth but not a theory of economic development. The growth process is only part of the overall of economic development and not the whole of the story. The process of development is not simply that of replication and accumulation and the growth of factors of production in the context of invariant social structures. Such a framework provides a mental fixation or predilection and has resulted in theories of economic development in the static framework of growth and consequently precludes an evolutionary framework.

The nation is a cultural part of the whole and as such, itself, enters into the processes of development as a variable. The evolution of the nation and nationalism were in fact quite significant and instrumental in the furtherance of economic development. Therefore the nation does not simply serve as the unit of observation, as a crucible, unrelated to the process but is itself an endogenous variable of economic development. And further, what is contained inside the territorial mark-off is not simply economic factor inputs but rather that the basic substance experiencing growth and development is really best covered by the concept culture It is the integrated totality, "that complex whole", first scientifically conceptualized by

Tylor, which best serves as the substance or clay of the process of economic development. The nation is not the overall substance but rather serves as a territorial cookie-cutter of culture and is of limited time span and historical relevance.

Consequently, it is the concept of culture as the basic substance of transformation and accumulation which should receive the primary focus in the conceptual framework of a general theory of economic development.[38] If this conclusion is correct, it would then logically follow that our theoretical framework of economic development be formulated in the conceptual framework of a scientific analysis of culture change and transformation. Culture change and transformation in a direction of continuous advance and increased complexity is also referred to in literature as culture evolution. In this study our methodology will be to use the anthropologists concept of culture, in its totality and evolution, as the basic framework to explain and analyse the processes of economic growth and development. Such an approach does not constitute a cultural theory but more correctly uses a theory of culture as the framework for a theory of economic development. We will call this methodology *cultural economics.*

REFERENCES

[1]The definitions offered by students in the area of economic development are indeed numerous and varied and reflect differing conceptualizations of the meaning of economic development: "Indeed, there are as many definitions of economic development and of the corollary concept of underdeveloped area as there are authors writing in the Field." Adamantios Pepelasis et. al., *Economic Development: Analysis and Case Studies* (New York: Harper and Row, Publishers, 1961), p. 3. "There is no traditionally established and clear cut notion as to what is meant by economic development" Harvey Leibenstein, *Economic Backwardness and Economic Growth* (New York: John Wiley and Sons, 1963), p. 8, and Sherman Robinson, "Theories of Economic Growth and Development," *Economic Development and Cultural Change*, 21 (October 1972), pp. 54-67, "A major difficulty in comparing theories of economic development is that two authors writing on the subject seldom mean the same thing by the phrase 'economic development'." p. 54. Aside from the succinct and brief definitions found in the many books, monographs and articles dealing with the subject matter of economic development, there have been several specific attempts at

conceptual clarification. For example: S.H. Frankel, "Some Conceptual Aspects of International Economic Development of Underdeveloped Territories "*Essays in International Finance* (Princeton, 1952), No. 14, which also appears in Frankel's *The Economic Impact on Underdeveloped Societies* (Cambridge: Harvard University Press, 1953), pp. 56-81; Everett E. Hagen, "The Process of Economic Development, "*Economic Development and Cultural Change* (April 1957), pp. 193-215; R. A. Shearer, "The Concept of Economic Growth," *Kyklos*, Vol. XIV, 1961, pp. 497-532; Robert d'A Shaw, "Rethinking Economic Development," *Headline Series*, (No. 208) New York: Foreign Policy Association, December 1971); Edgar Owens and Robert Shaw, *Development Reconsidered: Bridging the Gap Between Government and People* (Lexington: D. C. Heath and Company, 1972); Dudley Seers, "The meaning of development," in Nancy Bastor, ed., *Measuring Development* (London: Frank Cass Publisher; 1972); Denis Goulet, *The Cruel Choice: A New Concept in the Theory of Development* (New York: Antheum, 1971) especially pp. 332-4; Michael P. Todaro, *Economic Development in the Third World* (New York: Longman, Inc., 1977), pp. 50-69.

[2]"The first requirement of a scientific analyst is that he should clearly define the concepts he is utilizing." Gunnar Myrdal, "What is Development," *Journal of Economic Issues*, 8 (December 1974), pp. 729-736, p. 729. See for example: Earl Edward Eubank, "The conceptual approach to Sociology." pp. 47-63, in Harry Elmer Barnes and Howard Becker, eds., *Contemporary Social Theory* (New York: D. Appleton-Century Company, 1940), "The underlying thesis of this chapter is that the development of any science coincides with the development of its distinctive concepts." p. 47; also, by Eubank, *The Concepts of Sociology* (Baston: D. C. Heath and Company, 1931); and also, Herbert Blumer, "Science Without Concepts," *American Journal of Sociology*, 36 (January, 1931), pp. 515-33. In the annals of the evolution of the social sciences, perhaps one of the most noted examples of the point we are making would be the conceptualization of culture by Tylor in 1871. "The reason. . .is not only that Tylor possessed unusual insight and wisdom, but that he was deliberately establishing a science by defining its subject matter. That he made this definition the first sentence of a book shows that he was conscious of his procedure." pp. 149-51, A. L. Kroeber and Clyde Kluckhohn, *Culture: A Critical Review of Concepts and Definitions*. Vol. 47, Papers of the Peabody Museum of American Archaeology and Ethnology, (Cambridge: Harvard University Printing office, 1952).

[3]On a basic distinction between nation and nation-state, note: Karl W. Deutsch, *Nationalism and Social Communication* (Cambridge: The M.I.T. Press, 1966), pp. 104-5; and also, footnote 11, below.

[4]On this point note: Simon Kuznets, *Modern Economic Growth*, (New Haven: Yale University Press, 1966), pp. 16-19; *Economic Growth and Structure* (New York: W. W. Norton & Co., 1965), pp. 6-8; "State As a Unit in Study of Economic Growth," *The Journal of Economic*

History (Winter 1951), Vol. XI, pp. 25-41; "Measurement of Economic Growth," *The Tasks of Economic History* (Supplemental Issue of the Journal of Economic History), VII (1947), pp. 10-34; and also, Ingvar Svennilson, "The Concept of the Nation and Its Relevance to Economic Analysis" in E. A. G. Robinson, ed., *Economic Consequences of the Size of Nations* (London: Macmillan and Co., 1960), pp. 1-13; Norton Ginsberg, *Atlas of Economic Development* (Chicago: University of Chicago Press, 1961), pp. 3-5; and also Hugh G. J. Aitken, ed., *The State and Economic Growth* (New York: Social Science Research Council, 1959).

[5]"Practically speaking, the nation is taken as the unit of observation in the study of growth because it creates the statistics." Lane, "Units of Economic Growth Historically Considered," *Kyklos*, 15 (1962), pp. 95-104, p. 94.

[6]In other instances Kuznets gives more emphasis to the statistical and quantitative aspects associated with the nation as the basic unit, cf., for example, "The State as a Unit in Economic Growth," p. 27, but in *Modern Economic Growth*, emphasis is given to the decision-making nature of the national unit, p. 17, footnote 6.

[7]Boyd C. Shafer declares nationalism to be the ". . .strongest and most appealing group sentiment in the world today. . .", *Nationalism: Its Nature and Interpreters* (Washington, D. C: American Historical Association, 1976) p. 4., and pp. 44-58 for selected bibliography; and Karl W. Deutsch and Richard L. Merritt, *Nationalism and National Development : An Interdisciplinary Bibliography* (Cambridge: The M.I.T. Press, 1970) covering the years 1935-1966 and approximately 5,000 titles.

[8]"What is a nation? In the equilibrium theory from Marshall . . . to Samuelson. . . and till today, a country is treated as a compact bundle of factors of production. . ." Joan Robinson, "What are the Questions?," *Journal of Economic Literature*, 15 (December 1977), pp. 1318-1339, p. 1334.

[9]Hans Kohn notes in Louis L. Snyder, *The Meaning of Nationalism* (New Brunswick: Rutgers University Press, 1954), "But the historian will need the cooperation of many other disciplines. . .Professor Snyder has written the first introduction to such an interdisciplinary inquiry." p. ix. And also, Deutsch and Merritt, *Nationalism*, in their "Introduction" note: "In this research it very soon became apparent that no single scientific discipline and no single branch of humanistic scholarship was sufficient to deal with such problems." which is a reaffirmation of the basic position taken by Deutsch in his earlier bibliography (1956), p. 1.

[10]Hans Kohn, *Nationalism—Its Meaning and History* (Princeton: D. Van Nostrand Co., 1955) note in the preface that, "But nationalism is not the same in all countries and at all times," and, Boyd C. Shafer, *Nationalism—Myth and Reality* (New York: Harcourt Brace and Co., 1955), "The nationalism of each people has hence expressed itself differently and altered with time . . . .Consequently, because the thing

itself has differed and changed, the meaning given the word has varied with each language, each nationalist and with each period of time. Quite understandably, students, looking at it from different nations, different times, and for different reasons have defined it differently". pp. 3-4; and also, Louis L. Snyder, *The New Nationalism* (Ithaca: Cornell University Press, 1968).

[11]On the definitions and varied conceptualizations, briefly and with a good deal of selectivity, note: Louis L. Snyder, *The Meaning of Nationalism*, Carlton J. H. Hayes, *Essays on Nationalism* (New York: The Macmillan Company, 1926), "What is Nationalism?" pp. 1-29; Shafer, *Myth and Reality*, pp. 3-11; *Nationalism: A Report by a Study Group of Members of the Royal Institute of International Affairs* (New York: Augustus M. Kelley, Publishers, 1966), pp. xvi-xx, 1-7, 25-34; and Dankwart A. Rustow, "Nation," pp. 7-14, and Hans Kohn, "Nationalism," pp. 63-69, in David L. Sills, ed., *International Encyclopedia of the Social Sciences* (New York: The Macmillan Company and the Free Press, 1968), Volume 11; Guido Zernatto, "Nation : The History of a Word," *The Review of Politics*, 6 (1944), pp. 351-66.

[12]"The emergence of national states. . .was perhaps the most important political development of the early modern period." Herbert Heaton, *Economic History of Europe* (New York: Harper and Row Publishers, 1948), pp. 221-22. *Nationalism: A Report by a Study Group*, pp. 5-7; D. A. Rustow, "Nation", p. 11; Sam Darcy, *Late Afternoon for the Nation-State* (New York: Cromwell Books, Publishers, 1972), pp. 7-27.

[13]Two noted authorities, Hans Kohn and Carlton J. H. Hayes would concur, "The most important and best known are Carlton J. H. Hayes, *The Historical Evolution of Modern Nationalism*. . . and Hans Kohn's *The Idea of Nationalism*, which deserves to be regarded as the definitive history of the ideological origins of contemporary nationalism." Frederich L. Schuman, *International Politics* (New York: McGraw Hill Book Co., 1958), footnote p. 338. From Hans Kohn we have: "Nationalism as we understand it is not older than the second half of the eighteenth century. Its first great manifestation was the French Revolution which gave the new movement an increased dynamic force." *The Idea of Nationalism* (New York: The Macmillan Co., 1944), p. 3, 10, . . ., etc., and from the same source see also footnote 1, p. 579, which substantiates the claim that most historians have been in agreement on the point of dating modern nationalism circa, eighteenth century. Hayes is also in agreement on the point of dating modern nationalism: "The new nationalism appeared clearly and unmistakably in Europe in the eighteenth century, a century which was far more critical and self-searching than any earlier period of like duration in recorded history, a century which was peculiarly revolutionary." *The Historical Evolution of Modern Nationalism* (New York: The Macmillan Co., 1950), pp. 8-9. Also, "The use of the word nationalism to describe historical happenings before the eighteenth century is probably anachronistic" Shafer, *Nationalism—*

Myth and Reality, p. 5; and also, Edward Hallett Carr, *Nationalism and After* (London: Macmillan, 1967).

[14]"Only in the eighteenth century, through the simultaneous emergence of nationalism, democracy and industrialism. . ." p. vii, Hans Kohn, *The Idea of Nationalism*, and Carlton J. H. Hayes, *The Historical Evolution*, pp. 232-287.

[15]Frederick C. Lane, "Units of Economic Growth Historically Considered," *Kyklos*, 15 (1962), pp. 95-104. In this regard one may well raise a very important question: Should the explanation and scope of analysis be universalistic, that is, apply to more than one epoch and more than one economic system of an epoch? "This question—whether the projected theory should cover the growth of nations under industrial capitalism or under the industrial system, or, for that matter, should also encompass such earlier epochs as merchant capitalism, the agrarian empires of the East and the medieval town economy—is surely a major one. . . ." Simon Kuznets, "Toward a Theory of Economic Growth," in Robert Lekachman, *National Policy for Economic Welfare at Home and Abroad* (New York: Doubleday and Company, 1955), p. 71, and p. 64, and also note Lane's comments, p. 89. Raised another way, the question answers itself: Did the process of economic development have its origins in the eighteenth century with the start of industrialism? The origins of economic growth and development start with the origins and genesis of man's culture.

[16]Note Simon Kuznets, "The State as a Unit . . . " (1951), pp. 26-27.

[17]"With economic development, the size of the social unit grows." Charles P. Kindleberger, *Economic Development* (New York: McGraw-Hill Book Co., 1965), pp 30-33.

[18]Gunnar Myrdal, *Rich Lands and Poor* (New York: Harper and Brothers Publishers, 1957), pp. 60-61, notes the power of the new nationalism in liquidating the colonial empires during the post-WW II period. The American Revolution and American nationalism, circa two-centuries earlier, served the same basic function in the long-term process of economic development, note: Seymour Martin Lipset, *The First New Nation* (New York: Basic Books, 1963), p. 2, and, Herbert Aptheker, *The American Revolution* (New York: International Publishers, 1960), p. 23, cited in Charles H. Hession and Hyman Sardy, *Ascent to Affluence* (Boston: Allyn and Bacon, 1969), pp. 1, 42.

[19]On the issue of the transnational character of technology note: Kuznets, *Modern Economic Growth*, "And above all the problem must be faced whether modern economic growth, whose basic source is the application of a *transnational* resource like science and science-based technology, can be effectively studied in terms of national units," pp. 18, 286-94. Svennilson, "The Concept of the Nation and Its Relevance to Economic Analysis," by comparison tends to minimize the issue, pp. 12-13.

[20]Richard Hartshone, "The Role of the State in Economic Growth: Contents of the State Area" in Aitken, ed., *The State and Economic*

Growth, "*Location of a state within a culture area favourable to the development of the social characteristics enumerated may perhaps be the most important single factor for its economic growth.*" p. 321; Louis Jacques Zimmerman, *Poor Lands, Rich Lands* (New York: Random House, 1965), offers data for larger economic-geographical areas than that contained by the national unit in line with greater homogeneity, cf., pp. 27-29.

[21]"The modern nation state is one particular form of the territorial state." D.A. Rustow, "Nation", p. 11, *International Encyclopedia of Social Sciences*, Volume II; "The nation is a geographical unit cut out as a strip from the world map." Ingvar Svennilson, "The Concept of the Nation and Its Relevance to Economic Analysis," p. 1. Such limited territorial boundaries and economic discontinuities proved sufficient during the stage of economic development known as the Commercial Revolution. The nation state proved workable given an agrarian economy but has become increasingly out of step with the needs and requirements of a modern industrial society.

[22]"What can explain nationalism's surprising, and perhaps still growing, strength at a time when technology seems to have made it obsolete?" and. . . . "The whole thrust of the technological development of our time pushes beyond wars and beyond the economic fences of nation-states." Karl W. Deutsch, *Nationalism and Its Alternatives* (New York: Alfred A. Knopf, 1969), pp. 3, 190. Charles P. Kindleberger states: "The nation-state is just about through as an economic unit." *American Business Abroad: Six Lectures on Direct Investment* (New Haven: Yale University Press, 1969), p. 207. Arnold J. Toynbee notes: ". . . in this age national sovereignty spells mass suicide." and, "It seems fairly safe to forecast that, if the human race survives it will have abandoned the ideal and practice of national sovereignty.", "The Reluctant Death of Sovereignty," *The Central Magazine*, Vol. I, 3, (March 1968), pp. 28-33.

[23]Lester R. Brown, *World Without Borders* (New York: Random House, 1972), pp. 209-229, and, "The Interdependence of Nations," *Headline Series* (New York: Foreign Policy Association, October 1972), No. 212, pp. 13-16; U.S. Senate, Committee on Finance, *The Multinational Corporation and the World Economy* (Washington, D.C.: U.S. Government Printing Office, 1973), p. 8; and, George W. Ball, "Making World Corporations into World Citizens," *War/Peace Report*; Vol. 8 (October 1968), pp. 8-10, p. 9.

[24]"And, when the history of the late twentieth century is written, it will surely be said that it was the operations of industry that did more than anything else to undermine the overwhelming dominance of the nation-state over the condition of man for the last three centuries." Hugh Stephenson, *The Coming Clash: The Impact of Multinational Corporations on National States*: (New York: Saturday Review Press, 1972), p. 175. Also George W. Ball states: "While the structure of the multinational corporation is a modern concept, designed to meet modern requirements, the nation state is a very old fashioned idea and badly

adapted to our present complex world. Most nation states are totally inadequate as economic units. They are too small to provide efficient domestic markets in an age when the economies of scale make mass production imperative." "Multinational Corporations and Nation States," *The Atlantic Community Quarterly*, 5 (Summer 1967), pp. 247-53, 247.

[25]In 1945, Edward Hallett Carr, *Nationalism and After*, noted, "The nation is not a definable and clearly recognizable entity; nor is it universal. It is confined to certain periods of history and to certain parts of the world. Today—in the most nation-conscious of all epochs—it would still probably be fair to say that a large numerical majority of the population of the world feel no allegiance to any nation." p. 39. Consequently theories of economic development should be relevant and inclusive of all conceivable social aggregates and not simply the nation state. "Thus the unit which List studies is the nation state, and his theory of economic stages must be understood as applying only to nation states. This is an important aspect of his theory, since it was one of the chief reasons why later writers rejected it." p. 197, Bert F. Hoselitz, et al., *Theories of Economic Growth* (Glencoe: The Free Press, 1960).

[26]Shafer, *Nationalism: Its Nature and Interpreters*, p. 5; and Darcy, *Late Afternoon for the Nation-State*, pp. 178-255, "Summarizing then, it is evident that most of the countries of the world with inhabitants totalling a majority of the world's population have achieved nation-state independence only in the past twenty-five years, some only in the past decade." pp. 254-55.

[27]World-wide, in the proximate future, ". . . the balance still seems to be clearly in the direction of intensified and divinise nationalism." Simon Kuznets, *Postwar Economic Growth* (Cambridge: Harvard University Press, 1964), pp. 122-25.

[28]We base this conclusion on the continuum of the exponential advance of culture evolution and the underlying paradigm of logistic surges. Material and social technics, both, require transformation and structural change in order to maintain a continuum of long-term exponential evolution. We will develop and expand upon the "principle of similitude" in the course of this study.

[29]Morris B. Opler, "Cultural Dynamics and Evolutionary Theory," in Herbert R. Barringer, ed., *Social Change in Developing Areas* (Cambridge: Schenkman Publishing Co., 1965), ". . . Tylor introduced the definition of culture that most social scientists accept and repeat today. . ." p. 69; and. Milton Singer, "The Concept of Culture," *International Encyclopedia of the Social Sciences*, Vol. 3, pp. 527-542, p. 539.

[30]On the meaning of culture note: Alfred L. Kroeber and Clyde Kluckhohn, *Culture: A Critical Review of Concepts and Definitions*, Harvard University, Peabody Museum of American Archeology and Ethnology Papers, Vol. 47, No. 1 (Cambridge: The Museum, 1952) and the *International Encyclopedia of the Social Sciences* (1958), Vol 3, pp. 527-67 and their contained bibliographies as starting points. The

literature on the subject is well-surveyed and organized in the standard work by Kroeber and Kluckhohn. Actually if one goes beyond Part II of the study the total number of definitions could reach as high as three-hundred rather than one-hundred and sixty-four, note p. 149 and footnote 4a.

[31]On the "comprehensive totality . . . complex whole, totality, sum, sum total, all . . ." note Kroeber and Kluckhohn, *Culture*, pp. 43-46.

[32]Elman R. Service, "Cultural Evolution," *International Encyclopedia of the Social Sciences*, Vol. 5, pp. 221-228, p. 222.

[33]Whereas the Weber-Tawney thesis, as a case in point, represents a cultural theoretical framework and focuses on a cultural variable (religion) the theories of Veblen and Ayres in economics have focused on the Tylor conceptualization of overall culture. The emphasis on the whole of culture as the basis for the theoretical framework is also *modus operandi* of W.F. Ogburn in sociology and L.A. White in anthropology. Cultural refers to specific traits and parts; culture refers to the conceptual whole embracing and integrating the many cultural parts. In that the institutional school has focused on culture it is also viewed as an "holistic" methodology. Note, Allan G. Gruchy, *Modern Economic Thought* (New York: Prentice-Hall, 1947), especially pp. 18-28. Therefore while the many theories explaining the social aspects of economic development might be called cultural theories of development, it is the theoretical framework employing the Tylor conceptualization of the whole which we call a culture theory of culture evolution.

[34]Concerning the nature of man, Thorstein Veblen, *The Place of Science in Modern Civilization* (New York: Russell and Russell, 1961), noted both the innate and the cultural: "He is a creature of habits and propensities given through antecedents, hereditary and cultural, of which he is an outcome . . ." p. 79; and Clarence E. Ayres, "Veblen's Theory of Instincts Reconsidered," in Douglas F. Dowd. ed., *Thorstein Veblen: A Critical Appraisal* (Ithaca: Cornell University Press, 1958), pp. 25-37, while noting the biological ". . . such differences must have their taproots somewhere . . ." p. 25, Ayres nonetheless viewed human behavior in cultural terms, ". . . all human behaviour is a cultural phenomenon." *The Industrial Economy* (Cambridge: Houghton Mifflin Company, 1952), pp. 9-13, 79, and *The Theory of Economic Progress* (New York: Schocken Books, 1962), p. 89, *Toward A Reasonable Society* (Austin: University of Texas Press, 1961), pp. 71-86, and, "No other idea (culture) has made a greater contribution to our understanding of human nature." parenthesis added, p. 85.

[35]Note William F. Ogburn, "How Technology Causes Social Change," in Allen, *Technology and Social Change*, pp. 12-26, ". . . a variable cannot be explained by a constant" p. 13. During earlier periods culture change and biological change might both serve as causal agents, Ogburn, *Social Change*, p. 131, but during the modern period the biological factor appears as a relative constant and it is culture itself which serves as the variable, pp. 133, 141. This appears

as a central theme to Ogburn's work, the full title of which it should be noted is: *Social Change: With Respect to Culture and Original Nature.* What has changed ". . . is the cultural expression of human nature." p. 134.

[36]Joseph Spengler, "Theories of Socio-Economic Growth," in *Problems of Economic Growth* (New York: National Bureau of Economic Research, 1949), p. 88.

[37]Bert F. Hoselitz, *Sociological Aspects of Economic Growth* (Glencoe: The Free Press, 1960), p. 24, and also, Walter L. Johnson and David R. Kamerschen, ed., *Readings in Economic Development* (Cincinnati: Southwest Publishing Co., 1972), p. 54. While Hoselitz notes the importance of cultural variables he is not too optimistic concerning the origination of a general theory.

[38]"Most literature on development is nation centered. But the nation as an exclusive index of development presents grave difficulties. . . . The work already accomplished. . . would indicate that the time is ripe for a general re-evaluation of the genesis of the problem of development." Irving Louis Horowitz, *Three Worlds of Development: The Theory and Practice of International Stratification* (New York: Oxford University Press, 1966), p. x.

CHAPTER II

Normal Science and the Conceptualization of Economic Growth and Development

We have thus far presented the view that in order to clarify the conceptualization of economic development and growth it is important to first distinguish the substance which actually experiences growth and development. In reality it is culture which comprises the substantive nature of the processes of economic growth and development.[1] It is also our position that an improved conceptual framework of the process would aid in the further advance of a general theory of economic development.[2] We have argued that a correct conceptual framework for the process of economic development is to be found in culture and its evolution. The processes of economic development do not simply concern economic variables in isolation but rather are embedded in a culture matrix. Substantively it is Tylor's omnibus concept known as culture which experiences development and growth in the context of the process of economic development. Our analysis is therefore not simply one of cultural variables and their evolution but rather goes further and entails an integration of all such cultural variables into the overall conceptual whole known as culture. Consequently, our theoretical framework is not directed simply toward an explanation of the parts as *cultural* evolution but rather presents a view of the totality or the whole of *culture* evolution. In distinguishing between cultural evolution and culture evolution we draw attention to the premise that the evolution of the varied and many cultural parts can only be adequately understood in terms of the evolution of the whole, the whole known as culture. By comparison to our suggested framework of culture evolution let us now examine the conceptual framework of economic development as it appears in the current literature.

As we have already noted even the slightest perusal of the literature reveals a briar patch of conceptual confusion in that apparently no agreed-upon conceptualization of the processes of growth and development exists.[3] The conceptual polarity appearing in the literature runs the entire spectrum from the very simple on the one hand to the very complex on the other. About the most simplistic conceptualization of economic development would perhaps be found in conceptualizing the process as outward shifts of the efficiency locus better known as the transformation or production-possibility curve. General equilibrium theory of neoclassical economics, used by Gerald M. Meier in the field of international economics, demonstrates gains from trade derived from outward shifts of the production frontier.[4] Actually the term transformation curve is somewhat of a misnomer in that what is actually "transformed" for a given transformation curve is the quantitative composition of production in that more of one commodity is produced at the opportunity cost of less of another. Such a conceptualization does not even entail the transformation of a part, in terms of structural or qualitative change, let alone the culture matrix containing the whole of the process. In this theoretical framework, economic growth, indicated by outward shifts of the transformation curve, is offered as the conceptual equivalent of economic development.[5]

In the statics of pure trade theory there is actually no real shift in the transformation curve but rather the effect of trade produces a result "as if" the transformation curve had shifted when in actuality it did not. The forces of reciprocal demand, presented in the form of the Marshallian offer curve analysis, in determining improved terms of trade provide the basis for higher levels of total consumer satisfaction. Consequently, it is in the field of international economics, in pure trade theory, that we find the most simplistic conceptualization of the process of economic development. In the orthodoxy of the nineteenth century we find the basic theory of economic development contained in the static growth theory, or at best comparative statics, of comparative advantage. Consistent with the theory, trade was to serve as "an engine of growth," which was inferred to mean development.

As with culture, of which it is a part, the science of economics also periodically experiences structural change and evolution.[6] Keynesian economics, as an example of extraordinary science during the 1930's, not only provided an alternative to the neoclassical theory of trade and growth, but it was also subject to empirical quantification. Keynes the theorist was buttressed by Kuznets the empiricist, national income accounting, and the GNP concept. From this forward march in the advance and evolution of the science of economics it would be somewhat predictable that growth theories would evolve and that such theories would be accepted as theories of economic development. We speak here primarily of the Harrod-Domar type of theoretical construct and its many variations.[7] The conceptual framework that appeared during this period viewed percentage increase in incomes per capita as not only an indicator of the process of development but the process itself. It should be noted that there is a conceptual continuity contained in the neoclassical approach, as pure trade theory, and on into the Harrod-Domar framework in that both essentially treat economic growth as being the conceptual equivalent and synonymous with economic development. The two approaches differ in terms of the meaning given to economic growth but they do not differ from the focus and inference that economic growth and development are conceptual equivalents and synonymous. Both approaches consequently exclude the social and cultural as "noneconomic."

Others, however, do draw a distinction between growth and development and of the many possible ways of doing this, one way is to introduce normative criteria. But by introducing normative criteria the tendency is to make any attempt at conceptual agreement and clarity somewhat of an open-ended proposition. Zimmerman, as a case in point, defines economic growth in the sense of constant per capita income with an increasing population. By comparison, economic development is defined as the transition from economic growth to economic progress, the latter being defined as a long-term increase in per capita income.[8] More recently the tendency is to question the "progress" contained in such growth if it does not also generate higher rates of literacy and greater equality of income distribution. "In both the developing and developed worlds the call for the 'dethronement of GNP' as a major objective of economic activity was widely heard. In its place concern for the problem of poverty and equality became the major theme of the second development decade."[9] In contradiction to the classical and mainstream view that inequalities of income served as a necessary and favourable condition for economic development a more modern argument stresses that equity and social justice actually enhances rather than hinders development.[10]

Still in line with a similar questioning of GNP as a growth index of development there are those who would prefer to substitute the Physical Quality of Life Index (PQLI).[11] It is consequently not just growth but the form and direction of that growth toward an improved quality of life in three basic areas: life expectancy, adult literacy and infant mortality. While orthodox theory assumes that increased production leads to greater consumer satisfaction and welfare it appears evident, however, that increased production, as quantitative economic growth for the LDC's need not always manifest itself in an improved "physical quality of life" for the composite population. Consequently in the context of the PQLI conceptualization it is not just simple increases in quantitative production, as economic growth, which leads to greater consumer satisfaction but rather that higher levels of satisfaction are perhaps dependent upon qualitative changes in that growth.

While recognizing the importance of normative criteria and the idea of progress as goals to be achieved through the process of economic development, in our particular study, however, we will try to divorce normative issues and the idea of progress from our discussions of culture evolution and will concentrate primarily on economic advance. In this study economic development, as advanced technology and higher levels of energy control, is indicated by a quantitative increase in capacity. Economic development, in this sense of advance, provides the capacity for progress but human progress need not always be the outcome. On the banyan tree of culture evolution, Hitler's Germany represented a nation, for a given period in history, which had advanced to a very high level of economic development. The advanced level of economic development provided

Germany with a capacity for a high quality of life and sustained increase in economic growth. The clientele at Auschwitz (Oswiecim), however, might well have questioned the "progress" associated with the quality of life and equity of income distribution as provided by the Third Reich. Though we may not have agreed with Hitler's goals and policy objectives concerning equity and income distribution, as progress, Germany nonetheless at the time represented a nation at advanced stages of economic development. If WW II had ended differently we might have had a millenium of growth and development but under social conditions considered by many to be outside the realm of progress. However, in the context of the advance of economic production and energy control the Third Reich might still have been in the vanguard of economic evolution and development.

Consequently progress as such is not necessarily an assumed or natural outcome of the process of economic development but rather, and all the more, is something which has to be planned and worked for. Had Hitler had his way, some had even predicted such a possibility as a conceivable future drift of culture evolution, income distribution might have regressed in terms of an enlarged geni coefficient while at the same time it is also conceivable that energy control and technological change could have moved forward and at an exponential rate. By trying to divorce progress and the normative from our theory of economic development we do not endorse a laissez-faire policy but rather note even more the social necessity and responsibility to achieve "progress" as a direct outcome of planned policy. And in the achievement of such progress we need not impair future growth and development but, theoretically, can serve to enhance it.

It is our position then that culture evolution does not necessarily promote progress sui generis or autonomously and independent of man's control and direction. Progress is not necessarily an automatic or assured outcome of the process. Switching gears in our discussion and moving outside the realm of specific culture evolution (Hitler's Germany) and engaging the realm of general culture evolution (the earth as a whole) have we experienced progress in the long-term evolution of general culture? In 1850 world-wide population totalled 1.0

billion and a century later increased to approximately 3.0 billion. Of the 3.0 billion of the human species living on the earth at mid-twentieth century two-thirds and/or approximately 2.0 billion were bound in poverty characterized by malnutrition, illiteracy and other general conditions indicative of low living standards for the LDC's. After one century of modernization and exponential culture evolution man's "progress" was that he increased the numbers of humans on this Earth living under conditions of deprivation and squalor to approximately 2.0 billion. By 1950 man had increased the poverty population double to that of the total world-wide population which had existed in 1850. On a world-wide basis, then, have we had progress?

During the twentieth century the Lorenz curve, for world-wide income distribution, has moved in the wrong direction.[12] Consequently, for the world as a whole, we know that we can have economic development and culture evolution without necessarily experiencing progress for much of mankind. In that progress is not necessarily an automatic or natural result of the process of economic development, the trick is to use economic development to promote human progress. And while man's progress over the past century can be questioned and debated there is no question that general culture evolution has been manifest in a continuum of accelerated economic development. Economic development for the world as a whole has indeed taken place, but what is the phenomenon and how do we explain it? This study is an attempt to explain and conceptualize the process and, in so doing, we feel it is legitimate to divorce our discussions from the normative issues contained in the idea of progress.

We are arguing that economic development provides a capacity for progress, as a necessary condition, but it does not serve as a sufficient condition for achievement. Progress must first be defined and conceptualized by man; the concept of progress, itself, is a cultural relative in its genesis. Man must then design his culture for the achievement of that goal. Progress need not be an automatic outcome of the process of economic development. In his "age of uncertainty" man may "progress" himself to his own ultimate funeral in the form of a nuclear holocaust. Is it progress to build and add bricks to a structure doomed to collapse and thereby annihilate man in the process of his alleged progress? We are not subscribing to the current doomsday scenario presented by the "limits to growth" school of thought, among others, but rather we are noting that progress is not necessarily integral, inevitable or guaranteed result of the processes of culture evolution and economic development. Equity issues and the normative should be central in any discussion of policy objectives of the process but from a strictly theoretical analysis of economic development the normative issues associated with progress may tend to obfuscate and confuse the discussion of a phenomenon already difficult and complex.

If two nations are at the same advanced level of modern science, technology, and energy control, could we infer that they are at different levels of economic development given different uses of that capacity in terms of social equity and the quality of life. In comparing the United States with the Third Reich the scales of "progress" would hopefully, for most people, be decidedly in favor of the United States. The levels or stage of economic development, however, would have been quite comparable. Consequently, regardless of how we assess the "progress" of the Third Reich it was nonetheless representative of a culture at high levels of economic development. Why? If we move the whole social system upward what is the process and mechanism of that movement and how is it indicated and measured? The objective of our study is not to assess economic development as to progress, but rather as to process, and to analyze its advance as an evolutionary process of cumulative complexity. Normative issues aside, how then do we explain and empirically support and demonstrate the fact that some specific cultures are more advanced than others in terms of the processes of economic development. Our study therefore concerns economic development as cumulative advance and not progress though admittedly, and in the final analysis, it is the latter question which may be of greater importance.

Another way of drawing a distinction between growth and development would be to consider growth basically as an increase in size and development as changes in economic and social structure. Therefore, to some economists, economic growth represents essentially *quantitative* change in economic variables and economic development entails *qualitative* changes in both "noneconomic" as well as economic variables.[13] This broader view, as the qualitative, tends to move the conceptualization of the process of economic development away from the polarity of the simple to that of the more complex.

The methodology of the stages of economic development traditionally used by economic historians would be a way of introducing the qualitative, as a change in form and structure, into a conceptualization and theory of economic growth and development.[14] A stages' approach in analyzing changes in form and structure in a given direction is essential for an evolutionary analysis of economic phenomenon. With the introduction of the qualitative and a stages' approach we cannot avoid the introduction of the concept of evolution into an analysis of economic development. Said another way, if an analysis of economic development is to be evolutionary, it must embrace a stages' methodology. This is not to infer that a particular stages' approach, such as that employed by Marx or Rostow, is necessarily correct but that the method, itself, correctly used is essential for a scientific and evolutionary analysis of the process.[15] Modern evolutionists, such as Leslie A. White, do not endorse a unilinear or orthogenetic evolutionary process for specific culture evolution.[16] Ex post, we know that historically general culture evolution has moved through a paradigm of a sequential series of stages of development culminating in the currently most advanced stages known as industrialism. Ex ante, however, it is difficult to predict the future evolutionary path for general culture evolution. Also, concerning specific culture evolution, the path is not inexorably or inevitably a duplication of the same form and structure as those of specific cultures in the vanguard of general culture evolution. At this point in our study it is not our purpose to discuss the debits and credits of a stages' analysis but simply to note that a stages' methodology constitutes yet another alternative approach used to explain and conceptualize the process of economic development. Such a methodology stresses transformation of structure and form.

In the brief overview of the literature presented thus far we note that some economists exclude the social and the cultural, as the "noneconomic" from their analytical purview.

Other economists note that such "noneconomic" factors should be included in a theory of economic development but exclude such factors as variables for a variety of reasons, primarily perhaps, based on the difficulty of analysis.[17] By default these economists go back to a simplistic view of economic development as the economic growth of basic economic factor inputs. Others, being less timid in nature and engaging the domain of increased complexity, directly confront the social and cultural as endogenous and integral variables of their theoretical constructs. To this group of economists the "noneconomic" variables are very much economic in their import concerning the processes of economic development. "By *development* I mean the *movement upward of the entire social system* and I believe this is the only logically tenable definition."[18]

From this very brief review of a very large literature we note a spectrum of varying degrees of complexity concerning the current conceptualization of economic development. Can we conclude from all this that the more modern conceptualization as offered by Gunnar Myrdal has won the day and has emerged as the most advanced and *accepted* conceptualization of the process of economic development by the majority of economists?[19] Are we all institutionalists now? In this instance the wish is perhaps father to the thought. While we are in basic agreement with Myrdal's definition we disagree with the assumption that Myrdal's conceptualization dominates mainstream economics. On the contrary, as we will now argue and try to demonstrate, the majority of economists still subscribe to the more simplistic polarity of conceptualization and view the process of economic development as essentially one of economic growth. Mainstream economics still considers economic development in the quantitative frame of economic growth rather than in the qualitative frame of changes in social and economic structure. In order to explain our position we need a theoretical framework and currently discussion of the history or evolution of science, in our case economics, usually end up sooner or later in discussion of the Kuhnian matrix.[20]

In the Kuhnian framework the concept of "normal science" is crucial, and central. Normal science is the science practiced by the majority of scientists in a given discipline at a given moment of time; it is what scientists, as members of a given scientific community, normally do.[21] Normal science, however, is not static but in the dynamics of evolution experiences transformation as one disciplinary matrix (previously called paradigm) is transformed to the next in a sequential pattern of "gestalt switches."[22] The science practiced by a minority might be termed that of "extraordinary science" and as such represents an alternative disciplinary matrix to that manifest in the practice of normal science. To Kuhn extraordinary science does not constitute normal sicentific activity, in terms of what the majority of scientists normally do, but rather makes its appearance and is innovated during the exigencies of crisis. Extraordinary science practiced by a minority of scientists, represents an alternative view to that offered by the disciplinary matrix in dominance. Consequently, the disciplinary matrix of extraordinary science offers the option of a gestalt switch for the practitioners of normal science. The innovation of such an alternative disciplinary matrix as normal science constitutes a Kuhnian revolution in the development of science.[23]

It is our position that science is a social institution. Noting that science is a social institution serves to explain the difficulties of change and transformation.[24] In the Kuhnian framework extraordinary science is innovated as normal science given the exigencies of crisis. A given disciplinary matrix in dominance has a built-in stability which is difficult to budge and transform. When anomalies appear as empirical contradictions to results expected from a given disciplinary matrix and reach crisis levels, pressures are generated to innovate extraordinary science as the new disciplinary matrix in dominance. It is in this way that science, in its evolution experiences a Kuhnian revolution. Science apparently evolves in a paradigm of logistic surges underlying and leading to the overall exponential continuum.[25]

The disciplinary matrix in dominance, as the normal science of a given moment of time is dutifully recorded in textbooks and the leading journals and constitutes what the majority of economists learn as practitioners of normal science. In the process of professionalization the fledgling economist learns what he must do in order to become a scientist (economist). The economist becomes part of a community and basically behaves as the majority behaves. Science as a social institution molds his behaviour pattern in conformity to the majority. Those who swim against the stream are practitioners of extraordinary science and represent an alternative disciplinary matrix.

It is not quite correct to assume that if you ask a thousand different economists the same question you will get a thousand different answers.[26] It depends on the question. If for example the question is raised concerning the relevance of institutional analysis as an integral and substantive part of economic analysis, the majority of economists would answer in the negative. And such a negative response is not necessarily based upon systematic inquiry or specific knowledge of the Veblen-Ayres disciplinary matrix and, consequently, its rejection on scientific grounds but rather reflects that in their training the majority of economists by definition have absorbed the neoclassical synthesis. The neoclassical synthesis views the institutional approach as "...having withered away as an effective counterforce in economics. Who can explain it when a movement turns sterile?"[27] Learning the neoclassical synthesis, as normal science, means that the economist in his training learns to exclude the institutional and the cultural as integral parts of his theoretical explanation. The young economist learns the behavior pattern of exclusion long before he accumulates the necessary knowledge which would warrant such a judgment.

Practitioners of normal science may disagree on the solution of a given puzzle but they strongly agree as to which economic problems shall be submitted as puzzles to be resolved in the context of their given disciplinary matrix.[28] Say's Law as a case in point was part of the overall neoclassical disciplinary matrix and consequently the economic problem of unemployment was not viewed as a puzzle to be resolved by economists. For the practitioners of the normal science of economics the puzzle to be explained was not unemployment, but rather, the puzzle became one of explaining how supply created its own demand and generated full employment. The problem of unemployment was ultimately introduced as a puzzle to be resolved by economists with the innovation of Keynesian economics as the disciplinary matrix in dominance. Unemployment was not permeable as a puzzle given Say's Law and neoclassical economics as normal science.

All this is not to deprecate a given disciplinary matrix as normal science, nor normal science as a social institution. The function of normal science is to focus the full force of the scientific community on particular puzzles as delineated by the disciplinary matrix in dominance. If not for this the practitioner of science would see and look at everything and see and know nothing. Specialization was long ago noted as the fountainhead of economic advance and productivity and, consequently, in this sense, normal science provides a positive function. However, overspecialization can lead to rigidities of structure resisting change and transformation and in the process promote stagnation.[29] The introduction of different economic problems to be resolved as puzzles in the context of a given matrix requires the innovation of a new disciplinary matrix as normal science and such a gestalt switch would constitute Kuhnian revolution. A given or specific scientist will not usually make the switch. A new generation of economists is required which would be more permeable to the new matrix as normal science pressured by exigencies of crisis and anomalies inherent in the old orthodoxy.

Viewing science as a social institution is important in any understanding of the process through which economists have historically avoided the introduction of the obviously relevant problem areas into economic analysis. Normal science, functioning as a social institution, tends to establish boundaries and limits inquiry to the resolution of specific puzzles as delineated by the disciplinary matrix in dominance. Being an economist prior to the 1930's (not for all economists but for the majority) meant a process of professionalization whereby the fledgling economist, as a practitioner of normal science, learned and accepted neoclassical economics. Normal science as a social institution molds the behavior patterns of the economist, qua scientist, in terms of the questions raised and the answers given. Consequently the economist as technician learned the rigor of analysis of a normal science which avoided technological change, was consequently nonevolutionary and static, embraced Say's Law, assumed full-employment and perfect competition, accepted equilibrium analysis and excluded the social and cultural as integral variables of economic analysis. In that economic theory cannot be divorced from economic policy it is obvious that a disciplinary matrix devoid of the social, and the political would readily serve as a theoretical concomitant to the policy of laissez-faire.[30] Consequently political economy became more limited in its analytical purview and in its evolution came to be known simply as economics. To eliminate the social and the political from the theoretical framework would be quite compatible with the policy conclusion of no governmental regulation. Political intervention would be unnecessary and even detrimental to the successful operation of the economy.

All this came tumbling down with the "Great Crash" and the innovation of the welfare state. The economy malfunctioned under the policy guidance of laissez-faire. The associated anomalies and crisis of the period pressured the innovation of deficit spending and governmental intervention along with the concomitant theoretical framework known as Keynesian economics. Keynesian economics as extraordinary science during the 1930's became the normal science of the post-WW II period. Still it is to be noted that the Keynesian "Revolution" did not introduce the study of evolving social institutions, culture or technological change, into the accepted boundaries of economic analysis. Essentially Keynesian economics constitutes a static framework used to analyze quantitative, not qualitative, increases in income flows to achieve full-employment. The gestalt switch from Marshallian to Keynesian economics did not make normal science permeable to a theory of the processes of economic development, and consequently analysis and focus was still primarily directed toward economic growth. Keynes' theory was not that general.

The "Age of Keynes", however, did promote the invention and innovation of a growth theory known as the Harrod-Domar growth model. This theory was in its genesis basically oriented toward the growth problems of the advanced and mature industrial countries. Economists felt it legitimate to exclude the social and cultural as integral variables in that the mature countries had already achieved economic development. The problem, then, was one of essentially maintaining high and stable rates of economic growth.[31] While all this was taking place in the world of economic theory, the real world experienced "a great awakening" with the "end of empire." The need for a theory of economic development became apparent.

Although not designed as such, the Harrod-Domar growth theory experienced a conceptual metamorphosis and soon came to be interpreted by economists as the Harrod-Domar theory of economic development. "Harrod himself did not apply his system to the problems of underdeveloped countries, but that fact should not prevent us from doing so."[32] In that economists of normal science did the next best thing and used their theory of economic growth to explain the process of economic development.

A basic conclusion from all this is that given a theory of growth and the pressing need for a theory of development it is easy and even necessary to make the assumption that economic growth is synonymous with economic development. In that the majority of economists as practitioners of normal science subscribe to growth theory, the tendency is to conceptualize economic development as being synonymous with economic growth. As long as the neoclassical synthesis is retained as the disciplinary matrix in dominance the majority of economists will tend to conceptualize economic development in terms of economic growth. For the majority of economists to conceptualize economic development in the context of culture evolution as we suggest will necessitate a gestalt switch and the innovation of a new disciplinary matrix as normal science. Currently, however, the disciplinary matrix in dominance is the neoclassical synthesis and consequently, as a result, most economists conceptualize economic development as economic growth and do not introduce the "noneconomic" into their analytical purview.

As a reservation to our position some economists might note that the specific field of economic development is becoming increasingly more permeable to an institutional or cultural-type of analysis.[33] And this we would submit to as being correct. However it should be noted that the majority of economists have never really been preoccupied with the processes of development. Those mainstream economists who do venture into the field analyze economic development in the context of pure trade theory or in the growth-statics of a Harrod-Domar type model. If economists treat economic development from an institutional point of view, as the Myrdals and Galbraiths, they are by definition no longer practitioners of the neoclassical synthesis and normal science but rather serve as representatives of extraordinary science. Also, in addition, it should be noted, and a point which cannot be emphasized strongly enough, that all this is not to infer that growth theories are wrong per se but rather that they do not go far enough to include the noneconomic variables as legitimate puzzles to be analyzed and resolved within the boundaries of normal science. Growth theories are not complete theories of economic development.

Economists preoccupied with questions concerning economic development do not constitute the majority. Rather than having the field of economic development occupy center stage, as normal scientific activity of the majority, the number of articles submitted to the *AER* for example, and accepted, reveal a primary focus and interest outside the realm of economic development.[34] Social status, recognition as "applause" in the form of research grants, publications, promotions, pay increases and elevation to higher levels in the hierarchy of elites among the community of economists is not usually achieved or found in developmental economics. In the social pecking order among economists we find that economists specializing in economic development usually occupy a lower rung on that academic ladder.[35] Whether as a result of a "convenience of ignorance," or whatever, though the science of economics is over two-hundred years old, "The literature of development and underdevelopment is recent."[36] The processes of economic development, while emphasized in the literature by the practitioners of extraordinary science, have never really been the overriding concern or focus of the majority of the scientific community in the discipline of economics.

The orthodox economists of the mature nations seem to argue that economic development and modernization are really problems of the LDC's and that the problems of the mature countries are essentially those of growth and not of development and modernization which have already been achieved. This empirical reality is consequently offered as a legitimate justification for normal science in economics being concerned with a theory of growth rather than development. This infers that a theory of development is a scientific concern only of the Third and Fourth Worlds. By comparison, our analysis focuses on a general theory relevant to all stages of economic development. Economic development is an ongoing process and is related to the economic problems faced by the First and Second Worlds as well as the Third and Fourth. We are not arguing that the problems of the DC's and the LDC's are the same but that an identification of the relevant problems as puzzles to be resolved by science will be dependent upon a general theory of economic development. Economic development does not stop or terminate with an industrial revolution and modernization.[37] On the contrary, as we will demonstrate in this study, economic development in the context of general culture evolution is a continuous and ongoing process of acceleration and appears in the form of an exponential paradigm.

Currently it is not only becoming more common to question the usage of growth theory to explain, identify, and resolve the problems of the LDC but also, normal science and its associated growth theory in becoming increasingly subject to question in its relevance to problems of the mature DC's.[38] Our position is that a general theory of economic development is necessary in order to correctly identify and resolve the problems faced by the DC as well as the LDC. Therefore the new conceptualization of economic phenomena which we recommend is not simply for the LDC but concerns the DC as well. Normal science in economics still views current problems such as stagflation, resource depletion, pollution and ecology, urban decay, energy control, trade balances and the international monetary system in the framework of quantitative growth theory. Actually our current problems are primarily associated with the qualitative and the structural fed by an exponential evolution of technology and culture. These problems are precisely those problems avoided by the majority of economists as intellectual puzzles outside the boundaries of their matrix. Why economists take a head-in-the-sand approach and exclude the obviously important and relevant economic problems as puzzles of their disciplinary matrix is explained by the fact that the neoclassical synthesis is the normal science of the current period. In order to include the exponential evolution of science, technology and culture and the associated problems of economic production and social organization into the forefront and boundaries of economic analysis we must consequently introduce a new disciplinary matrix as normal science in economics. Our source of contention is that a general theory of economic development is not a sub-field of economics but constitutes the overall rubric for the field of economics in general. What we are saying here is that *there is a need for a restatement of the discipline of economics, manifest in normal science, which would include both the economic as well as the social and the cultural in the context of a new disciplinary matrix focusing on a general theory of economic development.*[39]

Usually it is not our material culture which malfunctions. Bridges stand, buildings do not collapse, computers work with precision and 747's usually fly quite well without accident. The basic economic problem of malfunction and anomaly is not therefore centered in material culture but rather centers in the social organization of an ongoing and expanding material culture. It is in the science of social organization that we see the malfunctioning of material culture as overproduction, stagflation, pollution and on. The "queen of the social sciences" is just that: a science of social organization. Unfortunately, the science of economics, as a basis for policy of social organization, be it of markets, a mixed economy or more toward economic planning, has lagged behind the physical sciences which provide a production of material goods seemingly of no end.

Also economists do not primarily concern themselves with the immediate and direct problems of physical production and energy control, such puzzles are usually left to the field of applied engineering. Adam Smith told us that the social organization of markets and prices, and therefore, laissez-faire, was the best policy direction: he did not propose material improvements, or the juggling of purely economic variables, in the production of a better steam engine. Theories in economics are primarily and ultimately concerned with the social institutions, as social technics, which best serve to organize the production of goods and services. Consequently, although certainly not always explicitly stated as such, discussions by economists are ultimately in behalf of free markets and laissez-faire versus regulations and controls of a mixed economy and beyond. It is ironic that economists of normal science deny the social connection of their discipline because that is precisely what economics is about; it is a science of economic policy as social organization.

Normal science in economics as it has evolved has primarily focused on the utilization of the social institution of the market as the best policy to promote the most efficient production and distribution of goods and services. In this sense, Keynesian economics was not that revolutionary in transforming this theoretical and analytical fixation; government's function was not to become the pump but simply to prime it.[40] The social technic of the market is taken as given and fixed and the rules of the game of normal science dictate that the economist not question the market system in terms of seeking alternatives but, rather, that economists of normal science primarily concern themselves with the "puzzles" of explaining how it works. Normal science in economics is geared toward the perfection and improvement of the market system; it does not seek or promote alternatives. It is in the context of the extraordinary science of a Myrdal or Polanyi that we note and find imperfection to the extent of seeking alternative social technics of social organization. Therefore, institutional evolution and transformation is an anathema to normal science in economics. Logically it would then follow that theory, analysis, and conceptualization concern primarily the static economic variables of economic growth to the exclusion of the social and the cultural that are involved in the dynamic processes of economic development. Therefore if one seeks a theory of economic development in the context of normal science one will find a theory of economic growth.

Consequently while on the surface we seemingly have a briar patch, as a tangled mass of conflicting concepts and definitions, underneath however we find a root cause for explanation and clarification. Though the literature reveals a spectrum ranging from the simple to the complex the conceptualization held to by the majority of economists, as practitioners of normal science, is obviously not a social or cultural view of the process of economic development but it is a conceptualization of economic development in terms of the quantitative growth of economic variables. The majority of economists during the current period either explicitly or implicitly treat economic growth as the conceptual equivalent of economic development. Consequently their theories of economic development are primarily theories of economic growth and not development.

Evidence that normal science in economics teaches, as current conventional wisdom, that economic growth is the conceptual equivalent of economic development is readily available in the literature. One of the best indicators of normal science during a given period is textbook treatment.[41] In the post-WW II period Samuelson and his textbook, enunciating the neoclassical synthesis as a continuity of the evolution of normal science in economics, have clearly triumphed. In Schumpeterian terms, while Keynes functioned as the inventor (with quite a few predecessors) Samuelson served as the innovator in the overall advance of the (social) technology of economics. The "Age of Keynes" was also the age of Samuelson's classic textbook of the period.[42] While there are many variations on the same theme, and many other textbooks replicate and duplicate Samuelson's work, Samuelson clearly stands as the Mill or Marshall of our current era of normal science. Samuelson and the learning of his basic textbook treatment stand as the *sine qua non* of normal science in economics today. An individual wanting to become an economist starts with Samuelson's basic text (or a reasonable facsimile) in his apprenticeship into the profession. We learn what we are taught.

And what do we learn? In Chapter 37, "The Theory of Growth," we find an attached "APPENDIX: Modern Discussions of Development Theory."[43] The "modern" discussions of theories of development focus primarily on the "neoclassical dynamics" or the Harrod-Domar growth model. Admittedly, in that Samuelson concludes that institutional economics has turned "sterile" it would be somewhat inconsistent to discuss the modern theory of economic development as provided by the Swedish economist, the Nobel laureate, Gunnar Myrdal.[44] This is also consistent with Samuelson's assessment of culture and custom as explanation in economic development which he appropriately, at least in the context of his textbook treatment, includes under the overall rubric of "Superficial Theories of Development."[45] All this leads to a foregone conclusion to be derived from Samuelson's text: "For decades now economists have been intensely interested in economic development. While they have developed no unified theory different from the basic growth models . . . they have added some special features to these models."[46] This standard textbook treatment then provides the foundation for economic analysis as to method, tools of analysis and basic principles to be applied in the more advanced courses in the curriculum of economics. In this way then, in the process of his technical training the economist learns to exclude the social and the cultural from his analytical purview.

Given this textbook introduction, the experience of most economists, and given the fact that economists who practice normal science would be the ones most likely chosen as contributors, we would expect the same basic conceptualization to prevail in our leading encyclopedias and dictionaries. *The International Encyclopedia of the Social Sciences*, as the leading encyclopedia of the social sciences, does after all represent somewhat of a consensus view. In checking Volume IV, p. 376, and under the heading: "ECONOMIC DEVELOPMENT," the reader is recommended to "*See* ECONOMIC GROWTH *and* STAGNATION."[47] Does not economic development rank as one of the most urgent and important economic issues of our time? Yet it does not receive independent and separate treatment in the leading encyclopedia of the social sciences. The subject of economic development is treated as being synonymous with economic growth and is generally melted into the *Encyclopedia*. For example: "Closely related to economic history is the rapidly expanding field of *economic development*, which covers both the theory of growth and the more practical application to the problems of less developed areas (*see* ECONOMIC GROWTH)."[48] Basic dictionaries also give support to the view that growth is conceptualized as being synonymous with economic development.[49]

Consequently, economic development is most frequently in the literature of normal science in terms of economic growth, that is, in terms of quantitative growth factors of economic production to the exclusion of socio-cultural or "noneconomic" factors. Given this predilection how then does the economist define economic growth? In that the Keynesian matrix is the normal science of the current period, definitions of economic growth primarily employ the GNP concept in one form or other. In terms of specifically defining economic growth itself, there is somewhat of a wide spectrum of definitions, again, running from the opposite poles of the simple to the more complex. The particular conceptualization of economic growth is then usually considered to be synonymous with economic development. Specifically, in terms of defining economic growth, we have on the rudimentary side of our spectrum the definition of economic growth simply as an increase in size in terms of an increase in production, not necessarily an increase in per capita production. In other words, " . . . a larger population gets an unchanged average income . . . ," thereby implying an increased aggregate size of economic production.[50] Others draw into their definitions the distinction of rising per capita income; in this view production must increase faster than population increases to warrant the designation of economic growth.[51]

And as we move further along the spectrum in the direction of a greater complexity of the definitions, we find others, for example such as Benjamin Higgins, drawing the distinction contained in the idea of sustained growth or some degree of continued increase in per capita income as a basic criteria for economic growth.[52] Higgins basically defines economic development in terms of economic growth; whereas by comparison it is our view that development entails technological and cultural transformation. Economic growth serves to indicate the process but is not the process itself. As we shall see, in terms of the subject matter of our next chapter economic growth may take place even for extended periods of time and on a per capita basis, via replication or through applying factor inputs of better quality such as more fertile land, within the context of a given overall gestalt of technology. Therefore, given Higgins' definition and conceptualization of economic development the assumption is made that economic development is synonymous with economic growth. Our conceptualization of economic development by comparison does not assume that per capita production increases alone are representative of the processes of development, that we do not develop simply by growing, but rather that development rests upon culture change and transformation in relation to the application of advanced levels of technology. Such a process is, in our view, characterized by many indicators, such as economic growth, productivity, energy utilization, as well as the social; and consequently in this view economic growth is a manifestation, a part of the process, and not its whole, in much the same way that increased body weight is a part but not the whole of human development and maturation. To this more expanded definition of economic growth, as we have noted, some add normative criteria and such considerations would, of course, add a considerable number of conceivable definitions to those given above.[53] And finally we reach the opposite pole in terms of the more complex definitions of economic growth, such as the one offered by Simon Kuznets in his *Modern Economic Growth*, and these definitions include the element of structural changes.[54] Therefore, with the introduction of the element of structural change we enter into somewhat of a twilight zone or a grey area between the definitions specifically of economic growth and definitions of economic development, for in addition to growth in a simplified sense we now add the element of transformation, and transformation is the crux of development.

Our concern in this study is to advance a general theory of economic development. This requires an historical or long-term perspective of the evolutionary sequence of economic development, that is, a generalized or universal conceptualization of growth and development applicable to all stages or epochs or levels of culture advance. Economic development as a phenomenon is not confined to one stage or level of culture advance but is a universal characteristic of culture evolution. Consequently, if we are to generalize, our definition must be applicable to all instances of economic growth and economic development and not just to one as exemplified by the modern experience. This does not preclude defining economic growth in terms of a particular epoch but simply that to generalize about economic growth in a universal sense from the empirical evidence of one epoch, such as the modern period of industrialism, and conclude that economic growth for all times and places exhibited similar characteristics, runs counter to basic rules of logic. To generalize from one-stage characteristics of economic growth for all stages reflects the same error in logic as it would be to conclude from the experience of one green apple that all apples are green and constitutes a basic fallacy. Our desire is to conceptualize economic growth in a way applicable to all epochs. Some are not so concerned and view economic growth as starting only with the modern period, and that economic growth is defined in terms of rapid and sustained change in production per capita which is, of course, only characteristic of modern period. Our view by comparison is that growth and development had their origins in the creation of the super-organic and that the origins of culture came circa one-million plus years ago. Each stage of economic development is characterized by a particular type of growth not only in terms of particular products, the bow and arrow versus the hoe, the plow, and the automobile, but also in the rates of production increase as well as the capacity for overall size. A hoe-type culture could never achieve the production of an automobile or the rates of growth (high and sustained) or the overall GNP total which is characteristic of cultures at the level of industrialism, but this does not mean that a hoe type culture is incapable of economic growth.[55] Its growth, however, would ultimately reach a logistic ceiling assuming the constraint of a fixed technology, as the gestalt of a hoe-type culture. Development by comparison entails the application of new technology and in the process transforms the hoe-type culture to a more advanced stage. Therefore, there are many differing types of economic growth and in each particular case serve as a characteristic of a particular stage or overall gestalt of technology. A generalized view of economic growth would have to take this basic observation into account; consequently we cannot define economic growth in a generalized sense in terms of sustained and high rates of increases in per capita GNP. For such a conceptualization of economic growth would only be relevant to the period of modern economic growth.

If we include in our definition of economic growth such criteria as "sustained increases in per capita product" and "sweeping structural changes" we are clearly defining economic growth as it is characterized by the modern period; we are looking at a particular type of economic growth which is a characteristic of and serves to distinguish the modern period marked by the overall technological gestalt of industrialism.[56] Therefore those who define economic growth in terms of sustained increases in per capita income, are stating that economic growth started circa mid-eighteenth century since it is only during the epoch of industrialism that economic growth took on these specific characteristics. However, if such a definition of economic growth is used in a general sense, we are by definition stating that economic growth did not take place prior to the eighteenth century but such a position is belied by the historical evidence of culture accumulation. A certain type of economic growth, modern economic growth, was ushered in via industrialism but economic growth in a universal sense is a cumulative characteristic of man's long historical past. Kuznets clearly draws this distinction but others do not and use the "high" and "sustained" and other criteria of modern economic growth in their definitions of economic growth as a generalized conceptualization and apparently apply it to all epochs.[57] This is not always explicitly stated but definitely implied by those who equate economic growth to economic development. It is no wonder then that we nurture a briar patch.

If we pursue such mental gymnastics in our definition of economic growth we are left in an awkward position: countries must experience economic growth to reach the take-off which then signals the start of sustained economic growth, but by definition we cannot have economic growth prior to the take-off since by definition economic growth entails sustained increases of product per capita and at high rates. For if it is assumed that underdeveloped or developing countries are in the phase of premodern growth they have as yet to achieve sustained growth. Therefore, sustained growth cannot as yet be characteristic of their economic growth at the current stage of their economic development. Evidence, however, bears out the fact that the developing countries are still growing, nonetheless, and hopefully may even be experiencing economic development.[58] Therefore our definition to be applicable and relevant to the developing countries should be toward the pole of simplicity and not restricted by criteria only applicable to the modern period. Certainly as a culture passes from a hunting and gathering situation to one of a neolithic orientation it has experienced economic development, or from the feudal type of social organization to that of merchant capitalism, and in the process it need not achieve "sustained" rates of economic growth. Such sustained growth is characteristic of modern industrialism. To say that economic development and growth only start with industrialism would be the equivalent of saying that biological evolution (development) only started with Homo sapiens.

Clearly then, our definition of economic growth, if historical perspective is desired, must be very broad in nature and in the direction of simplicity rather than complexity. "To be applicable to a number of economic epochs, economic growth might perhaps be defined as a sustained increase in population attained without a perceptible lowering of per capita product, i.e., in combination with either stability or rise in per capita product."[59]

Thus far, we have noted that a review of the literature indicates that economic growth is predominantly treated in normal science as being synonymous with economic development. But economic development as an evolutionary process entails movement from the primitive to the more advanced; it entails structural change and transformation. Economic growth is not just a phenomenon of the modern period but requires an interepochal conceptualization in historical perspective. Consequently, we have chosen the definition of economic growth most amenable to an interepochal or universal type of analysis.

We now confront a basic question: given economic growth, as so defined, is such economic growth synonymous with economic development as normal science in economics would lead us to believe? Do we experience economic development simply by growing? Or conversely can we have economic growth and little or no development? A basic position underlying this study is that economic growth on a long-term exponential continuum is a function of economic development. This is not to infer that growth and development are unrelated, on the contrary, in the context of cumulative and circular causation we will later in this study show that growth promotes development and development in turn promotes growth. However, and this is the point, economic growth, by itself, and without development will ultimately produce stagnation and appear as a growth curve in the form of the logistic or Gompertz configuration unless continuously fed and transformed by technological change and advance. In the realities of the empirical world can we find cultures experiencing economic growth and, at the same time, no development, and thereby give credence and support to our theoretical position? If this proves to be correct we can conclude that economic growth is not synonymous with development. And if this is correct, it then follows that theories of economic growth are not theories of development?

REFERENCES

[1]Actually we do not refer here to all of culture in a complete sense but to all the technics of social organization and economic production which collectively, and as a gestalt, comprise the "core of culture." It is the advance of the "core of culture" which is relevant to the processes of economic development. In later chapters we will clarify the distinction between the "core of culture." and culture. The "core of culture" is nonetheless a culture concept rather than cultural and consequently based upon thc Tylor conceptualization.

[2]Paul Streeten, "An Institutional Critique of Development Concepts," in *The Frontiers of Development Studies* (New York: John Wiley and Sons, 1972), pp. 117-128, and also, "A Critique of the 'Capital/Output Ratio' and its Application to Economic Planning," pp. 71-116. "It is not enough to point to biases, particularly if they are so plain. The interesting question is, how is it that they have such a strong grip on thought, in spite of their obvious faults." p. 59. On the sociology of knowledge note also, Gunnar Myrdal, *Asian Drama.* (New York: Pantheon, 1968), 3 Vols,, "The Beam in Our Eyes," Vol. I, pp. 1-47, and (Streeten) Appendix 3, Vol. III, pp.1941-2004. This of course leads us to T.S. Kuhn and the history of science and the smaller field of the sociology of knowledge currently called the sociology of science, being led by Robert K. Merton, *The Sociology of Science* (Chicago: University of Chicago Press, 1973), ed., Norman W. Storer; and also, S.B. Barnes and R.G.A. Dolby, "The Scientific Ethos: A deviant viewpoint," *European Journal of Sociology* 11 (1970), pp. 3-25.

[3]"No precise definition of development exists and there are many, sometimes conflicting, views of what is meant by the term." Kathryn Morton and Peter Tulloch *Trade and Developing Countries* (New

York: John Wiley and Sons, 1977), p. 13. Daniel R. Fusfeld, "Development of Economic Institutions" *Journal of Economic Issues* 9 (December 1977), pp. 743-784, ". . . there is no consensus among scholars about the meaning of those terms," p. 744. We have already noted this point, "Probably no technical term has been used by professional economists of this generation as enthusiastically (and ambiguously) as the term 'economic growth.'" p 313, Fritz Karl Mann, "Institutionalism and American Economic Theory: A Case of Interpretation," pp. 307-323, *Kyklos*, 13 (1960). And, to this we add our general theme concerning the importance of conceptualization, "It is important to select a definition, because the methods of achieving growth, variously defined, may differ, and the pros and cons of growth depend upon the choice of definitions." *The Promise of Economic Growth* (Washington, D.C.: Chamber of Commerce of the United States, 1960), p. 6.

[4]*The International Economics of Development* (New York: Harper and Row, 1968), and *International Trade and Development* (New York: Harper and Row, 1963) while the intellectual itinerary was scheduled, ex ante, for a dynamic passage, the destination ex poste, is that of comparative statics.

[5]"We can now extend the analysis to development problems by first interpreting a country's development in terms of outward shifts in its production frontier." p. 22 in G.M. Meier (1968) and p. 20 in G.M. Meier (1963) of the previous footnote.

[6]Dudley Dillard, "Revolutions in Economic Theory" *Southern Economic Journal* 44 (April 1948), pp. 705-724, speaks in terms of five basic revolutions, though not necessarily "revolutions" as used in the Kuhnian framework.

[7]Predictable in the sense of "simultaneous inventions" as noted by W.F. Ogburn and the "singletons and multiples" of R.K. Merton. On Cassel in relation to the post-WW II growth theories note: Gunnar Myrdal, *Against the Stream* (New York: Panteon Books, 1973) pp. 182-183, and the *Asian Drama*, Vol. III, pp. 1969, 3. Keynesian economics itself was predictable in that it also had many predecessors, for example, note: George R. Feiwel, *The Intellectual Capital of Michal Kalecki* (Knoxville: The University of Tennessee Press, 1975). Also, W.F. Ogburn and D.S. Thomas, "Are Inventions Inevitable?," *Political Science Quarterly* 37 (March 1922), pp. 83-98; William F. Ogburn, *Social Change* (New York: The Viking Press, 1950), pp. 90-102; and R.K. Merton, *Sociology of Science*, pp. 343-382.

[8]These basic distinctions form a general outline of the material covered in Louis Jacques Zimmerman's, *Poor Lands, Rich Lands: The Widening Gap* (New York: The Random House, 1965), pp. 19-20. Also, Zimmerman is not alone in associating progress with development, note: A.J. Youngson, *Possibilities of Economic Progress* (Cambridge: Cambridge University Press, 1959), pp. 3-23; and Colin Clark, *Conditions of Economic Progress* (London: Macmillan and Co., 1957); Norman S. Buchanan and Howard S. Ellis, *Approaches to Economic*

Development (New York: The Twentieth Century Fund, 1955), pp. 119-25; H.J. Habakkuk, "The Historical Experience on the Basic Conditions of Economic Progress," (from Leon H. Dupriez, *Economic Progress*) in Malcolm E. Falkus (Ed.), *Readings in the History of Economic Growth* (Nairobi: Oxford University Press, 1968), pp. 33-48. "Studies of this kind inevitably suggest a simple idea of development, equating it with growth and progress. The three concepts are not clearly distinguished in economic writing." Raymond Aron, *The Industrial Society* (New York: Frederick A. Praeger, 1967), p. 10. And also, J.B. Bury, *The Idea of Progress* (New York: The Macmillan Co., 1932), and Charles Van Doren, *The Idea of Progress* (New York: Frederick A. Praeger, 1967); and, Werner Hochwald, "The Idea of Progress: A Review Article," *Journal of Economic Issues* 7 (March 1973) pp. 47-59. And, Peter Lengyel, *Approaches to the Science of Socio-Economic Development* (Paris: UNESCO, 1971), "Such attempts can in fact not lead to much beyond impressions or crude indexes, made up of figures which are no more than arbitrary evaluations." pp. 14-15.

[9]Michael P. Todaro, *Economic Development in the Third World* (New York: Langman Inc., 1957), p. 95.

[10]Todaro, *Third World*, pp. 94-126; Gunnar Myrdal "Equity and Growth, "*World Development* 1 (November 1973), pp. 43-47; and "Growth and Social Justice," *World Development* 1 (March/April 1973), pp. 119-120.

[11]On this alternative index, note: Overseas Development Council, *The United States and World Development* (New York: Praeger 1977), pp. 147-179.

[12]Note: Zimmerman, *Poor Lands, Rich Lands,* where he utilizes the Lorenz curve analysis and shows the world-wide widening gap for the years 1900-1960. Also note: Irma Adelman and Cynthia Taft Morris, *Economic Growth and Social Equity in Developing Countries* (Stanford: Stanford University Press, 1973), in which the authors suggest that optimistic attitudes of greater income equality with growth ". . . has no basis in fact." p. 186, and "The frightening implication of the present work is that hundreds of millions of desperately poor people throughout the world have been hurt rather than helped by economic development." p. 193.

[13]This basic distinction occurs frequently in the literature: Charles P. Kindleberger, *Economic Development* (New York: McGraw-Hill Book Company, 1965), pp. 3, 15; Everett E. Hagen, *The Economics of Development* (Illinois: Richard D. Irwin, 1968), p. 29; Howard S. Ellis (Ed.), *Economic Development for Latin America* (London: Macmillan and Co., 1962), pp. 110-11; Robert W. Clower, et al., *Growth Without Development* (Evanston: Northwestern University Press, 1966); Ronald A. Shearer, "The Concept of Economic Growth," *Kykols* 14 (1961), pp. 497-532; Kenneth E. Boulding, "Toward a General Theory of Growth," *Canadian Journal of Economics and Political Science*

Vol. 19 (August 1953), pp. 326-40, p. 326; Barry E. Supple (ed.), *The Experience of Economic Growth* (New York: Random House, 1963), pp. 11-12; Benjamin Higgins, *Economic Development* (New York: W.W. Norton and Company, 1968), p. 106; Robert A. Solo, *Economic Organization and Social Systems* (New York: The Bobbs-Merrill Company, 1967), p. 358; Joesph Spengler, "Social Evolution and the Theory of Economic Development," in Herbert R. Barringer (ed.), *Social Change in Developing Areas* (Cambridge: Schenkman Publishing Company, 1965), p. 244; Roberto de Oliveira Campos, *Reflections on Latin American Development* (Austin: University of Texas Press, 1967), p. 68; Report by the Secretary General, *The United Nations Development Decade: Proposals for Action* (New York; United Nations, 1962), pp. 2-3; and also Salvatore Schiavo-Campo and Hans W. Singer, *Perspectives of Economic Development* (Boston: Houghton Mifflin Company, 1970), a distinction which constitutes a general theme of their book, pp. 3-5, 17; and Myrdal, *Against the Stream*, pp. 189-192; and Philip A. Klein, "An Institutionalist View of Development Economics," *Journal of Economic Issues* 9 (December 1977), pp. 785-807, pp. 787-789. We will return to this very important issue, the basic *qualitative* versus *quantitative* distinction, in the course of our analysis.

[14]Bert F. Hoselitz, *Theories of Economic Growth* (New York: The Free Press, 1960), pp. 193-238; Gerald M.Meier, *Leading Issues in Economic Development* (New York: Oxford Unversity Press, 1970), pp. 92-120, especially, 119-120.

[15]This is analogous to saying that if we are to reach the moon we must use rockets, using rockets per se however will not necessarily guarantee a successful moon landing. The use of a stages' approach will not in itself serve as a sufficient guarantee of a science of economic development but a general theory of economic development once achieved will contain a stages of economic development methodology as a necessary and integral part of the overall theoretical framework.

[16]Marshall D. Sahlins and Elman R. Service, eds., *Evolution and Culture* (Ann Arbor: The University of Michigan Press, 1960), note pp. ix-x, of foreword by Leslie A. White and Sahlins, pp. 12-44, and on Marx, p. 31. "General culture evolution is the successive emergence of new levels of all-around development." p. 28. General evolution fits neatly into the paradigm of logistic surges leading to the overall exponential. A paradigm relevant to general biological evolution, general evolution of transportation technics as well as many other phenomena, including general culture evolution. A stages' methodology is relevant to general culture evolution but not necessarily to specific. We know that, historically, while man's culture in general as a world-wide view has experienced metamorphosis and transformation that this process need not apply to a specific culture in its evolution.

[17]Even though economists may recognize "noneconomic" factors there is a tendency to disengage on the grounds of ignorance under the assumption that our current tools of analysis are inadequate to deal with the complexities of socio-cultural phenomena. Lionel Robbins, "The Dynamics of Capitalism," *Economica* 6 (March 1926), pp. 31-39, notes that, "The causes of material progress, equally with the causes of intellectual progress, interact in so complex a manner that scientific generalizations about them are a matter of the utmost difficulty. We neither possess the knowledge nor the capacity to elaborate laws of progress. . . . It is no reproach to economists that they have been content to leave the devising of sweeping generalisations to poets metaphysicians and amateur historians." p. 32, and cited by William L. Lockwood, *The Economic Development of Japan* (Princeton: Princeton University Press, 1954), pp. 503, 588; and on the same point, Conferences on Comparative Economic Growth and Structure, *The Comparative Study of Economic Growth and Structure* (New York: National Bureau of Economic Research, 1959), "Economic growth, as every serious student knows is closely associated with many noneconomic factors . . . these noneconomic factors cannot be ignored in studying economic growth." and yet within the same paragraph, "Our ignorance of the purely or predominantly economic aspects of economic development is still so great that the problem of integrating economic with noneconomic factors cannot yet be attacked with reasonable expectation of success." p. 4. Everett E. Hagen notes this basic problem in his "Turning Parameters into Variables in the Theory of Economic Growth," *The American Economic Review* 50 (May 1960), pp. 623-628. "Noneconomic factor must enter fully into the theoretical system as variables, with causal relationships flowing to as well from them." p. 623, ". . . A number of economists who are students of economic growth make generous reference to the importance of noneconomic factors," and, ". . . Having mentioned noneconomic factors they then proceed to ignore them and discuss development as though only economic factors bring it about." pp. 624, 625. For a citation of this reference as well as further discussion see Myrdal, vol. 3, pp. 1904, 1903-1912.

[18]Gunnar Myrdal, "What is Development?, "*Journal of Economic Issues* 8 (December 1974); pp.729-736, p. 729. This is the basic definition which Myrdal also uses in the *Asian Drama* and elsewhere in his prolific contributions to the literature. And what better covers the "entire social system" than Tylor's omnibus concept known as culture? But of course social systems can be dealt with in a variety of ways, for example: Peter Lengyel, *Approaches to The Science of Socio-Economic Development* (Paris: Unesco, 1971), "Social Systems and Cultural Dynamics," pp, 207-268, and on the references could go. Todaro, *Economic Development*, pp. 13-16, as a recent work in development economics also seems to endorse Myrdal's conceptualization, ". . . *development economics must be concerned . . . major economic, institu-*

tional and social transformation of entire societies in the shortest possible time.", p. 15

[19]For an optimistic assessment in this direction note Philip A. Klein, "An Institutionalist View of Development Economics," " . . . in the field of development economics the victory has been so complete that many economists fail to realize it. . ." p. 785. It should be noted that Klein's discussions concern the subdiscipline of development economics, as a part, whereas our concern is the entire discipline of economics as a whole, "What we have been suggesting is that in this field mainstream economists are institutional economists." p. 800.

[20]On the basic literature note: Thomas S. Kuhn, *The Structure of Scientific Revolutions* (Chicago: University of Chicago Press, 1970); Imre Lakatos, and Alan Musgrave, eds., *Criticism and the Growth of Knowledge* (Cambridge: The University Press, 1970) especially pp. 1-24, 231-278; and, Frederick Suppe, ed., *The Structure of Scientific Theories* (Urbana: The University of Illinois Press, 1974) especially pp. 135-151, 459-482. And although Kuhn primarily related his theoretical framework to the physical sciences many articles have appeared in recent years relating *The Structure of Scientific Revolution* to the evolution of the science of economics.

[21]On the concept "normal science" note, Kuhn *Scientific Revolutions*, pp. 23-42, 135-42; Lakatos, *Criticism*, pp. 242, 249; Suppe, *Scientific Theories*, p. 138.

[22]Originally Kuhn identified normal science by the concept "paradigm", however admitting to "Having lost control of the word . . .," Lakatos *Criticism*, p. 272, and since the term ". . . points to a central philosophical aspect of the book. . ." p. 234, and in order to overcome the confusion and ambiguities of the term paradigm, Kuhn decided ". . . to replace it with the phrase disciplinary matrix." Suppe, *Scientific Theories*, p. 463. Currently, normal science is characterized by the disciplinary matrix in dominance, p. 142. On the "gestalt switch" see Kuhn, *Scientific Revolutions*, pp. 111-135; and Benjamin Ward *What's Wrong with Economics*? (New York: Basic Books, 1972), pp. 95-107.

[23]In the history of economics, Keynes represented extraordinary science during the 1930's. During the post-WW II period Keynesian economics made the transition to normal science. In the literature the majority of articles dealing with the subject conclude that in the history of economics there has been at least one Kuhnian revolution; the example given is that of the Keynesian revolution.

[24]To our view Kuhn represents a transition, a bridge, from the history of science to that of the sociology of knowledge. Kuhn introduces a "sociological base" as a "community" of scientists but his basic work *The Structure of Scientific Revolutions* is not really a study of the sociology of knowledge. It is in the field of the sociology of science, as a subset of the sociology of knowledge, that we find science treated as a social institution. On this note R.K. Merton, *The Sociology of Science*; and Barnes and Dolby, "The Scientific Ethos," "The

substance of the approach is that science is treated as a social institution. . . .", p. 3. And also, Simon Kuznets, *Economic Growth of Nations* (Cambridge: Harvard University Press, 1971), ". . . the tremendous increase in the stock of useful knowledge, much of it traceable to growth of *science viewed as a social institution* devoted to the production of new tested and potentially useful knowledge." (italics added), p. 307.

[25]What constitutes a paradigm of general culture evolution (Ogburn and Hart) is also the paradigm of the evolution of science.

[26]Recall the response of economists concerning the wisdom of the Hawley-Smoot Tariff and the correspondence with President Hoover, note F.W. Taussig, "The Tariff Act of 1930," *The Quarterly Journal of Economics* 45 (November 1930), pp. 1-21, for mainstream analysis, and, Asher Isaacs, *International Trade: Tariff and Commercial Policies* (Chicago: Richard D. Irwin, 1948), for the consensus view of economists involving 1028 signatures and 46 states and 179 colleges, pp. 232-34.

[27]". . . Institutionalism withered away as an effective counter-force in economics." Paul A. Samuelson *Economics* (New York: McGraw-Hill Book Company, 1976), p. 847. And also Myrdal *Against the Stream*, what Kuhn calls normal science Myrdal refers to as mainstream or "establishment economics." pp. 1-3, and the tendency is for establishment economists to treat practitioners of the social and the cultural (the Myrdals and Galbraiths) as sociologists or journalists, pp. 14-15.

[28]On T.S. Kuhn and "puzzles" note, *Criticism*, pp. 1, 5.

[29]On the problems of overspecialization note, K. William Kapp, *Toward a Science of Man in Society* (The Hague: Martinus Nijhoff, 1961); and Sahlins and Service, *Evolution and Culture*, "The Law of Evolutionary Potential," pp. 93-122.

[30]Leo Rogin, *The Meaning and Validity of Economic Theory* (New York: Harper and Brothers, 1956); and, Dillard, "Revolutions in Economic Theory." ". . . the general finding is that the hypothesis is overwhelmingly confirmed." p. 706.

[31]There are many examples in the literature in which authors draw the distinction that economic growth is the problem of the mature countries and that economic development applies to the underdeveloped countries. "The more developed they become, the more relevant and useful does economic analysis become and the more effective are purely economic policies. Indeed for the highest subset, development economics merges into growth economics." George Dalton, "Economics, Economic Development and Economic Anthropology," *Journal of Economic Issues* 2 (June 1968), pp. 173-86, p. 179. The Harrod-Domar model extended the short-run analysis of Keynes into the long-run, note Gerald M. Meier and Robert E. Baldwin *Economic Development* (New York: John Wiley and Sons, 1959), pp. 100-118.

[32]Benjamin Higgins *Economic Development* (New York: W.W. Norton, 1968), p. 113. Even though the literature reveals reservation in terms of using growth theory as of economic development, this, of course, need not be the majority view nor need individual defer from so doing. "Strangely enough, however, the theory has found its principal field of application in the planning of development for underdeveloped countries." Albert O. Hirschman, *The Strategy of Economic Development* (New Haven: Yale University Press, 1963), p. 31, and also, in line with our overall discussion, "Growth Models and Development Processes," pp. 29-49; "This emphasis on the growth phenomenon per se implies that at least in the first instance the economist approaches the problem of economic development within the context of a theory of economic growth." Shearer, "The Concept of Economic Growth," p. 500. The literature is replete with examples which support the view of using growth theory as theory for economic development.

[33]The view of P.A. Klein, "An Institutional View of Development Economics," among others.

[34]"Report of the Managing Editor for the Year Ending December 1970," *American Economic Review* 61 (May 1971), p. 498; 64 (May 1974) p. 477; 65 (May 1975), p. 476; 66 (May 1976), p. 497; 67 (February 1977) p. 450. It should be noted that economic development is included in the overall classification of "Economic Growth; Development; Planning, fluctuations," which overall as a group usually scores quite low, let alone if the data were broken down further, specifically of economic development.

[35]Benjamin Ward, "What's Wrong with Economics?," p. 10.

[36]Anthony R. de Souza and Philip W. Porter, *The Underdevelopment and Modernization of the Third World*, Resource Paper No. 28 (Washington D.C.: Association of American Geographers, 1974), p. 5. And B. Higgins, ". . . the concentration of scientific interest in 'development' is fairly recent.," p. 9 in Lengyel, *Approaches to the Science*.

[37]According to Everett E. Hagen, *The Economics of Development* (Homewood: Richard D. Irwin, 1968), "There are less developed countries and more developed countries. But there are no developed countries. For there is no identifiable end point to the process of development. Development—that is, increase in productivity—may go on forever." p. 5, and we agree. Note also, P.A. Klein "An Institutionalist View of Development Economics," In that ". . . 'growth, development and evolution' are characteristic of *all* economies—not just those of the Third World". p. 802.

[38]Todaro, *The Third World*, pp. 10-13, and footnotes 4,5,7 and 8, p. 17, for references to some of the standard literature on the issue of the current crisis of economic theory and policy and "The limited relevance of 'traditional' theory". This literature is quite large and includes the more radical URPE as well as the more moderate institutional school and on into the realm of normal science itself. John G.

Gurley "The State of Political Economics," *The American Economic Review* 61 (May 1971), pp. 53-62, "... the assumptions and methods of economics are being challenged, almost as never before . . ." p. 53; John Hicks, *The Crisis in Keynesian Economics* (New York: Basic Books, 1975); Joan Robinson" . . . the evident bankruptcy of economic theory which for the second time has nothing to say on the questions that, to everyone except economists, appear to be most in need of an answer.", "The Second Crisis of Economic Theory," *American Economic Review* 62 (May 1972), pp. 1-10, p. 10; Allan G. Gruchy, *Contemporary Economic Thought* (Clifton: Augustus M. Kelley, 1972), "... increasingly irrelevant to the major issues of our times," pp. 1, v; and, E. H. Phelps Brown, "The Underdevelopment of Economics," *Economic Journal* 82 (March 1972), pp. 1-10, "... contributed so little toward the soultion of current problems . . ." p. 10. Perhaps one of the better discussions on the point being made here is found in Kurt Martin and John Knapp, eds., *The Teaching of Development Economics* (London: Frank Cass and Co., 1967), especially Dudley Seers, "The Limitations of the Special Case,' pp. 1-27.

[39]As Daniel Fusfeld notes, "Post-Post Keynes: A Shattered Synthesis," *Saturday Review* 55 (January 22, 1972), pp. 36-39, "The problems of the present indicate the path to the future. A reconstruction of economics—a new synthesis and a new paradigm is in order." p. 39. Keynesian economics is representative of a limited and static theory of economic growth whereas what is necessary to resolve and identify our current prablems is a more general theory of development as a new view of economic phenomena. John K. Galbraith does represent that "path to the future" and provides not simply static growth theory but "The General Theory of Advanced Development" *Economics and the Public Purpose* (Boston: Houghton Mifflin Company, 1973), pp. 38-51, to include the dynamics of technological change and economic evolution.

[40]"Everything then functioned very much as before but at a higher level of output, income and employment. The market remained as in the textbooks. . . . The neoclassical ideas escaped fundamental change. So viewed the Keynesian Revolution was a small revolution." Galbraith, *Economics and the Public Purpose*, p. 189.

[41]What in the past Mill and Marshall presented as the "principles" to be learned has been provided by Samuelson in the present. A reviewer of Marshall's *Principles of Economics*, noted that the work, ". . . 'will probably become for the present generation what Mill's *Principles* was for the last'" Quoted in John Maynard Keynes, *Essays in Biography* (New York: W.W. North and Company, 1963), p. 181 and cited by Dillard, "Revolutions in Economic Theory," p. 710. However, Samuelson's principles may not be that general, Dudley Seers notes: "The title of Samuelson's text should not be 'Economics' but 'The Economics of the United States in the 20th Century.' p. 16, "The Limitations of the Special Case."

[42]Others of course in addition to Samuelson were also helpful

in the innovation of Keynesian economics. For example note: John Kenneth Galbraith, "How Keynes Came to America,'. *A Contemporary Guide to Economics, Peace and Laughter* (Boston: Houghton Mifflin Company, 1971), pp. 43-59.

[43] Paul A. Samuelson, *Economics* (New York: McGraw-Hill Book Company, 1976), pp. 746-77.

[44]It is significant that Gunnar Myrdal as the leading economic theorist of economic development is ignored and not cited in the basic textbook treatment offered by the chief practitioner of normal science.

[45]Samuelson, *Economics*, pp. 764-766, and for a statement indicating the opposite polarity from that of a Gunnar Myrdal, note: "But putting stress on these noneconomic factors does not solve the problem of *explanation*." p. 765.

[46]Samuelson, *Economics*, p. 767.

[47]David L. Sills, ed., *International Encyclopedia of the Social Sciences* (New York. The Macmillan Company and the Free Press, 1968), 17 Volumes. The section dealing with economic growth, pp. 395-429 basically uses the concepts of growth and development as being interchangeable. And again, "The attempt to formulate a theory of growth applicable to such countries essentially may be viewed as another strand from the same basic framework of inquiry identified here as the post-Keynesian theory of growth."
(Gustav Ranis), pp. 414-415.

[48]*International Encyclopedia*, Vol. 4, p. 483. And though the fields of economic history and economic development are indeed closely related the tendency of the "new economic historians," using orthodox theory, is to view economic history from the vantage of growth rather than development. This also gives support to our contention that normal science in economics tends to view growth as the equivalent of economic development.

[49]Julius Gould and William L. Kolb, eds., *Dictionary of the Social Sciences* (New York: The Free Press of Glencoe, 1964), UNESCO, "*Economic Development* and *economic progress* are widely used synonymously with *economic growth* . . ." p. 221; others, implying that the terms are synonymous, ignore the concept economic development and simply define economic growth: J.L. Hanson, *A Dictionary of Economics and Commerce* (London: MacDonald and Evans Ltd., 1974); *The McGraw-Hill Dictionary of Modern Economics* (New York: McGraw-Hill Book Company, 1973); Christine Ammer and Dean S. Ammer, *Dictionary of Business and Economics* (New York: The Free Press, 1977); and this is also reflected in basic texts, Meier and Baldwin *Economic Development*, ". . . they are in essence synoymous." p. 2; and titles of standard works such as Rostow's which really represents a "stages of economic development" though the title is noted as *The Stages of Economic Growth*. To conceptualize economic development as economic growth is consistent with normal science as it has evolved since the

days of Adam Smith, note Lionel Robbins, *The Theory of Economic Development in the History of Economic Thought* (London: Macmillan and Co., 1968), ". . . I shall use it in relation to movements in real income per head. . ." pp. 3-5.

[50]For example: Norman S. Buchanan and Howard S. Ellis, *Approaches to Economic Development* (NewYork: The Twentieth Century Fund, 1955), p. 22; Zimmerman, *Poor Lands Rich Lands: the Widening Gap* pp. 19, 72 ff.; Meier and Baldwin, *Economic Development*, pp. 2-3; Kuzents, *Modern Economic Growth* p. 30, and Six Lectures on Economic Growth (Illinois: The Press of Glencoe, 1959), pp. 13-14. (We refer here to Kuznets' interepochal definition of economic growth and not his definition for "*modern* economic growth" as given in *Modern Economic Growth*, p. 1.)

[51]For example: Hagen, *The Economics of Development* p. 29; W. Arthur Lewis, *The Theory of Economic Growth* (Illinois: Richard D. Irwin, 1955), pp. 9-10; W.W. Rostow, *The Stages of Economic Growth* (Cambridge: Cambridge University Press, (1960) p. 69, *The Process of Economic growth* (Oxford: Oxford University Press, 1960), footnote No. 3, p. 81; Paul A. Baran, *The Political Economy of Growth* (New York: Monthly Review Press, 1967), p. 18. In this latter case it is interesting to note the agreement, in terms of treating growth as being synonymous with economic development, between a Marxist and the consensus opinion of the orthodoxy of anti-Marxists or non-Marxists. In all fairness, Baran does give a somewhat more general meaning to economic development; for example, his view on transformation (p. 3). But the essence of his definition of economic development is in terms of economic growth; in fact, he uses the two concepts interchangeably.

[52]See Higgins, *Economic Development*, p. 147; and also, Harold F. Williamson and John A. Buttrick, eds., *Economic Development* (Englewood Cliffs: Prentice-Hall, 1954), p. 7. This conceptualization of growth is also used interchangeably with development and prevails in the *International Encyclopedia*, especially pp. 395-408, Vol. 4, written by Richard A. Easterlin leaning heavily on Kuznets' definition in *Modern Economic Growth*, p. 1.

[53]We have already referred to some of this literature but in addition note: Eugene Staley, *The Future of Underdeveloped Countries* (New York: Harper and Row 1961), pp. 94-95; Wendell C. Gordon, *International Trade: Goods, People and Ideas* (New York: Alfred A. Knopf, 1958), p. 564; Peter T. Bauer and Basil S. Yamey, *The Economics of Underdeveloped Countries* (Chicago: The University of Chicago Press, 1965), p. 1; on these welfare considerations also note: Shearer, "The Concept of Economic Growth," pp. 507 ff.

[54]"We identify the economic growth of nations as a sustained increase in per capita or per worker product, most often accompanied by an increase in population and usually by sweeping structural changes." p. 1. This is a specific difinition for modern economic growth

taking place (circa) in the eighteenth century, and forward, for the mature countries achieving the stage of industrialism.

[55]"VIEWED IN THE BROAD SWEEP OF HUMAN HISTORY, Improvements in technology and resulting rise in per capita income have always been occurring everywhere." Everett E. Hagen, *On the Theory of Social Change* (Homewood: The Dorsey Press, 1962), p. 10. Nonetheless, Hagen refers to *economic growth* as the growth of the 18th and 19th centuries. Consequently what we refer to as "modern" economic growth, Hagen and others, refer to simply as economic growth.

[56]Such a view of economic growth is not characteristic of all nations today but only those nations which have entered the epoch of modern economic growth, i.e., industrialism. Support for this position is, of course, found in the works of Simon Kuznets culminating in his *Modern Economic Growth*, and, as we have noted, constitutes a part of his basic definition of modern economic growth, the phrase, ". . . a sustained increase in per capita . . ." This position is fairly well accepted in the literature, for example: Rostow's analysis as a case in point: "In a decade or two both the basic structure of the economy and the social and political structure of the society are transformed in such a way that a steady rate of growth can be thereafter regularly sustained." *The Stages of Economic Growth*, pp. 8-9. Therefore "regularly sustained" growth is the result of growth and development and not a characteristic of growth in a universal or generalized sense. It is a characteristic of the modern period: Phyllis Deane; "Long Term Trends in World Economic Growth," *Malayan Economic Review* XI (Oct. 1961), pp. 14-26.

[57]As we have already noted: Kuznets, *Modern Economic Growth*, pp. 1, 20. Others, as we have noted, use the basic elements of modern economic growth and apply this to their definition which is then equated to economic development and consequently imply a universality of application which is unwarranted. To include "sustained" and other criteria of modern economic growth in a definition is warranted (this is perfectly legitimate) if one desires to define modern economic growth or the stage or epoch of industrialism, but not for a universal or interepochal treatment of the concept. The definition offered by Kuznets (p. 20) excludes "sustained," "structural" or even "per capita" increases as necessary criteria of economic growth conceptually applicable to historical generalizations including a number of epochs.

[58]On the evidence that economic growth is currently taking place in the development world note: Maddison, *Economic Progress and Policy in Developing Countries*, especially Chapter I, and p. 269; also Lester B. Pearson, *Partners in Development* (New York: Praeger Publisher, 1969), pp. 23-52, and 358 ff; and also, Everett Hagen, *The Economics of Development* (Homewood: Richard D. Irwin, 1975) p. 20. For a less sanguine view on the "Development Decade," though still recognizing the fact that growth (however weak) is taking place in the

underdeveloped world, cf., Salvatore Schiavo-Campo and Hans W. Singer, *Perspectives of Economic Development* (Boston: Houghton Mifflin Company, 1970), pp. 137-38. Is such growth, however, indicative of economic development? Note for example Robert d'A. Shaw, *Rethinking Economic Development*, Headline Series, No. 208 (New York: Foreign Policy Association, 1971), "Disillusionment with the Decade of Development," pp. 3-15.

[59]Kuznets, *Modern Economic Growth*, p. 20.

CHAPTER III

Economic Growth and No Development

We have noted that practitioners of normal science in economics tend to treat growth and development as conceptual equivalents. Consequently, theories of growth are used as substitutes for theories of economic development. However, if a social aggregate used to delineate culture grows, will such growth also always be indicative of its development? In short, if a culture grows will it also develop as normal science leads to believe? If empirical reality indicates that a social aggregate does not necessarily develop simply by growing, this would also indicate that economic growth and development are not conceptual equivalents. Let us first note an analogy to the biological.

Growth not only takes place in terms of economic and social aggregates but is the basic characteristic of "almost all objects of human study"; analogies are often drawn to the biological.[1] "In a strict sense . . . "whereas *growth* might be defined as " . . . an increase in the amount of the organism's living matter or protoplasm . . . " *development* might be defined as the " . . . formation of new and complex structures out of the undifferentiated and apparently simple . . ."[2] If, for example, as a hypothetical case we were to take a six-month-old baby and increase the size of all his cells and the protoplasm therein, proportionately (a constant cost case), the result would be proportionate growth in terms of increased size but not a change in terms of transformation associated with development.[3] And if that were all, at the end of a decade of such growth we would simply have a very large baby; however, he would still be a baby and as such still be illiterate, unable to walk, and oblivious to all that maturation and development would bring.

Similarly, in the case of economic and social aggregates, though they may grow, they need not develop. Unfortunately, today many underdeveloped regions of the world, though they have grown and, as we have noted, are growing still further, are still in the baby stage of development. As the result of replication and duplication they have vast stores of illiteracy; they are big in size and have large populations and are getting bigger. However, they have not as yet experienced the take-off and drive to maturity into the industrialism of modernity. Recommending that they simply experience an increase in production (a view of the problem in terms of economic growth), even if on a per capita basis, which really says produce the same only more of it, does not really solve their problem of development which is essentially one of culture transformation and advance.[4] This chapter is directed toward the world of empirical reality to demonstrate that there can be economic growth and no development.

There are those who perhaps might state the converse. Hagen, for example, states: "Rise in per capita income is always accompanied by change in economic and social structure. There is no economic growth without some economic development."[5] Such a conclusion depends, of course, upon the definitions and concepts used in drawing the conclusion. Such a conclusion is warranted if one assumes economic growth to be of the nature of "indefinitely continuing growth" which would require therefore "continuing technical progress" (our economic development and noted by Hagen, p. 180). If, however, one refers to economic growth as "... merely to rise in per capita income ... "(Hagen, p. 29), then, to our view, such growth need not always entail economic development.

We will attempt later in our study to argue theoretically, as opposed to the simple empirical references of this chapter, that economic growth can take place, and for long periods of time, in the context of a given or fixed gestalt of technology or stage of economic development as a level of culture advance. This would be an example of economic growth in the context of invariant technology or no economic development. Economic growth could take place and for long periods through replication and increases in factor inputs but, ultimately, given the assumption of a fixed technology and therefore, no economic development, a logistic ceiling or plateau would develop in terms of the increments of economic growth. Traditional societies may therefore grow but ultimately will reach saturation and stagnation unless they experience economic development, conceptualized as a change in their overall gestalt of technology leading to a more advanced stage of economic development. On this basis, policy of the developing countries should ultimately be more directed towards technological change or economic development, rather than directing attention simply to economic growth per capita to the exclusion of development problems per se. Over the long haul on a interstage or interepochal basis, "indefinitely continuing growth" is a function of economic development. For it is true as Kindleberger reminds us "Growth without development—for example more and more steel in the Soviet Union or more and more coffee in Brazil leads nowhere."[6] Consequently, simple economic growth will not necessarily produce economic development, the two concepts though closely related are therefore not the same or synonymous. As in the world of biological evolution and development, a culture does not develop simply by growing.

But it is true, as Sidney Hook reminds us, that analogies do not really prove anything. Aside from our baby analogy, is there any empirical evidence from the real world of experience which would substantiate the view that economic growth can take place without necessarily resulting in economic development?[7] Empirical support to our position is given in the context of the Brazilian experience and the results of which are expressed quite well by Furtado:

> " . . . growth was in fact considerable . . . and continued for an entire century. Nonetheless, this growth occurred without any perceptible change in the inner structure of the economic system, nor did the occasional regressions bring about any structural change. . . . the slave enterprise had a tendency to grow in size only—that is, without undergoing any structural changes."[8]

Traditional societies, in the Rostovian sense of agrarian cultures in the phase of pre-Newtonian science and technology ultimately face a ceiling in their capacity for growth. But this is not to deny that such cultures, as the Brazilian case in point, can and do exhibit a good deal of growth even though the overall technological base is fixed and/or relatively constant. Indeed, such growth is in fact to be expected of a specific culture growing in the context of a satiated technology. After a slow start followed by a phase of accelerated economic growth, such culture in the perfection of its overall technology would ultimately experience satiation and stagnation.[9] Therefore, while one phase of a specific culture's growth might be considerable and reflected even in accelerated economic growth, such growth, however, need not indicate development but on the contrary represents an expected phase of the typical "*S*" growth curve of a culture growing but not necessarily experiencing long-term development.

The "*S*" growth curve as the logitsic and/or the Gompertz is the pattern of the typical agrarian culture which has yet to embark upon modernization or the take-off characterized by an industrial revolution. However, it is not agricultural production, per se, which serves as the limiting constraint, but, more specifically, agricultural production fed by a pre-science technology. The Industrial Revolution characterized a revolution in both agricultural as well as industrial production. MEG (modern economic growth) is indicative of a scientific epoch and is manifest in the application of science to both agricultural as well as industrial production. A system of slavery would tend to accentuate the basic logistic pattern indicative of an agrarian culture of pre-Newtonian science. The social institution of slavery characterized by legalized illiteracy would thereby serve to further prevent a breakthrough of the logistic ceiling by holding back the advance of education and science. Consequently, might we also use the growth and development experience of the ante-bellum South in the United States to serve as another empirical example to demonstrate economic growth and no economic development, as the above would imply.

The economics of slavery in the ante-bellum South currently ranks as one of the most frequently discussed issues in American economic history. The Conrad and Meyer article was responsible not only for a resurgence of interest in the economics of slavery but it also constituted an innovative breakthrough in a new methodology for analysis in economic history. Conrad and Meyer, in their seminal article as leaders and proponents of the new economic history and in their attempt to demonstrate the viability of the slave economy of the South (as well as perhaps the viability of neoclassical theory) have presented evidence in order to demonstrate that the system was profitable, " . . . according to an economic (as opposed to accounting) conceptualization of profitability."[10] But also, and as a result, there has been increased attention drawn to the relation between slavery and the economic growth and development of the South overall.

Before taking a closer look at the trees let us not lose sight of the forest. In our discussion of the economics of slavery we are not concerned specifically with the profitability issue, per se, but rather intend to use the overall issue of the economics of slavery to serve as: (1) primarily, an empirical example of growth and no development; and (2) another case in point to demonstrate the need of a general theory of economic development in the analysis of economic phenomena. Bearing these two overall purposes in mind let us now look at a few of those specific trees.

According to the new economic historians their methodology concerns a combination of theory and quantification, to recognize the " . . . intimate relationship between measurement theory."[11] The direction would be toward that of a more scientific analysis through rigorously defined concepts of economic analysis in order to resolve and clarify the basic issues of economic history. The new economic historians seem to imply that the traditional approach is mostly descriptive and lacks the theoretical rigor necessary for a systematic and scientific analysis. At the same time, it appears, however, that traditionally, economic history has always been quantitative. Redlich makes this point and so, apparently, does Fogel, "Economic history has always had a quantitative orientation."[12] What is new therefore is not quantitative measurement but rather the methods and theory used in obtaining the statistics. In this light, what is new about the economic history is the application of mainstream economic analysis (normal science) to historical economic phenomena. Consequently, the method is new but the theory is old. Perhaps instead of calling the approach to economic history "new" a preferable and more accurate alternative would be cliometrics or econometric history. Applying normal science to economic history tends to establish boundaries and limits inquiry to the basic economic factors of production. By so limiting the scope of questions to the "puzzles" delineated by mainstream economics one also limits the nature and dimensions of the answers.[13] Given the application of normal science one might surmise that the new economic historians are primarily concerned with showing the importance and relevance of quantitative economic growth rather than the qualitative processes of development which entail the dynamics of social and technological change. Traditionally, by comparison, the methodology was to use economic history as an analytical tool conceptualized in a social and institutional framework which would serve to improve upon and perfect the science of economics. Traditionally, the approach was to search for and to originate a theory of qualitative as well as quantitative change and economic evolution through the use of history as a basic tool of analysis. The direction was toward a theory of economic development rather than simply a theory of economic growth. The approach of the new economic historians, by comparison, is to take economic theory as given, established and perfected, and to then apply the theory to the study of economic history. The issue at stake is therefore not really numbers, statistics, quantification, but rather concerns the theory and methodology used by the new versus the traditional economic historians in the derivation of those numbers.[14]

In their attempts at "reinterpretation" have the new economic historians been successful, as one would expect from their methods, in more accurately stating and correcting the findings of the traditional economic historians? Unfortunately, as the new economic historians themselves readily admit, the expected results have not been achieved: "Rather than ending the controversy regarding the economics of slavery, the work of Conrad and Meyer intensified it."[15] The attempt by the new economic historians to clarify the issue of the economics of slavery has indeed, if anything, led to an increased debate discussion and apparently, at time, exacerbation. The current leading work in discussions of the economics of slavery, by the new economic historians, is the very scholarly and erudite work entitled: *Time on the Cross* (T/C).[16] However, the challenge issued by Fogel need not have been withdrawn, if such be the case, since it was taken up any way and with evident enthusiasm.[17] The basic work as the *fait accompli* to clarifiy and resolve the issue of the economics of slavery, apparently, has still yet to be produced. What then went wrong, "Why then, should they have written so flawed a work"?[18]

Certainly T/C cannot be faulted for its lack of effort or inputs of theory and science. There is to our view absolutely no contention of the integrity of scholarship nor the collective effort which Fogel and Engerman employed and directed. They embarked upon their query, the economics of slavery, energized by the full thrust of scientific economic analysis and theory. T/C represents an awesome display of scholarship, science and collective effort; this we do not question.[19] But effort and integrity of scholarship are not enough and may be in vain if the effort is misdirected by the wrong theoretical framework. This is not to state that neoclassical theory is wrong per se but it is incorrect to use a static theory (neoclassical) to analyze, understand and explain the dynamic processes of economic development.[20]

When results do not coincide with expectations there is a tendency in science to blame the scientist rather than the science that he uses. When the building collapses we tend to blame the carpenter, not his tools.[21] However, we would like to note that such an interpretation would primarily be offered by a practitioner of normal science. To him, given his acceptance and faith in the theoretical framework, the more probable conclusion would be that the science is correct but that the scientist is wrong in his application. By comparison, the practitioner of extraordinary science lacking a similar faith in the normal extraordinary science of the moment would tend to question not only the scientist but, more so, would seek alternative tools. We will argue that the mixed reaction to T/C and its failure to succeed was not based upon subpar scientists, for it is recognized that Fogel and Engerman are among the best and are established leaders of the new economic history. The problem concerns more that they used the wrong tools, as concepts and theory, in terms of what they tried to explain and clarify. Their conceptional and theoretical framework limited the scope of their analysis to the statics of the economics of slavery; the dynamics of slavery, however, were really beyond their analytical purview.

Problems of the dynamics of evolutionary economic phenomena are not contained within the boundaries of the neoclassical framework as "puzzles" to be resolved.

It is frequently noted that facts of the empirical world do not speak for themselves but that the facts chosen and their interpretation are a function of a given theoretical framework.[22] In the evolution of science we also note the process of circular and cumulative causation, in that facts and experience aid in the formulation of theory and theory in turn helps to delineate the relevant facts and phenomena which theory intends to explain and analyze. Consequently there is an interrelation between theory and history and Eli Heckscher's plea is recognized as warranted.[23] Consequently, the issue concerns not theory and its relevance to historical analysis but rather which theory is relevant. Which theory do we then use?

The German historical school, in establishing the traditional mold sought to originate a theory associated with the dynamics of social change and economic development through the reliance upon history in its formulation.[24] It sought the perfection and improvement of the science of economics. Traditionally, economic historians were concerned with an holistic or interdisciplinary methodology in the development of their theory. Therefore, whereas traditionally economic history served as an analytical tool used in the search and origination of theory, the new economic historians have, by comparison, laid out the claim that such theory exists and has existed for some time. The problem of the new economic historian is not the origination and perfection of theory, but rather the perfection of our interpretation of history. This according to the new economic historians, will be accomplished via the application of normal science in economics, as theory, to the study of economic history. For example in order to overcome the descriptive tendencies of traditional economic history Fogel draws attention to the importance of theory, and the answer as to which theory is straight-forward: "As it turns out, the theory required for the desired measurements follows rather directly from the economists' traditional analytic tools of supply and demand."[25] This methodological twist innovated by the new economic historians during the 1960's represents a veritable loadstone for students of the sociology of science. How can it be explained that whereas modern theories of economic development discussed during the post WWII period were moving in the direction of the social and the cultural, as explanation, the economic writing in the field of economic history resorted in their explanation to a theoretical framework of economic development which had historically evolved devoid of the institutional, the cultural, and the technological? We speak here of the static theory of neo-classical economics. Kenneth Stampp observes: "As a sheer guess their view of slavery may stem in part from a desire to make everything fit comfortably in a neoclassical behavioral model."[26] Consequently the new approach is not that new but resides within the " . . . conservative-consensus school of recent American historical scholarship."[27] What is new, then, about the new economic historians is that the application of their theoretical framework precludes an institutional and social analysis of economic history.[28] Given our discussions of the previous chapter, this would be the logical result that one would expect from the application of normal science in economic phenomena viewed in historical perspective.

Therefore the source of contention between the traditional and new approach resides not in the desire to use theory nor in its significance and importance. The distinction rests upon which theory is chosen. In incorporating the structural technological and institutional change the traditional approach also embraced a dynamic analysis, whereas the new economic historians by avoiding these isssues embraced the static. What is needed perhaps is a bridge of the two approaches, in terms of a theoretical framework which would be capable of integrating a static and dynamic analysis.[29] The issue will not be resolved, however by claiming and asserting, as the new economic historians do, that a static theory is relevant to the dynamics of the empirical world of economic development.

If the particular issue of economic history concerns economic growth and comparative statics then normal science in economics will do just fine as the theoretical framework. However if one discusses an issue of economic history relevant to economic development and evolution, a theory of static economic processes is not sufficient by itself in that analysis would require both the static and the dynamic. For example, in an analysis of biological evolution the functional relationships revealed by the study of the cadaver, and in the fields of histology, and physiology, are necessary parts of the overall evolutionary picture just as much as comparative anatomy. The important point, however, is the need to integrate the static into an overall dynamic framework. Neoclassical theory, by focusing on so many still shots, deprived us of the motion picture. Traditional economic history, of course, tried to present the motion picture. The traditional analysis of slavery which the cliometricians seem so intent on reinterpreting is primarily an analysis of slavery in the dynamics of the process of economic development. Slavery was traditionally analyzed as a social institution, as part of an overall social system. Slavery was not simply treated as a factor input of a given production function with technology held as invariant. It is in this context that some claim that the central issue in the slavery controversy is one of correctly conceptualizing economic development. As E.A.J, Johnson states: "It seems to me that Mr. Meyer is quite right when he points out that this controversy centers around the definition of development."[30] Louis Hacker also apparently supports this view: "It is this idea of socio-economic evolution as the key to development, that the more percipient critics of Conrad and Meyer have stressed."[31]

When we speak of the profitability of slavery do we define such profits in static, short-run terms or do we consider the profitability of the system in the context of long-run economic development? Of course, how we define profits (the conceptual problem again) is very important in concluding whether or not profits have accrued. It is true as Keynes reminded us that for the human organism, the long-run state of maximum entropy is uninteresting, it is the short-run that counts. Hewever, for the social entity, it is the long-run and the continued and sustained advance of culture and civilization which counts as the major concern. Certainly short-run gains, if at the opportunity cost of long-term economic stagnation, would indicate that the social system, slavery, was "unprofitable". It is this long-term veiw of profitability in terms of the overall process of economic development which is the primary concern of the traditional view of slavery.[32] Consequently, the issue of opportunity costs is not one of the statics of the short-term compartive yields of capital. The issue of opportunity costs of slavery is not to be measured in the short-run and static terms of the MEC (marginal efficiency of capital), but rather as the long-run opportunity cost of foregone industrialization and economic development.

It is in the sense of foregone industrialization that we can note the ultimate stagnation of the southern economy. This places our "puzzle" to be analyzed and resolved in the realm of the processes of economic development. But in order to deal with the evolutionary processes of development we need a theory of economic evolution. It is somewhat amazing that while on the one hand the new economic historians make a claim for "rigorously defined concepts of economic analysis" we find that nowhere in the literature do the new economic historians rigorously define economic development nor do they submit for critical review, a general theory of economic development. We raise the sixty-four dollor question: what is the conceptual and theoretical framework of economic development used by the new economic historians to achieve their alleged rigor of scientific analysis? Conclusions are reached concerning the nexus between slavery and the process of development but on what basis?[33]

Apparently, the new economic historians reach their conclusions regarding development in that they equate economic growth with economic development.[34] Nowhere perhaps in the literature of current economics is the distinction between growth and development more blurred, obfuscated and confused than that presented by the new economic historians. While Fogel and Engerman present a dazzling display of statistical virtuosity and inference they fail to produce the conceptual and theoretical rigor warranted for the acceptance of those statistics. Our concern is not found in a questioning of the data nor the issue of profitability in a static sense, and so on; enough of this appears in the literature.[35] Our primary focus and concern in this study is in the area of concept and theory. Our position is that while the southern economy was growing, 1840-1860, that this need not lead to the conclusion that economic development was also taking place and/or that it was not being retarded.[36]

In the first place was economic growth taking place in the southern slavocracy? Even those critical of T/C note that: "The general prosperity of the late ante-bellum era of southern history . . . are beyond serious dispute."[37] But from such a limited period of economic growth can we infer anything concerning long-term trends of development or even growth itself? Elsewhere, Fogel and Engerman, themselves, note: "Still since we do not yet possess data for the entire ante-bellum era, it is possible that the Southern performance during 1840-1860 was unusually good."[38] Given such a limited historical experience of economic growth is it warranted to draw any conclusions concerning the long-term process of development either ex-post or ex-ante? In that Fogel and Engerman do not present a rigorous or systematic conceptualization and theory of economic development, to conclude one thing or other about economic development is really stepping outside the boundaries of their analytical and theoretical purview, yet they willingly do so.[39] In this context it should be also recalled that the primary concern of the traditional interpretations of the economics of slavery, which T/C is so intent on reinterpreting, dealt primarily with the long-term process of economic development.

We concede that the economy of the South experienced growth during the period 1840-1860. The basic question then becomes, however, was such growth indicative of development? Also, not only does the issue concern whether or not slavery prevented economic development up to that time but, in addition, did the growth of the slave system make future development that much more difficult.[40] In order to answer these questions one must leave the domain of the static neoclassical theory of economic growth, or at best comparative statics, and engage a dynamic theory of economic development. We have argued that such a theory should be formulated in the conceptual framework of evolution. Given such an alternative theoretical framework, what are the basic issues and questions concerning the economics of slavery and why might one conclude that while the southern economy experienced economic growth that it need not have necessarily experienced economic development?[41]

Although others have, it is not our purpose to question, broadly, the correctness or incorrectness of T/C overall or the specifics in so far as the analysis is related and confined to economic growth. As previously stated, our source of contention centres specifically on the nexus which Fogel and Engerman try to construct between a strictly static analysis of economic growth and the dynamics of the processes of economic development. To be sure, the study of economic history concerns economic growth, but such economic growth as we have argued, does not take place in isolation and independent of the overall culture matrix. Consequently, there is a need for a conceptual framework of culture, and to introduce the dynamics, we concern ourselves not only with culture in a static framework but with culture and its evolution. It is through the analysis of culture evolution that one engages the processes of economic development. All this is of course outside the limited scope and boundaries of neoclassical economic analysis.[42] In that Fogel applies mainstream theory to the study of economic history one would expect that his focus would be primarily directed towards economic growth. To Fogel: "The new generation has not turned away from the traditional theme of its discipline. The central interest of the new economic historians is still the description and explanation of economic growth."[43] As we have noted, however, the traditional concern of economic history has not been simply with economic growth but rather has focused on economic development as well, and in so doing directed attention toward social and technological change and an interdisciplinary analysis. And while Gunnar Myrdal would not be correctly classified simply as an economic historian, in that his interests and scope of analysis are too far-ranging, he does nonetheless to our view incorporate the methodology of traditional economic history in the development of his theoretical framework. In the institutional tradition, Myrdal notes an holistic view of history: "But the central idea in an institutional approach is that history and politics, theories and ideologies, economic structures and levels, social stratification, agriculture and industry, population, developments, health and education, and so on, must be studied not in isolation but in their mutual relationships."[44] Might we conclude, then, that Myrdal is more prone to use history in the development of his theory whereas with the new economic historians the tendency is more to use mainstream economic theory to develop history?

In the institutional tradition, we note as a basic theme of our study that economic growth on a long-term exponential continuum is a function of culture evolution. Growth as replication and duplication cannot continue without changes in structure. Culture evolves and is transformed; it experiences change in structure with the innovation of advanced technology and higher levels of energy control. The process is best described and analyzed in the methodology known as the stages of economic development. General culture in its evolution appears as sequential pattern, as a series of stages, starting with the primitive and the hunting and gathering base of technology, and on to the currently most advanced stage known as industrialism. The essence of the process is the advance of useful knowledge applied to man's social organization and economic production. Currently, that knowledge is organized and produced through the social institution known as science. Consequently, the current stage of economic development (the stage of industrialism), is characterized by the application of science to economic production and social organization. It was through such a long-term process of culture evolution that mankind, circa mid-eighteenth century, finally engaged modern economic growth. Given the brief statement of our position, did the slave economy of the South impede or promote this long-term developmental process for the region as a whole?

Obviously the "puzzles" to be answered in such a theoretical framework are beyond the scope and methods of the new economic historians. For example, Fogel notes that "the cliometricians have downgraded the role of technological change in American economic advance . . ."[45] This is a fantastic position to maintain, in that a whole literature has appeared in the post-WWII period stressing the importance of technological change, not only to economic development, but to economic growth as well.[46] Douglass North, himself a leading proponent of the new economic history, states: "If the theory employed in economic history (and economic growth) continues to be restricted to the tools of traditional micro-macro economics, further advances in knowledge, are by the very nature of the theory, severely restricted."[47] For it is precisely in the area of technology as a variable (which neoclassical theory holds as invariant) that we find the necessary condition to avoid long-term economic stagnation. Again, Douglass North clearly states the position: "Among economic historians technological change has always held the pre-eminent position as a source of economic growth. Clearly, in the sense that man's productive capacity is always limited by the 'state of the art' this imposes at least an upper limit on output."[48] For it is obvious that given the assumption that technology is invariant that the slave economy of the South ultimately would stagnate. What we are saying here includes but goes beyond the "natural limits" of slavery and draws attention to the "cultural limits" of the system.[49] If we assume, as in cultural economics, that advances in technology are held to be key in the avoidance of economic stagnation, was the technological base of the southern economy, in fact, fixed or invariant during the ante-bellum period of economic growth?

In this context we must draw the distinction between the perfection and development of a given gestalt of technology to that of the transformation of a gestalt to the next higher level. It is the latter case of technological change which avoids stagnation and leads to a continuity of exponential economic growth via a sequential pattern of logistic surges. In the former case of technological change we find that in the perfection of a given gestalt ultimate stagnation is the result and it appears in the form of the logistic or Gompertz growth curve. The southern economy represents a case in which the given gestalt, an agrarian slavocracy, was being perfected but not being transformed to a higher gestalt, such as a culture characterized by industrialism.

For example, in the field of transportation technology, a continuum of the exponential growth curve, as measured in miles per hour, has been achieved by switching gestalts and not by the perfection of a given gestalt. The long-term development process in transportation technology appears as a series of logistic surges, starting with foot travel, on to animals, the railroad, the automobile, propeller-driven aircraft, jets, and ultimately to rockets. Technological change does take place in the confines of a given gestalt such as propeller-driven aircraft as the material technic was in the process transformed from that of vintage Wright Brothers to that of the P-38 of WWII fame. Ultimately, however, it is predictable that advances in propeller-driven aircraft, as measured in miles per hour, would symptotically approach a ceiling or plateau in the perfection of the gestalt. Basic to our study is the "principle of similitude" which states that growth cannot continue without a change in form or structure.[50]

What causes the change in form or structure, required for

continued growth, is the application of advanced technology. In terms of a given gestalt, the application of more advanced levels of technology, as applied useful knowledge, becomes increasingly limited. Consequently, any given gestalt, even though it experiences technological change in its perfection, must ultimately level off as the potential for adding new knowledge diminishes. In this way a given technic gradually becomes more and more impermeable to advances in useful knowledge. Though thousands of engineers try there is little more that can be done to improve upon the speed which can be obtained from propeller-driven aircraft. In order to maintain the exponential growth paradigm, the solution becomes not one of bigger and better propellers but ultimately is found in the transformation of structure and form from that of propellers to jets and on to rockets. In its perfection, a given gestalt ultimately satiates and stagnates and is manifest in the typical "*S*" growth curve.

Consequently, in the long-term development process as the upward movement from one stage of economic development to the next the importance of technological change appears not so much in the perfection of a given stage but rather in the transformation of one stage to the next higher level. The slave economy of the South represented a given stage of economic development, as a fixed gestalt (as with propeller-driven aircraft), and in this sense, as fixed technology, we conclude that the ultimate stagnation of the system becomes predictable. It is our position that technological change did take place in the southern economy but it did so in the perfection of an agrarian slavocracy rather than in the transformation of the overall gestalt of technology to that of industrialism.[51]

Just as the nymph stage in the life of a given insect precludes the existence of the flying stage so does the social institution of slavery cancel out the stage of development characterized by modern economic growth. Two stages of development cannot exist concurrently in the same structure be the structure social or biological, to have one means that you cancel out the other. It is obvious that if you have a nymph you do not have an insect with wings enabling it to take off and fly, for once, the insect flies it is no longer a nymph. If a social structure of an economy is characterized by the institution of slavery it is equally obvious, to our view, that such a structure precludes the take-off into modern economic growth. Slavery cannot serve as a social concomitant to the advanced material technics of modern industrialism. Let us explain why.

To begin with, the new economic historians, by comparison, see no apparent contradiction between slavery and economic development and industrialism. T/C in particular states: "... does not prove that slavery was incompatible with an industrial system or that slaves were unable to cope with an industrial regime."[52] But what is meant by an industrial system? According to Simon Kuznets, and as we have already noted, an industrial system is characterized as "... the current epoch of spreading application of science to processes of production and social organization ..."[53] Modern economic growth in turn is a function of such an industrial system. If the achievement of such an industrial system is dependent upon the advance of science and its application and if such a system is equated with advanced economic development to argue that slavery is compatible or not inimical to economic development and/or industrialism, as the new economic historians do, presents a difficult position to support and maintain. For if it can be explained as to why the slave system would not be permeable to the modern science and technology, characteristic of industrialism, it would then be fair to conclude that slavery was incompatible and/or inimical to economic development.

While Fogel and Engerman in T/C primarily draw their conclusion based upon urbanization we prefer to draw attention to the development of human skills and resources as necessary conditions for the innovation of industrialism.[54] T/C presents the view that slaves acquired a diversity of skills and were really not that limited by the system or their innate ability.[55] They argue that the "myth of black incompetence" is revealed by the fact that the slaves did actually acquire a diversity of skills which consequently served to prove that the slave did indeed have the prerequisite innate ability.

We also agree that the racial views of a Phillips or Fitzhugh are unwarranted. It was not innate deficiencies which deprived the slave of skills necessary for an industrial society but rather the problem was external and resided in, if we may use that word again, culture. Language skills constitute one of the most fundamental of all social technics in the process of economic development. And the evolution of knowledge into scientific knowledge is predicated not only in the spoken word but the written word as well. This fundamental and most basic language skill was not legally accessible to the slave. Elsewhere, Fogel and Engerman note: "The deficiency of education in the South has been well documented. The education of slaves was prohibited by law . . . "[56] In our cultural economics we present the view that the forward march of culture evolution requires a flexibility for transformation of both material and nonmaterial culture. The rigid and inflexible system of slavery cannot serve as a social concomitant to a material culture characterized by advanced industrial production. No nation has achieved modern economic growth, today, in the milieu of slavery and legalized illiteracy. High rates of literacy constitute the hallmark of modern industrial societies.[57] It is, consequently, incredulous that whereas a whole literature stresses the importance of education in the processes of economic development, Fogel and Engerman, in T/C, basically ignore this vital and fundamental issue and the role of legalized illiteracy.[58] In the context of cultural economics, the advance of useful knowledge and its evolution into science is the essence of the process of economic development. A system of legalized illiteracy is inimical and incompatible with such a process. Another related question presents itself: why was it necessary to make the education of a slave punishable by law? Why not educate the slave and thereby make the system permeable to advanced knowledge and technology?

A story making the rounds in the groves of Academe goes something like this: A graduate student, with a radical Marxist orientation, took an advanced seminar in economic history in one of the leading universities on the East coast and upon reading T/C concluded that the workers of the world should unite to reinstitute the system of slavery of the ante-bellum South in order to improve upon their working conditions and economic efficiency. Though the student, considering his predilections, obviously indicated confusion to begin with, T/C evidently did not help in basic clarification or resolution. T/C presents the system of slavery as an overall benign model of efficiency, profits and harmony.[59] Slave agriculture proved to be 35 percent more efficient than the northern counter part of free agriculture and the level of exploitation was not as bad as previously thought. In fact, according to T/C, the slave developed into sort of a team player, absorbed the Protestant work ethic, and became motivated by a system of rewards.[60] However, the conclusion of acquiescence on the part of the slave which would be derived from such a sanguine and salubrious situation is not supported by historical evidence.[61] Actually it was the pressure of insurrection which led to the reaction in the form of laws and legislation which made the education of the slave illegal.[62] Woodson notes a basic lesson to be learned by the South which we extend to authors of T/C as well: "The South has not yet learned that an educated man is a better laborer than an ignorant one."[63]

Another basic weakness in attempts of T/C to relate the institution of slavery to economic development is that the authors exclude the process of energy control and its interrelation with the overall processes of economic growth and development. This of course is explained by the fact that their theoretical framework excludes such a puzzle to be resolved and, consequently, as with technological change, culture evolution, and so on, the issue is basically ignored and avoided. In all fairness, we also note, not only does mainstream economic analysis not include energy control as an integral and endogenous variable of the overall theoretical framework, but the institutional school is also guilty of the same deficiency. The one social scientist, however, who clearly stands out in this area and who offers a theoretical framework inter-relating energy control and culture evolution is, of course, Leslie A. White.[64] White stands out, perhaps as the most prominent anthropologist of the twentieth century writing in the area of culture evolution. We will follow this lead and try to incorporate energy control into the theoretical framework of cultural economics.

Cultural economics, as with traditional economic history, hardly eschews the quantitative but, rather, supports and endorses statistical reference. Energy data as the quantitative, perhaps serve as the best empirical reference to support our position that general culture evolution appears as a paradigm of logistic surges leading to the overall exponential. Statistics on energy utilization reveal not only the quantitative, as growth, but also the qualitative, as development, in the transformation of form and structure. Over time man has advanced his control of energy as he switched energy gestalts from that of animal power to that of fossil fuels, and on to nuclear power and solar radiation. Each gestalt, however, by itself constitutes a limit or ceiling on the further advance of culture evolution and economic development. Again the issue for continued exponential economic growth and evolution is not the perfection of a given gestalt, for example animal power in the form of slaves, but rather the transformation of energy sources from that of animal power to that of fossil fuels and beyond.

On the issue of productivity and efficiency of the slave system, cultural economics focuses attention on the basic issue of energy control. Man's productivity is essentially based upon his capacity to control energy, and capital in the form of slaves rests upon one of the most inefficient energy converters and producers known to man, namely man himself. Man has the capacity to generate 1/10 to 1/20 horsepower. Consequently past civilizations based upon slaves as a form of capital (compared to capital in the form of machinery) were very limited in their capacity to utilize or control higher levels of energy, and therefore, their capacity for more efficient production.[65] Also, as the standard arguments go, slaves cannot fly, power a nuclear ship nor regardless of their total number be able to melt iron ore with their collective energy production.

However, it might be argued that the slave, of the antebellum South, conceivably could have acquired the prerequisite reading and writing as well as other skills characteristic of modern science and an advanced industrial system and, himself, use higher levels of energy as free and educated labour does today. But the southern slave system was predicated upon the ignorance and legalized illiteracy of the slave; education would have increased the pressures for manumission, voluntarily or through the force of rebellion and insurrection. And this had been the fear all along, and it was this fear which led to legalized illiteracy. Consequently the southern slave system could not have been permeable to an industrial system for to have educated the slave, a necessary condition for modern economic growth, would have meant the end of the slave system.

But facing the issue directly, what about industrialization itself? Did the South in fact industrialize? If so, the empirical reality of accomplished industrialization would refute the theoretical conclusion stated above. To begin with, no society has ever made the transition to industrialism, and modern economic growth, given the institutional setting of slavery. There is no historical precedent and Fogel and Engerman have offered none to prove otherwise. Hitler might have come close in providing empirical evidence to refute our basic hypothesis, that southern slavery could not have served as a social concomitant to an industrial society, but Fogel and Engerman have not.[66] And while it is recorded in the literature that some industrialization did take place in the South, it is also "... well known that Southern industrialization lagged behind that of the North ..."[67] Discussions concerning industrialization and the Southern economy revolve around various hypotheses as to why industrialization was retarded and not around the fact of retardation per se.[68] Starobin notes, that "... it must be understood that, in the long run, extensive industrialization would have been difficult, if not impossible, under a rigid slave system."[69] And in that slavery retarded industrialization it held back the long-term processes of economic development. In a long-term view, then, the real opportunity cost of slavery in the ante-bellum South was located in foregone industrialization and economic development. In T/C Fogel and Engerman offer the following: Preliminary work suggests that slavery both retarded industrialization and increased per capita income."[70] This supports our contention that growth can take place without development, a possibility which even Fogel and Engerman suggest, and which we have cited previously.[71]

But not only did the slave system of the South retard industrialization and development but the further growth of the system made it increasingly more difficult to transfrom that system. As the social structure of slavery became more perfected in its growth and development it became more rigid and inflexible and less and less permeable to the modern technology which would have brought about its transformation. As the southern economy of slavery became more specialized in the production of cotton it became more difficult to transform that system to higher stages of economic development. This result conforms to the "Law of Evolutionary Potential" as enunciated by Elman R. Service.[72] In fact, even after the structural and social rigidities inherent in the system of slavery were broken by the Civil War the South did not have its "take-off" until as late as the 1930's.[73]

The similarity to the current overall world-wide situation is striking; generally the agrarian economies, the developing countries, on the periphery are growing in an absolute sense, though usually slowly and grudgingly, but at the same time they are falling behind the industrial centers; the relative income/comparison in terms of world-wide income distribution indicates that the gap is widening. The basic distinction to be made here is that the ante-bellum North-East as with the industrial centers of the world today has its growth sparked by vast cultural changes in the direction of industrialism, to the advance of science and its application to production, whereas the ante-bellum South and the agrarian periphery of the current world economy exhibit relative institutional and cultural rigidity. Development entails qualitative changes of structure, of culture, and not simply the quantitative increases associated with economic growth. Prior to the Civil War was the gestalt of slavocracy of the agrarian South being reinforced and perfected or was a transformation toward industrialism taking place? While no longer considered to be our nation's number one economic problem the relative underdevelopment of the South still persists to this day.[74]

In this overall discussion of the economics of slavery, we hope to have demonstrated the importance of concept and theory in economic analysis. What we have been arguing for the science of economics, overall, is also relevant to the field of economic history in particular. For if theory, as a general theory of economic development, is applied to the field of economic history the "atmosphere" will indeed be "vibrant."[75]

In our search of empirical reality, another example of *Growth without Development* is manifest by the Liberian experience. Our example has a somewhat ironical relation to the southern slavocracy which existed in the United States in that free blacks became the colonial settlers (Americo-Liberians) who, ultimately, though a minority, dominated the political and social structure of Liberia and consequently their fellow black Africans as well.[76] However, the basic similarity to the southern economy of the ante-bellum U.S. is that Liberia has demonstrated a capacity for growth in the context of a rigid social, political, and economic structure. As we have noted, the basic rigidity of the overall gestalt does not preclude any social or culture change, or economic growth within a fixed overall gestalt. For it is to be noted that Liberia constitutes a prime example of an 'enclave' or 'dual' economy.[77] Consequently, though certain sectors of the overall economy may be developing this would not constitute a general overall assessment for the majority of the population (2/3) who live in tribal communities and who have their livelihood based upon subsistence agriculture, development possibilities for this group (2/3) are not too promising.[78] Consequently, we submit that Liberia serves as another empirical case in point to demonstrate *Growth without Development*.

It appears that many countries of the Third and Fourth worlds will experience economic growth during the current period. "Indeed, the estimates for the recent decade indicate substantial increases in total and per capita product for most underdeveloped countries."[79] However, the basic question which we raise is does such economic growth always serve as a valid indicator of economic development, are the two concepts necessarily synonymous? If not, then, theories of growth cannot be assumed to be theories of economic development. This chapter has provided instances from the empirical world to demonstrate economic growth in the context of little or no economic development. Therefore, even if the developing countries are currently experiencing economic growth they may simply be marking time, for the entrance into modernity (industrialism) is not governed by growth alone but growth coupled to ". . . major structural changes that must be made in order for the process of growth to continue on a sustained and adequately cumulative basis . . . a thorough transformation of a country's economic and social framework."[80]

REFERENCES

[1]Kenneth E. Boulding, "Toward a General Theory of Growth," *Canadian Journal of Economic and Political Science* 19, (August 1953),

pp. 326-340. For a questioning of the organic analogy, note, Ronald A. Shearer, "The Concept of Economic Growth," *Kyklos* 14 (1961), pp. 497-532, pp. 504-505. In our essay we do not view the organic analogy in terms of proof or empirical evidence, to infer that happenings in the biological prove the social, but rather in terms of clarification and as a tool to delineate the basic issues concerning growth versus development.

[2]J. Arthur Thompson and Patrick Geddes, *Life: Outlines in Biology* (London: Harper and Brothers, 1931) Vol. I, Chapter I, "The Characteristics of Organisms," pp. 15, 23-24, and also reprinted in Harlow Shapley, et al. ed., *A Treasury of Science* (New York: Harper and Row, 1963), pp. 285, 289 and cited by Shearer, "The Concept of Economic Growth," p. 503. "Economic development is a complex historical process in which economic and non-economic factors are closely interwoven . . ." ". . . Development is therefore not only economic growth, but growth plus change: social, cultural, and institutional, as well as economic." Paul Alpert, *Economic Development* (New York: The Free Press of Glencoe, 1963), p. 1.

[3]An example of a constant-cost situation in which all inputs are increased proportionately, product expands proportionately and technology is viewed as invariant; the whole process may be interpreted as simple replication. Note: Zimmerman, *Poor Lands, Rich Lands* (New York: Random House, 1965), pp. 72-100; Joseph Spengler in Barringer ed., *Social Change in Developing Areas* (Cambridge: Schenkman Publishing Company, 1965), pp. 244-245. Also, A.L. Kroeber, *Anthropology* (New York: Harcourt Brace and Company, 1948), ". . . there is serious doubt whether magnification as such, mere quantitative swelling-up, can be legitimately construed as progress." p. 303.

[4]This point of view is basic to this chapter and to our study in general; the idea that ". . . development signifies not only growth but historical change, movement from one social form to another. . ." Raymond Aron, *The Industrial Society* (New York: Frederick A. Praeger, 1967), p. 12.

[5]Everett E. Hagen, *The Economics of Development* (Homewood: Richard D. Irwin, 1968), p. 29.

[6]Charles P. Kindleberger, *Economic Development* (New York: McGraw-Hill Book Company, 1965), p. 3

[7]"At best an analogy can only suggest a plausible conclusion whose validity must then be established on other grounds." *Theory and Practice in Historical Study: A Report of the Committee on Historiography* (New York: Social Science Research Council, 1946), p. 108. (Cited by Simon Kuznets, "Measurement of Growth," *The Tasks of Economic History*, A Supplemental Issue of the *Journal of Economic History* (Supplement 7, 1947), pp. 10-34, p. 11.

[8]Celso Furtado, *The Economic Growth of Brazil* (Berkeley: The University of California Press, 1963), p. 56.

[9]While the typical "*S*" growth curve, as the logistic, ultimately reaches a saturation limit, the mid-portion of such a curve exhibits exponential

growth. On this note John de Solla Price, *Science Since Babylon* (New Haven: Yale University Press, 1961), pp. 105, 116, and, *Little Science, Big Science* (New York: Columbia University Press, 1963), p. 21.

[10]Alfred H. Conrad and John R. Meyer, "The Economics of Slavery in the Ante-Bellum South," *The Journal of Political Economy* 66 (April 1958), pp. 95-130. This has all mushroomed into a fairly sizeable literature which we will sample in our following discussions.

[11]Robert William Fogel and Stanley L. Engerman, *The Reinterpretation of American Economic History* (New York: Harper and Row, 1971), p. 7.

[12]Fritz Redlich, "'New' and Traditional Approaches to Economic History and Their Interdependence," *Journal of Economic History* 25 (December 1965). pp. 480-495, pp. 481-482. And Robert William Fogel, "The Reunification of Economic History with Economic Theory," *American Economic Review* 55 (May 1965), pp. 92-98, p. 92; and, Fogel and Engerman, *The Reinterpretation*, p. 7. Economic history, however, does not only entail an analysis of the quantitative but also includes the qualitative as "factual or empiricistic." Fritz Redlich, "Potentialities and Pitfalls in Economic History," *Exploration in Entrepreneurial History* 6 (Fall 1968), pp. 93-108, pp. 93-95. And Simon Kuznets, "Summary of Discussion and Postscript." *The Journal of Economic History* 17 (December 1957), pp. 545-555, states: "Clearly: many factors that loom large in the analysis of economic change cannot be reduced to measurable units." p. 548.

[13]On "The Scope of the 'New' History." see Lance E. Davis, "'And It Will Never Be Literature': A Critique," *Explorations in Entrepreneurial History* 6 (Fall 1968), pp. 75-92, "If . . . the term is narrowed to those questions amenable to economic analysis (and this definition would cover almost all of the work in the new history to date), the area is quite small indeed." pp. 76-83.

[14]On the numbers game and fact versus figures, see Herbert G. Gutman: *Slavery and the Numbers Game*: A Critique of Time on the Cross (Urbana: University of Illinois Press, 1975), especially pp. 174-176. Some might find the comments of John A. Hobson *The Social Problem* (London: Nisbet, 1901) pp. 231-34, relevant in this context. "Every bit of knowledge needs to be assayed by submission to the touchstone of the Universal before its value can be ascertained, or it can be set in relation to knowledge as a whole. The over-specialist has let slip the standard of knowledge, and is at the mercy of all sorts of private superstitions and illusions. Thus, with misspent scrupulosity, he squanders his labour on vain trifles, counting every bit of knowledge worth the pains it has cost, because he owns no standard of economy. Man is the measure of all things, and the specialist who has made himself less than a man can measure nothing." Cited by W.H. Richmond, "John A. Hobson: Economic Heretic," *American Journal of Economics and Sociology* 37 (July 1978), pp. 283-294, pp. 293-294.

[15]Fogel and Engerman, *The Reinterpretation*, p. 310.

[16]Robert William Fogel and Stanley L. Engerman *Time on the Cross: The Economics of American Negro Slavery*, 2 vols. (Boston: Little, Brown and Company, 1974). The meeting in September 1967 evidently reflected some exacerbation. "The subtle tension that marked the opening of the meeting gradually changed into mutual irritation." . . . "Faces flushed. Voices became strident" . . . Gesticulations became so aggressive that they were menacing." Vol. 2. pp. 16-17.

[17]Gutman, *The Numbers Game*, p. 174, 240. Another composite work, in addition to the many critical reviews, which questions and is critical of T/C and, as with Gutman, apparently takes up the challenge, would be Paul A. David et al., *Reckoning with Slavery: A Critical Study in the Quantitative History of American Negro Slavery* (New York: Oxford University Press, 1976).

[18]Gutman, *The Numbers Game*, p. 167.

[19]Note T/C, Vol. 1, pp. 3-12, 265-270; and Gutman, *The Numbers Game*, pp. 1-3.

[20]We will repeat this position in several instances and it is a view subject to question. For example: Ralph Andreano, *New Views on American Economic Development* (Cambridge: Schenkman Publishing Co., 1965), offers "Alfred Marshall's *Industry and Trade*: A Neglected Classic in Economic History," pp. 317-329, as a framework to analyze American economic development. Marshall's ". . . conception of economic history is not static; but on the contrary quite dynamic." p. 320. From Lance E. Davis, however, we find: ". . . much of economic theory is static, but history by its very nature is dynamic. . . oft-times static theory (the best set of tools in the economic workshop) may provide misleading dynamic results." in Ralph L. Andreano, *The New Economic History: Recent Papers on Methodology* (New York: John Wiley and Sons, 1970), p. 74. Andreano also notes that ". . . Marshall had a particular methodological approach to economic history: use the tools of modern economic analysis, quantify and then examine the rationality of past economic behavior." *New Views*, p. 319. Such is the methodology of the new economic history as well. We do not conclude that such methodology results in a "perversion of Economic History." W. Cunningham, "The Perversion of Economic History," *Economic Journal* 2 (1892), pp. 491-506, p. 491, but rather that the relevance of neoclassical analysis pertains to the statics or comparative statics of economic growth and that the methodology is not relevant to the dynamics of development. As with Keynes and Andreano we consequently do not deny the historical insights as provided by Marshall but we limit this contribution primarily to the area of an analysis of economic growth. We also extend this assessment to the contributions of the new economic historians.

[21]Thomas S. Kuhn, *The Structure of Scientific Revolutions* (Chicago: University of Chicago Press, 1970) p. 80.

[22]"The facts speak only when the historian calls on them: it is he who decides to which facts to give the floor, and in what order or context." p. 9, in Edward Hallett Carr, *What is History*? (New York:

Alfred A. Knopf, 1963), "The Historian and his Facts", pp. 3-35.

[23]Eli F. Heckscher, "A Plea for Theory in Economic History," in Frederic C. Lane and Jelle C. Riemersma, eds., *Enterprise and Secular Change* (Homewood: Richard D. Irwin, 1953), pp. 421-430. And as Lane and Riemersma point out, the question becomes not only which theory but also, how was the theory derived, p. 431.

[24]In comparison to the deductive logic of the classical school, "The historical school, in contrast, endeavored to use history and observation as implements in the reconstruction of economic science." Frank Amandus Neff, *Economic Doctrines* (New York: McGraw-Hill, 1950), p. 355. Pater Temin, *New Economic History* (Baltimore: Penguin Books, 1973), ". . . the study of historical cases was supposed to generate laws of economic behavior." p. 7. It is of course difficult to generalize about the German historical school since it comprised many writers and, also, as with its subject matter, evolved. At the same time, it cannot be doubted that one of the objectives of the German historical school was the attempt to discover laws of development of national economies . . ." Bert F. Hoselitz, ed., *Theories of Economic Growth* (New York: The Free Press, 1960), p. 194.

[25]Fogel and Engerman, *The Reinterpretation*, p. 149.

[26]Kenneth. E. Stampp in David, *Reckoning with Slavery*, p.30. and Douglas Dowd, ". . . the new economic history as an attempt to incorporate the methodology of neoclassical economics and procedures of econometrics with the materials and questions of economic history. . . "Slavery as an Obstacle to Economic Growth in the United States: A Panel Discussion, "*The Journal of Economic History* 27 (December 1967), pp. 518-560, p. 534. And,". . . new economic history has been assembled to introduce the reader to economic history as a form of applied neo-classical economics." Temin, *New Economic History*, p. 8.

[27]Harold D. Woodman, "Economic History and Economic Theory: The New Economic History in America," *The Journal of Interdisciplinary History* 3 (Autumn 1972), pp. 323-350, p. 327, 9. And, Gutman *The Numbers Game*, pp. 167-169.

[28]See Redlich, " 'New' and Traditional Approaches, "Traditionally economic history deals primarily with the development of economic institutions. . . The new approaches tend to deal primarily and directly with economic processes while more or less neglecting economic insitutions." p. 482. And, ". . . the crux of an econometric argument. . . requires a judgement concerning the interplay of institutions in the past. . . "Harry N. Scheiber, "On the New Economic History—and its Limitations: A Review Essay," *Agriculture History* 41 (October 1967) pp. 383-395, 385. The recent attempts to use neoclassical theory to analyze institutional change do not, to our view, resolve this theoretical and analytical lacuna on the part of the new economic historians. We refer here to Lance E. Davis and Douglass C. North *Institutional Change and American Economic Growth* (Cambridge: Cambridge University Press, 1971); Douglass C. North and

Robert Paul Thomas, *The Rise of the Western World* (Cambridge: Cambridge University Press, 1973); Douglass C. North "Institutional Change and Economic Growth," *The Journal of Economic History* 31 (March 1971), pp. 118-25; Lance Davis and Douglass North, "Institutional Change and American Economic Growth" *The Journal of Economic History* 30 (March 1970), pp. 131-149; Douglass C. North and Paul Thomas, "An Economic Theory of the Growth of the Western World," *The Economic History Review* 23 (April 1970), pp. 1-17. As Woodman, "Economic History and Economic Theory," states, "Modern economic theory is simply inadequate. . . By compressing all social relations into economic relations. . . they have distorted reality beyond recognition." p. 347.

[29]In later chapters we will show how cultural economics might possibly accomplish such an integration. Cultural economics does not eschew the static but incorporates the static into an overall dynamic theory of culture evolution.

[30]"Slavery as an Obstacle to Economic Growth in the United States: A Panel Discussion," *The Journal of Economic History* 27 (December 1967) pp. 518-560 "We are talking about the transformation of the economy." pp. 558-59. Whereas, to Conrad, ". . . it may mean a good wheat crop" p. 555, which is of course, to our view, simple economic growth.

[31]Louis M. Hacker, *The Course of American Economic Growth and Development* (New York: John Wiley and Sons, 1970), p. 163.

[32]Fogel and Engerman,". . .perhaps the strongest, aspect of the Phillips interpretation, is concerned with the relationship between slavery and the pace of Southern economic development.". . . Many scholars have followed. : . "*The Reinterpretation,* p. 319. On the view that the traditional concern was that of the "socio-economic evolution" of the South, as a whole, note also, Hacker, *American Economic Growth and Development,* pp. 160-166.

[33]As Fogel and Engerman, *The Reinterpretation,* note: ". . . we have also probed more deeply into the nexus between slavery and the development of the economy of the ante-bellum South." p. 310. On the "explicit theory" of economic development used by the new economic historians for their deep probing, see: Robert William Fogel, "The Specification Problem in Economic History" *The Journal of Economic History* 27 (September 1967) pp. 283-308, especially pp. 292, ff.

[34]This we would expect (recall our discussions of the previous chapter) from the application of normal science in economics to economic history. For exmple, Fogel and Engerman, *The Reinterpretation,* note ". . . processes central to American economic development." p.2, while most of their discussions and focus concern economic growth. Stanley L. Engerman, "The Effects of Slavery Upon the Southern Economy." *Explorations in Entrepreneurial History* 4 (Winter 1967), pp. 71-97, speaks of one of the central issues being economic development, p. 71, "retarded economic development. . . " p. 73, "to retard southern economic development. . . " p. 85, but then states as a basic

conclusion, "... slavery was consistent with a growing economy." p. 91. Most would agree with the conclusion but not as an answer to issue No 3, raised by Engerman on p. 71. In the discussions of the *JEH* (1967) to a question raised concerning economic development Meyer answers in terms of "Southern economic growth" and concludes, "That was really not in our purview" pp. 553-54, and, given the methods and theory of the new economic historians, we agree that economic development is beyond their analytical purview.

[35]Even though Fogel and Engerman are among the best carpenters in the business, they may have bent a few nails: David, *Reckoning with Slavery*, "egregious errors", every striking assertion... is cast into doubt," p. 339, "seriously flawed book" p. 8; and Gutman, *The Numbers Game*, "misleading ... contains frequent and important errors of all kinds in its use of quantitative... evidence," p. 2, "Such a world, even as measured by the flawed evidence that fills the pages of T/C, did not exist." p. 173. Richard Sutch, "The Treatment Received by American Slaves: A Critical Review of the Evidence Presented in *Time on the Cross*, *Explorations in Economic History* 12 (October 1975), pp. 335-438. "If the methodology is not to blame, then the fault must lie with the authors." p. 429, therefore present the position of a new economic historian who has faith in the tools but questioned the specific application.

[36]"Growth and development are *not* synonymous terms; they are related terms. The one may or may not imply the other; but they are not the same thing. The fact that the South grew between 1840-1860 has no necessary implications about development. Development implies structural change in the economy and a change in the nature of the society" Dowd, in *JEH* (1967) p. 552. And, Marvin Fischbaum and Julius Rubin, "Slavery and the Economic Development of the American South," *Explorations in Entrepreneurial History* 6 (Fall 1968), pp. 116-127, pp. 116-117, 126.

[37]David, *Reckoning with Slavery*, p. 349; and T/C, Vol.I, pp. 6, 251, 247-257.

[38]Fogel and Engerman, *The Reinterpretation*, p. 336. Recall our discussions of the logistic curve and John de Solla Price, the period 1840-1860 might be viewed, perhaps, as the exponential phase of the overall "*S*" growth curve, and consequently while the period appears as "unusually good", its structural rigidity meant ultimate stagnation.

[39]And while we could footnote this point at length, one quick reference: "The re-examination of slavery is part of a more ambitious effort to reconstruct the entire history of *American economic development* on a sound quantitative basis:" T/C, Vol 1, p. 6, italics added.

[40]This is, of course, a basic question facing the developing countries in general, and it is easy to relate the similarities between the ante-bellum South in the United States to other underdeveloped areas of the world today. "Both areas show the effects of a semi-feudal social and landholding system in restraining economic development in modern times and both show how stubborn such institutions are in

loosening their grip." Sanford A. Mosk, "Latin America Versus the United States," *American Economic Review* 41 (May 1951), pp. 367-383, note pp. 371-381.

[41]Though it is difficult to delineate the specifics of the conceptual and theoretical framework of economic development used by Fogel and Engerman in drawing their conclusions, they apparently have conceded our point; ". . . slavery could have retarded the economic development of the South even though the South actually experienced moderate, or even rapid, economic growth." *The Reinterpretation*, p. 334.

[42]" . . . cliometrics provides a set o tools which are of considerable help in analyzing an important but limited set of problems. Many vital issues in the economics of slavery lie beyond the range of these tools." T/C, Vol. 1, p. 9. And also,Lance E. Davis "The Scope of the 'New' Economic History," pp. 68-75, in Andreano, *The New Economic History*.

[43]Robert William Fogel, "The Reunification of Economic History with Economic Theory," *The American Economic Review* 55 (May 1965), pp.92-98, p. 92. By comparison, Chester W. Wright, "The Nature and Objective of Economic History," in Ralph L. Andreano, ed., *New Views* pp. 27-38, states: "The economic historian. . . is expected to cover the whole range of economic life and development. Its all-inclusive scope and its primary concern with the evolutionary development of the whole economic order chiefly distinguish economic history from applied economics." p. 27, and not only must the economic historian have the knowledge of the economist, but . . . "he must have some knowledge of the whole of the social and natural orders. . . " p. 30.

[44]Gunnar Myrdal, *The Asian Drama*, Vol. 1. p. x.

[45]T/C, Vol. 1. p. 7.

[46]Downgrading technological change is not even currently the view of normal science during the current period. We speak here of the seminal contribution of Rebert M. Solow, "Technological Change and the Aggregate Production Function," *Review of Economics and Satistics* 39 (August 1957), pp. 312-320. In that all do not agree, see: D. Jorgenson and Z. Griliches, "The Explanation of Productivity Change" *Review of Economic Studies* 34 (July 1967), pp. 249-283.

[47]D.C. North and L.E. Davis, *Institutional Change and American Economic Growth*, p. vii. However, in a previous and major work by Douglass C. North, *The Economic Growth of the United States* 1790-1860, (New York: W.W. Norton, 1966) the predilection was to ignore social change, "This is not the place for the theory of societal change . . ." pp. 7-8.

[48]Fogel and Engerman, *The Reinterpretation*, p. 163. For given the assumption of a fixed technology ". . . growth by flight from exhausted land cannot be continued . . . Eventually . . . there is nowhere new to go." p. 351 David, *Reckoning with Slavery*.

[49]The institutional school, in the Veblen Ayres tradition, gives support to this view; "*the culturally limited determinants of what in fact we choose actually to do*." Philip A. Klein, "American Institutionalism;

Premature Death, Permanent Resurrection," *Journal of Economic Issues* 12 (June 1978), pp. 251-276, p. 263.

[50]In the course of our study we will relate this principle to the overall exponential curve as provided by W. F. Ogburn and the underlying logistic surge as the basic contribution of Hornell Hart.

[51]Even T/C notes technological change within the overall fixed social system, Vol. 1. pp. 199-200. And Douglass North, *Growth and Welfare in the American Past* (Englewood Cliffs: Prentice-Hall, 1974), p. 75, and *The Economic Growth of the United States*, p. 8, on the importance of the cotton gin.

[52]T/C, Vol. 1, p. 5.

[53]Simon Kuznets, *Modern Economic Growth* (New Haven: Yale University Press, 1966), p. 487.

[54]Whereas Veblen conceptualized technology more in the realm of material culture, Ayres placed more emphasis on skills, as nonmaterial technology, serving as a concomitant to the material technics. Machines and man's material culture do not operate and function autonomously but require complex human skills and behavior patterns. In our conceptualization, technology is comprised of *both* material and nonmaterial technics.

[55]On the one hand the authors of T/C infer that slaves were not really that limited in the acquisition of skills and then on the other hand state: ". . . slaves were completely excluded from such choice professions as law, politics, and education." Vol. 1, p. 40. After looking at the statistics provided by T/C Gutman, *The Numbers Game*, concludes, "Any suggestion that urban slaves shared a common occupational structure with either free black workers or white workers or that slave artisans dominated the urban ante-bellum crafts is agregiously mistaken." p. 54, "It is impossible that 44 percent of Southern urban artisans were blacks in 1860." p. 9.

[56]Fogel and Engerman, *The Reinterpretation*, p. 337. Reformers of the time, however, conveyed the emotion and importance given to the issue of education, for example, from Garrison we have: "If I had children, rather than that they should grow up in ignorance, I would feed upon bread and water: I would sell my teeth, or extract the blood from my veins." Cited in Carter G. Woodson, *The Education of the Negro Prior to 1861* (Washington, D. C.: The Associated Publishers, 1919), p. 256. The economic structure of the South not only affected the education of the black population but also reduced opportunities for the white population as well, Douglass C. North, *The Economic Growth of the United States 1790-1860* (New York: W. W. Norton & Company, 1966), pp. 133-134.

[57]For statistics in support of the contention that advanced countries are characterized by low rates of illiteracy and that underdeveloped countries are characterized by high rates, note: UNESCO, Monographs on Fundamental Education, *World Illiteracy at Mid-Century* (Switzerland, 1957). And also, *Statistical Abstract of the United States (1968)*, pp. 866-867, for a range of illiteracy, in percent of the total,

from that of 1.5 USSR, 2.2 U.S., to Niger at 99.1. And that a correlation exists, still does not mean that we correctly understand basic causal connections and policy direction. See Mary Jean Bowman and C. Arnold Anderson, "Concerning the Role of Education in Development." pp. 246-279, in Clifford Geertz, ed., *Old Societies and New States* (New York: The Free Press of Glencoe, 1963). The development of human resources through education constitutes a primary necessary condition of the process of economic development but it is not sufficient by itself, and on this point and the importance of the overall social setting see Myrdal, *Asian Drama* Vol. 3, pp. 1546-1548; and, Micheal Todaro, *Economic Development in the Third World* (New York: Longman 1977), pp. 253-265.

[58]Today a sizeable literature has appeared which recognizes the importance of human resources in the developmental process: Fredrick H. Harbison, *Human Resources as the Wealth of Nations* (New York: Oxford University Press, 1973), Myrdal, *Asian Drama*, Vol. 3, pp. 1531-1828; F.H. Harbison, C.A. Myers. *Education, Manpower and Economic Growth* (New York: McGraw-Hill, 1964) and for basic bibliographical references and an introduction to the contributions of T.W. Schultz among others, see Gerald M. Meier, *Leading Issues in Economic Development* (New York: Oxford University Press, 1970), pp. 673-675; and Mark Blaug *The Economics of Education* (New York: Pergamon Press 1970), especially pp. 165 ff. And while the role of education in the process of economic development has yet to be adequately understood, to imply that a system of legalized illiteracy is compatible with an industrial system runs counter to the views expressed in the current literature. A position apparently overlooked in T/C is that "The principal institutional mechanism for developing human skills and knowledge is the formal educational system." Todaro, *Economic Development*, p. 235.

[59]T/C makes it all sound pretty progressive, but was the treatment that good? Note, Richard Sutch, "The Treatment Received by American Slaves," and Paul A. David and Peter Temin, "Slavery: The Progressive Institution," *Journal of Economic History* 34 (September 1974), pp. 739-783. Were the choices made by the slave free and voluntary as modern welfare economics requires as a basic and underlying assumption?

[60]T/C, Vol. 1, pp. 144-157, 147; Gutman, *The Numbers Game*, pp. 14-41.

[61]Rather than stress manumission, T/C stresses acquiescence and opportunities within the system, Gutman, *The Numbers Game*, p. 77. According to T/C, "The relative absence of rebellion thus posed a dilemma," Vol. 1, p. 242. However K. Stampp, in David, *Reckoning with Slavery*, notes: "Evidence of resistance is overwhelming in the sources on slavery . . ." p. 27; and, Wilbert E. Moore, *American Negro Slavery and Abolition : A Sociological Study* (New York: Joseph Okpaku Publishing Co., 1971), pp. 131-135; and also, Herbert Aptheker. *Negro Slave Revolts in the United States*, 1526-1860 (New York: International Publishers, 1939), for some of that evidence.

[62]C.G. Woodson, *The Education of the Negro*, "The Reaction." pp. 151-178. "The more alarming insurrections of the first quarter of the nineteenth century were the immediate cause of the most reactionary measures." p. 155, "Southerners of all types thereafter attacked the policy of educating Negroes." p. 159.

[63]Woodson, *The Education of the Negro*, p. 178. And also: Mary Jean Bowman, "Human Inequalities and Southern Underdevelopment," *The Southern Economic Journal* 32 (July 1965), pp. 73-102.

[64]Let us be clear at the outset that we do not endorse L.A. White's sui generis views nor his historical materialism. L.A. White is not frequently mentioned by economists but his name does appear upon occasion, see for example: Herbert R. Barringer, et al. ed., *Social Change in Developing Areas: A Reinterpretation of Evolutionary Theory* (Cambridge: Schenkman Publishing Co., 1965) p. 243, We will discuss L.A. White and his contributions in greater detail later in this study.

[65]"When all of the energy man needs to do his work must be taken from food and processed through his muscles a low limit necessarily applies to his standard of living." George Russell Harrison, *The Conquest of Energy* (New York: William Morrow and Company, 1968) p. 9. This is a brief statement of a subject which will be expanded upon in a later chapter of this study.

[66]On the Nazi concentration camp analogy see, Stanley M. Elkins, *Slavery, A Problem in American Institutional and Intellectual Life* (Chicago: University of Chicago Press, 1959); and also, Ann J. Lane, *The Debate over Slavery: Stanley Elkins and His Critics* (Urbana: University of Illinois Press, 1971).

[67]Robert S. Starobin, *Industrial Slavery in the Old South* (New York: Oxford University Press, 1970), p. 163, and also, Fred Bateman and Thomas Weiss, "Comparative Regional Development in Ante-bellum Manufacturing," *The Journal of Economic History* 35 (March 1975), pp. 182-208, where the North is divided into the East and West, it is still noted that the ". . . South ranked at the bottom in virtually every measure of manufacturing development." p. 189.

[68]See for example Bateman and Weiss, "Comparative Region of Development," pp. 185-189 and No 1, p. 186; and Harold D. Woodman, ed., *Slavery and the Southern Economy* (New York: Harcourt, Brace & World, Inc., 1966), "Part IV, Slavery and Economic Development," pp. 179 ff.

[69]Starobin, *Industrial Slavery*, p. 189, pp. 186-189.

[70]Vol. 1, p. 257, and Engerman, "The Effects of Slavery Upon the Southern Economy" (1967), ". . . if growth is equated with urbanization and industrialization, the South does compare unfavorably with the rest of the nation." p. 87, and evidently by growth Engerman means development?

[71]Recall, Fogel and Engerman, *The Reinterpretation*, p. 334. Also, "The Southern economy thus grew in the ante-bellum era, but it did not *develop* in the sense that the economy of the North did." David, *Reckoning with Slavery*, p. 351.

[72]Marshall D. Sahlins and Elman R. Service, ed., *Evolution and Culture* (Ann Arbor: The University of Michigan Press, 1960). "The more specialized and adapted a form in a given evolutionary stage, the smaller is its potential for passing to the next stage . . . Specific evolutionary progress is inversely related to general evolutionary potential." p. 97.

[73]Walt W. Rostow, *The Stages of Economic Growth: A Non-Communist Manifesto* (Cambridge: The University Press, 1961) dates the take-off for the U.S. during the decades preceding the Civil War, pp. 9, 38. For the South, however, the ". . . take-off can only be dated from the 1930's . . ." p. 67. While the U.S. prior to the Civil War had only one nation it had two different and clear-cut cultures, and the two different cultures accounted for the different levels of economic development. Therefore, in our view, to correctly analyze development the more appropriate social aggregate is culture and not the nation, and this, of course, is the basic premise of our first chapter.

[74]In 1938 President Roosevelt stated that, ". . . the South presents right now the Nation's No. 1 economic problem. . ." p. 1,*Report on the Economic Conditions of the South* (Washington, D.C.: National Emergency Council, 1938). "In 1938 the U.S. South was an underdeveloped area within the most developed country in the world." p. 166, Arthur Goldschmidt, "The Development of the U.S. South," in *Technology and Economic Development* (New York: Alfred A. Knopf, 1963), pp. 166-180. Also on the subject of regional disparities and that ". . . the core of the developmental problem is institutional." note, Douglas F. Dowd, "A Comparative Analysis of Economic Development in the American West and South," *Journal of Economic History* 16 (December 1956), pp. 558-574. Even though the 1940's marked an improvement over the 1920's the Southern percentages of 67 and 82 were still quite below the national average.

Per Capita Incomes by Regions, 1929 and 1947 as Percentage of National Per Capita Income

Region	*1929*	*1947*
Continental U.S.	100	100
New England	123	109
Middle East	136	118
Central	106	105
Northwest	79	104
Far West	127	118
Southeast	51	67
Southwest	68	82

SOURCE: *Survey of Current Business,* U.S. Dept. of Commerce, Sept. 1948, p. 17. (Cited by John V. Van Sickle, "The Southeast: A Case Study in Delayed Industrialization, "*The American Economic Review* 41 (May 1951), p. 389). That the problem is still with us and extends into the current period and that it has structural roots, note: William A.H. Nicholls, *Southern Tradition and Regional Progress* (Chapel Hill:

The University of North Carolina Press, 1960), and also, F.R. Marshall, "Some Rural Economic Development Problems in the South," *American Economic Review* 62 (May 1972), pp. 204-211.

[75]A basic critique of T/C concerns the lack of a correct theoretical and conceptual model: ". . . *Time on the Cross* transgresses the limits of the behavioral sciences by mechanically applying inappropriate models, and by seeking to wring from appropriate models various behavioral and attitudinal inferences that are quite unwarranted." David, *Reckoning with Slavery*, p. 340. And, ". . . the model of slave socialization in T/C is *static* and, therefore, *ahistorical*." Gutman, *The Numbers Game*, p. 7. and for the new economic history in general: "Economic analysis, using the tools of econometrics, is not enough and by itself capable of explaining causatively the process and structure of change and development." Louis M. Hacker, "The New Revolution in Economic History: A Review Article based on *Railroads and Economic Growth: Essays in Econometric History*, by Robert William Fogel," *Explorations in Entrepreneurial History* 3 (Spring 1966) pp. 159-175, 175. And while the use of the computer presents a positive potential [*Wall Street Journal* 28 (March 1974), and Gutman *The Numbers Game*, p. 2, No. 5] as the Sussex group reminds us, "Computer models cannot replace theory. The healthy reaction to computer fetishism is exemplified by the terse aphorism 'Garbage in, garbage out," H.S.D. Cole, et al. *Thinking about the Future: A Critique of the Limits to Growth* (London: Sussex University Press, 1973), p. 9. And Gunnar Myrdal, perhaps more kindly states "One will never get more from this magic box than one puts in." in Wilhe L. Oltmans, *On Growth* New York: G.P. Putnams, 1974) p. 237. T/C placed good theory into the magic box but the programming was not relevant to the processes of economic development.

[76]Robert Clower, et al. *Growth without Development: An Economic Survey of Liberia* (Evanston: Northwestern University Press, 1966), pp. 4-10. Americo-Liberians comprise about ". . . 5 percent of Liberians, control the country and govern the tribes. . ." p. 5, and to an advantage: "Our rough estimate is that fewer than 5 percent of the total income-receiving units in the economy receive more than 90 percent of total domestic income in money and in kind." p. 65. And, "The title of our book. . . is intended to emphasize a central feature of Liberian economy, namely, that enormous growth in primary commodities produced by foreign concessions for export has been unaccompanied either by structural changes. . . or by institutional changes . . ." p. vi and also, pp. 31-40.

[77]Ibid. pp. 4, 245, and the critical book review by Paul B. Huber, *The American Economic Review* 57 (June 1967), pp. 617-20, and note his reference also to p. 196 or the McLaughlin study as well as his view toward the "mistaken belief that political institutions in Liberia are static."

[78]Ibid., "Despite its rich resource base and its long association with the technologically most advanced country in the world, Liberia is thoroughly backward—politically, socially, and economically. About

two-thirds of its people live in tribal communities and receive the bulk of their livlihood from subsistence agriculture, principally from growing rice and cassava. . . . Less than ten percent of the population is literate. . . few advances have been made in transforming the subsistence sector of the economy, nor is significant progress in prospect. The economic backwardness of Liberia is attributable neither to lack of resources nor to domination by foreign financial and political interests. Rather, the underlying difficulty is that the traditional leaders of Liberia have not permitted those changes necessary to develop the society and economy." p. 4. This is similar to the view presented by Fabian Linden in the context of the ante-bellum South, 'Repercussions of Manufacturing in the Ante-Bellum South,' *North Carolina Historical Review* 17 (October 1940), pp. 313-331 and reprinted in Woodman, *Slavery and the Southern Economy* (1966), pp. 215-223.

[79]Kuznets, *Modern Economic Growth*, p. 461, and Benjamin Higgins, *Economic Development*, (New York: W.W. Norton & Company, 1968) ". . . underdeveloped countries as a class are not stagnant." p. 11. Higgins then notes the underdeveloped countries having high rates of economic growth; he might also have included, "The rate of expansion of the economy of Liberia during the decade preceding 1961 surpassed that of any other country in the world." Clower, *Growth without Development*, p. 23. Also, recall our references to Angus Maddison, *Economic Progress and Policy in Developing Countries*, (London: Allen & Unwin, 1970), and Lester B. Pearson, *Partners in Development* (New York: Praeger Publishers, 1969). And also, Everett E. Hagen and Oli Hawrylyshyn, "Analysis of World Income and Growth 1955-1965," *Economic Development and Cultural Change* 18 (October 1969), for a comparison of growth rates between the advanced and underdeveloped countries and for evidence that underdeveloped countries were growing during the decade of the 1960's.

[80]Kuznets, pp. 461-462 and his *Economic Growth and Structure* (New York: W.W. Norton, 1965), p. 23-30. "The transformation of an underdeveloped into a developed country . . . is a thoroughgoing revolution in the patterns of life. . . a revolutionary change in many aspects of life and must overcome the resistence of a whole complex of established interests and values." p. 30. For such changes ". . . in broad cultural terms" necessary for economic development note: Harry G. Johnson, *Economic Policies Toward Less Developed Countries* (Washington, D.C.: The Brookings Institution, 1967), pp. 44-45, and "Thus economic development and industrialization require the transformation of the society and the economy, and the transformation must be largely an internal one." p. 47. "In summary, the transition from a traditional to a modern industrial society requires a massive and far-reaching transformation in the cultural pattern of a people in the social and political structure as well as in the economic processes, in intellectual preconceptions and in the expectations of man." Charles H. Hession and Hyman Sardy, *Ascent to Affluence* (Boston: Allyn and Bacon, 1969), p. 11.

CHAPTFR IV

A Process of Transformation and Evolution

The conceptual framework used in our analysis and explanation of the process of economic development is culture evolution. Culture evolution is marked by culture transformation in the direction of higher levels of energy control. It is economic development as technological advance which serves as the core and dynamics of this overall advance and transformation of culture.[1] And while economic growth is interrelated with the process of economic development, economic growth by itself, as replication and without structural transformation, will ultimately lead to satiation and stagnation. Economic development is not simply a process of economic growth in terms of a unidimensional increase in quantitative size but entails qualitative and structural changes as well. "The time has come to take cognizance of the fact that economic development involves change—change in structure, function, resource allocation, which we sum up in the word 'transformation'."[2] Kindleberger certainly is not alone in this view, economic development is frequently interpreted in the literature as a process of transformation and references in support of this position are not difficult to find.[3] Culture as the substance experiencing economic development is transformed; a metamorphosis takes place as culture absorbs and accumulates new ingredients (technics), and assumes new structures and forms in the process. These qualitative changes in turn have their influence on the rates and magnitudes of economic growth. The process is circular and cumulative in that economic growth in turn provides a broader base for new technics to be created and absorbed in a culture of now larger size. Obviously, a culture at the level or stage of industrialism generates more in terms of new technics and is capable of absorbing and using more new technics than a culture at the neolithic level of culture accumulation or advance. The evolutionary process is both circular and cumulative in that development promotes economic growth and economic growth in turn is interrelated to the promotion of economic development.[4]

Economic growth alone, however, would run its course and stagnate if it did not experience a continuous stimulant for transformation embodied in the dynamics of technological change and advance. Therefore, if we are to analyze economic growth and its particular characteristics in a given historical context, we must relate that growth to a specific stage of economic development or level of culture advance. In this sense the characteristic quantitative features and structure of a given type of economic growth are primarily a function of technological change and the particular level of economic development. We draw attention, here, to characteristic differences between that of one culture accumulting in its growth more bows and arrows versus another culture replicating more and more automobiles. The nature, overall size, and rate of economic growth, would differ considerably in two such cultures and it is in this sense that we speak of growth as being primarily a function of culture evolution and a particular stage of economic development. In this context it is noted in the literature that only cultures in the stage of development known as industrialism are characterized by a specific type of growth known as modern economic growth (MEG).

If in assessing the speed of the jockey we assume no horse, though he evidently be seated on one, we do no better in economic analysis to theorize about economic growth in the context of invariant culture and technology. In short, as the speed of the jockey is a function of the horse, so is the rate and pattern of economic growth a function of culture evolution and the stage of economic development. A given type of economic growth is not a self-contained or autonomous (independent) phenomenon. That an economy is characterized by high and sustained rates of economic growth is explained by the fact that it is riding the horse of industrialism.

Consequently, a description and explanation of the process of transformation becomes central to any explanation of the overall process of economic development. This chapter, in focusing on transformation and evolution, constitutes an integral part of our overall objective viewed as the advance of a general theory of economic development. In the literature of economics, attempts to describe, record and explain the overall processes of transformation have traditionally been directed to the field of economic history. In the evolution of the science of economics it has been the field of economic history which has provided the methodology and analytical perspective for the process of transformation. Gide and Rist note that the first doctrine stressed by the historical school would be found in the "... process of transformation and of evolution."[5] And in that a theory of transformation derived from the study of economic history would provide the foundation for a theory of economic development we might also conclude: "ECONOMIC DEVELOPMENT IS THE GRAND THEME of economic history."[6]

In general terms it can be argued that economic history has much to offer for the science of economics.[7] But today, in the field of economic history, a polarization exists in terms of basic methodology. Consequently, the precise usage of economic history as a tool of analysis in the further advance and development of economics, is not that clear-cut. Toward the polarity of the new economic history, we have noted, that emphasis is directed primarily toward economic growth. Economic growth is then, in turn, conceptualized as the equivalent of economic development. It is in the traditional approach, however, rooted in the German historical school, that we find primary focus directed toward evolution and transformation and, therefore, the overall processes of economic development.[8]

In that the new economic history is based upon the application of neoclassical theory, and therefore relevant to the processes of economic growth, we find that the methodology represents a static view and seriously limits the scope for historical analysis of economic development. Such a critique must be somewhat legitimate and genuine in that it is presented not only by economists sympathetic to the traditional approach to economic history but, such a view, also emanates from the new economic historians themselves. Douglass C. North, an eminent leader of the new economic history, states: "What I do wish to concentrate on are the limitations imposed by the body of theory which is used in the new economic history—that is neoclassical economic theory."[9] Consequently that neoclassical theory places constraint or limitations on an analysis of economic history, in its exclusion of technological and institutional change, is not simply our view but also represents a basic critique of the cliometric approach offered by the cliometricians themselves.[10] Citing the limitations of a given matrix is relatively easy, making the corrections to override the limitations is, however, really the hard part.[11]

In that economic development is the grist for the mill of economic history, countless references could be cited as examples which relate economic history to the processes of "economic development". But given a conceptualization of economic development, as a process of transformation and evolution, we feel that the methodology of the German historical school, as the traditional approach, is the more relevant. When one shifts gears and moves from theories of economic growth to theories of economic development one also engages the methodology and theories of the economic development.

> "The sorts of models we have been examining thus far deal with growth as an ongoing process, i.e., with growth rather than with development. But there are theories which go beyond this task and try to account for successive changes in the rates of growth and in the structure of the economy, i.e., with development proper. The most notable are the so-called 'stages' theories derived from economic history . . ."[12]

If one recognizes that economic development is an evolutionary process then a stages approach becomes the relevant methodology.[13] Economic development as an evolutionary process is directional and reveals a transformation of one structure or form to the next in a sequential paradigm manifest in greater culture complexity and accumulation as well as higher levels of energy control.[14] Consequently a stages' methodology serves as a necessary and integral part of any general theory of economic development. The stages' methodology is in fact older than the science of economics, itself, and has had long-term historical continuity. The methodology was used even by Adam Smith but it is in the German historical school that we find its most extensive advance and application.[15]

However, one does not have to be overly perceptive to recognize that the stages' methodology has not been innovated by normal science in economics. "Economists have, on the whole, seen little usefulness in the various theories of economic stages."[16] In the first place, normal science in economics, as the neoclassical synthesis, provides for essentially a static analysis of economic phenomenon. Issues of the dynamics of transformation are outside the conceptual and theoretical boundaries of the overall framework.[17] By comparison, the dynamics of transformation and the processes of economic development are most relevant to a stages' methodology. In that the dynamics of economic development do not constitute the focus and concern of normal science in economics, the framework is not permeable to a stages' methodology.

This is not to infer that the stages' methodology has itself been perfected and is endogenously without flaws. Our position is not that the stages approach has been perfected but rather that it needs to be perfected. Consequently, while the approach constitutes the correct direction, assuming a focus on economic development, we also note that the practitioners have not always practiced with precision.[18] For example, it might be said that both Marx and Rostow, as practitioners of a stages' methodology are guilty of committing the unilinear fallacy. The unilinear fallacy entails the assumption, for all cultures, that once the evolutionary process is started that it continues as an inevitable and predictable sequential pattern of structural change leading to advanced stages of development. By noting the unilinear fallacy, economists then in turn reject the entire approach. "Almost all historians now recognize the limitations of such a linear conception of history and no longer attempt to classify countries according to stages of development."[19]

Modern evolutionists reject the unilinear argument by drawing the analytical distinction between *general* and *specific* culture evolution.[20] It is culture overall as general culture evolution, which embraces the whole of the earth and mankind, and which has experienced the evolutionary process of transformation from one stage to the next. One culture, then another, has assumed a vanguard position in the overall of general culture evolution. That is not to say that a specific culture will advance and evolve through the paradigm of stages characteristic of general culture evolution. That two-thirds of the world's population has been locked-in to stagnation and has yet to achieve MEG belies the inevitability of the evolutionary process for all (specific) cultures. That general culture evolution has appeared in a sequential pattern of economic stages does not mean that every given or particular culture will pass through the same stages on a road of continuous development. That the path for a given or specific culture is not unilinear does not disprove the existence of culture evolution and the stages of economic development. General culture evolution indicates that man's overall culture on earth has evolved. This evolutionary process has appeared, historically, as a sequential pattern of structural changes, as one stage of economic development has given rise to the next. A general theory of economic development cannot be devoid of the framework of economic development. A theory of economic development must therefore explain the process of transformation from one stage to the next.[21]

While the unilinear or orthogenetic argument can be discounted are there any other reservations or sources of confusion concerning the stages methodology?[22] We draw attention here to three problems basically centering on: (1) The correct "identification and classification of different economic stages;" (2) The issue of relative comparisons and the relation to the real world; and, (3) The theory and explanation of the "transition of an economy from one stage to the next."[23] The remainder of this chapter will be directed primarily to the first issue which basically concerns the correct delineation and description of the stages of economic development. Later chapter will deal with the second and third points cited above.

It is to be noted that the first issue concerning taxonomy and classification is not unrelated to the other issues. And of course third issue of theory, as a general theory of economic development, is the primary focus of our study. Economic historians who have tried to systematically describe and analyze the stages of culture evolution have served the same function as the taxonomists in the sphere of the study of biological evolution and development. For until biologists had classified and described the transformation and mutation they could not theorize as to cause.[24] Similarly a classification and description of the stages of economic development would be a precursor to any theoretical explanation of the process of economic development. We must first have a description of what has happened before we can explain why and how. Let us now, in our taxonomic itinerary of description of the stages of economic development, first engage the concept of evolution itself.

"The grand movement of origin, transformation and differentiation of our universe, our earth, and life itself is called evolution."[25] Economic development is but one aspect of the overall picture of evolution which would entail the *inorganic*, the *organic* and the *superorganic*. The inorganic evolved to produce the organic, the organic evolved to produce man and society evolved from man. Useful knowledge in the form of technics of social organization and economic production was accumulated and stored and then passed on through the vehicle of culture. Culture, the extrasomatic resine of society, the superorganic, may in this sense be viewed as man's social heritage.[26] It is in this light that we see the essence of economic development as being culture evolution. For without culture and its accumulation and transformation mankind would simply revert to the level of a raw animal.[27] The residue of social activity is accumulated and stored by culture; culture functions as a storage bank of man's accumulated knowledge and provides the mechanism or vehicle for passing this knowledge on from generation to generation. Culture provides a blueprint or code for human behavior and in this regard serves as man's social DNA. The greater part of the overall knowledge contained and stored by culture concerns matters or functions called economic, the activities concerned with making a living occupy most of man's energies and constitute the core of culture. In solving the basic core of economic problems man solves the problem of survival; the basic economic problems are consequently central, crucial and overriding. Therefore, our treatment of the stages of economic development is from the broad viewpoint of the evolution of the core of culture.

Evolution as a concept is applicable to " . . . many realms of thought in social and natural science and to philosophy in general."[28] In our context (economic development) we are concerned with culture evolution towards advance and this entails not only change with order and direction to higher and higher technological gestalts, as culture is transformed from one stage or level of development to another.[29] Evolution is change from one form to another, something evolves from something else and therefore general culture evolution has continuity.[30] Something does not evolve from nothing. Biological evolution (in the context of general evolution) rests upon a continuity of DNA but this need not preclude the extinction or lack of particular species (specific evolution) or dead-end evolutionary roads of stagnation exemplified by the nautilus and sturgeon. Similarly, it is general culture evolution which has the continuity and generates new forms; whereas the evolution of unique cultures (specific evolution) may not always exhibit continuity and therefore may not always give rise to new forms of culture. The basic point being made here is that culture is always changing. Such changes, however, need not always be representative of culture evolution in the direction of economic development; for this to take place the changes must be related to the advance and transformation of the overall gestalt of technology conceptualized as the core of culture.[31]

The views on culture evolution offered by anthropologists appear at first glance to be polar; the anti-evolutionists on the one hand (Boas, et al.) versus the evolutionists on the other (Tylor, Morgan, Childe, White, et al.) with the former being historically in the decided majority. White, however, as an evolutionist, in his foreword to the Sahlins and Service study (and elsewhere) feels in terms of prognosis, somewhat optimistically, though we hope with clairvoyance, that the future will reveal a tipping of the scales to the evolutionists. Compare the polar views on evolution:

> "The theory of cultural evolution, to my mind the most inane, sterile, and pernicious theory ever conceived in the

> history of science (a cheap toy for the amusement of big children) . . ."[32]

and,

> ". . . civilization itself is developed from low to high stages. . . . wherever there are found elaborate arts, abtruse knowledge, complex institutions, these are results of gradual development from an earlier, simpler, and ruder state of life. No stage or civilization comes into existence spontaneously, but grows or is developed out of the stage before it. This is the great principle which every scholar must lay firm hold of, if he intends to understand the world he lives in or the history of the past."[33]

On second glance the literature also reveals a possible reconciliation, "Evolution as a scientific doctrine—not as a farrago of immature metaphysical notions—is secure."[34] This view might also emanate from the "anti-evolutionists" who maintain that they are not against evolution per se but rather the specific underlying assumptions and theories developed during the nineteenth century.[35] In our analysis as we attempt to understand and answer basic questions concerning the evolutionary process, we do so in the context of overall culture in a universal sense rather than that of a specific culture or cultures. We will attempt to indicate the advance and general evolution of culture by various technological characteristics and will mark the advance (not necessarily always progress) through a series of stages or levels of culture development.[36] Boas, in this regard, stated the following:

> "If we should value progress entirely by the development of invention and knowledge, it would be easy to arrange the divisions of mankind and in order of progress, beginning with the simplest cultures of early Paleolithic man and leading up to modern civilization . . ."[37]

There are many ways of characterizing and describing the advance of culture in the form of techno-economic stages to demonstrate direction in the process of culture evolution and economic development. For example,

> " . . . human evolution (at least on its cultural side) may be divided into at least three grand techno-economic stages: a very long food gathering and collecting stage, a relatively recent food producing stage and the present-day industrial stage."[38]

Agreeing with such a general classification, we offer in our analysis four basic stages of economic development and culture evolution. After a very long period of hunting and gathering man entered into three basic culture revolutions. And while there are many ways of describing and classifying the stages of economic growth our emphasis is upon culture evolution and the characteristic techno-economic base, which we view as the core of culture.[39] "The hunting and gathering stage as "The Paleolithic or Old Stone Age covers all but 1/200 of human history," and marks in our classification the first stage of economic development.[40] In our framework we will deal with four basic stages of economic development:

I Hunting and Gathering
II The Agricultural Revolution
III The Commercial Revolution
IV The Industrial Revolution

The culture levels or stages are demarcated by revolutionary changes in the overall level of technology. And that while these culture revolutions were perhaps gradual and evolutionary in their genesis, they were revolutionary in their impact on the life of man in that they represented vast transformation of man's culture and social organization.

The *Agricultural Revolution,* starting circa 8,000-6,000 B.C., was marked by the domestication of animals and plants. The techno-economic changes associated with the new gestalt called the *Agricultural Revolution,* as opposed to the previous gestalt of hunting and gathering characteristic of the paleolithic period, gave rise to surpluses, expanded the size of total production and population or what in this study would be referred to as increased economic growth.[41] These changes coupled with metallurgical advances pressed for the need of new political organization and this development marked the origin of what has been called the "urban revolution," the development of cities, circa 4,000-2,000 B.C. the start of writing and the breakthrough into man's civilization.[42] The *Commercial Revolution* (merchant capitalism) circa A.D. 1400 was marked not only by overseas expansion and commercial innovation but also by the introduction of the nation-state and the interrelated improvements in controls, communication and centralization associated with national integration, the printing press (a major precursor for the advance of science and consequently the build-up for the advent of industrialism) and also by other characteristics, such as, for example, the changing values associated with the Protestant Reformation.[43] In the advance of culture evolution the *Commercial Revolution* served as a period of transition from that of the "traditional" culture with its agrarian base to the take-off into modern industrialism. In Rostow's analysis the "preconditions for take-off" were established during the Commercial Revolution and in the process the old form of culture in the mold of the "traditional society," the culture of pre-Newtonian science and technology, was transformed into the new form characterized by industrialism as culture entered the sphere of aerodynamics with its "take-off."[44]

The advance of useful knowledge, stored by culture, cumulated and grew along Ogburnian exponential lines and ultimately produced the scientific breakthroughs of the sixteenth and seventeeth centuries. Science as it grew over time was applied to production and social organization in a gradual and evolutionary manner but the results were indeed revolutionary. Industrialism, or the industrial system, as the major innovation, as the primary techno-economic characteristic of the modern period may be defined as:

> ". . . a concept used to designate a wide application of knowledge, based on empirical science, to the problem of economic and social technology. It is the adoption of the industrial system, combined with certain social and political concomitants, that is at the basis of the rapid growth of per capita income in some countries. And the industrial system dates from one and half to two centuries ago."[45]

Industrialism or the industrial system represents the current culmination of culture's cumulation of useful knowledge. Industrialism as the highest level in the stages of economic development is the apogee of culture advance yet achieved by man.

Also, in view of our definitions of industrialism and economic development, is industrialism synonymous with economic development? Almost, but not exactly; we feel that the question warrants distinction and clarification. Economic development in its universal conceptualization is applicable to all stages of economic development (general evolution) and is basically the process of advancing useful knowledge and applying such knowledge to practical ends, that is, man's production of goods and services and social organization. Consequently the conceptualization of industrialism, that is, science to economic production and social organization comes quite close to the universal definition of economic development used in this study. But there is, of course, a basic distinction, though the development and evolution of culture has extended into past history some one million plus years, it is only the modern period of the last two hundred plus years in which useful knowledge has been coupled to and fed by science. The application of science to production is characteristic of the genesis of a specific stage of economic development known as industrialism, and consequently has also been viewed as "the scientific epoch." However, it was only during the modern epoch characterized by industrialism that useful knowledge proliferated in an explosive manner through its copulation with science. Consequently, the process of long-term economic development as a function of general culture evolution, has always been fed by the advance of useful knowledge. However, it is only during the current modern period that such useful knowledge has been nurtured by science.

The epoch of industrialism signalized by the Industrial Revolution, circa mid-eighteenth century, marks the highest stage in the evolution of culture, though as we have noted, not necessarily the terminal point. The Industrial Revolution was unique to Great Britain and introduced new technics so advanced that the impact was revolutionary not only in the vast changes in material technics but it also entailed concomitant revolutionary changes in the non-material technics as well, in the form of new social, political and economic organization.[46] Industrialism was launched via the socio-economic system of capitalism, a net (not a dam) in the form of laissez faire was thrown across the stream of technology (laissez-innover) and the flow became torrential as culture became more and more permeable in its innovation of the new material and nonmaterial technics of production and social organization. After the initial Industrial Revolution in Great Britain many other industrial revolutions followed during the nineteenth and twentieth centuries in Continental Europe, the United States, the Union of Soviet Socialist Republics, and Japan with the characteristic increase in industrialization and urbanization—a transformation of cultures. Consequently, if underdeveloped countries are to ultimately cross the river to the nirvana of the highest levels of economic development yet achieved by man, they must cross on the bridge of industrialism.[47]

> "At long last, with the modern growth of scientific knowledge, man has arrived at a point where he consciously invents . . . the great upward curve of progress in technology of which man can rightly boast, therefore, is an evolution from unplanned discovery to planned invention."[48]

REFERENCES

1Since economic development and technological advance are amenable to measurement, though not necessarily direct measurement, we may indicate a direction toward higher levels of culture accumulation and advance. Given such a direction, and not merely change, we may then speak of culture evolution. However, while higher levels of energy control, consumption, economic growth, and education, for example, are all indicators of the process, they are results or manifestations of the process; they are not the process in and of and by themselves.

2Charles P. Kindleberger, *Economic Development* (New York: McGraw-Hill Book Company, 1965), pp. 168-190. And it should be noted that not everyone agrees as to precisely what is meant by transformation and structural change, cf., Fritz Machlup, *Essays on Economic Semantics* (Englewood Cliffs: Prentice Hall, 1963), pp. 73-96.

[3]We have already cited references to this view, however, in addition note: "Economic development. . . is simply the transformation of a backward, sometimes primitive, and always unproductive society into a modern and productive one." P.T. Ellsworth, *The International Economy* (New York: The Macmillan Company, 1964), "Economic development is that branch of economics concerned with cumulative changes in the arrangements or institutions by which social groups earn their livelihood." p. 5, Dudley Dillard, *Economic Development in the North Atlantic Community* (New Jersey: Prentice-Hall, 1967); "This specialized economists' approach needs to be modified. But such a change can be accomplished only by elaborating, point for point, a theory of economic growth within a larger framework of a theory of social transformation." John Friedmann, "Intellectuals in Developing Societies," *Kyklos* 13 (1960), pp. 513-544, p. 519; Everett E. Hagen, "The Process of Economic Development," *Economic Development and Cultural Change* 5 (April 1957), pp. 193-215; Wilbert E. Moore, "Industrialization and Social Change," pp. 299-370, "Economic development requires a variety of change in the structure of economic activities and in the norms governing them." p. 317 in Bert F. Hoselitz and Wilbert E. Moore eds., *Industrialization and Society* (UNESCO, 1963), ". . . it is essential to give explicit consideration to this structural transformation. . ." Bruce F. Johnston and Soren T. Nielsen, "Agricultural and Structural Transformation in a Developing Economy," *Economic Development and Cultural Change* 14 (April 1966), pp. 279-301, p. 297; "What is needed is a revolution in the totality of social, cultural and religious institutions and habits. . " p. 218, J.L. Sadie, "The Social Anthropology of Economic Development," pp. 210-220 in David E. Novack and Robert Lekachman, eds., *Development and Society* (New York St. Martin's Press, 1964).

[4]A good deal of the current literature is concerned with the causal relation of technological change to economic growth and development. Jacob Schmookler's analysis is an exception in that *Invention and Economic Growth* (Cambridge: Harvard University Press, 1966) draws attention to the relation between economic growth (demand), that is, the expansion of market size as a result of growth and its impact in terms of more invention. Schmookler questions Ogburn's exponential expansion, in a general sense, and specifically in terms of the assumption that increased numbers of inventions are primarily based upon the supply side, that is, that more elements of culture (supply) are primarily responsible for the generation of more inventions. By comparison Schmookler is less concerned with supply-push factors and, rather prefers a demand-pull type of analysis. Note, also William D. Nordhous, *Invention Growth and Welfare* (Cambridge: The M.I.T. Press, 1969), pp. 15-17, for comparisons between Schumpeter and Ogburn on the one hand and Schmookler on the other. It is interesting to note in this context that Ogburn was not completely adverse to a demand-pull type of causal explanation of invention. Note, William F. Ogburn and Meyer F. Nimkoff, *Sociology* (Boston: Houghton Mifflin Company,

1964), ". . . Demand as distinguished from need does, however, often account for the kinds of invention made." pp. 670-671. In any event, the point being made here is that the process is circular and cumulative, economic development and growth promotes invention and invention promotes economic development and growth, i.e., the forces of supply and demand are both in operation.

[5]Charles Gide and Charles Rist, *A History of Economic Doctrines* (Boston: D.C. Heath, 1948), p. 403. And, "History like the study of other countries and cultures is an education in structural change." Donald McCloskey. "Does the Past Have Useful Economics?" *The Journal of Economic Literature* 14 (June 1976), pp. 434-461 p. 447. On structural change and the new economic history see also, Douglass C. North "Structure and Performance: The Task of Economic History," *Journal of Economic Literature* 16 (September 1978),pp. 963-978.

[6]Gerald M. Meier and Robert E. Baldwin, *Economic Development: Theory, History, Policy* (New York: John Wiley and Sons, 1959), p. 140. Also, Carter Goodrich, "Economic History and Economic Development" in Easton Nelson, ed., *Economic Growth: Rationale, Problems, Cases* (Austin: University of Texas Press, 1960), pp. 3-16; and, Barry E. Supple, *The Experience of Economic Growth* (New York: Random House, 1963), pp. 3-46, and, "Economic History and Economic Underdevelopment," *Canadian Journal of Economics and Political Science* 27 (November 1961), pp. 460-478; and, A.W. Coats, *Economic Growth: The Economic and Social Historians Dilemma* (University of Nottingham, 1966); and R H. Tawney, "The Study of Economic History" *Economica* 13 (February 1933), pp. 1-21.

[7]On the view that the study of economic history can add to the science of economics, see Donald McCloskey, "Does the Past Have Useful Economics," *Journal of Economic Literature* 14 (June 1976), pp. 434-461.

[8]While all traditional economic historians would not necessarily endorse and fit the Veblen-Ayres mold of institutional economics, the Veblen-Ayres framework is nonetheless in the mold of traditional economic history. The influence of the historical school on institutional economics is well-recorded in the literature. See for example, Theo Suranyi-Unger "The Historical School," *International Encylopedia of the Social Sciences* Vol. 4, pp. 454-457; and, Edmund Whittaker, *A History of Economic Ideas* (New York: Longmans, Green and Co., 1943), pp. 732-740. Douglass C. North also notes the connection between the traditional economic historian and institutional economics: "The 'old economic historian,' the institutionalist of Veblen and C.E. Ayres' persuasion. . .," in "Structure and Performance," p. 974.

[9]Douglass C. North, "The New Economic History After Twenty Years," *American Behavioral Scientist* 21 (November/December 1977), pp. 187-200, p. 193. And, Nathan Rosenberg, *Perspectives on Technology* (Cambridge: Cambridge University Press, 1976), in spite of the basic orientation and genuine insights into technological phenomena provided

by the neoclassical economics. . . a deeper and richer understanding of these phenomena would involve a willingness to step outside of the limited intellectual boundaries of this mode of reasoning." p. 1.

[10]"The serious study of economic growth, in contrast to the cosmetic models provided by neoclassical theorists, entails theory dealing with population growth, technological change, the evolution of property rights, and a theory of the state." D. North "After Twenty Years," p. 195. And if such new directions are not pursued". . . we shall become as extinct as the giant sloth—a mere footnote in the history of economic thought" p. 195.

[11]In the context of current neo-institutional economics, the correction is to be achieved not by Veblenian rejection but rather through a synthesis. Note A.W. Coats, "Clarence Ayres's Place in the History of American Economics: An Interim Assessment,' in *Science and Ceremony* eds., William Brait and William Patton Culbertson, Jr. (Austin: University of Texas Press, 1976), pp. 23-48, 39, and, John Kenneth Galbraith *The New Industrial State* (Boston: Houghton-Mifflin Company, 1967), p. 402. Galbraith combines a static and dynamic analysis in his dichotomy of the overall into the market and planning systems. "The market system. . . does conform in broad outline to the neoclassical model." in his *Economics and the Public Purpose* (Boston: Houghton-Mifflin Company, 1973), p. 44. We also argue in the direction of synthesis and bridge building rather than a Tower of Babel in either direction, "On Avoiding Babel" see David Landes *Journal of Economic History* 38 (March, 1978), pp. 3-12.

[12]Kindleberger, *Economic Development* p. 54. Goran Ohlin notes that "Economists think of growth in terms of Marshallian continuity; historians are forced to periodize." "Reflections on the Rostow Doctrine," *Economic Development and Cultural Change* 9 (July 1961), pp. 648-649, 655. On the stages of economic development: Bert F. Hoselitz ,"Theories of Stages of Economic Growth" in *Theories of Economic Growth, ed., Bert F. Hoselitz* et al., (New York: The Free Press, 1960), pp. 193-238; N.S.B. Gras, "Stages in Economic History." *Journal of Economic and Business History* 2 (May 1930), pp. 395-418, and *An Introduction to Economic History* (New York: Augustus M. Kelley, 1969); and George Rogers Taylor, "Stages Theories of Economic History," in *Approaches to American Economic History*, eds., George Rogers Taylor and Lucius F. Ellsworth, (Charlottsville: The University Press Virginia, pp. 25-36, 125-126.

[13]Leslie A. White, "Evolutionary Stages, Progress, and the Evaluation of Cultures "*Southwestern Journal of Anthropology* 3 (Autumn 1947), pp. 165-192, notes, "If one simply refers to recognize and admit the existence of an evolutionist process in culture, then naturally he cannot admit to stages of development. For those who recognize that one form grows out of another, the concept of stages will be found useful as a descriptive, interpretative, and evaluative device. . . Stages are merely the succession of significant forms in the developmental process" p. 179.

[14]On the issue of direction and development note: "*Development* is any change that has a continuous direction and which culminates in a phase which is qualitatively new." Sidney Hook, p 118, in *Theory and Practice in Historical Study: A Report of the Committee on Historiography* (New York: Social Science Research Council), and also, *International Encyclopedia of the Social Sciences* (1968), Vol. V, p. 204. The direction of culture evolution is provided by technological advance, for example, as a statement of this often repeated theme, note, R.M. MacIver, *Society* (New York: Rinehart and Winston, 1961), pp. 556-557. Also, whether the change is gradual or revolutionary does not negate the evolutionary nature of the process. The changes of the Industrial Revolution though comparatively rapid in terms of historical perspective were nonetheless manifestations of the evolutionary process. Direction is an important ingredient of development (evolution) and this direction in the context of culture evolution is provided by technological change and is manifest in the stages of economic development. Ogburn and Nimkoff *Sociology* "Evolution is merely change in a given direction," p. 741; and Wilson Wallis, *Culture and Progress* (New York: McGraw-Hill Book Co., 1930, cited by Ogburn and Nimkoff. And also, for a similar cenceptualization of evolution, see Gerhard Lenski and Jean Lenski, *Human Societies* (New York: McGraw-Hill Book Company, 1974), p. 493 and in passim. The stages' analysis provides descriptive evidence to demonstrate the direction of culture evolution and development.

[15]On the historical continuity and the dating back to Aristotle, see Gras, "Stages," p. 397 and Hoselitz, "Theories of Stages," pp. 198-199, footnote 12. And on the relation between the historical school and a stages' methodology, "Among economists who developed theories of economic stages, the members of the German historical school were outstanding. . . " Hoselitz, pp. 193, 233, and, Howard D. Marshall, *The Great Economists* (New York: Pitman Publishing Corporation, 1967), "This repeated emphasis on a series of stages in the development of an economy as a part of the Historical School's approach . . . p. 192.

[16]Hoselitz, "Theories of Stages," p. 234. See also: Michael P. Todaro, *Economic Development in the Third World* (New York: Longman, 1977), pp. 51-55; Henry William Spiegel, *The Growth of Economic Thought* (Englewood Cliffs: Prentice-Hall, 1971), ". . . the so-called stages theories of economic development, which from then on, and for a long time were to obfuscate the study of economic history." p. 417. And on the leading work of the current period, we find that the reaction to Rostow's stages is more often negative than positive, cf., Simon Kuznets, "Notes on the Take-Off," *Economic Growth and Structure* (New York: W.W. Norton & Company 1965), pp. 213-235; Robert William Fogel, "Railroads and the 'Take-Off' Thesis : The American Case," in *Railroads and American Economic Growth* (Baltimore: The Johns Hopkins Press, 1964), pp. 111-146; and on the basic literature see: Gerald M. Meier, *Leading Issues in Economic Develop-*

ment (New York: Oxford University Press, 1970), pp. 92-120, especially p. 120.

[17]Again note Hoselitz, "Theories of Stages" p. 234 and his reference to the work by Herbert Giersh, "Stages and Spurts of Economic Development" in Economic Progress, ed., Leon H. Dupriez.

[18]According to N.S.B. Gras, in that though ". . . the execution may be faulty but the method is at least worthy of note." the solution rests not in the destruction of the methodology but rather in the Schumpeterian framework of "creative destruction." "We can serve ourselves best by testing and discarding old stages and inventing new ones." Cf., Gras, "Stages in Economic History," pp. 415, 418.

[19]Gerald M. Meier and Robert E. Baldwin, *Economic Development* (New York: John Wiley and Sons, 1959), p. 145.

[20]On this very, very important distinction, note: Marshall D. Sahlins and Elman R. Service, eds., *Evolution and Culture* (Ann Arbor: The University of Michigan Press, 1960), pp. 12-44; and which has been reprinted in, Robert A. Manners and David Kaplan, eds., *Theory in Anthropology* (Chicago: Aldine Publishing Company, 1968), pp. 229-250; and, Elman R. Service, "Cultural Evolution," *International Encyclopedia of the Social Sciences* Vol. 5, pp. 221-227, especially, pp. 223-226; and, Lenski and Lenski, *Human Societies*. Also, on the unilinear issue of culture advance: "To postulate certain stages in the process of cultural development as regards mankind as a whole does not necessarily imply that all people everywhere necessarily passed through all of the same stages or were likely to do so." Bidney, *Theoretical Anthropology* (New York: Columbia University Press, 1953). p. 222.

[21]In terms of theory and explaining the transition from one stage to the next ". . . and in applying this yardstick they make a poor showing indeed. . . . They all fail to contain models including the main variables which may be made accountable for a transition from one stage to the next." Hoselitz, "Theories of Stages,' p. 238.

[22]In terms of the unilinear issues are we possibly dealing with a straw man? For example, some maintain that an orthogenetic, unilinear view was never held in the first place: "Tylor and Morgan, and most ethnologists of their time as well, were concerned with the world-wide manifestation of cultural stages and not with the culture of a particular society . . . it seems doubtful that any of these evolutionists ever believed such manifest nonsense." Elman R. Service, *International Encyclopedia of the Social Sciences* (1968), Vol. V, p. 223; Bidney, *Theoretical Anthropology*, pp. 217, 222. L. A. White also argues along these lines, "Neoevolutionism is a misleading term . . we regret any such notion. The *theory* of evolution set forth in this work does not differ one whit in principle from that expressed in Tylor's *Anthropology* in 1881 . . ." p. ix, *The Evolution Of Culture* (New York: McGraw-Hill, 1959), L.A. White's position on the unilinear issue is clearly stated, for example, in his "Evolutionary Stages, Progress and the Evaluation of Cultures," pp. 170-171, he notes that evolution for cultures in accordance with a rigid sequence of stages is

not supported by empirical evidence and that all cultures need not go through the stone-bronze-iron sequence but that in an instance of a given or specific culture the bronze phase may be skipped, notably Africa, and the sequence may consequently be from stone to iron. This however, does not invalidate the ". . . evolutionists claim that *in the process of technological development* a bronze stage preceded that of iron." p. 171. A possible source of confusion of Boas et al. according to L.A. White would be ". . . the answer is simple, the Boas school has confused the *evolution of culture* with the culture history of peoples." in "Diffusion vs. Evolution," *The American Anthropologist* 47, (July-September, 1945), pp. 339-346, especially pp. 343, 345, and 354. To which others might concur, i.e., ". . .I think White is right in maintaining that some anthropologists have confused the evolution of culture with the culture history of specific peoples." Clyde Kluckhohn, "The Role of Evolutionary Thought in Anthropology" in *Evolution and Anthropology: A Centennial Appraisal*, Betty J. Meggers, ed., (Washington, D. C., The Anthropological Society of Washington, 1959), p. 145. For additional references on White's attack on the anti-evolutionists, note, footnote 9, in L.A. White's *The Evolution of Culture*, p. ix; his introduction in Sahlins and Service, *Evolution and Anthropology: A Centennial Appraisal*, and, for his overall collection, Gertrude E. Dole and Rebert L. Carneiro, *Essays in the Science of Culture* (New York: Thomas Y. Crowell Company, 1960).

[23]Note, Hoselitz, Theories of Stages, "p. 194, as the source of our focus, also cf., Simon Kuznets, *Economic Growth and Structure* (New York: W. W. Norton & Company, 1965), pp. 213-216.

[24]"It is undoubtedly no accident that the early suggestions of descent by change were made during the period when Linnaeus and others were developing a workable system for classifying living organisms," Herbert H. Ross, *A Synthesis of Evolutionary Theory* (Englewood Cliffs: Prentice-Hall, 1962), p. 2. This does not mean that a Linnaeus or the stages-type of economist will be completely correct in classification or description but that as theory then develops classification will improve and this in turn promotes additional improvements in the area of theory.

[25]Elman R. Service, *International Encyclopedia of the Social Sciences* Vol. 5, p. 221. For a basic work interrelating the physical (inorganic), the biological (organic) and the social (superorganic) see: Sol Tax, ed., *Evolution After Darwin* (Chicago: University of Chicago Press, 1960), 3 Vols. On evolution, cf., also Julian H. Steward, *Theory of Culture Change: The Methodology of Multilinear Evolution* (Urbana: University of Illinois Press, 1955) Also, Julian H. Steward, "Evolution and Process" in A.L. Kroeber, Anthropology Today: An Encyclopedic Inventory (Chicago: University of Chicago Press, 1953), pp. 313-315. Also, *Evolution and Anthropology: A Centennial Appraisal* (Washington, D.C.: The Anthropological Society of Washington, 1959), and, Hudson Hoagland and Ralph W. Burhoe, *Evolution and Man's Progress* (New York: Columbia University Press, 1962), also, Ralph Linton, *The Tree*

of Culture (New York: Alfred A. Knopf, 1961), Part II, "Evolutionary Processes," pp. 21-60. And also, from the point of view of economics, note, Stow Persons, *Evolutionary Thought in America* (New Haven: Yale University Press, 1950), Chapter VI, pp. 202-268, Joseph J. Spengler, "Evolutionism in American Economics, 1800-1946." These references are obviously quite selective and, of course, pertain to a limited area of a very extensive literature concerning the concept of evolution.

[26]"Society and culture are related but not synonymous. Society is the group in interaction and culture is the product." . . . "Society comes first and culture after. Culture issues from society in interaction. During the hundreds of thousands of years when *homo sapiens* was passing through his various development sequences, it may be logically assumed that at sometime he existed in society but without culture. . . . logically and historically society precedes culture." p. 128, Francis E. Merrill, *Society and Culture* (Englewood Cliffs: Prentice-Hall, 1961) based upon David Bidney, *Theoretical Anthropology* (New York: Columbia University Press, 1953), p. 104 in his chapter "Society and Culture," pp. 85-124, especially, p. 103 ff. and Lenski and Lenski, *Human Societies*, ". . . society is a form of social organization that has evolved, not once, but a number of times, independently and in widely separate animal lines. It is found not only among humans, but also among many species of mammals, birds, fish, and even insects." p. 7, and also, Kingsley Davis, *Human Society* (New York: Macmillan, 1949), p. 27 (cited by Lenski and Lenski).

[27]"Human society, without culture, would be reduced to the level of present day ape societies." p. 197, Harry Hoijer, "Language and Writing," in Harry L. Shapiro, ed., *Man, Culture, and Society* (New York: Oxford University Press, 1956). This is another way of saying that there can be no economic development if there is no culture; consequently as we add to culture (actually to the "core of culture" since not all of culture concerns economic development; we will clarify this issue later) we add to development—the idea of cumulative evolutionary change. "In this sense to go back five or ten thousand years, or even more, need not be irrelevant, and may well be a most illuminating exercise in the study of economic progress." Barry E. Supple, *The Experience of Economic Growth*, p. 27.

[28]*International Encyclopedia of the Social Sciences* (1968) Vol. 5. p. 202. And L.A. White, recognizes evolution to be ". . . one of the most basic and fruitful concepts of all of science." in Sahlins and Service, *Evolution and Culture*, p. xii.

[29]Culture always changes, "ALL CULTURES, even the simplest, seem to be in a continuous state of change." Ralph Linton, *The Tree of Culture* (New York: Alfred A. Knopf, 1961), p. 41. Also, Melville J. Herskovits states in Ralph Linton, ed., *The Science of Man in the World Crisis* (New York: Columbia University Press, 1945). ". . . yet changes constantly take place as generation succeeds generation, and new ideas, new alignments, new techniques come into thinking of its members. For no living culture is static." p. 143, and George M. Foster, *Tradi-*

tional Culture: and the Impact of Technological Change (New York: Harper and Row, 1962) p. 16. As culture evolves and changes, such changes may be of the nature of advance which to some is equated with progress, or such changes may be regressive or may even entail stagnation. In terms of social evolution, Herbert Spencer felt that possibly regression was as frequent as progression. Note: Leslie A. White, "Evolutionary Stages, Progress and the Evaluation of Cultures," *Southwestern Journal of Anthropology* 3 (Autumn 1947), pp. 165-192, pp. 177 ff. Our concern is with economic development and therefore with culture evolution which is in the direction of advance marked by higher and higher gestalts of technology. Perhaps, for a more meaningful discussion of change and direction in relation to the concept of evolution, note C. W. Lewontin, *International Encyclopedia of the Social Sciences* (1968), Vol. 5, pp. 202-209, and also, Sahlins and Service, eds., *Evolution and Culture*, p. 6 ff.

[30]"By evolution we mean a process in which one form grows out of another in chronological sequence; evolution is a temporal sequence of forms." p. 178, "Culture evolves; one form grows out of another. There is form and continuity in the culture process. . . . An evolutionary stage is simply one of a succession of forms in the developmental process. . . . We may properly speak of progress in cultural development not in the sense of more recent forms in the successive series but also in terms of higher and better." Leslie A. White, "Evolutionary Stages, Progress and the Evaluation of Cultures," p. 186.

[31]It is of course obvious that culture change is not predicated solely on technological change, as the invention, innovation and assimilation of new technics. But culture change in any direction and not simply related to the process of economic development, may be brought about through wars, natural disasters and on, i.e., the forces which we consider exogenous in the process of culture change. Exogenous though they may be, they are still relevant to the process of culture change. On this point note Evon Z. Vogt, "Culture Change," *International Encyclopedia of the Social Sciences* (1968), Vol. 3, p. 555. There is, consequently, a conceptual distinction between culture change and culture development.

[32]B. Laufer's review of: R.H. Lowie, *Culture and Anthropology* in *American Anthropologist* 20 (1918), pp. 87-91, p. 90, cited by L. A. White in his *The Evolution of Culture* (New York: McGraw-Hill, 1959), p. vii; "Evolutionism in Cultural Anthropology: A Rejoinder," *American Anthropologist* 49 (1947), p. 403.

[33]Edward B. Tylor, *Anthropology* (New York: D. Appleton & Company, 1881), p. 20, cited by White, *The Evolution of Culture*, p. vii a quotation which appears with regularity in the literature.

[34]Robert H. Lowie, "Evolution in Cultural Anthropology: A Reply to Leslie White," *American Anthropologist*, Vol. 48 (1946), pp. 223-233, p. 223.

[35]"Boas' critique was directed not against the principle of evolution as historical development, which he accepted but orthogenesis

of dominant English and American theory of the time." p. 101, Alexander Lesser, *International Encyclopedia of the Social Sciences* (1968), Vol. 2. And, Franz Boas, "The development of ethnology is largely due to the adaption of the evolutionary standpoint." *Race, Language and Culture* (New York: The Macmillan Company, 1940) and cited by Lesser. Also, on this point, note Bidney, *Theoretical Anthropology*, pp. 215 ff. who notes that Boas ". . . was not opposed to the concept of evolution within the context of a given culture or to the idea of limited progress within certain spheres of culture, such as technology." L.A. White, however, is skeptical and feels that evolutionists should not be lulled to complacency and argues that the Boas school is in opposition to any theory of culture evolution and not just those of Morgan, Spencer, et al., see: "Evolutionism in Cultural Anthropology: A Rejoinder,', pp. 402 ff., especially pp. 410-411. Robert H. Lowie in his "Evolution in Cultural Anthropology: A Reply to Leslie White," feels that: 'Professor White should relax. . ." p. 223, "It is unilinear evolution that the Austrians and the Boasians reject, but since White has latterly discovered that Tylor and Morgan are not unilinear evolutionists at all. . . what is the row about from White's point of view? It would seem then "he is right and we are right, and all's as well as well can be." p. 227.

[36]On the face of it perhaps many would call the advance of culture, progress, certainly this would be the case of L.A. White in his "Evolutionary Stages, Progress and the Evolution of Cultures," in the sense of being "better" and as something which can be measured by "objective standards." While our current opportunities for longevity, for leisure, for living standards undoubtedly represent "progress" over the caveman period we still need not conclude that the "Third Reich" was better, or progress, though it represented technological advance. Our advance in nuclear technology may lead us to progress right back to the stone age. At this point we may refer to the dinosaur analogy: Perhaps one way to explain the extinction of the dinosaurs would be that their bodies become too massive for their small brains to control; likewise, has man created a technological body too large for his brain to control and properly organize? If we evaluate progress based upon man's capacity for survival, man's conceivable ultimate destruction based upon technological advance could hardly be viewed as progress. "No author denies that technological *advance* occurs; the question, here. . . is whether the advance is progressive (i.e., for the better), "Van Doren, *The Idea of Progress*, p. 340. And also, Lenski and Lenski, *Human Societies*, pp. 79, 460.

[37]Franz Boas, *General Anthropology* (Boston: D.C. Heath and Company, 1938), p. 677. Apparently Boas was not opposed to evolution in the context of historical continuity and change of a particular culture or cultures but resisted attributing any universalism to the process. To Boas, "Cultures rather than culture became fundamental to the study of man." Alexander Lesser, *International Encyclopedia of the Social Sciences*, Vol. 2, "Boas, Franz," pp. 99-110, 102. Boas,

therefore, was more concerned with the historical approach or the analysis of unique cultures or specific evolution as opposed to general evolution, see also, David Bidney, *Theoretical Anthropology* (New York: Columbia University Press, 1953), pp. 215-223, "Boas was opposed to the assumption that there was one fixed formula for cultural evolution applicable to the past or to the future of all societies; but he was not opposed to the concept of evolution within the context of a given culture," p. 215. This may be the root of the conflict since the "traditional evolutionary concerns of anthropology" were more with the grand theme of general evolution as embodied in the writings of Tylor, Morgan and currently L.A. White. On this note Sahlins and Service, eds., *Evolution and Culture*, pp. 40-44.

[38]Robert J. Braidwood, *International Encyclopedia of the Social Sciences*, Vol. 4, 1965, p. 247. This is very similar to Ralph Linton's three basic mutations; pp. 48, 662-663, *The Tree of Culture* (New York: Alfred A. Knopf, 1955): (1) Use of tools, fire, and language; (2) Discovery of how to raise food; and (3) since the late 1700's (a) How to get power from heat, and (b) Discovery of the scientific method.

[39]As we have already noted, there are many ways of organizing man's past history in terms of stages of economic development. "The particular innovation selected and the length and scope of the epoch will be determined by the scholar's emphasis." Kuznets, *Modern Economic Growth* (New Haven: Yale University Press, 1966), p. 4, and, ". . . the distinction and definition of epochs in the long stretch of human life on this planet is partly a matter of judgment, dependent upon the scholar's interest." p. 3.

[40]J. Desmond Clark, "Hunting and Gathering," *International Encyclopedia of the Social Sciences* Vol. 7, pp. 9-15, p. 9. We find that even today remnant paleolithic conditions still prevail for large numbers of people when at the same moment of time other men of other cultures are exploring outer space. "There are perhaps about a million people in the world still securing at least a portion of their food supply simply by hunting, fishing, and gathering wild fruits, roots or other edible materials. . . Such food gatherers include the Eskimo, Pygmies, the Australian Aborigines, Bushman and certain aboriginal people of India." John J. Honigman, *The World of Man* (New York: Harper and Row, 1959), p. 299.

[41]Though the separation of horticulture and agriculture is warranted we have for purposes of simplicity of exposition included both under the overall rubric of The Agricultural Revolution. On the separation, cf., Lenski and Lenski, *Human Societies*, pp. 162-262. On the food gathering to the food producing transition in addition to Gordon V. Childe's *Man Makes Himself* (London: Watts, 1941), *Social Evolution* (New York: Henry Schuman, 1951), note, Graham Douglas Clark, *From Savagery to Civilization* (New York: Henry Schuman, 1953), and also, Linton, *The Tree of Culture*, pp. 61-169.

[42]The city evolved from the surpluses achieved through the domestication of animals and plants, cities, as such would be impossible if

culture were in a paleolithic stage or form. A city is defined by Linton on the basis of economic specialization, "It is a community which subsists by the exchange of manufactured products and services for food and raw materials." *Tree of Culture*, p. 118. But this break-through, a social invention, was highly significant for the advance of culture, "It represents a social invention which in its significance for the growth of culture is fully as important as any technological invention with the possible exception of food-raising." Ibid. Cities provided a capacity for population growth greater than that of the village and this population density and growth was further instrumental in the advance and evolution of culture. Note also, Robert McC. Adams, *The Evolution of Urban Society* (Chicago: Aldine Publishing Co., 1966), and Carl H. Kraeling and Robert M. Adams, *City Invincible* (Chicago: The University of Chicago Press, 1960).

[43]Simon Kuznets in his *Modern Economic Growth* points to the *major* innovation of the epic of merchant capitalism as being "over-seas expansion and the exploitation of contacts with the New World," and it is the major innovation which imparts unity to the epoch. But it is not to infer that we "can ignore everything else that is going on." pp. 2-5. Also on the other innovations of the period, note Clarence E. Ayres, *The Theory of Economic Progress* (New York: Schocken Books, 1962), pp. 137 ff. and to the special importance given to the printing press and movable type for the advance of know-ledge and science as well as its relation to the Industrial Revolution. On the *Commercial Revolution*, note also Lawrence Bradford Packard, *The Commercial Revolution* 1400-1776 (New York: H. Holt and Company, 1947), and Herbert Heaton, *Economic History of Europe* (New York: Harper and Row, 1948), pp. 213 ff.

[44]To Rostow, "The take-off is defined as an industrial revolution . . ." *The Stages of Economic Growth: A Non-Communist Manifesto* (Combridge: Cambridge University Press, 1968), p 57.

[45]pp. 238-239, Simon Kuznets, *Economic Change* (London: William Heineman, 1954). In our study we use industrialism as being synony-mous with the industrial system as defined by Simon Kuznets, note also, "Indeed, modern economic growth is, in substance, an applica-tion of the industrial system, i.e., a system of production based on increasing use of modern scientific knowledge." p. 15 and ". . . it means the applications to problems of production of modern scienti-fic discoveries and additions to the stock of tested knowledge." pp. 110-111, *Six Lectures on Economic Growth* (New York: The Free Press of Glencoe, 1959) and in passim, *Modern Economic Growth*, op. cit., for example: " 'modern economic growth' to describe the current epoch of spreading application of science to processes of production and social organization. ." p. 487, and which on p. 9, he also desig-nates as "the scientific epoch" to give emphasis to the crucial role of science. Also note Lecture II of his *Six Lectures*, "The Necessary Condition," pp. 29-35. Kuznets is of course not alone in his appraisal of the industrial system or what we in this study also call industrialism

or what Raymond Aron, *World Technology and Human Destiny* (Ann Arbor: The University of Michigan Press, 1963) calls an "industrial society" p. 59., and also note his *The Industrial Society* (New York: Frederick A. Praeger, 1967).

[46]The classic interpretation of the Industrial Revolution, Arnold Toynbee, *The Industrial Revolution* (Boston: The Beacon Press, 1956), draws attention to the fact that, "The essence of the Industrial Revolution is the substitution of competition for medieval regulations. . ." p. 58.

[47]The process of achieving industrialism, which is characterized, among others, by industrialization and urbanization through a series of stages, to us represents a process of qualitative transformation and not simply economic growth and consequently would be more correctly viewed as a process of economic development. On this score it is interesting to note, that Rostow's *The Stages of Economic Growth* emerged out of a query presented to him concerning ". . . The Process of Industrialization," p. ix. In designating his work as one of economic growth he conforms to the current dominant (though by no means universal) tendency to equate growth with development.

[48]Ruth Benedict, "The Growth of Culture," pp. 182-195, in *Man, Culture, and Society*, ed., Harry L. Shapiro (New York: Oxford University Press, 1960), p. 193. And David S. Landes, "The point, as we have noted, is that man can now order technological and scientific advance as one orders a commodity," in H.J. Habakkuk and M. Postan, eds., *The Cambridge Economic History of Europe* (Cambridge: Cambridge University Press, 1965), p. 585.

CHAPTER V

Energy Transformation as an Indicator of the Process of Economic Development

Of all the phenomena of the universe, few offer as much for intellectual excitement and direction, and need for further understanding as the concept of energy.[1] Energy constitutes the prime mover of the universe. The concept of energy embraces the entirety, the whole of the evolution of the physical, the biological, as well as the cultural. "Everything in the universe may be described in terms of matter and energy, or, more precisely in terms of energy . . .Energy is the basic and universal concept of science."[2] Energy and evolution, they go together. Energy transformation is the motor force of evolution, overall, and culture evolution marks the more recent manifestation of that process. Consequently, our analysis of economic development or evolution, is directed toward a part of the whole of evolution. The conceptual problem, which constitutes an important focus of our study, is certainly not unique to the social sciences nor with economic development in particular but constitutes a running battle in the evolution of science in general. Nowhere is this more evident than with the concept of energy.

> "Progress in science is a matter of seeing with new words."
>
> "The searching analysis of modern science is made possible by the use of devised concepts."
>
> "The striking contrast between Aristotelian and Galilean-Newtonian mechanics is due to the use of specifically devised concepts for explanation. Modern science is simply a symposium of such concepts."

> "Concepts pass in and out of currency as soon as they fail to do justice to the variety of experience. Whether an observation is explained or not is simply a matter of whether it can be reported adequately using the conceptual apparatus available. . . . To be a scientist is to know not only how to use the language created from these concepts, but also how and when to improve its vocabulary and syntax."
>
> "The spectacular progress of physics and chemistry during the nineteenth century can quite fairly be attributed to the acceptance of energy as a fundamental concept."[3]

Energy, as with the concept of economic development, is not a thing or physical substance. "Unseen and untouched, energy can only be imagined in the mind of man."[4] Energy, as with economic development, appears in a variety of forms capable of empirical verification. Therefore, when energy is analyzed in its manifestation, the usual approach is to discuss and analyze the form of energy, such as: mechanical; chemical; electrical; radiant; nuclear; and, thermal.[5] And from an analysis of the various forms of energy, science, as it evolves over time, improves upon the conceptualization of energy. But as with economic development as a concept, since energy as a concept has no physical substance, energy must be explained to be conceptualized. This process is circular, we observe and acquire empirical reference and description, we then explain and conceptualize, which then further provides the basis for more sophisticated and more scientific observation which then in turn aids in more scientific conceptualization and explanation.[6] Apparently, the conceptual problem itself entails an evolutionary process. This would therefore apply to the concept of economic development as well as that of energy. The process of conceptualization represents an unending running battle. Knowledge which man acquires is not finite but keeps growing and evolving—the concepts of energy and economic development are indicative of process of cumulation. Our scientific concepts are not fixed and finite but evolve with the advance of science. The mental power of Galileo, Newton, and Einstein has not resolved the concept of energy and neither have the efforts of Smith, Marx, Veblen, Schumpter, Keynes, Myrdal, or Kuznets resolved the concept of economic development. With the growth of knowledge we come to know that there is more to know, we improve upon our knowledge but we never complete it, and consequently though great as the contributions of these scientists may be, they simply constitute way stations along the infinite road of cumulative knowledge.

The formulation of a scientific conceptualization of energy is usually ascribed to Thomas Young (1807), though its origins might rightfully be considered as going back to the day when Galileo allegedly as a young man observed the swing of a pendulum and measured the time period of the arc by the beat of his pulse.[7] It is interesting to note how many of our major concepts in science are of such recent origin. For example, two central concepts of our study date from the nineteenth century, evolution (1859) and culture (1871). And while Darwin and Tylor had predecessors they are usually given credit concerning the formulation of these two very important concepts. It is of significance, however, that evolution and culture were both scientifically conceptualized *after* the birth of the science of economics, which is usually dated in 1776 with the work of Adam Smith. The science of economics was consequently born and nurtured in a scientific environment devoid of the conceptual framework of culture and its evolution.[8]

Energy and matter form the basis of the evolution of the universe and this entails the inorganic, the organic, and the superorganic. Consequently, basic to any general theory of evolution, in all its forms, would be an analysis of the interrelationship between energy and matter, "Indeed . . . Matter and energy, the two go dancing off together to form our cosmos . . ."[9] And in much the same way that we will argue in the course of our study, that technology and culture are not separate and unrelated entities but represent opposite sides of the same thing, useful knowledge, we find similarly that:

> "Mass . . . is the equivalent of energy in all its manifestations. Thus energy and matter are not the two faces of the universe, but simply two sides of the same face. Increases and decreases in energy, according to this theory, are always associated with a change in mass."[10]

The Janus countenance of the universe, one side being

energy and the other matter, is similar to the Janus countenance of useful knowledge which on the one side is represented by technology and on the other by culture. It is also to be noted that useful knowledge is not unrelated to the universe.

The universe is infinite and represents the entirety of what there is to be known, and useful knowledge, on the other hand, represents what man knows of the universe. Man through his usage of the tool of culture accumulates, and at an increasing rate, useful knowledge of the universe which in its application appears as the addition of new technics to the overall gestalt of technology. The universe of energy and matter represents what exists to be known and is infinite, and useful knowledge by comparison represents man's awareness of the universe of what is known of the infinite. This knowledge is accumulated and stored by culture. As culture evolves and advances through the process of technological change man comes to know more and more and consequently gains greater control of his universe through a greater control over energy. In gaining a greater control of energy man achieves a greater capacity for work and consequently higher levels of productivity and production. It is in this sense that man through his advance and transformation of culture also advances his control over energy and thereby provides a basis for higher levels of production and control over the environment. Consequently, in the process of culture evolution, man improves upon his standards of living not only in quantity, but quality as well, and it is this process which we conceptualize as the process of economic development.

Energy as a concept represents the all-embracing power of the universe.[11] In this sense energy may serve as an interconnecting conceptual and theoretical bridge between the physical, the biological and the social in an explanation of the overall of the process of evolution. For if man, as the biological, has evolved from the physical, and from man, society and culture, it is not completely beyond reason to assume the possibility of the discovery of general laws integrating and unifying the three basic areas of overall evolution: the inorganic, the organic, and the superorganic. Ultimately it probably will be found that such general or universal laws of evolution explaining the path of evolution through the inorganic, the organic, and the superorganic will have energy and its transformation as their core and focus. Consequently, if a schema explaining the all of evolution were ever devised, if such a Gordian knot were ever untied, it would perhaps have as its central thread the basic relationship between energy and matter.[12] And conceivably on this basis as we come to understand more and more of the physical and the biological in the context of energy control and transformation we will also enhance our understanding of the social and the cultural. Such thoughts of a grand design of evolution are indeed scintillating and stimulating to the intellect. The concern of our study, however, deals not with the whole of evolution, but rather with a part of the whole of evolution, in the conceptual framework of economic development and culture evolution. How then is energy related to economic development?

The concept of evolution concerns both quantitative and qualitative processes. The quantitative, as replication, duplication and reproduction, is characteristic of the growth process, and the qualitative, as structural change and transformation, is characteristic of the development process. In that nothing is done or moves in the cosmos without energy transformation, the evolutionary processes of economic growth and development are, consequently, also tied to man's control and advance of various forms of energy. Various forms of free energy provide man with a capacity to work. Work is required in order to maintain the existence, procreation, and further evolution of mankind. Energy and work are interrelated and interchangeable terms. The standard definition of energy which appears in the literature is: "Energy is the capacity to do work."[13] In advancing his control over energy, therefore, by definition, man advances his capacity to work. Consequently, labor productivity as a measure of man's capacity to do work is enhanced and advanced through higher levels of energy control.

But according to the Second Law of Thermodynamics the universe is moving from order to disorder and toward a uniform distribution of energy. Entropy is the thermodynamic measure of this wearing down process and indicates the amount of unavailable energy which exists in a system. Low entropy indicates an ordered form as free energy. High entropy results when free energy is used and disordered and is dissipated into the cosmos and in the process becomes bound or unavailable. But work must be continuously done, there is a need for more energy, if the evolutionary process is to continue. Life systems therefore must continuously struggle to overcome the entropic degradation inherent in various forms of energy. Entropic reversals, or negative entropy, are required in order for life systems to overcome the operation of a basic energy law of the universe.

Therefore as the physical universe moves from levels of low entropy to high entropy life systems must counteract and work in reverse, if they are to survive and endure in the evolutionary process. The Entropy Law is consequently basic to any discussion of evolution. And while the Entropy Law has penetrated and been accepted in the fields of the physical and biological sciences it has yet to really penetrate the social sciences. In the first place evolution per se is still yet to be fully accepted in the social sciences in general and this would prevail, especially so, in particular for economics. But on top of it all, it might also be noted that entropy is not that fully comprehensible even to all physicists let alone to individuals trained as economists.[14] Nicholas Georgescu-Roegen stands almost alone in his attempt to relate *The Entropy Law and the Economic Process*," . . . the thesis that I have endeavored to develop in this book, namely, that the basic nature of the economic process is entropic and that the Entropy Law rules supreme over this process and over its evolution."[15]

Mankind has two basic instruments with which to deal with entropic degradation in the struggle for free and available energy. Such energy as it is used to provide man with the ability to work and produce in order to maintain his existence, procreate, and evolve over time is converted into bound or latent energy. The two instruments which we refer to here are the *endosomatic* (or somatic) and the *exosomatic* (or extrasomatic.[16] In biological life, as the endosomatic, free energy is used not only to sustain the life of the organism and aid in its procreation but it is also necessary in order to achieve genetic mutation as a change in structure. In invoking the Marshallian biological analogy we argue that the same process of evolution is continued on in culture evolution as the exosomatic.[17] The replication process as the reproduction of economic goods concerns economic growth, whereas the genetic mutation of structural change appears in the form of the new technological change, and concerns the processes of economic development. "Exosomatic instruments enable man to obtain the same amount of low entropy with less expenditure of his own free energy than if he used only his endosomatic organs."[18] The exosomatic might also be called the superorganic or better yet, man's culture.[19] Consequently it is culture and its evolution which provides the most powerful instrument in man's quest for entropy reversals as negative entropy. And it is that process, the process of culture evolution, which we are focusing on in this study in its relation to energy transformation and economic development.

In that physicists would logically be the ones to deal with a systematic or scientific conceptualization of energy it is no surprise to find that the originators of the connection, that energy control relates to the advance of man's civilization, were physicists.[20] In anthropology, the social scientist who, clearly stands out in dealing with the issues we have noted and who relates the advance of energy control to culture evolution is Leslie A. White.[21] White also invokes the Entropy Law. "... the fundamental significance of culture cannot be understood without recourse to this great generalization of physics."[22]

Perhaps L.A. White represents an example of Ohm's Law concerning electrical energy as applied in the sphere of the social sciences. In that the flow of L.A. White's intellect, with high voltage levels of integrity and fidelity, from an extraordinary source of energy potential (his battery of brain cells), has met with a good deal of resistance (in attempts at divisive division) and while all this has generated a significant amount of heat, social scientists, in general, have yet to see the light. To those who have dealt with the concepts of energy and culture the connection between the two would be as obvious as tying the horse (energy) to the wagon (culture). Yet the idea of relating energy control and transformation to culture evolution is resisted by social scientists. And further, not only is the relation of energy to culture evolution resisted, but culture evolution, itself, is yet to be fully accepted. But as L.A. White notes, there is hope in that: "We are confident, however, that basic and fruitful concepts will eventually be accepted and exploited. After all, the science of culture is still very young."[23]

And while we recognize L.A. White's contribution to culturology and the importance of a science of culture, we do not necessarily, therefore, endorse or agree with either his historical materialism, as methodology and theory, or his sui generis view of culture evolution.[24] White takes a determinist view in his analysis of the relation between technology and culture. Culture evolution to L.A. White is explained in terms of culture, sui generis, and it is technology which serves as "The Basis and Determinant of Cultural Systems."[25]. Crucial in such a discussion would be the concept of technology employed. To L.A. White technology is found in material culture; technology so conceptualized does not substantively include nonmaterial culture. To say that the dominant force in explaining overall human behavior is contained in culture, and that consequently that culture also dominates in man's economic behavior is one thing. But to say that technological change in turn determines culture evolution is another. For if our desire is to explain culture evolution, and since culture evolution is a part of the overall of evolution which embraces the physical, the biological and the social, any explanation of the process of culture evolution must also take cognizance of the biological, the physical and the social. Therefore we must include man, as the biological, natural resources as the physical, and culture as the social; not as simply fixed parameters but as variables. To claim that culture advances sui generis presents, therefore, less than the complete picture. To negate man's role in the process transforms anthropology into a "dismal science" as much as the Malthusian framework transformed economics. For if man in the final analysis has no control over the process there is, indeed, no hope. That technology provides for the dynamics of culture evolution, analogous to genetic mutation in biology, we accept. But what then determines technology? The answer rests in the process of circular and cumulative causation. And given a circle where does one start? Technological change concerns a complexity of forces, inherent in an amalgam of the biological, the physical and the cultural. Consequently, while technological change dominates, one may legitimately raise the question, what in turn determines technology and its transformation?

In the course of this study we will present the view that technology represents the application of useful knowledge to the practical ends of economic production and social organization. Substantively technology represents the concretion of useful knowledge and appears in both social and material forms. Technology appears as a gestalt comprised of both material and social inventions and not simply the material. Consequently, what determines technology is what determines the advance and innovation of useful knowledge in the form of social and material technics. And therefore, though technology dominates in the advance of culture evolution there are a myriad of forces which in turn determine useful knowledge and its advance as well as its application in the form of the new technics of technology. In that the process of culture evolution is one of circular and cumulative causation it is difficult to say which variable determines which. Advances in useful knowledge in their application appear as technics of both economic production and social organization. Material culture, however, concerns only economic production and embodies tools and energy sources. Advances in useful knowledge therefore in changing technology also advance levels of productivity which generate higher levels of economic growth which in turn increase the capacity for capital formation. Such increases in income provide for greater commitments for education and science and in turn provide for the further advance of useful knowledge. And so the "wheel of economic development" spins, more and more knowledge begetting more and more knowledge. The essence of the dynamics of the process of economic development is consequently contained in the advance of useful knowledge which in its application takes on the form of man's technology.

Consequently, the control over energy advances with the advance in useful knowledge. In view of this, the advance of useful knowledge is the essence of the process of culture evolution and economic development. Not only does our energy base of natural resources increase with the advance of useful knowledge, for example, from coal to conceivably the deuterium of our oceans, but in addition our material tools for utilizing the expanded resource base advance as well. As long as man was limited to his own energy capacity of a very limited horse-power he was also limited in the size and scope of his tools and machines and consequently his capacity to do work.[26] As man advances useful knowledge he learns of new energy sources and how to control them, he can then improve upon his material technics which utilize such new energy sources. When man moves from animate to inanimate sources of energy control he therefore can advance from the axe to the bulldozer. All this adds to his productivity, his capacity and efficiency to do work, and consequently, his production of goods and services, or what is usually referred to as economic growth. Therefore, again our basic theme, economic growth on a long-term continuum is a function of economic development, and such culture evolution and transformation entails higher levels of energy control. Development will not be achieved simply through growth since without development or technological change, by itself, would ultimately lead to a logistic ceiling or limit.

As we advance useful knowledge, itself increasing at an exponential rate, we move through a series of logistic surges in our utilization of various energy sources such as those of wood, coal, petroleum, hydroelectric, and nuclear. It is in this way that the evolution of culture, as the extrasomatic, provides for an increased capacity to obtain new sources of free energy as the economy moves from fuelwood to coal and on to petroleum. As man uses such sources of free energy it is true that he produces the by-products of bound energy and waste. But, also, in the advance of culture and technology, and thereby higher levels of energy control, he also provides for a greater capacity to cope with and solve the waste problem. As man advances culture he promotes order to overcome the evolution toward disorder inherent in the physical universe.

The new sources of energy control provide for a similar exponential pattern of logistic surges in our transportation technology and our capacity to travel in miles per hour in the context of various technics of transportation. With the new forms of energy, the technics of transportation changed from that of our feet, to the horse (both animate and relatively inefficient) to the railroad, the automobile, the airplane, in the form of the propeller and then the jet, and then to rockets. As we do not grow simply by growing faster, we similarly do not increase our capacity to travel in miles per hour simply by running faster but such logistic surges in miles per hour are dependent upon our transformation of technics of transportation, which in turn are related to new energy sources. Our capacity to travel as well as our capacity for economic growth on a continuum is consequently dependent upon culture evolution. Culture, as it advances, transforms our energy sources as well, and in so doing increases man's capacity and efficiency to do work, be such work devoted toward such basic economic activities as transportation or building bridges or to such non-economic activity as the waging of war.

In his treatment of the relation between energy and culture evolution Leslie A. White presents the ". . . law of cultural development: *culture advances as the amount of energy harnessed per capita per year increases, or as the efficiency or economy of the means of controlling energy is increased, or both.*"[27] It would be legitimate to debate White's precise formulation of the "law" of cultural development. However it appears beyond debate, especially in view of the contributions of Leslie A. White and Nicholas Georgescu-Roegen, to deny the importance of the Entropy Law and the role of energy in its relation to the economic process.

And yet, even with such an obvious connection between energy control and man's capacity to do work, that is, specifically related to his capacity to produce goods and services, the economist has generally excluded energy control from the purview of his analysis.[28] Mainline theory of economic analysis has just recently (post WWII) made significant inroads into trying to understand the basic relationships between technology and economic development and growth; discussions similarly relating energy transformation to economic development and growth in any overall general theoretical framework have just recently, with the work of Georgescu-Roegen, begun to appear on the horizon. Though overlooked by mainline theory, energy control is nonetheless of fundamental importance in an understanding of the process of economic development and growth. It must be noted that energy as a commodity takes on the form not only of fossil fuels, such as petroleum, but also is related to our basic foodstuffs and grains, as well, which serve as stores of free energy to be converted and transformed.[29]

In a broad sense evolution on the earth has been the story of solar energy transformation.[30] Energy, as we have noted, is defined as the capacity or ability to do work and energy expended or released per unit of time is the definition of power. And, "The work performed by a power depends on this power and the duration of its action."[31] Man's capacity to perform work, to produce goods and services, during a set period of time is consequently a function of man's capacity to control energy. And it is the level or stage of economic development, or by the same token the stage of culture advance, which is the primary consideration in determining the energy plateau.[32]

Economic development, therefore, involves a process of moving from one energy plateau to the next through the advance of useful knowledge by adding new technics to the overall gestalt of technology. Continued economic development into the future is in turn regulated by man's control over energy, and again the circular nature of the process in that economic development promotes a higher energy plateau and a higher energy plateau aids in the process of further economic development.[33] In view of these relationships indicating that economic development is a process which increases capacity to control energy, it would then follow that one of the most relevant indicators of economic development would be that of the level of energy control.

We are now in a position to present quantitative measures of the descriptive analysis of the stages of economic development offered in the previous chapter. Figure V-I, "A Paradigm of Energy Control as Successive Logistic Surges" gives empirical support to the view that culture evolution advances exponentially with the underlying paradigm of logistic surges. Each particular energy gestalt can also serve to indicate a particular stage of economic development, note: Figure V-II, "The Stages of Economic Development and the Levels of Energy Control." It is in this way that we have attempted to combine both a description and measurement of the stages of economic development.

We have argued that energy transformation is relevant to all of evolution and, consequently, that energy transformation is also necessary for the processes of economic and social evo-

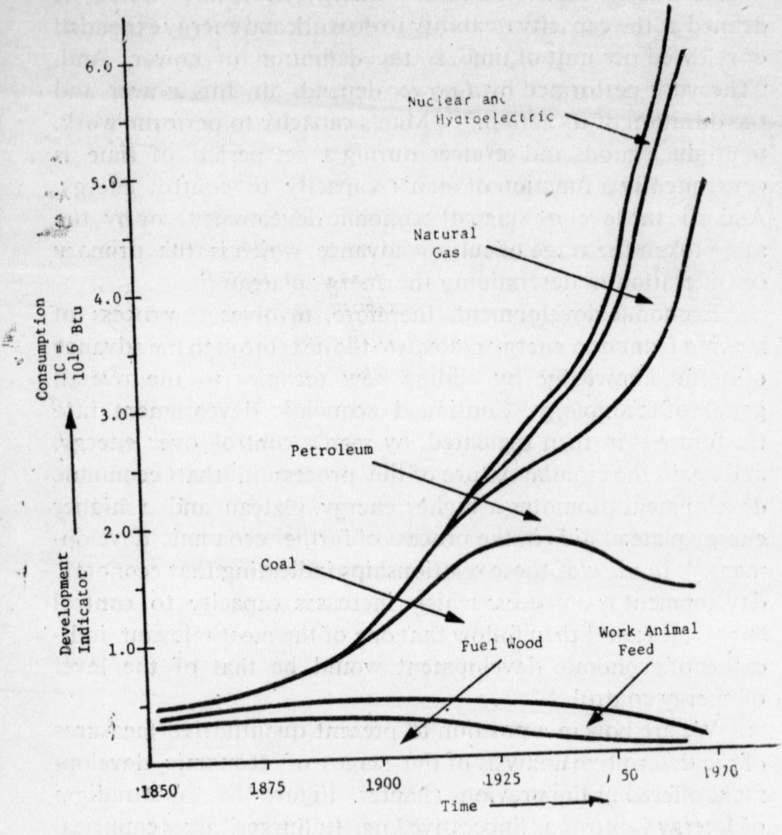

Fig. V-I. A Paradigm of Energy Control as Successive Logistic Surges, 1850-1970 (United States).

Source: Fisher, John C., *Energy Crisis in Perspective* (New York: John Wiley and Sons, 1974), pp. 157-172, and for the development indicator 1C=1016 Btu, see p. 15. Though the hydroelectric and nuclear gestalts are in actuality separate, the scale of presentation requires that they be treated as one, and also in view of the magnitudes, that wind and water be excluded (data plotted at 25 year intervals).

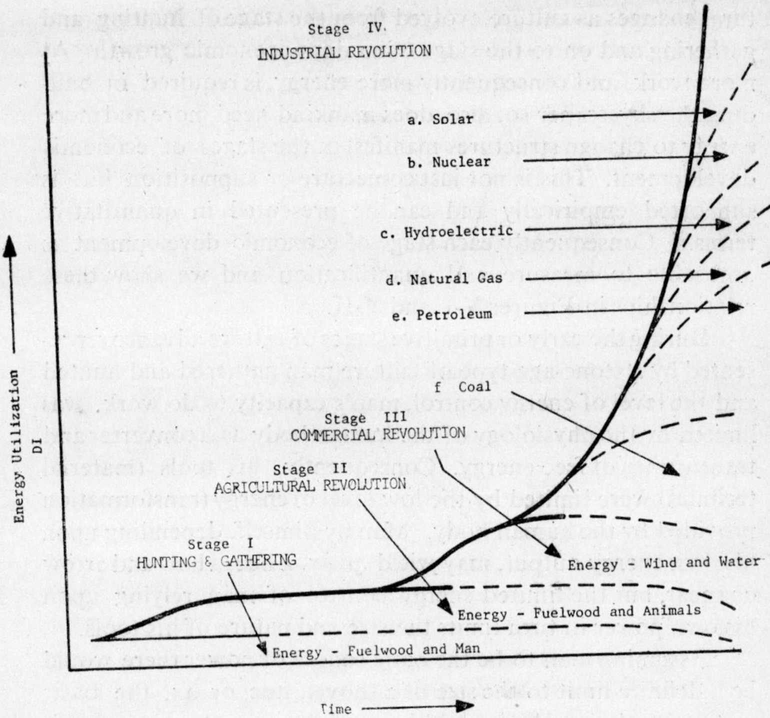

Fig. V-II. The Stages of Economic Development and the Levels of Energy Control.

lution. Work must be accomplished in order to achieve economic growth as replication, as more and more bows and arrows, cotton, or automobiles. But energy is not used simply for reproduction but entails mutation as well. In economic terms this is analogous to the work involved in transforming the structure of the economy. The matrix of the stages of economic development provides a methodology for describing these structural changes as culture evolved from the stage of hunting and gathering and on to the stage of modern economic growth. As more work, and consequently more energy, is required in building the skyscraper so, also, does mankind need more and more energy to change structures manifest in the stages of economic development. This is not just conjecture or supposition but is supported empirically and can be presented in quantitative terms.[34] Consequently each stage of economic development is amenable to measure and quantification and we show these relationships in Figures V-I, and V-II.

During the early or primitive stages of culture advance represented by a stone-age-type of culture man gathered and hunted and the level of energy control, man's capacity to do work, was limited by the physiology of the human body as a converter and transformer of free energy. Consequently, his tools (material technics) were limited by the low level of energy transformation provided by the human body. Man by himself, depending upon his own energy output, may wield an ax, a hoe, a bow and arrow or spear, but the limited energy control of man relying upon his own power in turn limits the size and nature of his tools.

Assuming man to be the basic source of power there would be a definite limit to the size of a shovel, hoe or ax, the basic material technics which could be used by man to achieve his practical ends. By transforming the energy level we remove limits on the material technics, machines and tools, which may be utilized for practical ends. With the new energy gestalt of petroleum we replace the shovel, hoe or ax and introduce, for example, the tractor, the immensely huge machines used in strip-mining and the 747. This is, of course, a basic theme of L. A. White but one which frequently appears elsewhere in the literature.[35]

The weapons and missiles (material technics) of early cultures, "the arm-, foot-, and mouth-propelled instruments," powered by man alone have been vastly transformed to the current guided missiles plus hydrogen bomb of modern military technology, a transformation predicated upon man's increased control over energy.[36] Each new energy plateau consequently opens the door to a wave of new material technics which in turn add to man's control over energy and all of which add to his capacity to perform work. Man by himself represents a relatively low level of energy transformation and at most can produce the equivalent of 1/10—1/20 horsepower.[37] Given such a low level of energy transformation man's capacity for population increase and economic growth was basically limited by the geographic and climatic conditions, the conditions of forage of the physical environment provided by nature.[38] Man broke through this ceiling on his economic growth through the advance of technology and the transformation of culture, that is, through the processes of economic development.

Culture evolution, as a process of technological advance, can consequently be viewed as a series of stages of economic development characterized by energy transformation. As the higher energy plateaus are reached the scope of material technics is increased and is reflected in man's movement from the hoe, to the plow, to the tractor and on. The higher energy plateaus reflect man's increased capacity to perform work and are reflected in increased productivity and economic growth. Therefore, an interrelated sequence exists in the "wheel of economic development:" advances in useful knowledge in the form of new technics added to the overall gestalt of technology represent technological change and provide a basis for increased energy control and transformation which in turn provides for a greater scope for inventing new technics, both material and nonmaterial, which in turn increase man's capacity for work, consequently his productivity, and thereby his economic growth. The circle of cumulative causation of the "wheel of economic development" is renewed with the genesis of new technics and their innovation.[39]

With the advance of culture, man learned to harness the energy of other animals; he learned to harness wind to the sails of ships, water to devices and machinery, and ultimately the big breakthrough—he learned to harness heat to power to machinery.[40] The statistics on energy consumption both for cultures and culture reveal this trend. The United States as an example of "cultures" in the vanguard of "culture" advance reveals this trend in energy consumption. In estimates of work output by sources of energy we find that human and animal sources constituted 65.4 percent of the total for the year 1850 and the inanimate 34.6 percent and that by 1950, just one century later, the inanimate sources by comparison accounted for 98.5 percent of the total.[41] It is then the structural and quality changes associated with energy transformation which have given man his current capacity for work inherent in modern economic growth.[42] In the process man developed, over time, the capacity to sustain large numbers of his own specie and today upwards of four billion people inhabit the earth as a result of culture evolution and the associated transformation of energy.[43] The populations of other warm-blooded, earth-roaming mammals such as the great herds of American bison, appear small by comparison and were limited in their collective size by the natural conditions of forage. As noted previously, the great human population densities of the twentieth century would obviously be impossible under paleolithic conditions of energy control.[44]

For the reasons given above we conclude energy levels to be basic indicators of the overall level of technological advance and economic development and consequently serve as quantitative indicators of the long-term trend of our development curve.[45] Harrison in his *Conquest of Energy* also reasons along these lines and gives numerical magnitudes to the various stages of culture in line with energy control and advance. Harrison views the evolution of culture in terms of basic energy plateaus, ". . Over centuries, men have climbed, usually very slowly, from one level of energy control to a higher level.[46] Economic development and culture advance may consequently be indicated by levels of energy control and this is what Harrison does. The period of hunting and gathering, which marks the first energy plateau, was followed by the second plateau characterized by agriculture and the domestication of animals; the second plateau marked a five-fold increase in man's energy control and capacity. A third plateau was reached with industrialism and this constituted, according to Harrison, an approximate fifteen-fold gain in energy when compared to the agricultural plateau. Industrialization with atomic fuels, as compared to fossil fuels, would represent an additional five-fold increase in man's energy control.[47] The first energy plateau is equated to *one*, the second (the Agricultural Revolution) plateau as a five-fold increase is equated to *five*, the third (industrialization with fossil fuels) at a fifteen-fold increase is equated to *seventy-five* and the fourth (industrialization with atomic fuels) estimated at *three-hundred seventy-five*. The estimates provided by Harrison indicate that as culture advances, through series of stages or technological gestalts, we achieve higher levels of energy control and that this advance has accelrated over time.[48] The view presented here that energy control and usage is correlated to culture change and advance and is by the same token a driving force propelling civilization is, of course, as we have noted, not a terribly new revelation.[49]

Also, in relation to our previous statements regarding the evolution of culture, the exponential or accelerating increases of culture discussed here apply to *culture* and not necessarily to *cultures*, that is, we are speaking of exponential advance in the context of general evolution and not specific evolution. An underdeveloped country hardly has an accelerating culture but rather has experienced the rigors of a logistic ceiling, in the confines of limited energy control, in its overall economic development. Therefore, while the acceleration of development is characteristic for culture in general, in a universal sense, we may find in a particular instance of a given culture, that is for a given underdeveloped region or country, that a ceiling may exist on the accumulation of technology and culture advance.[50] And that the ceiling of low levels of energy transformation and GNP/capita, and the associated high levels of illiteracy and as disease, exists, and as late the third quarter of the 20th century and for as much as 2/3 of mankind; we well know to be a fact.

In summary then, in relating energetics to the processes of economic development, it appears that mankind must continuously search out and control new forms of free energy. Entropic reversals, as negative entropy, are required for mankind not only to survive but to continue the evolutionary process in the form of structural change. The extrasomatic, as the superorganic or culture, has provided the basic overall tool whereby mankind has extended the limited energy control contained in his own organic structure as the somatic. The new structures of culture evolution are described and delineated through the stages of economic development as methodology. In this chapter we have attempted to show how a descriptive treatment of the stages of economic development can be quantitatively substantiated in the context of various forms of energy as the development indicator. It is energy, therefore, which constitutes the motor force behind the process of economic development and culture evolution. But how has mankind accomplished the remarkable feat of moving from one energy gestalt to the next? What is the process whereby mankind generates control over new energy gestalts and thereby provides for the required new levels of free energy? It is with such a focus that we will be able to explain the transition from one stage of economic development to the next and, thereby, the process of economic development. To answer the question concerning the theory of transformation, we must now change the concepts of knowledge, technology and culture and try to clarify their basic meaning and interrelationships. How is it that in the advance of useful knowledge we advance technology and, also, in the process promote the evolution and transformation of culture?

REFERENCES

[1]Of the several sources which one might refer to on the conceptual problem of energy, note: D.W. Theobald, *The Concept of Energy* (London: E. & F.N. Spon, 1966). Also: Morton Mott-Smith, *The Concept of Energy Simply Explained* (New York: Dover Publications, 1964); Bruce Chalmers, *Energy* (New York: Academic Press, 1963); and, Michell Wilson, *Energy* (New York: Time 1963).

[2]Leslie A. White, *The Evolution of Culture* (New York: McGraw-Hill Book Co., 1959), p. 3.

[3]Theobald, *The Concept of Energy*, pp. 175, 2,3,24 and xiv.

[4]Wilson, *Energy*, p. 9. That the concept of energy is real though it is not a thing or of specific physical characteristic or substance is one of the basic points made in Theobald's, *The Concept of Energy*, ". . . it may be objected, we cannot say what energy is like, although we can to some extent say what the electron or the molecule is like." The fact that energy is not a thing in the normal sense of that word does not mean that it does not exist and that it is not real . . ."

p. 177, and, "Energy has empirical reference, metaphysical substance has none." p. 177, and, "There is no structure for energy because energy is the fundamental concept of all physical interaction." p. 178. That the concepts of energy and economic development have no specific structure does not mean that they lack empirical reference or physical indication. As L. A. White and others maintain, nuclear explosions and high levels of GNP/capita reflect high levels of energy transformation, the former in the so-called physical world and the latter in the social.

[5]Note the preface to Chalmers, *Energy* and also, Fred Cottrell, *Energy and Society* (New York: McGraw-Hill Book Co , 1955), "Energy must be defined in terms of the ways in which it manifests itself . . . To do justice to the concept of energy would require treating each of its manifestations as it is treated by experts in that particular field." pp. 5-6.

[6]"A particular science will evolve its own language, its own scheme of concepts. Theories and the concepts embodied in them provide the language scientists use to report their observations. From time to time new observations cannot be reported satisfactorily, since the language of available theory is inadequate. The conceptual framework is then appropriately enriched or modified until the language is sufficiently comprehensive. The new observations can then be reported, they are then explained. . . . This process of evolution is naturally enough most obvious on the fringes of rapidly developing sciences such as nuclear physics." Theobald, *The Concept of Energy*, pp. 8, 10.

[7]The date when the concept energy "first entered the technical vocabulary of science" would be 1807 and was introduced by Thomas Young. Note, J. Clark Maxwell, *Theory of Heat* (London: Longmans, Green and Co., 1894), p. 91. Theobald, *The Concept of Energy*, p. 57, dates the first usage of the concept of energy in a scientific sense by Thomas Young in 1805 but this is perhaps a typographical error in that Theobald's reference is dated 1807, note, p. 85, and also, Wilson, *Energy*, pp. 12, 16. The existence of man's culture proximates one million years, yet it was only as recently as 1807 that he first scientifically conceptualized energy and only one century later that Einstein added his contributions leading to the ultimate breakthrough of the mid-twentienth century into the age of nuclear energy. Developments which again add support to the view that culture cumulates and advanccs at an exponential rate.

[8]The German physicist, Rudolf Clausius, conceptualized entropy and formulated the Entropy Law in 1865. As Allan G. Gruchy notes: ". . . economics was a well-established science long before evolutionary concepts had become a part of the intellectual furniture of most men. By origin and tradition the science of economics is therefore non-evolutionary." p. vii in David Hamilton, *Evolutionary Economics* (Albuquerque: University of New Mexico Press, 1970).

[9]Wilson, *Energy*, p. 9.

[10]Ibid., p. 143.

[11]Leslie A. White, as perhaps the leading proponent of culture evolution in the context of energy transformation, expresses this thought with: "Every event that takes place in the universe, whether it will be physical, biological, or cultural is an expression of energy, an instance of energy transformation. All cultural systems, therefore, like all physical and biological systems can be reduced to a common denominator: energy. Energy is a universal dimension of culture." "The Energy Theory of Cultural Development," pp. 139-146 in Morton H. Fried, ed., *Readings in Anthropology* (New York: Thomas Y. Crowell Company, 1959). Vol. II, p. 140. In another treatment of energy, by George Russell Harrison, *The Conquest of Energy* (New York: William Morrow & Company, 1968) we find ideas almost identical to those expressed by Leslie A. White: "Yet energy is every bit as important as matter. Neither can exist without the other. Unless energy is involved, no particle or galaxy can move, no creature come alive, no human think. Every physical occurrence, every mental or emotional experience, involves the interaction of energy with matter. Because of the tangibility of matter we speak of 'material' wealth, overlooking the fact that most wealth springs from energy control." p. 2.

[12]As Nicholas Georgesu-Roegecu notes: "It is physics again that supplies the only clear example of an evolutionary law: The Second Law of Thermodynamics, called also the Entropy Law." and, "Clausius seems to have thought of it in the same way, for he coined 'entropy' from a Greek word equivalent in meaning to 'evolution'." *The Entropy Law and the Economic Process,* (Cambridge: Harvard University Press, 1971), pp. 129,130.

[13]Note "Work, Energy, and Power," pp. 10-31, in Jerry B. Marion, *Energy in Perspective* (New York: Academic Press, 1974).

[14]On the difficulties, note N. Georgescu-Roegen, *The Entropy Law and the Economic Process*, pp. 4-5, and, "But—a fact hard to explain—loud though the noise created by the Entropy Law has been in physics and the philosophy of science, economists have failed to pay attention to this law, the most economic of all physical laws." p. 280.

[15]Ibid, pp. 283, xiii, ii, 18, 281, and passim, and also, Nicholas Georgescu-Roegen, *Energy and Economic Myths* (New York: Pergamon Press, 1976), especially, pp. 3-36, and, pp. 53-60.

[16]N. Georgescu-Roegen, Ibid., pp. 307-308, 11, and 348 ff. On the somatic and extrasomatic, see Leslie A. White, *The Evolution of Culture* (New York: McGraw-Hill Book Company, 1959), pp. 38-39.

[17]Note N. Georgescu-Roegen, *The Entropy Law and the Economic Process*, pp. 11, 281, on the Marshallian biological analogies. And L. A. White *The Science of Culture*, " . . . we may interpret the evolution of culture in terms of the same principles of thermodynamics that are applicable to biological systems." p. 39.

[18]N. Georgescu-Roegen, *The Entropy Law and Economic Process*, p. 307. "We economists call them capital equipment, but Lotka's term, *exosomatic instruments*, is more enlightening." Capital is indeed a very important part but it is only part of the whole of culture (recall our

discussions in Chapter I of this study) and it is relegated to the one-half of culture known as material culture.

[19]"This extrasomatic mechanism, this traditional organization of tools, customs, language, beliefs, etc., we have called *culture*." L.A. White, *The Evolution of Culture*, p. 38.

[20]The attempt to relate energy and civilization is therefore not original with L.A. White and on many occasions L.A. White notes his predecessors, see for example "The Energy Theory of Cultural Development," pp. 142-146, and also, *The Evolution of Culture*, especially pp. 39 ff.

[21]On L.A. White's contributions, note: Gertrude E. Dole and Robert L. Carneiro, *Essays in the Science of Culture* (New York: Thomas Y. Crowell Company, 1960), especially pp. 486 ff. for a bibliography of L.A. White's contributions, and also, the foreword by Harry Elmer Barnes, pp. xi-xlvi. In addition to *The Evolution of Culture* (1959) and *The Science of Culture* (1949), see also, *The Concept of Culture* (Minneapolis: Burgess Publishing Company, 1973), and, *The Concept of Culture Systems* (New York: Columbia University Press, 1975). According to Harry Elmer Barnes, " . . . Dr. White will probably go down in the history of anthropology as the outstanding protagonist and practitioner of cultural evolution in the middle third of the present century, if not in the whole century . . ." p. xxiv.

[22]P. 38, L.A. White, *The Evolution of Culture*, and, "Living systems are means of arresting and even reversing, the cosmic drift toward maximum entropy." p. 35. This is not to infer that culture negates the Entropy Law, on the contrary, culture in its function to concentrate energy ultimately reinforces the Second Law of Thermodynamics, see p. 39, footnote 19 where L.A. White addresses this issue.

[23]Fried, *Readings in Anthropology*, Vol 2, p. 146; and, Vol 1, where the following assessment of White appears: "A major defender of evolutionary theory in anthropology when most voices were raised in opposition, White has had the rare pleasure of seeing his once unpopular views taken up by many younger anthropologists." pp. 15-16.

[24]On "culturology," note L.A. White, *The Science of Culture*, pp. 115-117, 409-415, *The Evolution of Culture*, pp. 28-29, and, "Culturology,", Vol. 3, *International Encyclopedia of the Social Sciences* (1968), pp. 547-551.

[25]pp. 18-28, *The Evolution of Culture*. " . . . our theory of technological determinism." p. 28, "The technological factor is the basic one; all others are dependent upon it." p. 19. "The technological factor is therefore the determinant of a cultural system as a whole." *The Science of Culture*, p. 366. In the course of our study we will argue against this view, not in deference to ". . . the political passions of times." (See Marvin Harris, *The Rise of Anthropological Theory* (New York: Thomas Y. Crowell Company, 1968), pp. 637-639) but rather, that simply, in our view White is incorrect.

[26]L.A. White frequently draws attention to the interrelations between energy (E), tools (T) and product (P). Note *The Evolution*

of Culture, Chapter 2 "Enegry and Tools," pp. 33-57, especially, pp. 40-42; *The Science of Culture*, pp. 374-76, 40-54.

[27]*The Evolution of Culture*, p. 56, and also on the "law of cultural evolution" see "Energy and the Evolution of Culture" *American Anthropologist* 45 (1943) pp. 335-356, p. 338. On White's "Law" see Harris, *The Rise of Anthropological Theory*, p. 636, and, as a "research strategy" note: Betty J. Meggers, "The Law of Cultural Evolution as a Practical Research Tool" in Dole and Carneiro, eds., *Essays in the Science of Culture*, pp. 302-316.

[28]The concept of energy has not penetrated the normal science of main-line economic theory; it is not an integral part of the theoretical framework of economic analysis. This is not to say that energy, mostly as energy resources, does not enter into works presented as general surveys. Note, W.S. Woytinsky and E.S. Woytinsky, *World Population and Production* (New York: The Twentieth Century Fund, 1953), pp. 749-983, especially pp. 924-983 and, J. Frederic Dewhurst, *America's Needs and Resources* (New York: The Twentieth Century Fund, 1955), pp. 901-915, and also, *Europe's Needs and Resources* (New York: Twentieth Century Fund 1961) in *passim*. But attempts, such as we are making, to integrate the concept of energy into an overall theoretical though there are examples, such as, L.A. White, N. Georgescu-Roegen, framework are not too numerous and also, Fred Cottrell *Energy and Society* (New York: McGraw-Hill Book Company, 1955). If it is correctly argued that discussions concerning economic development cannot take place in the context of invariant technology we argue similarly for the inclusion of energy transformation.

[29]"Energy has become the world's most important economic commodity; more of it is bought and sold than any other item, although it is not always obvious that it is energy that is changing hands." Chalmers, *Energy*, p.v.

[30]"For more than four billion years before man appeared on earth, nature had been experimenting in the endless processes of evolution, building up ever more complex patterns of matter which guided the flow of energy into ever more diverse channels." George Harrison, *The Conquest of Energy*, p. 5. And, ". . the sun has been and is the earth's one energy source of any consequence. . . accounts for all our energy except for microscopic amounts that are from radioactive transformations in the earth itself." Eugene Ayres, *Energy Sources—The Wealth of the World* (New York: McGraw-Hill Book Company, 1952), pp. 1, 177 and 202. And, "The only known sources are the sun's radiation, nuclear energy (that is, fission and fusion), the energy associated with the rotation of the earth and the moon in their orbits, and the heat stored and generated in the earth (geothermal energy)," and, "It follows that at least at the present time and in the near future we will be dependent upon the energy that comes form the sun in the form of radiation," Chalmers, *Energy*, pp. 263-265. And, "Thus it is that all the activity on earth is carried on; and this available energy is directed by life and mind so as to enable us

to do all that we have yet found physically possible: We might sum up this available energy for the most part as the energy of chemical or molecular combination, the atoms having been rearranged into fresh molecules by solar light, so that they can thereafter release their stored energy in required directions." Sir Oliver Lodge, *Energy* (New York: John F. Rider Publisher, 1957), p. 44. And to relate solar energy transformation to the economic and the social, "Since the sun is the source of all life and energy on our planet, the flow of human economic activities can be represented as a cycle in the transformation of solar energy." Woytinsky, *World Population and Production*, p. 928.

[31]Woytinsky, *World Population and Production*, pp. 924-25. Cottrell, *Energy and Society*, pp. 5-8.

[32]"Culture is an organization of things in motion, a process of energy transformations. . . . It is an organization of energy transformations that is dependent upon symbolizing." L.A. White, *The Evolution Culture*, p.38.

[33]According to L.A. White, energy is perhaps one of the best indicators of culture evolution or economic development. Similarly, Harrison in his *A Conquest of Energy*, in passim, associates energy plateaus with the level or stage of economic development. This is not unreasonable in view of the fact that ". . The supply of energy is itself one of the principal factors influencing the rate of economic development." E.A.G. Robinson and G.H. Daniel, "The World's Need for a New Source of Energy," pp. 38-49, in *Peaceful Uses of Atomic Energy* (New York: United Nations, 1956), Vol. 1. p. 38. That energy consumption increases with the process of economic development and consequently serves as an indicator of economic development is recognized in the literature. "This great dramatic shift to mineral energy is the very basis of technological progress. One could almost concentrate the whole history of economic development into this simple transition: man power to animal power to machine power." J. Frederick Dewhurst and Gloria Waldron, *Power, Machines, and Plenty*, Public Affairs Pamphlet, No. 142, (New York: The Twentieth Century Fund, 1948) p. 9 (referred to by Zimmermann, *World Resources and Industries*, p. 58). "Economic development is largely a matter of adding to the horsepower available to assist the people who at present are poor because of the lack of it." E.A G. Robinson and G.H. Daniel, "The World's Need for a New Source of Energy," p. 47. Also, Manners, *The Geography of Energy*, pp. 15-21, and, John Davis, *Canadian Energy Prospects* (Royal Commission on Canada's Energy Prospects, 1957), pp. 13-56. And, ". . world energy consumption which has been growing at an accelerated basis, consequently for the universal conceptualization of culture, such a world-wide supply would be basically the equivalent of world-wide development and rising income." *New Sources of Energy and Energy Development* (New York: United Nations, 1962), pp. 17-20. As an indicator of culture advance or the stage of economic development, we must note the distinction between consumption and production or demand and supply. If we speak of the

supply (production) of energy on a world-wide basis, consequently for the universal conceptualization of culture, such a world-wide supply would be basically the equivalent of world-wide demand (consumption). However, for cultures, as a particular nation, the supply and demand for energy may differ by significant amounts. For example, in Kuwait energy *Production* per head in coal ton equivalents amounts to 359.27 compared to energy consumption per head of 1 54 Venezuela although not as extreme also offers comparable figures of 29.41 for production and 2.18 for consumption. It is energy consumption rather than production which more accurately indicates the level of development for a particular culture and it is energy consumption which most closely correlates with income per capita as well. Note, Gerald Manners, *The Geography of Energy* (London: Hutchinson & Co., 1964), p. 16. Therefore, ". . Energy consumption is the significant factor, and consumption need not be related to production in any particular area or region," Philip Sporn, *Energy: Its Production Conversion and Use in the Service of Man* (New York: The Macmillan Company, 1963), p. 35.

[34]On the general idea, note: Davis, *Canadian Energy Prospects*, pp. 15-16, and for empirical reference world-wide (culture): *Peaceful Use of Atomic Energy* (New York: United Nations, 1956), Vol. 1, *The World's Requirement for Energy: The Role of Nuclear Energy*, p. 10; and Joel Darmstadter, et al., *Energy in the World Economy* (Baltimore: The Johns Hopkins Press, 1971). No indicator is however perfect, there are also reservations to the use of energy as a basic indicator. Countries with a cold climate and large geographical areas tend to use more energy/capita and these factors are not related to the level of development. Also, energy indicates a capacity to do work and sometimes this is done inefficiently, for example, energy consumption/capita in the U.S. compared to Sweden and West Germany.

[35]"Without control over a supply of energy far superior to their own muscular force, men would have little use for machines and in fact could not build them." Woytinsky, *World Population and Production*, p. 925.

[36]On this note: Francis R. Allen, ed., *Technology and Social Change*, (Francis R. Allen), pp. 354-386, and (Hornell Hart), pp. 35-47, 223-237.

[37] On estimates of human energy converted into horsepower, note Woytinsky, *World Population and Production*, p. 925. L.A. White, *The Evolution of Culture*, pp. 41,45,. . ., etc., C.M. Ripley, "Twenty Men Equal One Horse,' *Power* (March 1947), pp. 104-105. Though the total energy released by the horse is greater man is considered to be a more efficient transformer, note, Cottrell, *Energy and Society* p. 21 and on the general issue, pp. vii, 6, 15-38. Consequently, as man added to his social heritage he also discovered additional sources of energy which he used to accomplish his work. Man by himself represents a limited and weak source of energy, Consequently, the social institution of slavery is not compatible with MEG. Simon Kuznets notes: ". . . Modern economic growth. . . not compatible

with. . . illiteracy or slavery. . . which prevailed in earlier times. ..." p. 247, "Modern Economic Growth. Findings and Reflections," *American Economic Review* 63 (June 1973), pp. 247-258, What mankind needs is not "human slaves' but "energy slaves" and such energy slaves are provided by MEG and the concomitant forms of energy, note: John McHale, *The Future of the Future* (New York: George Braziller, 1969), p. 210, and A.R. Ubbelohde, *Man and Energy* (New York: George Braziller, Inc., 1955), pp. 86-101, p 96 and passim, 110-111,. . . , etc.

[38]The land area per man would vary according to such conditions, for example: "The prehistoric inhabitant of a temperate climate was likely to need about one square mile of forest in which to forage for food sufficient for his family." Harrison, *The Conquest of Energy*, pp. 8-9, "Without abundant energy our standard of living would sink quickly to that of primitive man, and we would find the world immediately overpopulated." Ayres, *Energy Sources*, p. 128. The high population density of the modern period would of course be impossible given the energy plateau of the paleolithic period. "A great increase in world population without a great increase in per capita demand for energy is not plausible." Palmer Cosslett Putnam, *Energy in the Future* (New York: D. Van Nostrand Company, 1953), p. 231. On the subject of population growth and culture advance see also, Carlo M. Cipolla, *The Economic History of World Population* (Baltimore: Penguin Books, 1962).

[39]"Economic growth to meet these challenges can come about only by greater production and greater productivity. Both of these involve the extension and development of technology in which new, frequently very massive tools are employed, and which, as they grow in size and in sophistication, will require increasingly larger quantities of energy for their operation." Sporn, *Energy*, p. 51 and,". . economic growth consists essentially of increasing the average productivity of a labor force and this in turn is directly influenced by the quantity of energy which can be incorporated within the production process." Manners, *The Geography of Energy*, p. 15.

[40]Though steam has taken the wind out of the sails of man's ships, wind, though certainly of limited potential, is still not completely removed from the energy picture, note: Putnam, *Energy in the Future*, pp. 188-191.

[41]Note, Dewhurst, *America's Needs and Resources*, pp. 908-1116. And also, Fisher, *Energy Crisis in Perspective*, pp. 160-161. This trend is also manifest in universal culture, see Woytinsky, *World Population and Production*, pp. 929-931, for the world's supply of energy by sources, for the years 1880-1948. "The dominant technological development o' the past three centuries has been the large-scale and increasing substitution of inanimate for animate energy as the motive force for man's machines. . . It is this energy base that has made possible the whole complex of technological developments that constitutes modern industrial civilization." pp. 589-590, *International Encyclopedia of the Social Sciences* (1968), Vol. 15.

[42]On the relation of energy to economic growth, note: Dewhurst, Frederic J., "Relation of Energy Output to Production in the U.S., *Social Science*, Vol. 23 (October 1948), pp. 207-217; "It is no accident that the United States leads the world in the per capita consumption of inanimate energy, as it does in per capita income." in Dewhurst, *America's Needs and Resources*, pp. 901-915, 903; Edward S. Mason, *Productive Uses of Nuclear Energy: Energy Requirements and Economic Growth* (Washington D.C.: National Planning Association, 1955); E. S. Mason, "Energy Requirements and Economic Growth," *Peaceful Uses of Atomic Energy* (1956), pp. 50-76; Davis, *Canadian Energy Prospects*, pp. 19-45; Nathaniel B. Guyol, "Energy Consumption and Economic Development," in *Essays on Geography and Economic Development* (Chicago: University of Chicago Press, 1960), Norton Ginzberg, ed., pp. 65-77. and, Denis Hayes, *Rays of Hope* (New York: W.W. Norton & Company, 1977), "Energy and Economic Growth," pp. 140-151; and Joel Darmstadter, et. al., *How Industrial Societies Use Energy* (Baltimore: Johns Hopkins University Press, 1977). Also in relating energy to output, ". .there may be no upper limit to productivity or real income per capita and, hence, none to the demands per capita for the *output* of energy. But there does appear to be a limit to the quantity of energy output required for a quantum of real national income—a limit that is different for each economy and in some way characteristic of it." Putnam, *Energy in the Future*, pp. 453, 449-453. There is statistical evidence to show that, that for some countries, output of energy per unit of output of goods and services has tended to increase and then to have leveled off. This basic characteristic, when better understood, may ultimately be used as an indicator of various levels (gestalts) of economic development. The explanation at present is, however, not completely clear, note, also, Sam H. Schurr and Bruce Netschert, *Energy in the American Economy* (Baltimore: The Johns Hopkins Press, 1960), pp. 16-17 and 144-190; Hans H. Landsberg, and Sam H. Schurr, *Energy in the United States* (New York: Random House, 1968), pp. 57-61; Edward S. Mason, *Productive Uses of Atomic Energy*, pp. 55-58; and, Davis, *Canadian Energy Prospects*, pp. 23-24.

[43]Not only does a low energy level limit the absolute or total size of the population and its longevity but it also limits the size of the social unit as well, Cottrell, *Energy and Society*, pp. 23-25, and 166-168. On the general issue of relating population and energy control, note, Putnam, *Energy in the Future*, pp. 7-70. There is evidence to indicate that in addition to the quantity of human life (population data) that the probability of longevity of human life is also a function of economic development and culture advance. Note also: "Scientific and Social Aspects of Control over Aging" in Gerald Feinberg, *Consequences of Growth* (New York: The Seabury Press, 1977), pp. 41-62.

Period and era	*Average length of life from ancient to modern times (years)*
Early Iron and Bronze Age (Greece)	18
Circa 2000 Years Age (Rome)	22
Middle Ages (England)	33
1687-1691 Breslau	33.5
1838-1854 England and Wales	40.9
1900-1902 United States	49.2
1960 United States	69.7
2000	100-150

SOURCE: Louis I. Dublin, *Factbook on Man* (New York: The Macmillan Co., 1965), p. 394 and by the same author, *Length of Life*, p. 42 and in passim; referred to by Putnam, ibid., p. 25, and for the year 2000, Herman Kahn, *The Year 2000* (New York: The Macmillan Company, 1967), p. 56. Of course, our longevity figures represent estimates on the length of life in years but such a quantification of life reveals nothing of the quality of that life which has been the chief benefit of the advance of useful knowledge in the form of economic development.

[44]"It is the leitmotiv in this book that the three basic types of economic organization—hunting, agricultural, industrial—are accompanied by three corresponding ranges of economic and demographic levels at which human societies operate." Carlo M. Cipolla, *The Economic History of World Population*, p. 107.

[45]"This great shift to mineral, or 'mechanical', energy and the vast expansion in its use are the essence of technological progress. . . For the consumption of mineral energy is in a sense merely an index of the state of our technology." Dewhurst, *America's Needs and Resources*, pp. 909-910; "There are strong grounds, therefore, for taking the statistics of energy consumption to be a quantitative measure of economic progress." Davis, *Canadian Energy Prospects*, p. 20; "As a consequence of the close relationship between the use of energy and economic development, there is a high degree of positive correlation between the consumption of energy and the standard of living in a country." Manners, *The Geography of Energy*, p. 16; and also, Allen, *Technology and Social Change*, pp. 250-252; and, Nathaniel B. Guyol, "Energy Consumption and Economic Development," in Norton Ginsburg, ed., *Essays on Geography and Economic Development*, pp. 65-77.

[46]George Russell Harrison, *The Conquest of Energy* (New York: William Morrow and Company, 1968), p. 2.

[47]Actually, Harrison, in his overall treatment, refers to five energy plateaus; he distinguishes the "Atomic Age" in terms of nuclear fission (4th) and nuclear fusion (5th). Note pp. 4, 204 and chapters XII and XIII, and also, Sporn, *Energy*, pp. 4-5, 7, 52.

[48]On the accelerated use of energy and the exponential advance, and the impact of industrialism, "The records of production of the various fuels do not go back very far, but the curves rise so sharply that all production prior to recorded data can be ignored with a probable error of less than 1 per cent. We find that of all the fossil fuel recovered since the earth was created two billion years ago, more than 86 per cent has been produced and used since 1900," and, "The curve for combined production shows that all of the fossil fuel produced in the world up to 1900 would satisfy the present world economy only about five years." Eugene Ayres, *Energy Sources: The Wealth of the World*, pp. 25-27; "The story would resemble the fantastic. . . the effect has been cumulative, and energy, the common ingredient of all these activities, has gone on compounding both as to supply and demand." Davis, *Canadian Energy Prospects*, p. 20.

[49]For a limited sampling of support to this view, note the following references and in turn their references as well: ". . . the suggestion of Fair-grieve that human history is the story of man's increasing control over energy may not seem unreasonable." Zimmermann, *World Resources and Industries*, pp. 54-55; ". . . *it may be said that in its widest sense on its material side history is the story of man's increasing ability to control energy*." James Fairgrieve, *Geography and World Power* (London: University of London Press, 1941). p. 4; "the growth of man's dominion over matter through control of energy was and is likely to be a long-drawn out process. It extends back through history and prehistory to the very beginnings of humanity. Every important technical advance in the past has involved some new phase in the control of energy." A.R. Ubbelohde, *Man and Energy*, p. 13; and some of the repeated references to L.A. White, *The Science of Culture*, pp. 363-393; *The Evolution of Culture*, pp. 33-57; "The Energy Theory of Cultural Development" in M.H. Fried's *Readings in Anthropology*, Vol. II, pp. 139-146, "Energy is a universal dimension of culture," and culture, "is an extrasomatic mechanism for capturing free energy, harnessing it and putting it to work in the service of the human species." pp. 140-141.

[50]We have already discussed that issue in several instances, but again for Elman R. Service on this issue note: "Thus the culture of mankind generally is an evolutionary stage in the universal process, while particular societies differentiate into cultural generaand species, creating heterogeneity." *International Encyclopedia of the Social Sciences* (1968), Vol. V, p. 222 and, of course, his "Evolution: Specific and General" in .Sahlins and Service, eds., *Evolution and Culture*, pp. 12-44.

CHAPTER VI

The Dichotomy of Useful Knowledge

The stages of economic development reveal the basic fact that the advance of culture as a process of evolution was historically marked by a vast transformation of man's social and economic organization. We have described and distinguished the various levels or stages of culture advance or economic development with each stage characterized by its own particular overall gestalt of technology. Each level of technology, such as a neolithic culture, provides an extrasomatic structure which increases the capacity of man to harness more and more free energy. As more work is required with advances in economic development, higher and higher levels of energy control are required in order to maintain and continue the evolutionary process. But how does all this come about? Such an explanation requires a general theory of economic development and/or evolution. A general theory of economic development would entail an explanation of the dynamic process of transforming one stage to the next which basically means a transformation of the overall gestalt of technology characteristic of the particular stage in question.

What then is the mechanism of transforming the overall gestalt of technology? In attempting to answer this question we will first, in this chapter, direct our attention to a conceptual clarification of technology and culture in terms of their interrelation with useful knowledge. In our next chapter, we will engage circular and cumulative causation in the framework of the "wheel of economic development" and try to explain how the advance of useful knowledge, also, in the process promotes the advance of technology and the transformation of culture. In this chapter, however, we will try to establish the basic underpinnings of our theoretical framework by taking a closer look at culture and technology and their relation to useful knowledge. Useful knowledge is a protean concept of many forms, two of which are represented by the dichotomy of useful knowledge into the core of culture and the overall gestalt of technology.[1]

It is the purpose of this chapter to note the relationships between knowledge, culture and technology. In this context, an important distinction to be clarified is that whereas all knowledge forms the basis for all of culture and all techniques, it is only useful knowledge which forms the basis for the core of culture. Useful knowledge constitutes knewledge applied to the practical ends of economic production and social organization and takes on the form of technics. Consequently, it is technics and not techniques which are stored in the core of culture. And it is the integrated whole, as a totality, of all technics which comprises the overall gestalt of technology. Therefore; as we advance useful knowledge in the form of technics, we are also in the process transforming culture in that the core of culture is comprised of material and social technics. As heads and tails are the opposite sides of the same coin, so are the overall gestalt of technology and the core of culture the opposite sides of the same coin, the coin of useful knowledge. Useful knowledge manifests a dichotomy in terms of the core of culture on the one hand and the overall gestalt of technology on the other.

Consequently the dynamics of economic development concerns the process of culture advance but more specifically, however, the advance of not necessarily all of culture but rather the core of culture. Useful knowledge in its store is represented by the core of culture and in its application, as a whole, by the overall gestalt of technology. We emphasized in Chapter I, "The Crucible and Clay of Economic Development," that culture, as conceptualized by anthropologists along the lines of Tylor's definition, is the concept most properly suited to the actual substance (clay) experiencing the process of economic development. It is knowledge in turn which serves as the fountainhead of culture. And it is culture, our social heritage, which accumulates and stores this knowledge. Technology in turn represents the application of that knowledge toward man's practical ends and constitutes the dynamic element in the form of new technics, the social genes of mutation, of the process of culture evolution. If we are to explain culture evolution and not simply culture change we must do so in terms of elements within culture itself.

> "For to understand an activity is to know it as a concrete whole; it is to recognize the activity as having the source of its movement within itself. An understanding which leaves the activity in debt to something outside itself is, for that reason, an inadequate understanding."[2]
>
> ". . . it appears that an evolutionary economics must be the theory of a process of cultural growth as determined by the economic interest, a theory of a cumulative sequence of economic institutions stated in terms of the process itself."
>
> ". . . *ominus cultura ex cultura* . . . Cultural phenomena (including the economic) derive exclusively from other cultural phenomena and can be explained only in terms of other cultural phenomena."[3]

We will now attempt to show how useful knowledge on the one hand in its store takes on the form of culture and on the other hand in its application, or use, the form of technology. The overall gestalt of technology and the core of culture in their origins and genesis are of the same substance, that substance being useful knowledge. As we shall see later, the additions to useful knowledge in the form of new technics which when innovated form the basis of technological change constitute the dynamic element of culture evolution, that is, economic development. We consequently have through a tautological conceptualization, characterized culture change and evolution through technological change, not in the sense that technological change causes culture change, but that rather they are opposite sides of the same substance and to change one means to change the other. Consequently that to change one, technology, we change the other, culture. If we alter the dough we do not cause the bread to change but rather have changed the bread by definition, since the dough is the very substance of bread. Keynesian economics, though static, similarly embraces a taútological conceptualization but of income rather than of useful knowledge. The upper and lower loops of the circular flow of income view income on the one hand as factor payments and, on the other, as production. In changing production we also change the magnitude of factor payments. Similarly we note that in changing technology we also, in the process, change and transform culture, since that is what the core of culture is made of.[4] Given its importance as the dynamic factor of culture evolution, how has technology and technological change been treated in the literature by economists?

In the history of economic doctrine and prior to WW II, the main line of economic theorists treated technological change, by and large, as invariant.[5] Concern of economists toward questions of economic development was relegated primarily to the field of international economics. Theory on economic development became a subsidiary to theory on international trade and, consequently, economic development as such was more or less the expected outcome of the operation of comparative advantage and international specialization.[6] Historically, concern of main-line theory has been more with the optimum efficiency of allocation and later to full utilization (full-employment) of a given resource complex rather than to a change or transformation of the complex.[7]

The 1950's, however, marked a new direction, a watershed period, in which analytical attention of main-line economic theorists moved in the direction of technological change and was augmented under the leadership of Fabricant, Abramovitz and Solow.[8] A contradiction appeared when theoretical expectations were compared to actual empirical results; for a given period, marked by 1909-1949, Solow found that capital accounted for approximately 10 percent of the increased productivity, the residual of 90 percent was largely unexplained.[9] The residual of 90 percent as "a measure of our ignorance" could perhaps be reduced by altering basic assumptions, such as those pertaining to the quality of factor inputs, the role of economics of scale, and so on, and in the process break down the residual into more precisely quantifiable individual parts. However, such attempts purport a precision perhaps greater than that warranted by the methods of calculation and consequently might be assessed as falling "... short of success."[10] Even though a precise quantification as a *direct* measurement of technology and rates of technological change and the impact on growth and economic development may be an impossibility, this does not mean that we cannot *indirectly* indicate technological change through the measurement of various indicators or characteristics of technology and technological change. It is in the context of indirect measures of technological change that most economists currently concerned with economic growth support the proposition that technology is a very important factor, if not the most important factor, accounting for economic growth.[11] Such recognition of the importance of the technological factor is not only now the concern of the growth economist, as mainstream economics, but such emphasis is also a common concern of those economists currently engaged in the field of developmental economics.[12]

Again this emphasis upon technology is not meant to infer technological determinism. Our view is not one of simplistic technological determinism in terms of causation. In the first place we do not simply view technology as comprising material technics alone which are responsible for changes elsewhere; our view is that technology is the substance of what is being developed in the process of economic development. Technology is a complex whole and the overall gestalt entails the nonmaterial as well as the material. Technology is to development as dough is to bread. The question then becomes, what causes technology to change and this would require an answer and explanation in terms of a multiplicity of variables. In such a complexity of circular and cumulative causation it then becomes difficult to delineate and identify any single factor. While technology dominates, in terms of culture and economic development, what then dominates technology in its evolution and advance? If, as some do, we were to view technology as simply being the composite of material technics, a resistance to the view that technological changes (changes in the material sector) are the primary or key factors explaining change elsewhere would be warranted. Our view, of technology being both material and nonmaterial is rather not that technological, change *causes* economic development but rather that the advance of technology, the advance and application of useful knowledge, constitutes the *process* of economic development. This process manifests itself in greater energy control and consequently greater productivity and consequently greater magnitudes and rates of increase of economic growth. Therefore the issue in explaining economic development is not how technology causes economic development but rather how do we explain the advance of technology as a process in the advance and application of useful knowledge. To our view there can be no economic development without technological advance, in the same way that we have no transformation of the bread given a fixed dough. Culture accumulates and stores technics and consequently as we change our technics we change culture, and this represents our basic tautology. Consequently, while agreeing that we must focus on technological change if we are to explain the process of economic development, that is not to say that technological change determines the evolutionary process. In the last analysis it is man, interacting with a multiplicity of factors contained in his environment of culture plus physical resources, who generates new technics and in so doing determines the process.

A shift has taken place, in the field of developmental economics, to include in analysis not only the conventional factors of land, labor and capital, but, in addition, the factors of technological change.[13] All this does not imply a universal agreement, especially since we are dealing with the views of economists, for example: "Yet more important is the fact that the whole case for the progress of underdeveloped countries through technological advance is irrelevant. Modern technology is by its very nature not suitable to serve as a lever to raise *per capita* output in most underdeveloped countries."[14] Perhaps the rather strong statement by Brenner is due to an incorrect conceptualization of technology. Technology is not something fixed and rigid in terms of material and nonmaterial technics that are always the same for each stage of development regardless of cultures. The application of useful knowledge to production and social organization results in a myriad of varying technics spawned by different cultural and physical settings. To say that underdeveloped countries would develop through advancing their technology via the application of science to production and social organization is not to say that the resulting technics, especially in the nonmaterial sector of culture, will be or must be the same for all countries or that underdeveloped countries might not benefit through more labour intensive technics. To agree to the view that underdeveloped countries should not try to emulate the precise material and nonmaterial technics of the advanced countries does not negate the view that technology is of signal importance in the process of economic development. That a country should develop technics applicable to its cultural setting is recognized in the literature.[15] Though explanations and theory are not clearly given, enough evidence may be found in the literature to support the view that currently in the field of developmental economics technology is being assigned a position of prominence in the process of economic development. It is in addressing our query to a clarification of the concept of economic development that we are in turn, therefore, forced into theoretical explanation on the role of technology and technological change as well. That technology is important in relation to economic growth and economic development, most would agree; the question now becomes—what then is technology.

Economists frequently define technology indirectly in terms of changes in technology relative to the production function, "... a shorthand expression for *any kind of shift* in the production function."[16] Defining technological change in abstract and esoteric terms commensurate with the theoretical tools and analytical models currently employed by economists, as procedure, is relatively easy to execute; however, it does contain certain weaknesses.[17] Using the production function methodology to indicate the effects of technological change is okay insofar as it goes; the problem, however, is that such a treatment of technological change does not go far enough. Such an approach deals with a part but not the whole of technological change; technology in relation to the processes of economic development is far more complex. The isoquants of the production measure changes in the quality of production but this is only one aspect of the results of technological change. To measure technological change this way disembodies technological change from the whole of the culture matrix. Technological change is a complex process and among its many manifestations entails the quality of products, the creation of new products, leisure, shifts in the structure of production, as well as the more general social and cultural changes.[18] Economic growth in terms of simple residual quantity changes in production represents at best a partial indicator of technological change but it is not a direct measure of all technological change since the whole picture of technological change entails more than just the unexplained portion of economic production. If we define technological change in terms of some magnitude of a residual of economic goods, then it would follow that by definition, since we have equated technological change with a residual of goods, to change technology we simply increase the residual quantity of economic goods, a circular reasoning which really says nothing about how to change technology, how technology has changed or really if technology has changed at all.[19] For it has been noted that the residual approach has also been viewed as a "residual of ignorance." It has a catch-all air of enigma rather than a quantifiable reality in terms of being a direct measure of technological change. The correct procedure would be first to explicitly define the concept of technology, then to measure technology directly to achieve a quantifiable magnitude and then to determine the rate of the change of magnitude over time.[20] Why is this not done?

Attempts at explicit definitions of technology are numerous. For any complex phenomenon, such as culture, nationalism, social institutions and our economic development, there may be many definitions which may be essentially correct conceptually, and, if so, such definitions would be basically compatible and interchangeable.[21] This is to be expected since there are many words in a given language and the possible combinations border on the infinite. To drive one definition or to claim only one definition as being correct appears unrealistic. The truth is that due to the nature of language, many definitions for a given correct conceptualization would be the expected result. However, not all definitions are based upon the correct conceptualization and, consequently, not all definitions are correct, compatible and interchangeable. To the social scientist the issue is one of correct conceptualization rather than that of a single, unique and precise definition agreed to by all. Social scientists may realistically hope to agree on the former but may unrealistically hope to agree on the latter. Definitions of technology fit this general pattern and while there are many attempts at definition, they are evidently not all based upon the correct conceptualization. Definitions of technology run the full spectrum from the very simple view that material artifacts and tools comprise technology, to the more complex that technology comprises both tools and skills to the even more complex view that technology comprises the social as well as the material and not simply skills or the nonmaterial associated with tools.[22]

In our view, a correct conceptualization of technology would entail useful knowledge but in addition not simply the embodiment of useful knowledge but its application toward the practical ends of economic production and social organization. Also, and to us perhaps one of the most important conceptual distinctions in the whole of our analysis, is that the manifestations of the application of useful knowledge are of the form of material as well as nonmaterial technics. This means that technology in our conceptualization comprises not only machines and the associated skills, but also the concomitant social institutions. Technology substantively embodies the social as well as the material in its overall integrated gestalt as an organic whole.

The conceptualization of technology contained in the similar definitions offered by Schmookler and Mansfield does warrant merit in focusing on the social pool of knowledge but there are also shortcomings. The basic definition used by Schmookler and Mansfield states that, "Technology is the social pool of knowledge of the industrial arts," and conforms to a view prevalent in the literature that technology is in substance knowledge. We are not referring here to the effects or results of technology but rather its substance. To look at the results of technology we might look at changing production functions or extend to a time-series analysis to view changes in production per man hour, or productivity, as a basic indicator of technological change.[23] But to confine useful knowledge to the "industrial arts" is perhaps too restrictive in that agricultural technics are as much a part of technology as the industrial and that the paleolithic as one epoch of the pre-industrial period had technics which were not industrial. Also, "industrial" is perhaps more frequently associated with material technics whereas "practical" would be more appropriate to the view that technology is both material and nonmaterial. To counter this argument some might refer to the "industrial arts" as covering generally industry or productive labor and therefore in this sense would have greater historical relevancy. But using the word "industrial" is unduly confusing since "industrial" also is used frequently in the sense of manufactured goods and related to the epoch of industrialism. Consequently we prefer and will use in our definition "practical" rather than "industrial." And practical in this sense referring to those arts or technics related to economic production and social organization.[24]

A definition which more closely approximates our conceptualization in terms of knowledge and also by providing an additional emphasis on application would be that offered by Galbraith: "Technology—the development and application of scientific or systematic knowledge to practical tasks . . ."[25] In our conceptualization of technology we would like to emphasize the doing, the use, the application of knowledge to practical ends and not simply view technology as a store or "social pool." The store or reservoir function is provided by culture but technology relates to the application of the culture store of useful knowledge to the solution of man's unresolved practical problems associated with his economic production and social organization. Social inventions as well as material inventions are directed toward problem solving and in this sense constitute the application of useful knowledge in the solution of basic practical problems confronting man. Consequently we have referred to Galbraith's definition which draws attention to "application."[26]

Also, technology is not simply representative of technics to solve problems generated by the natural environment but rather that of the total environment which combines the environment produced by culture itself as well as that of nature. As culture advances man does indeed overcome problems of a hostile natural environment, but in so doing, culture itself as it advances generates many new problems in need of solution. Problems of depression, unemployment, ecology and pollution, population and nuclear proliferation are problems of culture advance; and these problems currently dominate those of the natural environment. Man has been so successful in solving the problems of natural environment that he now can live on the bottom of the ocean, in outer space and on other planets, but he finds it increasingly difficult to live with the exponential complexities of culture. In short, while technology is admittedly directed toward problems of an environment containing both natural and cultural factors it is the latter which tends to dominate more and more with the advance of culture and economic development.[27] In addition, we wish also to emphasize the role of culture as a store and accumulator of the useful knowledge which serves as the base for technology as well as to note further that technology, as with culture, is both nonmaterial as well as material.

Ogburn's *Social Change* is one of the leading studies to systematically note the basic dichotomy of culture into material and nonmaterial culture; however, not all agree as to the importance of this basic distinction. Kroeber argues that since material and nonmaterial culture are both in essence forms of knowledge that there is little significance in drawing a conceptual distinction.[28] Our entire analysis is based upon the predication that at root both material and nonmaterial culture (and technology) are of knowledge and consequently we agree with Kroeber in terms of origins and substance. But that knowledge in the process of concretion takes on the form of material culture on the one hand and on the other nonmaterial culture is a distinction of fundamental importance to our theoretical framework. For is not a basic problem of underdeveloped countries that the nonmaterial portion of their cultures has proved impermeable to the advance of modern technics? How can we deal with the problem of "cultural lag" without the basic distinction between material and nonmaterial culture. Also, while the theoretical significance of the distinction between material and nonmaterial culture is open to debate apparently no one denies that in actuality culture is, of course, so divided.[29]

In fact, one of the most celebrated dichotomies ever formulated in the history of the social sciences is the Veblenian distinction and dichotomy of culture into the technological (material culture) on the one hand and social institutions (nonmaterial culture) on the other. Veblen's dichotomy divorces social technics (nonmaterial culture) from the dynamics of culture evolution. In the context of our cultural economics, by comparison, our dichotomy is formulated from the starting point of useful knowledge which appears on the one hand in its store as culture and, on the other, in its application as technology. So conceptualized, both culture and technology are of the nature of the material and nonmaterial. Therefore our definition: Technology is the application of the culture store of useful knowledge to practical ends associated with economic production and social organization.[30]

If we assume, as we have, that knowledge is crucial to a conceptualization of technology and further that, "The stage of technology reached by culture is based on the central factor in cultural progress, namely, knowledge," we might then ask a basic question, what is knowledge ?[31]

Knowledge as we have tried to emphasize is a protean concept and manifests itself in many forms. Knowledge is man's awareness of his environment and is the result of learning. Knowledge in its substance is ". . . the body of truths or facts accumulated by mankind in the course of time . . . the sum of what is known."[32] Knowledge as that which is known is not only that knowledge which is warranted, verifiable, and useful but entails all knowledge, the entire spectrum from folk belief to positive science. Gossip, hearsay, folklore ceremonial religious ritual, and the knowledge of such arts as a headshrinking are all forms of knowledge.[33] Such peripheral knowledge might be classified in a variety of ways, for example, perhaps as, "small talk and pastime", "spiritual", "ceremonial" and "unwanted" but it is still knowledge.[34] Therefore since all these categories constitute knowledge we might then conclude that not all knowledge is useful or directed toward ends which are practical, that is, related to man's economic production and the concomitant social organization. At this juncture since we are concerned with *all* knowledge we are consequently dealing with *all* (or the totality) of culture. Later we will further distinguish between *all* knowledge and *useful* knowledge and *all* culture versus the *core* of culture. Not *all* of culture but rather the *core* of culture, concerns the dynamic process of economic development. Given a broad conceptualization of *all* knowledge, how is knowledge related to *all* culture?

Culture in line with Tylor's conceptualization of totality may be defined as : "the sum total of the social and political rules, technological inventions and economic institutions, the arts, shared beliefs and practices—that is the culture . . .[35] Culture so conceptualized as a complex totality may then be viewed in terms of the many functions associated with it. One function performed by culture is that it serves as vehicle for storing and accumulating knowledge and passing such knowledge on from generation to generation. Culture is man's social heritage; it represents an overall storage bank of man's accumulated knowledge.[36] The known in terms of social or public knowledge as distinguished from the knower or knowing is stored by culture. The social knowledge which is stored or accumulated by culture when used becomes the basis for man's techniques in fulfilling his basic objectives.[37] Carried further, culture in this regard may be viewed in its entirety as the superorganic which functions as an overall technique of man's survival and adaptation to his environment and as an overall means for the achievement of his wants and needs.[38] Culture is man's overall technique for establishing a continuity and accumulation of knowledge, the difference between man and (beast) other animals. Knowledge acquired through enculturation provides man with the means of knowing what to know to achieve his objectives.

Consequently, the protean nature of knowledge reveals a Janus countenance: on the one side viewed from its store, knowledge manifests itself 'as man's culture, as his social DNA, and on the other, in its use and application, as techniques. Therefore, when we speak of culture and techniques, we are merely taking two different views of the same substance—knowledge. A mountain, though it is one, gives the appearance sometimes of being different or of several forms depending on whether it is viewed from the northern or southern face. Language as a case in point portrays the Janus dichotomy of knowledge. Language can be viewed as a part of culture in its function as store of knowledge. In addition, viewed from its function as a tool or basic skill of communication, language may be thought of, in the sense of use or application of knowledge, as a basic technique.[39]

Up to this point our analysis has been basically concerned with *all* knowledge and *all* culture; we will now draw a distinction between *all* and *useful* knowledge. Since the objective of our study concerns economic development, we are concerned with *useful* knowledge and not *all* knowledge, with the *core* of culture and not all culture and with technics and not all techniques.

Useful knowledge is a part of the whole of knowledge, it is the knowledge which is amenable and applicable to practical ends; it is the knowledge relevant to economic production and social organization.[40] As we have noted, not all knowledge is useful, and while religious, ritual, ceremonialism, incantation, gossip, head hunting and shrinking all entail knowledge, skills and procedures and represent complex techniques, an advance of knowledge along these lines would not constitute a development of the practical arts.[41] It is the technics of economic production and the concomitant social organization which constitute applied useful knowledge associated with practical ends and which are necessary for economic development. That is not to say that such ceremonial techniques do not constitute important traits of a culture. On the contrary, they may even dominate a given culture, and this, of course, is a basic point, to the actual detriment of economic development and the advance of useful knowledge.[42]

Since all of culture is not related to the dynamic processes of economic development, we are censequently concerned only with useful knowledge as opposed to all knowledge, and it is this stock of useful knowledge which, in its store, constitutes the core of culture.[43] We are concerned with the store of useful knowledge relevant and applicable to practical ends.[44]

In this regard we view the core of culture as being concerned with more than just subsistence activities, which is the meaning of the phrase to some but consider it to include a broader area of other "economic arrangements" as well, that is, man's overall economic activity and concomitant social organization.

Carrying our argument further, who would deny that the

automobile is part of our technology; but the automobile is, also, part of our culture. Automobiles are a part of culture—material culture; they are also a part of the core of culture in that automobiles serve as a store of useful knowledge. Each generation does not start out fresh with bare wheels but rather we have the accumulated useful knowledge stored or embodied in the modern automobile to which we add and which consequently accumulates more useful knowledge.[45] Material artifacts of the core of culture in origin are based upon useful knowledge, a particular type of knowledge which when applied and innovated takes on a material form. Material culture can consequently be conceptualized as the concretion of useful knowledge.[46]

Useful knowledge when applied need not only manifest itself in its cultural store as material culture, it may also take the form of nonmaterial culture. As a case in point, institutions are a form of knowledge; they also represent nonmaterial culture; they are mechanisms for storing useful knowledge and aid in governing human behavior, human thought, values, attitudes and actions.[47] The concept, institution, is perhaps one of the most difficult of all in the social sciences to define and conceptualize.[48] We will simply refer here to a standard type definition as given by Shmuel N. Eisenstadt:

> "... institutions or patterns of institutionalization can be defined here as regulative principles which organize most of the activities of individuals in a society into definite organizational patterns from the point of view of some perennial, basic problems of any society or ordered social life."[49]

The social adjustment to a problem or need in the form of a social technic (institution) which may also be viewed then as a social invention has more frequently in the past evolved out of established practice and custom perhaps following from a chance innovation of a new social technic. The wave of the future inherent in the advance and development of the social sciences will be social inventions spawned more through scientific procedures and less dependent upon chance and serendipity, such an assumption underlies our "frictionless wheel of economic development." (We will develop this concept in a later chapter.)[50]

As members of society adjust to a particular social problem or need, the solution becomes routinized and passed on to succeeding generations in the form of institutions or social habits. Members of a given culture no longer have to re-think or re-solve the social problem in terms of starting anew. Useful knowledge, as with the automobile, is stored and embodied only this time by comparison in a social technic known as an institution. The solution, the "arrangement," "procedure," or "convention" is passed on; the knowledge of the social behavior pattern is transmitted via the institution.[51] In order for man to solve his basic problems of production and survival, social technics are of importance equal to that of material technics. As such, the institution may be viewed as a form of useful knowledge and serves the culture side of the dichotomy of knowledge in that it functions as a store of knowledge. Also, of course, we do not maintain that all knowledge passed on and transmitted through the institutional structure is useful and serves the practical tasks confronting man. For as we have previously noted, for example, the institutions of head hunting and shrinking.[52] Therefore not all institutions embody useful knowledge relevant to the core of culture.

We have looked at one face of knowledge in the form of its store in the material and nonmaterial elements of culture; we will not look at the other face of knowledge represented by technology. Culture stores knowledge which when used and applied provides man with techniques to achieve his desired ends and objectives, and as we have noted, not all these ends are of a practical nature in the sense of being related to the core of culture. To emphasize this point let us make a distinction between techniques and technics. In our distinction technics are specific techniques which are applied to practical ends and in their formation are based upon useful knowledge. A technique represents the application of any type of knowledge to a particular end, an end which may or may not be of a practical nature. A technic is the application of useful knowledge for a particular practical end. Techniques constitute the whole and concern all knowledge and technics by comparison are a part of that whole and concern useful knowledge; all are techniques but technics delineate those techniques directed toward practical ends.[53] We develop many techniques some of which are fairly complex and require a fair amount of knowledge and skill: snake charming, religious ritual, hobbies and games such as the playing of musical instruments, fly-casting, or chess, but such techniques are not necessarily directly associated with the promotion or advance of economic development. However, some techniques are of a practical nature and these in our analytical framework are called technics. The opposite face of technics, which in their integrated entirety constitute the overall gestalt of technology, would be the core of culture. And it is the advance of this core which constitutes the process of economic development.

Technics represent the application of useful knowledge stored by culture and are, themselves, part of culture and consequently may be either material or nonmaterial in composition. In this light, the automobile represents in its *store* of useful knowledge a material artifact of the core of culture, and in addition, viewed from the other face of knowledge as a material technic of transportation in terms of the *application* of that knowledge, represents man's technology. Therefore the automobile is representative of both faces of knowledge, on the one hand serving as a *store* it is part of material culture and on the other hand in its *application* as a material technic in man's overall gestalt of technology. Some regard only material technics as technology.[54] Is this view correct or conversely are we correct in arguing that technology comprises not only the material technics but nonmaterial technics as well?

Examples of the nonmaterial core of culture, which basically constitutes nonmaterial or social technics of the overall gestalt of technology are many, such as: language, skills, social and political organization, the factory system, money, the business firm, and the scientific method. Language certainly qualifies as a part of culture, it is a *store* of knowledge, and in its application provides a technic so fundamental that any culture, let alone culture at the advanced level of industrialism, could scarcely function without it. It is one of the most basic and fundamental of all nonmaterial technics.[55]

Skills in a more generalized sense constitute a very important part of man's overall technology. And while skills are perhaps most frequently thought of in conjunction with the tools of material culture, and the use of material objects, the skills themselves, are in actuality embodied in the population in the minds of men and are consequently nonmaterial forms of knowledge. In this sense, knowledge as skills embodied in the labor force provide a very important part of the overall of technology and comprise elements of nonmaterial culture. WW II was destructive of European plant and equipment and productive capacity, yet even given such vast destruction of its physical capital or material culture the rejuvenation of the European economy was remarkably quick. That Europe basically accomplished its reconstruction of wartime damage by the early 1950's shows the importance of nonmaterial technics (knowledge and skills) embodied in the labor force as a form of nonmaterial capital. Consequently policies promoting literacy and education are of fundamental importance in promoting economic development.[56]

Can we go further in our analysis, which stresses that nonmaterial as well as material technics comprise technology, by now including the more basic political and social institutions in the overall of technology. Many in the literature refer to material inventions and nonmaterial inventions, but there is a tendency then to view the former as technological inventions and the latter as social inventions. The implication being that social inventions are outside the realm of technology.[57] Therefore, while some social scientists concede the reality of social inventions, they do not make the logical next step to include such social technics in their conceptualization of technology. This tends to reinforce the view that technology is essentially material; whereas to our view it is both material and nonmaterial. Consequently in our study we refer to material and nonmaterial (social) technology rather than to speak of technology and social invention which to us implies that social inventions are not part of the overall of technology.

Using the institution of the city as a case in point to serve as an example, are we correct in assuming that social technics are integral parts of man's overall technology. The social invention known as the city is considered by some to be one of the most significant innovations in the long-term historical advance of culture.[58] Also in any analysis of the evolution of the industrial system would a correct analysis of its technology entail the steam engine alone and in isolation, or should we more correctly also include the concomitant social technics inherent in the factory system and thereby take into account in our analysis both the material and nonmaterial technics as an integrated whole.[59] Would it not be more correct then to view technology as an integrated whole of material and nonmaterial technics?

Sending such material artifacts of industrialism, as steam engines and railroad tracks or electric light bulbs to underdeveloped countries does not give them an industrial system. For an industrial system to function it requires both the material and institutional underpinnings. For such a system to be implanted in underdeveloped countries requires an integrated overall gestalt of technology, which is based upon the advance of useful knowledge to the level of science and its application to both the material and nonmaterial technics. We cannot really view the material technics in separation; material technics do not function by themselves but require nonmaterial technics as well if the overall system is to function. The Asmat of New Guinea use the canoe as an important means of providing transportation but the material technic, the canoe, as a means of providing transportation does not paddle itself, the paddling depends upon muscle and institution.[60]

For purposes of analysis we will conceptually identify the integrated whole of all material and nonmaterial technics as the overall gestalt of technology, and it is the overall gestalt of technology which constitutes the core of culture. With knowledge in the form of a gestalt and its association with culture we deal not with the separated branches of oak tree but rather with the integrated and interrelated branches of the banyan tree.[61] Such is the way of knowledge, culture and the integrated nature of the overall gestalt of technology. The gestalt of technology is more than just a simple addition of parts (technics) but constitutes an organic whole of functional parts in much the same way that we note that the overall music of a symphony is something more than just the addition of the tunes of the individual parts (instruments).[62] Each instrument played concurrently, though in separated rooms, would not produce a symphony; it is only when all instruments of the orchestra are played together in a single room, as an integrated gestalt, that the whole appears as a symphony. The organic whole as a totality is greater than the sum of its parts.

To be meaningful for an underdeveloped country, technology must consequently be viewed as an integrated totality to function, and these countries should therefore focus on the overall gestalt of technology as their objective and not merely isolated parts, for example, a steel mill or railroad line does not constitute industrialism. Industrialism concerns the totality, the overall, and conceptually we have presented this analytical objective in our core of culture and the overall gestalt of technology. And as we have already noted in several instances this is not to imply that all social or nonmaterial technics will be the same for all industrial systems (we do not even make this assumption concerning material technics) but that a nonmaterial technic must be provided concomitant with the material technic for the overall technology to function.[63]

Since we have assumed that technology contains material and nonmaterial technics, social institutions, related to practical tasks and, consequently, embodying useful knowledge, may then be considered as integral parts of the overall gestalt of technology.[64] This then implies that social institutions as social inventions may serve as dynamic factors of economic development and culture evolution.[65] As we have noted previously in the case of the city, social institutions, as social inventions, when innovated may serve as a dynamic factor or indepentent variable of significance for culture evolution and economic development. But more, in addition, we submit that one of the most dynamic forces of all in the whole expanse of the history of culture evolution and economic development has been of the nature of a social institution and not a material technic.[66] The most powerful and sustained thrust of cultural expansion has taken place during the epoch of modern economic growth which in turn was dependent upon an industrial system. The industrial system, as previously noted, was defined and conceptualized in terms of the application of science to production and social organization. Useful knowledge based upon scientific methods enabling man to consciously solve practical problems is the basic dynamic force behind the current sustained and high rates of expansion of material culture characteristic of modern economic growth. Practical knowledge is

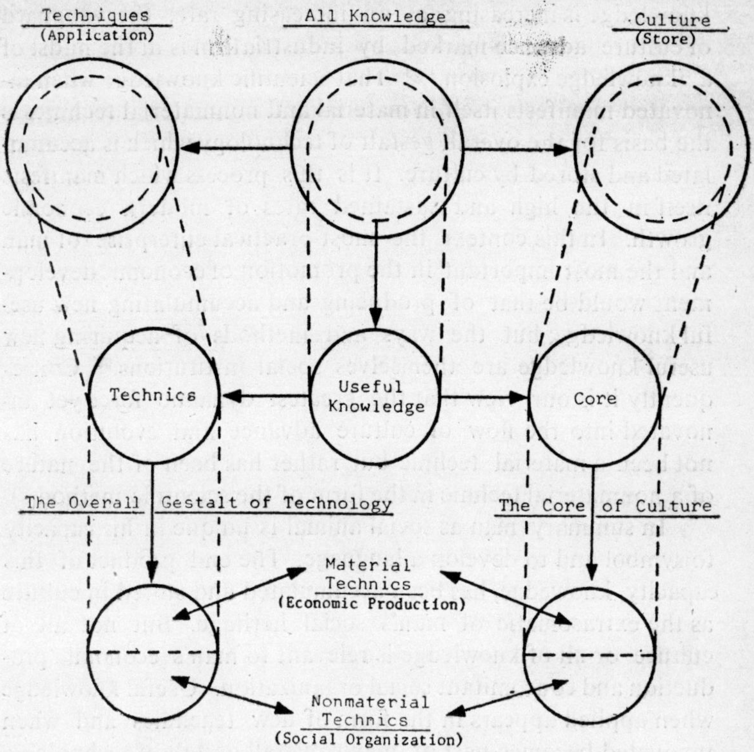

Fig. VI-1. The Dichotomy of Useful Knowledge.

now so organized that we can consciously and wilfully solve technical problems. No longer must we rely upon chance or serendipity as a source of new technics with associated periods of economic drought and stagnation.[67] Consequently, useful knowledge is increasing at an increasing rate; the vanguard of culture advance marked by industrialism is in the midst of a "knowledge explosion."[68] That scientific knowledge when innovated manifests itself in material and nonmaterial technics is the basis for the overall gestalt of technology which is accumulated and stored by culture. It is this process which manifests itself in the high and sustained rates of modern economic growth. In this context the most practical enterprise of man and the most important in the promotion of economic development would be that of producing and accumulating new useful knowledge; but the ways and methods of acquiring new useful knowledge are themselves social institutions.[69] Consequently it is our view that the greatest dynamic force yet innovated into the flow of culture advance and evolution has not been a material technic but rather has been of the nature of a nonmaterial technic in the form of the scientific method(s).

In summary, man as social animal is unique in his capacity to symbol and to develop a language. The end product of this capacity, knowedge, has been accumulated and stored in culture as the extrasomatic of man's social heritage. But not all of culture or all of knowledge is relevant to man's economic production and concomitant social organization. Useful knowledge when applied appears in the form of new teachnics and when innovated becomes part of man's overall gestalt of technology. Therefore, knowledge as a protean concept appears in many forms. On the one hand useful knowledge in its store appears as man's culture and as such is passed on from one generation to the next. Man interacting with culture and the physical environment applies the knowledge stored in culture to resolve the practical problems associated with production and survival. Thereby man generates the new technics of technological change, both social and material, and in the process promotes the dynamics of culture evolution and economic development. Consequently, technology and the core of culture are the opposite sides of the same coin, the coin of useful knowledge. To change one, technology, is to change the other, culture. In adding to technology man is consequently in the process, ipso facto, also transforming culture. The core of culture and overall gestalt of technology represent a dichotomy of the stock of useful knowledge, our protean concept (see Fig. VI-1 "The Dichotomy of Useful Knowledge") [70]

Consequently, in advancing useful knowledge, in the form of social and material technics, man in the process also transforms culture. This process is manifest in the form of the stages of economic development. Each stage results in and is indicated by higher levels of energy control and which provides man with an increased capacity for higher standards of living and greater control over the environment. Therefore it is the advance of useful knowledge which promotes the dynamics behind culture evolution. Higher levels of energy control, as a result of economic development, enables mankind to harness more and more free energy, and thereby to overcome the Entropy Law and the long-term processes of entropic degradation. The process has enabled mankind to service and provide for his practical ends, and it is this process, also viewed as culture (knowledge) accumulation and evolution, though far more complex and advanced,which continues on today. the process of advancing useful knowledge and its application to practical ends is the essence of culture evolution and the process of economic development.

But how does all this come about, how does man advance useful knowedge, and what are the variables to be considered in the process ? We will now enter the domain of circular and cumulative causation and consequently, engage the contributions and methodology, of the noted economist, the Nobel laureate, Gunnar Myrdal.

REFERENCES

[1]The word protean aptly covers the concept of knowledge, Richard R. Nelson, Merton J. Peck, and Edward D. Kalachek, *Technology, Economic Growth, and Public Policy* (Washington: The Brookings Institution, 1967) note that, "Knowledge is a protean concept." p. 8. One of the better sources to cover the subject matter of this chapter, briefly, and yet with a good substantive treatment as well as a quick introduc-

tion to the literature, would be Daniel Bell, "The Measurement of Knowledge and Technology," in Eleanor Bernett Sheldon, and Wilbert E. Moore, eds., *Indicators of Social Change* (New York: Russell Sage Foundation, 1968), pp. 145-246.

[2]Michael Oakeshott, *Political Education* (Cambridge: Bowes and Bowes, 1951), p. 9. Cited by S.H. Frankel, *The Economic Impact on Underdeveloped Countries* (Oxford: Basil Blackwell, 1953), p. 19.

[3]On the quotations, in the Veblen-Ayres tradition, note: Thorstein Veblen, *The Place of Science in Modern Civilization* (New York: Russell and Russell, 1961), p. 77; Clarence Ayres, *The Theory of Economic Progress* (New York: Schocken Books, 1962), p. 62 And, "What is true of Veblen's work in this respect is true of institutional economics in general—the fact that there is more often than not a general recognition of culture as the master principle of social analysis," Louis J. Junker, "Theoretical Foundations of Neo-Institutionalism," *The American Journal of Economics and Sociology* 21 (April 1968), pp. 197-213, p. 201; and Myron Watkins, "Veblen's View of Cultural Evolution," in *Thorstein Veblen: A Critical Appraisal*, ed., Douglas F. Dowd, (Ithaca: Cornell University Press, 1968), pp. 249-264.

[4]Consequently, our position is that, "Technological change involves cultural change." *Science and Technology for Development*, Vol. I, *World of Opportunity* (New York: United Nations, 1963), p. 193. For a possible reservation to this view, note Benjamin Higgins, *Economic Development* (New York: W.W. Norton & Company, 1968), "Economic Development Without Cultural Change," and uses the case of a cultural lag of a non-material sector of the Japanese culture, the feudal system, to support the view that, ". . . Here the argument seems to be that profound cultural change is not always necessary in order to achieve technological change and economic development." pp. 264-265. That we still have a capitalistic system in the U.S. today is true but to equate twentieth century capitalism with nineteenth century capitalism in terms of no change would be similar to the view that the current manifestations of the feudal system in Japan are the same as the feudal system in the pre-Meiji era.

[5]Jacob Schmookler in his, "Technological Change and Economic Theory," *The American Economic Review*, 55 (May 1965), pp. 333-345. In this article, as Zvi Griliches notes, Schmookler presents the view that, ". . . standard economics had no theory of technical change." p. 344, and also, his *Invention and Economic Growth* (Cambridge: Harvard University Press, 1966, "Unfortunately, neoclassical as well as classical economics seems better adopted to the analysis of replication than to that of technological change. Technological change is the *terra incognita* of modern economics." p. 3. Also it is interesting to note Schmookler's comments on replication in the context of no technological change which to us represents economic growth and no development. "While the analysis of a strictly replicating economy, that is, an economy without technological progress, is helpful in understanding many economic phenomena, its utility in the study of econo-

mic development is limited. The vast economic changes since the Stone Age, or for that matter during recent centuries in the West, were possible only because of technological progress." Ibid. On main line or standard theory and technological change note also ". . an invariant state of technology," Lester B. Lave, *Technological Change: Its Conception and Measurement* (Englewood Cliffs: Prentice Hall, 1966), p. 3. And also, Everett Hagen, *On the Theory of Social Change* (Homewood: The Dorsey Press, 1962), p. 51. And William D. Nordhaus, *Invention, Growth, and Welfare: A Theoretical Treatment of Technological Change* (Cambridge: The MIT Press, 1969), "The main inadequacy of existing theory lies in the theory of the firm. In the standard theory of the firm, the level of technology is assumed to be given," p. 3. Except for the heterodox such as Marx, Veblen, and Schumpeter, economists were preoccupied with issues other than technological change and economic development.

[6]J.R Hicks notes that, "Underdeveloped economics is a vastly important subject . . . If there is any branch of economic theory which is especially relevant to it, it is the Theory of International Trade." J.R. Hicks, *Capital and Growth* (New York: Oxford University Press, 1965), pp. 3-4. A view which would be in the tradition of Riccardo, Mill, Marshall and Taussig. "The opening of foreign trade. . . sometimes works a sort of industrial revolution in a country. . ." J.S. Mill, *The Principles of Political Economy* (London: Longmans, 1911) p. 351. We question comparative advantage not on its inherent logic or its relevancy to economic growth but rather present reservations to the theory in the context of economic development. Jonathan Hughes, in his *Industrialization and Economic History* (New York: McGraw-Hill Book Company, 1970) notes the failure of international trade to live up to its expectations and states: "Hence Mill's hypothetical history of economic development through international trade now strikes us as roseate, naive. Yet this was an article of faith until recently." p. 7.

[7]Abramovitz ". . . actually excluded from his survey models of the Harrod-Domar type on the grounds that they made no assertion about the likely development of the economy over time." F.H. Hahn and R. C.O. Mathews, "The Theory of Economic Growth: A Survey, "*The Economic Journal* 74 (December 1964), pp. 779-902, 779.

[8]The basic introductory literature on the subject would be: Murray Brown, *On the Theory and Measurement of Technological Change* (Cambridge: Cambridge University Press, 1966); Lester B. Lave, *Technological Change: Its Conception and Measurement* (Englewood Cliffs: Prenrice-Hall, 1966); Edwin Mansfield, *The Economics of Technological Change* (New York: W.W. Norton & Company, 1968); W.E.G. Salter, *Productivity and Technical Change* (Cambridge: University press, 1966). While Lave in the text of his book appears to give major credit to Solow he does notice the contributions of others preceding Solow, note p. 4, footnote p. 5. In this regard note, S. Fabricant, "Economic Progress and Economic Change," 34th *Annual Report of the National Bureau of Economic Research* (New York: 1954); M. Abramovitz

"Resource and Output Trends in the United States Since 1870," *The American Economic Review* 46 (May 1956), pp. 5-23. Also, the latter appears as Occasional Paper No. 52 (New York: The National Bureau of Economic Research, 1956). Also, Robert M. Solow, "Technical Change and the Aggregate Production Function," *The Review of Economics and Statistics* 39 (August 1957), pp. 312-320, Evsey D. Domar "On the Measurement of Technological Change, *The Economic Journal*, Vol. 71 (1961), pp. 709-729. Robart A. Solo, *Economic Organization and Social Systems* (Indianapolis: The Bobs-Merrill Company, 1967), "The Insignificance of Capital Accumulation," pp. 91-100. The above literature refers to a particular methodology of main-line theory in relation to the aggregate production function and the "residual of ignorance" discussions. Others during this period were also discussing technological change and the overall importance of science and technology in relation to economic growth and development but in the context of a different theoretical mold. Certainly this would apply to Simon Kuznets and constitutes a recurring theme in his many contributions to the literature. And in the Veblenian tradition, of course, Clarence E. Ayres, *The Theory of Economic Progress* (Chapel Hill: University of North Carolina Press, 1944).

[9]"With a magnificent wave of his hand, Solow named this 90 per cent *technological change*. In one mighty blow Solow cut the Gordian knot. . . No wonder the classical economists were wrong; 90% of the increase in productivity was neglected." Lave, *Technological Change: Its Conception and Measurement*, p. 4. Actually the 90% figure is a rounded one, Solow offered a figure of 87-1/2% as the residual representative of technological change. Note, "Technical Change and the Aggregate Production Function," (1957), pp. 316, 317 and 320.

[10]On the "measure of our ignorance" note, Abramovitz, *American Economic Review* (1956) p. 11, and, Solomon Fabricant, "Basic Facts on Productivity Change," *Occasional Paper No. 63* (New York: National Bureau of Economic Research, Inc., 1959) p. 22. An example of an attempt to give more precision to the residual and its component parts would be found in Edward F. Denison, *The Sources of Economic Growth in the United States and the Alternatives before Us* (New York: Committee for Economic Development, 1962 and *Why Growth Rates Differ* (Washington, D.C.: The Brookings Institution, 1967). In one instance, Denison, (*Economic Growth of the United States . . . .* p. 229) assessed the contribution of the advance of knowledge calculated as a residual, in its contribution to total output, to be of the magnitude of 20%. Moses Abramovitz notes, however, that, "Denison's attempt to attach numbers to these elements, however, still falls short of success. And this unfortunate fact is just the inevitable consequence of the present state of the art." ". . . But this assumption is based on no empirical evidence whatever and, as Denison makes amply clear, constitutes no more than his own sober judgment." In his review of Denison's *Economic Growth in the United States . . .*, which appeared in *The American Economic Review*, 52, (September 1962), pp. 762-782,

pp. 777, 775. And Brown, *On The Theory and Measurement of Technological Change*, "this particular method of measuring the components of technological progress is in its infancy in terms of conclusive results." p. 3. Even Denison notes, "I know of no way to estimate directy the contribution of the advance of knowledge and its application to the growth rate. This estimate is obtained as a residual." *The Source of Economic Growth in the United States* . . . (1962), p. 229. And Mansfield, *The Economics of Technological Change*, states that in terms of the effect of technological change on the growth rate: "All that can safely be said is that the effect has been substantial." p. 5.

[11]Kuzents' view on this is explicit and repetitive in his prolific contributions to the literature and has been referred to previously, but again: "Continuous technological progress and, underlying it, a series of new scientific discoveries are the necessary condition for the high rate of modern growth . . ." *Six Lectures* (1959), p. 29. Also, *Modern Economic Growth*, pp. 10, 18, 87, 157, 276, 286, 491, and on, in his *Economic Growth and Structure* . . . etc., Surendra J. Patel states, ". . . mainly from . . . accumulated technological advance." in his "Main Features of Economic Growth over the Century," *The Indian Economic Journal*, 11 (January-March 1964), pp. 287-303, p. 290. Gustav Ranis, ". . . the growing realization that growth cannot be explained simply in terms of larger quantities of constant quality inputs combining in known ways to produce output. Economists are reaching a real consensus. . ."*International Encyclopedia of the the Social Sciences* (1968) Vol. 4, p. 413. And Richard A. Easterlin, "The fundamental basis for this productivity growth has been technological innovation. . . "*International Encyclopedia of the Social Sciences* ((1968), Vol. 4, p. 398. And, Nathan Rosenberg in Melvin Kranzberg, ed., *Technology in Western Civilization* (New York: Oxford University Press, 1967), I, states that: "Although such studies have involved the use of statistical data of imperfect reliability and heroic simplifying assumptions, they nevertheless point forcefully and conclusively in the same direction; that is, that the great bulk of the historical increase in output per capita, . . . was due to raising the productivity of resources rather than to using more of them." p. 516. And, Alfred W. Stonier and Douglas C. Hague *Textbook of Economic Theory* (London: Longmans Green & Co., 1963), ". . . technical progress therefore turns out to be even more essential to economic growth than is capital accumulation." p. 534. And Edwin Mansfield, *Industrial Research and Technological Innovation* (New York: W.W. Norton & Company, 1868), "There is general agreement among economists and others that one of the most powerful forces influencing the American economy is technological change. . . " p. 1. And Odd Aukrust, "Factors of Economic Development: A Review of Recent Research," *Weltwirtschaftliches Archiv*, 93 (1964)' pp 23-43, "I believe it is generally accepted by now that growth models which assume 'constant techniques' must necessarily be unrealistic, since they abstract from what is, perhaps, the crux of the process of growth." p. 33 And Schmookler, *Invention and Economic Growth*, "that the

creation and diffusion of technological knowledge is at the heart of modern economic growth is now widely accepted." p. vii.

[12]C.P. Kindleberger (New York: McGraw-Hill Book Company, 1965) notes, ". . technical change is not just one aspect of growth in some systems but the central one." p. 134. Benjamin Higgins notes, "In all these theories pride of place is given to technological progress." p. 194. *Economic Development* (1968), p. 150 and ". . . generally lay primary stress on technological progress." p. 194. And, Bruce R. Morris, "Technological change has probably been the central fact in the development of the advanced countries." *Economic Growth and Development* (New York: Pitman Publishing Corporation, 1967), p. 264. And Henry H. Villard, "In the main but not entirely," but nonetheless " . . . overwhelming credit must still be given to 'improvements in technology' . . ." *Economic Development* (New York: Holt, Rinehart and Winston, 1963), p. 16. Ishrat Z. Hussain, "The difference between developed and under-developed countries lies in their technological level." *Economic Factors in Economic Growth* (Bombay: Allied Publishers Private Limited, 1967), p. 222.

[13]On this note Roberto de Oliveira Campos, *Reflections on Latin American Development* (Austin: University of Texas), p. 45, and Tom E. Davis, "Changing Conceptions of the Development Problem," *Economic Development and Cultural Change*, 14 (Oct. 1965), pp. 21-32; and, Stephen Enke, *Economics for Development* (Englewood Cliffs: Prentice-Hall, 1963), pp. 91-106.

[14]Y.S. Brenner, *Theories of Economic Development and Growth* (New Yotk: Frederick A. Praeger, 1966), p. 259.

[15]Wendell C. Gordon, *The Political Economy of Latin America* (New York: Columbia University Press, 1965); and, J. Baranson, "New Technologies for Developing Areas," *Bulletin of Atomic Scientists* (Sept. 1961), pp. 275-277.

[16]Solow, "Technical Change and the Aggregate Production Function: (1957), p. 312, Kindleberger, *Economic Development*: '. . . technical change is represented in the two-input-one-output production function. . .by a shift of the isoquants toward the origin." p. 134; and, Pepelasis, *Economic Development*, "Technological change. . . involves a change in the actual production function of a given enterprise." pp. 133-134; Brown, *On the Theory and Measurement of Technological Change*, pp. 9-28; and as basic methodology, Henry J. Bruton, *Principles of Development Economics* (Englewood Cliffs: Prentice-Hall, 1965), and, Edwin Mansfield, *Micro-economics: Theory and Applications* (New York: W.W. Norton & Company, 1979), pp. 511-530.

[17]"It is a simple matter to define a technological change in terms of changes in the characteristics of an abstract technology," Brown, *On the Theory and Measurement of Technological Change*, pp. 20, 12.

[18]"Technological change in Solow's model is neutral and disembodied, a kind of better air which changes nothing except the rate of production." Lave, *Technological Change: Its Conception and Measurement*, p. 25.

[19]Unfortunately, to define technological change as the unexplained portion of the increase in output per man is not very informative." Lave, *Technological Change: Its Conception and Measurement*, p. 17.

What goes under the rubric of technology and technological change? Treating technological change as a residual increase in productivity ". . . begs a complex question. One can say that technological progress consists of all the better methods and organization that improve the efficiency. . of both old capital and new. But this can be many things." Daniel Bell, "The Measurement of Knowledge and Technology," pp. 176-177 in Sheldon and Moore, eds., *Indicators of Social Change*.

[20]"This approach, however, has the disadvantage of treating technological change implicitly. An effect is measured—an increase in the productivity of inputs. . . But technological advance itself, which would seem to demand definition in terms of an increase in knowledge relevant to economic activity, is not treated explicitly." Richard R. Nelson, et al., *Technology, Economic Growth, and Public Policy* (Washington D.C.: The Brookings Institution, 1967), p.7.

[21]As we have noted, in several instances, a good example of this point would be the Kroeber and Kluckhohn study in that many of the definitions offered were compatible with Tylor's omnibus or holistic totality treatment of the concept. Consequently we also have Ogburn stating, "The terms, the superorganic, social heritage and culture have all been used interchangeably." *Social Change* (1922), p. 6.

[22]For general statements, note, Robert S. Merrill in the *International Encyclopedia of the Social Sciences* (1968), Vol. 15, pp. 576-589. A very authoritative study, Hans Singer et al., ed., *A History of Technology* (London: Oxford University Press, 1954), 5 Vols., defines technology as ". . . covering the field of how things are commonly done or made, extending it somewhat to describe what things are commonly done or made"

And further adding that ". . . Technology is an aspect of history and specially of social history." p. vii, Vol. I. This very broad conceptualization of technology is given a restricted interpretation in Vol. II, "Our work. . . is thus concerned mainly with the nature and evolution of processes, techniques and devices—in fact with technology proper and not with its social and economic repercussions. . . Thus regarded, these volumes are perhaps more in the nature of annals than of history proper." Vol. II, p. vi. On these points and the Singer, et al. study, note: *Technology and Culture* (Fall 1960), Vol. I No. 4, for the overall review of the Singer study and specifically the comments by Clement W. Meighan, "The Beginnings of Technology," pp. 334-339. This concerns our conceptual problem again, for given the ". . . statement of goals, it is manifestly unfair to criticize these volumes for their shortcomings in omitting much of the possible cultural interpretation of their data." Also in a general vein, note, John Joseph Murphy, "The Concept of Technology," pp. 6-9 in Daniel L. Spencer and Alexander Woroniak, *Transfer of Technology to Developing Countries* (New York: Frederick A. Praeger, 1967). And perhaps more in line with the conceptualization of technology being related to the social as well as material, note, W.F. Ogburn, "The Meaning of Technology." pp. 3-11, in Francis R. Allen, et al., *Technology and Social Change* (New York: Appleton-Century-Crofts, 1957). In summary: In terms of the various conceptualizations of technology we move from the simple to the more complex. "In the popular mind, technology is synonymous with machines of various sorts—the steam engine, the locomotive. . ." However, "Technology. . . is much more than tools and artifacts, machines and processes. It deals with *human work*, with man's attempts to satisfy his wants by human action on physical objects." pp.5-6, Vol. I in Melvin Kranzberg and Carroll W. Pursell, Jr., *Technology in Western Civilization* (New York: Oxford University Press, 1967). Also, W. Paul Strassman, *Technological Change and Economic Development* (Ithaca: Cornell (University Press, 1968), pp, 2-3.

[23]Note John W. Kendrick, *Productivity Trends in the United States* (Princeton: National Bureau of Economic Research and Princeton University Press, 1961). However, to deal with technology from the view of substance and not results or effects we must deal with knowledge. G. Warran Nutter, "On Measuring Economic Growth" *The Journal of Political Economy* (February, 1957), 65, pp. 51-63, "Technology is knowledge—in particular, knowledge of how to produce things." p. 55. Others giving emphasis to knowledge, skills, education—Brown, *On the Theory and Measurement of Technological Change* (1966), p. 2; Bruton, *Principles of Development Economics* (1965), p. 178 ff, Chapters III & IV; Salter, *Productivity and Technological Change*, pp. 13-26; and *A Dictionary of the Social Sciences* (UNESCO, 1964), treats the concept mainly in terms of a "body of knowledge," p. 716; Arthur Lewis, *The Theory of Economic Growth* (Homewood: Richard D. Irwin, 1955), pp. 164-200; Harvey Leibenstein, *Economic Backwardness and Economic Growth* (New York: John Wiley and Sons, 1957), pp. 135-146. Also specific examples among the many possible references using Simon Kuznets as a source, note, *Economic Growth and Structure*, pp. 60 ff., pp. 83 ff. and *Modern Economic Growth*, pp. 286 ff. and passim in which he focuses on "empirical," "useful," "tested" knowledge. And also, ". . . the standard definition, which is: 'the science or systematic knowledge of the industrial arts.' "*Science and Technology For Development* (New York: United Nations, 1963), Vol. I, *World of Opportunity* p. 33. And, Michael Michaelis, "Technology and Economic Implications of 3 Percent Growth," pp. 492-501, *The American Economic Review* (May 1968), pp. 493-494. Richard R. Nelson, et al. *Technology, Economic Growth and Public Policy*, pp. 7-13. On the Schmookler and Mansfield definitions note Schmookler, *Invention and Economic Growth*, p. 1, and Edwin Mansfield, *The Economics of Technological Change* (New York: W.W. Norton & Co., 1968), "Technology is society's pool of knowledge regarding the industrial

arts. p. 10 and Mansfield, *Microeconomics,* (1979), p. 9.

[24]"Technology in its, broad meaning connotes the practical arts." Robert Merrill, p. 576, *International Encyclopedia of the Social Sciences* (1968), Vol. 15 and Richard R. Nelson, et al., *Technology, Economic Growth and Public Policy,* "The stock of known technique for achieving practical results." p. 8.

[25]John K. Galbraith, *Economics and the Public Purpose* (Boston: Houghton Mifflin Company, 1973), p. 39, *The New Industrial State* (Boston: Houghton Mifflin Company, 1967), p. 12.

[26]Ohers also note "application" in their definitions: ". . . technology consists of accumulated knowledge, techniques and skills, and their application in creating useful goods and services. . ." J. Frederick Dewhurst and Associates, *America's Needs and Resources* (New York: The Twentieth Century Fund, 1955), p. 834; ". . ." technology is in some sense applied knowledge." Charles Van Doren, *The Idea of Progress* (New York: Frederick A Praeger, 1967), p. 341; an emphasis not ignored by Mansfield, ". . . knowledge regarding the application of these principles to production. . ." *The Economics of Technological Change* p. 10; and, "Technology may be defined as the body of knowledge accumulated by science and invention and available for application in the processes of production." Mary L. Fledderus and Mary van Kleeck, *Thechnology and Livelihood* (New York: Russell Sage Foundation, 1945). p. 9.

[27]In terms of the problem-solving objective some focus on man's natural environment. ". . . technology comprises all that bewilderingly varied body of knowledge and devices by which man progressively masters his natural environment . . ." T.K. Derry and Trevor I. Williams, *A Short History of Technology* (New York: Oxford University Press, 1961), p. 3. And for "A Soviet View," "Modern technology is the embodiment of the knowledge man has accumulated in his struggle to harness the forces of nature." p. 1, "The History of Technology As a Science and As a Branch of Learning: A Soviet View," *Technology of Culture,* 2 (Winter 1961), pp. 1-4.

[28]"A distinction often made between material and nonmaterial culture is mentioned here only as probably having no first-rate significance," A.L. Kroeber, *Anthropology* (New York: Harcourt, Brace and Company, 1948), p. 295. Kroeber evidently reasons (p. 295) that since they are both knowledge in origin, they are not basically different. "What counts is . . . the knowledge how to produce . . . It is this knowledge, concept, and function that get themselves handed down through the generations . . ."

[29]"The literal difference is of course obvious: physical objects as against institutions and ideas," (Kroeber), *Anthropology*, p. 295, and while Robert K. Merton does note certain confusions and difficulties associated with the basic distinction he also admits that: "No one denies that there are material and nonmaterial (abstractive) elements in culture." "Civilization and Culture" *Sociology and Social Research,* 21, (November-December, 1936), pp. 103-113, p. 106. And as with Kroeber, Merton

raises the query: "But does this alone suffice to render the distinction of sociological significance." p. 106. In any event, while some can question the theoretical significance the reality of material and nonmaterial culture is apparent; note, A.L. Kroeber and Clyde Kluckhohn, *Culture: A Critical Review of Concepts and Definitions*, Papers of the Peabody Museum of American Archaeology and Ethnology, Harvard University, Vol. 47, No. 1 (Cambridge: Published by the Museum, 1952) under the headings listed "material culture" and "implicit culture", p. 76, and for the definitions cited by Bose, Winston, p. 43; Herskovitz, p. 44; Reuter, Young, p. 60; Folsom, p. 64; and, Kluckhohn, p. 65. . ., etc.

[30]This would also be similar to the more broadly defined definition of technology offered by Emmanuel G. Mesthene, in *Program on Technology and Society*, Fourth annual report: 1967-68, Harvard University, " . . . we define technology as the organization of knowledge for practical purposes." p. 44. For a discussion of this definition and its weaknesses, as well as a critical attitude toward *laissez innover* and technology in general, note John McDermott, "Technology; The Opiate of the Intellectuals," *The New York Review of Books*, Vol. XIII (July 31, 1969), pp. 25-35, and p. 29 for McDermott's alternative definition.

[31]Francis E. Merrill and H. Wentworth Eldridge, *Culture and Society* (New York: Prentice-Hall, 1952), p. 100. And also, in the 1961 edition, Merrill states, "The basic element in technology is knowledge." p. 125. Perhaps a more popularized expression of the same thought by Alvin Toffler would be: "If technology, however, is to be regarded as a great engine, a mighty accelarator, then knowledge must be regarded as its fuel." p. 27, and, "knowledge is change"—and accelerating knowledge-acquisition fueling the great engine of technology, means accelerating change."p. 29, *Future Shock* (New York Random House, 1970).

[32]So defined in *The American College Dictionary*. This treatment of knowledge as consisting of awareness, acquaintance, cognizance on the one hand and as a body of facts or truths on the other (the knower and the known) is used also by Fritz Machlup, *The Production and Distribution of Knowledge in the United States* (Princeton: Princeton University Press, 1962), "*. . . that which is known . . .*" and the "*state of knowing*." pp. vi and 13 ff. In the course of epistemological discussions philosophers view knowledge in terms of "warranted belief . . . knowledge is belief," and that knowledge, ". . . is knowledge only *if belief in it is warranted*; i.e., if there is *sufficient reason for asserting that it is true*." pp. 3-4, W.H. Werkmeister *The Basis and Structure of Knowledge* (New York: Harper and Brothers 1948). Our concern at this juncture is with *all* of culture and consequently with *all* of knowledge and not knowledge in the sense of "verifiable truth" but rather any and all knowledge and its relation to culture. All knowledge includes gossip, myth, small-talk, and so on. These aspects of knowledge are part of *all* culture but do not constitute a part of the core of culture.

"There are ways of making it all knowledge regardless of the strength of belief in it or warranty for it." Machlup, *The Production and Distribution of Knowledge in the United States*, p. 23.

[33]Robert K. Merton, *Social Theory and Social Structure* (New York: The Free Press, 1968), "The term 'knowledge' must be interpreted very broadly indeed, since studies in this area have dealt with virtually the entire gamut of cultural products . . ." p. 510; British Association For the Advancement of Science, *Notes and Queries on Anthropology* (London: Routledge and Kegan Paul, 1951), p. 195.

[34]"Even a cursory survey is enough to show that the term 'knowledge' has been so broadly conceived as to refer to every type of idea and every mode of thought ranging from folk belief to science." Merton, *Social Theory and Social Structure* (1968), pp. 521, 510, 525, 550-52. And Machlup, *The Production and Distribution of Knowledge in the United States*, pp. 20-21.

[35]Elman R. Service, *International Encyclopedia of the Social Sciences* Vol. V, p. 222.

[36]"Knowledge has often come to be assimilated to the term 'culture . . ." Merton, *Social Theory and Social Structure* (1968), p. 521; Felix M. Keesing, "The story of cultural development can be seen from one facet as involving increased knowledge." *Cultural Anthropology* (New York: Holt, Rinehart and Winston, 1958), p. 321; Harry Hoijer, "Each generation takes over, by word of mouth and tradition the accumulated knowledge of their predecessors, add their own contributions as drawn from their experiences and observations, and pass the whole on to succeeding generations." in Harry L. Shapiro, ed., *Man, Culture and Society* (New York: Oxford University Press, 1960), p. 197; Groves and Moore definition cited in the Kroeber and Kluckhohn, *Culture*, p. 48, "Culture is thus the *social heritage*, the fund of accumulated knowledge. . ."; and, Lewis Mumford, "For only when knowledge and practice could be stored in symbolic forms, and passed from generation to generation, was it possible to keep each fresh cultural acquisition from dissolving with the passing moment or the dying generation." in Paul H. Oehser, ed., *Knowledge Among Men* (Washington, D.C.: Published by Simon Schuster in cooperation with the Smithsonian Institution, 1966), p. 131; and, George M. Foster, "Culture may be thought of as a memory bank where knowledge is stored . . . to guide us in situations in which we routinely find ourselves." *Traditional Cultures: and the Impact of Technological Change* (New York: Harper and Brothers, 1962), p. 19.

[37]We are concerned with social knowledge and not with the private accumulations of the genuis who is also a recluse and a hermit and whose knowledge dies with him not having been made public or social. On this, note Harvey Leibenstien *Economic Backwardness and Economic Growth* (New York: John Wiley and Sons, 1967), p. 136.

[38]On the view that culture functions as an overall technique of adaptation enabling man to survive and to cope with his mllieu, note the Kroeber and Kluckhohn study, *Culture*, p. 74 and pp. 55-58. And

also on the adaptive role of culture, note Robert L. Carneiro, *International Encyclopedia of the Social Sciences,* Vol. 3, pp. 551-554.

[39]To view language as a part of culture and knowledge is not uncommon, note, Harry Hojier in Shapiro, ed,, *Man, Culture and Society,* pp. 196-223 and also by Hoijer, ". . . language does not stand separate from culture but is an essential part of it." in Kroeber, *Anthropology Today,* pp. 554-573, p. 554. Language is also viewed as a tool, note the Singer study, *A History of Technology,* Vol. I, ". . . the most important of which is that characteristically human tool called 'language." p. v. And Kroeber and Kluckhohn, *Culture,* pp. 115-124.

[40]This would, of course, constitute a broad area of knowledge, "But all empirical knowledge, all scientifically tested information, no matter how abstract and remote it may seem, is potentially useful, potentially applicable in economic production. . . All empirical knowledge is thus potentially relevant to economic production." Simon Kuznets, in Lekachman, ed., *Notional Policy for Economic Welfare at Home and Abroad,* p. 60 or for another source of Kuznets', "Toward a Theory of Economic Growth," note, *Economic Growth and Structure,* pp. 1-81, p. 61 and pp. 84-85.

[41]Therefore on this basis our view is that not all knowledge is relevant or usesul in terms of economic development. On this basis Benjamin Higgins perhaps overstates the case when he notes: "The disheartening truth is that no aspect of human knowledge is completely irrelevant to the process of development." *Economic Development* (1968), p. 7. Undoubtedly Higgins' conceptualization of knowledge would be knowledge exclusive of gossip, incantation, and ceremonialism.

[42]Knowledge need not always be useful: "Many irrational practices or plain ignorance in both religion and magic—as well as in government and economics—play important real, as well as symbolic, roles in holding a culture together and making it work." Merrill and Eldridge, *Culture and Society* (1952) p. 92 and the study cited: Wilbert E. Moore and Melvin M. Tumin, "Some Social Functions of Ignorance," *American Sociological Review,* 14, (December, 1949). pp. 787-795. However, that much ceremonialism is nót concerned with man's practical objectives is also apparent, and in addition may also be negative in its retardation of the further advance of useful knowledge, "The Australian Arunta are a ceremonial people," and this tendency toward "ritualistic and ceremonial behavior" retards the 'drift or direction" of the material culture toward advance and accumulation. Merrill, *Culture and Society,* p. 101. This view of course is basic to Thorstein B. Veblen and his analysis of the imbecile and the ceremonial.

[43]"The cultural structure clusters about this body of matter-of-fact knowledge as its substantial core," Thorstein Veblen, *The Place of Science in Modern Civilization* (New York: Russell and Russell, 1961), p. 2. Also, on the "core of culture" as used elsewhere in the literature note: Julian H. Steward, *Theory of Culture Change* (Urbana: University of Illinois Press, 1955), ". . . the constellation of features

which are most closely related to subsistence activities and economic arrangements. The core includes such social, political, and religious patterns as are empirically determined to be closely connected with these arrangements." pp. 37, 6. And also, John J. Honigman, *The World of Man* (New York: Harper and Row, 1959), p. 299.

[44]We have previously noted a preference for "practical" rather than "industrial". Also, while some view the practical arts or to us practical technics as associated primarily with material culture, note Robert S. Merrill, "hunting, fishing, gathering, agriculture, animal husbandry, and mining through manufacturing, construction, transportation, provision of food, power, heat, light. . ." *International Encyclopedia of the Social Sciences* (1968), Vol. 15, p. 576, we would emphasize specifically, and explicitly, the nonmaterial technics or the social inventions associated with social organization, in addition to material technics, as being equally a part of the practical arts (technics) of man.

[45]On the view that each generation does not start out fresh, note, Pitirim Sorokin, *Contemporary Sociological Theories* (New York: Harper and Brothers, 1928). "Each new generation does not start anew with its own experience, but with the gathered experience of all previous generations which has been accumulating in the course of time. This is evident." p. 746.

[46]New economic goods form a part of material culture and embody material manifestations of additions to useful knowledge. ". . .material culture. . . means the tools and artifacts (hatchets to houses) used by mankind. As we have suggested, these physical things are merely the concretion of the truly cultural knowledge that is behind them." Francis E. Merrill and H. Wentworth Eldridge, *Culture and Society* (New York: Prentice-Hall, 1952), p. 91. This also applies to physical capital which represents another part of material culture and which also embodies useful knowledge. On changes in capital that embody technical knowledge, note: Robert M. Solow, "Investment and Technical Progress," pp. 89-104 in *Mathematical Methods in the Social Sciences*, 1959, Kenneth J. Arrow, et al., (Stanford: Stanford University Press, 1969), in which he questions that technological change is "disembodied" that ". . . It floats down from the outside. . . This conflicts with the casual observation that many if not most innovations need to be embodied in new kinds of durable equipment before they can be made effective." pp. 90-91. On this point by Solow note also the Lave study, *Technological Change: Its Conception and Measurement*, ". . .technological change might be embodied in new capital." pp. 35, 101-105. And for a much earlier statement note: Allan G.B. Fisher, "Capital and the Growth of Knowledge," *The Economic Journal*, 43 (Sept. 1933) pp. 379-389. "The major capital stock of an advanced nation its not is physical equipment: it is the body of knowledge amassed from tested findings and discoveries of empirical knowledge, and the capacity and training of its population to use this knowledge effectively. One can easily envisage a situation in which technologi-

cal progress permits output to increase at a high rate without *any* additions to the stock of capital goods." Kuznets, in Lekachman, *National Policy for Economic Welfare*, p. 39. Also on this point note the *Horndal-effect* in Zimmerman, *Poor Lands, Rich Lands: The Widening Gap*, pp. 104, 132, footnote 6, and 143.

[47]That institutions embody and are a form of knowledge, note, "By *knowledge* I mean all that man has learned. . . I include cultural institutions." Fred L. Whipple, *Knowledge Among Men*, Paul H. Oehser. ed. (New York: Simon and Schuster, 1966), pp. 177-178, and W.H. Hamilton, *Encyclopedia of the Social Sciences* (1932), ". . . the roots. . . run far back into the past and embody the knowledge. . ." p. 84, Vol. 8. Also note Keesing, *Cultural Anthropology*, and his reference to Malinowski, p. 321. In this context we often find in the literature references to "social knowledge," for example, note, W.A. Lewis, *The Theory of Economic Growth* (London: George Allen & Unwin 1955), pp. 164-200.

[48]On the difficulties note: Joyce O. Hertzler, *Social Institutions* (New York: McGraw-Hill, 1929), and Don Martindale's comments, *Social Life and Cultural Change* (Princeton: D. Van Nostrand Company, 1962), p. 49. And also, Charles Wolf, Jr., "Institutions and Economic Development," *The American Economic Review*, 45 (December 1955), pp. 867-883, p. 868, footnote 5.

[49]*International Encyclopedia of the Social Sciences* (1968), Vol. 14, p. 410. And also, Don Martindale, *Social Life and Cultural Change*, ". . . the standardized solutions to the problems of collective life. A group is a shared *strategy* of interhuman behavior, i.e., a plan of action intended to achieve defined objectives. Institutions are fixed elements of such strategies." pp. 32, 39. And also, Walton H. Hamilton, for a more general definition and less oriented toward problem solving: ". . . It connotes a way of thought or action of some prevalence and permanence, which is embedded in the habits of a group or the customs of a people. . . Institution fix the confines of and impose form upon the activities of human beings." *Encyclopedia of the Social Sciences* (New York: The Macmillan Company, 1932), Vol. 8, p. 84.

[50]On the social inventions, note, W.A. Lewis, *The Theory of Economic Growth*, p. 176. While many in the literature use the term, social invention, and our references could consequently be numerous, we briefly refer to Ogburn and Nimkoff, *Sociology* (Boston: Houghton Mifflin Company, 1964), for a succinct discussion as well as a listing of some of the more recent manifestations of social inventions, pp. 709-712.

[51]"Social institutions are the great conservers and transmitters of the cultural heritage." Francis Merrill, *Society and Culture* (1965), p. 361. It is in this sense that we view the institution as a store of knowledge and consequently view institutions as elements of culture.

[52]In the particular as to what denotes an institution, especially of the "imbecile" and ceremonial" variety, may be subject to debate.

In this instance we follow the lead of Linton who denotes head hunting as an institution. "It was maintained by the institution of head hunting." *The Tree of Culture* (New York: Alfred A. Knopf, 1955), p. 216.

[53]Although the two words are often used with little distinction, there is a distinction which we would like to make and which would be of importance for our theoretical framework. Originally from ". . .the Greek word from which technique is derived means indifferently art, skill, carft, trick, strategem, ruse." Harry E. Barnes and Howard Becker, eds., *Contemporary Social Theory* (New York: D. Appleton-Century, Company, 1940), p. 494. "In this sense there are techniques of every conceivable type of action. . . prayer. . . asceticism. . . thought. . . research. . . education. . . love. . . war. . ." p. 161, Max Weber, *The Theory of Social and Economic Organization* (Glencoe: The Free Press, 1957) and edited by Talcott Parsons referred to by Robert S. Merrill, *International Encyclopedia of the Social Sciences* (1968), Vol. 15, p. 577. And Lewis Mumford, "For the sake of clarity, I prefer to use technics alone to describe the field itself, that part of human activity wherein, by an energetic organization of the processes of work, man controls and directs the forces of nature for his own purposes." *Art and Technics* (New York: Columbia University Press, 1952), p. 15. And, Richard L. Meier, ". . . By the term 'technics' is meant the complete range of methods for transforming resources into goods and services. ' *Science and Economic Development* (New York: John Wiley and Sons and the Technology Press of Massachusetts Institute of Technology, 1956). To our view the distinction is that technology includes only technics and not all techniques and consequently that technology embraces only the core of culture but not the whole of culture. C.E. Ayres notes that: "No one supposes that the technological process is the whole of culture. . ." *The Theory of Economic Progress* (New York: Schoeken Books, 1962) p. 121.

[54] In the literature some confine technology to material culture, but this is not correct. A common error is ". . . the error of supposing that technology has to do only with things." Actually, ". . . technology is not 'things' but a form of human behavior." C.E. Ayres, *The Industrial Economy* (Cambridge: The Riverside Press: 1962) p. 311 and *The Theory of Economic Progress* (1962). "This absolute mutual contingency of skills and tools. . . as a function of huuan behavior." p. 108 Thomas P. Hughes in his review of Brook Hindle's *Technology in Early America: Needs and Opportunities for Study* in the *Journal of Economic History* 28 (March 1968), pp. 138-139 summarizes our view as to the error of limiting technology to material culture. "An historian of technology who limits himself to the artifacts might be likened to a political historian who did not go beyond such obvious manifestations as laws and constitutions."

[55]As Bronislaw Malinowski notes: "Speech is a bodily habit and is comparable to any other type of custom . . . Language thus is an integral part of culture; it is not, however, a system of tools but rather

a body of vocal customs," *Encylopedia of the Social Sciences* (1931), Vol. IV, p. 622. And as such, as a nonmaterial technic, language to us constitutes a part of the overall gestalt of technology. "It may seem odd that writing should be included in technology. But, after all, writing is a tool—an intellectual tool, if you will. It was the necessary instrument of exact science, the applications of which have revolutionized technology." V. Gordon Childe, *Social Evolution* (New York: Henry Schuman, 1961) p. 23.

[56]"Perhaps the important single element in a national integration program is educational reform, and in my view, the most important single element in educational reform is a determined literacy drive. . . To start on a national development program while leaving the population largely illiterate seems to me to be futile." Gunnar Myrdal, *An International Economy* (New York: Harper and Row, 1969), p. 186. Such an emphasis, which as we have already noted, is growing in the literature and, of course, would be basic to our analysis, which stresses the advance of useful knowledge as being the essence and fountainhead of economic development. And also, Nelson, et al. *Technology Economic Growth and Public Policy*, pp. 11-13, "The Embodiment of Technological Knowledge in the Labor Force."

[57] Kuznets is somewhat ambivalent on this issue and in many instances refers to technology and social inventions, and thereby tends to separate the technological from the social, rather than to the matetial and (social) nonmaterial inventions of the overall technology. For example: ". . . some innovations may be largely technological, the exploitation of the potential of growth provided by them usually require much social invention . . ." and, ". . . for the dominant views of and economic epoch are as distinctive and as important as the technological and social epochal innovation . . . raises sharply the stock of technological and social knowledge . . ." *Modern Economic Growth*, pp. 5, 12, 286. As we shall see, and soon discuss, in other instances Kuznets speaks in terms of "modern material and social technology" p. 477, and consequenty includes social (nonmaterial) technics in the overall conceptualization of technology. Meier and Baldwin, *Economic Development*, also note the importance of social technics but do not apparently treat social knowledge as an integral part of technology. "Social knowledge is just as important as technical knowledge, since development depends as much upon learning how to administer large-scale organizations, or how to create institutions that favor economizing effort and economic rationality as it does upon the knowledge of how to breed new seeds or learning how to build bigger dams," p: 298. Even Ogburn, as one of the outstanding authorities on the issue of technology and social change, is also ambivalent on the issue. On the one hand he defines technology as being material: . . . that is the material products of technology which is the implication of the word 'technology' in the title . . . In short it includes the material objects of culture." "Technology as Environment," in *William F. Ogburn on Culture and Social Change* (Chicago: University of Chicago Press, 1964),

ed., Otis Dudley Duncan, p. 79, and in Ogburn and Nimkoff *Sociology* (1964) we find social inventions classified under the heading: INNOVATIONS IN NON-TECHNOLOGICAL CULTURE," p. 709. Yet elsewhere we find: "Technology is therefore essentially social. We do not ordinarily think of technology as sociological. Rather we consider it as mechanical and belonging to the physical sciences," *Technology and Social Change* (New York: Appleton-Century-Crofts, 1957), p. 9.

[58]Recall Linton, *Tree of Culture*, p. 118 and also, V. Gordon Childe, "The Urban Revolution," *The Town Planning Review*, 21, (1950), pp. 3-17. And also, on the role of the city and urbanization, J.A. Ponsioen, *The Analysis of Social Change Reconcidered* (The Hague: Mouton and Company, 1969), pp· 127-136. In this context what also might be said for the importance of the social technic known as the nation as a concomitant nonmaterial technic to the early phases of the overall gestalt of industrialism.

[59]In his *Philosophy Manufactures* (London: William Clowes and Sons, 1835), Andrew Ure, in viewing the factory system notes the importance of the non-material or social technics. "To devise and administer a successful code of factory discipline, suited to the necessities of factory diligence, was the Herculean enterprise, the noble achievement of Arkwright." p. 15. And Ogburn in *Technology and Social Change*, F.R. Allen ed., "So also is *factory* or the *factory system* as a referent for the technology that has developed since the invention and use of the steam engine." p. 9.

[60]"Artifact and custom are equally indispensable and they mutually produce and determine one another." pp. 622, 626. Malinowski, *Encyclopedia of the Social Sciences*, (1931) Vol. IV.

[61]Linton, *The Tree of Culture*, p. v and Kroeber, *Anthropology*, p. 260.

[62]On "gestalt theory", as it is currently applied to the field of psychology, note: Solomon E. Asch, *International Encyclopedia of the Social Sciences* (1968), Vol. 6, pp. 158-175. "The problem that gestalt theory confronts is that of an extended event, whether an experience or an action, that cannot be adequately described as a sum of smaller, independent events." p. 158. Also, Arthur Spiethoff, "Pure Theory and Economic Gestalt Theory; Ideal Types and Real Types" in Frederic C. Lane and Jelle C. Riemersma, eds., *Enterprise and Secular Change* (Homewood: Richard D. Irwin, 1953), pp. 444-463.

[63]We have in several instances drawn attention to the basic fact that the U.S. and the U.S.S.R. have embraced an industrial system or the overall gestalt of industrialism in the context of very differing social technics. On this point note the statement by B.F. Hoselitz, pp. 27-58, in Willian B. Hamilton, ed., *The Transfer of Institutions* (Durham: Duke University Press, 1964). Also, Kuznets, *Six Lectures* pp. 110-114: and, Julian H. Steward, *Theory of Culture Change* (Urbana: University of Illinois Press, 1955), pp: 38-39; and, Higgins, *Economic Development* (1968), p. 258; and, J.M. Clark, in *Problems in the Study of Economic*

Growth (New York: National Bureau of Economic Research, 1949), pp. 40-42.

[64]We have noted previously that Kuznets is sometimes ambivalent on this issue, however, he does in several instances clearly state that social organization, i.e., social technics, are an integral part of the overall of technology: "And by technology we mean not merely the set of rules and devices of material production, but all types of devices and schemes—objectively described and adaptable by any qualified user —whether in the sphere of material production or social organization." in the *Problems in the Study of Economic Growth* (New York: National Bureau of Economic Research, Inc., 1949), pp. 17-18. And another statement by Kuznets on the issue, "The most important productive resource available . . . is the stock of technical knowledge embodied in tangible records and in the personal skills and habits of the population." "Measurement of Economic Growth," The Tasks of Economic History (Supplemental Issue of the Journal of Economic History), p. 12. Also recall *Economic Change* (1954), pp. 238-9, in which Kuznets states, ". . . a wide application of knowledge, based upon empirical science, to the problem of economic and social technology. . ." And also, in Lekachman, *National Policy for Economic Welfare at Home and Abroad*, ". . . they have adoped modern economic and social technology." p. 26. While a position taken by a social scientist somewhat earlier (1947, 1949) in his career need not always be adhered to Kuzents, in (1966), does seem to support the view that social technics are indeed a part of the overall of tecnnology, i.e., ". . . modern material and social technology." *Modern Economic Growth* (1966), p. 477. A.H. Johnson, *Whitehead's Philosophy of Civilization* (Boston: Beacon Press, 1958), notes that: "*There are techonological devices in realms other than the physical.* Social techniques, expressed in institutions, cannot be overlooked." p. 36. and also, Charles R. Walker, *Modern Technology and Civilization* (New York: McGraw-Hill Book Company 1662), pp. 2-3 Gunnar Myrdal in his criticism of social anthropologists states: "They seldom attempted, however, to develop their science into a social technology, which would have meant utilizing their assembled stock of knowledge about the social facts to prescribe how social change could be induced and controlled in a rational and wholesome way . . . The next stage in the development of cultural anthropology will necessarily be its orientation towards social technology." *An International Economy* (1969), p. 173. Also, George M. Foster in his *Traditional Culture, and the Impact of Technological Change* (New York: Harper and Row, 1962), "Perhaps the use of the term *sociotechnological* development would clarify our thinking . . . These nonmaterial changes are more subtle. Often they are overlooked or their significance is underestimated." pp. 2-3. And, "The social scientist . . . looks upon technological development as change in the patterns of culture and society." p. 9. And, Erich W. Zimmermann, *World Resources and Industries* (New York, Harper and Brothers, 1951), "Two categories of the arts may be distinguished: material or technical arts . . . and so-

cietal or institutional arts. . . The two groups of arts are branches of the same tree; they draw their strength from the same soil." pp. 31-32. And to us that soil is the soil of useful knowledge which is the basis for material and nonmaterial technics and which together comprise man's technology.

[65]In his "Cultural Lag as Theory," *Sociology and Social Research*, XLI (January 1957), pp. 167-73, Ogburn clearly states that the independent variable may be material or nonmaterial. See also, Ogbrn and Nimkoff, *Sociology* (1964), pp. 710-712. And while the main emphasis is apparently that it is the material culture which more likely than not serves as the pace-setter, Ogburn and Nimkoff note "The fact that technology is at present so powerful a cause of cultural lags, and consequently social disorganization, does not deny that other variables such as social inventions or population changes are creating lags also." p. 734.

[66]"But the most important invention of all had no direct industrial connection whatever: namely the invention of the experimental method in science. . . its full effect upon technics did not begin to be felt until the middle of the nineteenth century." Lewis Mumford, *Technics and Civilization* (New York: Harcourt Brace and Company, 1934), p. 132, and, "Out of this habit grew a new phenomenon: deliberate and systematic invention." p. 218. And the frequently cited quotation: "The greatest invention of the nineteenth century was the method of invention." Alfred North Whitehead, *Science and the Modern World* (New York: The Macmillan Company, 1925) p. 136.

[67]While a precise ordering of *the* scientific method might be difficult to come by, i.e., ". . . on one point I believe almost all modern historians of the natural sciences would agree. . . There is no such thing as *the* sciencific method." James B. Conant *Science and Common Sense* (New Haven: Yale University Press, 1951), p. 45, an offshoot of such methods is that man now enabled to consciously attempt and succeed at problem solving by systematic and fruitful methods, i.e., the prime case of the moon landing and return. And the more we solve the greater is our capabity to solve.

[68] What *is* unique about the modern era, however, is the rapidity, depth and constancy of the flow of new technology. ". . . technological progress has become systematic and dependable, and it comes not in a trickle but in a flood. . . In a certain sense the 'scientific attitude' is at the root of the whole thing." Richard T. Gill, *Economic Development Past and Present* (Englewood Cliffs: Prentice-Hall, 1963), pp. 17-18; and, Kuznets, *Economic Growth and Structure*, pp. 85-87. A view evidently endorsed by Easterlin, who, in discussing the "origins of modern economic development" states that: The answer would appear to lie in the virtual explosion in the stock of knowledge, and particularly scientific. . . in the past three centuries." *International Encyclopedia of the Social Sciences* (1968), Vol. 4, pp. 406-407. Wesley C. Simonton also gives an indication of the extent of this "knowledge explosion" by estimating that". . . one half of the scholarly material on hand

today had been produced since 1950 and that 80 percent of the scientists the world has known are alive today." *The New York Times*, Jan 24, 1965, p. 63:3. Basically the hypothesis is that "culture is a cumulative process; it gains momentum as it proceeds." Zimmermann, *World Resources and Industries*, p. 31. "The human store of knowledge is generally increasing at an accelerating speed. . ." Sol Tax, "Selective Culture Change." *American Economic Review* 41, (May 1951), pp. 315-323, p. 316, and "I think therefore, that we are allowed to state that scientific knowledge and technical power advance according to the law and rate of an increasing geometric progression or logarithmic function." Zimmerman, *Poor Lands, Rich Lands: The Widening Gap*, p. 139. The idea of culture advancing exponentially is of course basic to William F. Ogburn's *Social Change* and also note Ogburn and Nimkoff, *Sociology* (1964), pp. 666-672., and Hornell Hart, in *Technology and Social Change*, F, R. Allen, ed., pp. 27-55, and his annotated bibliography, p. 55 (Chapin, Chase, Merrill and Ogburn); and also on the acceleration and measurement of knowledge recall our reference to Daniel Bell, and also, no discussion would be complete without reference to the works of John de Solla Price. A goodly portion of our study will be devoted to a discussion of the very fascinating phenomenon of the "knowledge explosion" and the exponential rate of culture advance.

[69]"Moreover the way of knowledge is itself an institution. . . we can learn. . . to the extent allowed by our prevailing methods of inquiry." W.H. Hamilton, *Encyclopedia of the Social Sciences* (1932), Vol. VII. p. 88; and, ". . . Most modern technologies include not only traditions for making and doing things but also traditions for 'advancing the state of the art,' for producing new knowledge, processes, and products." Robert S. Merrill, *International Encyclopedia of the Social Sciences*, Vol. 15, p. 582. Perhaps the most practical of the technics would be those associated with the production of new knowledge. We readily recognize factories and industries associated with the production of material culture, i.e., consumer goods and capital plant and equipment we are now also coming to recognize the "knowledge industry" and the "knowledge factory." Note, Clark Kerr, *The Uses of a University* (New York: Harper and Row, 1966), pp. 87-91: and, Fritz Machlup, *The Production and Distribution of Knowledge in the United States* (Princeton: Princeton University Press, 1962); and Robert M. Hutchins, *The Learning Society* (New York: Frederick A. Praeger, Publishers, 1968), "Every educational system is a technology," p. 12, p. 74 and, "Modern educators are more like Henry Ford. In the economic realm we are dedicated to the mass production of goods; the corresponding term in the jargon of our subject is mass education," p. 75.

[70]"Whatever the source, the increase in the stock of useful knowledge and the extension of its application are of the essence in modern economic growth." Kuznets *Modern Economic Growth*, 286; and elsewhere, *Economic Growth and Structure*, pp. 83-92, p. 114, p. 60. . .,

etc. or stated more along the lines of a culture analysis, "Knowledge is the only truly crescive (i.e., growing) aspect of culture." Merrill and Eldredge, *Culture and Society* (1952), p. 86. Alfred Marshall, "Knowledge is our most powerful engine of production; it enables us to subdue Nature and force her to satisfy our wants." *Principles of Economics* (London Macmillan & Co., 1907) 5th edition, pp. 138-139 on the expansion of the Marshallian as well as the overall classical position, note, Lord Robbins, *The Theory of Economic Development in the History of Economic Thought* (New York: St. Martin's Press, 1968), pp. 70-94, after which Lord Robbins concludes: "After this surely there is little that need be said to emphasise the significance of knowledge to the processes of economic development." p. 94 Moses Abramovitz, *American Economic Review* (My 1956), pp. 13-14 and in Lekachman, *National Policy* p. 81. And Zimmermann, *World Resources and Industries*, pp. 9-10, "Knowledge is truly the mother of all other resources . . . The difference between neolithic man, who roamed the earth in misery and fear, and man today, who lives in relative comfort and security is knowledge. . . "

CHAPTER VII

The Wheel of Economic Development

It is our view that any theory or explanation of economic development must be interdisciplinary in method since we are dealing with the whole gamut and complexity of culture and its evolution, or more correctly, the "core of culture." We have discussed at length the basic position that: "Development is therefore not only economic growth, but growth plus change: social, cultural, and institutional, as well as economic."[1] In the history of political economy the cultural and social variables have traditionally been relegated to the realm of the so-called "noneconomic" analysis. Though historically ignored in mainstream economics, the noneconomic variables are, nonetheless, very important in the overall process of economic development. For it is becoming more and more apparent that what the economist has designated "noneconomic" factors are in their import on economic development very much economic. In this sense designating the cultural factors as "noneconomic" is a misnomer. Consequently, "Someone once quipped that economic development is much too serious a topic to be left to economists. . . . As the economic historian well knows, a full account of a nation's economic development embodies its entire cultural history."[2]

Evidence of an increased tendency, especially during the post-WW II period, to view economic development from an interdisciplinary or holistic methodology, as including the noneconomic or broadly speaking, cultural factors as well as the isolated economic, is amply provided in the literature.[3]

However, it should be noted that we are not referring here to practitioners of normal science. Mainstream economists still view economic development as being essentially economic, that is, economic growth in the context of traditional economic analysis and to the exclusion of the noneconomic. Those who do give place to the cultural and the social certainly do not treat culture or the so-called "noneconomic" variables in the same manner.[4] Also, many who do endorse the inclusion of noneconomic factors as essential to analysis turn about and justify their avoidance of an holistic approach on the grounds that interdisciplinary methodology is too primitive, that our lack of knowledge or ignorance in this area is too great.[5] Social scientists who repudiate an interdisciplinary analysis in the context of economic development may be correct in such a position; however, if a social scientist endorses an interdisciplinary approach, as an holistic or culture-type of analysis as being correct for an analysis of economic development, it would seem incongruous for that social scientist to then timidly disengage on the ground of ignorance. Should not our ignorance propel us as social scientists to break away and to achieve advanced levels of knowledge rather than to partake in a rigor mortis of our ignorance. If the problem is correctly viewed as cultural and interdisciplinary, if we are correct in the conclusion that we should analyze the noneconomic as well as the economic, let us see how and why, however rudimentary our methods. Is it not a porous intellectual position for those who do recognize the importance of interdisciplinary methodology in the analysis of economic development to then eschew such an approach on the basis (pretext?) of ignorance, claiming that the social sciences as such are insufficiently developed for such an endeavor? Usually a discovery of ignorance in the area of useful knowledge is taken as a plea for action to generate useful knowledge, to clarify the confusion, eliminate the ignorance, and to fill the gap.[6] Success, of course, may be a long time in coming but at least the effort should be made, ignorance is not an excuse for disengagement but rather should be a call to arms. We in this study accept the challenge of an interdisciplinary analysis on the grounds that not only is economic development a culture process but in addition that economic development cannot take place without culture change, more correctly, culture evolution.[7]

The methodology of our theoretical framework to explain this evolutionary process and to incorporate the "noneconomic" will rest upon the principle of circular and cumulative causation.[8] That causal relationships are circular results in cumulative effects that are either vicious or virtuous circles. Our schema basically concerns the circular relationships between technology and culture and that as technology changes it changes culture and that the new culture complex in turn generates new technics, and so on the circle spins.[9] If a new technic is not innovated, there is no change in technology and, consequently, no transformation of culture. However, such a case of culture stagnation does not negate the circular interrelationships of the causal factors involved and associated with economic development but simply demonstrates that economic development need not always be virtuous but can be vicious in terms of cumulative effects. The long-term process of general culture evolution has been virtuous and manifest in the exponential. For a specific culture, however, the vicious circle of stagnation may dominate and be reflected in economic stagnation and even decay and disintegration. Economic stagnation would, in a two-dimensional configuration, be represented by the asymptotic ceiling of the logistic and in three-dimensional configuration, by a cylindrical helix.[10]

The circulatory system of man's blood stream interrelating the heart and lungs via arteries and veins represents a circular interrelationship of blood flows, but cumulative effects in terms of the quality and quantity of the blood supply are limited. The circular relationships of the example provided by man's circulatory system constitute a static or functional analysis. Such a static or functional analysis has merit in biology (physiology) and also has its place in sociology, and anthropology, and economics in that such methodology clarifies the interrelationships of the parts. Given a still-shot picture, an analysis for a given moment of time, for a given culture or economy, how are the parts interrelated, how do they function, what are the circular interrelationships (the heart and lungs) of a given overall gestalt of technology? However, the study of biology is not restricted simply to physiology and the functional but also entails comparative anatomy and biological evolution. Before the biologist could conceptualize genetic mutation and biological evolution he had to first understand the interrelationships of functional parts. Consequently, scientific analysis in biology entails the static and functional as well as the dynamic. By analogy the social sciences are not simply concerned with the static but must also focus on the dynamic as well, especially if the analytical objective is economic development.

A stages-type of analysis of economic development not only concerns the dynamics of transformation but also has static or still-shot features as well. A stages analysis also entails a description of the functional parts of a particular gestalt of technology for each given stage of economic development. For a given moment of time, a stages analysis shows how the social and the economic, the cultural parts, are functionally interrelated in the sense of circular causation. In the context of a particular stage of economic development for a given moment of time, a particular overall gestalt of technology represents a X-sectional slice of the three-dimensional configuration of culture; the parts are casually related in a circular manner and analysis is static and functional. This provides a theoretical buttress for a dynamic analysis which is concerned with the mechanism of transition, an explanation of the movement from one stage to the next. We will approach this problem in the course of this chapter in the context of the "closed" and "open" wheel of economic development. The closed wheel representing the static and functional and the open wheel being the case in which the environmental composite of culture and natural resources proves permeable to new technics. It is in the case of an open wheel of economic development that the spiral of culture advance moves out of the realm of the cylindrical helix to a variation of the conical. Therefore, though the factors of economic development are causally interrelated in a circular way, in both a closed and open wheel of economic development, it is the latter case which embraces circular causation with positive cumulative effects.

Let us recapitulate the analysis which we have presented up to this point. At heart of the matter is useful knowledge, knowledge amenable to the practical ends of economic production and social organization. When we speak of an advance in terms of economic development, what we are really viewing in essence is an advance of man's useful knowledge.[11] But such knowledge is of no import for economic development unless applied to the practical ends of economic production and social organization and innovated as such. It is when so used that such knowledge becomes an integral part of the overall gestalt of technology. Technology in the form of material and nonmaterial technics, in its store, represents thecore of culture and, consequently, the advance of this core can be demonstrated by the advance of technology. We call this advance the process of an economic development. Moreover, if we change technology we also in the process change and transform the core of culture; clearly we have a tautology and this constitutes our basic circular relationship. In this way we see that technology is the endogenous variable contained within our framework of analysis and is a factor of historical continuity capable of indicating the directional advance of economic development.[12] In this light, technology does not cause economic development but is its very essence.

If such a view of the relation of technology and economic development be correct, it would then follow that to analyze and explain the process of economic development we must explain the process of the invention and discovery of new technics and their innovation since it is this process which constitutes the advance of technology. Since our conceptualization of technology stressed the application of useful knowledge to the practical ends of man, our explanation, our theory, of the process of economic development would have to include : (A) An explanation of the process of dicovering and inventing new technics, (B) An explanation of the process innovating the new technics; (C) How such an innovation would be integrated into overall gestalt or technology and, (D) How the change in technology would affect the culture transformation and cumulation; and to complete the circle, how such changes in culture cumulation (D) are related to the formation and genesis of new technics (A). Therefore, changes in technology are related to changes in culture and culture in turn as it accumulates and is transformed is related to changes in technology.[13] Whatever the source of causation or origin of the new technic, its addition to the overall gestalt of technology is viewed as a necessary condition for economic development

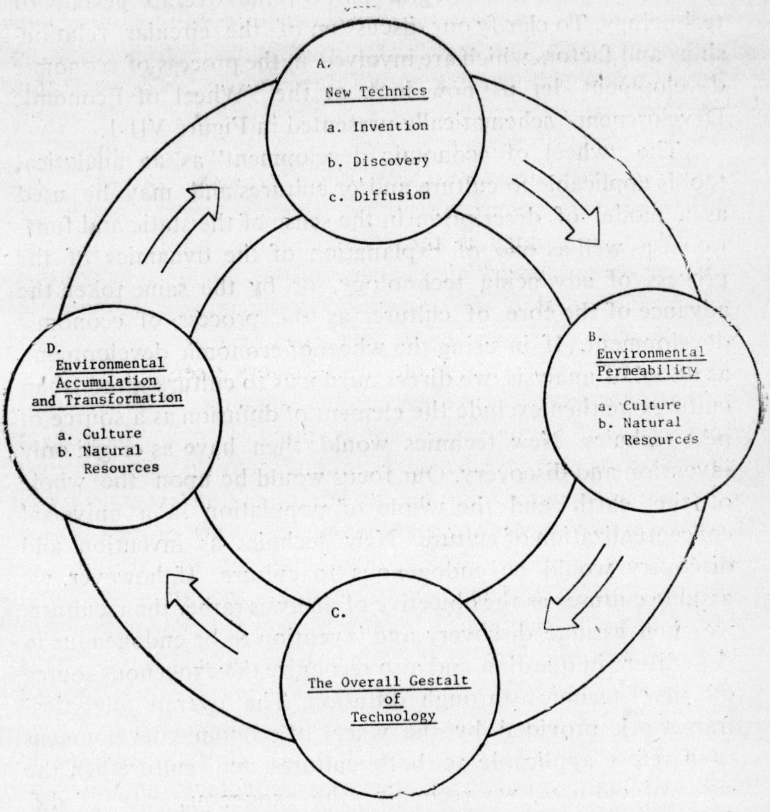

Fig. VII-1. The Wheel of Economic Development.

or positive culture cumulation.[14] The new technics which for a specific culture may have their genesis in invention, discovery, or diffusion, need not be innovated and therefore do not constitute a sufficient condition for economic development by themselves. Economic development takes place when the new technic becomes an integral part of the overall gestalt of technology. To clarify our discussion of the circular relationships and factors which are involved in the process of economic development let us now look at the "Wheel of Economic Development" schematically presented in Figure VII-1.

The "wheel of economic development" as an analytical tool is applicable to culture and/or cultures and may be used as a model of description in the sense of the static and functional as well as one of explanation of the dynamics of the process of advancing technology, or by the same token the advance of the core of culture, as the process of economic development. If in using the wheel of economic development, as a tool of analysis, we direct our focus to culture rather than cultures we then exclude the element of diffusion as a source of new technics. New technics would then have as origin only invention and discovery. Our focus would be upon the whole of the earth and the whole of population in a universal conceptualization of culture. New technics as invention and discovery would be endogenous to culture. If, however, we assume cultures as the objective of analysis rather than culture, we then assume discovery and invention to be endogenous to the culture in question and also recognize the exogenous source of new technics through diffusion. The overall analytical framework provided by the wheel of economic development is therefore applicable to both cultures and culture. In the case of cultures, we recognize the exogenous case of diffusion as a way in which new technics are introduced to a particular culture and in the case of universal culture the process is completely endogenous and we consequently exclude diffusion as a source of new technics. In both cases, however, that of culture as well as cultures, it is the new technic and its innovation which is crucial to the process of economic development and culture evolution.

New ideas in the form of material or nonmaterial technics, are initiated by man through invention or discovery endogenously for a given culture and are presented to other cultures through the process of diffusion. The *New Technics* (A) do not automatically become part of the productive process, that is, *The overall Gestalt of Technology* (C), but require innovation. The *New Technics* (A) represent the increment, and *The Overall Gestalt of Technology* (C) is the summation or total of those increments, the accumulation past and present in the form of an organic whole, which have become effective and actual integral parts of the processes of production. *The Overall Gestalt of Technology* (C) represents, consequently, the level of technological advance; it represents the sum total of a country's accumulated technology (assuming the analysis to be one of culutres) and is indicative of the stage or level of economic development. Whether or not the *New Technics* (A) are actually used, are innovated, and become an addition to *The Overall Gestalt of Technology* (C) is dependent upon the environment to which the new technic is exposed. Is the total environment of both culture and natural resources, represented by *Environmental Permeability* (B), permeable to the new technic? Are the social and economic factors favourable for its innovation? Many inventions (technics) do work but excessively high costs may prove prohibitive and deter innovation. Are the reflections of basic social institutions in the attitudes and values of the population favorable, such as, for example, birth control technics of prophylaction and abortion which are available but not always innovated and replicated. Are the psychological factors associated with personality and motivation (also, of course, function of culture) favorable and conducive to the innovation of the new technic? In the economic sphere, in the sense of integrating orthodox economic analysis into the wheel of economic development, what of the level of capital accumulation, the levels of effective demand, the size of the market, the skills and size of the labor force, the existing level of technology embedded in the culture, characteristics of the natural resource base and the underlying infrastructure of transportation and educational facilities? Also, are the entrepreneurs as the Schumpeterian innovators available, is the motivation both private and public necesary for innovation in existence? The element of innovation is crucial and without which economic development does not take place. That the innovators necessarily be a profit-seeking entrepreneur as the Schumpeterian model suggests is an assumption perhaps more relevant to the past experience of Western Europe and the United States and less applicable to the current realities of the underdeveloped countries today.[15]

To determine the causal factor which actually brought about a change in the gestalt of technology is difficult. Since we are dealing with a circle the "locus of the evolutionary impulse" might be anywhere. To ask what caused the sequence of invention and innovation might be answered in terms of the cultural setting itself, or an accident or chance occurrence, serendipity, or economic growth and effective demand or increased market size. Or it might be due to changed social values (Weber and his analysis concerning the role of religion in economic advance) or it might be the result of profit seeking and dynamic entrepreneurship. The dynamic force of change and innovation of a particular technic might well have been in a particular case and for a particular culture a profit-seeking entrepreneur. While Schumpeter's schema is relevant to a particular or specific culture having such profit-seeking entrepreneurs and is applicable to our wheel of economic development as explanation, it does not apply to culture in the sense of a universal or generalized theory explaining economic development. Where does the circle start? Ultimately it is in the mind of man that the change is made, that the new technic is formed and innovated, but even here, one may well question what programmed man's brain to result in such behavior and once again we return to the concept of culture. However, it should be noted that this does not negate the fact that additions of new technics to effective processes of production constitute a necessary condition for economic development. What we are saying here is that the "causal" locus of this increment may be difficult to delineate and locate due to the circular nature of the whole precess.

Also is the natural resource base adequate, not only arable land and minerals but climate and topography; negative conditions in the area of natural resources may make certain new technics, especially those derived from diffusion and for a culture in the earlier stage of economic development, inoperable. The natural resource base may serve as a barrier to the innovation of a new technic such as the construction of canals or airfields in cultures with high mountainous terrain at topography or the innovation and development of hydroelectric power in a desert such as the Sahara. Consequently the environment to which we submit the new technic may prove impermeable due to unfavorable conditions in the area of natural resources.

If the new technic passes through the given environmental setting of culture and natural resources and is innovated we then have addition to *The Overall Gestalt of Technology* (C). With this change in technology we have now established the basis for *Environmental Accumulation and Transformation* (D), that is, changes in the form of transformation and cumulation of the given environmental situation of culture and natural resources which existed prior to the innovation of the new technic.[16] As the new technic becomes a part of the overall gestalt of technology and is replicated, culture is transformed and there is generated in the process an increased capacity for additions to material and nonmaterial culture as well as an accumulation and transformation of the resource base. When we think of natural resources the tendency is to view depletion rather than accumulation, but in reality, as with culture, natural resources accumulate and are transformed with the advance of useful knowledge. This is not an unusual interpretation.[17] While it is true that specific resources are subject to depletion and even outright destruction with the advance of technology, resources in general (the overall resource base) tend to accumulate with advance in technology.

The culture represented by (D), *Evironmental Accumulation and Transformation* may for a given moment of time be viewed as a specific culture's accumulated store of useful knowledge and provides a basic seed bed for the nurture and generation of *New Technics* (A). As new technics are added and accumulated the given culture provides a more fertile ground in its capacity to produce *New Technics* (A). Whether the *New Technics* (A) come as a flood or a trickle is a function of the stock of useful knowledge accumulated and stored in given culture, that is, the level of economic development as represented by *Environmental Accumulation and Transformation* (D). The basic factors associated with the production of new technics may or may not be available and in sufficient quantity for a given culture. Such factors are dependent, primarily, upon the level or stage of economic development. Science or pre-science as method of inquiry, the level of energy control, the levels of literacy and education, a free versus authoritarian society, capital accumulation, productivity, market size and effective demand, are some of the factors influencing the generation of new technics and are, themselves, functions of the stage of economic development. Obviously, using Rostow's terminology, a traditional society characterized by pre-Newtonian sciences would not be able to produce a flow of new technics comparable to a culture which had achieved a take-off and the stage of modern science in its economic development.

Consequently, the flow of *Technics* (A) for a given culture is primarily a function of the level of economic development. The view is consistent with Ogburn's theory of the exponential advance of culture. The greater the accumulation of elements, technics, of a given culture, the greater would be the probability of new combinations as invention and discovery in the form of new technics. Knowledge begets knowledge and at an exponential rate. The grudging slowness of invention and discovery during the paleolithic period in which simple flaking and chipping technics did not change for thousands of years compared to the knowledge and invention explosion of the current period of industrialism serve as basic examples. For a specific culture, economic development is not inevitable in that even if the new technics are presented (either endogenously through invention and discovery or exogenously through diffusion) they need not be innovated due to the lack of culture permeability which is, itself, also a basic function of economic development. The current cultures of Japan and Western Europe would be permeable to the technics of mass production but such premeability would not be the case for the cultures of the Eskimo or Bushman. However, though for a specific culture it need not take place, economic development pre-supposes an advance of technology as a necessary condition. If no technological advance occurs, there is no advance in economic development though there may exist a potential for economic growth. Economic growth if it occurs would be based upon replication and the increase in factor inputs and not technological change, and would basically represent an increase in size of what already is in existence. Even though economic growth based upon replication could spread and endure for long periods of time (our previously cited cases of economic growth and no development), ultimately, such growth would lead to a logistic ceiling or state of stagnation inside the constraint of invariant technology.[18]

While such a schema, as presented in the wheel of economic development, is indeed very general and rudimentary, it importantly does focus attention on the nature of the process of economic development. The process of economic development is essentially that of an expansion of useful knowledge and its application to the practical ends of economic production and social organization which results in the accumulation and transformation of culture. Economic development is not simply conceptualized as increased quantities of goods and services. Economic growth is a characteristic and a result, a manifestation and indicator of technological advance or economic development, but it is not the process itself. Economic growth on a long-term continuum as the exponential is a function of economic development, for without technological advance economic growth ends in a saturation and stagnation and the logistic. As method, in offering the overview contained in the wheel of economic development, we have presented the whole in order to better understand the parts.[19] Correct conceptualization of economic development in its entirety or whole in the presentation of a general framework is a foundation for the further elaboration of theory and for a proper focus on future research tasks. In our framework as we look more closely in detail at the variables (A), (B), (C) and (D) we generalize less and become more and more specific and relevant to a particular culture in question.

Still, however, more in the context of broad generalization, let us note some specific features of our variables (A), (B), (C) and (D). *New Technics* (A), in the context of the economic development of a particular culture, are generated by invention, discovery and diffusion.[20] Since the social heritage, the *Environmental Accumulation and Transformation* (D), is different for each culture we would expect the inventions and discoveries produced by each culture, to be different. However, the greater the homogeneity of cultures, the greater the homogeinity of *New Technics* (A), not only in form but in the rate and quantity of production of new technics as well. Also, *New Technics* (A) submitted to a culture for acceptance in the form of diffusion would usually more readily take place between more homogenous cultures, further adding to their homogeneity.[21]

New Technics (A) are crucial for culture cumulation not in the sense of the "locus of the evolutionary impulse," since the causal factor of change in a system of circular causation may be located anywhere, but as a necessary condition for economic development. That invention and discovery constitute the source of culture advance is a basic axiom. It is the explanation of the process, however, which is subject to debate and controversy.[22] What caused the new technic to appear when and how it did? Innate capacity, economic demand, public policy and private policy toward research and development, culture accumulation, resource accumulation, or the lack of resources are all possible explanations for the genesis of the new technic. Our point is that in a circle of causation, the precise locus of the particular cause behind the new technic is difficult to determine. As the fountainhead of the process, the genesis of the additions to useful knowledge embodied in the new technics deserves more attention than it currently receives in the literature, not only by economists, but by the social sciences in general.[23] As a general proposition, inventions and discoveries are basically the result of an interaction between man, culture, and the physical environment.[24] In comparison, man has changed relatively little biologically during the period of the accelerated changes in culture of the past 10,000 years; it is consequently the factor of culture which serves as the independent variable.[25] Man's innate capacity has not varied but has, by comparison with culture, remained relatively constant over time. Man serves as a catalytic agent in the process of culture accumulation and transformation in that his biological nature is not much altered in the process. However, as man experiences enculturation in the context of a culture in the advanced stages of scientific knowledge, his personal store of knowledge accumulates and, consequently, his capacity to create or discover new technics increases. Therefore, while man's brain has not been altered much in recent times in a physical sense, the capacity of that brain has been greatly increased as a result of enculturation in the context of advanced levels of culture. In this regard we may then also view the brain of man as an independent variable subject to change and transformation, and not simply as a constant. In recent times, man's brain, as a computer, has been relatively fixed in its physical substance but over time the enculturation process has programmed that computer in a more complex and sophisticated manner providing man's brain with an increased capacity for problem solving and for the development of new technics. Man gives life to culture. Without man culture ceases to accumulate; without man we would lack the dynamic agent of culture cumulation and transformation generated by new technics. It is the mind of man which is then a necessary condition for culture evolution, and with the advance of culture the mind of man becomes programmed with more and more useful knowledge. We are, therefore, obviously not advocating some form of technological or culture determinism but rather, once again, draw attention to the circle. Man's brain as a dynamic agent generates new technics which become the elements accumulated by culture, and as culture advances and is transformed, man's brain becomes more effectively programmed via the enculturation process and, consequently, the process increases the capacity of man's brain to develop new technics, which again advances culture, and on the circle spins.

Certainly, then, the stage of economic development, or the overall accumulation and store of useful knowledge would be a primary focus in any explanation of inventive capacity and activity. Cultures in the stage of pre-science versus science, a neolithic culture versus one of industrialism would hardly be of similar capacity for the generation of *New Technics* (A). In these discussions it is apparent that we cannot deny the importance of culture. If we feel that man's capacity to invent depends basically on his mastery of the known and if we take "knowledge as a parameter of invention", we must consider that what is known is basically what is stored by culture.[26] Man's acquisition of such knowledge is accomplished via enculturation which is itself, as a process, largely determined by culture, our

Environmental Accumulation (D). These areas of analysis present interesting questions and much must be done to clarify the forces behind the generation of *New Technics* (A) but at least, to our view, this would constitute a correct direction for inquiry.[27]

The process of creating *New Technics* (A) is consequently a complex cultural process dependent upon many factors: the innate; the psychological; the social; the economic, and the political; the stock of useful knowledge and the level of culture cumulation; public and private leadership; the education and skills of the population; the forces of the market as supply and demand; attitudes toward R and D; and on. There is a shrinkage, however, in that a larger stock of useful knowledge fed by discovery results in the production of a smaller stock of inventions and of these inventions not all are innovated.[28]. The degree and extent of the replication of the *New Technics* (A) which are innovated is not the same in all cases, nor is their impact and significance, for example, the ball point pen versus the printing press. But even if *New Technics* (A) are available, it is all for nought unless innovated; the "wheel of economic development" does not spin a spiral of cumulation unless innovation takes place. "An invention, when applied for the first time, is called an innovation. Traditionally economists have stressed the distinction between an invention and an innovation on the ground that an invention has little or no economic significance until applied."[29]

Innovation is the synapse of economic development connecting inventions (*New Technics*) on the one hand to the actual production process (*The Overall Gestalt of Technology*) on the other. In our schema, ". . . at the link where innovations transform new technological knowledge into production reality . . ." we introduce the new elements of culture, the new technics, into our overall *Gestalt of Technology* (C).[30] But it should be noted that the process of innovation is complex; it is complex because it is fundamentally a cultural process. Innovation entails not only the initiative of the innovator but other propitious factors as well, the conditions presented by our overall *Environmental Permeability* (*B*).

The innovator is necessary, since it is ultimately the human agency which activates the process, both from the view of invention as well as innovation, but it is culture and the natural resource base which conditions the innovator to behave as he does.[31] It is not just man, but man in a particular environmental setting of culture and natural resources who does the innovating. Also, that while, "Cultural change is accumulative . . ." we also note that, " . . . cultural change is selectively accumulative."[32] As the Douglas fir pushes upward to the sun, new branches are added and old branches atrophy and fall off. Culture, as it grows and accumulates, selectively adds new technics (automobile), and old technics (horse and buggy) are eliminated. Therefore, even granting that man serves as the ultimate agency of innovation, culture serves as a selective screen, allowing certain inventions to be added and applied and others not; it is in this sense that we speak of the permeability of culture. Even if the innovator desires to innovate the *New Technics* (A), itself a culturally conditioned process, the *Environmental Permeability* (B) embodied in culture and the natural resource base may present conditions which are impermeable to the new technics and consequently prevent innovation.

Environmental Permeability (B) involves two basic factors; (1) culture; and (2) natural resources. First let us look at culture and its composition in relation to the permeability of new technics and their innovation.[33] Conditions of material and nonmaterial culture may be unfavorable and consequently may screen out attempts at innovation. Is the material structure and social organization of the economy adequate for the application (innovation) of the new technic? We refer here to such factors as: the level and quality of capital accumulation; educational facilities; the size of the market or the level of effective demand; transportation facilities; ancillary services and products; and on, characteristics of the basic level of economic development and culture advance. Consequently, though the new technics are available, especially via the route of diffusion, many cultures are unable to innovate such technics due to the overall low level of their stage of economic development.

However, in discussions explaining why available technology is not diffused to underdeveloped countries, the obstacles to *New Technics* (A) are perhaps most frequently treated in the literature in terms of nonmaterial culture, that is, the social or institutional structure of a given culture. This is usually viewed as the basic problem of underdeveloped countries since the advanced material technics and scientific breakthroughs are already in existence though yet to be innovated into their *Overall Gestalt of Technology* (C).[34] One might say then, in this regard, that the interplay between the given institutional structure and the *New Technics* (A) is of fundamental importance in the advance of economic development and growth in the underdeveloped world.[35] In many underdeveloped countries today the social and political institutions buttress the favored position of an established elite. Such groups favor for one reason or other retention of the status quo, and serve to function as a dam against the flow of *New Technics* (A), whether such technology is of an internal endogenous creation or through the more available external source of diffusion.[36] What such countries need is in an overall sense the innovation of the nonmaterial technics associated with scientific methods and attitudes. With the methodology of scientific inquiry such countries may then develop the many material and nonmaterial technics relevant for solving their own problems, given their specific culture and natural resource base. The basic need, then for the LDC is that the technics of scientific methods be incorporated as integral parts of their *Overall Gestalt of Technology* (C). The vanguard of culture advance has shown this to be the key of the industrial system, that is, the spreading application of science to processes of economic production and social organization. The discussion here points to a central problem facing the underdeveloped countries, the problem of culture diffusion. Not necessarily the diffusion of specific social institutions or material technics, but rather the diffusion of scientific attitudes and methods to enable the underdeveloped countries ultimately to produce (invent and discover) their own relevant *New Technics* (A) to solve their own basic problems in the context of their own cultural setting.[37]

In our discusssion of innovation we have essentially stressed cultural factors, but in considering the permeability of the environment to new technology we must also include the role played by the natural resource base. An important limiting factor on the advance and acceptance of *New Technics* (A) would be that of natural resources. In cultural explanations of economic development primary focus is usually directed toward cultural variables to the exclusion of natural resources.[38] Natural resources are, however, relevant and should not be completely excluded from discussions of growth and development.[39] In the early stage of culture advance, given the primitive levels of technology and energy control, man found it difficult to control and adapt to the existing environmental conditions. Consequently, unless the climate was favorable, the game abundant, and the soil fertile, a given population found it difficult to procreate, survive and grow. On this basis perhaps we might say that resources are a much greater limiting factor in the earlier stages of economic development and progressively diminish in importance with the advance of culture. In a general sense, the availability and supply of resources as a factor will always be a necessary condition for development in that propitious resource conditions ameliorate the process of development. And, the processes of development, in the advance of useful knowledge, in turn, expand the dimensions of our resource base. The process, contained in our "wheel of economic development is circular; resources promote development and development promotes resources. While culture (in a universal sense) in the stage of industrialism might suffer from short-run shortages and depletion of specific resources, such as coal and petroleum, the overall resource base in the long run, as a general proposition, is a function of knowledge, and, consequently, unlimited in supply. In terms of technology man cannot ignore natural resources, both in the creation of new technics and their innovation, but it might be correct to say that as culture advances it is culture as social organization which dominates our attention more and more, in the formation and innovation of new technics rather than a given resource base.[40] For advanced countries the major problems are not really associated with a finite natural resource base. Though resources admittedly constitute, at times, a very serious short-run problem, the more fundamental and at times intractable problems concern those generated by culture increasing at an increasing rate. Therefore, with the advance of culture and economic development, it is culture which dominates man's environment and which presents man with the greatest problems in need of resolution. By comparison, natural conditions and resources as a part of the overall environment to which we direct our new technics become relatively of lesser importance. And also, as we have tried to emphasize, with the advance of culture, natural resources become less of a limiting factor since what we consider to be a natural resource is itself a function of technology and culture.[41] With the advanced culture, the problem is no longer one of primarily overcoming harsh environmental conditions provided by the physical world and limited resources; this mankind has done. The problem of the modern period is, more pointedly, primarily one of generating new technics, both social and material, to keep pace with an accelerating culture.

If the environmental complex of culture and natural resources proves permeable to the innovation of the *New Technics* (A) we then have additions of new technics to the *Overall Gestalt of Technology* (C), the core of culture. It is at this juncture that the new technic becomes an effective and actual part of the processes of production or social organization. *The Overall Gestalt of Technology* (C) represents the existing integrated sum total of all material and nonmaterial technics accumulated and innovated, and if we add to this level, we then have a change in the total of technics or in the level of technology. It is at this juncture that the new technic appears as a change in technology. *The Overall Gestalt of Technology* (C) represents a structural, organic whole, and not just an aggregation of parts; similarly, an orchestra is not just a collection of various musical instruments but rather a collection of various instruments in an integrated way to function as an overall gestalt. It is this overall integration of material and nonmaterial technics which provides the basic overall technology characteristic of each stage of economic development.[42]

Consequently, *The New Technics* (A) represents a potential change in technology, but to be of significance, to be considered as an actual change in technology, for the purposes of economic development and culture evolution, such technology must be innovated. A change in technology takes place when a new element, a new increment in the form of a new technic, has been added to the overall gestalt, such a change produces many significant results; it is the forward step in the process of economic development.

In the first place, the core of culture changes; it accumulates and is transformed. Since the opposite side of the gestalt of technology is the core of culture, to change one is to change the other. In the process of economic development culture accumulates and receives an addition to its store of useful knowledge. As the new technics are replicated and spread throughout the economy these qualitative changes produce quantitative results and provide the economy with a greater productive capacity which is manifest in economic growth.[43] Without such qualitative changes inherent in technological change, the limits of economic growth are restricted. Until a culture (an economy) can accumulate useful knowledge to the level commensurate with an industrial system, such an economy cannot hope to achieve the high and sustained rates of growth, as well as high levels of GNP/capita characteristic of modern industrial economies. Our position is that in order to comprehend the process of economic growth, one must first comprehend the process of economic development. Economic growth by itself does not guarantee a change in technology or a change in structure, but, as noted previously, economic growth may take place independently of technological change and may simply lead to a bigger size of what already exists. This constitutes a basic theme of our study: a country does not develop simply by growing.[44] And conversely, exponential economic growth on a long-term continuum requires economic development. Therefore even if, as a social scientist, an economist is basically only interested in economic growth, he cannot completely exclude the complex cultural nature of the process of economic development. Consequently, the maintenance of economic growth on a long-term exponential continuum entails and requires an analysis of the "noneconomic" as well.[45]

Assuming the innovation of specific material technics, the new level of technology achieved by adding the technics to the *Overall Gestalt of Technology* (C) not only adds to material culture and consequently to greater cultural accumulation as well as transformation, per se their simple addition, but also the new machines, the new products, the new material technics themselves also generate pressures for further culture change. The innovation of the automobiles, for example, served as a fountainhead for a myriad of additional material technics and ancillary services manifest in: highways service stations; rubber, synthetics; petrolium; and on. In this sense, as a material technic, such as the

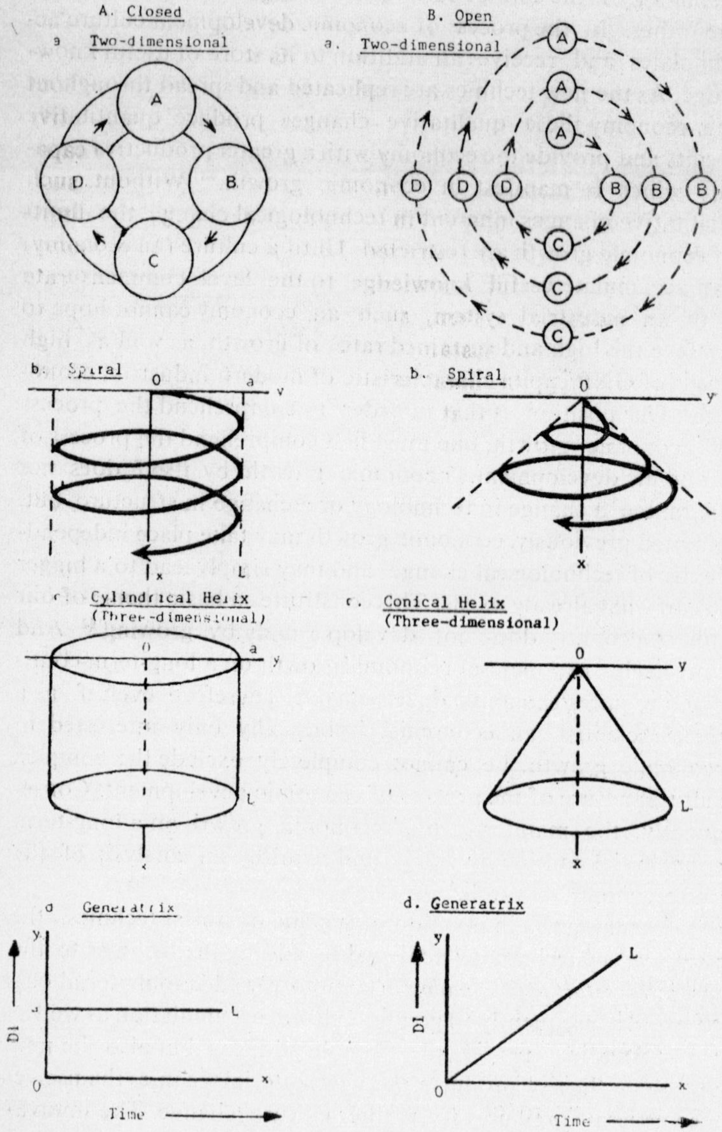

Fig. VII-2. A Closed and Open Wheel of Economic Development.

automobile, generates new technics, we may then view the automobile as a causal agent of further culture change, both social and material. But also, the addition of a new material technic such as the automobile represents. ipso facto, a change of culture. Since technology is the oppoiste side of the core of culture, the introduction of the automobile, as a new technic (material) of transportation, thereby in itself, constituted a change in culture. The innovation of the automobile, consequently, by itself, constituted a change in culture as well as technology (recall our dichotomy of useful knowledge). In this perspective the automobile does not cause culture to change but rather the innovation of the automobile was a change in culture since,as a material technic, it constitutes the very substance of the core of culture. However this is certainly not to deny that the automobile caused and resulted in many additional social and material changes of culture perhaps of equal or even greater significance (for example, the moving assembly in the context of mass production) as culture reacted to, and accommodated to, the new material technic.

Also, the *New Technic* (A), the incremental technic, need not be a material technic, as represented by our example of the automobile, but may also be nonmaterial, for example a new institution or an institutional modification ; the nation, supranationalism, or scientific methods, but the processes and results are basically the same.[46] Once the material or nonmaterial technic has been successfully innovated and passes through the barriers associated with *Environmental Permeability* (B), it is assimilated into *The Overall Gestalt of Technology* (C). Changes are then initiated, though the new technics vary in importance and significance, and appear as culture accumulation and transformation.[47] Since the resulting change in technology is not only of cultural significance but may also in many instances alter the content, size and dimensions of what is considered to be the natural resource base we speak in terms of the accumulation and transformation of both culture and natural resources, categorized as the totality of *Enviromental Accumulation and Transformation.*[48]

Following through with the circular nature of the process, the *Environmental Accumulation and Transformation* (D) then provides added stimulus and capacity, economic growth being one such factor, for the generation and production of more *New Technics* (A) and consequently the movement along the circle, the wheel of economic development, starts anew with return to our starting position, the *New Technics* (A). Also, the new situation achieved in *Environmental Accumulation and Transformation* (D) creates a new cultural and resource situation for *Enviromental Permeability* (B) in the sense of a changed screen of different conditions through which additional new technics attempt to pass. For instance, a culture which through the process of accumulation and transformation has reached the stage of industrialism currently our highest stage of culture advance, offers a very porous screen to new technics. A neolithic culture, by comparison, which not only is limited in its capacity to generate new technics offers little in terms of cultural permeability. What we are saying here is that the advance of useful knowledge progresses at an exponential rate and that those countries which are developed, and at higher stages of economic development, tend to develop faster than those countries at lower stages of economic development. More developed countries have an advantage in the production and innovation of useful knowledge. In terms of potential for develoment it is consequently better to be developed than underdeveloped.

Thus far we have pointed to some of the perhaps more obvious circular interrelationships involved in the process of economic development. If there are a lack of *New Technics* (A) and/or if the situation presented by the *Environmental Permeability* (B) is rigid and lacks the permeability necessary for innovation the circle remains closed and the wheel of economic development does not spin. This is schematically presented in Figure VII-2 "A Closed and Open Wheel of Economic Development." Figure VII-2 (A) represents a vicious circle in terms of a "closed" wheel of economic development and invariant technology. Figure VII-2 (B) represents the case of an "open" wheel of economic development, as a virtuous circle, with an expanding and changing technological base. By adding the element of time to the circle of cumulative causation of culture change we move from the realm of two-dimensional to three-dimensional analysis or from the realm of plane to solid geometry, and from statics to dynamics. The path of culture represented by the three-dimensional configuration of culture accumulation and transformation, over time, appears as a spiral or helix. How else would a circle move over time if not in the form of a helix or spiral?

If technology is assumed to be invariant or constant and that New Technics (A) are not innovated, the "closed" wheel of economic development would appear in its temporal path as cylindrical helix. In the diagram, the *OY* axis represents a development indicator (DI), such as economic production or energy consumption and the *OX* axis represents the time dimension. The development curve, as the generatrix, would be of the form of a straight, horizontal line *aL*, in Figure VII-2, A (d). This would represent a path of no economic development, no technological change and no cultural transformation. The situation is one of economic stagnation with a three-dimensional configuration over time equivalent to that of a cylindrical helix.

If, however, the screen provided by the setting of culture and natural resources proves propitious and permeable, we then have the basis for a synapse and an open wheel of economic development and technological change. The configuration of the spiral as it expands over time is one of a conical helix. This is schematically presented in Figure VII-2, B, with the generatrix or development curve *OL*. By adding time to our wheel of economic development, as the circle of cumulative causation of culture change we move from the realm of two-dimensional to three-dimensional analysis or from the realm of plane to solid geometry, and from statics to dynamics.

But we know that the wheel of economic development does not spin smoothly and without friction. The addition of new technics requires adjustment and synchronization into the overall gestalt of technology. As new technics are added and innovated the response and adjustment by the rest of culture is not perfectly integrated and synchronized. This lag in time periods of adjustment by the various interrelated parts of culture has been conceptualized as a cultural lag. We will now focus on the theory of cultural lag and will suggest, in the next chapter, how the problem of a cultural lag might be overcome and thereby, in the process, generate a frictionless wheel of economic development.

REFERENCES

[1]Paul Alpert, *Economic Development* (New York: The Free Press, 1963), p. 1.

[2]Gerald M. Meier and Robert E. Baldwin, *Economic Development: Theory, History, Policy* (New York: John Wiley and Sons, 1957), p. 119, pp. 119-124.

[3]For example, Joseph J. Spengler, "Theories of Socio-Economic Growth," *Problems in the Study of Economic Growth* (New York: National Bureau of Economic Research, 1949), "Of all the theories or explanations of the course of growth . . . that which runs in terms of culture (broadly defined) . . . is logically the most adequate albeit the most difficult to formulate effectively." p. 88. And also by Spengler, in Herbert R. Barringer, *Social Change in Developing Areas*, (Cambridge: Schenkman Publishing Company, 1965), "In the light of what has been said, economic development is a cultural evolutionary process." p. 268. And also, Moses Abramovitz, in Bernard F. Haley, ed., *A Survey of Contemporary Economics* (Homewood: Richard D. Irwin, 1948), p. 177, and also, in Robert Lekachman, ed., *National Policy for Economic Welfare At Home and Abroad* (New York: Russell and Russell, 1961), p. 84, and Simon Kuznets, "Much as one may regret leaving the shelters of the accustomed discipline, it does seem as if an economic theory of economic growth is an impossibility, if by 'economic' we mean staying within the limits set by the tools of the economic discipline proper . . ." pp. 72-74, p. 73; and *Problems in the Study of Economic Growth*, "Indeed one is tempted to say that economic growth is not essentially an economic problem." p. 16. Benjamin Higgins, *Economic Development* (New York: W. W. Norton and Company, 1968), "Twenty years ago the majority of the economic profession tended to regard interdisciplinary social scientists as the 'lunatic fringe.' Today . . . cross-disciplinary inquiries show signs of becoming 'standard economics.'" p. 224, "The day will no doubt arrive when the distinction between 'economic' and 'social' development will disappear from the literature." p. 405. Also, Lyle W. Shannon, *Underdeveloped Areas* (New York: Harper and Brothers, Publishers, 1957), pp. 196-200. And Bernard Okun and Richard W. Richardson, *Studies in Economic Development* (New York: Holt, Rinehart, and Winston, 1961), pp. 334-416. And Adamantios Depelasis, *Economic Development* (New York; Harper and Brothers, 1961), pp. 161-176, "The process of economic development is not restricted to economic change but is essentially a transformation of the human agent and his social environment within which economic activity unfolds." p. 161. And, Helio Jaguaribe, *Economic and Political Development* (Cambridge: Harvard University Press, 1968), "Development is a total social process, and only for methodological convenience or in a partial sense can one speak of economic, political, cultural, and social development." p. 4. Bert F. Hoselitz, "Economic Growth and Development: Noneconomic Factors in Economic Development," *American Economic Review*, 47 (May 1957), pp. 28-41; Everett Hagen, "The Process of Economic Deve-

lopment," *Economic Development and Cultural Change*, V (April 1957), pp. 193-215; P. T. Ellsworth, "Factors in the Economic Development of Ceylon," *The American Economic Review*, 43 (May 1953), pp. 115-125. George Dalton, "Economics, Economic Development and Economic Anthropology," *Journal of Economic Issues*, 2 (June 1968), pp. 173-186. J. Baranson, "Development as a Scientific Discipline," *The American Journal of Fconomics and Sociology*, 26 (April 1967), pp. 127-134; John P. Owen, "Methodology in Economic Development, A Comparative Analysis," *The Southern Economic Journal*, 23, pp. 126-133; Manning Nash, "Some Social and Cultural Aspects of Economic Development," *Economic Development and Cultural Change*, 7 (January 1959), pp. 137-150; John E. Sawyer, "Social Structure and Economic Progress: General Propositions and Some French Examples," *The American Economic Review*, 41 (May 1951), pp. 321-329. Gunnar Myrdal, *Asian Drama* (New York: The Twentieth Century Fund, 1968), 3 Vols., especially note Vol. 1, pp. 26-31, "A Plea For an Institutional Emphasis" and of course the stress on the noneconomic as well as the economic is characteristic not only of the *Asian Drama* but Myrdal's other works as well, cf., *Rich Lands and Poor* (New York: Harper and Brothers, 1957); Simon Kuznets melts this general assumption in his numerous contributions to the literature, explicitly however, cf., *Economic Growth and Structure* (New York: W. W. Norton and Company, 1965), pp. 120-122; Everett Hagen, *On the Theory of Social Change* (Homewood: The Dorsey Press, 1962); David C. McClelland, *The Achieving Society* (New York: The Free Press, 1962); W. A. Lewis, *The Theory of Economic Growth* (London: George Allen and Unwin, 1955); W. C. Gordon, *The Political Economy of Latin America* (New York: Columbia University Press, 1965) George M. Foster, *Traditional Cultures and the Impact of Technological Change* (New York: Harper and Brothers, 1962); James Sydney Slotkin, *From Field to Factory* (Glencoe: The Fress Press, 1960); Bert F. Hoselitz *Sociological Aspects of Economic Growth* (Glencoe: The Free Press of Glencoe, 1960); Ralph Braibanti and Joseph J. Spengler, eds., *Tradition, Values, and Socio-Economic Development* (Durham: Duke University Press 1961); A. Vermenlen and C. Sanders, *A Study in Development: Institutional Aspects of Economic Growth and Social Development* (Netherlands: Rortterdam University Press, 1970); Irma Adelman and Cynthia Taft Morris, *Society, Politics, and Economic Development* (Baltimore: Johns Hopkins Press, 1967); Roberto de Oliveira Campos, *Reflections on Latin American Development* (University of Texas Press, 1967); Salvatore Schiavo-Campo and Hans W. Singer, *Perspectives of Economic Development* (Boston: Houghton Mifflin Co., 1970); Raul Prebisch, *Towards A Dynamic Development Policy for Latin America* (New York: United Nations, 1963); and on the similarities of the Latin American "structuralists" and the American "institutionalists," note, James H. Street, "The Latin American 'Structuralists' and the Institutionalists: Convergence in Development Theory," *Journal of Economic Issues*, 1 (June 1967), pp. 44-62; John H. Kunkel, *Society and Economic Growth* (New York: Oxford University Press, 1970); Joseph A.

Raffaele, *The Economic Development of Nations* (New York: Random House, 1971); Richard J. Ward, *The Challenge of Development* (Chicago: Aldine Publishing Co., 1967); C. E. Black, *The Dynamics of Modernization* (New York: Harper and Row, 1966); Chester L. Hunt, *Social Aspects of Economic Development* (New York: McGraw-Hill Book Co., 1966); Robert T. Holt and John E. Turner, *The Political Basis of Economic Development* Princeton: D. Van Nostrand Company, 1966); Irving Louis Horowitz, *Three Worlds of Development* (New York: Oxford University Press, 1966). This listing obviously could go on and on, but two fairly recent, general works, also including the cultural and the "noneconomic" and noting their importance would be: Clarence Zuvekas, Jr., *Economic Development* (New York: St. Martin's Press, 1979); and, Michael P. Todaro, *Economic Development in the Third World* (New York: Longman, 1977).

[4]For example, Gunnar Myrdal and Gerald M. Meier represent polar opposites in terms of theory and methodology, yet we find that Gerald M. Meier, *The International Economics of Development* (New York: Harper and Row, 1968) does not exclude the cultural or institutional from his analysis, "Not only is this vital for economic change in itself, but also for political and socio-cultural advances which may be the necessary preconditions of economic progress." p. 220, but still such recognition of the importance of the socio-cultural factors does not seem to find its way into Meier's basic theoretical framework of his first forty pages. Apparently no one doubts that the social factor is important in an analysis of economic development, Peter T. Bauer and Basil S. Yamey, *The Economies of Under-Developed Countries* (Chicago: The University of Chicago Press, 1957), ". . . it is clear that the economic progress both requires and causes significant changes in social institutions . . ." p. 68. If Bauer and Yamey are correct on this issue, and we feel that they are, how then may we justify the exclusion of social change from our theoretical and analytical purview of economic development?

[5]Lionel Robbins, "The Dynamics of Capitalism," *Economica* (March 1926), pp. 31-39, in line with this view, notes: "The causes of material progress, equally with the causes of intellectual progress, interact in so complex a manner that scientific generalisations about them are a matter of the utmost difficulty. We neither possess the knowledge nor the capacity to elaborate laws of progress. . . . It is no reproach to economists that they have been content to leave the devising of sweeping generalisations to poets, metaphysicians and amateur historians." p. 32. This is cited by William W. Lockwood, *The Economic Development of Japan* (Princeton: Princeton University Press, 1954), pp. 503, 588. And, "Economic growth, as every serious student knows, is closely associated with many noneconomic factors . . . these noneconomic factors cannot be ignored in studying economic growth." And yet within the same paragraph we find: "Our ignorance of the purely or predominantly economic aspects of economic development is still so great that the problem of integrating economic with noneconomic

factors cannot be attacked with reasonable expectation of success." *The Comparative Study of Economic Growth and Structure* (New York: The National Bureau of Economic Research, 1959), p. 4. Everett E. Hagen notes this basic problem in his "Turning Parameters into Variables in the Theory of Economic Growth," *The American Economic Review*, 50 (May 1960), pp. 623-628. It is Hagen's view that "Noneconomic factors must enter fully into the theoretical system as variables, with causal relationships flowing to as well as from them." p. 623. ". . . A number of economists who are students of economic growth make generous reference to the importance of noneconomic factors." ". . . Having mentioned noneconomic factors, they then proceed to ignore them and discuss development as though only economic factors bring it about." pp. 624, 625. For a citation of this reference as well as further discussion, note, Myrdal, *Asian Drama*, 3, p. 1904, pp. 1903-1912. And also, Braibanti and Spengler, eds., *Tradition, Values, and Socio-Economic Development*, pp. 141-142, and pp. 57-113.

[6]The words of Robert K. Merton, which he used in the context of relating technology to the worker, are also very appropriate here: "To suspect the full measure of one's ignorance is a first step toward supplanting this ignorance with knowledge." *Social Theory and Social Structure* (New York: The Free Press, 1957), p. 562.

[7]Such a view is not universally accepted, note, James C. Abegglen's, *The Japanese Factory* (Glencoe: The Free Press, 1958), Higgins *Economic Development* (1968), "Economic Development Without Cultural Change," pp. 264-265. Japan is used as a case in point to demonstrate economic development without profound cultural change, but perhaps such a conclusion is based up on too restricted a view of culture and what is meant by cultural change. To us, that certain feudal traits of Japanese culture resisted transformation and change with advances in technology and increased industrialization exemplifies a cultural lag but not that culture as a whole was not changing, and in the case of Japan, drastically. That remnants of a feudal system were retained does not mean that social organization or nonmaterial culture stood still, especially in terms of the new role of the state and nationalism as Japan embarked upon industrialism and industrialization. That there was a feudal carry-over is recognized, G.C. Allen, *A Short History of Modern Japan* (New York: Frederick A. Praeger, Publishers, 1963), pp. 167-168; Alpert, *Economic Development*, pp. 21-25. In this context we think of Thorstein Veblen's *Imperial Germany* (New York: The Macmillan Company, 1915) and "The Opportunity of Japan," pp. 248-266, in Leon Ardzrooni, ed., *Essays in Our Changing Order* (New York: Augustus M. Kelley, 1964); and, Reinhard Bendix, pp. 27-68, in Richard P. Dore, *Aspects of Social Change in Modern Japan* (Princeton: Princeton University Press, 1967); and Douglas F. Dowd, "Technology and Social Change: Japan and the Soviet Union," pp. 283-301 in Douglas F. Dowd, ed., *Thorstein Veblen: A Critical Reappraisal* (New York: Cornell University Press, 1958). At first glance this gives one the impression, "All of this, as Veblen saw

it, was the pouring of the new wine of modern industry into the old bottle of feudalism." Dowd, p. 286, but as Dowd points out the old bottle, the "Spirit of Old Japan" was a plastic bottle of flexibility and subject to the pressures and forces inherent in technological change, i.e., "But the progress of the industrial technology carries as its price the adaptation of the society to a new institutional framework, one stimulating the development of commercialism and individualism, and emphasizing the cash nexus." p. 291. For in the modern period of Japan we see the introduction of science, industrialism and industrialization and to us this represents dramatic and drastic cultural change. E. Herbert Norman, *Japan's Emergence as a Modern State* (New York: Institute of Pacific Relations, 1940), "Among the most remarkable phenomena which marked the Meiji Restoration and subsequent years was the speed of the transition from a feudal into a modern industrial society." p. 11. And G.C. Allen, *A Short History of Modern Japan*, "... to introduce applied science and industrialism ..." p. 169. And Ogburn, *Social Change*, "Japan has made remarkable changes in her culture within a few decades." p. 131. And, Edward Norbeck, Economic Change and Japanese Social Organization," pp. 337-353, in Gertrude E. Dole, *Essays in the Science of Culture*, (New York: Thomas Y. Crowell Company, 1960), "The Japanese response has been astounding, the most rapid and drastic cultural change conjointly involving a large number of human beings ever to occur under conditions of internal peace in the recorded history of the world." pp. 337-338.

[8]For a discussion of this methodology note Gunnar Myrdal, *Asian Drama*, Vol. III, pp. 1843-1940, and footnote 1, p. 1844 for additional references, note also, *Rich Lands and Poor*, pp. 16-21. Our analysis, cultural economics, will use circular and cumulative causation in the context of the "wheel of economic development."

[9]Charles P. Kindleberger discusses this problem somewhat in his *Economic Development* (New York: McGraw-Hill, 1965), pp. 18-39, in noting the debate over whether it is the social and cultural which cause the economic or whether the economic causes the social and cultural, and apparently concludes in favor of a circular relationship rather than one-way causation. "Economic development changes attitudes, as well as being the result of changed attitudes." p. 38. It is difficult to establish which factor causes which, in a circle where is the starting point?

[10]That the effects need not be cumulative and that the effects may produce "low-level equilibrium" or stagnation, cf, Myrdal, *Asian Drama*, Vol. III, p. 1844, footnote 3, p. 1845 footnote 1, and pp. 1870-1878. On the cylindrical helix note Figure VII—2, "A Closed and Open Wheel of Economic Development."

[11]And again, Simon Kuznets' *Economic Growth and Structure*, "That the accumulation of empirical and tested knowledge is at the base . . . a truism." p. 61. "We, therefore, need a theory of the production and accumulation of empirical knowledge, even if for years to come this may mean nothing more than an attempt to learn

about the processes involved and the factors that seem important. . . . It may be better to call explicitly for a theory of production of such knowledge as an indispensable focus. . . ." p. 62. Also, Allan G.B. Fisher, "Capital and Growth of Knowledge, " *The Economic Journal*, 43 (September 1933), pp. 379-389." . . . economic progress which rests upon growth of knowledge . . . It was mainly extensions of knowledge . . . which led to the second stage . . ." pp. 379, 380, 381, and 383. And further, "At the simplest level of explanation, all economic change is the result of two factors: new knowledge . . . and the effective use in the production of goods and services of that knowledge." R.M. Hartwell *The Causes of the Industrial Revolution in England* (London: Methuen & Co., 1967), p. 21. And Hagen, *On the Theory of Social Change*," . . . two steps: The discovery of new knowledge . . . and the incorporation of that knowledge in the productive proceses." p. 11 and Chapters 2 and 12. Also note, on the emphasis on the growth of knowledge, C.E. Black. *The Dynamics of Modernization* (New York: Harper and Row, Publishers, 1966), and, Kenneth E. Boulding *The Meaning of the Twentieth Century* (New York: Harper and Row, 1964).

[12]Yale Brozen, "Determinants of the Direction of Technological Change." *The American Economic Review*, 43 (May 1953), pp. 288-302, "Since technological change is primarily an endogenous variable, perhaps we economists should no longer take technological change as an externally determined given in our models," p. 301.

[13]"Modern technologies are culture producing as well as culture-using socio-cultural systems." Robert S. Merrill, *International Encyclopedia of the Social Sciences*, Vol. XV, p. 582. Also, Robert A. Sole, "The Meaning and Measure of Economic Progress," *Technology and Culture*, 9 (July 1968), pp. 388-414, p. 388; and, Higgins, *Economic Development*, p. 346, point No. 4. Also, while our treatment of culture is certainly broader than simply economic growth, Jacob Schmookler catches the point which we are trying to make here of the circular relationship between technology and culture. "That the creation and diffusion of technical knowledge is at the heart of modern economic growth is now widely accepted. On the other hand, it also seems intuitively obvious that economic growth itself somehow effects the growth of technology." *Invention and Economic Growth* (Cambridge: Harvard University, 1966), p. vii.

[14]Without technological change, the innovation of new technics, a culture could not maintain economic growth on a continuous basis but would enventually reach saturation and stagnation. Continued technological advance, that is continued economic development, is a necessary condition for continued economic growth. Cf. Simon Kuznets, *Six Lectures on Economic Growth* (Glencoe: The Free Press of Glencoe, 1959), "The Necessary Condition," p. 29-35.

[15]Some go so far as to say that Schumpeter's "Theory of Economic Development" is in actuality not applicable or relevant to the current underdeveloped countries. Cf., H.W. Singer, *International Development*:

Growth and Change (New York: McGraw-Hill Book Co., 1964), pp. 55-56.

[16]On the view that cultural change is accumulative and on the nature and process of accumulation, cf.. F. Stuart Chapin, *Cultural Change* (New York: The Century Co., 1928), especially Chapter II.

[17]For example, statements by Davis and Woytinsky give support to this view: "most of the natural resources used in a modern economy are man-made and can be expected to grow with the progress of science," and "our resources are very large and rapidly growing larger." in Lekachman, ed., *National Policy for Economic Welfare at Home and Abroad*, pp. 158, 164. "This effective geographic environment is determined by our skills in using it; it is, therefore, related to the development of technology. The environment is enlarged by new knowledge and new skills. . .Human evolution is doubly dynamic; man and the geographic environment react upon each other, and both terms are transformed." Abott Payson Usher, *A History of Mechanical Inventions* (Cambridge: Harvard University Press, 1954), p. 2. But perhaps the best statement on the point being made here is contained in Zimmerman's *World Resources and Industries*, more recently revised, as W.N. Peach and James A. Constantin, *Zimmerman's World Industries and Resources* (New York: Harper and Row, 1972).

[18]"The stationary state of classical economics is an economy in which only replication occurs, and any isolated society which elected to enlarge its technological capacity only by replication would tend to approach that state." Schmookler, *Invention and Economic Growth*, p. 3.

[19]In speed reading it is a well-known fact that it is easier to assimilate the parts of a book granting the knowledge of the whole. In short, it helps to have an overview of the book before attempting to understand the parts. In solving a jigsaw puzzle it is much easier to assemble the parts given a knowledge or overview of the whole picture than it is to derive the whole by piecing together the parts and having no conception of the whole. In short, the parts appear meaningless without a conceptualization of the big picture.

[20]For a comparison of invention and discovery note Chapin, *Cultural Change*, pp. 344-346. Our usage of diffusion is rather simple and refers to technics that are brought to a given culture from other cultures. Diffusion, perhaps, accounts for the greater part of any given culture's social heritage. On the more simple view note Ogburn and Nimkoff, pp. 662-664 and on the complexities and the associated term, acculturation, note: A.L. Kroeber, *Anthropology Today* (Chicago: The University of Chicago Press, 1953), pp. 621-631.

[21]On the view that for any given culture only a small fraction of the totality of its accumulated store of knowledge is due to locally invented elements (technics), note, Ralph Linton, *The Study Man* (New York: D Appleton-Century Company, 1936), pp. 326-327, referred to by Ogburn and Nimkoff, *Sociology* (1964), pp. 662-663.

[22]"The addition of cultural forms that accumulate is the result of invention and discovery. That culture grows by means of inventions is

of course universally recognized." W.F. Ogburn, *Social Change*, p. 80.

[23]For a "...selective summary of the literature on the economics of invention.." note, Richard R. Nelson, "The Economics of Invention: A Survey of the Literature," *The Journal of Business*, 32 (April 1959), pp. 101-127. It is not that significant contributions have not been made by economists, but rather that we should have more of them. For example: *The Rate and Direction of Inventive Activity: Economic and Social Factors*, The National Bureau of Economic Research (Princeton University Press, 1962), and, of course, Jacob Schmookler, *Invention and Economic Growth*.

[24]H.G. Barnett, *Innovation: The Basis of Cultural Change* (New York: McGraw-Hill Book Co. 1953) notes that "...all innovations come from two major sources...the cultural history that is available to the innovator..." and, "...the natural man himself, his physical and mental attribute, as a thing or other part of the inescapably given universe of phenomenon." p. 10. Also, as we have already noted, Barnett treats invention as basically being synonymous with innovation, "Beyond this purpose no significance should be attached to the differential employment of 'invention' and 'discovery.' Both are names for innovations." pp. 7-10. In our study, however, while we draw a distinction between invention and innovation, we do recognize that inventions are in origin the result of the interaction of the physical or biological nature of man and culture and consequently are in agreement with Barnett on the basic point being made here. Ogburn and Nimkoff, *Sociology* (1964), are also in apparent agreement here and stress three basic factors: the existing level of accumulation of culture traits; demand; and mental ability. In mental ability, emphasis is given to the upper reaches of the normal curve indicating inherited inventive ability, pp. 670-671, interacting with culture. And also, Chapter 5, pp. 80-102 in William F. Ogburn, *Social Change*.

[25]This constitutes a basic and underlying assumption throughout Ogburn's *Social Change*, note especially pp. 117, 133, 141-142 and 372-377. "Therefore, there appears to be for this period no correlation between cultural changes and biological changes. Cultural evolution is thus not to be accounted for by biological evolution." p. 141. But even if we note mental ability and the biological, we still, of course, must face the cultural situation. Given a large enough population we should expect a given percentage with the mental ability necessary for inventive activity, and consequently, if little or no inventions are forthcoming, we must look to social organization and culture for explanation. Note, Robert A. Solo, *Economic Organization and Social Systems* (Indianapolis: The Bobbs-Merrill Company, 1967), p. 115, and pp. 131-134, for the idea, *ceteris parabis*, that the larger the population, the larger the pool of creative talent and that the utilization of that "...creative potential is a function of social organization." That in the future the innate may also be a variable and subject more to the force of culture evolution, note Gerald Feinberg, *Consequences of Growth* (New York: The Seabury Press, 1977) especially pp. 126-143.

[26]Solo, *Economic Organizations and Social Systems*, p. 116.

[27]With a possible few exceptions, such as the Veblen-Ayres tradition of mainstream institutional thought, Marx and, also, Schumpter, and such offshoots as W. Rupert MacLaurin, "The Sequence from Invention to Innovation and Its Relation to Economic Growth," *The Quarterly Journal of Economics*, 67 (February 1953), pp. 97-111, the inquiries in the area of invention were usually conducted outside the field of economics and more so by anthropologists and sociologists, e.g., S.C. Gilfillan, *The Sociology of Invention* (Chicago: Follett Publishing Co., 1935). However, as economists become more concerned with technological change, a trend which we have already noted in several instances of our study, they also will become more interested in inventive activity, note, *The Rate and Direction of Inventive Activity*, pp. 3-4. Also, since at root of the process of invention is the formation of new ideas which represent additions to useful knowledge, what needs to be done is to integrate the whole field of the sociology of knowledge, itself considerable in its literature, with the study of economic development. This would again give emphasis to the eclectic nature of "the wheel of economic development" in that the sociology of knowledge becomes important in analyzing the origins of new technics, how (D) is related to (A), and also, how these ideas are accepted and innovated (B). For ultimately this may constitute one of the most crucial areas for analysis in the field of economic development, a point noted by Gunnar Myrdal, *The Asian Drama*, Vol. I, for "A Plea for a Sociology of Knowledge" and "The Beam in Our Eyes," pp. 5-35.

[28]Note, p. 31, Simon Kuznets, *Six Lectures on Economic Growth* (New York: The Free Press of Glencoe, Inc., 1959).

[29]Mansfield, *The Economics of Technological Change*, p. 99. This Schumpeterian distinction is usually adhered to by economists: Kindleberger, *Economic Development* (1965), pp. 137-139; Eill, *Economic Development* (1967), pp. 18-19; G.F. Gay, "The Diffusion of New Technology," *Natural Institute of Economic Review*, Number 48 (May 1969), pp. 40-83, p. 40; Robert Higgs, *The Transformation of the American Economy, 1865-1914*, (New York: John Wiley and Sons, 1971), p. 43. Some economists tend to treat the two as equivalents, Williamson, *The Growth of the American Economy*, pp. 4-6; and as we have also noted among anthropologists, Barnett, *Innovation: The Basis of Cultural Change*, pp. 7-10, although other anthropologists do draw the distinction, Linton, *The Tree of Culture*, p. 43. Though the same individual or institution may in a certain instance be responsible for both the invention and innovation we feel that the processes of invention and innovation are distinct and consequently in our study draw a distinction between invention and innovation. While for analytical purposes, perhaps, a distinction is in order, it is, of course, obvious that both invention and innovation are of importance for the process of economic development. "The process of innovation, which is the actual adoption of new techniques in the process of production, is fully as important to industrial growth as the invention itself." Shepard B. Clough and

Theodore F. Marburg, *The Economic Basis of American Civilization* (New York: Thomas Y. Crowell Company, 1968), p. 43.

[30]At this point in our theoretical schema, with the innovation of a new technic accomplished, we may rightfully speak of technological change. On the quotation as well as three factors of basic importance to Simon Kuznets in the process of innovation, note, *Six Lectures on Economic Growth*, pp. 31-32.

[31]Traditionally to the economist, the businessman or entrepreneur served as the innovator, today, however, ". . .businessmen are not the only innovators or organizers in economic life. The state is a center of economic decision, an agent of investment, and a carrier of change in the same way and, in some places, to a greater extent than is the business firm." Moses Abramovitz in Lekachman, ed., *National Policy for Economic Welfare at Home and Abroad*, p. 81, and Michael Shanks, "Government as Innovator," *The Innovators: The Economics of Technology* (London: Cox & Wyman, 1967), pp. 102-190.

[32]Chapin, *Cultural Change*, p. 203.

[33]Our concern is more with factors which retard the innovation of new technics and not with the time lags which develop between the genesis of a new technic and its actual innovation. On the time lag between invention and innovation, note, Mansfield, *The Economics of Technological Change*, pp. 100-106 and also Shanks, *The Innovators*, which was directed this basic problem: "My basic message can be summed up in a few sentences. There is a wide gap in every country between the knowledge of new products, processes and techniques and the successful application of that knowledge in industsy," p. 9.

[34]". . .it is generally viewed as a social problem originating in the failure of social institutions rather than in the lack of technical knowledge." Kuznets, *Economic Growth and Structure*, p. 2; and *Measures for the Economic Development of Underdeveloped Countries* (New York: United Nations, 1951), pp. 28-34.

[35]"The interplay of technology and institutional changes is thus of the essence of economic growth that take place within the framework constituted by some epochal innovation." Kuznets, *Modern Economic Growth* p. 5, and in discussing the problem of small nations, Professor Kuznets, also notes, "The main premise of this paper is that the proper framework of social institutions, capable of continuous and relatively painless adjustment and, in fact, social invention, is an indispensable prerequisite for modern economic growth," "Economic Growth of Small Nations." p. 32. Also, E.A.G. Robinson, ed., *Economic Consequences of the Size of Nations* (New York: St. Martin's Press, 1960), pp. 14-32. ". . .it must be applications of knowledge, whether they are embodied in industrial processes per se or in management and in human development. Indeed, as I shall emphasize later, the interplay of technological and institutional changes is of the essence in economic growth." Michael Michaelis, "Technology for Society" *The American Economic Review*, 58 (May 1968), pp. 492-501, pp. 493-494, and Charles Wolf, "Institutions and Economic Development," *The American*

Economic Review, 45 (December 1955) pp. 867-883.

[36]"That not everybody in developing countries desires economic development; the rich and privileged, the army, the landlord, politicians and civil servants may be quite content with things as they are . . ." Adrian Moyes and Teresa Hayter, *World III* (New York: The MacMillan Company, 1965), p. 33. Vested interests holding back technological change need not always be of an economic elite, for example the Luddites. Nor need the base always be economic; other attitudes such as religious beliefs may also retard the penetration and innovation of new technics. Also, vested interests of a controlling elite need not always hold back technological advance but may in many instances promote specific and selective types of technological change, if perhaps such changes increase their power and position. Rostow argues similarly that "a new elite" may serve a positive role as a necessary condition in process of promoting modernization. "It would be widely agreed that a new elite—a new leadership—must emerge and be given scope to begin the building of a modern industrial society." *The Stages of Economic Growth* (Cambridge: Cambridge University Press, 1968), p. 26.

[37]"Where it has been learnt, human beings are experimental in their attitude to material techniques, to social institutions, and so on. This experimental or scientific attitude is one of the preconditions of progress. The greatest progress will occur in those countries where education is widespread and where it encourages an experimental outlook. "*Measures for the Economic Development of Under-Developed Countries* (New York: United Nations, Department of Economic Affairs, 1951) p. 13. Whereas the Commercial Revolution endogenously established the preconditions for take-off for Western Europe, "The more general case in modern history, however, saw the stage of preconditions arise, not endogenously, but from some external intrusion by more advanced societies." Rostow, *The Stages of Economic Growth*, p. 6. Diffusion, from the advanced cultures to the underdeveloped, however achieved, consequently, plays an important role in the economic development of underdeveloped countries. "Perhaps the most numerously observed cases of cultural inertia are due to difficulties of diffusion of culture." Ogburn, *Social Change*, p. 194. And, undoubtedly, while certain specific material and nonmaterial technics may be of an advantage in the process of economic development, we are concerned at this point and give specific focus to the diffusion of scientific attitudes and methods.

[38]"A cultural theory of growth seeks its explanation within the culture itself, attaching relatively little weight to the purely material environment which (within limits) is or can be given shape by culture." Joseph Spengler, "Theories of Socio-Economic Growth" in *Problems in the Study of Economic Growth*, p. 89. And, Robert L. Heilbroner, ". . . we can attribute to a lack of physical resources only a subsidiary role in causing underdevelopment," and, " . . economic underdevelopment is not so much a reflection of nature as of human attitudes and institutions." *The Great Ascent* (New York: Harper and

Row, 1963), pp. 34, 36.

[39]Natural resources embodied in the soil-climate complex, mineral resources and the topographic structure are not always excluded from discussions concerning growth and development. For example, note the statements by Lane and the general concurrence by Kuznets, in Lekachman, *National Policy for Economic Welfare at Home and Abroad*, pp. 92-93, 98, and passim, i.e., pp. 114-116. Also, Abbot Payson Usher, *A History of Mechanical Inventions*, pp. 1-10 and Joseph J. Spengler, ed., *Conference on Natural Resources aud Economic Growth* (Washington, D.C. : Resources for the Future, 1961); and, Norton Ginsberg, ed., *Essays on Geography and Economic Development* (Chicago; University of Chicago Press, 1960).

[40]"In its simplest terms, technology is man's efforts to cope with his physical environment—both that provided by nature and that created by man's own technological deeds. . . " Kranzberg, *Technology in Western Civilization*, Vol. I. p. 4. And on the point that natural resources constitute less of a limiting factor with the advance of culture, note Betty J. Meggers, "Environmental Limitation on the Development of Culture," *American Anthropologist*, 56 (October 1954), pp. 801-824, pp. 815-816. The more successful man becomes in advancing culture and technology the greater his capacity to cope with the physical environment, i.e., the moon landing, and, consequently, the factor of natural resources becomes progressively less important as a limiting factor with the advance of culture. "Climatic and land conditions, as obstacles to human effort, are much less forbidding today than in the past. . . are less important today than they may have been in periods of more primitive technology." Simon Kuznets, *Economic Change* (London : William Heinemann, 1954), p. 228. For a more detailed discussion of the point being made here, note, John H. Adler, "Changes in the Role of Resources at different Stages of Economic Development," in Spengler, ed., *Conference on Natural Resources and Economic Growth*, pp. 48-73, on the "declining importance of resources." In our schema, the wheel of economic development, the role of resources is more ameliorative and permissive in the context of *Environmental Permeability* (B) and perhaps more casual in the context of *Environmental Accumulation and Transformation* (D) in which resources as a part of the overall environment are perhaps casual in the relation to the generation of *New Technics* (A). Available resources may aid in the development of new technics conducive to their exploitation, or a weak resource base may be instrumental in advancing knowledge along the lines of synthetics pp. 55-57.

[41]Recall our comments in footnote 17 of this chapter. In addition : " 'Economic resource' is a concept relative to a given state of technology." Kuznets, *Economic Change*, p. 229, and, ". . . one may argue that the natural-resource potential is a function of the changing stock of technological knowledge." Kuznets in Lekachman, *National Policy for Economic Welfare at Home and Abroad*, p. 36. "But these limits are not absolute, as is presumed by the geographic determinists.

The limitations of resources are relative to the position of our knowledge and of our technique. The limits of both actual resources and potential resources recede as we advance. . ." Usher. *A History of Mechanical Invention,* p. 9, and on the general issue for further discussion, note, Higgins, *Economic Development.* pp. 209-223. Some anthropologists, in the context of culture determinism, conclude : "Finally, in dealing with cultures in general, or with culture as a whole, the factor of environment may be considered a constant and therefore disregarded in explanation of the culture process." L. A. White, *International Encyclopedia of the Social Sciences,* (1968), Vol. 3, p. 548. And some economists, in their growth models, exclude resources (land) from their analysis, R. F. Harrod, *Towards a Dynamic Economics* (London : MacMillan & Co., Ltd., 1960). p. 20.

[42]Each stage in our stages' analysis is characterized by its overall technological gestalt. V. Gordon Childe also characterized his stages by their technological features. "For the purposes of this work, all societies can be divided into a few very abstract types, and these then arranged in a hierarchy that is also, in some degree, a chronological sequence . . . The latter factors provide bases for classifying societies into groups which are also stages in a temporal sequence." V. Gordon Childe in Charles Singer, ed., *A History of Technology* (London: Oxford University Press, 1954), Vol. I, p. 40.

[43]"Changes in technology, then, are the critical instruments enabling man to utilize his resource environment more efficiently and to generate the increase in productivity which is at the heart of the process of economic growth." Nathan Rosenberg in Kranzburg, ed. . . *Technology and Western Civilization,* Vol. I., 516. While perhaps defying precise quantification it may be fair to generalize concerning the impact of technology in terms of "the numerous histories of technology which have been written provide strong qualitative evidence of the tremendous impact upon productivity of various technological developments." Richard R. Nelson in Walter W. Heller, *Perspectives on Economic Growth* (New York : Random House, 1968), p. 192. "As Velben would put it, in the long run there can be no economic growth with economic change or development." And, "Economic growth is in the final analysis a matter of technological advance . . " Allan G. Gruchy, "Veblen's Theory of Economic Growth," in Douglas F. Dowd, *Thorstein Veblen : A Critical Reappraisal* (New York : Cornell University Press, 1958), pp. 151-176, pp. 156, 160.

[44]We are certainly not maintaining that economic growth is unrelated to technological change and does not in fact stimulate technological change but rather our view is that economic growth by itself is not a sufficient cause; economic growth is not synonymous with economic development. Consequently, we agree that, "The reciprocal relationship must be stressed. We have so far emphasized that impact of technological change generating a rapid rate of economic growth. It is equally true that a rapid rate of economic growth, with its consequent expansion of markets, is one of the

strongest possible encouragements to technical innovations." Nathan Rosenberg in Kranzberg, *Technology in Western Civilization*, Vol. I, p. 522, and this would also constitute the emphasis of Schmookler in his *Invention and Economic Growth*.

[45]The view that a strict economic analysis of economic development may be an impossibility is not new and certainly not new to Douglas F. Dowd, e.g,, ". . . the process of economic development does not appear to be reducible to the neat categories conventional economics." "The Economics of Slavery in the Ante Bellum South : A Comment," *The Journal of Political Economy*, 66 (October 1958), pp. 440-442, p. 442. And also: ". . . it is not possible to explain economic change by previous economic conditions alone. For the economic state of a people does not emerge simply from the preceding economic conditions, but only from the preceding total situation." Joseph A Schumpeter, *The Theory of Economic Development* (Cambridge : Harvard University Press, 1959), p. 58.

[46]"The modern evolutionist . . finds no need to insist that the initial loci must always be in the same sector of culture." *International Encyclopedia of the Social Science* (1968), Vol. 5, p. 226. Usually, scientific methods are more easily applied and accepted in the area of material rather than social technics, and as a consequence, as a generalized proposition, material technics usually lead in the process of culture accumulation and the social lags. The proposition that the material culture usually leads and dominates is the view of Ogburn, note *Social Change*, pp. 268-280; it is usually the nonmaterial or adaptive culture which adapts and lags in relation to the material. But Ogburn concedes that the nonmaterial may also lead in the process. (Indeed, it is conceivable that a change may first occur in the nonmaterial culture and later the material culture be adjusted to such a change." pp. 268-269. "Ogburn puts more stress on cases where material factors change first and cultural factors adapt, but he points out that it is also possible for nonmaterial factors to start the process of change." Etzioni, *Social Change*, p. 407. And also, S. Herbert Frankel, *The Economic Impact on Underdeveloped Societies* (Cambridge: Harvard University Press, 1955), pp. 18-19. In any event, whether the new technic is material or nonmaterial, such new technology and its innovation is a necessary condition for cultural accumulation in line with the economic development. The precise cause of the change in terms of the "locus of the evolutionary impulse," is, however, difficult to determine.

[47]The molecules (technics) which bombard our substance, our clay (culture) need not all be of the same size or significance. While it would be difficult, quantitatively, to measure what constitutes a major innovation, there certainly is a difference in weight of impact and significance between such technics as language, writing, the printing press, the steam engine, the automobile, the jet airplane, the city, the nation, science and nuclear power on the one hand to a new type of fountain pen or razor blade on the other. "Inventions vary from one

to another as to their social effects. Some are quite negligible in their effects, for instance a new type of safety razor blade. The great majority of inventions have slight use and little social significance." Ogburn in Allen, ed., *Technology and Social Change*, p. 23. For examples and analyses of major inventions, note, pp. 107-241.

[48]Schumpeter noted ". . . development consists primarily in employing existing resources in a different way, in doing new things with them, irrespective of whether those resources increase or not," p. 68, *The Theory of Economic Development* (Cambridge : Harvard University Press, 1959). We agree, and at this point add that technological changes not only make for more efficient usage of an assumed given supply of resources, but, in addition, lead to an accumulation and transformation of the resource base itself.

CHAPTER VIII

The Theory of Cultural Lag

In our attempt to explain economic development in the context of culture evolution we have focused on the advance and innovation of useful knowledge as the essence of the process.[1] In our dichotomy of useful knowledge, as a protean concept, we have noted that such knowledge appears on the one hand in its application in the form of technology and on the other hand, in its store, as culture. Therefore, the advance of technology also results in the advance and transformation of culture as well. Consequently, an explanation and analysis of the process of adding technics, as the new elements of culture mutation, becomes central in any theory of the process of economic development. In the context of circular and cumulative causation we have presented the wheel of economic development as an analytical framework to simplify and explain the complex process of the origination and innovation of new technics. However, if the wheel of economic development spins, does it always spin without friction? If a new element is added to the overall gestalt of technology, how does culture react in its adjustment to the addition in the form of a new material or social technic? Are the new technics of adjustment perfectly synchronized to the newly added technics of transformation? Does the wheel of economic development spin with friction generated by varying rates of adjustments to the newly innovated technics? In the literature an analytical framework to deal with this problem has been provided by W.F. Ogburn; we speak here of the theory of cultural lag.

The general idea of cultural lag has, itself, evolved over time. Certainly, the Veblenian dichotomy which juxtaposed the technological, as material culture and the dynamic, to the ceremonial, as nonmaterial culture and the static, would represent a classic case of cultural lag. And while Ogburn claimed not to have read Veblen on the issue, the similarity between the Veblenian dichotomy and the Ogburnian cultural lag theory is obvious.[2] Origin aside, it was Ogburn nonetheless who gave specific and explicit formulation in terms of what has since become known as the theory of cultural lag. The term, cultural lag, was first used by Ogburn when he was a professor of economics and sociology at Reed College (1914), and was first published in *Social Change* (1922) under the chapter heading: "The Hypothesis of Cultural Lag."

> "The thesis is that the various parts of modern culture are not changing at the same rate. Some parts are changing much more rapidly than others; and that since there is a correlation and interdependence of parts, a rapid change in one part of our culture requires readjustments through other changes in the various correlated parts of culture . . . where one part of culture changes first, through some discovery or invention, and occasions changes in some part of culture dependent upon it, there frequently is a delay in the change occasioned in the dependent part of culture. The extent of this lag will vary according to the nature of the cultural material, but may exist for a considerable number of years, during which time there may be said to be a maladjustment."[3]

Is the problem of maladjustment due to the inherent nature of material and nonmaterial culture which lends itself to faster rates of acceleration which is not inherent or characteristic of nonmaterial culture? The classic case of cultural lag usually offered in the literature is that material culture moves forward at rates of acceleration faster than those of nonmaterial culture. The independent variable is most frequently presented as part of material culture, viewed as technology and the adaptive culture as the dependent variable in the form of nonmaterial culture. The question becomes: "Is the nonmaterial culture similarly accumulative resulting in increased cultural base?"[4] As we have previously noted, A. L. Kroeber is apparently in accord with the view that material culture alone is cumulative and additive and that the nonmaterial is not. By comparison, Kroeber assumes the social to be substitutive rather than accumulative. Hornell Hart in turn asserts that both the material and nonmaterial accelerate and accumulate in the context of general culture evolution. Let us now review and assess these arguments.

Culture overall, as opposed to cultures, has always advanced in the paradigm of the exponential curve, the system of industrialism just marks a higher stage of increased acceleration. It is not difficult to empirically support the view that material culture, as part of the overall, accumulates and with acceleration. However, it is not that evident that nonmaterial culture or the social also is additive and accumulates, let alone with acceleration. Consequently, there is a predilection, perhaps, in the form of the concept of cultural lag which to many (in a restricted usage of the concept) implies that material culture accelerates and accumulates whereas the nonmaterial does not, and consequently the culture lag. It is therefore not unreasonable for Kroeber to assert as he does that the material sector or technology accumulates whereas the nonmaterial does not and is by comparison in its advance more of the nature of substitution and replacement rather than being accumulative or additive.[5]

In separating the biological from the sociocultural Kroeber draws the basic distinction that,

> ". . . the process of cultural development is an additive and therefore an accumulative one, whereas the process of organic evolution is primarily a substitutive one."[6]

However, from the assumption on the one hand that the biological is substitutive and the cultural additive it would then be inconsistent in another instance to conclude, as Kroeber does, that such a large and integral part of culture evolution, as nonmaterial culture, is simply substitutive and not accumulative since he is of the opinion that culture, overall, is accumulative.[7] It may be closer to the truth to say that the evolution of both material and nonmaterial culture in the context of general culture evolution entails accumulation as well as substitution, and with acceleration.

Nonmaterial technics, as well as the material, tend to accumulate in two basic ways: in one sense accumulation takes place through proliferation and diversification, and in another sense through the reproduction of a given technic as more and more are added in the replication of the technic. As culture evolves it becomes more complex as it adds more and more material and social technics in terms of a proliferation of new technics, in the long parade of the advance of useful knowledge. This would be analogous to the proliferation of life into many varied forms, in terms of genetic mutation, in the process of general biological evolution. Culture accumulates in its evolution not only through development and changes in structure in the proliferation and addition of new technics but, also, such new technics in turn replicate and grow. Such growth and replication of the newly added technic in turn serves as another source of culture accumulation. As we have noted the evolutionary process concerns both growth (replication) and development (transformation). A new social technic, the welfare state and deficit spending, replaced and substituted for the social organization and policy of laissez-faire. Over time, the welfare state spawned new social technics manifest in agencies, budgets, bureaucracy and in the process accumulated through proliferation and replication as society tried to keep pace with the increased complexities of industrialization.

To assume however, that nonmaterial technics are only substitutive would be to infer a constancy of social institutions which are conceivably replaced but do not increase in number and function in the sense of proliferation. To assume that culture has historically contained only a given number of institutions represents a static type of reasoning. Did culture in its origins start with a given and fixed set or number of social technics which have simply been substituted for or replaced or has culture accumulated in the proliferation and diversification of new social technics? Institutions are viewed in some instances in terms of institutional areas, such as the family, religion, government and on. Consequently, in this context, one might argue that the overall institutional structure, as the whole of institutions, remains constant or fixed. Change is only then of the nature of replacement and substitution in that, for example, one form of government or religion replaces another. However, it was not that the Protestant religion replaced that of Catholicism, but rather that the religion in turn experienced proliferation in the form of many sub-species of the new Protestant religion. In the process culture was transformed and accumulated. No one apparently would make the assumption of a fixed set or number of material technics, consequently, why should this be assumed for the technics of nonmaterial culture?

Since inventions may be social as well as material, one might conclude that man has over time, interacting with his cultural reservoir of useful knowledge, added numerous and new social technics to the overall gestalt of technology; for instance, where could one find the city, money, nationalism, the welfare state, full-employment, science, the IMF, and on, during the paleolithic period of hunting and gathering. The proliferation of material technics entails the need for concomitant social technics as additions to the overall gestalt of technology as a necessary condition for the proper functioning of the proliferation and accumulation of new and varied material technics and, vice versa.

No one apparently doubts that there is accumulation in the material sector, but the material sector also exhibits substitution and replacement. Just as the IMF replaced and substituted for the international gold standard so has the automobile replaced and substituted for the horse and buggy. We start with four wheels, add to this a carriage and a horse, substitute an internal combustion engine, add a concrete or asphalt road, and we have an additive, cumulative process producing differing and alternative vehicles of transportation. However, in the process culture also experiences losses as new material technics serve as substitutes or replacements for less efficient technics. The horse and carriage in its demise represents a cultural loss for an advanced culture such as the United States and was replaced or substituted for by other material technics serving as transporation.[8] Consequently, we substitute one material technic for another but the new technic, such as the automobile as replacement or substitution, overcomes the loss of culture of the horse and buggy through an even greater accumulation of culture. This takes place not only through the improvements in the automobile and the ancillary services that it requires, but also, through the proliferation of other new technics, both material and nonmaterial, with the automobile serving in this sense as a leading sector.[9] With the automobile we add to the technics of mass production with the technic of the moving assembly line innovated by the Ford Motor Company circa early twentieth century and as a result we now have a capacity for production and replication to glut our highways and cities, as never before, with four-wheeled material artifacts in numbers never attainable under conditions of horse-and-buggy technics.[10] Therefore, while culture experiences losses with the advance of material technics through substitution and replacement, the overall process is additive in that the accumulation of material culture advances with the advance of technology. This explains why technology is so intimately related to higher levels of economic growth and standards of living in that it creates new products as well as more efficient methods of production with higher levels of energy control and all of which results in an increased capacity for growth and accumulation. Although, not as frequently recognized, the same basic process of substitution and accumulation, as exemplified in the material sector, prevails in the nonmaterial sector as well.

A good example of substitution and accumulation in the nonmaterial sector of culture is provided for by the institution of money.[11] In the evolution of our banking structures we observe that not only does one form or structure replace and ultimately give rise to another but each new form grows and accumulates in its development along the lines of increased complexity. As with the coral reef both material and nonmaterial culture are additive and accumulate; but unlike the coral reef the material and nonmaterial technics of culture also experience in their evolution changes in structure and form as a metamorphosis. Both the social and material technics of culture demonstrate a capacity to absorb and accumulate more and more knowledge. Just as knowledge accumulates and is additive in the evolution from the horse and buggy to the Galaxie Ford, so also do we see a similar additive and accumulative process of knowledge as its concreted form changes in increased complexity from that of the international gold standard to that of the IMF. Banking in its evolution passed from the goldsmith or money changer and cash holder to deposit banking as assets were increased through loans, and banks thereby created money when deposits became greater than cash. With the advance of culture and economic development, national banking evolved into varying structures and forms, with the Bank of England and the Federal Reserve System of the United States serving as examples of proliferation.[12] National banking in turn evolved into international banking with the new technic known as the international gold standard during the nineteenth century. These nonmaterial technics in national and international banking were integral parts of the accumulation and development of the overall gestalt of technology characteristic of the stage of economic development known as industrialism. The unique first-time experience of this transformation and revolution in methods of production and social organization came to be known as the Industrial Revolution. The Industrial Revolution, which centered in Great Britain, unleashed forces of production which led to the evolution, circa 1870's of a vast world-wide multilateral network of trade. However, the 1870's was also the period when the major trading countries of the world followed the lead of Great Britain (1816) and went on a monemetallic gold standard.[13] The evolution of new technics of material culture mainfest in the trade and transport of more and more economic goods (material culture) saw also the evolution of concomitant nonmaterial technics in the field of international banking. With the "unfolding of the fan" the enlarged multilateral network of world trade, which evolved, was held together by the glue of convertibility and credits inherent in the international gold standard. The international gold standard, however, was relatively short-lived and there developed a need for replacement and substitution as the glue turned to water during the Great Depression of the 1930's and the interrelated disintegration of the world-wide trading network.[14]

Our discussion of the evolution of the international monetary system could continue along similar lines to also include the demise of the Bretton Woods System during the early 1970's and its replacement by the floating rate system of the current period. The point being made here, however, is that the processes of culture evolution which include substitution and replacement as well as accumulation and addition apply to both material and nonmaterial culture. As parts of material culture accumulate and accelerate we also note that similar processes prevail in the evolution of the social and vice versa. As a general characteristic of culture evolution we find that changes in form and structure in one area require concomitant changes in structure and form elsewhere. The lack of response in adjustment, known as a cultural lag, leads to crisis and chaos and/or stagnation. Such maladjustment pressures for a new structure or form, as a gestalt switch, as adaptive culture responds in its adjustment to the dislocation wrought by the innovation of new elements into the overall gestalt of technology.[15]

To further reinforce the point being made here, that whereas standard textbook treatment explains the demise of the international gold standard in relation to the equilibrating forces of income and price changes, inherent in a fixed rate system, we might further extend explanation to include changes in structure. In the context of culture and structural change the retention of the gold standard until as late as 1931 represented a cultural lag which led to maladjustment and the malfunctioning of the world economy during the period of the Great Depression. The changing structure of the world economy in the material sector had required concomitant changes in the structure and form of the international monetary system. Pressures for adjusting the cultural lag through the creation of a new international monetary system to replace the defunct gold standard appeared in the crisis wrought by the economic chaos and stagnation of the period.[16] In the immediate post-WW II period this lag was adjusted to by the innovation of the new social technic in the form of the IMF.

A systematic study covering the structural changes of the period and which resulted in the demise of the international gold standard is contained in the standard work by William Adams Brown, Jr.[17] Brown attempts to reverse the standard textbook procedure which rests explanation upon mainstream theory by using historical analysis as a guide to explanation, that is, to look at the international gold standard more in terms of actual practice and less in terms of theory.[18] The key, according to Brown, for the successful operation of the pre-war system was the single-center idea of the nineteenth century international banking edifice, the beating heart of which was London. This constitutes the central theme of Brown's study.[19] According to Brown the salient structural feature of the pre-war system was that the world's international credit system had but one center—London. The viability of the structure depended upon the economic domination and supremacy as well as upon stable banking conditions at the center. The diffusion of industrialism, and also, therefore, industrialization, to other nations broke down the British hegemony and the foundations of the structure were removed; the single center gave way to a multiplicity and the system crumbled. Brown's analysis is consequently very amenable to the methodology of *cultural economics* and basically shows that as culture advances and becomes more complex, new problems arise and that these problems require not only new technics in the material sector but institutional adjustment as well in the form of new social technics—exit the international gold standard, enter the IMF.[20] The IMF represents a new social technic, a social invention, an addition, a greater accumultion of useful knowledge applicable to international monetary affairs. The IMF represents a prime case of the application of science to social organization, as social technology, in order to resolve the friction inherent in a cultural lag. And since the IMF also substituted for the international gold standard, it may be viewed as both substitution and accumulation.[21] Consequently, as the material technics advance and accumulate, we also see accumulation in the area of concomitant nonmaterial technics, and vice versa. A substantive explanation would be that at base they are both in their origins and genesis representative of useful knowledge, and since useful knowledge accumulates, the same result would be expected of both material and nonmaterial technics. That material and nonmaterial technics are in actuality manifestations of useful knowledge is fundamental to our study, it is also a basic assumption made by Kroeber. To our view this contradicts and is inconsistent with Kroeber's position that the nonmaterial sector of culture does not accumulate.

While Kroeber recognizes a literal distinction between material and nonmaterial culture, that is, ". . .physical objects as against institutions and ideas. . ." he does not feel that they function differently in culture, consequently, the distinction is of "... no first-rank significance."[22] What really is of importance and significance is "...the knowledge how to produce and use them...It is this knowledge, concept and function that get themselves handed down through generations, or diffused into other cultures, while the objects themselves are quickly worn out or consumed."[23] We could not agree more with the proposition which states that at base both material and nonmaterial cultures are in essence forms of knowledge. However, if there is no distinction between material and nonmaterial culture, since they are both representative of knowledge as Kroeber maintains, why then draw a distinction in another context to maintain that one form of knowledge manifest in material culture accumulates and is additive while useful knowledge in another form, manifest in the nonmaterial sector of culture, simply replaces or is substitutive. Since a most fundamental characteristic of knowledge is its accumulation, would it not also logically follow that since both the material and nonmaterial sectors of culture are of knowledge that both would therefore accumulate as well. In the context of our dichotomy of useful knowledge, we argue that both material and nonmaterial technics are predicated on the base of useful knowledge; that both are characterized by both substitution and accumulation; and, that the distinction between material and nonmaterial technics is not just a literal one but one of considerable significance for analytical and theoretical purposes. It should be noted that discussions in the literature concerning material and nonmaterial culture do not concern the actual existence of the dichotomy, a literal and real distinction exists because in actuality there is a material and nonmaterial dichotomy in culture. The discussions over material and nonmaterial culture concern the significance of the dichotomy for analytical and theoretical purposes associated with culture evolution. The significance of the dichotomy is well recognized in the literature of developmental economics. The basic problem of a lag in social technics commensurate with modern technology is central to any meaningful analysis of the problems facing underdeveloped countries. Not so well understood, however, is that economic development is an ongoing process and relevant to mature countries as well, and that the European economy, as a region, must also innovate in the area of social technics, primarily in the area of supranationalism, in order to make the culture of Western Europe more permeable to the latest in modern material and nonmaterial technics.

In conclusion, then, we agree with Hornell Hart in the position that both material and nonmaterial technics accumulate and are additive. However, as we will demonstrate later, in that knowledge accumulates and with acceleration, the same exponential characteristic also prevails for nonmaterial culture, as the social, as well as for the material.[24] Consequently, the problem of a cultural lag cannot be explained and accounted for by the intrinsic nature of nonmaterial culture, for if our social structure is not also characterized by additive processes of accumulated we would forever be foredoomed and never able to resolve the problem of cultural lags. But if nonmaterial culture is also permeable to useful knowledge, and if useful knowledge is also characterized by acceleration in its accumulation, we must look elsewhere in our accounting of cultural lags.

A few more points are in need of clarification in relation to the accumulation of nonmaterial technics. As we do not state that all cultures necessarily accelerate in their accumulation but rather that acceleration is characteristic of universal culture in general, we also do not state that all of material culture accumulates uniformly either for a particular culture or culture in general. We have noted that some material technics far from accelerating may stagnate or even decline and constitute culture losses in their disappearance.[25] The same applies for social institutions, some accelerate, some stagnate and change little and others hopefully, such as head hunting, are lost. Overall, however, culture accumulates and with acceleration in that losses are more than covered by the innovation of new technics. The new technics are, themselves, representative of an accumulation of useful knowledge and produce an even greater capacity for culture to accumulate and with acceleration. New technics proliferate and/or substitute and replace in the context of general evolution or they may improve, refine and perfect in the context of specific evolution. Therefore all material technics or all the nonmaterial technics of culture do not have to accumulate as a necessary condition for the overall accumulation of culture.[26]

Another issue to be more clearly understood in an analysis of cultural lag in addition to the fact that nonmaterial culture as well as material culture accumulates and with acceleration, is the issue of the concomitant nature of social and material technics. In various instances we have made the assumption that new technics are added as a whole, that consequently the nonmaterial exists along with the material, and, vice versa. Techonology to be functional and operational appears in the form of the integration of the whole or the gestalt of interdependent social and material technics. Culture development, as the addition of new technics, does not take place in separated halves, one part material and the other social, but rather the new technic, if it is to be operable and is to function, must exist as an integrated whole or gestalt of its own of material and nonmaterial parts, a fertilized egg. A fertilized egg to be operational exists as a gestalt containing both female and male parts.

We may give an underdeveloped country a Boeing 747 but it will never get off the runway if that country's airport is without the concomitant social technics. Similarly the steam engine as a material technic of textile production could not have been innovated in the context of the domestic system, but, rather, was concomitant to the social technic known as the factory system.[27] Economic development as a process is basically a social process, and, consequently, material technics to function need concomitant social technics. But also, conversely, social technics need concomitant material parts.[28] In the solution of basic economic and social problems man devises new technics, and whether the new technics are essentially material or nonmaterial they cannot be innovated without the necessary concomitant social and/or material technics being in existence, they simply could not function.

At this point we must distinguish between a specific or individual gestalt and the overall gestalt of technology. Each specific technic has its own individual whole or gestalt of material and nonmaterial parts (technics). Material technics such as a telephone, an airplane, or a computer need concomitant material technics such as wires and telephone poles and airfields, but in addition they also need social technics if the specific technic is to function and be operable. The overall gestalt of technology, by comparison, is really one big technic, a technic of culture as a whole, it is the core of culture. For the overall technic to function, which is really the technic of culture, an holistic concept, there is consequently the need of material and nonmaterial parts (technics). The overall gestalt of technology is somewhat analogous to Durkheim's "organic solidarity" concept. We view the overall gestalt of technology as the core of culture which is an integrated whole of all specific material and nonmaterial technics and serves as the basic characteristic of a given stage of culture advance. In any event, the material and nonmaterial technics must be concomitant, either for a specific gestalt or the overall gestalt, if the technology is to function and be operable.[29] That man was able to apply power to machines in the production of textiles was not just a function of the material technics of the Industrial Revolution but was also due to the fact that concomitant social institutions had evolved concurrently and were in existence. That the material technic of the steam engine was able to function and was innovated as it evolved demonstrates that concomitant social institutions in the ultimate form of the factory system were evolving and were also in existence. This is not to infer that social technics will be the same for all social systems using modern material technics but rather that social institutions capable of performing the necessary concomitant social functions must be available for the specific technic to function as a gestalt.

Man, as an organic gestalt or whole, could not function given the heart of a lemur any more than our modern industrial societies could function with the banking structure of the Fuggers of Augsburg. Man needs a functional part called a heart but the heart must be concomitant to other parts of the organic whole if the overall gestalt known as man is to function. The overall gestalt is consequently a structural and integrated whole and not just an aggregation of parts. Homo sapiens is not just a random summation or unrelated aggregation of cells, organs and tissues but rather an integrated, organic whole which becomes known as man. And analogous to the organic whole of biological life, as the integrated gestalt known as man, in the social life, since the days of Tylor, we have come to conceptualize culture in an holistic sense as a gestalt. In our analysis we have called the integrated whole of material and nonmaterial parts of the overall gestalt of technology, the core of culture. Culture is an holistic concept.

Consequently, if such a conceptualization is correct, we would then expect accumulation not only in the material sector of culture but in the social sector as well, in that the sectors are integrated as a whole, if one sector accumulates the other would be expected to accumulate as well. And, this we submit to be the actual case, such as, the multinational corporation, the IMF, the welfare state, and nationalism, are all examples of institutions demonstrating accumulation concomitant to the accumulation taking place in the material sector. We might, therefore, continuing with such an holistic schema of economic development, predict that while economic integration and supranationalism need not be an inevitable occurrence for underdeveloped nations of small size in the areas of Latin America, Africa, and elsewhere, that rather such an innovation will be a necessary condition for the permeability of those cultures to modern industrial technics. This is not to infer that the social technics providing for integration will or should be the same for Latin America, Africa, or Europe, but rather that ultimately a new technic of political organization (a new concomitant heart providing for better circulation), providing for a larger market size and capable of absorbing modern industrial technics, must be innovated if the organic whole of culture, the overall gestalt of technology, is to advance. And such an advance marks the process of economic development and culture evolution. It is for this reason that though modern material technics are actually available to underdeveloped countries through imports, they are not diffused into the overall gestalt of the underdeveloped country's technology due to the lack of concomitant social technics. Even assuming that an underdeveloped country has sufficient foreign exchange or could secure the necessary credits with which to make the purchase of a sufficient amount of advanced material technics in the form of imports those technics would not be operable without the necessary concomitant social technics. Usually in those rare instances when the financing of the importation of material technology is resolved we find the underdeveloped country also importing foreign social technics in the form of foreign technicians and foreign corporate organization. Such a solution does not necessarily therefore transform the overall gestalt of the underdeveloped country to industrialism but rather marks the genesis of a dual economy and foreign enclaves. Given the necessary foreign exchange it is relatively easy to import a bulldozer or the latest IBM computer, both of which may be acquired almost instantaneously; however, the concomitant social technics of education, individual skills and social organization are the difficult parts to acquire and take time to achieve since they constitute a learning process but they are necessary if the overall advanced gestalt of industrialism is to be innovated and to prove operable. Since the material technics of modern industrialism have been invented and are actually in existence their lack of diffusion and spread to the underdeveloped countries is primarily explained by the lack of the necessary concomitant social institutions.[30] Therefore, for a material technic to be actually applied and innovated, for it to be operable and to function, and since the overall process is essentially social, the necessary concomitant social technics must also be in existence.

And now a very legitimate and obvious question: If it is correct that both material and social technics are additive and accumulate, and if it is also correct that social and material technics tend to be concomitant and integrated as a gestalt, how then do we explain the cultural lag hypothesis of Ogburn?[31] How can a cultural lag exist if the material and nonmaterial technics must both be in existence for the overall technic to function?

Even though concomitant technics for a specific gestalt serve as necessary conditions for the operation and the functioning and for the actual existence of a given gestalt, this does not preclude a cultural lag in the context of concomitant technics. Though the overall technic exists as a gestalt this does not mean that it is operating smoothly and does not exhibit areas of malfunction. Parts of the whole might lag behind in the development of the whole. For example, in the specific gestalt of railroad technology, bigger and more powerful engines may develop and advance faster than the breaking system or tracks of sufficient stability and strength or faster than the social concomitants which develop over time, such as the Interstate

Commerce Act of 1887 in the context of the experience of the American economy. In a static sense for a given moment of time we have noted that technics operate as gestalts and that many technics, both material and nonmaterial, are necessary as functional parts for a specific gestalt, suce as the gestalt of the automobile and its production, to prove operable. It is not correct to conclude from the fact that since the totality or gestalt of material and nonmaterial technics must actually be in existence for the gestalt to be operable, that this necessarily negates the possibility of a cultural lag. Such a conclusion ignores the fact that cultural lag does not concern the static, or a given moment of time, but rather deals with the dynamic or rates of change of adjustment over intervals of time. To say that certain technics(parts) are necessary for the specific gestalt to be operational and to exist is to assert a functional point of view, a cross-section for a given moment of time, and this is what we have done. However, there is no reason to assume in the context of culture evolution, which entails movements over time, that concomitant technics need necessarily move forward in a perfectly synchronized manner devoid of lags. Therefore though concomitant technics are interdependent and integrated in a functional whole they are still subject to lags in development and innovation.[32]

For the material technic of the automobile to be operable we need wheels, a motor, a steering mechanism, brakes and on; they are concomitant technics of the automobile. Without the wheels or without the motor the material technic known as the automobile would not function. In the production of the automobile the specific gestalt entails as necessary conditions the material technics required to produce the automobile, as well as the technics or parts of the automobile itself, plus the concomitant nonmaterial technics. For a given moment of time of these parts exist in the very existence of automobile production as the heart and lungs and circulatory system exist in an operational and viable biological organism. For without the integration of the concomitant technics, automobile production as such would be nonoperational, it would not function and consequently could not exist. This is not to say that the development and evolution of concomitant technics is perfectly synchronized.

In the development and growth of a biological organism (assuming a normal and healthy body), as the cells undergo differentiation into tissues and organs in ontogeny, they tend to grow in a synchronized and interdependent manner as regulated by genetic controls. This is provided for by the biological DNA. However, in the social sphere there is no such integrative agency of synchronization and, consequently, there is no necessary reason for technics, though integrated and concomitant, to grow and develop together in perfect synchronization. Consequently, though the wheels, brakes, and motor as material technics are concomitant to the automobile and that though they grow and develop together they need not develop in a synchronized manner but one or the other may (in all probability—will) lag or lead the others for a given interval of time.[33] Also, the same might be said for the concomitant social technics of automobile production specifically among themselves or collectively as they may lead or lag behind the material sector.

In a static sense, for a given moment of time, and for a specific gestalt such as that of the automobile to prove operable there must be in existence the necessary material and nonmaterial technics. However, this does not preclude a cultural lag which as theoretical explanation is not a static concept but rather is concerned with changes over time. Given the concomitant technics of the automobile there is no reason to assume that the technical problems associated with the development of the motor, or the wheels or highways, or the concomitant social technics will all advance in a perfectly synchronized manner and be devoid of cultural lags but rather in all probability they will advance at varying speeds of development.[34] Technological breakthroughs of concomitant material or nonmaterial technics associated with the automobile need not necessarily be synchronized in their development over any interval of time. Though the concomitant technics are not precisely synchronized in the evolutionary development of the automobile as concomitant technics they are, however, integrated and as such must continue to develop for the continued overall development of automobiles. The lack of development of a specific technic which serves as a crucial part of the whole will limit or place a ceiling on the development of the whole.

In this way the whole malfunctions and stagnates with the lag of one of its parts. The Galaxie Ford would not prove operational given the engine or brakes of the Model A. This is similar to the logic behind the law of diminishing returns in that we limit the continued advance of the whole by holding one factor constant. Given one fixed factor we ultimately reach a plateau or ceiling for the whole. If the two-cylinder, two-horsepower engines of the earlier automobiles had been retained and not improved upon, we would have limited the advance of the overall technic known as the automobile. Consequently the engine as a technic is concomitant to the automobile; it is an integrated functional part of the whole. Therefore, though they need not be perfectly synchronized, the integral parts of the whole must continue to develop and overcome the lags in their development if the specific gestalt as a whole, such as the automobile, is to continue to develop and grow as well. This would constitute a basic characteristic of technics which we wish to distinguish as being concomitant.

The relationship and interdependence of concomitant technics as part of a gestalt can be thought of as occurring at various levels. The specific gestalts constituting canals, railroads, automobiles, aircraft, and on, collectively at the next or higher level, comprise the overall of transportation technology. Transportation, overall, can also be viewed as a gestalt and therefore of both material and nonmaterial technics, and consequently subject to a variety of cultural lags. In addition to transportation, there are other major functional areas, such as banking, energy, education, business organizations, government. Certain functional areas are considered part of material technology, such as transportation and energy and directly related to economic production. Other functional areas such as government, business organizations and banking, are directly related to social organization of that economic production. Together the material technics of economic production and the concomitant nonmaterial technics of social organization comprise at the highest level of integration, or what has been called in this study, the overall gestalt of technology.

At the highest level of integrating concomitant technics of material and social technology we therefore need energy control to advance along with transportation, along with business organization, along with banking, and on, as social and material concomitants of the whole in order for the whole to function.[35] Consequently, a cultural lag in a major functional can lead to the stagnation or malfunctioning of the whole. Therefore, the new technics invented and innovated in the wheel of economic development must be synchronized in order to prevent cultural lags and the malfunctioning of the whole of the core of culture. In economics this level of analysis would be analogous to the malfunctioning of the entire economy.

It is truly a marvel that biological forms, as organic wholes, are able to accomplish the miraculous and almost unbelievable feat of synchronization in the growth and development of concomitant parts. The complexity and wonder of the parts, such as the eye, the brain, the heart, the circulatory system, the nervous system in their particular growth and development and, yet further, given the assumption of a healthy body, that they grow and develop with synchronization to produce the gestalt of the body as an organic whole. Can society ever hope to achieve such a healthy body or must it always experience cultural lags or must it always malfunction to produce a sick economy characterized by crisis, chaos, and/or stagnation. In order to answer this question we must look at the basic cause of cultural lags and to do this we must once again return to our dichotomy of useful knowledge and the wheel of economic development.

The cause of a cultural lag is not that nonmaterial culture is not additive or accumulative. In our dichotomy of useful knowledge we have noted that both material and nonmaterial culture are potentially permeable to useful knowledge. In the next chapter we will argue that culture evolves along an exponential curve which envelops an underlying paradigm of logistic surges. This paradigm, as structure, characterizes both material and nonmaterial culture. Consequently, social technics can lead and serve as the independent variable and material technics can lag and serve as the dependent variable and "adaptive culture."[36] However, that while the social might lead and the material lag, during the current period of modern economic growth it is fairly obvious that the major cultural lags are of the nature whereby we find material culture outracing the social.[37] Again this is not because the nonmaterial is incapable of accumulation and with acceleration, for if this were so we could never really overcome the problem of cultural lags. But rather that currently we find that material culture accelerates and accumulates at faster rates. But why is this so?

This raises a fundamental question concerning cultural lag: if our assumption is correct that both material culture and nonmaterial culture are at base, useful knowledge, should not a greater synchronization prevail, should not the horse of nonmaterial culture gallop more apace with the horse of material culture? What is the basic explanation of the fact that nonmaterial culture tends to lag behind the material during the current period of culture evolution characterized by industrialism? The key for explanation and resolution of the problem resides in "The Place of Science in Modern Civilization."[38] The epoch of industrialism is characterized by the application of modern science to economic production and social organization and therein lies the answer.

In the context of the dichotomy of useful knowledge, we have noted that all technics are at root useful knowledge. It should also be noted, however, that additions to useful knowledge are of heterogeneous sources, such as: serendipity, change and random processes, as well as what might be called systematic scientific methods and procedures. In addition, even if a new technic is discovered or invented by man or made available to a specific culture via diffusion, the new technic is of no consequence to culture evolution and economic development unless innovated. Therefore, the spectrum of the source or genesis of the new technic as well as the possibility of adoption is wide and heterogeneous. At present it is material culture which is more susceptible and amenable to the application of more scientific procedures than would be so for nonmaterial culture, the sector of social technics or institutions. Therefore problem solving (the new technic) is more systematically achieved and more predictable in the material sector as well as being more easily innovated. The process of problem solving with the use of scientific methods and procedures in the material sector has been institutionalized in its ready acceptance for cultures in the stage of industrialism. This is perhaps the basic explanation for the sustained modern economic growth and development associated with industrialism. The genie which man has let out of the bottle and which has ushered in the dynamic thrust of modern times is the genie of science. However the acceptance of applying systematic and predictable knowledge to social problems for the genesis of new (social) technics has by comparison tended to lag over time.[39] When in the future we apply science to the social technics with the same vigor and institutionalized acceptance that we now do in the material sector we will have come the full circle. At such a point our theoretical framework contained in the *wheel of economic development* could then rightfully be called a *frictionless wheel of economic development*.[40] And in the process there would be innovated the means whereby man could increase his capacity to resolve the more urgent and pressuring cultural lags and in the process to then more closely synchronize the accumulation of the material and social technics in the overall gestalt of technology.

> "The future of civilization depends upon the invention of better methods of social invention, or, in other words, a radical speed-up in the development of genuine social science."[41]

REFERENCES

[1]Again it is not our position that the concept of evolution dominates or is fully accepted in the social sciences. Anthropology has perhaps been more permeable to the concept than has sociology and with mainstream economics being least permeable of all. Note: Gerhard Lenski and Jean Lenski, *Human Societies: An Introduction to Macrosociology* (New York: McGraw-Hill Book Company, 1974), p. 24, No. 26 and also, pp. 76-93 and passim. In economics, those who dealt with technological change and change in structure did not always endorse the concept of evolution. Joseph A. Schumpeter in his *The Theory of Economic Development* (Cambridge: Harvard University Press, 1959), notes: "But the evolutionary idea is discredited in our field. . . To the reproach of unscientific and extrascientific mysticism that now surrounds the evolutionary ideas, is added that of dilettantism. With all the hasty generalizations in which the word 'evolution' plays a part, many of us have lost patience." pp. 57-58.

[2]For Ogburn's comments on Veblen note, Otis Dudley Duncan, *William F. Ogburn on Culture and Social Change* (Chicago: The Univer-

sity of Chicago Press, 1964), ". . .I had never read him on this point." p. 87.

[3]William F. Ogburn, *Social Change* (New York: Dell Publishing Company, 1966), pp. 201-202, 199-280 and passim; and "Cultural Lag as Theory," *Sociology and Social Research*, 41 (January-February 1957), pp. 167-174, also appearing in Duncan, ed., *William F. Ogburn*, pp. 86-95; and Hornell Hart, "The Hypothesis of Cultural Lag: A Present Day View," in *Technology and Social Change* (New York: Applenton-Century-Crofts, 1957), pp. 417-434; William F. Ogburn and Meyer F. Nimkoff, *A Handbook of Sociology* (London: Routledge and Kegan Paul, 1968), pp. 595-603 and passim; James W. Woodward, "A New Classification of Culture and a restatement of the Cultural Lag Theory, "*American Sociological Review*, 1 (February 1936), pp. 89-102; John Mueller, "Present Status of Cultural Lag Theory," *American Sociological Review*, 3 (June 1938), pp. 320-327; and, Joseph Schneider "Cultural Lag: What is It?" *American Sociological Review* 10 (December 1945), pp. 786-791; and A.J. Jaffe, "Ogburn, William Fielding," *International Encylopedia of the Social Sciences* (1968), Vol. 11, pp. 277-281.

[4]Ogburn, *Social Change*, p. 273.

[5]"But there is the difference that each art, or for that matter, each philosophy or religion, very largely has to begin all over again, whereas each of the intermittent periods of discovery in science can begin, and generally does begin, just about where the last one left off. Science and in the main technology, are evidently accumulative by nature, while philosophy, religion, art—and empire and nationalism tend to be strongly substitutive: a new product replaces an old one." A.L. Kroeber, *Anthropology* (New York: Harcourt, Brace and Company, 1948), p. 303. The reference to Kroeber was cited by Hornell Hart, "Acceleration in Social Change," in Francis R. Allen, et. al., *Technology and Social Change* (New York: Appleton-Century-Crofts, 1957), p. 35. In certain instances even Ogburn seems to give support to Kroeber on this issue: "The phenomenon of selective accumulation is centainly true of material culture, but it may not be true for other parts of culture, such as religion, science, art, law and custom. Customs may be only slightly accumulative. "*Social Change*, pp. 73-79, especially pp. 77-78.

[6]Kroeber, *Anthropology*, p. 297. Birds substitute wings for legs, and man, in the cumulative, sociocultural process, adds an airplane. "In sum, it represents an accretion to the stock of existing civilization. . ." p. 5. It should be noted that Kroeber used this distinction not only to support the contention that nonmaterial culture was substitutive and not accumulative but also, to clarify the roles of the organic and the superorganic in culture evolution. "Once the broad implications of the distinction which this example illustrates have been grasped, many common errors are guarded against." p. 5. "Without sure grasp of this principle, many of the arguments and conclusions in the present volume will lose their significance." p. 6 and, "The relation between what is biological and what is sociocultural has just been said to be a sort of central pivot of anthropology. . ." p. 7.

[7]Kroeber agrees that, overall, culture accumulates, "All in all, the verdict of history confirms such a judgment." and, ". . .it does seem clear that in an over-all sort of way the sum total of culture of mankind has pretty continuously grown in bulk through history," *Anthropology*, p. 297. In looking at the parts however, Kroeber feels that the nonmaterial sector does not accumulate whereas in comparison in the material sector there is a ". . .persistent tendency for technology and science to grow accumulatively," p. 304. Kroeber perhaps is in error in assuming that the material sector (to which he relegates technology and science) alone accumulates since material technics do not function alone, by themselves, in a social vacuum but need concomitant, social technics if they are to be operable. It is in this sense that we assume that if the material technics accumulate with culture evolution and economic development so then do the nonmaterial technics.

[8]It is our view that substitution and accumulation occur in both the material and nonmaterial sectors of culture. Therefore material technics are also subject to substitution and displacement as they are replaced by new material technics: "Displacement occurs when a trait disappears from culture. The log cabin. . .Horse-drawn vehicles, the icebox. . . commercial sailing ships have been displaced largely from western ways of life." And, to the point: "Much displacement arises from the appearance in culture of what is perceived to be a more satisfactory substitute for a given trait." in John J. Honigman, *The World of Man* (New York: Harper and Row, 1959), pp. 233-234. Note, also, Kroeber, *Anthoropology*, pp. 374, 378.

[9]The idea that the introduction of a given new technic will lead to a proliferation of additional technics and, consequently, culture accumulation and transformation, is analogous to the leading sector concept as used by Walt W. Rostow in his *The Stages of Economic Growth* (Cambridge: The University Press, 1961), and his examples, such as the railroad during the take-off stage and the automobile during the stage of high mass-consumption. In the process of innovation and replication of the railroad we experience a culture loss in terms of canals, but overall the railorad added more to culture than was lost and consequently the impact on the whole was one of accumulation. Certain canals were more successful than others and exhibited staying power, for example, the Erie, but canals as a technics of transportation reach a logistic ceiling, and then gradually begin to disappear. In the process they are substituted for by more efficient alternative methods such as the railroad and the automobile. The automobile serves as a prime case of a leading sector and produced not only concomitant material and nonmaterial technics but also wrought great social change as well. Note Francis R. Allen, ed., *Technology and Social Change*, pp. 107-132, and for similar processes and results for motion pictures, radio and television, aviation, and atomic energy, pp. 133-241. The petroleum industry had its origins with Colonel Drake and the drilling of the first well at Titusville, Pennsylvania in 1859, and grew concomitant to the automobile used as a technic of transportation. But then the petroleum industry took on its

own momentum and in turn led to a proliferation of many new technics, and today, the petro-chemical industry literally entails thousands of new products. But petroleum is just one example, there are many others. As we view the new products, the new machines, the new energy sources, as well as the concomitant and commensurate social technics of the twentieth century, alone, as compared to previous periods, we see culture accumulation and with acceleration.

[10]Though we may dispute the rightful individual title concerning the invention and innovation of the moving assembly line, it was still the Ford Motor Company that served as the innovator. On the dispute, note, John K. Galbraith, "Was Ford a Fraud," in *The Liberal Hour* (Boston: Houghton Mifflin Company, 1960), pp. 140-165. "The most spectacular of the Ford contributions to mass production was the steadily moving assembly line. Of this, Sorenson avers, Ford, so far from being the inventor, was for a long time a skeptic." p. 152.

[11]On the evolution of money as an institution we refer to Robert Triffin, *The Evolution of the International Monetary System: Historical Reappraisal and Future Perspectives* (Princeton: Princeton Studies in International Finance, No. 12, 1964), reprinted in, Robert Triffin, *Our International Monetary System* (New York: Random House, 1968), the latter being dedicated to: "Pierre Teilhard de Chardin and Jean Charon, and their inspiring vision of the evolutionary process." In *Our International Monetary System*, Triffin notes that, "Money like all other human institutions is the prey of an evolutionary process that has always eluded the attempt of 'conservatives' to stop it, and of 'radicals' to deflect it too widely from the trajectory imparted to it by the momentum of past decisions and accidents." p. viii. The basic evolutionary pattern which Triffin discerns is: "Its major theme is that the gradual assertion of man's control over his physical environment is marked, in the monetary field, by the gradual displacement of 'commodity money' by man-made 'fiduciary money'," pp. x, 165 ff.

[12]The banking structure of the United States evolved from the first Bank of the United States, to the second Bank of the United States, to the National Banking Act of 1863-64, and on to the Federal Reserve System. One system substituted for another and represented greater complexities and accumulations of useful knowledge. That the social technics need not be precisely the same for each nation is evident from the empirical record in that the American banking structure is federal and more pluralistic than the European unitary counterparts and reflects unique historical occurrences in the context of given cultures. Note George Rogers Taylor *Jackson versus Biddle* (Boston: D.C. Heath and Company, 1949), pp. v-vi. The point being made here is that as culture advances it is not only the material sector which accumulates and becomes more complex, in its additive nature, but this applies to the social sector as well. What is being said here in terms of money and banking might also be said in terms of the evolution of the business firm to the current level of the multinational corporations. Also, the same might be said of our basic trading institutions as they evolved

from the fair, the staple, the auction, the commercial league, the joint-stock and regulated companies, and on to the nation state of mercantilism and industrialism, and on to the current trend toward regionalism and supranationalism. These basic institutions were formed during certain stages of culture advance, the new nonmaterial technics (Category A of our wheel of economic development) were produced in the context of a given culture setting (Category D). "All were instruments of trade growing out of the condition existing at their time of origin." Asher Isaacs, *International Trade: Tariff and Commercial Policies* (Chicago: Richard D. Irwin, 1948), p. 44. Isaacs speaks in terms of the fact that: "These institutions—remnants, reminders, and survivals of which exist today—must not be thought of as succeeding one another. They ran somewhat concurrently and even came into conflict at times." p. 31. Such a view does not negate evolution but rather is a statement of the reality of the process and one which we have noted. That a sturgeon and man, a state bank and the Federal Reserve, a partnership and the multinational corporation, exist concurrently is not a negation of evolution but is indicative of the proliferation and diversity inherent in the process.

[13]This, of course, is based upon the empirical evidence provided by Folke Hilgerdt's classic study concerning multilateral trade. Note. "The Case for Multilateral Trade," *The American Economic Review*, 33 (March 1943), pp. 393-407; William R. Allen and Clark Lee Allen, eds., *Foreign Trade and Finance* (New York: The Macmillan Company, 1959), pp. 426-440; and, *The Network of World Trade* (Geneva: League of Nations, 1942). And for the international gold standard, on which the literature is considerable, note, William Adams Brown, Jr., *The International Gold Standard Reinterpreted 1914-1934* (New York: National Bureau of Economic Research, 1940), 2 Volumes.

[14]"The period of 1914 to 1945, bordered by two world wars and bisected by a catastrophic depression, can surely be described as one of disintegration of the world economy and declining world trade, under any reasonable definition of these terms." Gottfried Haberler, "Integration and Growth of the World Economy in Historical Perspective," *The American Economic Review*, 54 (March 1964), pp. 1-22, p. 6. New technics were invented during the Bretton Woods' discussions and were directed towards the rejuvenation of the sector of international trade and finance. Some of the social inventions presented during the post WW II period were actually innovated, such as the IMF, GATT and the IBR & D, and others were not, for example, the ITO and Keynes' bancor.

And to support the contention that the international gold standard was relatively short-lived, "The international gold standard is by no means such an old and venerable institution as most seem to believe. It is a monetary system constructed by Great Britain after the disorders of the Napoleonic Wars: it developed into an international gold standard after the Franco-German war in the beginning of the seventies." Gustav Cassel, *The Downfall of the Gold Standard* (Oxford:

Clarendon Press, 1936), p. 1. "The international gold standard is essentially a ceation of the second half of the nineteenth century." T.E. Gregory, *The Gold Standard and Its Future* (New York: E.P. Dutton and Co., 1932), p. 1. On the history of the gold standard as an international institution, note, R.G. Hawtrey, *The Gold Standard in Theory and Practice* (London: Longmans, Green & Co., 1933), pp. 59-86; Edwin Walter Kenmerer, *Gold and the Gold Standard* (New York: McGraw-Hill Book Co., 1944), pp. 45-132. Usually it is given a life span neighboring on the four decades between the 1870's and WWI, but J.B. Condliffe, *The Commerce of Nations* (New York: W.W. Norton and Co., 1950), felt it to be even less, "The period during which the gold standard was fully operative is less than twenty years, from 1897-1914." p. 362.

[15]As anomalies in the framework of T.S. Kuhn and *The Structure of Scientific Revolutions* pressure for a "gestalt switch" in the evolution of science, so do economic and social pressures of maladjustment pressure for gestalt switches, as new technics, in the overall evolution of culture. The evolution of science, as an evolution of knowledge, follows the same paradigm as general culture evolution. We refer here to the paradigm of logistic surges leading to the overall exponential.

[16]According to Ogburn ". . . there are certain events which cause cultural lags to crumble." p. 92, Duncan, *William F. Ogburn*. Among those forces for ". . . breaking down cultural lags . . ." Ogburn points to wars and revolutions. pp. 92-93.

[17]*The International Gold Standard Reinterpreted 1914-1934* (New York: National Bureau of Economic Research, 1940), 2 Volumes.

[18]"The main scientific questions which we try to answer are not: What was the *theory* of the functioning of the gold standard . . ." but rather, "What was the *practice* . . ." p. x, "We determined to follow a method of historical analysis . . ." p. xii, "The book is an example, whether successful or not the reader will judge, of the use of history as an instrument of analysis." p. xxvii, Vol. I.

[19]"The central theme is the progressive decentralization of the world's international credit system and the economic changes responsible for it." p. xx. Pages xx-xxvi present a synopsis of Brown's position and explanation of the centralization and decentralization of the world's credit system from 1914-1934. "We have come to the conclusion that the most outstanding characteristic of the financial world in which the gold standard functioned before the war was that it had one center." p. xv, and, "The most striking single feature of the pre-war gold standard system was the highly integrated world banking structure centered in London and operating on the basis of the strong international creditor position of Great Britain." p. 774, Vol. II. For additional references to this crucial point, in the context of Brown's analysis, note also, pp. x, xi, xiv, xvi, xvii, 27, 29, 133, 139, . . ., etc., a point which is repeated throughout his work. This basic position of a single center also appears in Brown's "Gold as a Monetary Standard 1914-1919." *Journal of Economic History*, IX (1949), pp. 39-49.

There were, of course, other financial centers in existence during the nineteenth century but "they, were, however, subordinate to the single financial center in London." p. 47.

On the issue of a single center not all would agree, ". . . but the picture of a single center in the pre-war world is an exaggeration to say the least." Melchior Palyi, "The Meaning of the Gold Standard: A Review Article," *The Journal of Business*, 14 (July 1941), pp. 294-314, p. 297; "All too often . . . the pre-1914 gold standard has been described in terms of the operations of the Bank of England alone . . ." Arthur I. Bloomfield, *Monetary Policy Under the International Gold Standard 1880-1914* (New York: Federal Reserve Bank of New York, 1959), p. 10. And, not all disagree, "To an extent not always realized today, the international economic organization of the nineteenth century was centered on and directed from England. The international gold standard was in effect a sterling standard. London was the commercial and financial heart of the whole system." Ragner Nurkse, *International Currency Experience*, League of Nations Publication (Princeton: Princeton University Press, 1944), p. 195. Problems associated with WWI, the Great Depression and the spread of the process of industrialization splintered the single center into three centers—Great Britain, the United States, and France—created problems of divided responsibility toward divergent ends when unity of command was needed. And in Brown's analysis it was the problems associated with the break up of the nucleus which brought about a disintegration of the gold standard, note, pp. 1051-69 on the "nature of the disintegration."

[20]The basic point here being that as a culture experiences growth and development, the additive and accumulative features are not restricted to the material sector alone but apply to the nonmaterial as well. J.S.G. Wilson in his "Banking," *The International Encyclopedia of the Social Sciences* (1968), Vol. I, notes: "The demand for larger banking is generally a concomitant of economic growth . . ." p. 516. As culture grows and develops, overall, the institutional sector grows and develops as well and this entails change not only as growth but development as well, i.e., transformation. Also as we increase our useful knowledge of banking technics (a process of development) we also aid in the process of further adding to overall economic growth and development, the circular and cumulative causation contained in our wheel of economic development. And as we add to our material technics, such as the steam engine, we also need concomitant social technics such as the factory system and concomitant and commensurate advances in banking technics, transportation technics, political technics, and on. In short, there is a need for an integrated growth and development of the parts in order for the overall whole or the gestalt of technology to function and develop. "A prior condition not only of growth but also of the integration of an economy and its financial institutions (without which larger units could scarcely emerge) is the development of adequate transport facilities and communications,"

ibid. And as the overall gestalt of technology grows and develops, over time, man, interacting with culture, acquires an increased capacity to generate additions to useful knowledge, and when applied and innovated adds new technics, both material and nonmaterial, which are characterized by both replacement (substitution) and accumulation.

[21]Not all technics necessarily experience substitution, accumulation and transformation. For obviously, technics also become a part of culture losses, such as tribal governments and bows and arrows. Also some, though they are still in use, do not experience any great accumulation or transformation, such basic tools as the hammer and ax, the sturgeons of the material world. Concerning nonmaterial culture it is our view that though social institutions need not always accumulate, we submit as a basic proposition that social institutions are nonetheless capable of cumulation.

[22]"Do they function with significant difference in culture? The answer seems No. . . . we may forget about this distinction." Kroeber, *Anthropology*, pp. 295-96. The position, that both material and nonmaterial technics are at root, knowledge, leads Kroeber to conclude that an ax may be considered to be sort of an institution, "In fact we can almost conceive of the ax as an institution . . ." p. 295. To our view, even though both material and nonmaterial technics are in essence made up of useful knowledge this does not lead to the conclusion that material technics, such as an ax, are institutions. Though an ax needs institutional buttresses for the whole or gestalt of the ax technic to function and be operable it is still nonetheless by itself a material technic. And that boys and girls are both of protoplasm we submit to be true but we beseech that there is a difference of significance for analytical purposes. To assume that the distinction between material and nonmaterial culture is of no significance is to assume away the theoretical case of cultural lag. And is cultural lag, a scientific concept which is now even part of our very language (check any dictionary), of no analytical significance and so easily done away with?

[23]Kroeber, *Anthropology*, p. 295.

[24]Note, the previously cited "Acceleration in Social Change," in Allen, ed., *Technology and Social Change*, pp. 27-55, especially pp. 35 ff. "The evidence for acceleration in nonmaterial culture is, however, clear." p. 35, "The principle of cultural acceleration applies to political institutions as well as to mechanical inventions. Social organizations, as well as machines, are developed through the uniting of previously existing elements into new working combinations. The validity of this theory may be verified by checking it against the facts of political history." p. 428.

[25]Ogburn, *Social Change*, pp. 73-79.

[26]"The rate of displacement rarely equals the pace of origination plus borrowing. . . . Instead of constancy, however, culture manifests a cumulative tendency." Honigman, *The World of Man*, p. 236.

[27]In such an instance, for a given culture, in that conceivably the

material technic has not been innovated we may more properly speak of a cultural delay rather than lag. Ogburn noted that Queen Mary, who died in 1953, never used a telephone and spoke of delay rather than lag in such a case, ". . . the failure to adopt a new invention is a delay—not a cultural lag." Duncan, ed., *William F. Ogburn*, p. 89.

[28]Modern social technics of government, for example, could not be operational or function today without the vast underlying matrix of concomitant material technics, such as, buildings, transportation and communications systems, telephones, typewriters, computers and on. Nonetheless though institutions of government require concomitant material technics, to be operational, they are still classified as non-material technics. It is for this reason that we refer to the core of culture in terms of the overall "gestalt" of technology.

[29]"Changes in the scale and character of the organizations by which economic activity is carried on are a necessary concomitant of modern technology. . . . Thus the scale of the units and the size and life of capital investment required by the technology of modern economic growth . . . forced a shift from personal ownership-management units to the large-scale corporation." Simon Kuznets, *Economic Growth and Structure*, pp. 101-103. And also by Kuznets, *Six Lectures on Economic Growth,* and his idea of "The industrial system and its social concomitants . . ." pp. 110-113. Also on the "Social Aspects" of industrialization, note, Wilbert E. Moore, *The International Encyclopedia of the Social Sciences* (1968), Vol. 7, pp. 263-270, especially pp. 267-269. Also, Joseph A. Kahl, "Some Social Concomitants of Industrialization and Urbanization," *Human Organization*, 18 (Summer 1959), pp. 53-74, for additional references pp. 71-74 and for Durkheim's, *The Division of Labor in Society* and his "organic solidarity," pp. 68-70.

[30]There are of course many reservations to such an interpretation. Some contend, and rightly so, that in underdeveloped countries where capital is expensive and labor abundant it may not always be the wisest policy to import material technics from the advanced countries where labor is short and capital is relatively abundant, note, John P. Powelson, *Latin America* (New York: McGraw-Hill Book Company, 1964), p. 280. By the same token we do not necessarily infer that underdeveloped countries should import foreign institutions, some contend that alien foreign institutions may also not be the best in terms of solving the problems of underdeveloped countries. "In broad outline the theme is that . . . to large degree the economic lag and the political instability are a result of the manner which these alien institutions have played their role." Wendell C. Gordon, *The Political Economy of Latin America* (New York: Columbia University Press, 1965), pp. 2, 10 . . ., etc. Gordon's view simply reinforces the institutional problem and specifically notes the exogenous Spanish source. However, granting the reservations as presented by Powelson and Gordon and others, and assuming *ceteris paribus* conditions, we tend to agree with perhaps what is the prevailing view in the literature on development economics, that the problem for underdeveloped countries is not primarily in material

technology but rather is located in the sector of social institutions. "The problem of underdeveloped countries in current discussion . . . is generally viewed as a social problem, originating in the failure of social institutions rather than in lack of technical knowledge." Simon Kuznets in Lekachman, ed., *National Policy for Economic Welfare at Home and Abroad*, p. 99. Also, on this issue note Gunnar Myrdal and especially the *Asian Drama* which rests upon the theme of social and institutional change as a central focus of the problem of economic development. In *An International Economy* (1956) Myrdal set the stage for his later (1968) three volume, *magnum opus*, "The Stage Set for a Great Human Drama," p. 210 and in which he notes: "*To prepare the way for economic development such countries need initial reforms of the social structure on a vast scale*; without them there will be no national integration and so no economic development." p. 171.

[31]Charles J. Erasmus, *Man Takes Control* (Minneapolis: University of Minnesota Press, 1961), presents a similar view: "The very fact that a society *has* a given technology is sufficient evidence that it is ready for it; technological development can hardly advance beyond the limits set by the social environment." p. 312. Erasmus consequently and expectedly, takes a dim view toward the theory of cultural lag. "Known to scientists as cultural lag, this idea persists with ramarkable tenacity at the popular as well as the professional level. Its tenacity is probably partly explainable by its usefulness to many social scientists as a justification for their own professional existence." p. 311. Perhaps Martindale also overstates the case against cultural-lag theory. "Why has the cultural-lag theory persisted in the face of all the criticism which over the years has been raised against it? This can only be attributed to the powerful wish by contemporary man to retain the doctrine of progress in the teeth of apparently fatal objections to it." *Social Life and Cultural Change*, (Princeton: D. Van Nostrand Company, 1962), p. 23. Elsewhere Martindale appears more favorably inclined toward the cultural-lag theory, "The theory (cultural lag) formulates a number of interesting problems that merit study and that are suggestive of the kind of empirical work that might be done to test its validity. This is more than can be said for some of Ogburn's critics, who place themselves in the position of being rejectors and detractors of his work without even bothering to test empirically the many hypotheses easily deducible from Ogburn's formulation of the process of social change." Don Martindale and Elio D. Monachesi, *Elements of Sociology* (New York: Harper and Brothers, 1951), p. 581.

[32]John Kenneth Galbraith, *The New Industrial State* (Boston: Houghton Mifflin Company, 1967) who also as we have already noted, conceptualizes technology as, ". . . the systematic application of scientific or other organized knowledge to practical tasks." p. 12 and in addition notes (again, p. 12) the difficulty of applying knowledge to the whole of automobile production and that in reality we build the whole by accumulating knowledge in the parts which are integrated in the whole. If this view is correct, it would then logically follow that the parts or

technics need not grow in a perfectly synchronized manner, but, rather, are subject to leads and lags even though they are concomitant technics of a specific gestalt such as that of automobile production.

[33]The invention of the automobile was the result of the evolution of relevant elements of the whole. The functional parts of the automobile evolve over time, cf., F. Stuart Chapin, *Cultural Change* (New York : D. Appleton-Century Company, 1928), p. 336, for a good diagramatic presentation of this point.

[34]To speak of a lag of one technic (part) of the automobile behind other technics of the automobile, such as, the wheels, engine and brakes, that one technic moves faster than the others and, consequently, that the pace of development of the other parts must move faster in order to catch up to the other more advanced parts, as a cultural lag, may be viewed by some social scientists as an incorrect usage and interpretation of cultural lag. However, Ogburn, himself, did note in the case of the automobile as an example that the material technics known as highways and parking structures which would also be analogous to our railroad trains and tracks. Note, Allen, ed., *Technology and Social Change* p. 8, and, Duncan, ed., *William F. Ogburn*, pp. 86-87.

[35]This reasoning then is not only applicable to specific gestalts such as that of automobile production but is relevant to the overall gestalt of technology as well. At the level of political economy there are many integral parts of the whole, such as transportation, credit and banking, communication, government, the production of goods and services. . . ., etc., in that a limit in the development of one part would consequently place a ceiling on the advance of the whole. "An interesting question is the part played by transportation, and, lately by communication inventions in the evolution of states in size. . . . When the transportation techniques used are poor, such as human muscle, the nation or empire cannot be very large. The stage of the transportation systems sets a limit somewhere on size. "William F. Ogburn, ed., *Technology and International Relations* (Chicago : University of Chicago Press, 1949), p. 8. As another example and in the context of the European political economy the retention of the outmoded nation state would serve as a limit on the overall advance or economic development of the region. The stagnation of a part, a social institution, a political technic known as the nation state, must give way to change and supranationalism if the whole is to continue to grow and develop. Also on this issue note : Hornell Hart, "Technology and the Growth of Political Areas," in William F. Ogburn, ed., *Technology and International Relations*, pp. 28-57, "Transportational inventions and discoveries are inextricably part of much more inclusive cultural developments. . . . Far more significant and useful results can be obtained by more fundamental analysis of cultural change in its more inclusive aspects." pp. 56-57, and, "Instead of regarding the individual transportational invention as the cause, and the predictive symptom, of subsequent political growth, do the facts of past cultural development require us to

recognize such inventions as inseparable parts of technological progress, which must be studied as a whole before any reliable and useful predictions and principles of action can be derived?" p. 28.

[36]On the point that either the material or social can lead, not only the material, in the formation of a cultural lag, note, Duncan, *William F. Ogburn*, pp. xvi, 132-133, and Hornell Hart in Allen, *Technology and Social Change*, p. 422.

[37]The major one being the acceleration in material technology of nuclear missile capability which has not been matched by our capacity to govern. Another major cultural lag occurs in world-wide economic development. The movement toward a New International Economic Order does not focus on applied engineering for material culture but rather is concerned with new social structure for the world economy.

[38]This constitutes, perhaps, Veblen's best essay, note, Thorstein Veblen, *The Place of Science in Modern Civilization and Other Essays* (New York: Russell & Russell, 1961), pp. 1-32. Veblen did not however feel that social organization would be permeable to science (matter-of-fact) but rather that social institutions absorbed "worldly knowledge" and therefore were static and not dynamic. In the framework of *cultural economics*, and specifically with the dichotomy of useful knowledge, the view presented is that both material and social technics are potentially capable of absorbing scientific knowledge and, therefore, that social institutions, as well as material technics, can also serve dynamic functions.

[39]On this general issue, compare the willingness of the Ford Motor Company to accept the material technic of the moving assembly versus their willingness to accept the social technic known as a trade union or in the international sector, the steam ship and screw propeller versus the League of Nations. The social sciences are to begin with of much more recent vintage than the physical sciences. For in order to have science applied to the social sector, we must first more fully develop the social sciences, and then gradually over time to have the social sciences become more and more accepted as tools used in the invention of new social technic. Such social acceptance and institutionalization is not inconceivable, one need only reflect how recent and how difficult it was for science to emerge in the physical world, for example, with the trials and tribulations of Galileo (1564-1642), Tycho Brahe (1546-1601), and Giordano Bruno (1548?-1600). Social acceptance of science to social organization, however, is not only conceivable, but, as we have noted in several instances, it is already manifest in such nascent experiments of the process as deficit spending, the IMF and EEC. On "the problem of social invention," note, Francis, E. Merrill, *Culture and Society* (New York: Prentice-Hall, 1952), pp. 110-113.

[40]Hornell Hart has presented a good deal of systematic thought on this basic issue and focuses on the cultural lag between the material and the social especially in the context of the atomic crisis. "Our crisis may well be formulated in terms of the lag of social science behind material science. But if we are to have any realistic hope of bringing

social science to bear effectively on the solution of the world crisis, it is necessary that we obtain first at least some small degree of scientific understanding of the nature of cultural lag itself." Allen, ed., *Technology and Social Change*, p. 417. And while Hart has written a good deal on this we refer specifically, in addition, to "Atomic Cultural Lag." *Sociology and Social Research*, 32 (1947-48), pp. 768-775, pp. 768-769. We accept Hart's reasoning in the specific area of atomic crisis but we in this study attempt to apply our analytical tools to the more generalised issue of economic development. In the context of our wheel of economic development, the acceptance of the application of science to social organization will not only add to the creation and invention of new social technics but will aid in culture permeability or the innovation of such technics and in so doing more smoothly synchronize the advance of material and nonmaterial culture, i.e., a frictionless wheel of economic development. Science, as the invention of invention, needs greater acceptance in the social sector equivalent to that now given in the material sector of culture.

[41]On this general theme note the "Successive-Emergence Theory of Intellectual Progress," first suggested by Auguste Comte. cf., Allen, ed., *Technology and Social Change*, pp. 512-516, and for the quotation note above (Hart), p. 512.

CHAPTER IX

Exponential Culture Evolution and Paradigm of Logistic Surges

We have noted in our previous chapter that culture does not accumulate and advance without friction. And though cultural lags are characteristic of the process of culture evolution it is to be noted that culture, nonetheless, does accumulate. Cultural lags do not negate the exponential nature of general culture evolution. Cultural lags represent relative short-run problems, in the very long-run, and again in the context of general and not specific culture evolution, cultural lags tend to be adjusted and melt away. "In the long perspective of history, though lags are not visible because they have been caught up. They are visible phenomena largely at the present time."[1] We now come to an interesting part of our anaysis of the processes of economic development. The focus of this chapter is directed toward structure, what can be said concerning the structure of general culture evolution? Historically though the wheel of economic development has spun with at times under tremendous stress and strain in the adjustment of cultural lags, it still has spun. If we ultimately override cultural lags in the long-run and our wheel of development spins what then is the resulting structure or paradigm of the process of economic development and culture evolution? Of the conceivable alternative paths, note figure IX-1, "Possible Alternative Paths of the Development Curve" we will argue in this chapter that the long-term path of culture evolution is exponential and envelops the underlying paradigm of logistic surges.

The fundamental contribution of Ogburn has been in the

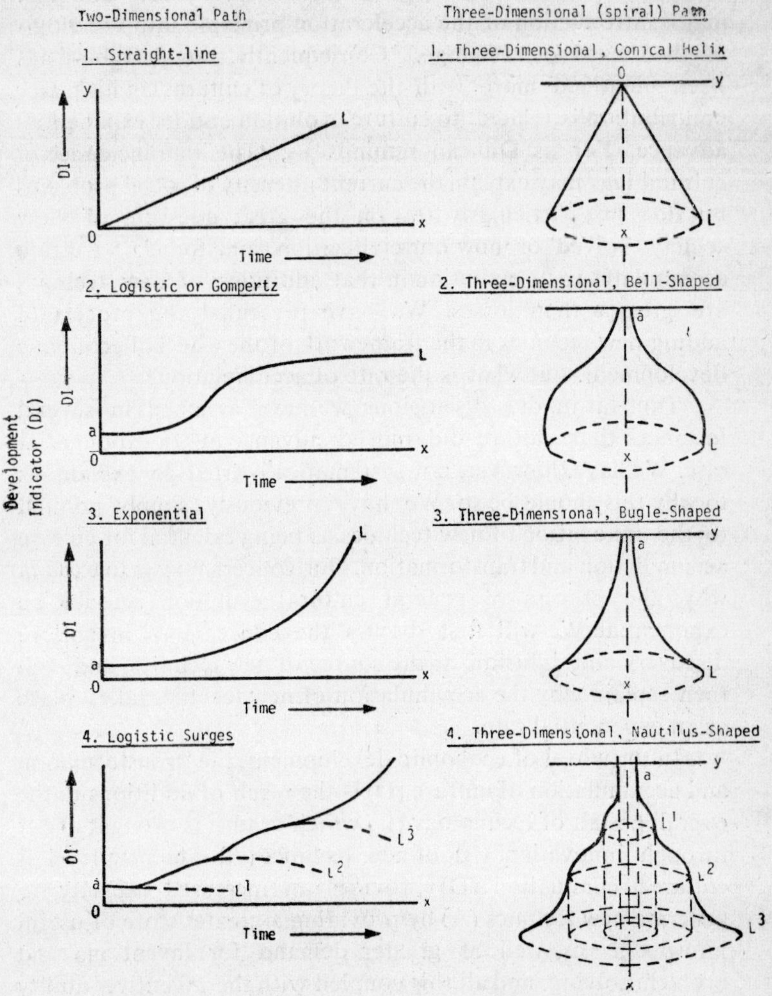

Fig. IX-1. Alternative Paths of the Development Curve

overall area of culture evolution and in his application of the anthropologist's conceptualization of culture (Tylor's) to sociology.[2] And in this regard Ogburn provided, "The first major introduction of the acceleration principle into sociological theories of social change."[3] Consequently, though Ogburn has been identified more with the theory of cultural lag his major contribution is related to culture evolution and its exponential advance. For as Duncan reminds us, "The high incidence of cultural lags may explain the current intensity of social problems but does not particularly bear on the great question of 'how society evolved' or 'how our civilization came to be'."[4] Culture accumulates in its evolution in that additions of new technics are greater than losses. We have presented the process of adding new technics in the framework of the wheel of economic development. But what is the rate of accumulation?

Thus far in our discussions we have assumed in several instances that culture did indeed advance at an exponential rate. We have, however, not systematically tried to explain as to why this should be so. We have previously simply pointed to the innovation of new technics as being essential for culture accumulation and transformation. Our concern now is to explain why the process of general cultural evolution should be exponential. We will first discuss the concepts of invention, discovery and diffusion, as the source of new technics, and will then explain why the accumulation of new technics takes place at an exponential rate.

In the wheel of economic development, the transformation and accumulation of culture (D) is the result of additions to the overall gestalt of technology (C) which in turn is brought about through innovation (B) of new technics (A). The new level of culture accumulation (D) provides an increased capacity to generate new technics (A) by providing a greater store of useful knowledge as well as greater demand for inventions and problem solving, and all this coupled with the inventive ability of the population.[5] A culture accumulates through new technics; these technics are potential additions to the store of useful knowledge, which when innovated become integral parts of the overall gestalt of technology. New technics are distinguished by their source of either the endogenous, as the intra-culture invention and discovery, or the inter-culture source of diffusion.[6]

Although not always treated in precisely the same way it is generally recognized that culture accumulation is based upon invention and discovery, our new technics, which then spread to other cultures through diffusion or internally, in a given or specific culture, through replication.[7] Although distinctions may be drawn in that an invention is the creation of something new, that is without prior existence, as to be found in a new "combination of existing and known elements of culture," for example (an internal combustion engine), whereas a discovery is a newly-found awareness of something that already exists (the double helix), both are endogenous ways in which to add new elements to the cultural store of knowledge and consequently in our study are both referred to as new technics.[8] And, of course, fundamental to our analysis would be that such new technics, the elements of culture accumulation, may be either material or nonmaterial.[9] Whether a new element of useful knowledge, the new technic, which accumulates in a specific culture as a store of knowledge, is in origin a discovery or invention, or is received through diffusion, is in itself a conceptual problem and the distinction may not always be that easy. In this study our overall concern is culture evolution and economic development, and we have noted that culture accumulates and is transformed by new elements (be they by invention or discovery) which we have called new technics. Most would agree that culture accumulates and is transformed by the flow and innovation of new technics but why is that flow and innovation assumed to be exponential?

Ogburn's theory of exponential culture evolution rests on the position that inventions provide the basis for culture accumulation.[10] Accumulation occures when more new elements, as inventions, are added to the culture base than are lost. The enlarged culture base provides a potential for exponential evolution in that invention is in actuality a combination of existing elements. These elements accumulate and, as with compound interest, knowledge begets knowledge. Probability dictates that the geometric progression, marking the advance of invention, is manifest in exponential culture evolution.[11]

A stages-type of analysis as we have presented previously clearly fits the Ogburnian exponential framework in that earlier or primitive stages of economic development and cultural evolution would be characterized by fewer inventions and slower rates of culture accumulation.[12] Primitive cultures have little capacity to generate new elements (our technics) when compared to the scientific-industrial complex of cultures marked by the stage of economic development known as industrialism. Overall statistical date related to culture accumulation and technological change empirically bear out Ogburn's theoretical position. Empirical support appears not as direct measures of the process but rather as indirect indicators of the results. And as we have already noted, one of the best overall indicators would be that of energy consumption. And not just that we consume more energy in an exponential paradigm with the advance of culture, but that the structure and form of energy changes as well.[13] How does one level or even budge Ogburn's theortical mountain?

The Ogburnian theory of culture and social evolution and the hypothesis of cultural acceleration is at variance with the conclusions reached by a number of economists. In assessing Ogburn's exponential accumulation Schmookler notes: "Few ideas have proved so intuitively attractive with so little foundation in either logic or evidence."[14] Whereas the sociologist might be more prone to explain in the context of emphasizing social forces the economist is by the same token more prone to atomistic reasoning as explanation.[15] The main-line economist has generally been traditionally molded in an intellectual environment supporting a more anthropocentric view whereas the sociologist and anthropologist by comparison are generally, though not always, more oriented towords the social and cultural as explanation.[16] The sociologist and anthropologist would be more inclined to say that culture molds the behavior patterns of the rugged individualist and the economist traditionally that the rugged individualist molds culture. In the framework of circular and cumulative causation both positions are possibly correct.[17] It would then be more consistent for the sociologist and anthropologist to tend to view the acceleration of inventions as perhaps inexorable and inevitable, a view not quite accepted by academicians nurtured in training as economists.[18] As we have already noted, economists have only recently engaged the study of technological change, and consequently the study of invention as well. However, while in part overcoming his past inertia to the extent to at least examine the issue of economic development the economist is still reluctant to develop new tools of analysis and relies upon traditional economic analysis as methodology to examine the processes of invention and technological change. We question the logic of substituting for an Ogburnian-type framework of social and cultural change, traditional economic analysis which as a theoretical framework was traditionally formulated to exclude these elements from its purview. This is not to deny the inherent logic and validity of traditional theory insofar as it was and is applied to restricted areas concerning market analysis but rather to deny the logic of applying such strict and rigorous economic analysis to problems such as inventions and technological change which are essentially sociocultural in nature. Economists, using traditional tools of economic analysis, have engaged the study of inventions, inventive activity, and technological change.[19] The basic weakness of these studies is that at best the conclusions are based upon partial evidence in that the analysis of invention is restrictively relegated to economic analysis whereas in reality inventions are basically of culture in terms of origin, substance, and effect.

There are two conceivable approaches which might be used to analyze and indicate the exponential accumulation of culture. We might on the one hand look at the flow of new technics and view the advance of culture evolution from the vantage of *inputs.* Or we might view the results of the process as the end product of innovation and assess or measure the process in terms of *output.*[20] Hornell Hart tends to look at the *output* side of the ledger and presents empirical results of the process to indicate acceleration of culture and technology. On the output side, the empirical evidence for general culture evolution appears to clearly indicate an exponential accumulation of technology and culture. What is more subject to question in the literature concerns the input side as the process of inventive activity. For example, Sanders apparently does not question the fact of culture acceleration but rather questions the procedure of equating culture acceleration with that of inventions.[21]

Although there are currently, apparently, no direct measures of inventive activity might we still nonetheless surmise a general pattern (as distinguished from direct numerical quantification of specific magnitudes) as would be theoretically expected from the results of such activity. This is the basic approach of Hornell Hart, in that if technology and culture, as results, accumulate exponentially, such acceleration tends to support the "principle of invention by combination" which infers an acceleration of invention.[22] That all new technics are not innovated is a reasonable assumption but the fact that in actuality technology and culture accumulate with acceleration also infers that innovation has kept pace with the exponential pattern.[23] And in our framework, the wheel of economic development, if technology (C) and culture (D) accumulate with acceleration, as a result of innovation, it would then follow that the sources of accumulation (the new technics), which feed the development process, also, must increase at faster and faster rates. Though the potential for accumulation offered to culture in the form of new technics is greater than that actually innovated does not refute the hypothesis that patterns of inputs of inventive activity, as with outputs of technology and culture, might be those of acceleration. Since the overall of culture and technology grows at an exponential rate, should not the elements of addition, the new material and nonmaterial technics, also be advancing in a similar exponential pattern though not necessarily at the same rate or of the same magnitude or qnantity.

Therefore in that culture and technology, as outputs of the process of innovation, accumulate with acceleration it is inferred that the inputs of invention also accelerate as well. However, instead of looking at our circle from the vantage of outflow or output, let us take a reverse spin and view the process from the side of inflow or inputs. Instead of looking at the results of the exponential addition of new technics let us now look at the new technics from the vantage of inputs. Why not, for example, try to directly measure inventive activity from the input side to determine and verify the rate of accumulation? Such an approach would involve a variety of conceptual problems and the associated difficulties of definition and measurement. What precisely constitutes an invention, and what should be included in the overall classification?[24] Should social invention, discoveries and science be included in the conceptualization of invention?[25] Given the conceptual difficulties and the very nature of inventive activity most apparently agree that a direct measure of inventive activity is not possible.[26]

However, if we are correct in our assumption that new technics (inventions) are in essence manifestations of useful knowledge, it would then follow that changes in the stock of knowledge would also serve to indicate changes in inventive activity and the rate of invention. But we have already noted that knowledge is a protean concept and, consequently, in the nature of its many forms defies direct measurement.[27] Nonetheless, that while direct measures of the advance of the whole, as the entire stock of useful knowledge, are not available we do find in the literature studies which indicate an exponential advance of knowledge.[28] If science as such an important part of the whole of useful knowledge is advancing exponentially, cannot we infer that the whole is also accelerating.

Derek J. de Solla Price notes the "law of exponential growth" in the context of scientific journals as well as the actual numbers of scientific papers found in those journals. Based upon empirical evidence in the form of statistical and numerical indicators of the growth of science the conclusion is that:

> "All of these show with impressive consistency and regularity that if any sufficiently large segment of science is measured in any reasonable way the mode of growth is exponential . . . . The law has, however, several remarkable features, and from it a number of powerful conclusions can be drawn. Indeed, it is so far reaching that I have no hesitation in suggesting it as the fundamental law of any analysis of science."[29]

Given our current tools of analysis conclusive answers must be viewed with caution, but Price does provide empirical evidence in support of his contentions.[30] Basically Price supports the position that science has historically advanced in the exponential mode of growth. From the vantage of the past record of culture evolution then, the evidence presented by Price tends to support the exponential theory of Ogburn.[31] Price, however, apparently questions the continuity of the exponential advance of science into the future and is of the opinion that a point of inflection has been reached and that the overall pattern will be that of the logistic rather than ongoing acceleration. To our view, by comparison, the Ogburn-Hart position, as well as the Veblen-Ayres tradition in economics, goes even further and would support the position that the exponential accumulation of science and culture will continue on into the proximate future as a basic "Law of Progress."[32] Price, in contradiction, feels that ultimately the exponential advance of science will reach saturation and level off. This constitutes a suggested "second basic law of the analysis of science: all the apparently exponential laws of growth ultimately must be logistic."[33] However, we will develop the position in the remainder of this chapter that there are no compelling reasons to assume that science, overall, cannot continue to grow exponentially. Given the assumption of continuous changes in structure, as a series of logistic surges in the various fields of science, the resulting path could conceivably be one of ongoing exponential acceleration.[34]

But these discussions concern the future and prognosis. The fact remains that at least up to the present the historical record indicates that on the input side science has advanced exponentially.[35] In terms of output, the evidence is also clear that in the context of general culture evolution, both culture and technology have advanced with exponential accumulation. Indeed, Hornell Hart, who has provided empirical evidence in support of culture acceleration is apparently correct when he states: "The reality of acceleration in technological growth can scarcely be doubted by any intelligent person who is acquainted with the facts."[36] Consequently, the evidence indicates that both from the *input* side, as knowledge and science, and from the *output* side as technology, that the accumulation has been exponential. Therefore, Ogburn's exponential accumulation of culture is not just hypothesis, or supposition but, given the empirical evidence, is vindicated and apparently stands as theory. Though the synapse between theory and the empirical evidence represents a difficult connection to prove conclusively, the logic of Ogburn's theory and explanation coincides with the expected results of exponential culture accumulation.

Given Ogburn's theory as being correct, that general

culture evolution is marked by acceleration, that knowledge begets knowledge, that new elements as the new technics of invention and discovery are added to the overall of technology to produce exponential accumulation, how can it then be explained that all cultures do not follow the exponential paradigm? How can it be maintained that culture advances exponentially when two-thirds of the world's population are locked into the logistic and experience secular stagnation? For the LDC world the historic pattern of economic development has been in the form of the logistic and not the exponential. In the Kuhnian framework how do we then explain the unexpected result, the anomaly of the logistic.

If the process once starts, and if knowledge begets knowledge, why does it stop and reach satiation in the context of certain specific cultures? Given the phenomenon of "simultaneous" inventions, as a universal characteristic of cultures everywhere, that the process of invention appears to be inexorable and continuous, what then stops it? At first glance in the context of the wheel of economic development the most obvious answer would reside in culture permeability. Though a given culture be continuously bombarded by new technics, environmental permeability may not permit penetration. The composite environment of culture and physical resources may serve as a dam, rather than a net, and hold back the inevitable and inexorable flow of new technics in their innovation. But the issue before us is more complex and not so easily explained. In the process of providing our answer we will also hopefully provide a more fundamental and penetrating analysis of the structure and nature of the evolution of knowledge. More is involved than simple culture permeability, for even if we were to assume, for example, that the culture and the physical environment proved propitious and permeable would the end result necessarily be exponential, as Ogburn and others lead us to believe?

Let us back track a bit. The underlying assumption behind our general theory is that knowledge in its advance provides the basis for the dynamics of culture evolution and economic development. Our own basic ignorance of the history of the idea and its evolution prevents our giving full pride of place to the true originators but certainly one of the recognized and most penetrating intellects to have dealt with the issue before us would be Thorstein Bunde Veblen.[37] In terms of method, in trying to understand the advance to knowledge and its structure, let us look at the whole before trying to understand the parts. And who would be better at the "holistic" than Veblen?

Whereas others also dealt with knowledge and the whole of culture, Veblen's originality pushed all this a bit further and applied the concepts to the processes of economic development and evolution. Veblen's famous dichotomy split culture into the technological or material on the one hand and the ceremonial or social, as the nonmaterial, on the other. Matter-of-fact knowledge, science, has the capacity to accumulate and with acceleration; "wordly wisdom," by comparison as ad hoc knowledge, does not accumulate and stagnates. According to Veblen it is the former type of knowledge, as the matter-of-fact, which is funneled into technology and explains the dynamic characteristics of technology. And it is the latter type of knowledge, worldly wisdom, which is absorbed into the social or institutional structure and accounts for its static nature. Therefore at root, Veblen's famous dichotomy was founded upon the capacity of different sectors of culture to absorb different types of knowledge. And this basic dichotomy has been characteristic of all stages of economic development in the long-term evolution of culture. "The Place of Science in Modern Civilization" is that the advance and application of science serves to promote the dynamics of economic evolution and constitutes the core of culture.[38]

Apparently Veblen's conceptualization of technology did not include social technics. Veblen argued that social institutions as the ceremonial and the static lagged behind the dynamic sector of material culture, especially machinery.[39] Social technics did not manifest the dynamic tendencies of accumulation and acceleration in that they were not permeable to the matter-of-fact type of knowledge. Ayres, however, went beyond this and tended to move mainstream institutional thought toward a conceptualization of technology to include the social as well as the material.[40] With *cultural economics* we have carried the mainstream institutional conceptualization of technology to its logical conclusion which would be a culture-conceptualization of technology.

Therefore, technology does not simply comprise material technics but given an holistic or culture conceptualization would include both the material and the social as an organic totality or gestalt. Whereas Ayres perhaps implied that social institutions as social organization might comprise integral parts of technology, our conceptualization explicitly states that social institutions, as social technics, are integral parts of the overall of technology. Technology, in the framework of the dichotomy of useful knowledge, is the opposite face of the core of culture and, consequently, has as integral parts the non-material as well as the material. It would then follow, a basic hypothesis, that if both social and material technics are potentially permeable to useful knowledge (Veblen's matter-of-fact), we would then expect that the same evolutionary process and structure would prevail for both material and nonmaterial culture. That is not to say that the material and social would move with synchronization and at the same rate of acceleration but rather that the process and resulting structure would be the same. We speak here of the process of advancing useful knowledge and the resulting structure of logistic surges leading to the overall of exponential acceleration.

Given our culture-conceptualization of technology and, further, the assumption that useful knowledge is not thwarted in its advance and application and is allowed to freely penetrate in the form of new social and material technics, would we not expect even more so that *all* cultures would advance along an exponential path of accumulation. What then holds it back to produce the logistic? Given the assumption that the culture is permeable to the new knowledge could the end result be logistic rather than exponential? We will now argue that this is indeed the case.

Now assuming that nothing prevents permeability, what inhibits the continuity of the exponential and bends it to produce the logistic is the ceiling imposed by the limits of perfectability. What limits the capacity for any specific technic to grow and develop exponentially, is that ultimately we satiate the possibilities for further improvement and perfection. If it is correct to assume that a specific technic grows and develops and is transformed because it has the capacity to absorb advances in useful knowledge, it then follows that to cut off the flow of knowledge, for whatever reason, we also cut off the process and capacity for continued growth, development and transformation. In so doing we then produce the logistic or typical "*S*" curve configuration. What terminates the flow in this case is not the lack of culture permeability but rather that for any given or specific technic the result is satiation or stagnation in its perfection.

Given the propeller driven aircraft of 1903, vintage Wright brothers, there was plenty of room for improvement. In the post-WWII period, though thousands of engineers might try, there was an obvious limit as to what could be accomplished in the confines or structure of propeller driven aircraft. Using miles per hour as the development indicator (DI) the data clearly reveal the logistic.[41] It is our position that the growth and development path for any specific technic, either material or nonmaterial will be of the form, the structure, of the logistic. Consequently, whether the specific technic be of the form of propeller driven aircraft, canals, or a particular industry such as textiles, or an energy resource such as petroleum, or even as the overall gestalt of technology in the form of a specific stage of economic development, the end result is a growth and development curve of the logistic and/or Gompertz configuration.

In order to identify and delineate the point being made here we will refer to this principle, that any technic satiates in its perfection, as the *Hopi Indian Syndrome*. Ogburn noted in explaining stationary societies, that given the technics, as equipment and methods used by the Hopi Indians in corn production, that modern scientific agriculturalists could not improve upon the end results.[42] Therefore even though we freely admit to new ideas, as new elements or technics, we ultimately satiate the possible ways of improvement of a given technic. Therefore, for a given or specific technic, the Hopi Indian Syndrome prevails, and we find ultimately that there are limits in perfection. Has our world of theory gone topsy turvy, are we now trying to maintain that ultimately the inevitable path for knowledge as it is concreted into material and nonmaterial technology is the logistic and not the exponential?

For the remainder of the chapter we will argue that both configurations are correct manifestations of the path of culture evolution and the process of economic development. It is correct to assume that each specific technic, as a given gestalt, satiates in its perfection. But we refer here to *specific* evolution, *general* evolution by comparison has the configuration of the exponential.[43] The solution of ongoing exponential evolution rests not in the perfection of a given gestalt but rather in the transformation, as a "gestalt switch," of a given technic to the next level as a logistic surge.[44] We have already drawn attention in many instances to the fact that the exponential curve of development is really an overall curve covering the underlying structure of logistic surges. Empirical manifestations of the paradigm of logistic surges appear in transportation as a series of gestalt switches from foot travel on to jets and rockets. In energy development the paradigm of logistic surges also appears as the basic structure underlying the exponential. Therefore, the evolutionary process of economic development entails both the perfection and satiation of given structures and forms as well as to the genesis of new forms and structures. The point being that exponential growth requires periodic structural changes, as new forms, in order to be maintained on an ongoing continuum. In the literature this is referred to as the "principle of similitude."[45] Now that we have presented somewhat of an overview let us once again look at some of the specific parts Let us look once again at the world of experience to provide empirical details as the muscle and flesh for our skeletal structure of theory.

For example does a particular or specific stage of economic development develop and grow in the configuration of the logistic as our above explanation would lead us to believe.

Rostow, in his stages' analysis, views a "traditional society" as constituting a ceiling or limit on economic growth.[46] A traditional society characterized by pre-Newtonian science represents a given level or stage of economic development (a given overall gestalt of technology) having a limit or ceiling on its economic development and growth. With a given or fixed overall gestalt of technology economic growth through replication and duplication would ultimately lead to saturation and stagnation, the logistic curve and the realities of Ricardian diminishing returns.[47]

In neoclassical theory a declining MP curve can be overcome by a shift in the entire curve brought about by technological change. But as we have noted, that for a given technic, even if such a technic is viewed as a stage of economic development, the possibilities for continued technological change are limited. Consequently, in that the potential for technological change for a given stage is finite and that technological change will ultimately cease, as the gestalt satiates in its perfection, we conclude, that, ultimately, the Law of Diminishing Returns will prevail. If, for example, the overall gestalt of technology is marked by hunting and gathering and fixed, economic development is also limited to that stage, and once the material and nonmaterial technics have been replicated or duplicated, economic growth in turn would ultimately reach a saturation point. To break the ceiling imposed upon economic growth and to advance along the road of economic development man had to transform the hunting and gathering gestalt to a higher level, to a new gestalt of greater energy control, and this was accomplished with the invention, discovery and innovation of the new technics of farming and animal husbandry. Continued growth and development was consequently predicated not only on the perfection of the old structure (hunting and gathering), but also, on the genesis of an entirely new structure or form in the context of the Agricultural Revolution. But such a transformed culture, Rostow's traditional society with its agrarian base, represents in itself a new ceiling on economic growth, a given overall gestalt of technology ultimately limiting economic growth unless it is transformed to the next stage of economic development. The transformation of the traditional society in the context of the European experience was accomplished through the establishment of certain "preconditions" (our stage No. III—The Commercial Revolution) which in turn paved the way for the further transformation of culture to the "take-off" or the Industrial Revolution. The new gestalt, characterized by industrialism, has provided man with a capacity for sustained economic growth in the flux of continuous culture transformation fed by the dynamics of modern science.

It should be noted that in the context of a traditional society, though the overall gestalt as a level is fixed, this does not imply a completely unchanging or static society in terms of economic growth and development within the confines of its

overall technological limitations (recall our discussions concerning the antebollism South).[48] A given overall gestalt of technology viewed as an overall technic, as one big technic of culture, becomes more developed as it grows and is refined and perfected over time, in a way similar to that of a particular material or social technic, for example: such as the steam engine or steam powered railroads, or propeller driven aircraft or the gestalt of the textile industry as a whole.[49] We improve the material technic, such as a steam engine, over time, but ultimately a saturation point is reached in terms of speed, efficiency and power. This, of course, is not to deny the growth and development of the technic (engine) over time but rather to note the inevitable ceiling and limit.[50]

Changes are always taking place in a given culture. These changes may lead to a greater perfection and development of a given technological gestalt, such as the role of the cotton gin in the transition from tobacco to cotton as it led to the development growth and perfection of the plantation-slavocracy in the South. However, such development and growth (specific evolution) of a given gestalt, as it specializes and adapts, leads to a dead-end evolutionary path of stagnation as would be the case with the sturgeon in the context of biological evolution. Greater adaptation and specialization of a given technological gestalt leads to greater rigidity and inflexibility and the given culture tends to prepetuate itself and resists (becomes more impermeable) to new technics of transformation.[51] And, as we have noted, a specific culture which consigns energy conversion to the human machine is indeed limited in its capacity for growth and development. As a general hypothesis: the retention or maintenance of a given stage of economic development, in terms of perfecting a given gestalt of technolgoy, places an ultimate limit or ceiling on economic growth and development.

Therefore while a specific culture is always in a state of flux ongoing economic development of a culture, on a continuum and in line with the process of general culture evolution, entails direction toward higher stages of economic development and not simply change. Economic development on an exponential continuum, on a scale of higher and higher levels of technology, entails the transformation of gestalt at low energy levels to gestalts of higher energy levels and not just development and growth within the context of a given gestalt. In this context, developmental policy for underdeveloped countries should not be for the development, refinement and perfection of a given gestalt, but rather for focusing on the issue of greater flexibility and permeability to new technics to aid in the transformation to a more advanced level of technology, a more advanced gestalt, which appears in the new structure of a higher stage of economic development.

Such a view is, of course, completely counter to the Ricardian theory of comparative advantage, the Ricardian assumptions being that through specialization and perfection, by becoming more efficient in the context of a given gestalt, a society may achieve economic development on a continuum. The emphasis is not on the transformation of given gestalt to a higher level but rather the perfection of a given gestalt through greater specialization. In the confines of the logistic such a policy may conceivably lead to a good deal of growth but ultimately such growth will reach a saturation and stagnation. Staunch supporters of the classical position such as Jacob Viner, consequently, support the view that industrialism and industrialization are not necessary conditions for economic development but rather that the key is to be found in more efficient agriculture. In part such a view is correct if the assumption is made that efficient agriculture will be achieved if the culture in question ultimately embraces industrialism, but this is clearly not what the classical school or Jacob Viner had in mind. It is to developmental economists such as Myrdal and Prebisch that we must turn for theoretical buttresses supporting institutional and structural changes leading to industrialization as necessary conditions of economic development. And such would also be the conclusion given the methodology of *cultural economics*. The idea of a new structure serving as a prerequisite for economic development is also manifest in the movement of the 1970's directed toward a new International Economic Order.

The Southern economy in the United States as it developed and grew, also developed and perfected and solidified its basic social institutions and material technics and as a result became more intransigent to political and social change. As a given overall technological gestalt becomes perfected and as it develops it becomes more difficult to generate and innovate new technics, analogous to the specific gestalt of propeller driven aircraft. As we move to a new overall gestalt of culture and/or as we move to jet aircraft the potential for a whole new variety of technics presents itself. However for a given, fixed gestalt represented by a specific stage of culture or in the instance of a particular material technic, such as propeller driven aircraft, a period of exponential increase would then be followed by saturation and inevitably a plateau. But not only does a fixed gestalt limit the new technics generated from endogenous sources but it in all probability would tend to make the culture less permeable to new technics from the source of diffusion.

Such a culture is then all the more likely to stagnate and not to experience a continuance of economic development. And the stagnation or lack of development could conceivably continue for long periods in that such cultures may be viable and endure and may maintain populations though at constant or lower living standards. Given the fixity of the overall gestalt such a culture would approximate a plateau of saturation as its structural walls become more rigid to change and less permeable to new technics. The wheel of economic development, consequently, no longer spins an expanding spiral, the wheel becomes closed and saturation and stagnation set in, a situation for which the two-dimensional growth configuration is a logistic curve and the three-dimensional configuration a cylindrical helix.

Therefore, by viewing the overall exponential pattern intrinsically as a series of logistic surges we see that while culture as a whole thereby has accelerated, such need not be the case for all cultures. For if a given culture is confined to a given stage of economic development by its incapacity to transform its technological gestalt, the result will be the logistic pattern and stagnation. Consequently, the Ogburn-Hart framework is amenable to an explanation of both the exponential advance of culture as well as the possible stagnation and deterioration of cultures.[52]

Given the analysis and theory of this chapter we are now in a better position to discuss and explain the logistic surges inherent in the evolution of culture and manifest in the stages

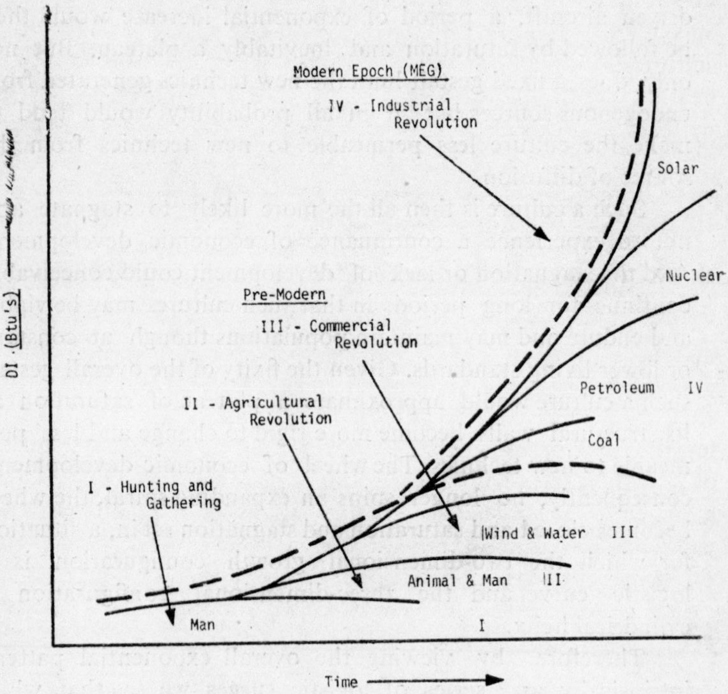

Fig. IX-2. The Exponential Evolution of Culture and the Stages of Economic Development.

of economic development. In figure IX-2, "The Exponential Evolution of Culture and the Stages of Economic Development", we have a composite presentation of our analysis and framework and similar to the graphic presentation contained in Chapter V, "Energy Transformation as an Indicator of the Process of Economic Development." We have also noted two major divisions, the modern epoch (MEG) and the pre-modern epoch. The latter embracing a good deal of time and little culture accumulation and the former which exhibits a good deal of accumulation within much shorter time span. This pattern is precisely the expected result, given the assumption of exponential culture evolution. The pre-modern epoch would embrace the three basic stages: I, The Hunting and Gathering; II, The Agricultural Revolution; and III, The Commercial Revolution.

These stages, historically, might be distinguished by a variety of development indicators, by the types and sources and levels of energy control, by the types of tool, by the growth and size of population, by its capacity for economic growth, with each stage representing a particular gestalt of technology.[53] Each stage would be characterised by a particular type of growth in terms of the quantity of growth as well as its quality.[54] The material technics of the hoe and plow as products and as tools would not be available in a stage I (hunting and gathering) type of culture in the sense of a fixed gestalt but rather as they were invented and innovated would mark the transformation of a stage I level of economic development to stage II. If our objective is to elevate the living standards of the two-thirds of mankind living in conditions of underdevelopment, and if we agree that living standards are determined by the production, availability and distribution of goods and services, the way to achieve this growth on a continuum is through a continuum of economic development.

In short, if an underdeveloped country wishes to push its production frontier out far enough to achieve the standards of living of the advanced countries, it can only do so through economic development, that is, the process of transforming the gestalt of technology to the overall gestalt characterized by industrialism. We have, of course, noted that underdeveloped countries may grow and develop as "traditional societies" but such growth is not open-ended and has a ceiling or limitation imposed by its limited technology. Consequently, the economic growth of a "traditional society" must come to a dead-end and that dead-end or plateau in economic growth would take place far short of the economic growth and living standards characteristic of cultures in the stage of industrialism. We consequently in the process might "perfect" the gestalt of a traditional society but such a gestalt is limited in its capacity to generate economic growth and further economic development.

To simply grow is not enough since growth by itself is not sufficient for economic development. Economic growth on a continuum of higher and higher levels is consequently a function of economic development and such growth will not be achieved simply by growing but is a function and characteristic of economic development.[55] Consequently, sustained rates of growth of GNP per capita and at high levels characteristic of cultures in the modern stage of industrialism will not be achieved by underdeveloped countries, regardless of the intensity of effort, the magnitude of resources, or the magnitudes of factor inputs applied to such an endeavor unless the culture in question has achieved the stage of economic development characterized by industrialism.[56] Consequently, if we are to elevate the levels of production of the underdeveloped world commensurate with the developed, we must raise the level of technology which serves as the basic constraint or ceiling on economic growth for the LDC's.

That technology is the basic limiting factor of continuous economic growth is also recognized in the literature.[57] And we have tried to explain how and why. Growth as a long-term continuum is characteristic of the process of economic development and if development stops, that is, if advances in technology are not forthcoming, growth will reach a ceiling or limit. Growth by itself will not produce development but rather, itself, will produce the logistic pattern; in short we do not develop simply by growing.[58] In the framework of the "principle of similitude" we again note that ongoing growth requires structural change. In the overall path of economic development and general culture evolution, growth on an exponential continnum requires a change in structure manifest in the transformation of one stage of economic development to the next.

Consequently, we view economic growth as a characteristic, as an indicator and a necessary condition for the process of economic development but not as a sufficient condition for the process of economic development itself. The process of economic development entails additions to useful knowledge in the form of new technics which are stored in the core of culture and used and applied in the overall gestalt of technology. As a result culture is transformed to higher levels of economic development, and the overall magnitude, the quantity and quality, of economic growth serves as an indicator or a manifestation of the process. The additions to useful knowledge as new technics take on material and nonmaterial forms and consequently as culture advances so does the quality and quantity of economic growth.

Culture has been in existence for hundreds of thousands of years and over time its advance has been exponential. The same holds true for economic growth which indicates the extent of culture accumulation.[59] The basic idea of "... *cultural acceleration* ... to take place in faster and faster, in steeper and steeper surges," consequently applies to economic growth as well.[60] For the early periods of culture advance the quality and quantity changes associated with technological advance were extremely slow, such as the casual breaking of stones as tools which was followed by the more refined chipping and flaking. These technics lasted for thousands of years without much change as to quality or the quantity of accumulation. Early technics concerning fire, tools, language, methods of hunting, gathering, producing, social institutions ... and on, were slow in advancing.[61] However, man's culture was not standing still and even during the earlier stages of growth it was gradually transformed and added to, though at very low rates of acceleration. And while the process was very slow and gradual, a characteristic of the early phase of an exponential pattern, and would give the appearance of constant levels of growth or no growth, growth and accumulation were in actuality taking place. In view of the almost constant nature of the growth curve during the earlier periods of cultural accumulation and growth some economists view economic growth as basically only a characteristic of the modern period and define it as such.[62]

Therefore, while one may point to the very gradual nature of changes associated with growth and development in the early stages of culture advance, the new technics while slow in their coming did accumulate and that accumulation vastly transformed the quality of man's life; and finally circa 10,000 years ago, man achieved through culture advance the dawn of civilization. Over time new technics were formulated and innovated, these new technics were additions to useful knowledge, not necessarily fed by science but still useful knowledge in the sense of how to organize, how to get things done, how to survive.[63] Chance, serendipity, trial and error were all at the fountainhead of early changes in technology; the stream was small and the flow was erratic. Since economic development deals with in essence the advance of useful knowledge, important threads in the evolutionary fabric certainly would have the development of the technics of language, writing and the printing press, but even here and as we have stressed all along in our analysis, the process of economic development entails not one specific gestalt in isolation but rather the integration and summation of all specific gestalts into the core of culture or the overall gestalt of technology. It is not simply a matter of looking at the major specific gestalts such as the printing press or the steam engine but to look at the interaction and interrelation of all the parts of the whole in the totality which we call the overall gestalt of technology.[64] And continuing in this vein, since the process of economic development is essentially a social one we cannot lose sight of the fact that the overall gestalt is comprised of material and nonmaterial technics, since without the necessery social institutions (as well as the concomitant material technics) the printing press and the steam engine would not have been operational.

Eventually what culture built up to as it accumulated more and more useful knowledge was the advent of science, the Scientific Revolution of the sixteenth and seventeenth centuries. Useful knowledge now accelerated in its cumulation in that the social institution of science provided more efficient and systematic methods for its production. As science evolved it was gradually in turn applied to man's basic problems of economic production and social organization.[65] Increasingly science came to lead the flow of new technics and as a result new technics were consequently produced at an accelerated rate; science-led technology is a dominant characteristic of the modern stage of economic development. Technology is as old as culture and as we have noted is essentially the application of useful knowledge to the practical ends of man associated with his economic production and social organization. Over time the advance of technology aided in the promotion of more systematic and organized knowledge and in turn this advanced technology still further, i.e., our circular wheel of economic development. Gradually knowledge came to be derived not just from experience and observation but its source came to be more closely tied to the experimental and the theoretical and subject to verification. As a gradual evolutionary process such knowledge increasingly found its way into the resolution of problems of economic production and social organization. Technology, as we have noted, has had the evolutionary continuity. Technology, and not science, is really the opposite of the core of culture and as with the core of culture is in essence useful knowledge. Therefore, useful knowledge also has the evolutionary coutinuity but up until the Scientific Revolution of the sixteenth and seventeenth centuries such knowledge was not derived from science, but after this period, the methods and results of science became increasingly important in the propagation of new useful knowledge (new technics) which in turn serves as the basic factor of culture accumulation and transformation. As a result, the dynamic thrust today behind technology, and consequently economic development, is that of science. Therefore, whether technology led science or science led technology as causation explaining the rapid acceleration of economic development during the eighteenth and early nineteenth centuries, the Industrial Revolution, is debatable, the end result has been a science-led technology. And upon this, that currently we are in an age in which science leads technology; there is consensus. The upshot is that for cultures in the vanguard of culture advance (in the stage of industrialism) science feeds technology, and consequently a stage which Simon Kuznets notes might even be called "the scientific epoch."[66]

Economic development is a process of advancing useful

knowledge and applying such knowledge to man's practical problems associated with economic production and social organization. Consequently, one of man's most practical and productive activities would be that of developing science which represents a more efficient technic or means to generate more useful knowledge, the fountainhead of economic development. Science serves as a method to more efficiently advance such knowledge and over time the evolution of such methods has produced a body or stock of knowledge known as science or scientific knowledge. In problem solving, such a stock of knowledge plus the use of scientific methods adds to man's capacity at problem solving not only in providing answers but in the more precise delineation of the questions and problems themselves. Problem solving while not perfect has become more predictable and systematic, in the early 1960's man predicted a moon landing within a decade and he was able to do just that. As culture advances it generates many new problems in need of resolution but the advance of culture to the level of the gestalt of industrialism also provides man with means or new technics (especially science) to solve these problems. Consequently the evolution of culture, by providing man with the invention of the method of invention in the form of science, the technic of science as method and as a stock of knowledge, has greatly increased man's capacity to generate new technics and to further advance his overall gestalt of technology; consequently, the relative trickle of pre-modern technological change has now turned to a flood.[67]

However, the flow of new technics (A) is only one part of the wheel of economic development. For technological change to occur, there must be innovation, that is, culture and the base of natural resources must be permeable to the new technic. The concomitant social organization to the evolution of science and its first-time application to production was the social organization, the economic system, which came to be known as capitalism. The Industrial Revolution, the first-time, unique experience, introducing industrialism to Western Europe and the world was delivered via the vehicle of capitalism.[68] A market system and the *laissez-faire* philosophy of the period provided a net (not a dam) across the stream of technology, the net of *laissez-innover*, and as a result the flow became torrential.

Economic Development and culture advance moved into high gear as the social acceptance of the application of science to production became gradually, over time, institutionalized in the economic system known as capitalism.[69] The upshot of the process is that, whereas in the past, periods of growth and development reached protracted ceilings of saturation and stagnation in that new technics were slow and erratic in their genesis, we now have entered the modern period in which growth has become sustained in that growth is now propelled by a continuous flow of new technics. New technics are currently being fed more and more by science and in addition their innovation has become more and more socially accepted and institutionalized (at least for material technics of economic production) and that as a result man has developed the nascent capacity for sustained economic growth and development.[70]

In summary, the view presented above is that culture has advanced exponentially in an evolutionary process of transformation and appears as a series of successive stages of economic development. In the literature, this sequential paradigm is referred to as a process of "escalation" or successive "logistic surges." While the actual path, therefore, is not smooth but is composed of a series of "*S*" curves increasing in their steepness, the overall path, as represented by an envelope curve containing the paradigm of logistic surges, is exponential.

> "*Throughout the entire sweep of history and prehistory, the power of human beings to achieve their basic purposes has been increasing at accelerating speed with local and temporary stagnations and setbacks. This long-run acceleration has taken place through a series of logistic and Gompertz surges, having higher and higher rates of increase.*[71]

The process of economic development, which is in essence the process of advancing useful knowledge, serves as the core of culture and provides for the dynamics of economic evolution. Consequently, the process of economic development appears ongoing and unending. Economic growth, which represents a residue of culture cumulation, did not simply start with the modern epoch but has had long-term historical continuity starting with the very origins of culture. Economic growth as replication and as a basic indicator of the process cannot continue without underlying structural changes which appear as the paradigm of logistic surges. Consequently, *cultural economics* as theory, buttressed by empirical realities, is in support of the principle of similitude which states that growth cannot advance as an ongoing continuum without structural change. But is it always going to be ongoing with exponential acceleration? Or is *Mankind at the Turning Point* as some maintain? Are there compelling reasons to assume that for future generations of mankind that the exponential of general culture evolution must inevitably be transformed to the logistic? Or even if not inevitable, should we plan and create the logistic, and limit economic growth, to avoid a doomsday denouement? Let us now address ourselves to these questions.

REFERENCES

[1]Otis Dudley Duncan, ed., *William F. Ogburn on Culture and Social Change* (Chicago; University of Chicago Press, 1964), p. 95.

[2]"Ogburn's main contribution to sociology was in the field of culture and cultural change; to him this was the heart of sociology." Vol. 11, p. 280, *The International Encyclopedia of the Social Sciences* (1968), A. J. Jaffe; "*Social Change* . . . seems to have been the first major work by an American sociologist in which the anthropological concept of culture was prominently employed." Kroeber and Kluckhohn, *Culture: A critical Review of Concepts and Definitions*, p. 15 (Also referred to by Duncan, *William F. Ogburn*, p. xxi); Ogburn himself, while recognizing cultural lag as a significant theory, felt that: "My contribution has been largely in the factor of exponential accumulation and also in the development of the factor of invention.", Duncan, p. xv, and also, "Indeed, the importance of culture has forced a reorientation of many of the most important concepts of sociology and even the consideration of a redefining of sociology.", Duncan, p. 16. Also note on the issue of Ogburn's contributions, Otis Dudley Duncan, "An Appreciation of William Fielding Ogburn," pp. 94-99, *Technology and Culture*, Vol. I (Winter 1960), p. 96. And, "The only part of the theory that has been criticized is the concept of cultural lag—criticisms based, I think, upon distortions and misunderstandings. However, the concept of cultural lag is not a fundamental part of the theory of social evolution." Ogburn, *Social Change*, p. 374.

[3]Hart's assessment, note, Allen, *Technology and Social Change*, p. 55, and further noting that Ogburn "cited the idea from Robert H. Lowie's, *Culture and Ethnology* . . " And also, "When sociologists speak of *Cultural acceleration* they mean underlying tendency of discovery, invention, and diffusion to take the place faster and faster, in steeper and steeper surges." p. 28.

[4]Duncan, *William F. Ogburn*, p. xvi William Fielding Ogburn, *Social Change* (New York: Dell Publishing Company, 1966), pp. 392-393.

[5]These are the three factors emphasised by Ogburn and Meyer F. Nimkoff, *Sociology* (Boston; Houghton Mifflin Company, 1964), (1) the existing body of knowledge of the cultural base, (2) demand, and, (3) mental ability, pp. 666-672. Also, Ogburn, *Social Change* (New York: The Viking Press, 1950). pp. 80-89, 378. Consequently it is not completely correct, as Jacob Schmookler maintains that Ogburn " . . seeks the causes of invention exclusively . . ." in the ". . . useful combination of pre-existing elements." *Invention and Economic Growth* (Cambridge: Harvard Univeraity Press, 1966), p. 60, in that Ogburn did give credit to demand and mental ability. But it would not be incorrect, perhaps to say that Ogburn places primary emphasis on the pre-existing level of culture as it would also be correct to say that primary emphasis by Schmookler is in the area of economic demand. Schmooler states: " . . Ogburn and his followers have emphasised the dependence of new inventions on the prior art to the point where the whole process takes on an inevitable character . . that the new knowledge gained from one moment to the next causes the supply curve to shift (exponentially) rightward. By contrast Gilfillan and the present writer have stressed factors on the demand side." in *The Rate and Direction of Inventive Activity : Economic and Social Factors* (Princeton: Princeton University Press, 1962), pp. 197-198.

[6]On the issue of diffusion, note, Ralph Linton, *The Study of Man* (New York: D. Appleton-Century Company, 1936), pp. 324-346. "The comparatively rapid growth of culture as a whole has been due to the ability of all societies to borrow elements from other cultures and to incorporate them into their own." p. 324, and, John J. Honigman, *The World of Man* (New York. Harper and Row, 1959), pp. 209-232, and in the literature diffusion sometime includes both the internal (primary) and external (secondary), p. 210. Ogburn and Nimkoff also follow this practice, "The transference of culture traits from one area to another or from one part of culture to another is called diffusion," *Sociology*, p. 662. In our study in order to distinguish the intrinsic or endogenous sources of new technics from the exogenous, or adventitious, we refer to diffusion in the "secondary" sense to cover the inter-culture spread of new technics and refer to the intra-culture spread of new technics as replication or duplication. An innovation of a new technic by the U.S.S.R. which was invented or discovered in the U.S. would be an example of diffusion, an innovation of a new technic in Vermont though invented and innovated in New York

would be an example of replication. There is conceptual distinction between "primary" and "secondary" and calling both diffusion only adds unnecessarily to confusion. As Honigman notes: "Usually the term 'diffusion' is used to designate this second type of cultural transmission," p. 210, and, "The process by which elements are transmitted from one culture to another is diffusion," p. 209, which more closely approximates how Ogburn uses diffusion in his *Social Change*, pp. 88-89.

[7]"Discovery and inventions are the obvious starting points . . . since it is only by these processes that new elements can be added to the total content of man's culture, "Ralph Linton, *The Study of Man*, p. 304; Melville J. Herskovitz, *Man and His Works* (New York: Alfred A. Knopf. 1952), pp. 492-504; Ogburn, *Social Change*, p. 50.

[8]We distinguish here, for a given culture, between endogenous sources of new technics (invention and discovery) and exogenous sources (diffusion). "The terms *invention* and *discovery* both carry the further implication of being elements which have originated within the bracket of a particular combined society and culture," Linton, *The Study of Man*, p. 305, and, "The process by which culture elements are borrowed, commonly known as diffusion," p. 304. Linton and others note the difficulty of clearly distinguishing between invention and discovery add consequently there is a tendency to lump inventions and discoveries under some overall heading. Honigman, *The World of Man*, notes the difficulties of distinction, pp. 194-196 and places both invention and discovery under the overall heading of "origination," perhaps to give emphasis to the endogenous nature of both, that both "have originated within" (Linton above). "The process by which new elements of culture are discovered or invented or distinguished from their circulation within or between communities will be called origination," p. 194. Ogburn tended to use invention and discovery, "The word, 'invention', as used here, carries a broad meaning and covers not only the concept of mechanical invention but also discoveries in applied science." in Duncan, *William F. Ogburn*, p. 65, and *Social Change*, p. 378. However, since for a given culture not only invention and discovery, but diffusion, as well, represent different potential sources of culture accumulation and therefore should be distinguished, they also may be considered collectively as new elements of useful knowledge for a given culture, and consequently, in our schema, are collectively referred to as new technics. On the distinction between invention and discovery, note Irving H. Siegel, "Scientific Discovery and the Rate of Invention," in *The Rate and Direction of Inventive Activity*, pp. 441-457. "Discovery is the act of wresting a secret from nature; and a secret that is won is a discovery. More specifically, a discovery may be a 'new' fact, principle, hypothesis, theory or law concerning natural (including human) phenomena that are observable directly or through their effects . . . . Invention may be regarded as purposeful and practical contriving based on existing knowledge . . . that has a signi-

ficantly novel feature." pp. 441-442, and, the reservation by Thomas S. Kuhn, ibid., pp. 451 ff. And also, for invention as making something new and discovery as coming up with something that has existed, note Fritz Machlup, *The Production and Distribution of Knowledge in the United States* (Princeton: Princeton University Press, 1962), pp. 162-163. In any event though distinctions are often attempted concerning invention and discovery the results are not that clear. In our analysis in order to overcome the difficulties of distinction we refer to both invention and discovery as new technics since whatever the source, invention, discovery or diffusion, it is the new technic, which as the additive element serves as the basis for culture accumulation and transformation.

[9]Ogburn defines invention as: " . . . a combination of existing and known elements of culture, material and/or a nonmaterial, or a modification of one to form a new one," *Social Change*, p. 378. Honigman, also treats inventions as both material and nonmaterial, "Unemployment insurance, land-lease, zoning, cooperatives, collective bargaining, and workmen's compensation schemes were all inventions," *The World of Man*, p. 197. We have noted this point previously, that social technics, and not only material technics, may be viewed as inventions. Consequently we have in this study considered new technics as both material and nonmaterial and consequently, in addition, a conceptionalization of technology to include both the social and material. In many instances Simon Kuznets notes a distinction between material and social inventions, but specifically a pointed discussion by him of the issue would be *The Rate and Direction of Inventive Activity: Economic and Social Factors*, pp. 19-43, in which he views the problems of definition and measurement of inventions concerning the material universe. But he nonetheless does recognize, "We thus exclude social inventions, new methods of including human beings to compete and cooperate in the social progress . . ." p. 19, And though he notes, "The effects of social inventions on economic productivity are obviously major and profound . . . "but for statistical and analytical reasons he concludes that material and social inventions " . . . can hardly be treated together," p. 19.

[10]Ogburn's four variables used in his theory of culture evolution are: invention; accumulation; diffusion; and, adjustment. This is similar but not the same as our four variables in the wheel of economic development. (A) new technics; (B) environmental permeability; (C) the overall gestalt of technology; and (D) environmental accumulation and transformation. On Ogburn's four variables note, *Social Change*, p. 377.

[11]On exponential culture accumulation Ogburn states: "This accumulation tends to be exponential because an invention is a combination of existing elements, and these elements are accumulative," and, that the cultural base increases lead to more than increases in a fixed ratio in that more elements lead to greater and greater possible combinations, "The reason lies in the definition of an invention as a combination of existing elements, and as the existing elements

increase, the number of combinations increases faster than by a fixed ratio," and, consequently, "The functional relationship between the size of the cultural base and the number of new inventions plus the tendency for cultural elements to accumulate helps to explain how our civilization came from simple beginnings to what it is today," *Social Change*, pp. 381, 382 and 385. Also, note, Ogburn and Nimkoff, *Sociology* (1964), pp. 659-660, 666-670.

[12]Ogburn in his *Social Change*, notes, "In prehistoric times cultural evolution was very slow; perhaps so slow as to be invisible over four or five generations . . . " p. 384, and, "there are more inventions in the United States today (per unit of population and per unit of time) than among the Eskimo, not because the people of the United States have any more inherent mental ability, but for the reason that we have a larger cultural base . . ." p. 382.

[13]If it were not for the quality and form changes (the result of new technics being innovated or what is also called technological change) energy could not be continuously produced on a long-term exponential paradigm but would reach a logistic ceiling. Recall our discussions of chapter V, above, "Energy Transformation as an indicator of the Process of Economic Development." Perhaps the name most frequently associated with empirical evidence for the acceleration principle would be that of Hornell Hart, note the sources so frequently referred to in this study, Allen, ed., *Technology and Social Change*, "Technological Acceleration and the Atomic Bomb," *American Sociological Review*, 11 (1946) pp. 277-293; and the general summary statement by Merrill, *Culture and Society*, (1952), pp. 583-587.

[14]Schmookler, *Invention and Economic Growth*, p. 59; and Barker S. Sanders, in *The Rate and Direction of Inventive Activity: Economic and Social Indicators*, "The theory seems untenable to me," pp. 63-68, p. 68. Sanders does not seem to question the acceleration of culture but rather whether or not such an acceleration is indicative of inventive activity.

[15]On atomism note Marc Tool, *The Discretionary Economy* (Santa Monica: Goodyear Publishing Company, 1979), pp. 45-46 and references to Harry K. Girvetz, *The Evolution of Liberalism* (New York: Collier Books, 1963).

[16]"The advantage in studying social evolution or emphasizing accumulation is seen in that it destroys the ethnocentric myth and egotistical fantasy that man created his civilization. Much truer is the idea that he inherited it." Ogburn, *Social Change*, p. 381. Leslie A. White carries this view to its extreme, note, "Ikhnaton: The Great Man vs. the Culture Process," *Journal of the American Oriental Society*, 68, pp. 91-114; "Man's Control over Civilization: An Anthropocentric Illusion," *The Scientific Monthly* 66 (March 1948), pp. 235-247.

[17]Rather than placing major emphasis on one-way causation, our methodology places major emphasis on circular causation, the process of interaction between culture and man. Man serves as a physical catalyst in the genesis of new technics and the new technics in turn

cause culture accumulation and transformation. Culture evolution in turn provides man's brain (analogous to a computer) with higher levels of programming and therefore greater inventive capacity which in turn promotes further advances in culture evolution. However, during the period of the last 10,000 years, the Agricultural Revolution forward, the genetic composition of biological man has remained relatively constant; whereas, culture has evolved with acceleration. In that a constant, the biological nature of man, cannot explain a variable, explanations of culture evolution tend to place primary emphasis on culture itself and its internal dynamics. Consequently, the sociologist and anthropologist tend to view cultural processes as the dynamic agency of causation. It is still nonetheless correct that mind of man, the computer, serves, as the catalyst, but that the computer is programmed by and large by culture. A genius raised by wolves will theoretically produce snarls and clawing but not a theory of relativity. Such a view concerning the nurture and behavior of wolf children represents a reasonable supposition, but, evidently, not an established fact. Note William F. Ogburn and Nirmal K. Bose, "On the Trail of the Wolf-Children," *Genetic Psychological Monographs* 59 (1959), pp. 121-191.

[18]The data on all these studies point the same conclusions—that is a given invention or discovery had not been made by the persons who actually did make it the logic of the developing culture would have caused someone else to achieve the same end." Linton, *The Science of Man*, p. 153. A. L. Kroeber supports the position of simultaneous inventions, *Anthropology* (1948), pp. 341-343, and consequently gives a " . . . recognition of super-individual of forces—historical agencies or social currents transcending personalities," p. 343, which, of course, is consistent with Kroeber's "The Superorganic," *American Anthropologist* 19 (April-June 1917), pp. 162-213, p. 200, which evidently inspired Ogburn (p. 85), *Social Change*, pp. 83-86, 90-102 and based upon the frequently cited study by William F. Ogburn and Dorothy Thomas, "Are Inventions Inevitable? A Note on Social Evolution," *Political Science Quarterly* 37 (March 1922), pp. 83-98. Also in support, note, Robert K. Merton, "The Role of Genius in Scientific Advance," *The New Scientist*, November 2, 1961, pp. 306-308 and also, Derek J. de Solla Price, *Little Science, Big Science* (New York: Columbia University Press, 1963), pp. 65-70 and his additional references. Schmookler takes exception to the "sociological determinist" concerning the simultaneous and inevitable nature of inventions, cf., *Inventions and Economic Growth*, pp. 189-195. In Jewkes, et. al., *The Sources of Invention*, in reference to simultaneous inventions, the following appears: "This is a highly plausible line of reasoning but some of the links in it are weak." p. 227. The Ogburn-Kroeber-Merton view on simultaneous invention deals with probability, given certain conditions of culture and physical environment certain events (inventions) are highly probable, so much so that they are considered to be inevitable. If the earth had no water then no boats would be forthcoming, however, given man, given culture, given lakes, rivers and oceans, we then conclude

that man would inevitably invent material technics to serve as floating devices for transportation. And that given boats and steam engines that steam boats become an inevitability as evidenced by Fulton (1807), Jouffroy, Rumsey, Stevens and Symmington (1802). This is countered by Schmookler's "genus and the individual," and that to some people "all Chinamen look alike." (*Inventions and Economic Growth*, p. 191). To Schmookler the steamboats which were invented were different and consequently we are in actuality discussing different inventions and not simultaneous inventions. "Whatever 'the' steamboat may mean, those of Fulton, Jouffroy, Rumsey, Stevens, and Symmington were different steamboats," p. 191. However, if the material technics invented by Fulton, Jauffroy, Rumsey, Stevens, and Symmington, were not all steamboats, and therefore examples of simultaneous inventions, what then were they?

[19]Note R. R. Nelson, "The Economics of Inventions. A Survey of the Literature," *The Journal of Business* 32 (April 1959), pp. 101-127, in which he notes that " . . . Demand and cost factors play major roles . . . . Much of the data on relative rates of technological progress can be explained in this fashion," p. 101. And from *The Rate and Direction of Inventive Activity: Economic and Social Factors*, "Almost all the papers in this volume were written by economists and tend to reflect the economists interest in economic growth and in problems of efficiency," and so that, " . . . may be fitted into a more or less classical economic analysis. . . . They are attempts to analyze inventive activity with the traditional tools of economic analysis," pp. 7-8. In the same study Schmookler notes: "The problem may be stated in the parlance of traditional economics . . . and, ". . . the problem before us is the relative influence of changes in (1) demand conditions and (2) supply conditions on the production of inventions," pp. 197-198.

[20]"The logic of measuring inventions in terms of technological progress, as the resultant of invention is quite as justifiable as the attempt to measure it in terms of inputs. . . . Both are used by science," Sanders, *The Rate and Direction of Inventive Activity*, p. 63.

[21]Sanders questions the view that we will be able to measure invention directly but rather may simply have to settle with various indicators as second-best solutions, "Some Difficulties in Measuring Inventive Activity," in *The Rate and Direction of Inventive Activity*, pp 53-90. Sanders notes: "In reality, Hart and his followers have never attempted to measure inventions, Hart is merely trying to establish the thesis that man's technological and cultural progress has accelerated over time." p. 64. "Hart believes that in measuring the rate of technical change he is measuring the rate of invention . . ." pp. 65, 75-76. And while apparently not questioning the fact of culture acceleration, pp. 64-65 Sanders does not accept the Ogburnian theory, pp. 67-68, as explanation.

[22]On the "principle of invention by combination" and that "invention consists of a new combination of old elements," note, Allen, *Technology and Social Change*, pp. 48-49. And while not the

complete story Hart notes, "... the rate of invention increases acceleratingly because the number of elements ready to be combined keeps multiplying in geometric ratio." p. 51.

[23]"Each invention is a candidate for an innovation, but only a small proportion of inventions is adopted," note, Simon Kuznets, *Six Lectures on Economic Growth* (Glencoe: The Free Press, (1961), p. 31, and also, *Economic Growth and Structure* (New York: W. W. Norton & Company, 1965), pp. 61, 85-92.

[24]As Schmookler notes: "We do not even have an agreed upon set of terms." *Invention and Economic Growth,* p. 3 and, "If an invention cannot be defined, what becomes of the attempts to classify inventions." John Jewkes, et. al., *The Sources of Invention* (London: Macmillan & Co., 1958), p. 14. "In studies aiming to determine trends in inventing, an important prerequsite is a precise definition of what one is trying to measure." (Sanders) *Rate of Inventive Activity*, p. 75, and to which Schmookler adds, "While it is not entirely clear just what Sanders means by invention, inventiveness, or inventive activity, in preferring direct measures of inventive input and out to patent statistics his logic is impeccable.", p. 78. On the overall problem, note Simon Kuznets, "Inventive Activity: Problems of Definition and Measurement," pp. 19-51.

[25]Schmookler, who relies upon patents as an index, excludes the nonmaterial technics from his analysis for the obvious reason, "But a nonphysical or rather a purely human means for attaining a result physical or otherwise, is not patentable." *Invention and Economic Growth*, p. 6 and that a "system" is non-patentable, p. 7. And whereas Schmookler excludes science, Ogburn includes science "... means the discovery of reliable and precise knowledge," as part of his conceptualization of invention, "Limitations of Statistics," *American Journal of Sociology* 40 (1934), pp. 12-20, p. 20. Schmookler, in his *Invention and Economic Growth* basically conceptualizes invention as "... operationally the term denotes an idea which would be patentable ..." p. 196, and consequently is not concerned with the whole of technological change, "Our focus has been on invention, not technological progress in its entirety." p. 175.

[26]*In the Rate and Direction of Inventive Activity*, Kuznets, "No efficient measures of the output of inventive activity are available now." p. 47, and, Sanders, "In my opinion none of the measures used to date is satisfactory, even as a crude measure of inventiveness as such or inventive activity," p. 53, although some would question a concensus Gilfillan notes: "All the economists at this conference seem to agree that an index of inventive output, i.e., successful invention, is much needed but impossible to obtain. Not knowing it was impossible I prepared one. . . ." p. 83.

[27] "We had better not lengthen the list of meanings that can be attached to the phrase 'stock of knowledge,' especially since none of the concepts is practically operational, let alone suitable for numerical measurement." p. 123, Fritz Machlup, *The Production and Distribution*

of knowledge in the United States, also, pp. 44-45, 123-125, 187, 375-376. And Schmookler, "I am only emphasizing that other knowledge possesses an identical quality, and while this quality merits study, it will elude measurement." *The Rate and Direction of Inventive Activity*, p. 49. And from Kuznets, *Economic Growth and Structure*, "If we wish to take stock of all the tested knowledge that is potentially useful in economic production . . . the view must be wide indeed. . . . No such inventory is possible with the tools generally available. . . ." p. 85.

[28]For example, the works of Derek J. De Solla Price, *Science Since Babylon* (New Haven: Yale University Press, 1961) and *Little Science, Big Science* (New York: Columbia University Press, 1963), indicate that at least up to the present, that science has advanced exponentially. Also, Henry W. Menard, *Science: Growth and Change* (Cambridge: Harvard University Press, 1971). And if science, as the fountainhead of the process advances exponentially, what might also be said of invention and technology. "But in the broad terms considered here, the drift of invention from mechanical into other lines must surely be controlled by the state of fundamental science." pp. 5-6, William N. Parker, "Economic Development in Historical Perspective," *Economic Development and Cultural Change* 10 (October 1961), pp. 1-7.

[29]*Little Science, Big Science*, pp. 4-5, and *Science Since Babylon*, pp. 92-124.

[30]Apparently not all would agree, Schmookler as a case in point while offering no evidence to the contrary claims that anyone accepting the "evidence" of Price is easily satisfied," *Invention and Economic Growth*, pp. 60-61. Price's reputation is nonetheless secure, note: Ina Spiegal Rosing and Derek de Solla Price *Science, Technology and Society* (Beverly Hills: Sage Publications, 1977), and, " . . . when the International Council for Science Policy Studies was founded he became its first president. He has published about two-hundred scientific papers and six books . . . ." p. 605. Also, Karl W. Deutsch, John Platt, Dieter Senghaas, "Conditions Favoring Major Advances in Social Science," *Science* 171 (5 February 1971), pp. 450-459, in noting the 62 major inventions and innovations of the twentieth century (1900-1965) provide a listing of the contributing social scientists. To make the listing once is commendable, note J. Schmookler, No. 12, p. 451, but Derek John de Solla Price made it twice, No. 23, p. 452 and No. 55, p. 454.

[31]The following statement is by Price but it could also have been written by Ogburn, "The exponential law is the mathematical consequence of having a quantity that increases so that the bigger it is the faster it grows." *Science Since Babylon*, p. 100.

[32]Clarence E. Ayres, *The Theory of Economic Progress* (New York: Schocken Books, 1962), pp. 119-121; "That these processes . . . will continue and accelerate is as likely as anything in the realm of human affairs can ever be," and, "The progressive acceleration of technological advancement, which we know to be the fact . . ." *The Industrial Economy* (Cambridge: Houghton Mifflin Company, 1952), p. 57-58, 401.

[33]*Little Science, Big Science*, p. 30. To Price this "basic law" applies to the "growth of science as a whole," in that, "... saturation is ultimately inevitable: it is far too approximate to indicate when and in what circumstances saturation will begin." p. 31. But the point being that "... exponential growth eventually reaches some limit ..." p. 20, and though difficult to predict with certainty that "Scientific doomsday is therefore less than a century distant." p. 19, it is inevitable according to Price that science will ultimately "... approach the critical point making its senile limit." p. 23, "The new era shows all the familiar syndromes of saturation." p. 32. "... probably during the 1940's or 1950's, we passed through the midperiod in general logistic growth of science's body politic." p. 31. And when "... the civilization is saturated with science. This may be regarded as an ultimate end of the completed Industrial Revolution," *Science Since Babylon*, p. 113.

[34]To further clarify and to aid in the understanding of the point being made here we draw attention to Fritz Machlup and his discussions concerning the "subject of the effect of the flow of inventions upon the ease of making further inventions," in his "The supply of inventors and inventions," *The Rate and Direction of Inventive Activity*, pp. 143-169, (156-157). Machlup draws a dichotomy between two schools of thought, the acceleration school "... the more that is invented the easier it becomes to invent still more," and the retardation school. "... the more that is invented, the harder it becomes to invent still more." Machlup's conclusion is that neither is supported by reason or evidence, "There is no *a priori* reason why the possibilities of technological development should be either narrowly limited or virtually limitless. Nor is there any legitimate basis for inductive inferences." We, however feel that logic and evidence support both schools of thought, that both schools are relevant and applicable to the process of culture evolution: acceleration being applicable to *general* culture evolution and retardation (saturation) being relevant to the areas of *specific* culture evolution.

[35]"We are living in what has been called the explosion of science, a period in which our rate of accumulating knowledge about the world and universe around us is galloping ahead more than 100 times as quickly as at the turn of the century ... The reality of this explosion is not difficult to discover qualitatively or quantitatively." And the editors, Sir Bernard Lovell and Tom Margerison, of *The explosion of Science: The Physical Universe* (New York: Meredith Press, 1967), are apparently in agreement with Price as they state, also in the foreward, that "Clearly, in due course, the scientific explosion must burn itself out."

[36]Allen, *Technology and Social Change*, p. 48. It is indeed difficult to understand how and why the resistance by some to the acceptance of evidence of such an obvious phenomenon as exponential growth. Not only has the principle of acceleration been stated systematically, and with evidence, by social scientists but human experiences and day-to-day living continuously confirm the fact. We can scarcely escape the reality

and our popularized sources of information continuously relay home the exponential pattern, for example, *Time* (January 1970), p. 53 for figures in terms of billions of passenger-miles per year for the years 1930-1970, showing the very rapid acceleration as we move from the Ford Tri-Motor of 1928 to the Boeing 747 or the 1970's. Could the Wright brothers have conceived that the flying machines innovated at the turn of the century would evolve by the 1970's into material technics capable of a moon landing and speeds in excess of 20,000 miles/hour or provide man with the capacity to produce 10 billion passenger miles by 1950 and an estimated 379 billion by 1980. "The idea of exponential curves—the acceleration of doubling rates of all kinds—has now become commonplace." Daniel Bell in Sheldon and Moore, eds., *Indicators of Social Change*, p. 148.

[37]Although, Tylor also noted the importance of knowledge in the processes of culture evolution, "*. . . largely due to his faculty of gaining new knowledge . . .*" in Herbert R. Barringer, et al., eds., *Social Change in Developing Areas* (Cambridge: Schenkman Publishing Company, 1965), p. 77 and passim, especially Morris E. Opler, "Cultural Dynamics and Evolutionary Theory", pp. 68-96. And, also the "law of three stages" by Auguste Comte, 1. the theological or fictitious, 2. the metaphysical or abstract, and 3. the scientific or positive stage, note *International Encyclopedia of the Social Sciences*, Vol. 3, pp. 200-206. But it was Veblen who directed attention of the processes of culture evolution to that of economic evolution. Whereas Tylor, Comte and Veblen all had precursors, it might be said that Tylor introduced scientific anthropology, and Comte scientific sociology and Veblen scientific evolutionary economics.

[38]"The cultural structure clusters about this body of matter-of-fact knowledge as its substantial core." p. 2, "The modern schema of culture comprises a large body of worldly wisdom, as well as of science." p. 20. And, "These two divergent ranges of inquiry are to be found together in all phases of human culture." p. 18, Thorstein Veblen, *The Place of Science in Modern Civilization and Other Essays* (New York: Russell & Russell, 1961). The points we are noting here concerning Veblen's theory of culture evolution are melted into his overall contributions, however a good starting place and summary statement is contained in his famous essay, "The Place of Science in Modern Civilization," pp. 1-32. That particular essay is considered by some to be Veblen's best and apparently Veblen, himself, agreed, cf., Joseph Dorfman, *Thorstein Veblen and His America* (New York: Augustus M. Kelley, 1961), p. 447.

[39]This is clearly a nascent theory of cultural lag, see, Charles Susskind, *Understanding Technology* (Baltimore: The Johns Hopkins Press, 1973), p. 82, and, "Veblen, Thorstein," *The International Encyclopedia of the Social Sciences*, Vol. 15, pp. 302-307, "Veblen analyzed . . . social processes in terms of culture lag." p. 304.

[40]On material and nonmaterial culture, see Ayres, *The Industrial Economy*, (Cambridge: Houghton Mifflin Company, 1952), pp. 50-51, and *Toward a Reasonable Society* (Austin: University of Texas Press,

1961), pp. 78-85, where on p. 85 he argues against a "false polarization" as the separation of nonmaterial culture from material culture. Consequently, it is incorrect to treat the "technological appurtenances" . . . "as external" . . . "to the social structure . . ." Ayres, "The Role of Technology," p. 281. Therefore, Ayres states. ". . . technology—the tool using aspect of human behavior—is not something separate and distinct from the societal network of personal relationships." . . . "All tool-using is social." *Reasonable Society*, p. 77. "Indeed, it is as a form of social organization that technology is most important." *The Industrial Economy*, p. 53. Nonetheless, Ayres did not consider institutions to be integral parts of technology: "Institutions are functionally different from technological patterns." *The Industrial Economy*, pp. 61, 42-50. To Ayres ". . . the peculiar quality of these particular foci of activity is unquestionably ceremonial." *The Theory of Economic Progress* (New York: Schocken Books, 1962), pp. 182, 177-202.

[41]Hornell Hart provides, in many instances, statistical evidence in support of this position. For example, Allen, ed., *Technology and Social Change*, p. 33.

[42]Over time, given a specific technic, there is a tendency toward perfection as we reach the saturation point in improvements. "Yet when the Hopi culture of corn was studied by our modern scientific agriculturalists there was no improvement that could be suggested, assuming their existing equipment. Indeed, their agricultural methods were considered the best under the circumstances." Otis Dudley Duncan, *William F. Ogburn: On Culture and Social Change* (Chicago: University of Chicago Press, 1968), p. 46. Such a society becomes stationary and stagnates in that there is a limit on its growth unless new elements (technics) are introduced to transform the overall gestalt to the next higher level.

[43]By now the reader should be aware of our many references to the distinction between general and specific culture evolution as presented by L. A. White and Sahlins and Service.

[44]The "gestalt switch" is central to the Kuhnian framework and serves as a necessary condition for the continued advance and evolution of science. Note, Thomas S. Kuhn, *The Structure of Scientific Revolutions* (Chicago: University of Chicago Press, 1970), pp. 111-135; and Benjamin Ward, *What's Wrong with Economics*? (New York: Basic Books, 1972), pp. 95-107.

[45]On the "principle of similitude" or "structural differentiation," note: Daniel Bell, "The Measurement of Knowledge and Technology," in *Indicators of Social Change* (New York: Russell Sage Foundation, 1968), E. B. Sheldon and W. E. Moore, eds., pp. 149-152; and, also by D. Bell, *The Coming of Post-Industrial Society* (New York: Basic Books, 1973), pp. 172-174.

[46]"But the central fact about the traditional society was that a ceiling existed on the level of attainable output per head." W. W. Rostow, *The Stages of Economic Growth: A non-Communist Manifesto* (Cambridge: Cambridge University Press, 1960), p. 4. A stage, therefore, may be

characterized by its overall technological gestalt and if such a gestalt is not transformed to new gestalts of higher energy control a saturation level will be reached in terms of its capacity for economic growth. "There are a number of reasons why in the absence of an accelerating rate of technical progress an eventual retardation should be regarded as inevitable." W. A. Cole and Phyllis Deane, in H. J. Habakkuk and M. Postan, eds., *The Cambridge Economic History of Europe* (Cambridge: Cambridge University Press, 1965), Vol. VI, Part 1, p. 47. "The technology existing at a given point in time sets limits on how much can be produced with a given amount of inputs." Edwin Mansfield, *The Economics of Technological Change* (New York: W. W. Norton & Company, 1968), p. 12. And, given our broad conceptualization of technology to include the social as well as the material, "As we shall emphasize throughout this book, economic progress of the poorer countries cannot proceed in a continuing and self-sustaining fashion unless it is preceded, accompanied, and followed by changes in the social and economic structure of these countries. . . . Economic development is thus growth plus change." Salvatore Schiavo-Campo and Hans Singer, *Perspectives of Economic Development* (Boston: Houghton Mifflin Company, 1969), pp. 3-4, and, "For development is not merely economic growth: it is growth accompanied by structural social and economic change." p. vii. Consequently, without the transformation of a given overall gestalt, the accumulated material and nonmaterial technics, to a new gestalt of higher levels of energy control, economic growth could not advance on a continuum but rather would reach saturation. Stated conversely, and, "To put it differently, a sustained high rate of growth depends upon a continuous emergence of new inventions and innovations." Simon Kuznets, *Six Lectures* (Glencoe: The Free Press, 1961), p. 33. And such a "continuous emergence" of new technics will not take place in the context of a given overall gestalt of technology (specific evolution and saturation) but rests upon the transformation of the overall gestalt (general evolution and acceleration). And ". . . *some* structural changes, not only in economic but also in social institutions and beliefs, are required, without which modern economic growth would be impossible." Simon Kuznets, *Economic Growth of Nations* (Cambridge: The Belknap Press, 1971), p. 348.

[47]"What is lacking is a more or less regular flow of innovation on a scale capable of defeating Ricardian diminishing returns . . ." W. W. Rostow, ed., *The Economics of Take-Off into Sustained Growth* (New York: St. Martin's Press, 1963), p. xxiii.

[48]Rostow's statement in this regard would also be quite applicable to the antebellum southern economy. "The conception of the traditional society is, however, in no sense static; and it would not exclude increases in output. Acreage could be expanded; some ad hoc technical innovations, often highly productive innovations, could be introduced. . . .productivity could rise. . .or the discovery and diffusion of a new Crop." *The Stages of Economic Growth*, p. 4.

[49]On the logistic pattern of production, for particular technics and particular industries, note Simon S. Kuznets, *Secular Movements in Production and Prices* (Cambridge: The Riverside Press, 1930), pp. 11-44: "Thus our illustrations show that the number of important inventions within an industry with an unretarded supply of raw materials tends to diminish over time." (p. 30); ". . .the number of operations to be improved is limited and gradually becomes exhausted." (p. 31); consequently inventions "gradually approach a stable level, the level of perfection." (p. 34); and consequently since technological advance (Kuznets, however, also considers population changes and changes in demand as factors of change pp. 5-11) dominates the process, the result is a "retardation of industrial growth. . .that with rare exception these data indicate a diminution in rate of growth, a definite approach to stability or even decline." (p. 35). On the mathematical curves "embodying these assumptions" note his comments on the Gompertz and the logistic, pp. 64-67. The 1930 study cited above was an outgrowth of "Retardation of Industrial Growth," *Journal of Economic and Business Activity*, Vol. 1 (1928-1929), pp. 534-560, (reprinted also in his *Economic Change* (London: William Heineman,) 1954, pp. 253-277. Also, many other similar examples of the logistic pattern could be given: for railroads, Alfred J. Lotka, *Elements of Mathematical Biology* (New York: Dover Publications, 1956), pp. 368-369; Alvin H. Hansen, *Business Cycles and National Income* (New York: W.W. Norton and Company, 1964), pp. 62-63; for mineral production and the prevailing pattern, S.G. Lasky, "Mineral Industry Futures Can be Predicted," *Engineering and Mining Journal* (August 1951), pp. 60-64, and, "Mineral Industry Futures Can be Predicted-II," *Engineering and Mining Journal* (September 1955), pp. 94-96.

[50]"The same tendency to slackening improvement and retarded spread has been observed in the history of such an important single invention as the steam engine." Kuznets, *Economic Change*, p. 272. "But the efficiency of a tool cannot be increased indefinitely; there is a point beyond which improvement of any given tool is impossible. . .the improvement of any tool or machine approaches closely, if it does not reach, a limit." Leslie A. White, *The Science of Culture* (New York: Farrar, Straus and Company, 1949), p. 375. And further, White states, "The energy factor may be increased indefinitely; the efficiency of tools only within limits." p. 376.

[51]This is similar to "The Law of Evolutionary Potential" of Elman R. Service in Sahlins and Service, eds., *Evolution and Culture*, pp. 93-124, specifically stated p. 97. Note also, perhaps closer to the point being raised here, the "Principle of Stabilization," in that, "Specific evolution means increasing adaptation to an environment, which is to say that it ultimately becomes nonprogressive." p. 95.

[52]Some evidently question such an interpretation, Sanders notes, ". . .Ogburn's theory of invention is far from validation. It fails completely to explain why some cultures prove much more dynamic than others, irrespective of the extent of the cultural base. It fails to account

for plateaus that are frequent in the course of any art or even for an entire culture complex." *The Rate and Direction of Inventive Activity*, p. 67. Also note William F. Ogburn, "Stationary and Changing Societies," *American Journal of Sociology* 42 (July 1936), pp. 16-31. To Ogburn the "conception of a stationary society is one where the cultural pattern does not change. . .there is social movement, but not cultural change." There are no new cultural traits (our new technics) to experiment with and perfection and saturation are achieved, pp. 17-18. By comparison, "a changing society is changing because new elements are introduced." p. 18. Hart also noted that ". . .the history of culture shows many examples of stagnation and of deterioration in culture. . . .It is only over the long run, and on the whole, that cultural change can be said to accelerate persistently." Allen, *Technology and Social Change*, pp. 54-55.

[53]"After about a million years of cultural development, during which time cultural systems were activated almost exclusively by energy from the human organism, a radical change took place: solar energy was harnessed in the form of plants and animals." Leslie A. White, *The Evolution of Culture* (New York: McGraw-Hill Book Company, 1959), p. 281. Certainly this would constitute the major distinction between our stages I and II. Also, the tools would be different, in quality, the rate of producing those tools in quantity would also vary, the capacity to sustain and propagate populations would also vary, and consequently, such factors could then serve to indicate the various gestalts or levels of economic development.

[54]"It would also be widely acknowledged, however, that the character, scale, and capacity for growth of an economy are closely related to the whole society of which it is a part." W.W. Rostow, *The Process of Economic Growth* (Oxford: Oxford University Press, 1960), p. 20.

[55]This would be analogous to man's efforts in the specific area of transportation and measuring growth in miles per hour. The overall pattern is exponential but this was achieved not by simply perfecting one technic of transportation but rather by adding new technics as individual gestalts (the railroad, the automobile, the airplane. . .,etc) which individually were characterized by the logistic but in the process of "escalation" or "logistics urges" produced the exponential. Hart repeatedly in his discussions of the acceleration of culture refers to transportation in particular, note, Allen, *Technology and Social Change*, pp. 32-34; "Logistic Social Trends," *The American Journal of Sociology* 50 (March 1945), pp. 337-352, p. 344, "Acceleration and the Atomic Bomb," *American Sociological Review* 11 (June 1946), pp. 277-293, pp. 284-285.

[56]Underdeveloped countries cannot produce certain goods and services since they lack the technological maturity. Rostow's stage "The drive to maturity" is defined in terms of the level of technological advance. "This is the stage in which an economy demonstrates that it has the technological and entrepreneurial skills to produce not everything, but anything that it chooses to produce," *The Stages of Economic*

Growth, pp. 10, 59-72. A country in the stage of "the drive to maturity" has the technological capacity to produce what the most advanced countries are capable of producing if it were only to devote the necessary resources to its production. Such is not the choice or option of the underdeveloped countries. Rostow's breakdown of the modern epoch into the various stages, such as the "drive to maturity," while useful to clarify the point being made here, is nonetheless vague and difficult to quantify. Our preference for the modern epoch would be to use sub-stages delineated by the various specific and quantifiable energy gestalts, such as coal, petroleum and on.

[57]A very limited sampling of which reveals: ". . .a continuous and large rise in product per unit of labor is possible only with major additions of *new* technological and related knowledge," Simon Kuznets, *Six Lectures*, p. 29. "The state of technological knowledge limits what can be done with labor, capital and resources; what can be produced and how it can be produced." Richard R. Nelson in Walter H. Heller, ed., *Perspectives on Economic Growth* (New York: Random House, 1968), p. 189; "The response of the European economy to the new reasons for transformation, and consequently its capability for continued economic growth, will be the main theme of this study." ". . . 'uniform progress' without transformation can be regarded only as a highly abstract and theoretical conception." Svennilson, *Growth and Stagnation in the European Economy* (Geneva, United Nations, 1954), pp. 27, 7, 20-21. . . etc., and also, Svennilson's discussion of Gustav Cassels "uniformly progressive state," p. 5, and its relation to "technical progress;" "The technology existing at a given point in time sets limits on how much can be produced with a given amount of inputs." Edwin Mansfield, *The Economics of Technological Change* (New York: W.W. Norton & Company, 1968), p. 12. And Everett Hagen, "Viewed in the Broad Sweep of Human History, Improvement in technology and the resultant rise in per capita income have always been occurring everywhere. . . continuing economic growth—is obtained only by continuing improvement in techniques or products." *On the Theory of Social Change*, pp. 10, 12; "At low levels of technical knowledge there are severe limits to the extent to which output per man could be increased by more capital accumulation." Harvey Leibenstein in W.W. Rostow, ed., *The Economics of Take-Off into Sustained Growth* (New York: St. Martin's Press, 1963), p. 186; ". . .when one considers the nature of premodern methods of production it seems doubtful that greater capital, education and other quality inputs per worker, within the framework of that rudimentary technology, would have yielded the immense and continuing rates of productivity improvement characterizing modern growth." Richard A. Easterlin, *International Encyclopedia of the Social Sciences*, Vol. IV (1968), p. 406; "At a constant level of technological knowledge output per worker can be increased. . .but only to a certain extent. . .in the absence of new technological knowledge, sooner or later these possibilities would be exhausted." Nelson, Peck and Kalachek, *Technology Economic Growth and Public Policy*, p. 16. Recalling our discussions of

the Entropy Law, another way of viewing the level as a regulator of growth would be in terms of energy control, a country cannot move from a very low level of per capita income to very high levels without increases in energy control. And also, energy control and consumption, the capacity to do work, is a function of advanced levels of technology. "Large differences in income are associated with large differences in energy intake, and we may take it for granted that no country at this stage of history can enjoy a high per capita income without becoming an extensive consumer of energy." Edwards S. Mason, *Energy Requirements and Economic Growth* (Washington, D.C.: National Planning Association, 1955), p. 9. "The thesis of the book is simple. It is that the energy available to man limits what he *can* do and influences what he *will* do," and, "The thesis that theenergy available to man determines what man *can* do means that energy sets a limit. The idea that energy influences what man *will* do implies that within the limits so set the supply of energy is also a factor at work influencing choice." Fred Cottrell, *Energy and Society* (New York: McGraw-Hill Book Company, 1955), pp. 2, 9. "*A Society system may so condition the operation of a technological system as to impose a limit upon the extent to which it can expand and develop, when this occurs, cultural evolution ceases.*" Leslie A. White, "Energy and the Evolution of Culture," *American Anthropologist*, 45 (July-September, 1943), pp. 335-356, p. 348.

[58]This is not to deny the importance of economic growth as a necessary condition and as an aid in the process of economic development and as we have noted in numerous instances (vide ante) a circular relationship exists between economic growth and development. However, economic growth, by itself, if only based upon replication and duplication or increased factor inputs, will eventually level off and reach a limit. Economic growth by itself does not guarantee new technics and their innovation.

[59]We are not discounting cyclical movements around the long-term trend generated by depressions or wars which would shift the exponential curve and present a short-term discontinuity. We refer here to the overall secular trend, the behavior of economic growth in its long-term continuity, as having the exponential pattern. On the shifting of the expected exponential pattern, and using energy sources as an indicator, note, *Peaceful Uses of Atomic Energy* (New York: United Nations, 1956), Vol. 1, *The World's Requirements for Energy: The Role of Nuclear Energy*, p. 11. And also, Hornell Hart, "Depression, War, and Logistic Trends," *American Journal of Sociology*, 52 (September 1946), pp. 112-122. On the secular long-term trend viewed as a path of "dynamic equilibrium," note, William Fellner, *Trends and Cycles in Economic Activity* (New York: Henry Holt and Company, 1956), ". . . strong common-sense foundations" contained in "These fundamentals might lead one to expect that output should also be continuously rising . . ." p. 13. These fundamentals include a continuously expanding technology, (our basic ceiling constraint) "In spite of some lost arts, it is reasonable to assume

that our technological and organizational skills are *continuously* increasing" p. 13. And while not omitting the price-behavior or resource-mobility requirements of sustained growth, ". . . the main theme of the book . . ." is that, "Sustained economic growth requires qualitative adequacy as well as quantitative sufficiency of technological and organizational improvements, that is, of new skills." p. v. We agree with his supposition that though sectors of a particular economy achieve logistic patterns that such a flattening need not materialize for the economy (United States) as a whole, pp. 9-10, and p. 7 footnote No. 2. Such a view has a qualification, for in order to hold true we must speak of culture in a universal sense and not particular cultures (United States). While it may be realistic to assume that for culture as a whole or general culture evolution, that the long-term trend will be exponential this need not apply to specific culture evolution (cultures such as the U.S., U.S.S.R. and Japan) and that the long-term trend for a particular culture may well be a flattening or the logistic and even after it has embraced the gestalt of industrialism.

[60]The definition of cultural acceleration is by Hart which we have already referred to and constitutes the basic definition of cultural acceleration used in this study, note, Allen, ed., *Technology and Social Change*. p. 28, and note reference to the acceleration in cutting-tool efficiency as a prime example, pp. 28-30.

[61]This story has of course been well recorded, some of the basic works: Charles Singer, et al., *A History of Technology* (Oxford: Oxford University Press, 1954); T. K. Derry and Trevor I. Williams, *A Short History of Technology* (New York: Oxford University Press, 1961); and, Abbott Payson Usher, *A History of Mechanical Inventions* (Cambridge: Harvard University Press, 1954). "To appreciate the sluggishness of discovery and invention in prehistoric or early historic times, and down to the present day in most parts of the world, it is essential to realize that our own civilized conditioning to a technological environment has made this appreciation extremely difficult." Singer, (Vol. I), p. 60, (H. S. Harrison).

[62]We have already noted this point, that economic growth did not start from nothing circa, 1750, its acceleration increased perhaps but the principle of accelerated growth as such goes back to the start of culture. Sustained and high levels of growth perhaps started circa, 1750, but accelerated growth on an inter-stage basis or as a characteristic of general evolution began with the beginning of culture. The characteristics of such economic growth, such as specific products or rates of increase would change over time and be representative of a given gestalt. Consequently modern economic growth represents not the historic continuity of economic growth but only the type of growth characteristic of cultures which have embraced industrialism. Everett E. Hagen, *On the Theory of Social Change* (Homewood: The Dorsey Press, 1962) notes these points yet nonetheless defines economic growth in terms of the modern period: "Change at such a pace may be termed *economic growth*." p. 10. "The characteristic which distinguishes the modern

period in world history from all past periods is the fact of economic growth. It began in Western Europe . . ." W. A. Cole and Phyllis Deane, *The Cambridge Economic History of Europe* (Cambridge: At the University Press, 1965), H. J. Habakkuk and M. Postan, eds., Vol. VI, part (1), p. 1. As noted earlier, those who define economic growth in terms of "sustained rates" are limiting economic growth to the current stage of industrialism known as modern economic growth. Whereas our view is that economic growth, in a universal conceptualization and on an interepochal basis, is a function of culture evolution and economic development and, consequently, starts with the birth of culture.

[63]"One is to marvel at the high degree of technological attainment achieved without guidance from anything worthy of the name of science. Progress in technology, though exceedingly slow, was cumulatively astonishing in its extent." Singer, et al., *A History of Technology*, Vol. II, p. 774.

[64]This conceptualization of the process is similar to the method known as System Dynamics. "The basis of the method is the recognition that the *structure* of any system—the many circular, interlocking, sometimes time-delayed relationships among its components—is often just as important in determining its behavior as the individual components themselves." Meadows, et al., *The Limits to Growth* (New York: Universe Books, 1972), p. 31.

[65]The chicken and egg controversy concerning whether technology led science or science led technology is really not a controversy if viewed from the perspective of general culture evolution, for clearly technology precedes the advent of science. It is, of course, clear that technology has the long-term continuity in that its genesis was in the origins of culture. In that the scientific evolution is a phenomenon of the sixteenth and seventeenth centuries, technology as such predates science. "We repeat the obvious fact that technology is older than science . . . The only thing we can say with some assurance is that technology emerged before science." Robert Bruce Lindsay, *The Role of Science in Civilization* (New York: Harper and Row, 1963), pp. 198, 204. The controversy is related to the dramatic change in technology associated with the Industrial Revolution during the eighteenth century. Was the causal agent the fact that craftsmen and technological changes spurred on the scientific or were scientists and the stock of scientific knowledge the causal agents in the great technological changes of the period? Arguments can be found in support of both sides of the controversy. Concerning discussions of the issue in the literature we find: E. A. J. Johnson, "Industrialization and Economic Growth: Problems in Methodology," *Journal of Economic Issues* I (September 1967), pp. 219-230, questions the view presented by David S. Landes, that "Indeed, if anything the growth of scientific knowledge owed much to the concerns and achievements of technology." *The Cambridge Economic History of Europe*, Vol. VI, Pt. 1, p. 293. While recognizing the close alliance during the late nineteenth century Landes felt that Industrial Revolution" . . . the gap went from technology toward

science rather than the other way . . . when one speaks therefore, of the marriage of science and technology, one really refers to a complex liaison, which was not consecrated at a moment in time but developed slowly and unevenly, and varies to this day from country to country and industry to industry. There are still areas of production that must rely heavily on inspired empiricism. Nonetheless, it was the second half of the nineteenth century that first saw close systematic ties between the two . . ." p. 550. And further along these lines Edward S. Mason, *Economic Planning in Underdeveloped Areas: Government and Business* (New York : Fordham University Press, 1961), notes, "The early developments in industrial technology were undertaken not by men of science who discovered the practical application of general principles by skilled artisans and tinkerers working in the eighteenth century equivalent of a twentieth century garage." p. 32. Referred to by Gunnar Myrdal, *Asian Drama* (New York : The Twentieth Century Fund, 1968), Vol. I, p. 695, a position which Myrdal evidently supports. And, "Indeed, according to historians, little practical use was made of scientific knowledge until the middle of the ninteenth century . . . the inventions that provided the basis for the industrial revolution were invented by practical men and based upon observation, art, and common sense." Mansfield, *The Economics of Technological Change*, p. 11. By comparison, John Jewkes, et. al., *The Sources of Invention* (London; Macmillan, 1958) note that "In the nineteenth century there was apparently a stronger link between science and invention and a more closely knit society of men concerned with technical progress than is frequently supposed." p. 71. "But to speak of this century as the 'age of science' and of the nineteenth century as the 'age of empiricism' is far too bold a statement to contain the whole truth. Watt's steam engine was based on prior scientific knowledge . . ." p. 69. And on the steam engine, the symbol of the great breakthrough of the Industrial Revolution as man for the first time harnesses heat to power, Simon Kuznets states that, ". . . Watt's revolutionary changes in the steam engine represent essentially the application of scientific work and a scientific approach . . . In that sense the steam engine was the earliest major science-based invention . . ." *Modern Economic Growth* (New Haven : Yale University Press. 1966), p. 10 and also, *Economic Growth of Nations* (Cambridge : The Belknap Press, 1971), p. 330, footnote No. 4. This view is supported by milton Kerker, "Science and the Steam Engine," *Technology and Culture*, 2 (1961), pp. 381-390. In any case, the picture of steam engine technology that emerges is certainly more subtle than mere empiricism operating in the dark, far from the light of science," and, ". . . the conclusion is inescapable, almost obvious that the steam engine is a product of the age of science and is derived from science." pp. 384, 387. The Kerker article also appears in Thomas Parke Huges, *The Development of Western Technology Since 1500* (New York : The Macmillan Campany, 1964), and to which Lands notes : "There is no doubt some truth in this, though how much is impossible to say."

Ibid., p. 333, which is a more tractable statement and accommodating to the science-led view of technology than that which appears on p. 294, footnote No. 1 and views which Landes restates in his *The Unbound Prometheus* (Cambridge: Cambridge University Press, 1969), pp. 61, 104.

[66]*Modern Economic Growth*, p. 9, and also, "In these days it is hardly necessary to emphasize that science is the base of modern technology, and that modern technology is in turn the base of modern economic growth." This view also appears frequently in the literature, for example in the *International Encyclopedia of the Social Sciences* (1968), "In a fundamental sense, modern economic growth is a creature of the scientific revolution, for it reflects man's growing knowledge of natural phenomenon and the power thereby attained to mold his environment to his needs." (Easterlin), Vol. IV, p. 396; "Science now precedes technology . . . by the end of this century the further development of technology may be almost completely based upon the advances in scientific knowledge," Vol. 15, (Schilling), p. 594; ". . . one general trend is manifest : the ever closer marriage of science and technology . . . Beginning in the middle of the nineteenth century, however, a close alliance develops . . . the autonomous flow of scientific discovery fed a widening stream of new techniques." Landes, *The Cambridge Economic History of Europe*, Vol. VI, pt. 1, p. 550. Robert A Solo takes a view similar to Landes in that he questions the science-first supposition, ". . . between the rapid progress of science and of technology there was no clear connection." However, he does note the important role currently played by science, ". . . to an unprecedented degree in recent decades, the data of science are being accumulated and are being systematically utilized by trained professionals in order to solve problems of technology . . . Most important is the exploitation of the knowledge of competencies of science for the task of advancing the practical technologies." in *Economic Organizations and Social Systems* (Indianapolis: Bobs-Merrill, 1967), pp. 129, 116-118, 128-130; also, on the basic issue of science and its relation to technology, note: Peter F. Drucker, "The Technological Revolution : Notes on the Relationship of Technology, Science, and Culture," *Technology and Culture* 2 (1961), pp. 342-351. *In Summary* : "In our time technology has become almost synonymous with the application of scientific knowledge to practical ends. To us it seems that science is the source, the parent, of technology. Up to the end of the period treated in this volume, that is up to the end of 1500, and perhaps much later, it would be more accurate to say that technology was the parent of science. But from the rather indeterminate period usually called the Renaissance, natural phenomenon came to be more and more systematically observed. Moreover, knowledge of nature was ever-increasingly elicited by experiment, which is another word for controlled observation—a far more rapid and reliable way of extending knowledge. The rise of the use of experiment and recession of empiricism from technology will become increasingly evident as these volumes proceed." Charles Singer.

A History of Technology, Vol. II, p. 774.

[67]"Technological progress is not, of course, a new phenomenon in human history . . . What *is* unique about the modern era, however, is the rapidity, depth, and constancy of the flow of new technology. Past progress—like past economic development in general—was sporadic, uneven, and slow. Now, increasingly as the years go by, technological progress has become systematic and dependable; and it comes not in a trickle but in a flood." Richard T. Gill, *Economic Development : Past and Present* (Englewood Cliffs: Prentice Hall, 1967), pp. 17-18. "This cognitive tie between science and practice accelerated enormously the pace of invention." Landes, *The Combridge Economic History of Europe*, Vol. VI, pt. 1, p. 552. And also, Gunnar Myrdal, *Asian Drama*, Vol. I, pp. 700-705, for a reaffirmation of our view on the current relation of science to technological advance, and also, the Ogburnian exponential pattern.

[68]The industrial Revolution used here as David S. Landes does, is written in the upper case. *The Unbound Prometheus*, p. 1. to distinguish the eighteenth and nineteenth century experience in Great Britain from industrial revolutions, lower case, which took place elsewhere and later during different time periods.

[69]This study is directed toward an analysis of economic development in terms of "what is" and not "what ought to be," and consequently we assess the social of institutional setting in the context of its permeability to new technics. Capitalism may be questioned in many ways but not that it was not dynamic, on the contrary, that it was perhaps too dynamic in that the flood of new technics was if anything too rapidy and consequently too disruptive in that there were severe difficulties in adjustment. The fact remains, however, that capitalism in its origins represented the dynamic vanguard of culture advance and it accomplished this rapid flow of technology in the social environment of laissez-innover. Specifically how the social setting through which the new technics must pass is analyzed may be debated but that it is a warranted subject of analysis, given the field of inquiry as economic development, should, at this stage in the development of the social sciences, be beyond debate. Given the general institutional setting of capitalism should not infer a perfect homogenity of cultures. David S. Landes, *The Unbound Prometheus*, pp. 48-80, in his analysis of the Industrial Revolution discusses the British leadership in terms of social heterogeity in comparison to the Continent, differences which worked to the advantage of the British. Such as : "More than any other in Europe, probably, British society was open . . . barriers to mobility were lower . . ." p. 48, ". . . British commerce of the eighteenth century was, by comparison with that of the Continent, impressively energetic, pushful, and open to innovation." p. 52, "This readiness to abandon old ways for new, to place profit above craft pride . . . an orientation to the market . . . No where was the response to profit and loss so rapid . . . ." p. 54. What distinguished the British economy, as we have already had several

occasions to remark, was an exceptional sensitivity and responsiveness to pecuniary opportunity." p. 66, and in his discussion ends up with the current theoretical position (which we obviously endorse) that economic growth entails more than just the quantity of factor inputs but the "quality of inputs as well." p. 80.

[70]This does not mean that we have perfected our problem solving capacity. Obviously, there are currently many unresolved problems: cancer, unemployment, inflation, economic development, wars, to name a few, and assuming knowledge to be infinite, this will always be the case. But over time man's capacity for problem solving will increase, more and more of man's problems will prove tractable and amenable in a predictable fashion to man's science. "The point, as we have noted, is that man can order technological and scientific advance as one orders a commodity." Landes, *The Cambridge Economic History*, Vol. VI, Part I, p. 585. Consequently, whereas other overall gestalts were known for their ultimate rigidities and stagnations, industrialism as the gestalt fed by science, is known for its continuous flux and sustained growth.

[71]Hornell Hart, "Acceleration and the Atomic Bomb," *American Sociological Review* 11 (1946), pp. 277-293, especially, pp. 281, 290-91, and also, by Hart, "Human culture develops through a series of growth surges . . . Both in pre-history, over the long sweep of history and in modern times the slopes of logistic surges show a tendency to increase acceleratingly." in Depression, War, and Logistic Travels," *American Journal of Sociology*, Vol. 52 (September 1946), pp. 112-122, p. 122. And also, Palmer Cosslet Putnam, *Energy in the Future*, (Princeton ; D. Van Nostrand Company, 1953) pp. 277-282. On the "escalation" note Derek J. de Sola Price, *Little Science, Big Science* (New York : Columbia University Press, 1963), pp, 24-25, and for his reference to Gerald Holton, "Models For Understanding the Growth and Excellence of Scientific Research," in Stephen R. Graubard and Gerald Holton, eds., *Excellence and Leadership in Democracy* (New York; Columbia University Press, 1962), pp. 94-131.

CHAPTER X

Mankind at the Starting Point

On the one hand, then, we have those who support technological advance as the key to progress, not that technology need always be positive in each particular as to results, but that technological advance over the long run has provided a necessary condition for the further evolution and advance of man's culture and civilization.[1] We have tried to explicate this process by focusing on the concept and theory of economic growth and development. In the framework of cultural economics we have tried to show that the essence of the process concerns the advance of useful knowledge which is concreted, in its application and innovation, as technics of social organization and economic production. The overall gestalt of technology, as the totality of material and nonmaterial technics, constitutes the core of culture and the advance of which, as the process of economic development, provides for the dynamics of culture evolution. Culture, as the extrasomatic or the superorganic, provides an overall tool whereby mankind increases his capacity to control more and more free-energy and, consequently, to overcome the discipline embodied in the Second Law of Thermodynamics interpreted as the movement toward maximum entropy. In the process of economic development and culture evolution man gains control over higher levels and forms of energy and which, by definition, increases his capacity to do work. As man applies more energy over time he gains more power to reverse the long-term physical tendency toward entropic degradation. In transforming energy man increases his capacity to do work, a basic definition of the economic process, and in so doing man provides the motor force, the power, for culture evolution. The structure of this process appears as a paradigm of logistic surges underlying the exponential curve of culture evolution and economic development. The process is of value in that man advances his culture and civilization as a necessary condition for the promotion of further human development.[2]

On the other hand, and in contradiction, there are those at the opposite polarity who predict a catastrophic doomsday precisely because of the exponential curve of culture cumulation.[3] It appears intuitively obvious that ongoing exponential growth cannot continue in a finite system, a closed system, categorized and conceptualized as the "spaceship earth." Again, mankind appears at the cross roads.[4] As with Jevons, and in the Malthusian framework, it is predicted that the accelerating industrial processes will outrun a depleted base of finite resources. The paradox of exponential growth cannot long exist in a finite world. Are there compelling forces or reasons which are unalterable and which would lead us to conclude that an ongoing exponential process of economic growth and development will inevitably lead to a doomsday denouement? And if the result is not in the form of an inevitable doomsday, are the negative feedbacks of "growthmania" that extensive and overriding to force a choice, as policy, for a no-growth or steady-state economy.[5]

Though the conceptual and theoretical framework varies, it seems that most economists would endorse the policy orientation of more economic growth in opposition to the no-growth syndrome. A policy direction of more growth marks at least one instance in which institutional and mainstream economists can find living space and both dwell in the same room in terms of a similar policy goal and objective. Man will solve his socio-economic problems basically through the vehicle of more growth and not less. The mainstream position oriented toward more growth as a solution to our current problems is well-documented in the literature.[6] However, we do not infer that *all* mainstream and/or heterodox economists support the pro-growth position. As cases in point, Georgescu-Roegen, Boulding, Spengler and Heilbroner, among others, all of influence, and high reputation, and among the top scholars in economics, have made contributions to the anti-growth literature.[7] The reasons for questioning continued growth are many and they are diverse, and the conclusions reached in the literature do not all point to the doomsday finale.[8] And while the concepts and theories differ, as with the pro-growth group, those of the anti-growth predilection primarily argue that ongoing exponential growth cannot continue in a finite "spaceship earth." In the context of a closed system the focus is on finite energy and resources.

> "The central dilemma of all cornucopian premises is, of course, how to sustain an exponential increase of anything —people, mineral products, industrialization, or solid currency—on a finite resource base."[9]

To grow or not to grow, that is the question. Let us first assess some of the "not-to-grow" arguments. The Club of Rome stands in the vanguard of the limits to growth school of thought, basically we refer here to the works of Forrester, Meadows, and Mesarovic. This school of thought will receive our primary attention. Not because they represent the only anti-growth matrix but, rather, because of the brevity of our exposition and plus the fact that they are perhaps the most well-known. And while the Club of Rome was not necessarily the first to blow the whistle on the growth and ecological crisis, they blew it the loudest and with the clearest clairvoyance of impending disaster. To begin with what is the concept and theory of growth and development used by the Club of Rome in their analysis of exponential growth on a finite planet? In that we have just discussed the concept and theory of economic growth and development, for the past nine chapters in the framework of *cultural economics,* the issue is right down our alley. We will now try to show how *cultural economics* as a general theory of growth and development is relevant and applicable to one of the most pressing and serious problems of our time—the limits-to-growth issue.

First, in our discussion and analysis, we will assume that man will ultimately achieve a zero population growth (ZPG) and that such an achievement will be the result of increased growth and development. In advanced countries the historic exponential pattern of population growth is being bent toward the logistic and/or Gompertz configuration. Demographic predictions are, admittedly, subject to caution. But we submit, that given the assumption of ZPG, there is no reason to assume that compelling forces will necessitate zero economic growth (ZEG) and/or that we should reorient our basic policy toward a steady-state economy.[10] It is not our position to maintain that growth in its present structure and form can continue its exponential path but, rather, that given a change in the structure of growth that there are no unalterable or compelling reasons to assume that a limit to growth prevails. And/or that such a leveling of growth is inevitable or even desirable. Economic growth as it currently takes place in the form of more and more automobiles, powered by the internal combustion engine and the energy source of petroleum, plus the associated accumulation of waste and pollution, obviously cannot continue. However, that is not to say that economic growth, overall, in a general sense, as opposed to a specific type of growth, cannot continue and with exponential acceleration. This view is supported historically, by empirical evidence and predicated on structural change fed by the advance of technology. We speak of growth to be sure but qualitative growth rather than simple quantitative growth and/or replication. Historically, economic growth in a general sense has not been homogeneous or undifferentiated but has continued exponentially precisely because such growth has manifest a change in structure. We have referred to this previously as the process of "structural differentiation" and, also, as the "principle of similitude."[11] Therefore, we will argue that ongoing exponential economic growth is possible given the assumption of ongoing economic development.

In analyzing the conceptual and theoretical framework of the Club of Rome let us first start with the conceptual side of the limits to growth issue. Concerning the literature it should be noted that the problem is conceptualized as no-growth. Rarely do we find a suggested policy direction or goal in the conceptual framework of no-development. For while it is easier to accept the position of no-growth, it grates upon the ears and seems intuitively incorrect to be anti-development. But as our analysis has tried to show, growth and development are interrelated, we cannot hold back economic growth if we have continuous development. And economic development, in turn, is apparently fed by the inexorable flow of new knowledge rooted in the biological nature of man interacting with his physical and cultural environment. Also, while this inexorable process prevails for general culture evolution it need not, as we have noted in many instances, be inevitable or inexorable in the context of specific culture evolution. Therefore if economic development is ongoing, as the process of technological change, the results in the form of economic growth will also prevail in terms of the exponential and in the paradigm of logistic surges.

Next and still dealing with the conceptual problem we will now address the views of Mesarovic on the concept of economic growth as presented in *Mankind at the Starting Point*. For if we are to limit something, we must first clarify what it is we intend to limit.

> "Hence, unqualified arguments 'for' or 'against' growth are naive; *to grow or not to grow is neither a well-defined nor a relevant question until the location, sense, and subject of growing and the growth process itself are defined*."[12]

Conceptually, Mesarovic notes (p. 2) that economic growth is not a thing but a process, and to this we certainly agree. Mesarovic distinguishes economic growth in terms of two basic processes, the first type being that of "organic growth" and, the second, that of "undifferentiated growth." And it is the second type of growth of simple replication, as more and more undifferentiated growth, which cannot continue, "It is irrefutable that the second type of growth is cancerous and would ultimately be fatal."[13]

Mesarovic argues that whereas organic growth is to be preferred and can yet be experienced, it is undifferentiated growth which will have to stop. Mesarovic presents his organic analogy (p. 5) in order to overcome a weakness of the Meadows, study, *The Limits to Growth*, which viewed growth as being undifferentiated for the globe as a whole. Mesarovic by comparison, argues in favor of organic growth which infers that growth rates will be different for different regions of the globe with some being faster, others slower.[14] A homogeneous view of the system on a global scale such as provided by the Meadows' study is misleading. Mesarovic argues that organic growth is characterized by some parts growing faster than others in an organic whole viewed as an overall system of balanced growth.

Therefore, according to Mesarovic, the growth problem is still conceptualized on a global basis but not in homogeneous terms but, rather, in the context of heterogeneous problems of growth inherent in various regions.[15] Originally, in the earlier stages of analysis, Forrester concluded little hope for the underdeveloped world.[16] By comparison, Mesarovic apparently argues that the underdeveloped world in the proximate future can grow but that the industrialized regions should "... put a stop to further overdevelopment by accepting limits on a per-capita use of finite resources."[17] Ultimately, however, as with the oak tree leveling in its organic growth, the global picture presented is one of stable equilibrium.[18] Such a steady-state of global organic growth will not be achieved automatically but requires a "master plan" to function as a sort of biological DNA applied to the social.[19] And if not, then doomsday, and Mesarovic speaks, apparently, in terms of a time span of fifty years. And Mesarovic concludes "... the time that can be wasted before developing such a global system is running out. *Clearly, the only alternatives are division and conflict, hate and destruction.*"[20]

In the first place we feel that Mesarovic is conceptually wrong in his usage of the organic analogy. The organic analogy is useful in a static or functional framework in that it shows the interrelation of functional parts and, consequently, is amenable to a "systems" or "holistic" or "interdisciplinary" methodology. Institutional economics has been moving in this direction for some time now and we concur, obviously, with the methodology. And in reference to the processes of biological evolution, the organic analogy also serves to delineate and clarify the dynamic processes of growth and development. Consequently, we endorse the organic analogy for the static as well as the dynamic. Mesarovic is in error, however, in that his organic growth is relevant to specific development and evolution but not to general. Again that very important distinction of modern evolutionists, such as L.A. White and Sahlins and Service, is relevant. As we have noted, biological or culture evolution of the specific type must satiate and follow the logistic, such as Mesarovic's oak tree, D'Arcy Thompson's whale, and Hart's propeller driven aircraft. It is the process of overall or general biological evolution, however, which follows the path of the vine and appears in the paradigm or form of logistic surges.[21] Therefore organic growth related to the process of general culture evolution appears as the exponential and not the logistic. And again, ever since Galileo, who perhaps first drew attention to the "principle of similitude," the proposition holds that growth can be ongoing given a continuous change in structure.[22]

Therefore, while Mesarovic argues that differentiated growth, as organic growth, still produces the logistic we argue that it is precisely because of differentiated growth, viewed as changes of form and structure, that mankind can maintain the exponential on a continuum. The organic growth eludad to by Mesarovic is really related to changes within a given structure, the oak tree, and not to changes of the structure. But as we have tried to show it is the latter case, as general evolution, which constitutes the relevant process, be it biological or of culture. General evolution is related to changes of structure as one form is transformed to the next. Specific evolution, by comparison, concerns the growth and perfection of a given form such as the oak tree. Consequently, what will fix it all is inherent in the agency of social and cultural mutations, and we speak here of the agency downgraded and derided by the limits to growth school as the "technological fix."[23] It is the advance of useful knowledge, that when applied and concreted in the form of technological innovation, that provides the essence of the dynamics of the process of general culture evolution. And it is this process, which we contend, that is ongoing and potentially of no limit.

If for example, we observe the growth of man's population on earth, some areas experience more rapid rates of growth than others. Population growth is consequently analogous to Mesarovic's organic growth and, ultimately, it must satiate and follow the logistic curve of the oak tree But this is because we cannot drastically change the structure and form of the human body. Given a fixed structure and finite space, be it lilies in the pond, railroad tracks and a fixed territory or mankind's population on earth, there is a finite limit to the process of growth as simple replication of numbers. In the process, such exponential growth is transformed into the logistic. We do not argue that population growth can or even should continue exponentially.

That zero population growth will ultimately be achieved, as an assumption, serves as a necessary condition for ongoing and unlimited economic growth and development. Population growth must level off precisely because we cannot change the structure of Homo sapiens.

However if the size and structure and body weight of Homo sapiens could be reduced to that of the typical nerve cell in the brain, one human skull could contain the whole world-wide population of several billions of human beings.[24] In that biological evolution takes eons of time, the required and necessary transformation of the structure and form of Homo sapiens is not possible. Whereas the structure and form of the human body is fixed and rigid and must be taken as given, such is not the case, however, with the structure and form of economic growth and development. The rapid transformation of technology and culture witnessed during the twentieth century in areas of transportation, production, energy, communications, and on, appear as nothing short of fantastic.[25] The material technology of today borders on the science fiction of yesteryear.

Given the fixed structure and technology of the horse and buggy as transportation, mankind simply could not have experienced the growth of transportation to the point of several hundreds of billions of passenger miles as exists today. The growth in transportation, as measured by passenger miles, has been made possible not by replicating more and more horses but rather by switching gestalts from that of horse and buggy on to railroads, the automobile and the large commercial jets of the current period. The limited energy level, itself, inherent in animal power would have limited the capacity to do work and provide for increased passenger miles to the magnitude currently achieved with our advanced technics of transportation. Given horse and buggy technics, however, our capacity for transportation, measured in passenger miles, would have long since satiated in a veritable dung heap of enormous and catastrophic proportions.

Given the assumption of ongoing structural change, as a paradigm of logistic surges, continued exponential growth appears to be, conceptually, possible. Nonetheless, it also seems intuitively obvious that such exponential growth, that even if conceivable conceptually, given the fixity of the resource base provided by the "spaceship earth" cannot continue. Must not the doubling process of gobbling up more resources and energy, and producing the residue of more and more waste and pollution ultimately and inevitably come to a grinding halt? In that concept and theory tend to advance, together, in the framework of circular and cumulative causation, let us now engage theory, as we build our case against the limits-to-growth hypothesis.

The theoretical framework of the limits-to-growth school is found in the Malthusian contribution.[26] It was the exponential advance of population which placed pressure on a finite and limited base of agricultural production. The discipline inherent in the Law of Diminishing Returns produced the Malthusian prediction of crisis and inevitable doomsday. But the Malthusian framework was wrong in the nineteenth century context and it is equally wrong in the twentieth. The historic process of economic development has revealed that the solution to the problem of population override resides in technological change and the structural transformation of culture. And although Malthus lived and wrote during the dawn of the era marking the greatest technological breakthrough yet achieved and known to mankind, Malthus failed to make the connection. Malthus "...stood at the brink of a new century and failed to anticipate that the succeeding two centuries would show the greatest scientific gains in history—a chastening fact, well to keep in mind as one listens to the voice of the modern computer as it sings out the same Malthusian dirge."[27]

Culture in its evolution has cancelled out the weak assumption that nothing could be done to remove the causal roots of the impending crisis situation predicted by Malthus. The long-term process of economic development and growth has provided both the cause and cure for the population explosion. The record of the nations currently at stage of advanced MEG reveals population growth rates in the form of the logistic. The ultimate bending of the world-wide exponential population growth, we venture to say, will therefore reside in more growth and development and not less. The way to fully insure a continuity of the world-wide population explosion will be, indeed, through a policy of no-growth for the LDC. Perpetual economic stagantion will only perpetuate the world-wide population explotion.

And while representing a continuity of the Malthusian mentality, the Club of Rome, via the Mesarovic presentation, does not advocate laissez faire and opts for some mysterious "master plan," the basic policy inference is of a dismal nature. In that the essence of the problem is that of finite resources and in view of the fixed dimensions of the "spaceship earth" the problem will forever defy resolution. The crux of the crisis is consequently beyond mankind's capacity to solve. Resources are fixed and finite and, consequently, in the Malthusian tradition, there is nothing which can be done to solve the problem.[28] The recommended policy direction of no-growth or steady-state stagnation represents an *adjustment* to an insoluble problem; it does not, however, purport to solve the problem. Though we now stroke the canvass with a computer the picture painted is again of the dark and dismal Malthusian hue.

But mankind can do better, he need not simply adjust, the problem is subject to solution. In contradistinction to the doomsday soothayers, and the Malthusian framework, the Veblen-Ayres tradition as the "Law of Progress" offers, not simply an adjustment, but rather a possible solution. The consistent position of mainstream institutional thought has been that resources are not finite but rather continuously evolve and expand.[29] Natural resources are not static and finite but are subject to the dynamics of transformation in that they are a function of knowledge and technology.[30] Perhaps the best single source to further develop the Ayresian position of unlimited resources would be the updated version of the Zimmermann classic.

> "The concept of inexhaustible resources from the land and the sea is totally consistent with Professor Zimmermann's functional concept of resources. The 'neutral stuff' is available in sufficient quantity, and man's knowledge, the premier resource, makes it possible to convert and adapt the stuff to satisfy human needs. And man's knowledge is not consumed in use but expands with use—awareness of this simple truth is man's best hope for the future."[31]

We have, of course, referred to this basic theme frequently in our study and repeatedly emphasized the hypothesis that the advance of useful knowledge represents the essence of the processes of economic development and culture evolution.[32] But more, in explaining how this process takes place and in describing its structure, *cultural economics* has drawn attention to the Ogburn-Hart conrtibution which adds to the Veblen-Ayres framework and which provides for the crucial combination of the exponential and its underlying paradigm of logistic surges.[33] The basic proposition set forth by Galileo prevails in the "principle of similitude" in that ongoing growth is possible on a continuum given the condition of structural change.[34] Consequently, it is obvious that the resource of petroleum, as an energy gestalt, is definitely finite and limited and will ultimatly phase out in the decay of the logistic. Our overall resource base, however, will continue to expand as it has historically; resources, overall, do not decrease with long-term economic development and growth but experience exponential expansion in their evolution.

In the transformation of energy resources from fuel wood to fossil fuels and on to nuclear fusion and solar energy man continuously provides for higher levels of energy control. And, therefore, through economic development and culture evolution, by drawing upon more and more free energy mankind, in the process, overcomes the long-term tendency towards entropic degradation. The problem of continuous exponential economic growth concerns not the finite nature of resources but, rather, the issue is one of perfecting and improving upon our social organization in order to efficiently use a resource base potentially infinite in supply. In that the growth problem is really a problem of transition and the provision for efficient and smooth switches of energy and resource gestalts, the focus, should be on social organization and not the figment known as fixed resources. Ayres was correct all along.[35] And while negative offshoots such as the heat problem may ultimately prove interactable or difficult that is not to conclude that the problem is of the nature of finite resources. A potential heat contingency reinforces the view that the problem resides in the results of using resources potentially infinite in supply.[36]

All this is not to infer that we can go on with the replication of economic growth as it now takes place and that we can ignore negative consequences of waste, heat dissipation and pollution as well as be indifferent to conservation. Not that economic growth as it now appears in its current structure can continue, it cannot, nor that even if it could that it should. Galbraith is not alone in arguing for qualitative growth as opposed to the simple quantitative. Keynes also argued that economic growth, as we now know it, will not and evidently should not continue.[37] Given *cultural economics* we have tried to demonstrate in the context of concept and theory that accelerated magnitudes of ongoing growth are conceivable and possible given the assumption of continuous change in form and structure. And while it is not possible to predict the precise forms and structures of specific material and social technics, which will be derived from the future drift of culture, there are no compelling reasons to assume that the process of advancing useful knowledge as a series of logistic surges leading to the overall exponential, need ever be terminated by the constraint of finite resources.

In order to further clarify our point, that the earth in its limited spatial and physical dimensions does not constitute a finite limit of resources, and therefore of economic growth, as well, let us conceptualize the problem in the framework of what might be called a kaleidoscope analogy. The elements of earth appear as the bits and pieces comprising a huge kaleidoscope in which the general pattern and structure of economic growth and development is continuously capable of change to new forms and structures. Though a kaleidoscope, as with the earth, represents a finite entity in its physical dimensions, the patterns and structures which can be derived are infinite. In the case of culture evolution, however, the elements of innovation as the bits and pieces of knowledge (which determine resources) are not fixed and constant in number and form but are constantly changing and increasing over time. Invention it is to be recalled is the process of combining existing elements to form new structures as new technics. Given inexhaustible sources of energy the motor force to twist, turn and shake our kaleidoscope earth to produce new forms and structures is also infinite and unending. It is argued in the literature that nuclear fusion and solar energy do indeed provide the potential for an inexhaustible energy.[38]

> "The proceedings. . .present energy as the key that can unlock virtually every door of scarcity. If we can secure an inexhaustible source of energy, then the doom thesis will turn out to be invalid: we will never run out of natural resources."[39]

To our view useful knowledge will continue to accelerate in its accumulation and also that this accumulation will manifest itself in material culture as more economic growth. In this regard we do not treat economic growth as a statistic of uniform and homogenous dimensions representing production per capita correlated inexorably to increased pollution, ecological destruction and resource exhaustion. Economic growth need not simply be conceptualized as more and more cars and electric can openers. Growth, assuming technological change and culture evolution, entails not just proliferation and simple quantitative replication and increase, but growth can entail structural and quantitative changes as well. Given a leveling of the population we too would hope for a leveling or a zero-growth rate of specific consumer durables as well as substitution, such as more efficient and less polluting transportation systems; however, this does not infer a zero-rate of economic growth over all. As we further advance and explore and learn of space, as we move from Galileo's simple telescope, low in cost and resource utilization, the advanced complexity of technics (material and nonmaterial) associated with Cape Kennedy and Houston, we see not only great, even unbelievable, quality changes but also tremendous quantitative changes as well.

The dollar measurement of economic growth as we move from Galileo's telescope to Cape Kennedy would be a billion fold. The space authorities achieved such an increase in economic growth not simply by producing one-billion telescopes but rather through the qualitative changes associated with economic development and culture evolution and the development of new and complex tools of space exploration as well as for science overall. We would not like to inhibit or retard such economic growth, growth which leads not necessarily to more pollution and waste of resources, as would be the case of the automobile, but rather a type of economic growth which leads to advances in science and useful knowledge. Such material growth if thwarted and held back would also hold back the advance of science. In short what we are saying is that the answer to the growth question apparently lies more with a redirection of growth rather than that of no growth in that our continued conquest of knowledge will require larger accumulations of material buttresses.

And this need not always entail larger physical size but entails greater qualitative inputs which are more expensive and are, consequently, statistically reflected in measurements of economic growth or GNP per capita. For example, though the modern stereo set or the transistor radio may be physically smaller than their counterparts of the 1930's, and consequently may use even less in terms of resources, they do contain great qualitative changes and usually are more expensive in price per unit. Therefore, we have a type of economic growth, not necessarily of size or bulk, but rather of qualitative input which is reflected in higher levels of GNP per capita.

The analysis thus far assumes that a continuous flow of new knowledge, itself dependent upon structural change and the paradigm of logistic surges, is required for continued economic growth. Therefore, a possible upper limit or asymptotic ceiling on knowledge, itself, would also pose a constraint on continued exponential economic growth. Also, whereas transportation as specific functional area of the overall of culture evolution is perhaps ultimately limited by the speed of light, we are assuming that no such physical constraint appears concerning general culture evolution in that in essence we are dealing with the advance of knowledge and knowledge is infinite. Consequently, let us now look at the fountainhead of the process of economic development and culture evolution, do limits of useful knowledge exist and, thereby, provide for a bending of our exponential growth curve to the logistic?

Consequently, if it could be demonstrated that science itself will saturate and reach a ceiling in the future would not the same pattern then prevail in terms of culture advance. If science to production is the key to the dynamics of the modern period, is there any reason to assume that science, as a whole, will follow an "*S*" curve pattern and thereby lead economic development and growth along a similar path?

To begin with, that which accumulates in the process of culture evolution is infinite in scope; the dimensions of knowledge are infinite.

> Contrary to the nineteenth-century of science as a bounded or exhaustible field of knowledge whose dimensions would eventually be fully explored, we now assume on openness to knowledge which is marked by variegated forms of differentiation. . .a proliferation which was the consequence of the additional 'branching' of the field.[40]

It was a previously held view that we came to know more that there was then less to know. Currently, however, we find that as we advance the frontiers of new knowledge we find not finality but rather an expansion of the dimensions of what there is to know. The horizons of knowledge recede with scientific advance rather than come closer. As we come to know more we know that there is more to know and that we may never know it.

The branching and differentiation and specialization as more new knowledge begets more knowledge also accounts for the current "explosion" (more correctly acceleration) of knowledge as each new discovery, as each new field of inquiry leads to many more. The development of the field of molecular biology and the discovery of DNA have not closed the doors to knowledge about the evolution of life in the sense of completion or finality, any more than did Darwin's efforts during the nineteenth century but, rather, have shown how many new doors there would be to open. New knowledge shows how much we do not know and indeed, how much more we need yet to know and may never know.

> . . .In this view the world is not exhaustible, quite the contrary. It precisely never can be exhausted; there is more, infinitely more, to be known and we may never know it.[41]

But even granting the point that knowledge itself is unlimited our means for acquiring such knowledge may not be and consequently the lack of such a capacity could produce the end result of saturation and a ceiling on man's accumulation of science.

Derek J. de Solla Price, for example, contends not necessarily that knowledge is subject to limitation but rather that our means of acquiring knowledge will reach saturation, that we will reach a saturation in the numbers of scientists and therefore also of science.[42] However, saturation in scientists or in particular methods of science need not saturate science as a whole. Though particular fields or areas of science will undoubtedly follow the logistic, the overall of science will, to our view, follow the exponential. For example, one would expect, ultimately, that scientific journals and articles as a method or technic of communicating and accumulating scientific knowledge will run their course and achieve a plateau, as would be expected for other individual parts of the whole of science, but this need not lead to a limitation on man's overall capacity to acquire new knowledge though scientific methods in general.[43]

It should be noted that scientific journals and the articles contained therein serve as indirect indicators but not direct measures of the advance of science. Therefore, to say that scientific journals, abstracts and articles, as specific technics of science will satiate is one thing, to infer that the general evolution of science will satiate as a result is another. Ultimately, it is predictable that scientific journals and articles as technics of presenting and storing science will ultimately satiate as might also be said of the automobile, the internal combustion engine and petroleum as technics of transportation. But that is not to say that scientific inquiry and production of new knowledge, overall, must satiate given the perfection and satiation of a specific field or technic of science. The continued exponential growth of science will require continuous changes in the structure of science as well as the invention of new technics to present, store and organize that knowledge.

New methods and technics for discovering new technics of science as well as the store of science are themselves functions of the advance and level of useful knowledge. Such methods and technics are conceivably themselves unlimited since they themselves are functions of a knowledge marked by unlimited dimensions. Granting that ultimately men's total population will predictably level off in the future, a very reasonable assumption though not precisely predictable in terms of when and at what level, this will represent a finite entity in the quantity of scientists. But the quality of those scientists need not by comparison reach saturation and finite limits in that man has the unlimited capacity to devise new tools and methods as aids in the acquisition and generation of new knowledge, and in addition, also has at his disposal an unlimited capacity of energy control since energy control itself is also a function of useful knowledge and its advance.[44] Consequently, even assuming that the population will level off and ultimately reach a plateau and, therefore, a finite number of scientists we need not, however, assume a finite limit for man's capacity to generate and accumulate scientific knowledge. Therefore, since there is no limit to knowledge in its substance, and since there is no limit to man's tools and means of energy control in that tools and energy are both functions of knowledge, which is itself unlimited, there is theoretically no limit on man's capacity to generate and accumulate scientific (useful) knowledge.

Given the assumption that the stream of useful knowledge in its source is endless, that the fountainhead is infinite in supply, is the reservoir, the store of knowledge (our culture), infinite in capacity as a container? Culture advance and evolution entails not only the flow of knowledge but its innovation as well. Is the area to which useful knowledge is to be applied also infinite? We have conceptualized culture as the store of knowledge. Is there anything which will limit the size of the container of culture such as the limited size of our earth? Prior to the twentieth century our gestalt of technology has been applied to the earth and its immediate atmosphere but now with the penetration of outer space and the moon landing we have opened the solar system and beyond. We need no longer fear being bound by a finite earth of finite resources saturated by man's culture, the universe stands before us. There is consequently no overriding reason to assume a logistic curve for the advance of science and knowledge based upon a limited area of application.[45]

In that resources and energy are potentially inexhaustible in supply and in that there appear to be at present no limits to the acquisition, application, and store of useful knowledge there are, consequently, no compelling reasons to assume that the current exponential phase of culture advance and economic development will eventually reach a point of saturation. Theoretically man's capacity for economic development and economic growth is unlimited. Simon Kuznets observes that:

> "Difficult as it is to imagine unlimited growth in any social process, there are no inherently *compelling* reasons for the rate of growth of per capita product to decline. In the light of our earlier discussion, technological and other limitations on the *supply* side can hardly be viewed as an important factor.[46]

And, finally, that there are "no inherently compelling reasons" to assume that unlimited economic growth and development will necessarily be thwarted does not infer that the forces propelling culture forward are inexorable and inevitable and that culture acceleration in the direction of infinity will always be the case. That unlimited culture acceleration will continue toward infinity rests upon *ceteris paribus* assumptions. Nuclear annihilation, for example, a very real possibility, as well as some unforeseen natural calamity could conceivably arrest such an advance. Therefore, while our theoretical prophecy of unlimited economic growth and development can be so, it need not be so.[47] Exogenous forces, such as wars or natural calamities, are by definition and theory not endogenous or built into the system of culture evolution. Consequently, such forces do not provide compelling reasons to warrant the conclusion of ultimate and inevitable collapse or cataclysm. It may all come crashing down someday but it need not. And, especially, it need not collapse due to a finite earth and the figment of finite resources.

To grow or not to grow is consequently not the relevant question.[48] The question is really how to improve upon the quality of economic growth potentially unlimited in its advance. The issue of limited resources diverts attention from the real and primary problem area, the area of social organization.[49] S. Fred Singer correctly states the problem: "The growth versus no-growth controversy is largely a red herring; the real issue is whether the price system can do the job of guiding the necessary adjustments or whether centralized decision making is called for."[50] The problem is one of essentially adjusting to ongoing exponential economic growth and development through continuous transformation directed toward the perfection of the social structure. The issue is one of how to promote an efficient and perfected social organization to serve as a concomitant to resources potentially infinite in supply. The mechanism and process used in the perfection of the social structure is the same as that used in the perfection of the material sector; we speak here of the application of science to social organization. Such a process, though in a nascent stage of evolution, already exists and we note examples of specific social inventions such as the Constitution of the United States, the Treaty of Rome and the EEC, the IMF and overall, the organization of markets and laissez faire and the science of Adam Smith and, also, the deficit spending and the mixed economy associated with the science produced by John Maynard Keynes and others. These social technics were not of prior existence awaiting to be discovered under a rock, so to speak, but were created and invented by man through the application of useful knowledge. Such a process and, its results has sometimes, incorrectly, been referred to as "social reform" but this incorrectly gives the connotation of the application of emotion rather than science. Such a process should more correctly be designed as "social perfection" through the application of science, rather than "social reform." The process of social perfection is the same process as is used in the perfection of both parts of culture known as the material and the social. In the context of modern economic growth the process is that of applying science to *both* economic production as well as social organization. While the process is accepted in general it has been institutionalized more in the area of perfecting material technics such as tools, machines, buildings and energy control rather than that of the social structure. There has been, relatively speaking', a cultural lag and resistance toward the application of science to social organization.[51]

Viewed in this perspective, then, perhaps the major basic problem of the future advance of culture, stated as a general theoretical proposition, is consequently, not finite resources but rather would be that of cultural lag. More specifically the problem concerns the synchronization of changes in the institutional sector to those in the material. Theoretically, a wheel spun in a vacuum will spin forever, but in the real world, however, we find friction. Given certain assumptions, our wheel of economic development could spin indefinitely; it may, however, come to a grinding halt if the institutional or non-material lags too far behind. The culmination and fruition of industrialism in the context of economic development will be when man employs a balanced application of science to both social organization and economic production. When man applies science not only to material technics but to social technics as well, and with similar resolve and efficiency, culture will then advance along the spiral of "a frictionless wheel of economic development."[52] Such a system will expand exponentially and theoretically without limit.

Therefore, the problem is essentially one of synchronization. The basic mechanism of synchronization appears as the application of knowledge (science) in problem solving. But since this is basically our conceptualization of technology, what we are really saying, then, is that the "technological fix" will provide for the overall panacea. But it should also be realized that *cultural economics* clarifies the concept of technology as well as the technological process as substantively including *both* material and social technics. By comparison, when Garrett Hardin in, "The Tragedy of the Commons" draws attention to certain problems that have "no technical solution" the inference is that technology is material and not social.[53] To Hardin the propagation of the position of "no technical solution" connotes "courage" whereas to our view it connotes an incorrect conceptualization of technology. For it should also be observed that Meadows, Mesarovic, Daly, Brown, et al., while on the one hand they apparently deny the "technological fix," on the other hand they have all noted the importance of social policy and even some form of social planning as a means of adjustment to our current growth and development problems.[54]

Social solutions are frequently interpreted as nontechnological but in the context of our dichotomy of useful knowledge we argue that social technics constitute integral and substantive parts to the overall of technology. In the literature the distinction which we are describing here is sometimes referred to as "hardware" in relation to the physical and material and "software" in relation to the social or nonmaterial. In that the "software" technology must catch up to the "hardware" technology, "Our highest futures priority lies with social invention—the revaluation and redesign of our social forms and possibilities.[55]

Therefore, adjustment through technological change as the "technological fix" means the invention and innovation of *both* material and social technics. The solution to the crisis situation of the 1960's and 1970's in the areas of economic growth, energy and resources will require additions and accumulation (not stagnation) in both the material and nonmaterial sectors of culture. In the material sector, as examples of important areas in need of improvement, there is a need for substitution and new technics to replace the automobile and the internal combustion engine, more rapid transit and light-rail systems, and of course the big areas of new material technology in the promotion of fusion and solar energy.[56]

On the social side of the ledger, which represents the more difficult and lagging sector of technological change, there is need of more efficient social organization of what already exists and is in use but, also, there must be innovated more efficient mechanisms of transition as we shift from one logistic curve to the next. A question arises as to whether or not capitalism, as the overall rubric of social organization, is up to the challenge and is capable of providing for the necessary adjustments to the current crisis situation. Will resolution take place through a further perfection of the system of capitalism or is there a need for the innovation of a new and alternative socio-economic system? It is our optimistic view that the answer resides decidedly in a further perfection of the structure rather than in the innovation of some new and revolutionary structure as a gestalt switch. However, this does not mean a rigid structure of no change in terms of transformation and evolution.

Capitalism has historically served as a social concomitant to a material sector experiencing exponential accumulation of goods and services. Capitalism has not stood still, for had it not experienced a transformation of structure in its evolution it would have long since stagnated and declined given the discipline dictated by the principle of similitude. Not, certainly, that the system has been perfect, and did not experience friction and periodic collapse, but that it proved operational and that culture in the long run did advance exponentially. And, importantly, that it did so in the millieu of democratic institutions.[57] Equity and normative considerations, aside, the system of capitalism has provided the necessary overall, social concomitant to the exponential advance of the economic processes. The price system worked in the setting of laissez-faire, as well as laissez-innover, to promote the logistic surges, as one structure was innovated and substituted for another, in both material and nonmaterial culture. We speak here of technological advance in the areas of transportation, energy control, monetary systems, business and labor organization, and on. Given the system of capitalism, as the base of overall social organization, both material and social technics proved porous and permeable to the dynamics inherent in the application of modern science. The price system worked and was rather remarkable in its dynamics. Consequently, the exclusion of the price system as a mechanism of adjustment represents a major weakness of the MIT model. "No useful economic model is complete without some account of adjustment mechanisms. The very important adjustment mechanism which is central to the whole economic idea is the mechanism of the price system. The MIT model nowhere recognizes that this mechanism comes into account."[58]

In the U.S. economy and that of Western Europe and Japan the market mechanism and prices will continue to play important and dynamic roles of adjustment in the overall economic process. However, as the study of economic history reveals, the past experience of the market system has not always been in accord with textbook predictions. Anomalies appeared in various forms which indicated that sometimes pain rather than pleasure was being maximized through the long-run processes of adjustment. In the long-run it is perhaps true that such anomalies and cultural lags would ultimately melt and be adjusted through the price and market mechanism. But Keynes has taught us, however, that in the long-run the human condition of maximum entropy has proved uninteresting. In that technology is currently advancing so rapidly and with it pollution and depletion, our adjustment mechanism embodied in the overall social organization must be more responsive to short-run crises situations. Therefore, something must be added to the adjustment mechanism inherent in the market and prices in terms of a more immediate and instantaneous short-run response We can no longer exclusively afford the luxury of the long-run as the waiting period for solution. Consequently, there is apparently the need for a further change of the social structure of capitalism in the direction of what might be called indicative planning.[59]

If it had been for basic changes in its structure capitalism would have long ago stagnated in its evolution. Capitalism would not have kept pace and could not have served as a social concomitant to a material sector experiencing exponential expansion. The anomalies inherent in the massive unemployment and the Great Depression of the 1930's generated a crisis situation which pressured a transformation of the social structure from that of laissez-faire to that of the mixed economy and the welfare state. Once again the social structure is under pressure for further transformation and evolution only this time brought about by the crisis inherent in the anomalies of the 1960's and 1970's.

Therefore, in addition to the private entrepreneur to serve as the innovator, to provide for the new technics of structural change, we now speak of the government and its vital role as innovator in the economic process.[60] And while problems associated with current attempts at indicative planning might be cited to indicate avoidance and rejection, the alternative in the form of the unmitigated market process is also replete with what has been described broadly as "market failures."[61] Our first steamships, automobiles and airplanes also failed in one way or other, but ultimately these technics were perfected with the application of advanced knowledge and science. The same process of perfection will prevail with the technic of economic planning.

Recall the first ventures at space exploration attempted by the United States and how American hearts sank with despair at the collapse and explosion of the rocket on the pad. To get to the moon, however, we had to use rockets, no one disputed this point; the problem was one of perfecting and improving upon, rather than rejecting, the technic of space rocketry. Also, if mankind wishes to reach for the moon on earth, if mankind wishes to resolve his socioeconomic problems of unemployment, inflation, stagflation, conservation, pollution, poverty, solar energy, and on, it will require a further centralization and increased complexity of our social nervous system. We feel that the required and necessary synchronization of the economy will be achieved though a more active participation of the government in the future development of the economy and that this will mean a further advance toward some form of economic planning. And again, this is not to preclude or negate the monetary and fiscal policies and theories inherent in the neoclassical synthesis but, rather, that such policies must be advanced and further integrated into some form of overall national planning directed toward perfecting a structure of quality economic growth and development.[62]

And finally, in these discussions it should be noted that not only would a policy of limiting economic growth exacerbate global conflict and be completely out of touch with the problems faced by underdeveloped countries, but if our analysis and theory are correct, and if the process of economic growth and development is in essence that of advancing useful knowledge and science, a ceiling on growth and development will, consequently, place a ceiling on the advance of mankind's culture and civilization. And this we do not wish to do. Mankind is at the starting point; the civilization of mankind constitutes only one percent of the overall experience of culture evolution.[63]

The civilization process of mankind has, consequently, just started and with the advent of the Scientific Revolution of sixteenth and seventeenth centuries we are truly looking at the dawn and sunrise and not the sunset. Through the processes of economic growth and development mankind increases, with acceleration, the capacity to gobble up more and more of the infinity of knowledge and with bigger and bigger bites. The motor force to do all this work is generated by higher and higher levels of energy control, itself, a function of the advance of useful knowledge and technology. Culture, then, in its evolution becomes the extrasomatic tool whereby man overcomes the long-term movement toward entropic degradation.

The limits to growth school has not correctly conceptualized the process of economic growth and development. They fail to understand that economic growth is a manifestation and concretion of the advance of useful knowledge and serves as a necessary condition for the continued advance of culture evolution. In the late nineteenth century, during the era of Charles Darwin and early theories of evolution, it was perhaps difficult to imagine, conceptually, a transmutation and evolutionary biological process which started from one-celled simplicity and which was ongoing to achieve the multicellular complexity known as man. Approximately one hundred years later, it is perhaps equally as difficult, by comparison, for man to conceptualize and imagine his truly explosive position in relation to his advance of knowledge and his growing control over energy. Culture, increasing at an exponential rate and without conceivable limitation, is no easier in this regard to comprehend than the concept of infinity.

It has taken man a long time to advance culture to its current stage of economic development but the process is only at the very early beginning in the long-term advance of useful knowledge. We are now standing on the shores of the infinite sea of knowledge and our toes are scarcely wet. Mankind is at the starting point and not the turning point. We no longer have the world to conquer; it is now the universe. Such an undertaking has the dimensions of infinity and of no limit.

REFERENCES

[1]Marc Tool writing in the Veblen-Ayres tradition focuses on this issue, cf., "A Social Value Theory in Neoinstitutional Economics," *Journal of Economic Issues*, 11 (December 1977), pp. 820-843, and, *The Discretionary Economy* (Santa Montica: Goodyear Publishing Company 1979). Marc Tool's contribution reinforces the work of Gunnar Myrdal in the area of value *vis-a-vis* economics, and explicitly stated by Clarence E. Ayres, *The Theory of Economic Progress* (New York: Schocken Books, 1962), "Economics is nothing if it is not a science of value," p. 208.

[2]An interesting exchange of views on the no-growth issue, finite resources and the Ayresian "Law of Progress" appears in the literature: Joseph J. Spengler, "Limits to Growth: Biospheric or Institutional?," in *Science and Ceremony*, (Austin: University of Texas Press, 1976), William Breit and William Patton Culbertson, Jr., eds., pp. 115-133, and, Baldwin Ranson, "The Limits to Growth: Is Ayres's Position Unwarranted?," *Journal of Ecocomic Issues*, 13 (September 1979), pp. 655-669. Has Ayres led us astray by focusing on the social structure rather than finite resources?

[3]For a good discussion of the exponential problem in the context of the doomsday scenario, cf., Dennis L. Meadows, et al., *The Limits to Growth* (New York: Universe Books, 1972), pp. 1-87. On the general approach note the "system dynamics" of Jay W. Forrester, "Counter-intuitive Behavior of Social Systems" appearing in both the *Technological Review* 73 (January 1971), pp. 53-68 and *Technological Forecasting and Social Change* 3 (1971), pp. 1-22. The article just cited represents somewhat of a condensed version of his *World Dynamics* (Cambridge: Wright-Allen Press, 1971). Another statement of Forrester's systematic analysis of global growth and collapse appears in the "Report for the Club of Rome's Project on the Predicament of Mankind," i.e., Dennis L. Meadows, et al. *The Limits to Growth* (New York; Universe Books, 1972). Using computer simulation technics, a picture of an ecological cataclysm, circa, one-hundred years, is projected on the world growth horizon. *Limits to Growth* is a literal attempt at "blowing the whistle" in order to make man realize before it is too late and he does not have too much time) that he cannot continue on with the senseless plunder, pollution, destruction, and exhaustion of his planet earth. "*We can thus say with some confidence that, under the assumption of no major change in the present system, population and industrial growth will certainly stop within the next century.*" *Limits to Growth*, p. 126, "... the limits to growth will be reached sometime within the next one hundred years." p. 23. "*The basic behavior mode of the world system is exponential growth of population and capital followed by collapse.*" p. 142. The argument is presented that rather than have the current system run its course and in the process decrease world population (death and famine) through an oversaturated planet that man should intervene, before it is too late, and plan a transition toward some state of global equilibrium. The argument is put forth that in order to avoid catastrophe, man should intervene and plan a transition (on the idea of transition, note, *World Dynamics* " . . the transition from a world of growth to a world in equilibrium. ." pp. 5, 112, 126. . ., etc., *Limits to Growth* ". . . to join us in understanding and preparing for a period of great transition—the transition from growth to global equilibrium." pp. 24, 191, 193 and in passim) toward some form of global equilibrium, a planned stationary state (on the nature of global equilibrium," note, *Limits to Growth*, pp. 154-184, defined, p. 171. "The question is only a matter of when and how growth will cease, not whether it will cease." *World Dynamics*, p. 68. In short, " . . exponential growth cannot continue indefinitely." p. 2, "Forces within world system must and will rise far enough to suppress the power of growth." p. 5, "Exponential growth rates do not continue forever." p. 68, and *Limits to Growth*, pp. 45-87, "But virtually no one will argue that material growth on this planet can go on forever." p. 153 and in passim). The *ceteris paribus* assumptions of their argument rest upon continued population and capital expansion in the context of finite resources. "By now it should be clear that all these trade-offs arise from one simple fact—the earth is finite." pp. 86, 54-69,

and ". . . physical resources . . . are the ultimate determinants of the limits to growth on this earth." p. 45, and, *World Dynamics*, "The modes of behavior of interest in this book encompass the interactions that occur when exponential growth collides with a fixed environment." p. 68, and "But the reservoir is limited. Exponential growth cannot continue." p. 124. And also, Dennis L. Meadows, et al., *Dynamics of Growth in a Finite World* (Cambridge: Wright-Allen Press, 1974) and Mihajlo Mesarovic and Eduard Pestel, *Mankind at the Turning Point* (New York: E.P. Dutton & Co., 1974)

[4]As with an earlier statement by William Stanley Jevons, *The Coal Question* (London: Macmillan and Co., 1865) the question of ongoing growth and depleted resources has recurred: E.M. East, *Mankind at the Crossroads* (New York: Scribner's, 1923); E.A. Ross, *Standing Room Only* (New York: Appleton, 1927); Fairfield Osborn, *Our Plundered Planet* (Boston: Little Brown and Company, 1948), and for additional references, W.N. Peach and James A. Constantin, *Zimmerman's World Industries and Resources* (New York: Harper and Row, 1972), pp. 553-558, and their citation of Wilma Belden Fairchild, "Renewable Resources: A World Dilemma. Recent Publications on Conservation," *Geographical Review* (January 1949), pp. 86-89.

[5]Herman E. Daly, *Toward a Steady-State Economy* (San Francisco: W.H. Freeman and Company, 1973), for a more compromising position, note, Mancur Olson and Hans H. Landsberg, eds., *The No-Growth Society* (New York: Norton, 1973). In the preface to Warren A. Johnson and John Hardesty, eds., *Ecocomic Growth vs. The Environment* (Belmont: Wadsworth Publishing Company, 1971) we find: "In a finite world no positive growth rate can be maintained forever; it is a physical impossibility. This principle as applied to population growth, is rapidly gaining acceptance. It is the purpose of this volume to argue that an analogous conclusion regarding economic growth is also inevitable. . ." For economists, who have been trained in the arts of profit maximization and growthmanship, acceptance of such a policy direction would require a completely new reorientation concerning the processes and objectives of economic growth and development. "Progress and growth, the ideals that have been so much a part of the American dream, must be replaced by the ideals of balance and stability." p. 3. But in addition the view to some is not simply zero growth but actually minus growth. "A static GNP at the current $1 trillion level will only keep environmental destruction from increasing. An actual reduction in GNP is called for if the detrimental effects of man's economic activities are to be minimized." p. 94.

[6]Max E. Fletcher, ed., *Economics and Social Problems* (Boston: Houghton Mifflin Company, 1979), Adherents to the no-growth position currently make up only a small part of the general public and probably an even smaller proportion of professional economists, p. 283. To our view both mainstream and institutional economists support the position of unlimited growth. On the mainstream position (briefly): Robert M. Solow, "Is the End of the World at Hand," in *The Econo-*

mic Growth Controversy (White Plains: International Arts and Sciences Press, 1973), Andrew Weintraub, et al., eds., pp. 39-61; Wilfred Beckerman, *Two Cheers for the Affluent Society* (New York: St Martin's Press, 1974); William D. Nordhaus and James Tobin, "Growth and Natural Resources" in *Economics of the Environment* (New York: W.W. Norton & Company 1977), Robert Dorfman and Nancy S. Dorfman, eds., pp. 400-403. And the other basic works of rebuttal to the Club of Rome studies: H.S·D Cole, et at., *Models of Doom* (London: Sussex University Press, 1973), and John Maddox *The Doomsday Syndrome* (New York: McGraw-Hill 1972). On the institutional economist's views, cf., Ranson, "The Limits to Growth" and Spengler's "Limits to Growth." "Institutionalists have been guilty, along with most orthodox economists, of neglecting biospheric constraints on the current and the prospective state of human existence." Spengler, pp. 126-127.

[7]On this account we have already cited Spengler, "Limits to Growth;" and in addition, Nicholas Georgescu-Roegen, "The Entropy Law and the Economic Problem," and Kenneth E. Boulding, "The Economics of the Coming Spaceship Earth," in *Toward a Steady-State Economy*, Daly, ed., pp. 37-49, and 121-132; and also Robert L. Heilbroner, *An Inquiry into the Human Prospect* (New York: W.W. Norton, 1975), "The industrial growth process. . . will be forced to slow down, in all likelihood within a generation or two, and will probably have to give way to decline thereafter. . . we must anticipate the commencement of a new era of stationary total output and (if population growth continues. . .) declining materials output per head in the advanced nations." p. 129.

[8]Lester R. Brown, *The Twenty-Ninth Day* (New York: W.W. Norton and Company, 1978), "Some will view the changes in prospect with alarm, even in the doomsday terms. Others, including the author, believe that the problems outlined in this book are manageable but that managing them satisfactorily will require an exceptional exercise of political will and human ingenuity." p. 11.

[9]Preston Cloud, "Mineral Resources in Fact and Fancy," in *Toward a Steady-State Economy*, Daly, ed., pp. 50-75, p. 58.

[10]The solution to the population problem will ultimately be achieved through further economic growth and development, cf., Beckerman, *Two Cheers for the Affluent Society*, p. 193. And Clarence E. Ayres, *Toward a Reasonable Society* (Austin: University of Texas Press, 1961), ". . .all our experience of problem-solving points toward the probability that the population problem can and will be solved." p. 244. (Note Spengler, "Limits to Growth," p. 124, and footnotes 50, 51 and 52).

[11]Recall our references to Daniel Bell, "The Measurement of Knowledge and Technology," in *Indicators of Social Change* (New York: Russell Sage Foundation, 1968), E.B. Sheldon and W.E. Moore, eds., pp. 149-152, and *The Coming of the Post-Industrial Society* (New York: Basic Books, 1973), pp. 172-174, and also, "Mediating Growth Tensions," *Society* 15 (January/February, 1978), pp. 34-48.

[12]Mesarovic and Pestel, *Mankind*, p. 3. "In other words, we need

to know what is meant by 'growth,' and in what sense that growth is considered as desirable or undesirable. Growth, after all, is a process not an object; it cannot be pointed at physically, like a chair or table, for the sake of explication; rather, it must be conceptually defined." p. 2. "Put in another way, we should not tackle vast problems with half-vast concepts." Daly, *Toward a Steady-State Economy*, p. 51. Also, cf., a review of *Limits to Growth* entitled "Limits to Misconception," *Economist* (March 11, 1972), pp. 20-22, in that many of the issues raised by the limits-to-growth school would be resolved given a clearer conceptualization of the processes of growth and development which are involved. As we have also tried to maintain, man cannot provide billions and billions of passenger miles in transportation given horse-and-buggy technics. We have maintained that there is a limit to the growth and development of such a particular gestalt but from this do we infer a limit on the growth and development process overall. We feel that discussions concerning the pros and cons of growth, development and ecology are unnecessarily confused by a lack of proper clarification and basic understanding of the concepts and processes involved. For example, Shepard B. Clough, *The Economic Development of Western Civilization* (New York: McGraw-Hill Company, 1959), states that, "Desirable as economic growth may be, it cannot be expected to continue indefinitely, to infinity. It creates certain counterforces to curb it." pp. 14-15. Clough then goes on to list some of the standard factors usually referred to in such discussions, such as population and resources, and concludes in support of his position, "In no case in history has there been a straight-line progression of economic expansion; no society has attained and maintained economic primacy permanently." p. 15. Clearly the views of Clough concern cultures or specific culture evolution rather than general culture evolution. It is not our view that economic growth and development as processes necessarily continue indefinitely in the context of a given culture, but rather our analysis concerns that of general culture evolution.

[13]Mesarovic and Pestel, *Mankind*, p. 55.

[14]A position frequently presented in the Mesarovic and Pestel, *Mankind*, study is that "*. . .a path which leads to a solution is that of organic growth.*" p. 7, 9, 18, 54, 56, 70, 87, 144, 146, and passim.

[15]For critique by Mesarovic and Pestel of the homogeneous view of the global or one-world problem as offered in this Meadows study, cf., *Mankind*, pp. 36-59. It was perhaps the one-world view of the Meadows study which led Gunnar Myrdal, among others, to note: "All this loose talk about planetary and global solutions is humbug." in *On Growth* (New York: G.P. Putnam's Sons, 1974), Willem L. Oltmans, eds., p. 233.

[16]Another conceptual issue, and incidentally one of confusion as treated by the limits-to-growth school, would be related to the meaning of industrialisation. J.W. Forrester reaches rather harsh, perhaps more correctly, "dismal," conclusions concerning the economic advance of underdeveloped countries. "There may be no realistic hope for the

present underdeveloped countries reaching the standard of living demonstrated by the present industrialized nations." "Counterintuitive Behavior of Social Systems," *Technological Forecasting and Social Change* Vol. 3, Number 1 (1971), pp. 1-22, 19. This theme is continued in Forrester's *World Dynamics*, 6, p. 12 and he observes still further: "From the long view of a hundred years hence, the present efforts of the underdeveloped countries to industrialize may be unwise." p. 12. We might perhaps just as well advise a patient suffering from a respiratory ailment that he would live better and longer if only he would stop breathing. However, the Club of Rome by comparison and somewhat more optimistically notes that: "We recognize that World-equilibrium can become a reality only if the lot of the so-called developing countries is substantially improved, both in absolute terms and relative to the economically developed nations. . ." *Limits to Growth*, p. 191, and "We unequivocally support the contention that a brake imposed upon world demographic and economic growth spirals must not lead to a freezing of that status quo of economic development of the world's nations," for such policy could be taken as ". . .a final act of neocolonialism." p. 194. If this latter view is correct in that we cannot accept a "freezing of the status quo" does this not realistically lead to the conclusion of further culture evolution and the spread and advance of industrialism to the underdeveloped world? (M. King Hubbert, *Energy Resources*, (Washington, D.C.: U.S. National Academy of the Sciences, 1962), seems on first glance to reaffirm the position of J.W. Forrester, "Hence, so long as the world depends on fossil fuels as its principal sources of industrial energy, there appears to be little ground for the humanitarian hope of significantly improving the standard of living by industrialization of the underdeveloped areas of the world." pp. 132, 137, however, this is not to say that given sources of energy other than fossil fuels, such as nuclear, or fission and fusion energy, ". . . the dream of improving the standards of living of all the races of man no longer appears so visionary." p. 133. And it is to be noted that ". . .for all present purposes, nuclear energy may be regarded as being essentially inexhaustible in terms of human usage." p. 133. But even as late as 1974 we still find J.W. Forrester, incredibly, stating: "The less-developed countries may be better able to sustain their traditional goals and values than are the developed (overextended) countries." . . ."We may find that the assumed dedication of the underdeveloped countries to economic growth is largely in the minds of economists, government, bureaucrats, and businessmen in the developed countries who have been trying to push their own values and goals onto the less-developed countries." in Oltmans, *On Growth*, p. 226.

[17]Mesarovic and Pestel, *Mankind*, p. 69.

[18]Though the *Mankind* study by Mesarovic and Pestel dealt with regions and the Meadows' *Limits to Growth*, a homogeneous one-world, the end result of organic growth is still ultimately that of global equilibrium and that was also the position presented in Forrester's *World Dynamics*. The argument is put forth that in order to avoid

catastrophe, man should intervene and plan a transition (on the idea of transition, note, *World Dynamics*, ". . .the transition from a world of growth to a world in equilibrium. . ." pp. 5, 112, 126. . ., etc., and from the *Limits to Growth*, ". . .to join us in understanding and preparing for a period of great transition—the transition from growth to global equilibrium." pp. 24, 191, 193 and in passim) toward some form of global equilibrium, a planned stationary state (on the nature of "the state of global equilibrium," note, *Limits to Growth*, pp. 156-184, defined, p. 171. For the oak tree analogy, for the setting in of "tapered" organic growth which for the oak tree, ". . .even after a life time of 150 years, grows about 3 inches per year," *Mankind* p. 8. For a similar biological growth pattern, cf., D'Arcy Wentworth Thompson, *On Growth and Form* (Cambridge : Combridge University Press, 1959), 2 Volumes, for example, p. 173, Vol. 1.

[19]The Mesarovic-Pestel position is not on one-world but a diversified world reaching global equilibrium in a balanced system of organic growth. Balanced growth is not inherent in the system but requires a master plan. "Such a 'master plan' is missing from the processes of growth and development of the world system," *Mankind*, pp. 7, 143-157.

[20]On the quotation, Mesarovic and Pestel, *Mankind*, . 157, and on the time span, ". . .a period of fifty years. . .this coming half-century. . ." p. 17. Whereas, Baldwin Ranson uses in his discussions, "The Limits to Growth," the long-run time span of 500 years. "We think it reasonable to say that the long run includes the next 500 years or less." p. 656.

[21]Again note Sahlins discussion of "Evolution: Specific and General," in Marshall D. Sahlins and Elman R. Service, eds., *Evolution and Culture* (Ann Arbor: University of Michigan Press, 1960), pp. 12-44. We endorse the vine rather than the tree analogy but perhaps Sahlins is in error Diagram 1, p. 17 in depicting the end result as being, according to the diagram, a 45° linear, straight line whereas to our view the vine of general evolution is encased by the exponential. Specific evolution, as the phylogenetic, of fish entailed a much longer time span than did that of mammals, as a case in point. Earlier logistic surges are longer in time span and shorter in development, whereas later logistic surges are shorter in time span (*x*-axis) but longer in development (*y*-axis); the result is exponential not, therefore, linear.

[22]"No institution that undergoes a change in size does so, *if it is to survive and adapt*, without changing its form and shape. It was Galileo, more than 350 years ago, who laid down this principle." Daniel Bell, "Mediating Growth Tensions," p. 37.

[23]Discussions of the "technological fix" appear frequently in the literature, cf., Daly, *Towards a Steady-State Economy* pp. 67-69.

[24]Note Carl Sagan, *The Dragons of Eden* (New York: Random House, 1977), "The human brain (apart from the cerebellum which does not seem to be involved in cognitive functions) contains about ten billion switching elements called neurons." p. 40. And if we reduced

our size still further to the level of the DNA molecule and its fundamental building block, the nucleotide, "But the book of life is very rich; a typical chromosomal DNA molecule in a human being is composed of about five billion pairs of nucleotides." p. 23. But since by comparison we assume man's size and structure to be fixed there must ultimately be a bending of population growth from the exponential to that of the logistic and, therefore, ultimately ZPG.

[25]"Scientific knowledge and technological innovation are increasing at an exponential rate. . .for the more technologically complex a society becomes, the more easily it can generate and absorb new information and techniques. . .The change in the rate of technological innovation is equally impressive. In the first three hundred years after the invention of firearms, the improvement in the original product was so slow that Benjamin Franklin gave serious consideration to arming the Continental Army with bows and arrows. In contrast, only ninety years passed between the first successful steamphip and the disappearance of sails from warships, and fifteen years after the first flight of Orville Wright there were 2,600 planes and 300,000 men in the Royal Air Force." Warner R. Schilling, *International Encyclopedia of the Social Sciences* (1968), Vol. 15, pp. 594-595. Continued on into the present as advances in computers, atomic energy, space travel, and on, we find that the futures' books and predictions of the past have become the facts of the present which now border on the unbelievable and the fantastic.

[26]The Malthusian theoretical framework appears in Forrester, *World Dynamics*, for example, and carries on into the works of Meadows et al., and Mesarovic and Pestel. On the Malthusian connection, as "Malthus in, Malthus out" cf., H.S.D. Cole, *Thinking About the Future*, pp. 5-13, 137-158. Malthus, it is interesting to note, also influenced both Darwin and Keynes.

[27]Paul A. Samuelson, *Economics* (New York: McGraw-Hill, 1976), 10th Edition, p. 731.

[28]The finite resource argument appears central to all no-growth arguments, and not simply those of the of Club of Rome: "Surely any extended study of this issue will remind growth men of the obvious possibility that modern rates of growth cannot continue forever in a world with finite resources and capacity to absorb wastes." Olson and Landsberg, eds., *The No-Growth Society*, p. 12. Daly, *Toward a Steady-State Economy*, ". . .we must revise our economic thinking so that it will be more in conformity with the finite energy and resource limits of the earth. . ." p. vii. The finite resource position appears ad infinitum (truly without limit) in the Club of Rome literature, from Forrester, "The question is only a matter of when and how growth will cease, not whether it will cease." *World Dynamics* p. 68. In short, ". . . exponential growth cannot continue indefinitely." p. 2, "Forces within the world system must and will rise far enough to suppress the power of growth." p. 5, "Exponential growth rates do not continue forever." p. 68; and *Limits to Growth*, pp. 45-87, "But virtually no one will argue that

material growth on this planet can go on forever." p. 153 and in passim. The *ceteris paribus* assumptions of their argument rest upon continued population and capital expansion in the context of finite resources. "By now it should be clear that all these trade-offs arise from one simple fact—the earth is finite.", pp. 86, 54-69, and ". . .physical resources. . . are the ultimate determinants of the limits to growth on this earth." p. 45, and, *World Dynamics*, "The modes of behavior of interest in this book encompass the interactions that occur when exponential growth collides with a fixed environment." p. 68, and, "But the reservoir is limited. Exponential growth cannot continue." p. 124. And, Mesarovic, *Mankind*, ". . .can be narrowed only if global 'unity' and Earth's 'finiteness' are explicitly recognized." p. ix, "But we have discovered that these essential resources are by no means infinitely available." p. 12, ". . .man's erroneous assumption that Natures' supporting system was inexhaustible. . ."p. 15.

[29]Thorstein Veblen, *Absentee Ownership* (New York: Augustus M. Kelley, 1964), ". . .nor, indeed, is there any promise of its reaching anything like a final state of stability and finished growth in the calculable future; for the reason that the state of the industrial arts which underlies it are forever unstable." p. 230, ". . .this mechanisation has in recent times been going forward at a constantly accelerated rate, and it is still in progress, with no present promise of abatement or conclusion." p. 251. And Clarence E. Ayres, *The Industrial Economy* (Cambridge: Houghton Mifflin Company, 1952) "what constitutes a natural resource is determined by the state of the industrial arts and not vice versa." p. 86. ". . .what the natural resources of any society are conceived to be is determined by the technology of that society." p. 85, And, *The Theory of Economic Progress* (New York: Schocken Books, 1962), pp. 84, 112-113, and on. And also consistent with the Veblen-Ayres tradition Marc Tool, *The Discretionary Economy*, pp. 93-96, and Baldwin Ranson, "The Limits to Growth."

[30]To undermine the Malthusian conceptualization of fixed resources by noting that resources are in actuality a function of knowledge and technology is not only characteristic of those writing in the Veblen-Ayres tradition: "Recognition of the possibility of technological progress clearly cuts the ground from under the concept of Malthusian scarcity (an absolute limit to natural resources). Resources can only be defined in terms of known technology. . . .The notion of an absolute limit to natural resources availability is untenable when the definition of resources changes drastically and unpredictably over time." Harold J. Barnett and Chandler Morse, *Scarcity and Growth* (Baltimore: The Johns Hopkins Press, 1963), p. 7. And also, Henry Wallich, "Eco-Doom: The Limits to Credulity, "*Business and Society Review* (Summer 1972) Number 2, pp. 103-105, "Historical experience, which *Limits* ignores, so far suggests that the development of natural resources tends broadly to keep pace with the demand for them." p. 105. And Kenneth E. Boulding, "The Wolf of Rome," *Business and Society Review* (Summer 1972), p. 106-109, "Available natural resources at any one time, however,

are a function of human knowledge. . .This is perhaps the weakest link, at least in Forrester's short-run chain." p. 107. And, Harold J. Barnett, "Forrester's model is unsound in basic structure. He fails to build in feedbacks whereby societies utilize knowledge to overcome resource depletion and pollution." *Journal of Ecomomic Literature* 10 (September 1972), p. 853, add also, on the technology-resource connection, Nathan Rosenberg, *Technology and American Economic Growth* (New York: Harper and Row, 1972,) pp. 18-20.

[31]Peach and Constantin, *Zimmermann's World Resources and Industries*, quotation p. 551, and also, especially, pp. 3-108, 553-558, and, also Marc Tool, *The Discretionary Economy*, p. 90.

[32]Though many books deal with the subject matter of our study one of the more outstanding works in this area by one of the more outstanding economists of our era would be: Kenneth E. Boulding, *The Meaning of the Twentieth Century* (New York: Harper and Row, 1964). Boulding in his intellectual itinerary does indeed travel widely. In *The Meaning of the Twentieth Century*, Boulding analyzes the "second great transition in the history of mankind . . ." (p. 1), the transition from ". . . civilized to post civilized society . . ." (p. 2), the latter term referring to a technological or developed society. Emphasis in this particular study by Boulding is upon the advance of knowledge and in this regard is similar to our conceptualization of the process of economic development. In particular, note Chapter II, "Science as the Basis of the Great Transition," pp. 27-53. "The great transitions in the state of mankind, both the first and the second, may be identified primarily with the changes in the state of human knowledge. . . ." p. 27. In certain instances Boulding has noted the finite qualities of the "spaceship earth," for example, "It is clear that accumulation cannot proceed forever. The day must come, in the course of economic development, when income can grow but capital cannot. In the case of raw materials we will reach that stage very quickly." Kenneth E. Boulding, "The Consumption Concept in Economic Theory," *The American Economic Review* 35 (May 1945), pp. 1-14, p. 3. This theme is continued in his "The Economics of the Coming Spaceship Earth," in which he compares the unlimited dimensions of the "cowboy economy" with the closed earth represented by the limited resources contained in a "spaceman economy" and stresses the need for new economic principles and attitudes toward growth and consumption. But in this article he does note the possibility of a closed system, a system of recycling in which it is possible ". . . to concentrate diffused materials if energy inputs are allowed . . ." that is, an anti-entropic technology could conceivably be successful in terms of the resource issue (p. 7). He carries this point forward in *The Meaning of the Twentieth Century*, and while he certainly does not advocate waste and pollution in the interval before the achievement of such an anti-entropic technology the implication is that such as anti-entropic technology may be invented and innovated and is indeed a real, though not certain, possibility. ". . . it would seem wise to make the most pessimistic assumptions possible, and for man at this stage to make a

concerted and deliberate effort to avoid the waste of his exhaustible resources . . ." p. 150, and, "Fortunately there are signs that this vision is too dismal and that an anti-entropic technology is on the way—that is, one which will concentrate diffused material rather than diffusing the concentrated." p. 142. "These problems may be hard to solve but I know of no proposition that says they are insoluble. We may, indeed, be very close to the solution of the problem of material entropy and continued energy import." p. 149.

[33]On the issue of logistic surges it is Ogburn who more pointedly refers to Hart and not the other way around. "Hart concludes that cultural phenomena grow in logistic surges, one *S* curve follows another." Ogburn and Nimkoff, *Sociology* (1964), p. 670. And though Hart in turn has given recognition to Ogburn's general theoretical formulation, "Depression, War, and Logistic trends," *American Journal of Sociology* 52 (September 1946), pp. 112-122, p. 122, footnote No. 7, it is Hart to our view who provides the basic evidence concerning logistic surges as explanation. The "exponential principle" is basically explained by the fact that, "As the accumulation became larger, more innovations were made and the stock of existing knowledge piled up faster. The speed seems to have been accelerated so that the movement became faster as the body of knowledge got larger." Ogburn and Nimkoff, *Sociology* (1964), p. 667, and, "As to the future, the prospects are for continued rapid changes unless a considerable disorganization should occur, for the accumulation of knowledge continues." p. 695. It is also to be remembered that Ogburn's theoretical case applies to general culture evolution and not specific evolution (cultures). Ogburn noted this point and alluded to a weakness on the part of anthropologists. "In general they abandoned the explanation of culture for the attempt to explain cultures." *Social Change*, p. 375.

[34]Recall our previous reference, Bell, "Mediating Growth Tensions," p. 37; and also, Kenneth D. Wilson, *Prospects for Growth* (New York: Praeger Publishers, 1977), as another source of the Bell article.

[35]Consequently, we concur with the conclusions reached by Ranson, "The Limits to Growth," and that the problem resides in the social structure and technological change, not finite resources. Meadows, *The Limits to Growth*, takes the polar opposite view: "Faith in technology as the ultimate solution to all problems can thus divert our attention from the most fundamental problem—the problem of growth in a finite system—and prevent us from taking effective action to solve it." p. 154. The conclusion of the limits-to-growth school is that technological innovation and advance will not by itself preclude ultimate collapse, note, Meadows, Chapter IV, "Technology and the Limits to Growth," pp. 129-155. "The application of technological solutions alone has prolonged the period of population and industrial growth, but it has not removed the ultimate limits to that growth." p. 141, ". . . this behavior mode occurs if we assume no change in the present system or if we assume any number of technological changes in the system." p. 142. But if technological advance in both social and material technics

can give us an inexhaustible supply of energy and resources and solve the problem of environmental pollution, and assuming ZPG, then the process of culture evolution is unlimited. "Any human activity that does not require a large flow of irreplaceable resources or produce severe environmental degradation might continue to grow indefinitely." Meadows, p. 175.

[36]Heilbroner, *An Inquiry into the Human Prospect* among others, for example, cf., footnotes 13, 14, p. 51, draws attention to the heat problem, pp. 50-56. Paul R. Ehrlich and Anne H. Ehrlich, *Population Resources Environment* (San Francisco: W. H. Freeman and Company, 1972), "The ultimate limits to the use of energy . . . come not from its shortage but from the problem of dissipating the heat to which all useful energy is eventually degraded." pp. 69, 61, 234-236. For an excellent general discussion on "The Prospects for a Limitless Future," cf., Gerald Feinberg, *Consequences of Growth* (New York: The Seabury Press, 1977), and specifically on a more optimistic analysis of the heat issue, pp. 72-73, and footnote 10, and the implications for the harnessing of solar energy.

[37]Perhaps a basic fear of those supporting the zero-growth position is that man cannot continue to grow in the context of what we might call the San Simeon syndrome related to the life-style of William Randolph Hearst. John Maynard Keynes addressed himself to this issue in his "Economic Possibilities for Our Grandchildren," *Essays in Persuasion* (New York: W. W. Norton & Company, 1963), pp. 358-373, as he reversed the procedure and for a change looked at the long-run, as he took the "wings to the future" and contemplated economic life one-hundred years hence, and noted the distinction between absolute needs and those needs ". . . which are relative in the sense that we feel them only if their satisfaction lifts us above, makes us feel superior to, our fellows." p. 365. Keynes felt that such consumption, based not on absolute needs but rather on the San Simeon syndrome, would conceivably subside in the future. Though foul over fair might reign a while longer, "Avarice and usury and precaution must be our gods for a little longer still." p. 372. The future would see a victory of fair over foul. Perhaps in the future "We shall be able to rid ourselves of many of the pseudo-moral principles which have hag-ridden us for two hundred years by which we have exalted some of the most distasteful of human qualities into the position of the highest virtues. . . . The love of money as a possession . . . will be recognized for what it is, a somewhat disgusting morbidity, one of those semicriminal, semi-pathological propensities which one hands over with a shudder to the specialists in mental disease." p. 369. Therefore, if we assume a structure of social institutions supporting absolute needs, the economic problem—scarcity, if you will, would be capable of resolution ". . . the *economic problem* may be solved or be at least within sight of solution, within one-hundred years." p. 366.

[38]For example, Denis Hayes, *Rays of Hope* (New York: W. W. Norton & Company, 1977). But still the problem of heat remains, is the

globe cooling off or heating up? Note "Heat: The Ultimate Limit," pp. 16-18. Heat dissipation constitutes perhaps an ultimate problem, as the speed of light, perhaps, places a limit on transportation technology. But certainly the areas of energy utilization and heat dissipation will not constitute immediate problems in the context of Mesarovics time span of 50 years (*Mankind*, p. 17) and even not, apparently, in Ranson's "The Limits to Growth," suggested 500 year period of prognostication (pp. 656,660).

[39]Maurice Goldsmith, Han Waalwijk, and Niels Wiedenhof, eds., *A Strategy for Recources* (Amsterdam: North-Holland Publishing Company, 1977), p. v.

[40]Daniel Bell in Sheldon and Moore, eds., *Indicators of Social Change*, pp. 171-173.

[41]Ernan McMullin, "Limits of Scientific Enquiry," in Jacinto Steinhardt, ed., *Science and the Modern World* (New York: Plenum Press, 1966), pp. 37-84. p. 84, McMullin infers, and, admittedly, he may be correct, that whereas knowledge itself may be unlimited, man's capacity to acquire such knowledge may not. "I am not about to claim that scientific enquiry is nearing its end, nor even to maintain that it must have a term at some finite time in the future. My aim is a modest one really: to argue that some limits on the future progress of scientific inquiry are possible and certain among them probable. The aim is modest, yet if achieved, it would challenge one of the most pervasive convictions of twentieth century man: that the progress of science is likely to remain the steady and inevitable affair it seems recently to have become." pp. 37-38. McMullin does not argue that knowledge itself is finite: "But Darwin introduced a theory of evolution . . . immediately a vast domain of history opened to scientific inspection, a domain so complex, so extended, and contingent in its present-day remains, that the future task of biology seemed almost endless." p. 57, and "By the 1920's even the physicists were hesitant to claim any sort of finality for their basic theories . , . . " p. 58, but rather that man's methods or the nature of man himself may impose limitations upon man's ability or capacity to acquire knowledge. Along similar lines note, Eugene P. Wigner, The Limits of Science," pp. 757-765 in Herbert Feigl and May Brodbeck, eds., *Readings in the Philosophy of Science* (New York: Appleton-Century Crofts, 1953), ". . . its limitations are in the human intellect, in its capacity for interest and learning, in its memory and facilities for communication. All these are surely related to the finite span of the human life." p. 759. However, it would perhaps be fair to state, that while our capacities to acquire knowledge may be subject to limits, most would agree that knowledge itself is basically unlimited. "Perhaps the most unique characteristic of modern science is the generally accepted thema of the unlimited possibility of *doing* science, the belief that nature is inexhaustibly knowable." Gerald Holton, ed., *Science and Culture* (Boston: Houghton Mifflin, 1965), p. xxiv.

[42]This constitutes our interpretation of his *Science Since Babylon* and *Little Science, Big Science*, and similar to McMullin and Wigner in

that there may be natural limitations, of one form or other, preventing man from promoting an unlimited advance of science.

[43]This is discussed by Derek J. de Solla Price who also describes the phenomenon of the "invisible college" as a new technic to cope with the problem of the knowledge explosion as an alternative to journal articles to accumulate and transmit scientific knowledge, *Little Science, Big Science*, pp. 62-91, 85. One particular technic of science as a method for accumulating and transmitting knowledge may become saturated (scientific journals) but to our view this need not mean an overall saturation of man's scientific means (technics) to acquire new knowledge. Our basic position is that conceivably new technics (invisible colleges, greater team efforts, better tools . . ., etc.) could continuously be devised without limit since such technics themselves are a function of knowledge, itself, unlimited in scope and dimension. It has been through culture evolution as a process of advancing knowledge that man has been able to add to his limited biological capacities with which he senses the outer world. He has expanded his range of sound frequency and the limits of sight; he has, via computers, expanded his capacity to calculate, record and remember and most of these advances have come since the advent of the industrial revolution. Though man and his culture have existed for at least one-million plus years these developments are primarily of the last 200 years, and, consequently, the modern period, rather than marking a culmination, really marks the start of a great penetration by mankind into the vastness of knowledge. On this, briefly, note "Man Plus" and "The New Symbiosis" in McHale, *The Future of the Future* (New York: George Braziller, 1969). pp. 98-148.

[44]There are ways to compensate for a fixed number of scientists. Certain paths of inquiry may require greater co-operative research and team effort ". . . we should not forget that while it is true that relativity theory could not have been conceived by teamwork, the structure of the George Washington Bridge and probably even that of the Hanford nuclear reactors, could not have been thought out by a single individual . . . . Success of this may mean that the limitations of 'our science' which were described above are limitations only for individualist science." Wigner, "The Limits of Science" in Feigl, *Readings in the Philosophy of Science*, pp. 764-765. Also, as in the past with the building of Gothic cathedrals over centuries and generations of men, ideas and knowledge may also be accumulated through team efforts spanning several generations and further compensate for a fixed population of scientists. On the issue of an unlimited demand and supply of energy: "In a maturing economy there may be no upper limit to productivity or real income per capita and, hence, none to the demands per capita for the *output* of energy." Palmer Cosslett Putnam, *Energy in the Future* (Princeton: D. Van Nostrand Company, 1953), p. 453. Of course, continued advances in energy control are dependent upon continued technological change, Eugene Ayres and Charles A. Scarlott, in their *Energy Sources—The Wealth of the World* (New York:

McGraw-Hill Book Company, 1952) note that given a fixity of current methods "... the outlook ... would be dismal" but assuming transformation and the advance of new technics, the picture changes. "But man's resourcefulness continues on and becomes more potent with each passing decade. Because of this the future is bright. We cannot know what the solutions to the energy problem *will* be, but we do know what some of the solutions *could* be." p. 279. And, Fred Cottrell, *Energy and Society* (New York: McGraw-Hill Book Company, 1955), "It is obvious that it is not lack of a source of energy which limits man's activities .... Thus the amount of radiant energy is so far in excess of man's present ability to convert it that it cannot be considered to limit human behavior. Energy-imposed limits stem from the particular means by which energy is converted into particular forms desired by man at a particular time and place." pp. 15-16. And while M. King Hubbert, *Energy Resources* (Washington, D.C.: U.S. National Academy of Sciences, 1962) notes, "The resources of fission energy, uranium and thorium, and of fusion energy, deuterium or heavy hydrogen, are quite as exhaustible as the fossil fuels, but the quantities are so large that it is doubtful if any significant diminution of the total reserves could be effected by industrial uses within the next thousand years. Hence, for all present purposes, nuclear energy may be regarded as being essentially inexhaustible in terms of human usage." p. 133.

[45]"The stock of tested knowledge therefore concerns a much wider realm than has yet been exploited by mankind, and theoretically the *application* of knowledge can tap an area that extends far beyond our planet. . . in these days of interplanetary travel discussions we cannot dismiss the possibility of extending processes of economic production beyond the confines of the earth." Simon Kuznets, *Economic Growth and Structure* (New York: W. W. Norton & Company, 1965) p. 88. "Before our rockets and our telescopes lies a universe that a billion years of earthman's exploration will not exhaust." McMullin, Limits of Scientific Inquiry," op. cit., p. 37. Also, McHale, *The Future of the Future*, especially pp. 175-195. While social scientists of a liberal predilection in the United States point to the opportunity costs incurred in foregoing priorities on earth, and perhaps rightly so, and deride the billions being spent for space exploration, it should be noted, however, that such exploration is a logical step in the overall advance of culture. And it is general culture evolution which ultimately provides a given culture with advances in productivity and economic growth which serve in turn as necessary conditions for the improvement in human welfare.

[46]*Six Lectures on Economic Growth* (New York. The Free Press of Glencoe, 1959), p. 38. To suggest that ultimately there may be weakening on the demand side, as Kuznets does, p. 38, as, however, not to argue in terms of limited resources (supply). Demand for automobiles and our current overall pattern of growth will obviously slacken but not our demand for more quality growth, higher levels of science and energy control and new patterns and structures of growth and deve-

lopment to be derived from our kaleidoscope earth. And also, in part as a reaction to the pessimism associated with a stagnation economics of the classical and Marxian schools of thought, "as far as potential technological change is concerned, there is no proximate limit to economic growth. That a social process, like the economic growth of a nation, has no finite limit would seem, on the face of it, an absurdity . . . . it emphasizes the point that the growth potential that follows from progress in science and technology has no upper limit. . . one wonders how, in the light of the advance in science and technology during the last two centuries, the premise of a technological limit upon productive capacity in the long run can be retained." *Economic Growth and Structure* (New York: W. W. Norton & Company, 1965), pp. 87-89. Everett Hagan in his *The Economics of Development* (Homewood: Richard D. Irwin, 1968), states, "For there is no identifiable end point to the process of development. Development . . . may go on forever." p. 5, and, "There is no technical or economic reason why growth should not continue indefinitely . . . . But it is worthwhile to make the point forcefully that the process being studied in this volume is potentially an indefinitely continuing one." pp. 39-40. And looking at a specific culture, the American economy, Richard T. Gill, assuming continued technological acceleration, concludes, ". . . that there do not at the moment appear to be any fundamental obstacles preventing the American economy from supplying a continued increase in output per capita, and at rates comparable to those of the past." *Economic Development : Past and Present* (Englewood Cliffs: Prentice-Hall, 1967), pp. 76-78. W. W. Rostow also notes that ". . . the flow of modern science and technology may offer the potentiality of fending off Ricardian diminishing returns indefinitely . , ." pp. 9-10 in *The Economics of Take-Off into Sustained Growth* (New York: St. Martin's Press, 1963), and also, "The Past Quarter-Century as Economic History and the Tasks of International Economic Organization," *The Journal of Economic History*, 30 (March 1970), pp. 150-200, p. 196.

[47]There are many variables which could be introduced in terms of predicting that continuous technological advance "need not be so." For example, Gerhard Lenski and Jean Lenski, *Human Societies* (New York: McGraw-Hill Book Company, 1974), pp. 470, ff., "Looking Ahead," in which the authors present their basic imponderables, including that of a "nuclear holocaust."

[48]By comparison, Ronald G. Ridker, "To Grow or Not to Grow: That's Not the Question," *Science* 182 (December 1973), pp. 1315-18, argues that both positions are wrong.

[49]Robert M. Solow states ". . . really my complaint about the Doomsday School. It diverts attention from the really important things that can actually be done, step by step, to make things better." In *The Economic Growth Controversy*, Weintraub, ed., p. 61; Feinberg, *Consequences of Growth*, ". . . is a diversion from the more important choices . . ." p. 65; and in a radical vein, Marx also drew attention to the Malthusian diversion, cf., Maddox, *The Doomsday Syndrome*, pp. 40,

45 and, the following. "The hatred of the English working class against Malthus—the 'mountebank-parson' as Cobbett rudely calls him—is therefore entirely justified. The people were right here in sensing instinctively that they were confronted not with a *man of science* but with a *bought advocate*, a pleader on behalf of their enemies, a shameless sycophant of the ruling classes," quotation appearing in H.S.D. Cole, *Thinking About the Future*, p. 143.

[50]S. Fred Singer, "The Price System as a Control of Growth," *Society*, 15 (January/February, 1978), pp. 44-48, p. 48. Note also, Herbert N. Woodward, *Capitalism Can Survive in a No-Growth Economy* Stamford: The Brookdale Press, 1976), in which he argues, counter to the usual position stressing the growth oriented nature of the system, that business does not need growth and that Capitalism can be effective in a "slow growth and no-growth society," p. 26, passim.

[51]This is more correctly so at the macro level. John Kenneth Galbraith, Economics and the Public Purpose (Boston: Houghton Muflin Company 1973) argues that at the micro level, science to social organization is a characteristic of the "planning system" and accounts for its dynamics and power. For an interesting study on the connection of the corporate structure and science, cf., David F. Noble, *America by Design: Science, Technology and the Rise of Corporate Capitalism* New: Alfred A. Knopf, 1977).

[52]While the period of modern economic growth is characterized by science to social organization, the process is yet to be perfected but many recommended its further advance. *Economics*: "In a fundamental sense, economic modern growth is a creature of the scientific revolution, for it reflects man's growing knowledge of natural phenomena and the power thereby attained to mold his environment to his needs. Whether it will prove possible to contain the disruptive effects of its spread within a framework of nation-states would seem ultimately to depend on whether progress in social science can match that in natural science. . . . If, therefore, one turns from the question of the origins of modern economic development, which lie in the growth of natural science, to that of the future outlook, much would seem to turn on the prospect for comparable progress in social science." pp. 396, 407, *International Encyclopedia of the Social Sciences* (1968), Vol. IV, Richard A. Easterlin, *Anthropology*, ". . . that in due course of time a successful, *modus vivendi* is going to be worked out, in which the advantages of modern science and modern technology will be combined with social systems which are really adjusted to them, and which work . . . . But the main line of scientific development now is actually not in the development of more machines and more atomic fission . . . but for a steadily advancing understanding of human beings . . . for developing techniques by which we can produce well-adjusted and satisfied populations." Ralph Linton, *The Tree of Culture* (New York: Alfred A. Knopf, 1961), pp. 673-674. *From Sociology:* Perhaps one of the better references in support of this general theme would be Francis R. Allen, ed., *Technology and Social Change* (New York: Appleton-

Century-Crofts, 1957), and one to which we have referred to so frequently. And, Hornell Hart, "The future of civilization depends upon the invention of better methods of social invention, or in other words, a radical speed-up in the development of genuine social science," and, "If social science is the most promising instrument for speeding up the development of democratic international controls, is not a valid science of social science methods the most promising instrument of improving science." pp. 512, 515. And we should not forget others in sociology, going from Comte to Ogburn. In a book approximately dedicated to Lester Frank Ward, Harry Elmer Barnes, ed., *The History and Prospects of the Social Sciences* (New York: Alfred A. Knopf, 1925) Barnes notes that, " . . . the only hope of a successful and efficient utilization of the remarkable contributions of science and technology to human society lies in a persistent and organized effort to develop those social sciences which alone can serve to guide man toward an ever more safe and adequate exploitation and control of the increased power which natural science and technology have placed at his disposal." p. xix-xx. Also note, "Lester Frank Ward: The Reconstruction of Society by Social Science," by Harry Elmer Barnes, in Harry Elmer, ed., *An Introduction to the History of Sociology*, (Chicago: University of Chicago Press, 1948), pp. 173-190. "It has been the contention of Sociologists from Auguste Comte and Lester F. Ward to Sorokin that the chief justification of sociology is the guidance it can furnish to public officials and private citizens relative to building a better social order." pp. ix, xi. and "Confirming to the above criteria and objectives of useful knowledge in general, sociology is of ultimate importance only in so far as it furnishes the basis for an intelligent and efficient control of the social process and a progressive improvement of human culture and social institutions." p. 785. "Insofar as scientific knowledge of man, society, and culture develops, and is applied to the problems caused by social changes, planning in these sectors will be successful and we shall increasingly achieve the harmonious social adjustment for which we strive." Ogburn and Nimkoff, Sociology (1964), p. 763. While our discussion could admittedly go on ad infinitum, just one more reference (Delbert C. Miller): "In this stream of culture, the future calls for imaginative social scientists who can match the science of modern technology. Tested knowledge is needed to guide social relations so that the patterns of living are consistent, integrated and meaningful. Adaptation to unplanned change is not enough. Creative social change is possible and becoming ever more necessary. Man, the transformer of physical and social environment, has come of age." in Allen, ed., *Technology and Social Change, p. 250.*

[53]Daly, *Toward a Steady-State Economy*, pp. 132-134 for the reference to Jerome B. Wiesner and Herbert F. York, "National Security and the Nuclear-Test Ban," *Scientific American*, 211 (October 1964), pp. 27-35. When Wiesner and York refer to "no technical solution," p. 35, they clearly refer to the "hardware" produced by science and techno-

logy. For in the domain of the "software" as social invention the conclusion is: "We are optimistic, on the other hand, that there is a solution to this dilemma. The partial nuclear-test ban . . . is truly an important first step toward finding a solution in an area where a solution may exist." p. 35.

[54]For Meadows, *Limits to Growth*, on the limits to the "technological fix", "Numerous problems today have no technological solution." See pp. 149-150, 129-155. Technology to Meadows concerns material technics and not social, p. 148, in that "political and social institutions" are outside the realm of technology. Preston Cloud also notes that the solution is not to be found in technology but will require ". . . new social patterns and wise legislation." p. 59, Daly, *Toward a Steady-State Economy*.

[55]John McHale, *The Future of the Future* (New York: George Braziller, 1969), p. 11. And Feinberg, ". . . the stages of growth that remain may transform our civilization from its present form, into a very different one that is preferable to human life." *Consequences of Growth*, p. 3.

[56]"The purpose of U.S. energy policy should be the managing of a transition" from a world of cheap imported oil to a more balanced system of energy sources . . . Conservation and solar energy, in our view, are much to be preferred." Robert Stobauch and Daniel Yergin, "Toward a Balanced Energy Program," *Challenge* 24 (September/October 1979), pp. 3-11, p. 3.

[57]The basic value premises of Gunnar Myrdal, as enunciated in *Rich Lands and Poor* (New York: Harper and Brothers, 1957), "The value premises which determine my viewpoint are the desirability of political democracy and of equality of opportunity." p. xix, and also by Myrdal, *An International Economy* (New York: Harper and Brothers, 1956), pp. 9-16, 336-340, and footnote 1, p. 365; and, Paul Streeton, ed., *Value in Social Theory* (New York: Harper and Brothers, 1958); and in the continuity of the work by Ayres and Myrdal, again we refer to Marc Tool, *The Discretionary Economy*.

[58]Carl Kaysen, in Oltmans, ed., *On Growth*, pp. 68, 66.

[59]Many others in the context of the limits-to-growth issue have reached a similar conclusion, for example, Brown, *The Twenty-Ninth Day*, pp. 305-310, Robert L. Hailbroner, *The Worldly Philosophers* (New York: Simon and Schuster, 1972), pp. 279-307, especially, 299-301, and, also, by Heilbroner advocating economic planning, *Beyond Boom and Crash* (New York: W.W. Norton and Company, 1978). Would such voluntary planning also be what Masarovic and Pestel have in mind with their reference to a "master plan" or "blueprint", p. 7, *Mankind at the Turning Point?*

[60]It is interesting to note how closely Hornell Hart's "logistic surges" is related to Joseph A. Schumpeter's "Creative Destruction," *Capitalism, Socialism and Democracy* (New York: Harper and Brothers, 1950), pp. 81-86, ". . . the history of the apparatus of power production from the overshot water wheel to the modern power plant, or the history of transportation from the mailcoach to the airplane." p. 83.

And although Schumpeter stressed the evolution of capitalism and structural change, "the essential point to grasp is that in dealing with capitalism we are dealing with an evolutionary process . . . Capitalism . . . never can be stationary." p. 83. But he gave emphasis to the dynamics of the entrepreneur as innovator. Government can and has also played a similar role, i.e., the T.V.A. and the Manhattan Project as cases in point. In the context of indicative planning the government's role, as innovator would be greatly increased.

[61]We speak of the collapse and disintegration of laissez faire during the interwar period, for example Ingvar Svennilson, *Growth and Stagnation in the European Economy* (Geneva: United Nations, 1954), and, further, on the historic problem of unemployment plus the ecology crisis of the current period, note Kenneth Arrow in Benjamin M. Friedman, ed., *New Challenges to the Role of Profit* (Boston: D.C. Heath, 1978).

[62]In John K. Galbraith, *Economics and the Public Purpose* (Boston: Houghton Mifflin Company, 1973), the economy is split into the dichotomy of the planning system versus the market system. At the micro level of the firm and in the context of the *New Industrial State*, the large corporation owes its dynamics and power to its capacity to organize and plan, especially of scientific knowledge, for its own interest and not necessarily always that to the public. The next step is to have planning take place at the macro-level.

[63]In that culture has been in existence for approximately one-million years and that the Agricultural Revolution started circa 8000 *B.C.*, the period of civilization marks only one per cent of mankind's total culture experience. Note Leslie A. White, *The Concept of Culture* (Minneapolis: Burgess Publishing Company, 1973), p. 60.

CHAPTER XI

Cultural Economics

Our study is directed toward the advance of a general theory of economic development founded in the conceptual framework of culture evolution. Culture used in the sense of a totality or gestalt as first formulated, scientifically, by Tyler in 1871.[1] The process of economic development constitutes the dynamics as well as the core of culture evolution. And, in explaining the process of economic development, the focus is on the advance of useful knowledge which in its application and innovation appears as technology and in its store as culture. So conceptualized, technology and culture appear as opposite sides of the coin of useful knowledge; to change one (technology) is, therefore, to change and transform the other (culture). The methodology is therefore to explain economic phenomena and the process of economic development in the framework of culture evolution and we call this methodology—*cultural economics.*

But *cultural economics*, as the explanation of the process of economic development in the context of general culture evolution is not that new, it is our view, also, the basic thrust and focus of mainstream institutional thought in economics as the Veblen-Ayres tradition.[2] It is also our position that Veblen and Ayres have originated and provided for a nascent and rudimentary general theory of economic development. Economic evolution, of Veblen and Ayres, was to be explained in the conceptual framework of culture evolution:

> "...it appears that an evolutionary economics must be the theory of a process of cultural growth as determined by

> the economic interest, a theory of a cumulative sequence of enonomic institutions stated in terms of the process itself."
>
> ". . .*omnis cultura ex cultura* . . . Cultural phenomena (including the economic) derive exclusively from other cultural phenomena and can be explained only in terms of other cultural phenomena."[3]

For the social sciences in general others have also relied upon the conceptual framework of culture and its evolution in the formulation of their theories. Ogburn, for example, conceptualized the process of social evolution in the context of general culture evolution:

> "It is culture. Social evolution becomes then cultural evolution; and the evolution of groups since glacial times is part of the evolution of culture."[4]

The application of the anthropologists' culture to the issue of social evolution has been considered to be Ogburn's seminal and unique contribution as an American sociologist.[5] In our attempt to explain the processes of economic evolution, the Ogburnian methodology of using general culture evolution as a means of explaining social evolution appears as especially relevant.[6] Consequently, the use of culture evolution to explain economic development and evolution is not only basic methodology of Veblen and Ayres, but also provides the conceptual framework for Ogburn as well.

In addition to Ogburn (sociology), and in line with the development of the holistic and interdisciplinary methodology embodied in our study, emphasis has also been placed upon the contributions of Simon Kuznets (economics) and Leslie A. White (anthropology). Simon Kuznets does not represent mainstream institutional thought. Kuznets does not explicitly or directly refer to Veblen or Ayres nor their concepts and theory. Kuznets has basically served as a statistician or fact gatherer, in the context of national income accounting, to provide empirical buttresses for Keynesian, rather than Veblenian, economic theory. And though the quantitative methods of Kuznets ran counter to the orthodox theory of the early 1930's, Kuznets became the paragon of economic orthodoxy and the conventional wisdom of the post-WW II era.[7] Nonetheless, Kuznets' contributions might also be interpreted as providing a connecting link between the neoclassical and Keynesian on the one hand and the institutional on the other.[8] Whereas Picasso used paint to depict the modern epoch, Kuznets presents his picture of modern economic growth and the dynamics of the associated structural changes via the medium of numbers and statistics. In his concept and analysis of MEG, Kuznets combines growth as the quantitative with structural changes as the qualitative.[9] In this sense, then, it might be argued that Kuznets provides a bridge between the statics of growth theories of neoclassical economics on the one hand and the dynamics of institutional theories of development on the other.

And while to our knowledge Kuznets does not refer explicitly to Tylor or to culture and its evolution, as such, the basic framework is implicit in his analysis. The major innovation of MEG, as the scientific epoch, is that of applying science to economic production and social organization. But in that the dichotomy represents a split between material culture (economic production) and nonmaterial culture (social organization), the analysis provided by Kuznets is, therefore, not only explicitly of cultural and social variables but it is also, implicitly of the whole of culture as conceptualized by Tylor. Therefore, while Kuznets might be thought of more as an empiricist in the tradition of W.C. Mitchell, Kuznets also provides theory and explanation concerning the dynamics and qualitative aspects of MEG. And that theory we submit is implicitly based upon Tylor's totality of culture split into the dichotomy of social organization and economic production. In addition the emphasis, by Kuznets, on the stock of knowledge and the place of science in modern economic growth, as the scientific epoch, would certainly be relevant and compatible with institutional economics as well as the subject matter of this study.

Though not necessarily endorsing his historical meterialism nor his *sui generis* predilections, but in that our concern is that of general culture evolution, how can the contributions of Leslie A. White be avoided? According to Harry Elmer Barnes, "... Dr. White will probably go down in the history of anthropology as the outstanding protagonist and practitioner of cultural evolution in the middle third of the present century, if not the whole century. . ."[10] Mainstream economics, as the neoclassical synthesis, and even mainstream institutional economics, as the Veblen-Ayres contribution, have historically avoided energy control and the Second Law of Thermodynamics. By comparison, energy is the motor force behind the process' of general culture evolution constitutes an integral part of L. A. White's theoretical framework. We have tried to embody and integrate the contributions of L.A. White, with special emphasis on energy transformation, into the overall matrix of *cultural economics*.[11]

Consequently, *cultural economics* intent on modifying and advancing the Veblen-Ayres matrix, as a general theory of economic development, is pulled by the intellectual troika of Kuznets, Ogburn and White. We have not treated these social scientists as being sacrosanct; this has not been an exercise in exegesis for either Kuznets, Ogburn or White.[12] A basic problem in economic analysis is to expand its scope. Institutional economics in general, and Veblen and Ayres in particular, represents a methodology whereby the theoretical matrix of economic analysis would contain as integral and substantive parts, the social and the cultural. The crux of the battle is to introduce the social and cultural into the mainstream of economic analysis, and Veblen and Ayres and other hard-nosed institutionalists have fought this battle in the trenches.[13] The integrative concept to bring this about, and which Veblen and Ayres focused on, is culture.

In this context, Kuznets implicitly uses culture and its evolution and explicitly deals with the phenomena of economic growth and development. Ogburn and White, by comparison, explicitly deal with culture evolution but implicitly deal with the phenomena of economic growth and development. It is with Veblen and Ayres that the two processes are tied together explicitly. Explicit treatment is directed to both culture evolution and the processes of economic growth and development. And this study via a synthesis of Kuznets, Ogburn and White attempts to modify the Veblen-Ayres matrix in order to advance their general theory of economic development. *Cultural economics* therefore represents a continuity of the long-term struggle to introduce the social and the cultural into the matrix of normal science in economics. Conceptually, culture comprises the capability to provide for the future unity and synthesis of the social sciences. Veblen was prone to endorse the view: " 'Anthropology is destined to revolutionize the political and the social sciences as radically as bacteriology has revolutionized the science of medicine'."[14]

If mainstream institutional economics was also concerned and focused upon culture and its evolution, how then does the Veblen-Ayres tradition differ from the *cultural economics* of this study as an explanation of the economic process? A brief comparison might be of merit in order to further clarify what is meant by *cultural economics.* Although many distinctions could be noted, we will focus on three major areas dealing primarily with technology, structure and energy.

Perhaps the major distinction would rest with the conceptualization of technology. *Cultural economics* treats social technics in the form of social institutions as integral and substantive parts of overall technology. And while technology is of course central to mainstream institutional economics Veblen and Ayres were not that clear on conceptualization. Whereas Veblen bordered on the polarity of material culture, Ayres tried to move the concept of technology toward the polarity of social organization. But certainly not Veblen, nor even Ayres, ever explicitly included social institutions as integral and endogenous parts of technology.[15] Whereas it might be said that Veblen and Ayres have a culture-view (Tylor's) of the economic process they have, only, a cultural view of technology. They did not conceptualize technology in terms of culture which would have placed both the material and the social on equal footing as a gestalt or totality. An holistic or culture-view of technology, as presented in the context of *cultural economics,* includes both material and social technics. Social institutions are consequently integral and endogenous to the whole of technology. Therefore, given this conceptualization, the overall gestalt of technology can be viewed as the opposite side of the core of culture in the dichotomy of useful knowledge.[16] To change one (technology) is to change the other (culture) and the process of culture transformation is thereby explained in terms of its own substance.

In terms of the troika, L.A. White would approximate more

the Veblenian polarity material culture in his conceptualization of technology. And while Ogburn is not always that clear, and at times even conceptualized technology in terms of material technology to him, apparently, does include the social and even the institutional.[17] Social institutions as technology would be provided for by Ogburn's reference to the factory system in his overall treatment of technology.[18]

But it is Kuznets, even more so than Ogburn, who has provided for the explicit treatment, as used in *cultural economics,* to include social institutions as integral to technology. If the dynamics of technology rests upon, as Veblen maintained, the matter-of-fact (scientific) knowledge, why should the process only prevail for material technics? By characterizing the scientific epoch of modern economic growth as the innovation of science to both economic production and social organization Kuznets provided the basic insight used in the formulation of the dichotomy of useful knowledge.[19] And whereas the Veblen Ayres dichotomy is really that of culture split into material technology, as the dynamic and the nonmaterial of social institutions as the static, the dichotomy used in *cultural economics* entails the split into technology and culture. Consequently, technology in the context of cultural economic entails not only the material but entails social technology as well. All of this is not to shortchange the two leading neo-institutional economists of the current period; Myrdal and Galbraith also apparently include social technology in their overall conceptualization of technology.[20]

A good example of the point being made here would be provided by the social technic, the social institution, known as nationalism. To Veblen there is no mistake, and in line with his general treatment of institutions and their inherently imbecile nature, we find the following: "Born in iniquity and conceived in sin, the spirit of nationalism has never ceased to bend human institutions to the service of dissension and distress. In its material effects it is altogether the most sinister as well as the most imbecile of all those institutional incumbrances that have come down out of the old order."[21] However, Gunnar Myrdal treats nationalism as a social technic instrumental in breaking the yoke of colonial bondage and the establishment of national independence and integration.[22] Nation-state building and nationalism are prerequisite social technics necessary for the take-off into industrialization and MEG.

Both views are correct and exemplify the fact that technology, both social and material, can be positive as well as negative. The path of nationalism, as with all specific technics, is the logistic. Veblen's assessment of nationalism is more relevant to nature stages of the social technic in the form of the supernationalism of Western Europe characteristic of the 1930's. But nationalism not only services the imbecile but it also performs vital positive and dynamic functions, as a social technic, during the transitional period as culture evolves from the stage of economic development known as the Agricultural Revolution on to the Industrial Revolution. For mature industrial countries the next logistic surge in the process of general evolution will not be in the more intensified supernationalism but rather in the social structure of supranationalism as the regionalism, for example, embodied in the EEC.

Another good example in support of the position that social institutions can be dynamic (as well as static), and referred to so frequently in this study, would be provided for that of science itself. Science is a social institution.[23] *Cultural economics* argues that the essence of the process of development is to be found in the production and advance of useful knowledge. And the institution of science secures methods, as social technics, to produce more and more useful knowledge faster and faster than ever before. However, we are not maintaining that the material and social structures of culture are currently of equal porosity to the penetration of science. *Cultural economics* conceptualizes the achievement of the permeability of the social structure, to science, on an equal footing to that of the material structure, as a frictionless wheel of economic development.

And while Veblen and Ayres speak of culture accumulation with acceleration and even note the exponential as the "law of progress" they really do not analyze the resulting and underlying stucture. *Cultural economics* has added and integrated the contributions of Ogburn and Hart in order to provide a clearer picture and understanding of the form and structure of general culture evolution. The structure is that of an overall exponential curve encompassing an underlying paradigm of logistic surges. That structure is supported by empirical evidence and reinforces and verifies the "principle of similitude." That ongoing exponential growth cannot continue unless there is a change in structure can be substantiated by evidence from the real world. *Cultural economics* also combines the structure of logistic surges with the work of Sahlins and Service in their distinction between specific and general culture evolution. Each technic, in its given form or structure, be it propeller driven aircraft, the international gold standard, or even the overall gestalt of technology as a given stage of economic development, exemplifies specific evolution and is manifest in the logistic. It is the paradigm of logistic surges as the switching of specific technics which underlies the exponential and constitutes the path of general culture evolution. The change of structure as transformation is, consequently, fundamental and represents the crux of the process of economic development.

But in order to change a structure there is a need for power which might be defined as the application of energy over time. The motor force to change the structure, as a necessary condition of the process of economic development, is contained in energy. Nothing moves or is transformed in the cosmos without the use of energy, yet this aspect of the process of economic development had by and large not been incorporated by Veblen or Ayres into their matrix. The application and use of energy serves as a necessary condition for both specific and general culture evolution. Without the transformation of energy from one gestalt to the next, culture would be locked into specific evolution and would reach satiation in the development and perfection of a specific stage of economic development. General culture evolution requires the continuous transformation of energy from one level to the next. The higher levels of energy control are achieved through the advance of useful knowledge which enables man to invent and discover the new sources of energy required to perpetuate the exponential advance of culture and civilization. Therefore mankind has utilized more and more energy through the process of general culture evolution and, thereby, has overcome the long-term movement toward entropic degradation. And while this has been duly noted by L.A. White and incorporated into *cultural economics*, it has not been emphasized as endogenous or integral to the theoretical matrix of mainstream institutional economics.[24]

Also we feel that *cultural economics*, as a theoretical framework, is not only pulled by the intellectual troika of Ogburn, Kuznets and White but is also dependent upon many others in many disciplines and we have attempted to document this view in the course of our study. Also *cultural economics* is not only dependent upon other disciplines, but it melts, integrates, and combines the disciplines in a truly interdisciplinary manner as with scrambled eggs and not in a multidisciplinary sense of a beef stew in which each ingredient or discipline retains its own identity. The theoretical framework of *cultural economics* serves as a blender of the sciences called social· And mybe that is where we have been heading anyway. Kenneth E. Boulding, in stating his "growing dissatisfaction" with the state of economic theory finds himself:

> . . . gradually coming under the conviction, disturbing for a professional theorist, that there is no such thing as economics—there is only social science applied to economic problems.
>
> . . . we are, I believe, on the threshold of a new attempt at integration in the social sciences.[25]

In addition, not only is it possible to integrate the basic disciplines into the overall framework of *cultural economics* as we have done with the specific examples of sociology (Ogburn), economics (Kuznets), and anthropology (White), but also, we could synthesize in the framework of *cultural economics* a good deal of the scientific knowledge which has accumulated within the limited confines of economics itself.[26] It should be recalled that knowledge follows the evolutionary pattern of the banyan tree, rather than that of the oak tree, and consequently allows for cross-fertilization.

Let us now recapitulate, given the theoretical framework of *cultural economics*, how then do we explain and conceptualize the process of economic development? Briefly and in summary, in this study the process of economic development has been conceptualized in the context of a theory of general culture.[27] It is in the sense of culture serving as a store of knowledge of man's social heritage as well as a guide to man's activity and behavior that we have drawn the biological analogy and refer to culture as man's social DNA. The essence of the process is the advance of useful knowledge.[28] We have categorized useful knowledge into a basic dichotomy: that on the one hand, in its store, useful knowledge takes on the form of culture, and when that stock of useful knowledge is applied to problems of social organization and economic production, it takes on the form of technology. Therefore, we have the protean nature of useful knowledge and our basic tautology, that on the one face the form of useful knowledge may be viewed as culture and on the other as technology. Culture and technology appear in material as well as social forms and structures. The automobile as a store of useful knowledge serves as a form of material culture and, as a material technic, serves as a form of material technology. The social institution known as the nation state, as a store of useful knowledge, serves as a form of nonmaterial culture. As a nonmaterial technic, as a social invention, it also serves as a form of social technology. Consequently, to transform technology is also in substance to transform culture; they are opposite sides of the same coin—the coin of useful knowledge. Therefore, we have explained general culture evolution in terms of its own substance and ingredients.

New technics are the new elements which are added to culture and which in the process of innovation bring about the accumulation and transformation of culture. Whereas techniques represent the application of knowledge in a general sense and would include ceremonial or useless knowledge, technics, by comparison represent the application of useful knowledge or knowledge which is relevant to man's social organization and economic producation. The integration and aggregation of these technics as an organic whole comprise what we have conceptualized as the overall gestalt of technology.[29] It is the overall gestalt of technology (the opposite side of which would be the core of culture) which serves as the basic characteristic of a given stage or level of economic development. The theory of economic development which we present, using the framework of *cultural economics*, is consequently an explanation of the transformation of one given overall gestalt of technology to a higher level. The power to generate the structural transformation, as one stage of economic development gives rise to the next, is inherent in the form of new energy gestalts originated through the process of economic development. The basic mechanism for that transformation is the innovation of new technics.

Culture, man's social heritage, is continuously bombarded by the new technics which man invents and discovers. As the elements of the ocean continuously bombard and transform the coastline so do the new technics bombard and transform culture. As the skyline of New York was transformed from tepees to skyscrapers with the addition of new technics, so was transportation technology transformed from that of foot travel to rocket travel, and our energy source from that of fuelwood to fossil fuels and our tools from that of the hoe to that of machines and the overall gestalt from that of hunting and gathering to that of applying science to economic production and social organization. The new technics, for a specific culture, are derived from either invention, discovery or diffusion and may be material or nonmaterial. Fundamental to *cultural economics*, then, would be conceptualization of technology which would entail the nonmaterial as well as the material. While such a dichotomy has been by and large accepted in terms of the concept of culture, technology, itself, frequently has been conceptualized as material culture to the exclusion of the nonmaterial.[30] To our view the technics of technology may comprise social organization as well as economic production and, consequently, we speak of social technics (the factory system) as well as material technics (the steam engine).

To function technology requires concomitant material and social technics. These technics, however, need not advance in a synchronized manner. In fact, culture has historically evolved in a lopsided manner and this phenomenon has been conceptualized by Ogburn as a cultural lag. The most usual pattern being of the nature in which the material technics advanced faster than the social. Therefore, in culture evolution some parts of the organic whole grow faster than others. Such cultural lags are manifest in the periodic malfunctioning of the whole of culture or the aggregate economy.

In the case of biological evolution, the organic whole of the biological structure does not experience such a lack of synchronization in the developmental process. In biological growth and development of a given organism, the process of ontogeny is governed and controlled by nature's code of life in the form of DNA which gives out instructions to maintain a synchronized and coordinated pattern of growth and development for a given organism. A specific individual in his biological growth and development (given a healthy and normal body) experiences a coordinated and synchronized growth and development of his functional parts.

Man in his social growth and development, however, has no such agency, as yet, to perform the function of synchronization. It is in the future development and evolution of the social sciences that mankind will produce the agency of social organization, as social technology, capable of synchronizing the forward exponential advance of material and nonmaterial culture. Mankind, thereby, in the process will alleviate the most basic type of cultural lag. Given the innovation of the technic of the science to the nonmaterial sector of culture with the same enthusiasm as has been institutionalized in the material sector of culture, man would thereby in the process have innovated a "frictionless wheel of economic development."[31]

Fundamental to an understanding of the process of economic development would be the recognition that the process is both circular and cumulative. As noted previously, this constitutes a basic contribution of Gunnar Myrdal. We have incorporated the circular nature of the process in the framework of our "wheel of economic development," in which new technics are innovated in the framework of circular causation. We have delineated the circular sequence under four headings: New Technics (A); Environmental (Natural Resources and Culture Permeability (B); The Overall Gestalt of Technology (C); and, Environmental (Natural Resources and Culture) Accumulation and Transformation (D). The environment of natural resources and culture must prove permeable to the new technic if it is to be innovated and if it is to become part of the overall gestalt of technology.

The new technics serve as many drops of rain which produce changes in the stream of technology—however, these drops do not always make their way into the stream; they are not always innovated. But given the innovation of the new technic and, consequently, technological change, we then set in motion the forces of culture accumulation and transformation.

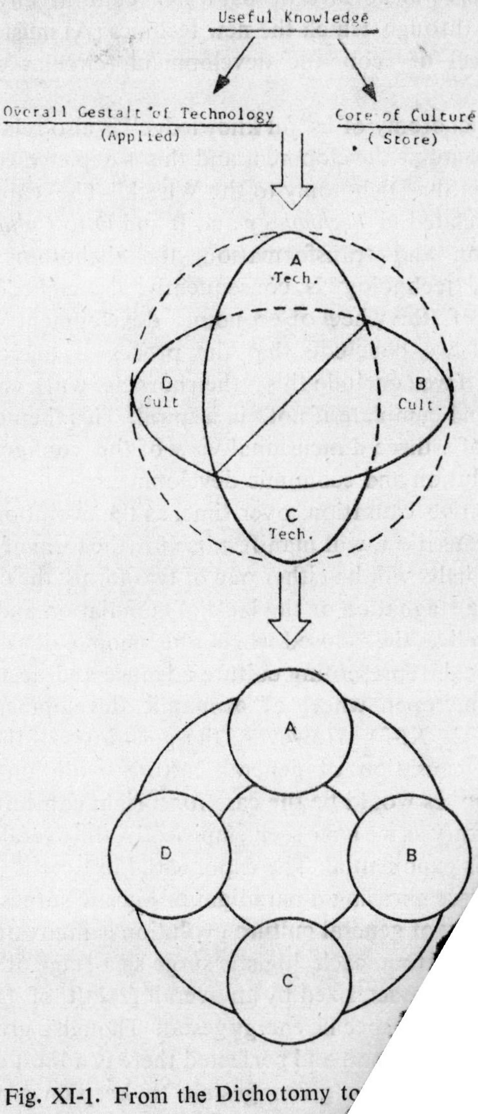

Fig. XI-1. From the Dichotomy to

The circular process not only generates a greater capacity for new technics (A) but also in the process the cultural permeability (B) is also transformed in that a new cultural environment is created through which the new technics (A) must pass, and so the wheel of economic development (circular causation) spins.[32]

The "dichotomy of useful knowledge" is also related to the wheel of economic development and this is depicted in Figure XI-1, "From the Dichotomy to the Wheel." The categories A and C are related to *Technology* and B and D to *Culture* and its accumulation and transformation; the dichotomy between culture and technology is, consequently, also embedded in the framework of "the wheel of economic development." But, in addition, if we conclude that the process is one of circular causation—if we conclude this—then how else will a circle move over time and cumulate if not via a spiral? This then offers the possibility of a three-dimensional view of the configuration of culture evolution and economic development.

Cumulative causation, over time, as the evolutionary path of circular causation, will manifest itself in the form of a helix or spiral. This helix will be either one of two forms: the cylindrical representing stagnation or the lack of cumulation and develop-
ent as well as the "closed wheel of economic development,"
the conical, representing culture advance and accumulation
ell as an "open wheel of economic development" (note
es XI-2, XI-3). However, the generatrix of the helix of
tive causation of general culture evolution is not a
line as would be the case for a right conical helix, for
ntrary as we have seen empirically, the overall develop-
is exponential. The exponential in turn is really an
rve encasing a paradigm of logistic surges.

of general culture evolution is innovative in the
ting each logistic surge as a stage of economic
racterized by an overall gestalt of technology
specific energy gestalt Though a given gestalt
on and perfected there is a limit or ceiling
a given gestalt to keep on growing and
process of economic development, as
just the perfection or improvement of
he gestalt must be transformed to a

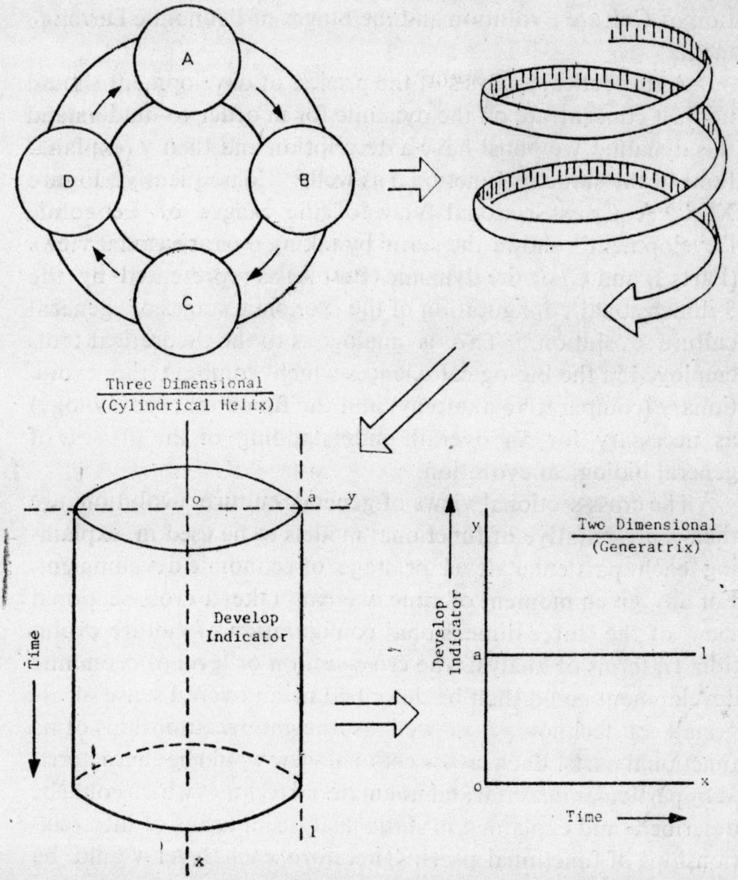

Fig. XI-2. The Closed Wheel of Economic Development.

higher level as indicated by energy consumption and control. The overall three-dimensional configuration of the dynamic process of economic development as it accumulates over time is represented by Figure XI-4 "A Three-Dimensional Configuration of Culture Evolution and the Stages of Economic Development."

A theoretical analysis of the process of development should not just concentrate on the dynamic for in order to understand the dynamic we must have a description and theory (explanation) of the static or functional as well.[33] Consequently, Figure XI-5 "A Cross-Sectional View of the Stages of Economic Development" shows the static by taking cross-sectional views (Parts B and C) of the dynamic (Part A) as represented by the 3-dimensional configuration of the economic stages of general culture evolution.[34] This is analogous to the theoretical tools employed in the biological sciences which combine the evolutionary (comparative anatomy) and the functional (physiology) as necessary for an overall understanding of the process of general biological evolution.

The cross-sectional views of general culture evolution are then representative of functional models to be used in explaining each particular level or stage of economic development. For any given moment of time we can take a cross-sectional view of the three dimensional configuration of culture evolution. In terms of analysis the cross-section or level of economic development could then be described in an overall sense of its gestalt of technology as well as the interrelationships of its functional parts. Each cross-sectional view would be characterized by particular material and nonmaterial technics which could be described and explained in static analysis in terms of interrelationships of functional parts. Therefore each level would be characterized by differing capacities in terms of economic growth as an overall magnitude as well as a rate. The type of economic growth for each level would also vary in terms of the specific goods and services produced. Each cross-sectional level would rely upon particular types of energy sources. Such descriptive material concerning the static or functional analysis of each cross-sectional level of cultural advance would be integrated and synthesized into the framework of the "closed" wheel of economic development, that is, our static model for a

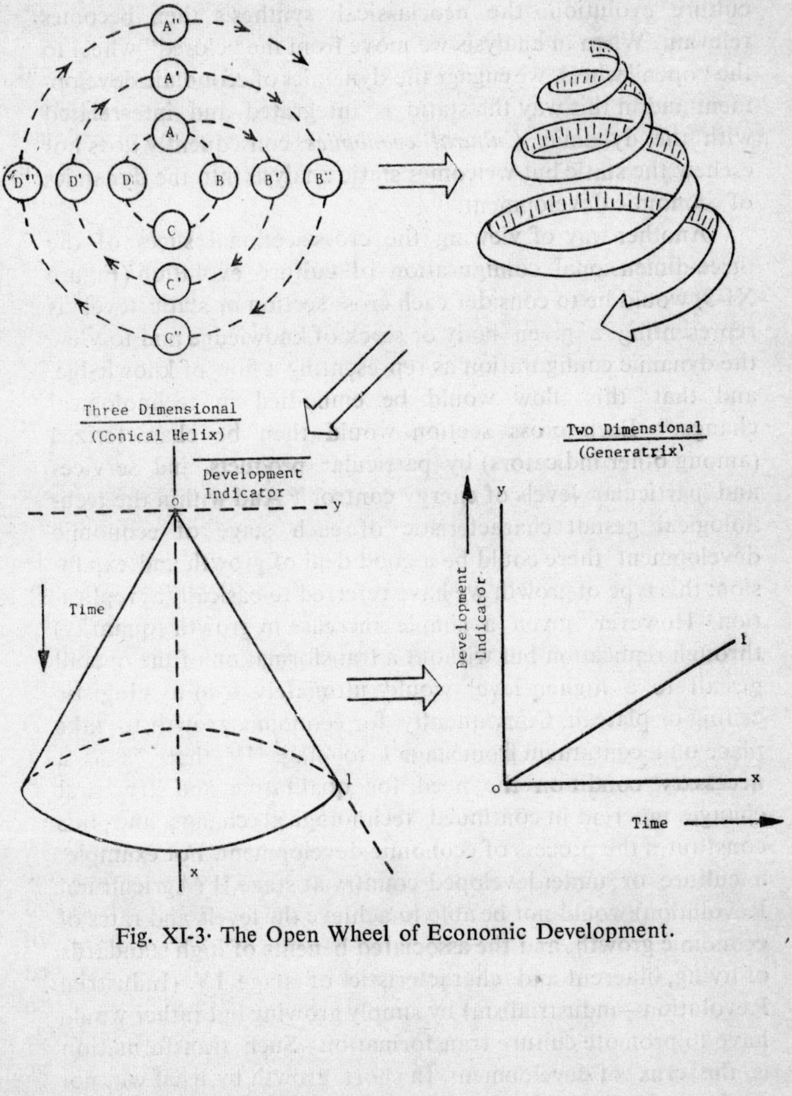

Fig. XI-3· The Open Wheel of Economic Development.

given level of economic development at a given moment of time. Theory in economics, as the neoclassical synthesis, provides for an explanation of such functional relationship and short-run policy directions. Given such a static, cross-sectional slice of culture evolution, the neoclassical synthesis then becomes relevant. When in analysis we move from the "closed" wheel to the "open" wheel, we engage the dynamics of economic development and in this way the static is integrated and interrelated with the dynamic. *Cultural economics* consequently does not eschew the static but welcomes static analysis into the dynamics of economic development.

Another way of viewing the cross-sectional slices of the three-dimensional configuration of culture evolution (Figure XI-5) would be to consider each cross section or static level as representing a given body or stock of knowledge and to view the dynamic configuration as representing a flow of knowledge, and that this flow would be embodied in technological change.[35] Each cross section would then be characterized (among other indicators) by particular products and services and particular levels of energy control.[36] And within the technological gestalt characteristic of each stage of economic development there could be a good deal of growth and expansion; this type of growth we have referred to basically as replication. However, given a simple increase in growth (quantity) through replication but without a transformation of the overall gestalt to a higher level would ultimately lead to a logistic ceiling or plateau. Consequently, for economic growth to take place on a continuum from stage I to stage IV there is as a necessary condition the need for qualitative and structural changes inherent in continued technological change and this constitutes the process of economic development. For example. a culture or underdeveloped country at stage II (Agricultural Revolution) would not be able to achieve the levels and rates of economic growth, and the associated benefits of high standards of living, inherent and characteristic of stage IV (Industrial Revolution—industrialism) by simply growing but rather would have to promote culture transformation. Such transformation is the crux of development. In short, growth by itself will not produce development but will rather produce a ceiling of saturation. Given the principle of similitude, economic growth

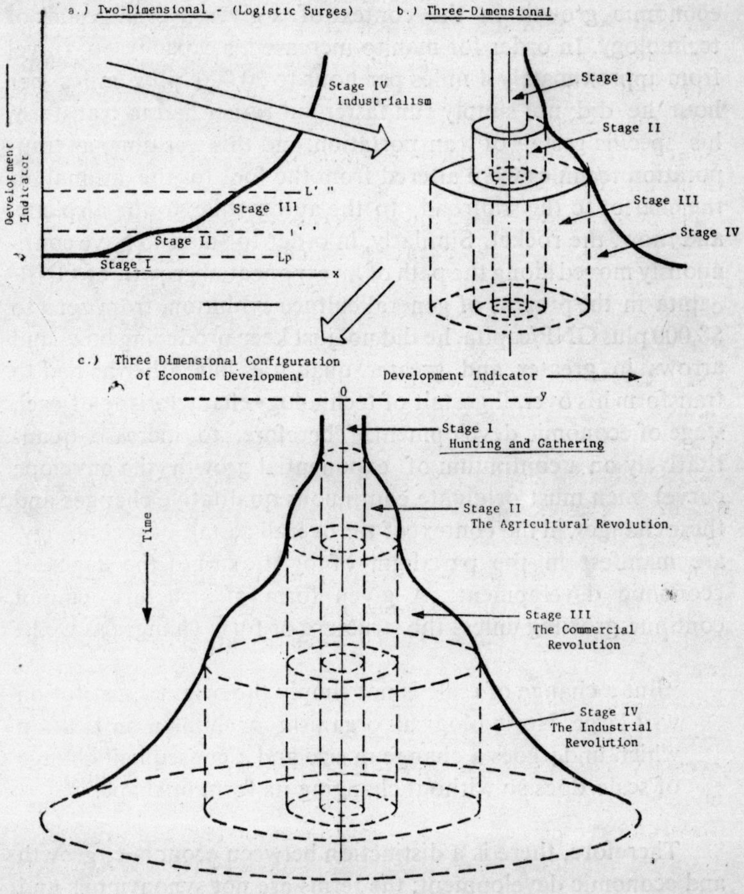

Fig. XI-4. A Three-Dimensional Configuration of Culture Evolution and the Stages of Economic Development.

as the quantitative cannot continue and be ongoing without structural (qualitative) change.[37]

In our study, using the analytical tool of logistic surges, we have given support to the basic position that there is a limit to economic growth in the context of a given overall gestalt of technology. In order for man to increase his capacity to travel from approximately 4 miles per hour to 20,000 plus miles per hour he did not simply run faster but rather had to transform his specific gestalt of transportation; and this was done as tranporation technics were altered from the foot to the animal, to the chariot to the railroad, to the automobile, to the airplane, and now, the rocket. Similarly, in order for man to have continuously moved along the path of an exponential growth of GNP/capita in the process of general culture evolution, from zero to $8,000 plus GNP/capita, he did not just keep producing bows and arrows in greater and greater quantities but rather he had to transform his overall gestalt of technology characteristic of each stage of economic development. Therefore, to increase quantitatively on a continuum of exponential growth (the envelope curve) man must originate continuous qualitative changes and these changes, in the context of the overall gestalt of technology, are manifest in the paradigm of logistic surges, the stages of economic development. A given form of structure cannot continue growing unless the structure or form changes as well:

> "But a change of scale is not simply the original institution writ large. No biological organism or human institution which undergoes a change in size and a consequent change of scale does so without changing its form or shape."[38]

Therefore, there is a distinction between economic growth and economic development; the terms are not synonymous and should be conceptually clarified and we have attempted such a clarification in the course of our study. And further, conceptual clarity is not just an end in itself but is necessary for scientific analysis, and consequently we have tried to show that the distinction between economic growth and economic development is of analytical and theoretical significance.

In summary then, given our conceptualization of economic development, in which we have used *cultural economics* as

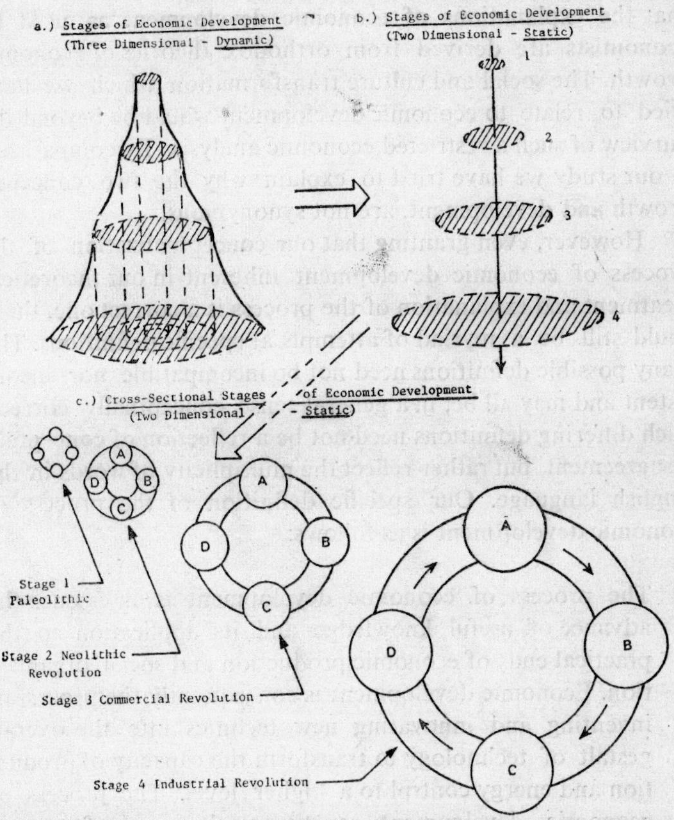

Fig. XI-5. A Cross-Sectional View of the Stages of Economic Development.

method, how then do we define the process of economic development?[39] In general, as we have previously noted, economists of the mainstream predilection tend first to define economic growth and then to use the definition as being synoymous with economic development.[40] Perhaps this is due to the fact that the explanations of economic development as used by economists are derived from orthodox theories of economic growth. The social and culture transformation which we have tried to relate to economic development would be beyond the purview of such a restricted economic analysis. By comparison, in our study we have tried to explain why the two concepts, growth and development, are not synonymous.

However, even granting that our conceptualization of the process of economic development inherent in our theoretical treatment and explanation of the process is a correct one, there could still be a myriad of attempts at specific definitions. The many possible definitions need not be incompatible nor inconsistent and may all be, in a general sense, conceptually correct. Such differing definitions need not be a reflection of conceptual disagreement but rather reflect the multiplicity of words in the English language. Our specific definition of the process of economic development is as follows:

> The process of economic development is in essence the advance of useful knowledge and its application to the practical ends of economic production and social organization. Economic development is consequently the process of inventing and innovating new technics into the overall gestalt of technology to transform the capacity of production and energy contrpl to a higher level. The process of economic development constitutes the core of general culture evolution and accounts for the accumulation and transformation of culture as manifest in the paradigm of the stages of economic development.

This concept of economic development has been implied in the course of our study and the conceptualization grew as we attempted, more and more, to explain the process. In so doing as we come to understand the concept more correctly we are then in a position to offer a more correct and specific definition of the concept. And the better our theory the better our conceptualization and the better our conceptualization the more we can improve upon and reinforce our theory. It is in this frame that we offer a definition of economic development, a definition which would lack full meaning and significance unless the reader is familiar with the analysis and theoretical framework of the study and its underlying assumptions and that the reader would have some understanding of the theory of economic development upon which the definition is based. Also, in our specific definition of economic development we use other concepts, for example, such as technology, and our definition would be conceptually incorrect if one were to insert into our definition a preconceived notion of technology conceptualized as material culture alone to the exclusion of the nonmaterial. A succinct and specific definition, then, appears as the tip of the iceberg above water, our study in its entirety serves as the whole mass of the iceberg and the substance upon which our conceptualization of economic development rests. There are many definitions of economic development which appear in the literature, though while lacking the same conceptualization of economic development as specifically presented in our study, would still be compatible and consistent with our conceptualization. Theory in developmental economics is moving in the direction of the cultural and the social and this reflects a differing conceptualization of the process from that which had been historically associated with strict economic analysis. Definitions conceptually compatible with our analysis and theoretical framework would embrace the social, and not simply the economic, as a magnitude or quantitative replication, since to our view the process is conceptually one of technological change and culture transformation. Definitions of economic development which we would view as incorrect and conceptually incompatible would be those which conceptualized the process as one of simplistic increases in quantitative economic variables devoid of the qualitative and the cultural and of course the evolutionary.[41]

And finally, before ending our study, several issues remain to be discussed: one concerns the mind of man versus the *sui generis* view of culture evolution; still another concerns value and human development; and still another concerns the issue of evolution, itself, as a generalized concept embracing the inorganic, the organic, and the superorganic. L.A. White, as perhaps one of the leading evolutionists of the modern period, in the social sciences, supports the view that the process of culture evolution is *sui generis.* We have certainly endorsed the need for a science of culture or what L.A. White calls culturology. And though such a science would require an explanation of culture evolution characterized by advances in technology and energy control; we do not, however, endorse the historical materialism, technological determinism or *sui generis* predilections of Leslie A. White.[42]

Is man simply a part of a materialistic and mechanistic process of culture evolution of which he has no control? Does culture determine and control man who submits as a passive agent, or is man the active and dynamic agent of culture evolution and as such does he have the power to control and regulate culture, and, thereby, to control his own destiny? To Leslie A. White:

> Culture thus becomes a continuum of extra-somatic elements. It moves in accordance with its own principles, its own laws; it is a thing *sui generis*. . .culture is not determined by man. . .the culture process is *culturally* determined. . .[43]

While at first glance the *sui generis* view of culture evolution seems without foundation the idea does appear to have some credibility. For example, did man control inorganic evolution or did the inorganic evolutionary process of matter and energy, *sui generis*, produce the physical environment? And from that physical environment who would argue that man controlled or was responsible for the dynamics of organic or biological evolution and thereby produced himself?[44] Carrying such thinking further, and over to culture as the superorganic, or the extra somatic, it is understandable that some would feel that man is subject to inexorable and inevitable forces and, consequently, is not really in control or the dynamic agent responsible for change, but rather is controlled by the processes of culture evolution. Hornell Hart, for example, has expressed the view.

> To many who have studied it, social change appears like a super human culture stream, moving forward on the shoulders of a countless multitude, driven and deflected by uncontrollable forces. . .the Gargantuan culture structure moves along on the shoulders of a countless multitude, driven and deflected by forces of which they are almost utterly ignorant?[45]

For while man was able to control the addition of parts, perhaps in the form of better bridges, roads, buildings, and particular social technics as well, would anyone ever venture to say that he knew what he was doing or where he was going or that he was in control in terms of general culture evolution? Was he ever in control, was he ever really cognizant of the "complex whole" as a collection and integration of these parts, both social and material, as culture evolved over time? Therefore, while it might be said that man controlled somewhat the evolution of the parts, he never controlled general culture evolution as a whole since this was beyond his conceptual framework.[46] During the earlier stages of economic development, man never really knew as he added the separate parts, as he innovated new technics, that he was transforming the overall gestalt nor did he have any idea as to where that gestalt was going in its evolution.

Has not the process of general culture evolution been one of spontaneous evolution as culture evolved, seemingly by itself, through the stages of economic development, as one overall gestalt of technology was transformed to the next? Would anyone submit that man was cognizant of or rationally in control of the overall process which brought about the Industrial Revolution let alone the Neolithic Revolution?[47] Even assuming that man was in control of adding the parts or elements of culture, as the new technics of invention and discovery, was he ever really in control of the whole as an integrated gestalt, the "complex whole" as culture is currently conceptualized?[48]

Does man have the ability and capacity to control culture evolution or will culture evolve along some predetermined path irrespective of what man does? Granted that man serves as a necessary condition for culture evolution, an assumption made by L.A. White, and also, granted that man serves somewhat as a catalyst (we have also drawn this analogy) does man, the catalyst, only serve as an activator of the process and without which the process does not take place, or does man, in addition, also serve as the dynamic agent responsible for accretion and transformation?[49]

As a result of the process of economic development, man is able to achieve higher levels of energy control and thereby in the process extends the limits of his capacity to originate new social and material technics. Man is not only capable as a catalyst of starting the overall machine (culture) in its operation, but in addition is capable of changing the very nature of the machine he has activated. Culture in its origins required man but man as such (biologically) in his origins did not require culture but came to use culture, as the superorganic evolved, to his advantage.[50] Without man culture could not have been originated; without man culture could not exist. Man is the life-blood of culture. For if man were destroyed and eliminated culture would no longer exist or be viable and only a lifeless residue of material artifacts would remain. Consequently, it is to man and his power of thought, creativity, and origination, that culture owes its dynamics and its very existence and life.

To question man's capacity to fully control general culture evolution in the past is not to deny man the potential for ultimate control in the future. Leslie A. White, however, denies man this capacity, "man does not and cannot control his culture or direct its course."[51] If Carlyle were with us would he also add such a science of culture, as culturology, to the dismal science of Malthusian economics?

A materialist and determinist explanation of culture evolution, such as the *sui generis* as offered by L.A. White, with its implied inevitability, serves somewhat as an opiate to the mind in that such an explanation tends to lull the intellect to sleep in thinking that some great mechanistic machine of culture evolution will lead continuously and inexorably along some predeter-minded path to progress.[52] Is it correct to assume that nothing can be done? Is not such a conclusion the basis for the policy directive of laissez-faire? By comparison, the whole impetus behind cultural economics is precisely to better understand the processes of culture evolution in order that mankind might better control culture evolution for the furtherance of human development.

Cultural economics, by comparison to the *sui generis* explanation of culture evolution, stresses the advance of useful knowledge manifest and concreted as new technics, both material and nonmaterial. Innovated in the form of technological change, such technics serve as the dynamic cause of culture evolution. Rather than a mechanistic or deterministic material technology acting *sui generis* with energy, it is ultimately then the mind of man in the invention of new technics which serves as "the locus of the evolutionary impulse" explaining economic development and culture evolution.[53] Culture provides man with an overall technic for the store and accumulation of new knowledge. Culture provides man with an overall technic to increase his capacity to invent and discover and thereby to add new technics of economic production, social organization and energy control. Culture, in its evolution, serves the function, the instrumental function, of promoting the human life process.[54]

In opposition to the *sui generis* position, many social scientists argue not only that man can control culture evolution but, in addition, that man must control and regulate culture evolution if he is to survive. It is in this context that we have noted the potential of a "frictionless wheel of economic development," a result basically derived from the greater application of science to social organization.[55] It is in this sense that *cultural economics* conforms to Tyler's position that,

> To impress men's minds with a doctrine of development, will lead them in all honour to their ancestors to continue the progressive work of past ages. . . .Thus, active at once in aiding progress and in removing hindrance, the science of culture is essentially a reformer's science.[56]

We use reform in the context of *cultural economics*, not as policy based upon emotion and feelings of self-righteousness, but rather policy guided by science and directed by the motivation of improvement in the sense of perfection. Policy as directed by science in order to perfect man's social technics in much the same way that we now use science to improve and perfect the material technics of medicine, of travel and transportation, of our buildings and bridges, and the like, of our material sector; let us now use science to perfect our social technics with the same enthusiasm which we have thus far shown for the material.[57] However, not only in the sense of perfecting specific material and nonmaterial technics, as specific and individual parts, but also, to synchronize and perfect the overall gestalt of technology as an integrated whole. In addition, that man seeks not simply to control the overall gestalt in order simply to control the problems of economics production and cultural lags, as ends in themslves, as economic production for the sake of economic production, but also to fulfill the age-old quest for reform. The whole conglomerate effort of science to economic production and social organization should be directed toward the promotion of the ultimate objective, the objective of human development and human welfare.[58] The perfection of specific material and nonmaterial technics and the perfection of the overall gestalt of technology are to function not as ends in themselves, but rather, as necessary conditions for the goal of improving and perfecting man as an ongoing process on a longterm continuum.

The achievement of such a goal will not be by chance and predetermined, inexorable forces of evolution but, assumes, that man does have capacity to control and plan the future path of culture evolution. Whereas the historic forces of inorganic and organic evolution can possibly be viewed as inexorable, the evolutionary realm of the superorganic and the cultural is not predetermined but, rather, can be controlled by man.[59] By comparison, the *sui generis* view perceives of man being controlled by cultural systems. Such a path is unidirectional and does not take into account circular and cumulative causation in the sense that man is not only a product of culture but is culture producing as well.[60] And while L.A. White certainly recognizes that man produces culture, such production, however, is not simply conditioned by culture but is *determined* by the cultural system.[61] The framework of *cultural economics* certainly would be supportive to the position that man's origination of new technics is strongly conditioned by culture. But *cultural economics* would also be in support of the position that man is capable of rising above that conditioning process; that man can ultimately take control of the culture which he has created. Man is capable of programming his own computer, the cerebral cortex, and for his own advantage.

If man can control and if man should control culture evolution, "which direction is forward?"[62] We must now discuss an issue avoided throughout most of our study, the issue of value. Mainstream institutional economics has pursued two basic paths of social inquiry: 1. the development of a general theory of economic development; and 2. a theory of value. And while Veblen was of the predilection that a scientist should employ "idle curiosity" his curiosity was not always that idle. Veblen applied his general theory of development in his critical and value-oriented analysis of industrial capitalism; throughout Veblen's work, value judgments were *implied*. The Dewey-Ayres combination thrust the issue of value judgments, *explicitly*, to front-row-center stage. Ayres stated: "Economics is nothing if it is not a science of value."[63]

In the tradition of mainstream institutional economics, *cultural economics* is also directed towards a general theory of econo mic development. However, in order to clarify and better focusaon our subject matter, and for a variety of other reasons, we heve thus far argued for a separation of value from the theor itical explanation of the process of economic development. We w ll now argue that a general theory of economic development and the issue of value are intimately related, and that, in the final analysis, the two issues cannot be divorced.

We agree with Marc Tool, that the issue of value judgments can be directly addressed and answered through scientific inquiry.[64] The value of the economic process is that it serves the instrumental function, as a necessary condition, for the continued advance and promotion of human development as the life process. Advances in economic production and energy control serve not as ends in themselves but only insofar as such technological advance provides for increased capacity and potential for the furtherance of the human life process. As John Ruskin so eloquently noted years ago in *Unto This Last*, it is not the cold vein of metallic ore which is of value, but the "Veins of Wealth" are those conducting the warm bloodstream of human life, ". . .the true veins of wealth are purple—and not in Rock but in Flesh—perhaps even that the final outcome and consummation of all wealth is in the producing as many as possible full-breathed, bright-eyed, and happy-hearted human creatures."[65]

To assert the direction of human development as the ultimate goal is not to engage a "final term" nor to disengage the means-ends-means continuum. The ultimate goal of human development, as value, does not represent finality of station but constitutes an ongoing journey of continuity. The concept of value represents a continuum manifest in technological advance which in the framework of *cultural economics* appears as the continued advance of the core of culture.[66] And by focusing on human development (ends) we do not deny the means-ends-means continuum in that technological advance and culture evolution (means) promotes human development (ends) which in turn serves as the means for the further advance of culture, and on the wheel of circular and cumulative causation spins The process of man advancing culture, in turn advancing man in turn advancing culture represents circular and cumulative causation and offers the potential for ongoing human development on an exponential continuum.

What must be done in the further perfection of the continuum is to develop and improve upon a concept and theory of human development. Human development and welfare must be conceptualized in gestalt and holistic terms and to include the social, cultural, and psychological, and not simply in terms of more and more economic goods. And as the concept and theory of human development improves over time, culture can be more systematically controlled, designed and planned to fulfill the objective of human development which in turn would promote higher levels of culture evolution. Culture evolution could then be directed more and more toward fulfilling the basic needs of human development as a continuous process in the evolution of the human potential.

Homo sapiens has gone through two basic stages in his evolution and development. The first stage concerned biological evolution and if that were all, given a basic fixity of the organic structure, there would have been a finite ceiling placed on the path of man's future evolution and development. Homo sapiens overcame the limits to his future development, which were inherent in the logistic of his biological structure, through the evolution of the extrasomatic or culture. In order for man to continue the development process, given the principle of similitude, a new structure became necessary. That new structure

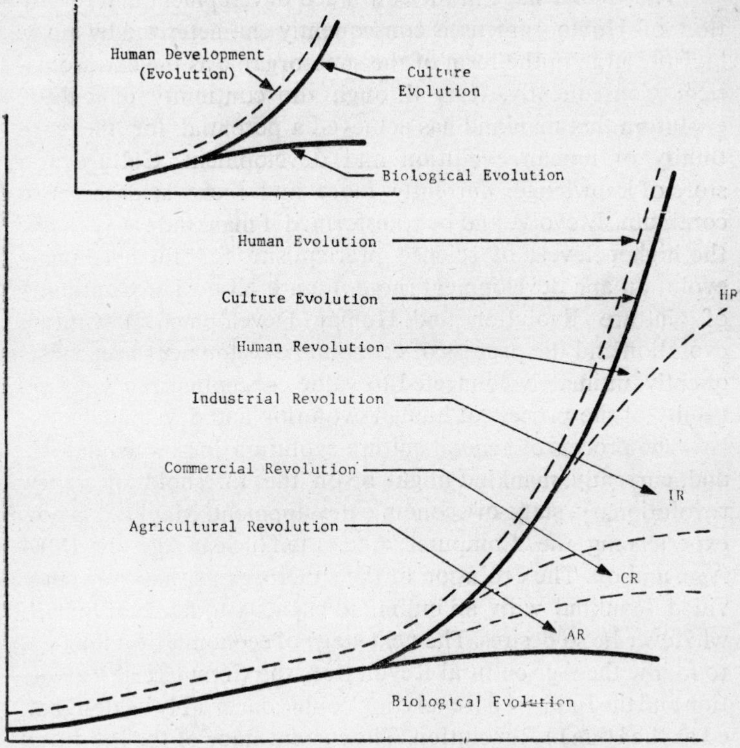

Fig. XI-6. The Continuity of Culture Evolution and Human Development.

was provided for in the evolution of the superorganic or culture. Through the superorganic, as the extrasomatic, mankind achieved higher levels of free energy, not as an end it itself, but as increased capacity for higher levels of human development.

The second stage in the continued development and evolution of Homo sapiens is consequently characterized by a new logistic surge in the form of the superorganic as the extrasomatic.[67] Consequently, it is through the continuity of culture evolution that mankind has achieved a potential for the continuity of human evolution and development. Culture as a store of knowledge, currently more and more science, must continuously evolve and be transformed if mankind is to achieve the higher levels of science prerequisite for further human evolution and development (note, Figure XI-6 "The Continuity of Culture Evolution and Human Development"). Culture evolution and the process of economic development are, consequently, intimately connceted to value conceptualized as a continuity of the process of human evolution and development.

The process of general culture evolution does not stand still and, currently, mankind might be on the threshold of a new revolutionary stage of economic development. Mankind is now experiencing the Computer Age, the Nuclear Age, the DNA Age, and on. The evolution of the superorganic has now provided mankind with an unlimited capacity to make of himself whatever he so desires. The next stage of economic development to follow the Agricultural Revolution, the Commercial Revolution and the Industrial Revolvtion could conceivably be designated as the Human Revolution. The current stage of the Industrial Revolution, as modern economic growth, is characterized by the application of science to economic production and social organization; human development is assumed to be achieved indirectly in the context of human welfare as more and more econonic goods. In the oncoming stage as the Human Revolution, and consistent with the value of human development, the overall gestalt of technology would be characterized by the application of science not only to economic production and social organization (yet to be perfected as a "frictionless wheel") but, in addition, science would be applied *directly* to the process of human development as well. Human evolution in its further perfection would no longer be achieved indirectly as an assumed by-product of economic production but would be submitted directly to a science, concept and theory, of human development. The social structure (superorganic) could then be molded and planned with this basic value in mind.[68] This is not to foresake economic production and higher levels of energy control which provide the underlying buttresses of material and nonmaterial culture required for human evolution. Economic development and growth serve as necessary, but not sufficient, conditions for further human development and evolution. Culture evolution must now be planned, controlled and directed through the application of science, not simply for the further advance of goods and services, but to directly focus on the furtherance of human development. The road ahead provided for by the continuity of culture evolution is in the direction of the application of more and more science, not only to perfect economic production and social organization, but science, directly and specifically, applied to the problem and process of human development.

> "This process, human evolution, must eventually be brought under human control. Here mankind will meet the greatest challenge of its biological and cultural histories. To deal with this challenge successfully, knowledge and understanding evolution in general, and of the unique aspects of human evolution in particular are essential."[69]

For all this to come to pass, if mankind is to control and direct culture evolution, there is a need then for further understanding and the advance of science.[70] Fundamental to such an understanding would be to recognize that our discussions thus far concerning economic development and culture evolution go under the general overall rubric of evolution, evolution as a generalized concept embracing the inorganic, the organic, and the superorganic. This presents the possibility of the existence of universal laws of evolution which apply and are relevant to the inorganic, the organic, and the superorganic on a continuum. In that the organic evolved from the inorganic and the superorganic from the organic, there perhaps exist universal laws explaining the continuity of the evolutionary process. Basic to evolution is the idea that one form grows out of the previous, therefore, there conceivably are universal laws and principles concerning the explanation of the process through which the organic grew out of the inorganic and the superorganic out of the organic. We speak here of the development and understanding of intrinsic universal laws and principles which apply to the inorganic, the organic and the superorganic on a continuum of evolution.[71] If so, we might learn basic principles to apply to culture evolution through the study of overall evolution as an overall process. The social sciences might benefit from an integration of the physical, biological, and social sciences, and the resulting cross-fertilization of thought and ideas addressed to the problem of overall general evolution.[72] This line of thought is expressed schematically in Figure XI-7, "The Rubric of Evolution and the Synthesis of Science", to show how the overall process of evolution might serve as an integrative concept for the whole of science in much the same way that the concept of culture serves to integrate the social sciences. The conceptual framework of evolution in some form of "systems way of thinking," tied-in with energy transformation might serve as a means through which to promote the unity of science.[73] The physical sciences (inorganic) plus the biological sciences (organic) plus the social sciences (superorganic) could conceivably be integrated through the universality and interconnecting principles of evolution. Such a synthesis of the three major fields of science would aid in the further clarification of the concept and theory of evolution. Such an improved upon understanding of evolution might then in turn help to integrate economics into the social sciences in an holistic sense. The objective would be to formulate a truly interdisciplinary approach, not simply multidisciplinary, for the social sciences in general and for economics in particular. The social science which exibits the greatest lag and most strongly resists the conceptual framework of evolution is economics. This is indeed unfortunate in that economics, as the "queen of the social sciences" is most strongly relied upon in the derivation of social organization as policy at the macro-level. Such an attempt at integration and synthesis would indeed press upon the mind of man the full weight of the exponential rate of growth of knowledge. Of course to point to the form and substance of which a key is to be made is one thing, to make such a key is another. But still, it logically follows that if we are to control

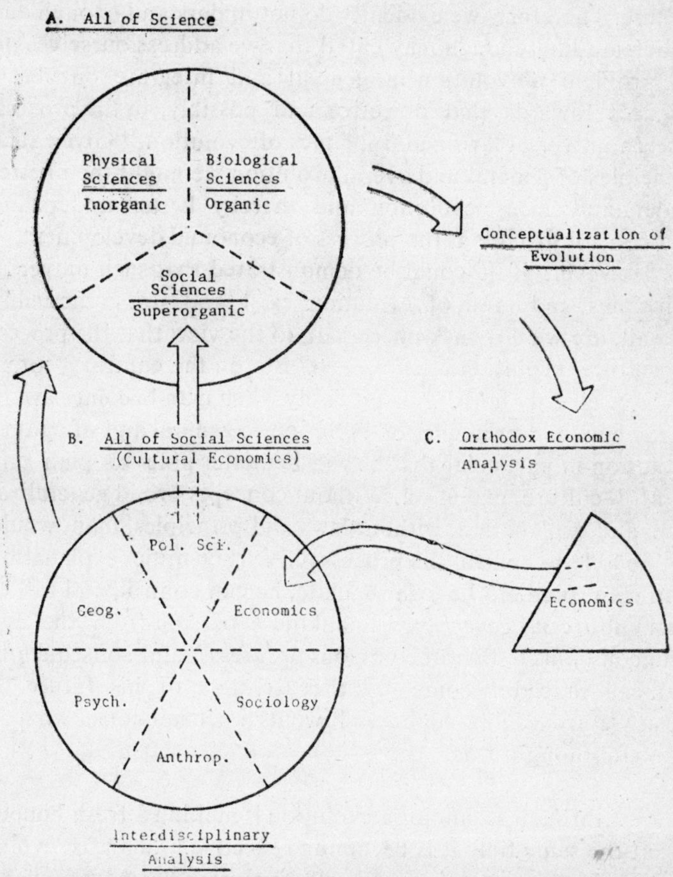

Fig. XI-7. The Rubric of Evolution and the Synthesis of Science.

culture evolution, we must understand culture evolution, not in a complete or finite sense (an impossibility, perhaps, assuming knowledge to be infinite) but rather to understand enough to control. And today who among our social scientists would state that we are in control of our overall technology and culture. Therefore, we evidently do not understand enough and understanding enough may entail that we address ourselves to the problem of evolution in general and integrate our basic sciences towards that objective and possibly, in the process, discern universal laws and principles of evolution.[74] Given such principles of general and overal evolution we might then better understand culture evolution and thereby better understand and control its core as the process of economic development.

However, if it could be demonstrated that such universal principles and laws of evolution exist and do in actuality prevail, are we not back once again to the view that the process of culture evolution is *sui generis*? But on the contrary, for as we have already noted, it is precisely when man becomes aware of the laws and principles of evolution in general and of culture evolution in particular that he will be better able to plan and control culture evolution. Without concepts broad generalization, and explanation, without laws and principles, man would not be able to control the process. Given scientific explanation man can predict, he can regulate, he can control, and rather than culture *sui generis*, ". . .mankind is passing from the age of unconscious to that of conscious progress," and consequently man can indeed become ". . .the architect of his future."[75] What we are saying here, and what a tremendous, what a powerful thought it is:

> ". . .through technology, evolution is making a fresh bound, at the same time it is becoming reflective. . .man is evolution become conscious of itself. Evolution has now to make its own choice."[76]

We close our study with the often-cited (by us as well) passage from Tylor's *Anthropology* concerning the concept of evolution, that indeed, "This is the great principle that every scholar must lay firm hold of, if he intends to understand either the world he lives in or the history of the past."[77] But further, that the concept of evolution, that the story of transformation concerning the evolution from unlimited gases and space to the solar system and earth to the evolution of life and man and then ultimately to culture, is perhaps one of the most stimulating concepts ever posed by the intellect of man, in need of study and further clarification. With *cultural economics* as part of that overall effort—we accept and welcome the challenge.

REFERENCES

[1]Tylor's conceptualization of culture still prevails: "Tylor's omnibus conception of culture is still the basis of most modern anthropological theories of culture, although the conception has been refined and developed in different directions." Milton Singer, *International Encyclopedia of the Social Sciences*, ed., D.L. Sills, Vol. 3, p. 539; ". . . Tylor introduced the definition of culture that most social scientists accept and repeat today . . ." Morris E. Opler, in *Social Change in Developing Areas* (Cambridge: Schenkman Publishing Company, 1965), ed., H.R. Barringer et al., p. 69. Reading the standard work by A.L. Kroeber and Clyde Kluckhohn, *Culture: A Critical Review of Concepts and Definitions*, (Cambridge: Harvard University, 1952), one might conclude from the many definitions presented that no consensus view, with continuity exists. However, in L.A. White's review of the Kroeber and Kluckhohn study, *American Anthropologist* 56 (June 1954), pp. 461-468, p. 462 he notes conceptual clarity and continuity in reference to Tylor. Nonetheless social scientists do not use the concept culture consistently in the same way, cf., Louis Schneider and Charles Bonjean, ed., *The Idea of Culture in the Social Sciences* (London: Cambridge University Press, 1973).

[2]Allan G. Gruchy, *Modern Economic Growth* (New York: Prentice-Hall, 1947), for example discusses "Cultural vs. Formal Economics," pp. 18-28, note also "The Institutional School," *International Encyclopedia of the Social Sciences* (Vol. IV), pp. 462-467, "*Veblen's Cultural Economics*" . . . which he described as "evolutionary" or "cultural economics" . . . p. 462. Though not in exactly the same tradition, Kenneth E. Boulding, "Toward the Development of a cultural Economics," *Social Science Quarterly* 53 (September 1972), pp. 267-284, also uses the term and directs attention toward a "cultural economics." In our study cultural economics represents a modified Veblen-Ayres matrix and is directed toward the advance of a general theory of economic development.

[3]On the quotation note: Thorstein Veblen, *The Place of Science in Modern Civilization* (New York: Russell & Russell, 1961), p. 77; and Clarence E. Ayres, *The Theory of Economic Progress* (New York:

Schocken Books, 1962), p. 96. "What is true of Veblen's work in this respect is true of institutional economics in general—the fact that there is more often than not a general recognition of culture as the master principle of social analysis." Louis J. Junker, "Theoretical Foundations of Neo-Institutionalism," *The American Journal of Economics and Sociology* 27 (April 1968): 197-213, p. 201.

[4]William F. Ogburn, *Social Change* (New York: The Viking Press, 1952), p. 377.

[5]As noted previously in our study, "Ogburn's *Social Change* . . . seems to have been the first major work by an American sociologist in which the anthropological concept of culture was prominently employed." A. L. Kroeber and Clyde Kluckhohn, *Culture: A Critical Review*, p. 15. And again, "Ogburn's main contribution to sociology was in the field of culture and cultural change; to him this was the heart of sociology." *International Encyclopedia of the Social Sciences*, Vol. 11, p. 280.

[6]"Ogburn's work, however, does provide relevant guidelines to the appropriate ways of helping the underdeveloped countries undergo social and economic transformation: his conception of the interrelation of all parts of culture implies that the problem must be attacked on a very wide front, and his insistence on the inherent continuity of social trends in a society suggests that these trends be taken into account when trying to effect socioeconomic change." A. J. Jaffe, *International Encyclopedia of the Social Sciences*, Vol. 11, p. 280.

[7]On the heterodox phase, note Simon Kuznets "Static and Dynamic Economics," *The American Economic Review* 20 (September 1930), pp. 426-441. "The early clash between the classical and historical schools was followed by a no less acrimonious discussion between the adherents of the inductive and of the deductive methods. At present, statistically minded economists are lumped together into the quantitative school as opposed to the neoclassical." p. 426.

[8]In this study we have noted Kuznets' contributions to a social and cultural analysis of economic phenomenon. Robert Fogel by comparison, as a leading exponent of the new economic history which is essentially based upon neoclassical theory and devoid of the social and cultural, also claims inspiration from the work of Simon Kuznets "for as Simon Kuznets (whose work, perhaps more than that of any other scholar, has inspired the new economic history) has frequently pointed out, there is an intimate connection between economic measurement and economic theory." Robert Fogel, "The Reunification of Economic History with Economic Theory." *American Economic Review* 55 (May 1965), pp. 92-98, 96. Simon Kuznets has the unique capacity to please both the neoclassical and institutional economist.

[9]Recall the basic definition of economic growth used by Simon Kuznets, *Modern Economic Growth* (New Haven: Yale University Press, 1966), p. 1, which stresses growth plus structural change.

[10]Gertrude E. Dole and Robert L. Carneiro, *Essays in the Science of Culture in Honor of Leslie A. White* (New York: Thomas Y. Crowell

Company, 1960), foreword, pp. xi-xlvi, p. xxiv.

[11]And again, that is not to accept the views of L.A. White on historical materialism and technological determinism in his explanation of culture evolution *sui generis*.

[12]Certainly, *cultural economics* would be amenable to the view that economic theory itself is subject to accumulation, transformation and evolution, apparently no scholar will ever provide the definitive work in an absolute sense and we have taken this attitude in our treatment of Ogburn, Kuznets and White. Myrdal notes: "We regard the generalizations making up our 'theory' as highly tentative and often conjectural. Many will challenge them; it is healthy that they should." *Asian Drama: An Inquiry into the Poverty of Nations* (New York: The Twentieth Century Fund, 1968), Vol. I, p. 30.

[13]Both W.F. Ogburn and E.A. Ross started out in economics but found greener pastures in sociology. On the difficulties experienced by E.A. Ross, note William E. Spellman, "The Economics of Edward Allsworth Ross," *American Journal of Economics and Sociology* 38 (April 1979), pp. 129-140. "The intellectual climate in economics was not conducive to critics of the classical theory as Veblen was to find in his academic odyssey, and as numerous economists, including Ross were to discover," pp. 131-132. On the difficulties faced by Ayres, note "An Intellectual's Portrait." pp. 3-22 in William Breit and William Patton Culbertson, Jr., ed., *Science and Ceremony* (Austin: University of Texas Press, 1976). And while Ayres excelled as a teacher and scholar, and as one of the outstanding theorists of institutional economics during the post-WWII era, his recognition was less than enthusiastic. As Galbraith notes in the foreword, "I proposed that he be made a distinguished fellow. . . . My case was dismissed without argument." p. viii. And while Keynes was made Lord John Maynard Keynes, and Samuelson and Friedman Nobel laureates, Ayres was made anonymous.

[14]"Why Economics is not an Evolutionary Science," *The Place of Science in Modern Civilization* (New York: Russell & Russell, 1961), pp. 56-81, p. 56. And Clarence E. Ayres, "Institutionalism and Economic Development," *Social Science Quarterly* 41 (March 1970) pp. 1036-1054, ". . . a unified field theory exists in embryo at least . . . its germ has been present in the theory that was implicit in Veblen's work . . . That germ is the later nineteenth-century concept of culture which Veblen absorbed during his formative years and which has since become the foundation-concept of all twentieth-century social thinking." p. 1041.

[15]To Ayres, "Institutions are functionally different from technological patterns." *The Industrial Economy* (Cambridge: Houghton Mifflin Company, 1952), pp. 61, 42-50. To Ayres ". . . the peculiar quality of these particular foci of activity is unquestionably ceremonial." *The Theory of Economic Progress* (New York: Schocken Books, 1962), pp. 182, 177-202. In the context of cultural economics institutions may perform instrumental as well as ceremonial functions and therefore be integral, as social technology, to the overall gestalt of technology.

[16]Therefore, in the framework of cultural economics, useful know-

ledge (science) can penetrate social technics (institutions) as well as material technics. Whereas, by comparison, to Veblen it is only the material technics which are permeable to the matter-of-fact (science) and such knowledge is dynamic and accumulates. Worldly knowledge, however, penetrates the social structure (institutions) and accounts for its static nature and ceremonial function. Note: Thorstein Veblen, *The Place of Science in Modern Civilization* (New York: Russell & Russell, 1961), pp. 1-31.

[17]On the one hand, Ogburn leaned toward a material conceptualization," ...technology—that is, the material products of technology, which is the implication of the word 'technology' in the title.... In short it includes the objects of material culture." in Otis Dudley Duncan, ed., *William F. Ogburn: On Culture and social Change* (Chicago: University of Chicago Press, 1964), p. 79. Elsewhere, "The Meaning of Technology," pp. 3-11, in *Technology and Social Change* (New York: Appleton-Century-Crofts, 1957), ed., Francis R. Allen, Ogburn clearly introduces the social into his conceptualization of technology. Note also the comments by Stanley A. Hetzler, *Technological Growth and Social Change* (New York: Frederick A. Praeger, 1969), pp. 94-95.

[18]"So also is *factory* or the *factory system* as a referent for the technology that has developed since the invention and use of the steam engine." p. 9 in Allen, ed., *Technology and Social Change*.

[19]Simon Kuznets frequently refers to "social technology," for example, "...the potential of material and social technology..." p. 254, in "Modern Economic Growth: Findings and Reflections," *American Economic Review* 63 (June 1973). pp. 247-258; and, "we are trying to identify the units that exploited the growth potential of modern material and social technology." *Modern Economic Growth* (New Haven: Yale University Press, 1966). p. 477. "And by technology we mean not merely the sets of rules and devices for material production, but all types of devices and schemes—objectively described and adaptable by any qualified user—whether in the sphere of material production or social organization." pp. 17-18, *Problems in the Study of Economic Growth* (New York: National Bureau of Economic Research, 1949).

[20]In addition to Myrdal and Galbraith, Eugene Staley also conceptualizes technology in a broader sense to include social technology as well as material technology, "...technology in a broadened concept that includes social technology..." and, "...this older and narrower concept of technology is, I hope, giving way to a newer broader concept that includes social technology.", and stresses the need for such social technology in his "Technology and Developing Nations," in C.S. Wallia, ed., *Toward Century 21* (New York: Basic Books, 1970), pp. 135-142, 136, 138.

[21]Thorstein Veblen, *Absentee Ownership and Business Enterprise in Recent Times* (New York; Augustus M. Kelley, 1964), "National Integrity," pp. 11-39, and 38-39. Also, "There appears to be no other or further attribute or capacity...of the modern nation except this moral and legal license to resort to violence at will." p. 13.

[22]Gunnar Mrydal, in *Rich Lands and Poor* (New York: Harper and Brothers, 1957) states: "In the era of awakened nationalism in the underdeveloped world the colonial system is now doomed..." p. 60, and, "Nationalism, as I have suggested, has an important function to fulfiil in welding together the masses and inspiring them to a common purpose and a unified policy..." p. 68.

[23]"By 1945 Merton had laid down an approach which identified science as a social institution..." pp. 9-10, to Barry Barnes, ed., *Sociology of Science : Selected Readings* (Baltimore: Penguin Books, 1972).

[24]In sociology, Ogburn and Hart, also, did not discuss energy transformation. Yet, as we have noted, statistics on energy utilization provide empirical support to Ogburn's general culture evolution, as the exponential, and Hart's underlying paradigm of logistic surges.

[25]Kenneth E. Boulding, *A Reconstruction of Economics* (New York: John Wiley and Sons, 1950), p. vii. Also in this regard, the comments of Stanley A. Hetzler, *Technological Growth and Social Change*, pertaining to his own study would also be applicable to ours: "The failure of traditional concepts to explain a rapidly changing social world calls for a redirection of effort, for the opening of new avenues of inquiry. This book represents such an attempt." p. 3. And similarly Robert A. Solo, *Economic Organizations and Social Systems* (Indianapolis: The Bobs-Merrill Company, 1967), "It has been precisely this stepping from one conceptual structure to another that has constituted the 'crises' of all the social and natural sciences. Today, again, economics confronts the phenomena of an unfamiliar sort. Using their established conceptual apparatus, economists attempt to deal with the new problems of growth and development, but neither microeconomics nor macroeconomics will do. A new framework must be devised." p. 357. And Daniel Fusfeld, "The Conceptual framework of Modern Economics" *Journal of Economic Issues* 14 (March 1980). pp. 1-52. "If intellectual history is a reliable guide we appear to be at one of those large turning points in the development of ideas in which a new view of the world and human behavior and new ways of explaining things are appearing." p. 43.

[26]It is our position that such diverse theories as embodied in the works of Adam Smith, Schumpeter, Marx, Keynes, Veblen, Galbraith and Myrdal are capable of synthesis into one overall matrix, including the static and the dynamic and in the framework of culture evolution. In future studies we will attempt such a synthesis in the context of *cultural economics*.

[27]And again, on general culture evolution as distinguished from specific culture evolution, note, Marshall D. Sahlins and Elman R. Service, *Evolution and Culture* (Ann Arbor: The University of Michigan, 1960). "General cultural evolution is the successive emergence of new levels of all-around development," p. 28, which fits neatly into the framework of logistic surges (Hart) and to which we have added, in terms of the stages of economic development, the successive logistic surges of the overall gestalts of technology. "The objectives of general

evolutionary research are the determination and explanation of the successive transformations of culture through its several stages of overall progress." p. 29. Therefore it is not just simply the perfection of a given overall gestalt of technology (the core of culture) but the transformation of a given gestalt to a higher stage of economic development manifest in a new structure and higher levels of energy control.

[28]In our study as a focus or primary orientation we have attempted to integrate the advance of useful knowledge into a systematic overall theoretical framework of economic development and consequently to show how the advance of useful knowledge is related to technological change and culture evolution. "We cannot, therefore take the stock of knowledge for granted; we must learn whatever we can about the causes of additions to and changes in it; we must have some theory of its production and accumulation." and, "We therefore need a theory of the production and accumulation of empirical knowledge, even if for years to come this may mean nothing more than an attempt to learn about the processes involved and the factors that seem important...any student who has ever concerned himself with economic growth of nations almost inevitably makes assumptions relating to the progress of knowledge and its effects on economic production. It may be better to call explicitly for a theory of production of such knowledge as an indispensable focus for direct and continuous concern..." Simon Kuznets in Robert Lekachman, ed., *National Policy for Economic Welfare at Home and Abroad* (New York: Russell and Russell, 1961), pp. 60-61. And, "If the present interest in economic growth stimulates effective work on the growth and application of knowledge, this will surely be among the most important debts which economics and the social sciences will owe the problem of economic development." (Moses Abramovitz), p. 82. This basic theoretical emphasis on useful knowledge is not only the view of Simon Kuznets (note, the sources which we have so often given reference, *Six Lectures on Economic Growth, Economic Growth aud Structure*, *Modern Economic Growth* and his more recent, *Economic Growth of Nations* and on the latter note, pp. 307, 322-323, 326, 329, 332, 333, 349, but is held by others as well. In addition to Kenneth E. Boulding, *The Meaning of the Twentieth Century*, pp. 27-29, 107, note also, Everett E, Hagen, *On the Theory of Social Change* (Homewood: The Dorsey Press, 1962), especially pp. 12-18. C.E. Black in his holistic analysis of modernization, *The Dynamics of Modernization* (New York: Harper and Row, 1966), places a similar emphasis on knowledge and science (his analysis of economic development, pp. 18-24, is somewhat more orthodox and traditional). " 'Modernization' as it is used here refers to the dynamic form that the age-old process of innovation has assumed as a result of the explosive proliferation of knowledge in recent centuries." and, "The accumulation of knowledge, and the methods of rational explanation by which it is achieved, is no doubt the most generally recognized aspect of modernization...it lies at the center of the process," and in terms of change of societies, "The ultimate source of this change is the growth of knowledge..." pp. 7, 11, and 47.

"The only moment in the life of an individual or a people in which the distinction of true humanity may be worthily bestowed on them is that in which something new is added to the stock of knowledge or experience. When men or nations originate they live and grow; when they cease to do that they decay and die. This has been true from the beginning." "Otis T. Mason, *The Origins of Invention* (Cambridge: The M. I. T. Press, 1966), originally published 1895, p. 410 All this (and more could be added) is not to infer, of course, that the social scientists cited above would necessarily agree with our particular analysis of useful knowledge and its advance but, rather, that they would in all probability agree that the advance of knowledge is central and, consequently, should be analyzed and explained and its role clarified.

[29]As we have noted one musical instrument does not make an orchestra, and while some instruments are perhaps of greater importance it is the integration of the whole which makes the reproduction of the symphony possible. And while certain technics of the overall gestalt of technology are perhaps of greater importance than others it is the integration and aggregation into an operational whole as a gestalt which enables man to produce his symphony of economic development. Technics of production and social organization do not operate in isolation as separate parts but require the functional whole, in the form of the overall gestalt of technology in order to be operable. That it is difficult to discern or understand the whole or totality does not negate the logic that in order to understand and explain the interrelationships of the parts we must first understand the whole. For as Joseph A. Schumpeter, *The Theory of Economic Development* (Cambridge: Harvard University Press, 1959), has noted, "Because of this fundamental dependence of the economic aspect of things on everything else, it is not possible to explain *economic* change by previous *economic* conditions alone. For the economic state of a people does not emerge simply from the preceding economic conditions, but only from the preceding total situation." p. 58. And Robert A. Solo, *Economic Organization and Social Systems*, "The economist needs a conceptual framework that will encompass the whole of a society, enabling him to take into systematic account the diverse elements relevant to the organization of coherent, effective social action and (hence) fundamental economic change." p. 359. Also, note, Arthur Spiethoff, "Pure Theory and Economic Gestalt Theory: Ideal Types and Real Types," in Frederick C. Lane (ed.), *Enterprise and Secular Change* (Homewood: Richard D. Irwin, 1953), pp. 444-463.

[30]Currently, there is a growing recognition that technology entails more than just material technics. A good deal has been contributed by the Harvard Program on Technology and Society to the literature on the issue of technology and social change, on their literature. note, *Harvard University Program on Technology and Society 1964-1972: A Final Review* (Cambridge: 1972), especially pp. 245-264 for their publications and Emmanuel G. Mesthene, *Social Change* (Cambridge: Harvard University Press, 1970), pp. 96-124. Their definition is consistent and

similar to the one used in our study, in that Mesthene defines "...technology as the organization of knowledge for the achievement of practical purposes," p. 25, and that technology is considered to be more than just tools, "At the Harvard Program on Technology and Society, we construe the term as including more than hardware alone." p. 24. As an example, Emmanuel G. Mesthene, "How Technology Will Shape the Future," *Science*, Vol. 161 (July 12, 1968), pp. 135-143, notes the importance of knowledge and the knowledge industry in—the references to Daniel Bell and his "Post-Industrial Society," "Our age is characterized by a deliberate fostering of technological change and, in general, by the growing social role of knowledge." p. 137, and, "...argues, in turn, for the importance of the social sciences," p. 138 and, "...there is a need for further institutionalization of the function of transferring scientific knowledge to social use." p. 139.

[31]As we have noted in many instances, a cultural lag can be the result of any combination of the material and social such as cars (material) versus highways (material) or the A-bomb (material) versus government (nonmaterial) but it is the latter type of lag, where the material apparently advances faster than the nonmaterial or social which more frequently prevails and receives greater attention. It is in this context, the "frictionless wheel of economic development," that man should devote greater energy and material resources into the development of his social technology. We do not assume that every attempt at applying science to the social sector will prove an unmitigated success, any more than we can assume unmitigated success in the material sector, but rather that science and scientific methods will hold the key for unltimate success. For it must be remembered that though early attempts at applying science to material technics to place a man on the moon met with spectacular failure, man ultimately through his science triumphed and achieved his goal of a moon landing. And consequently, while reaching for the moon is no longer considered fantasy, to assume that man has control over war and nuclear holocaust still is. In this regard many express fear and anxiety, "In the face of these tasks and these costs of failure and considering the lag of the social behind the physical sciences, it is easy to give in to a feeling of frustration and adopt an attitude of defeatism." Our study, however, is directed toward showing a way out; we are optimistic and we tend to agree with Olaf Helmer, *Social Technology* (New York: Basic Books, 1966), in that, "...such a pessimistic outlook is unwarranted." p. 4.

[32]While Simon Kuznets does not present the case for circular and cumulative causation as explicitly as does Gunnar Myrdal or as we have done in the framework of our "wheel of economic development," he frequently alludes to the process: "The foregoing discussion has repeatedly suggested long chains of sequence within the pattern of modern economic growth: one being from additions to the stock of useful knowledge and science to technological innovation, to growth in productivity, to changes in structure of production, to changes in other aspects of economic structure, to changes in political and social

structure and beliefs and back again to changed conditions of life and work, with their effects on demand; another being from science to technology, to innovation, to more learning, to more science and so on—all qualified by economic and social conditions that determine how widely the innovation will be applied and hence how much new knowledge will be acquired and what new tools will be created for further advance of knowledge, science, and technology." "*Economic Growth of Nations*, p. 350.

[33]The conceptual distinction between statics and dynamics has been obfuscated by the many differing definitions which appear in the literature, on this note. Fritz Machlup, "Statics and Dynamics: Kaleidoscopic Words," *The Southern Economic Journal*, Vol. 26 (October 1959), pp. 99-110, which also appears as "Static and Dynamics: Kaleidoscopic Words," (sic) in *Essays on Economic Semantics* (Englewood Cliffs: Prentice-Hall, 1963), pp. 9-42. To Simon Kuznets, "The major preoccupation of dynamic economics is the study of changes in social phenomena which take place in the course of time. . .The task of dynamic economics is first and foremost that of ascertaining the exact course of social changes, and of arriving, if possible, at some general traits of these changes whether in one and the same social phenomenon in the course of time, or in the relations among the various social phenomena." "Static and Dynamic Economics," *The American Economic Review* 20 (September 1930), pp. 426-441, p. 432. Also note the similar conceptualization by Mitchell and Veblen in Machlup, pp. 92, 93-90. We feel that a static analysis can be integrated into a dynamic analysis and, indeed, that such an analysis is necessary and interrelated to a dynamic explanation. Taxonomy, description, and functional relationships must first be delineated (static analysis) before we can possibly achieve an explanation or theory of dynamics involved in changing one form to the next. In the study of general biological evolution we note that in the development of theory a Linnaeus (1707-1778) precedes a Darwin (1809-1882): And moving from the realm of biological evolution to that of culture evolution we note that it was the historiographers, the scholars, who described and characterized cultures of the distant past who provided later-day social scientists with the differing forms of culture which then had to be explained in terms of processes of change. In this context the stages of economic development had to be described as static and functional entities before social scientists could attempt to explain the processes of transformation. And as we know more in terms of theory and the processes of economic development we will in turn be able to more accurately delineate the stages of economic development. In our analysis we have attempted to combine the static and the dynamic into our overall theoretical framework under the assumption that both are necessary for explanation. A cross-sectional view of our three-dimensional configuration of culture evolution (a still-shot picture), for a given moment of time and assuming technology as being invariant, will still entail theory and explanation concerning the functional parts and their interrelationships for any

given culture and we have presented such a static case in our "closed" wheel of economic development. The dynamic analysis concerns our "open" wheel of economic development (a motion picture) with the assumption of technological change and consequently culture transformation. Note Figure XI-5 "A Cross-Sectional View of the Stages of Economic Development."

[34]"Descriptions of cultures in terms of their elements are valuable mainly as a basis for comparative studies which may lead to the establishment of valid classification of cultures and the discovery of genetic relationships between them. . .determination of culture content is an absolute prerequisite to all effective studies of these dynamics. . . To understand cultural processes we must both know content and observe this content in action." Ralph Linton, *The Study of Man* (New York: D. Appleton-Century Company, 1936), pp. 300-301.

[35]Such a view looks at the process of advancing knowledge as a series of logistic surges and is similar in some ways to the "Successive-Emergence Theory of intellectual progress" as presented by Auguste Comte. "Comte formulated a conception of society based on a belief in a law of three stages. Society was regarded as a dynamic social unity fulfilling itself through a series of evolutionary stages, the theological, metaphysical and positive. It was this thought from, not merely the type of economic or political organization, which expressed the fundamental principle of social solidarity in each epoch." Delbert C. Miller in Francis R. Allen, et al., ed., *Technology and Social Change* (New York: Appleton-Century-Crofts, 1957), pp. 95-96, 513. The unified application of the stock of knowledge as a totality (social solidarity) would be similar to our concept of the overall gestalt of technology. That this approach to a stages-type of analysis was not completely original with Comte but possibly originated elsewhere (Saint-Simon), note, *International Encyclopedia of Social Sciences* (1968), Vol. 3, p. 201. Also, as an interesting side note concerning evolutionary thought in general: "Comte, it should be noted, posited a theory of cultural evolution through fixed stages, but still adhered to the non-evolutionary theory of the fixity of species in the realm of biology," David Bidney, *Theoretical Anthropology* (New York: Columbia University Press, 1935), p. 86.

[36]Primitive man had a limited selection of goods and services at his disposal. "The food of lemurs, anthropoid apes, and present-day forest pygmies is very much alike: it consists in the main of fruits and nuts, small birds and eggs, honey, grubs and and insects. It seems highly probable, therefore, that Lower Paleolithic man lived on much these same viands." Hornell Hart, *The Technique of Social Progress* (New York: Henry Holt and Company, 1931), p. 122. The goods, tools, clothing, food were changed not only in quantity but in quality as well as man moved upward on the ladder represented by the stages of economic development. On the theme of relating the scales or standards of living with the stages of economic development, note pp. 122-146. Consequently, man cannot acquire the conglomerate of goods and services character-

istic of industrialism unless he achieves that stage of economic development and this then entails culture transformation and not simply the growth and replication of that which already exists.

[37]*On the quantity-quality issue:* This theme is touched upon frequently by Simon Kuznets, note, *Economic Growth and Structure* (New York: W.W. Norton & Company, 1965), "Finally, consideration of the wide range of factors involved in the economic growth of nations should also draw attention to qualitative aspects of economic growth, which often elude us in quantitative economic analysis." pp. 120-122, and from his *Modern Economic Growth* (New Haven: Yale University Press, 1966), "Modern economic growth is distinguished by the fact that the rate of rise of per capita product was due primarily to improvements in *quality*, not quantity of inputs—essentially to greater efficiency or output per simple unit of input, traceable to increases in useful knowledge and better institutional arrangements for its utilization." p. 491, this is continued in his *Economic Growth of Nations* (Cambridge: The Belknap Press of Harvard University Press, 1971). For example, note Chapter II in which he raises the question of inputs versus productivity which he answers in the summary chapter, pp. 303-345, in favor of productivity as he concludes: Since per capita man hours and material capital grew so little, and since the growth of per capita product was largely the result of a high growth rate of productivity, improvements in quality of labor and capital—improvements not caused by an extra input of resources—were responsible for the high rate of growth of per capita product to characteristic of modern economic growth. These 'costless' improvements are connected with the tremendous increase in the stock of useful knowledge, much of it traceable to growth of science viewed as a social institution devoted to the production of new tested and hence potentially useful knowledge." p. 307; as Gunnar Myrdal points out, qualitative explanations do not preclude quantitative evidence, and certainly while Kuznets, as a case in point, gives recognition to the qualitative one could hardly say that he avoids the quantitative: "If anything, his approach induces the institutionalist economist to press harder for research than can give quantitative precision to his theories and bring them to the empirical test." Myrdal, *Asian Drama*, Vol. I, pp. 3C-31; and also Kenneth E. Boulding, "Mere accumulation is not enough. Economic Development does not consist merely in the piling up of things, but in the accumulation of new kinds of things." *The Meaning of the Twentieth Century* (New York: Harper and Row, 1964), p. 116; Hession and Sardy, *Ascent to Affluence*, note that ". . .the essence of the process of economic development is fluidity or flexibility in the techniques of production or resource allocation. . . economic development is not a mere matter of quantitative expansion in the use of economic resources." p. 3; J. Frederic Dewhurst, et al., *America's Needs and Resources* (New York: Twentieth Century Fund, 1955), "Such quantitative measures, however, fail to suggest the tremendous qualitative alteration that technology has brought in the way we live. . ." p. 835, Gustav Ranis, *International Encyclopedia of*

the Social Sciences, Vol. IV, "Whether or not we accept these statistical findings matters less than the growing realization that growth cannot be explained simply in terms of larger quantities of constant quality inputs combining in known ways to produce output." p. 413; and Salvatore Schiavo-Campo and Hans W. Singer, *Perspectives of Economic Development* (Boston: Houghton Mifflin Company, 1970), "Yet as most development economists would agree, a theory of economic development has not emerged. . .For development is not merely economic growth: it is growth accompanied by structural social and economic change." and, "Economic development is thus *growth plus change*." and, "As we have noted, a distinction should be made between the terms 'economic growth' and 'economic development.' . . . 'economic growth' applies to income increases within the existing social and economic framework, the term 'economic development' includes the notion of structural change on the economic or social level or both." pp. vii, 4, 17; and Veblen via Allan G. Gruchy, "As Veblen would put it, in the long run there can be no economic growth without economic change or development. A theory of economic growth is more therefore a theory of economic development." and, "Economic growth is, in the final analysis, a matter of technological advance. . ." in Douglas F. Dowd, *Thorstein Veblen: A Critical Reappairsal* (New York: Cornell University Press, 1958), pp. 156, 160; and, Raymond Aron, *The Industrial Society* (New York: Frederick A. Praeger, Publishers, 1967), "The contrast between development and underdevelopment is qualitative and not quantitative, although it can be expressed in figures." p. 54; also, Gerald M. Meier, *Leading Issues in Economic Development* (New York: Oxford University Press, 1970), "Development is taken to mean growth plus change; there are essential qualitative dimensions in the development process that may be absent in the growth or expansion of an economy through a simple widening process." p. 6; and also, in the framework of the White-Sahlins distinction between specific culture evolution or phylogenetic proliferation and quantification and general culture evolution or the realm of energy transformation and qualitative change, "Cultural systems extend themselves quantitatively by multiplication or reduplication. . .Cultural systems expand qualitatively by developing higher forms of organization and greater concentrations of energy." Leslie A. White, *The Evolution of Culture* (New York: McGraw-Hill Book Company, 1959), p. 39.

[38]This idea is referred to in the literature as the "general principle of similitude" or "structural differentiation." "The concept of structural differentiation, as derived from Durkhein and Max Weber, and elaborated by Talcott Parsons and his students is probably the key sociological concept today in the analysis of crescive social change." Daniel Bell in Eleanor Bernert Sheldon and Wilbert E. Moore, ed., *Indicators of Social Change* (New York: Russell Sage Foundation, 1968), pp. 149-152. "But what has been so marked and pervasive a feature of economic life now begins to appear in the once simple structures of educational and intellectual life. The growth of a university from 5,000 students is

clearly not just a linear increase in size but a massive upheaval in structure as well." p. 152.

[39]Economic growth may be specifically defined in terms of a given stage of economic development such as industrialism, and this is perhaps most frequently the case, but our analysis primarily concerns general culture evolution and consequently our definitions of economic growth and economic development concern all epochs or stages of economic development and are therefore universal. In this regard we have chosen (recall our previous discussions) as a possible definition of economic growth the one offered by Simon Kuznets in his *Modern Economic Growth*, "To be applicable to a number of economic epochs, economic growth might perhaps be defined as a sustained increase in population attained without a perceptible lowering of per capita product, i.e., in combination with either stability or rise in per capita product." p. 20. In this conceptualization growth is viewed as a quantitative increase in size of what already exists, a replication process, and one in which population increases do not result in lower per capita product or if population is constant that per capita product increases. In either case economic growth represents an increase in absolute size and magnitude. However since such growth would ultimately reach a logistic ceiling, given no technological change or culture transformation, we have come to view long-term economic growth as a function of economic development. Economic growth as a long-term exponential continuum is a function of the logistic surges, or, stated another way, the process of transforming the overall gestalts of technology. It is the latter process, the process of economic development, which we will now attempt to define.

[40]Previously, we have reviewed the spectrum of definitions of economic growth appearing in the literature running from the simple to the complex (the complex definitions relate to the modern period and consequently include per capita GNP increases which are "sustained" and which also include "structural" changes as well). The more complex definition of economic growth provided by Kuznets, *Modern Economic Growth*, p. 1, and which is relevant to the modern epoch of an industrial system is frequently used by other economists as a definition of economic growth, in general, which is then inferred to be the conceptual equivalent of economic development in a universal sense covering economic development for all stages and levels. We have attempted in our study to demonstrate the errors and inconsistencies in using such a definition of economic growth in a universal sense.

[41]We have previously reviewed the literature in terms of specific definitions, and consequently, at this point, will exclude those definitions of economic development in terms of economic growth but will rather simply present a few more definitions compatible with our conceptualization and therefore associated with culture transformation: Gunnar Myrdal, *An International Economy* (New York: Harper and Row, 1969), "Within this framework a great number of other social changes must take place, and in the cumulative process of adjustment

they are all interdependent, being causes as well as effects, the entire social system must be moving." p. 186 and which is more explicitly stated in Myrdal's *Asian Drama*, Vol. 3, pp. 1866-1870 and to which we have already referred; and, H.W. Singer, *International Development: Growth and Change* (New York: McGraw-Hill Book Company, 1964) and which Paul G. Hoffman notes: "Built into his analysis is the conviction that development is a total process in which not one aspect of human life, education, health, and aspiration can be ignored." p. ix; and Salvatore Schiavo-Campo and Hans W. Singer, *Perspectives of Economic Development* pp. 4, 5, 7, 17, . . ., etc., "The change involves society as a whole, and it is not limited to the more obvious changes implied in different rates of growth of various branches of economic activity." p. 4; and, Stanley A. Hetzler, *Technological Growth and Social Change* (New York: Frederick A. Praeger, Publishers, 1969), "Technology forms the root system of the whole complex known as *Western civilization*.', p. 17, and "Socio-Technics: A New Set of Hypotheses for Development," pp. 152-184, "From the viewpoint of this water, social change, technological advancement, and mechanization are, in a broad sense, synonymous." p. 184 and "It is the production technologies . . . which . . . are the very essence of development." p. 152, and Joseph A. Raffaele, *The Economic Development of Nations* (New York: Random House, 1971), "Economic development is a dynamic process or raising political, economic, and social capacities from the resources that are available to the nation in the long run," and, "Economic development is a social process involving an interaction between rising human capacities and their employment, on the one hand, and an environment and institutions that are favorable to them on the other." pp. 8, 377; and, Robert A. Solo, *Economic Organization and Social Systems*, "Economic progress has been conceived here as occurring through the development and application of superior techniques." p. 131. And Lenora Stettner, "Survey of Literature on Social and Economic Effects of Technological Change," in Jack Stieber, ed., *Employment Problems of Automation and Advanced Technology* (New York: St. Martin's Press, 1966), pp. 451-479, "By definition techonlogy is very retarded in the less developed countries . . ." p. 455; and, also Michael P. Todaro, *Economic Development in the Third World* (New York: Longman, 1977), "Development, in its essence, must represent the entire gamut of change by which an entire *social system*. . ." p. 62; and, Clarence Zuvekas, Jr., *Economic Development* (New York: St. Martin's Press, 1979), "Growth versus Development" and Not by Economics Alone," pp. 8-14.

[42]On L.A. White and the *sui generis*, which really runs as a recurring theme in his contributions to the literature, note, in his *The Science of Culture*, "Ikhnaton: The Great Man vs. the Culture Process," pp. 233-281, "The Locus of Mathematical Reality," pp. 282-302, and, Man's Control over Civilization: An Anthropocentric Illusion," pp. 330-359. And in his *The Evolution of Culture*, pp. 10-16, and in R.W. Sellars, ed., *Philosophy for the Future*, "Ethnological Theory," pp. 357-384, and, "Culturological vs. Psychological Interpretations of Human Behavior,"

"*American Sociological Review*, 12 (1947), pp. 686-698. Leslie A. White's advocacy of a science of culture, as culturology, is predicated upon the *sui generis* view of culture evolution, that culture processes are understood by analyzing culture per se to the exclusion of man, i.e., that man is essentially irrelevant to the process of culture evolution. While L.A. White views man as essentially irrelevant "a consideration of the human organism . . . is irrelevant, "p. 164," . . . the individual is irrelevant to an explanation of the culture process." p. 165, "As a matter of fact, the most effective way to study culture scientifically is to proceed as if the human race did not exist." p. 290, *The Science of Culture*, this is not to infer that man does not serve as a necessary condition for culture but that culture evolution takes place independently of man and beyond his control. For behind it all is the symbol, without symboling we do not have man nor do we have culture. "Man is unique: he is the only living species that has a culture. . . We thus define man in terms of the ability to symbol and the consequent ability to produce culture." *The Evolution of Culture*, p. 3. Therefore we may assume that if no man then no culture or civilization, but actually White defines man in terms of culture, that Homo sapiens the beast became Homo sapiens the human with the evolution of culture. A good summary statement by White would be: "We see culture as a vast continuum, a stream of cultural elements—of language, tools, utensils, beliefs, customs, and attitudes—that flows down through time. Culture was of course brought into existence by man—by countless human individuals —and it could not continue without them. But we do not need to consider man at all. . . in an explanation of culture change. For purposes of scientific interpretation, the culture process may be regarded as a thing *sui generis*; culture is explainable in terms of culture." *The Science of Culture*, p. 181. Culture is not only the superorganic or the extrasomatic but apparently has a life of its own, it grows and advances in the context of laws of its own dynamics. "Culture is an elaborate mechanism . . . Culture is therefore a thermodynamic system in a mechanical sense. . . Culture is thus a dynamic system capable of growth. . . A cultural tradition is therefore a dynamic system (powered by natural forces which it harnesses) that behaves and grows in terms of its own principles and laws. It may therefore be explained on its own level . . . It may be regarded as a system *sui generis*." pp. 166-167, 367. Man apparently enters White's framework as a material agency through which culture invents and discovers, rather than having man invent and discover, it is culture operating through man. White speaks in terms of the "Culture Determinants of the Mind," pp. 146-189. "The minding in its form and content is determined by culture. The individaul mind is a function of the cultural system that embraces it. What it does, what it believes, thinks and feels, are determined not by the individual but by the circumambient culture." p. 184. White consequently rejects explanations of culture dynamics in terms of the human mind. The thesis which he states (p. 161) "that man has created culture . . . that the culture process is to be explained in terms of the individual," is rejected, man is not the prime mover of the sociocultural process, note, p. 175, and ". . . we cannot explain the culture in terms of the individual mind; cultural systems can only be explained in cultural terms." p. 185.

[43]R.W. Sellars, ed., *Philosophy for the Future*, p. 374.

[44]Though the ultimate answer may rest elsewhere, our discussions of the *sui generis* concern man versus culture and do not really concern theological explanations of creation and evolution. Although such discussions do sometimes enter the literature, this has not been our focus or purpose, not, Leslie A. White, "Ethnological Theory," pp. 357-358, "Outside the priesthood, Dr. David Bidney has recently undertaken to introduce God and free will into ethnological theory: "Man under God, controls his own cultural destiny and is free to choose and realize the ends he would achieve." p. 358. In answer to which David Bidney might also introduce Morgan into the priesthood and for whom L.A. White may be regarded as a patron saint, ". . . Morgan's work is vitiated finally by the fact that he brings in God and Providence to account for the emergence of civilization . . . for Morgan a science of culture does not preclude acknowledgement of divine Providence and the role of contingent human efforts in bringing about the historical development of culture, "*Theoretical Anthropology*, p. 213. And while such a debate could go on *ad infinitum*, note White's answer concerning Morgan and divine Providence, p. xxviii in his introduction to Lewis H.Morgan, *Ancient Society* (Cambridge: Harvard University Press, 1964), and also, "Morgan's Attitude Toward Religion and Science," *American Anthropologist*, Vol. 46 (1944), pp. 218-230. On the issue of theology and evolution, note Robert T. Francoeur, *Perspectives in Evolution* (Baltimore: Helicon Press, 1956), and also, Sol Tax, ed., *Evolution after Darwin* (Chicago: University of Chicago Press, 1960), Vol. III, pp. 1-40, and Rheinhold Niebuhr, pp. 30-38, in *A Book That Shook the World* (Pittsburgh: University of Pittsburgh Press, 1958). And for further discussions on the issue, we simply recommend the name: Pierre Teilhard de Chardin.

[45]Hornell Hart, *Technique of Social Progress* (New York: Henry Holt and Company, 1931), pp. 539, 511. Although Hart notes the *sui generis* supposition he does not actually support it.

[46]Some would argue that since the cultural environment basically determines human behavior, it thereby determines choice as well. Our view would be that though culture strongly conditions behavior and presents the basic alternative, that man still, nonetheless, is capable of making a choice among the alternatives. Culture determines the limits in which the choice among alternatives is made. Therefore, if culture has not advanced knowledge to the point where culture is scientifically conceptualized and its evolution accurately explained the choice of control is not available to man as an alternative among other choices. This, of course, is not to say that mam lacks the power of ultimately controlling culture and his own destiny or that culture evolution is *sui generis* but that in order for man to control culture evolution he

must first correctly understand and conceptualize the process. Consequently, the option or choice of controlling culture evolution will increase as man further advances the accumulation of science concerning the processes of culture evolution.

"Primitive man is generally unaware of the existence of microbes and thus has no symbols with which to designate, describe, and comprehend them. Nevertheless, microbes influence him and he may die because of them .... By contrast, civilized man is aware of the existence of microbes and is able to formulate very elaborate statements about them. Microbes today constitute a part of or are represented in man's symbolic environment. This fact is undoubtedly of great significance. To have symbols for microbes means to be aware or conscious of them, to comprehend them. It also means that microbes may possibly be controlled and subordinated to human purposes." Alfred R. Lindesmith and Anselm L. Strauss, *Social Psychology* (New York: The Dryden Press, 1956), p. 79. Similarly, mankind must clarify the concept of evolution and explain if he is to control it.

[47]Phyllis Deane, *The First Industrial Revolution* (Cambridge: Cambridge University Press, 1965), notes that: "The first industrial revolution occurred in Great Britain is of particular interest in that it occurred spontaneously, without the government assistance which has been characteristic of most succeeding industrial revolutions." p. 2. If spontaneous, then how can one maintain that man controlled it? In addition, not only was it spontaneous as a phenomenon but man still a full century later was just beginning to make the first attempts at conceptual clarification. The Industrial Revolution started circa mid-eighteenth century. The Toynbee lectures dated circa 1880's. Not only did man not really understand the Industrial Revolution during the late nineteenth century but some argue that he still has yet to grasp its full meaning. On this latter point note the excellent collection of readings to which referred frequently, Philip A. M. Taylor, *The Industrial Revolution in Britain: Triumph or Disaster*? (Boston; D. C. Heath and Company, 1958).

[48]L. A. White, *The Concept of Cultural Systems*, defines the parts, such as social institutions, agriculture industry, manufacturing, mining, labor organization, scientists, as vectors, and "Culture and cultural vectors grow by themselves, . . .culture is a process *sui generis*." p. 67, 58-78. Therefore, L. A. White would deny the "anthropocentric illusion" that man is in control of even the parts (vectors), let alone the whole.

[49]Does man simply serve as a catalyst, as the yeast activating the brew of culture evolution, or does he have the additional capacity of adding the basic ingredients and thereby in the process control the accretion and transformation? L. A. White frequently refers to man as a catalyst but evidently in the sense of being an activator rather than transformer, ". . . he is so to speak, the catalyst that makes the interactive culture process possible." R. W. Sellars, *Philosophy for the Future*, p. 374, and, "The human nervous system is merely the catalyst that makes the cultural process possible." *The Science of Culture*, p. 302,

note also, pp. 181, 294, . . ., etc.

[50]This is similar to the old chicken-and-egg controversy, as to which comes first, man or culture. Such a controversy is conceptual at root in that the answer depends upon how man is defined, as to whether man is defined in biological or social terms. Biological evolution tells us that eggs precede chickens in that reptiles precede birds. By comparison, the generalized view of the evolutionary sequence leading from the inorganic to the organic to the superorganic reveals biological man obviously precedes cultural man. L. A. White defines man in terms of culture, "Man and culture originated simultaneously; and this by definition" *The Evolution of Culture*, p. 5, and infers that without culture we have Homo sapiens the beast but not Homo sapiens the human. In a statement of mitigated culture determinism White notes: "The behavior of man as a human being—as distinguished from his non-symbolic, primate behavior—is an expression of the interaction of the human organism and the extra-somatic cultural tradition. Human behavior is, therefore, a function of culture as well as of a biological organism." *The Science of Culture*, pp. 146, 161. "It is the symbol which has transformed man from a mere animal to a human animal." p. 35. Biological man evolved, lived in societies, developed tools and further developed biological man (note. p. 226 (1949), L. A. White) and gradually in the process evolved his capacity to symbol as he developed his language and powers of thought and meaning. In this sense then man as such precedes culture or perhaps as L. A. White would say, biological man precedes cultural man. "Neurological evolution in a certain line or lines, of anthropoids culminates eventually in the ability to symbol. The exercise of this ability brought culture into existence and then perpetuated it." (1959), p. 6, "It is obvious of course, that culture has emanated from the organisms of human beings: without the human species there would be no culture", (1949), p. 164, "To be sure, the symbolic faculty was brought into existence by the natural processes of organic evolution." p. 32, And once culture comes into existence (created, originated by man) it serves as an overall technic with which man increases his capacity for thought and origination and consequently his capacity to add to his store of knowledge, and thereby, in the process becomes more human and less bestial, a supposition subject to reservation, i.e., Auschwitz.

[51]Leslie A. White, *The Concept of Cultural Systems* (New York: Columbia University Press, 1975), p. 8.

[52]In certain instances L. A. White associates culture evolution with progress, note, "Evolutionary Stages, Progress, and the Evaluation of Cultures" *Southwestern Journal of Anthropology*, Volume 3 (Autumn 1947), pp. 165-192. For example: "Stages, progress and the evaluation of cultures are merely three aspects of one single issue: evolutionism or anti-evolutionism." p. 170. Which infers that culture evolution entails advanced stages and therefore progress as well and consequently that since culture moves forward *sui generis* so does progress; therefore, that progress is inevitable. Elsewhere we find White to be less optimistic.

"Technology builds but it may also destroy. The belief and faith that civilization . . . simply cannot go down in destruction because such an end would be too monstrous and senseless, is but a naive and anthropocentric whimper." *The Science of Culture*, p. 391. Therefore White seems to say that as long as culture exists it will inevitably progress, *sui generis*, but he qualifies this by also saying that the continued existence of culture is not, however, inevitable.

[53]It is noteworthy that included among the group stressing the mind of man and the dynamics of ideas would be Tylor and Morgan. For a discussion on this point note Morris E. Opler, "Cultural Dynamics and Evolutionary Theory," in Barringer, *Social Change in Developing Areas*, pp. 68-96, and to which we have already referred, and add: "The preeminence of mind and its stimulus value for the development of all other aspects of culture are fundamental premises of Tylor . . ." especially pp. 77-81. And on Morgan, pp. 81-92, and for an interesting point, in the context of the concept of technology as offered by L. A. White and that of *cultural economics*, made by Opler concerning Morgan: "Plainly, as he conceives it, technology and social institutions both 'register' or afford a clue to the evolutionary level or degree of progress. Neither is the prime mover; both are aspects of a more inclusive process." p. 88, and, "Time and again Morgan subordinates both the institutional and the technological to intellect." p. 90. And Hornell Hart notes that ". . . instead of technology being the basic cause of change, our analysis regards creative thinking as being primary." Allen, *Technology and Social Change*, p. 422 and also, his *Technique of Social Progress* (New York: Henry Holt and Company, 1931), "The Power of Individuals to Alter the Social Fabric," pp. 511-540. We also find evidence in the writing of Kuznets to support the "mind of man" supposition, ". . . additions to knowledge are largely the products of the free inquiring mind. . . . This assumption of the *free* mind is both a qualification of the hypothesis and a partial explanation of the impressive development of tested knowledge during the last two centuries. . . . Given this continuous play of the free mind . . ." *Economic Growth and Structure* (New York: W. W. Norton and Company, 1965), p. 88. But many others stress the mind of man as a basic focus in explaining culture dynamics: "All human progress is at bottom mental progress; all changes must go through the human mind." Edwin R. A. Seligman, *The Economic Interpretation of History* (New York: Columbia University Press, 1949), p. 148; "In the last analysis, reversal or modification of cultural trends is possible because human freedom involves a circular concept of cultural causality—rather than a linear one—according to which man is the efficient cause of the cultural process and culture in turn affects man." Bidney, *Theoretical Anthropology*, p. 17, "In the last analysis we must fall back upon man in society in a given environment as the ultimate source of his culture." p. 114; "Culture therefore is not a force operating by itself and independent of the human factors. There is a tendency to reify culture—that is, to endow it with life and treat it as a thing. . . . The basis for culture is found in the human mind,

and the physical manifestations have meaning only in term of these mental patterns. Ideas are the real foundation of culture." Francis E. Merrill, *Society and Culture*, (Englewood Cliffs: Prentice-Hall, 1969), 4th edition, pp. 84-85; A. L. Kroeber and Clyde Kluckhohn, *Culture: A Critical Review of Concepts and Definitions* (Cambridge: Harvard Printing Office, 1952), Papers of the Peabody Museum of American Archeology and Ethnology, Vol. 47, note that, "Goldenweiser's main point is an extension of this argument: culture change could not occur were it not for the creative activity of concrete individuals." p. 110, ". . . every element of it would be found to have had its beginning in the creative act of an individual mind. . . . An analysis of culture . . . leads back to the creative mind." p. 103; and Charles R. Walker, "For it is not to be forgotten that he (man) is the prime creator of all the sciences and all the technologies . . ." *Technology, Industry, and Man* (New York: McGraw-Hill Book Company, 1968), p. 2; And Joseph J. Spengler "Theory, Ideology, Non-Economic Values, and Politico-Economic Development," in Ralph Braibanti and Joseph J. Spengler, ed., *Tradition, Values, and Socio-Economic Development* (Durham: Duke University Press, 1961), "It is my thesis that the state of a people's politico-economic development, together with its rate and direction depends largely upon what is in the minds of its members. . . . The content of men's minds is looked upon as the potentially dynamic element, as the source whence issue change and novelty, in a world or universe that is otherwise essentially passive," pp. 4-5, "Mind, . . while largely the product of cumulated past events, at any moment is possessed of great autonomy . . ." p. 42; Ferdinand Lundberg, *The Coming World Transformation* (New York: Doubleday and Company, 1963), "The larger physical and biological events are beyond the control of man, and at most can be somewhat anticipated modified, and anthropocentrically utilized in certain respects. But on the social and cultural level man is the center, the agent as it were of environing change. . . . It is not the culture, then, that invents, but man, although man works with materials given to him by the culture on the basis of motivations stimulated in him by his environment . . . contrary to what White says, man can change his culture." p. 73, 77-78, 85. "Ideas, whether those of art and science, or those embodied in practical appliances, are the most 'real' of the gifts that each generation receives from its predecessors. The world's material wealth would be quickly replaced if it were destroyed, but the ideas by which it was made were retained. If, however, the idea were lost, but not the material wealth, then that would dwindle and the world would go back to poverty. And most of our knowledge of mere facts could quickly be recovered if it were lost, but the constructive ideas of thought remained; while if the ideas perished, the world would enter again on the Dark Ages." Alfred Marshall, *Principles of Economics* (London: Macmillan and Co., 1922), p. 780 cited by Lord Robbins, *The Theory of Economic Development in the History of Economic Thought* (New York: St. Martins's Press, 1968), pp. 93-94.

[54]L. A. White, *The Concept of Cultural Systems*, alters his previous

position on the function of culture, pp. xi, 9. The function of culture is not to service the needs of this "puny primate," pp. 9-13. Function in an ultimate sense cannot be answered, but functions of cultural systems are ". . . acts performed, the processes executed, by the system." p. 13.

[55]We have referred enough to this issue, Sheldon and Moore, "Toward the Measurement of Social Change: Implications for Progress," in L.H. Goodman, ed., *Economic Progress and Social Welfare,* also note, "And despite our expressed misgivings . . . Apparently, we are becoming a national society committed to some form of directed social change. Thus a viable marriage of social science and national policy formulation may well be required." p. 186.

[56]p. 453, Edward B. Tylor, *Primitive Culture* (New York: Henry Holt and Company, 1874), Vol. II, p. 453, cited also, in Barringer, ed., *Social Change in Developing Areas,* p. 80.

[57]In this context we have often referred to Keynesian economics as an example of the usage of the social sciences as a tool to perfect (reform) our social technics. Another excellent example is found in the area of the technics of international monetary organization; we speak here of Robert A. Triffin and the application of science to improve a basic institution of importance, i.e., money. As man's control over his physical environment has advanced with the advance of culture and science, so will he advance his control, his capacity to perfect and reform his social institutions. Money evolved, "The very birth of money was not only unplanned, but even unnoticed." *Our International Monetary System* (New York: Random House, 1968), p. viii, and over time as we develop the social sciences we will increase our capacity to consciously control and thereby reform and perfect our international monetary system. It is in this sense that we associate the social science with reform as perfection through conscious control. As we have perfected our material technics through the application of science so let us perfect the social. "The displacement of national fiduciary reserves by international fiduciary reserves should similarly be viewed as one aspect of the adjustment of the former tribal, feudal, and national institutions through which this control could previously be asserted, to the ever-changing realities of a more and more interdependent world. *Both phenomena Should be viewed in a vaster historical perspective: the long march of mankind toward its unity and a better control of its own fate.*" p. 179.

[58]"The concept of a cultural evolution independent of man is as fallacious as the notion of an actual human nature independent of culture. In the last analysis, culture is not a reality *sui generis,* but an instrument or function of man, and its significance and value must be measured by its utility in promoting the psychocultural evolution of man in the interests of human welfare." D. Bidney, *Theoretical Anthropology,* p. 84. This is of course not to deny that the meaning of the concepts of human development and human welfare is far from clear and in need of scientific conceptualization and clarification. We feel in addition that

not only is there a need for clarification but that such a clarification is possible and can be achieved in much the same way as we have attempted concerning the concept of economic development. "Human destiny need no longer be merely an affair of hopes and fears. In principle, it can be rationally defined on the basis of scientific knowledge, and rationally be pursued by the aid of scientific methods. Once greater fulfilment is recognized as man's ultimate or dominant aim, we shall need a science of human possibilities to help guide the long course of psycho-social evolution that lies ahead." Sir Julian Huxley, in Sol Tax, ed., *Evolution After Darwin*, Vol. I, p. 21.

[59]"If we wish to work towards a purpose for the future of man, we must formulate that purpose ourselves. Purposes in life are made, not found. . . .The future of progressive evolution is the future of man. The future of man . . . must be guided by deliberate purpose . . . . Progress is a major fact of past evolution . . . It may continue in the future, but it is not inevitable; man, by now become the trustee of evolution, must work and plan if he is to achieve further progress for himself and so for life." Julian Huxely, *Evolution: The Modern Synthesis* (New York: Hafner Press, 1974). pp. 556-578, pp. 576, 577, and 578. "Thus the process of development and change in social systems is fundamentally distinguished from the evolutionary processes of other biological systems by the existence of will and the ability to select purposively and consciously some particular *path* for change. . . In short, rather than natural selection, socio-economic systems have the capability to develop and evolve through time by a constrained process of what can be termed *volitional selection*." Richard Chase, "Structural-Functional Dynamic in the Analysis of Socio-Economic Systems: Adaptation of Structural Change Processes to Biological Systems of Human Interaction," *The American Journal of Economics and Sociology* 39 (January 1980), pp. 49-64, p. 50.

[60]David C. McClelland, "If our study of the role of achievement motivation in society does nothing else, perhaps it will serve to redress the balance a little, to see man as a *creator* of his environment, as well as a creature of it." *The Achieving Society* (New York: The Free Press, 1961), pp. 391-392. Marc Tool, *The Discretionary Economy* (Santa Monica: Goodyear Publishing Co., 1979), "a person is both product and producer of culture," pp. 47, 52, 53, . . . etc. Tool's "normative theory of political economy" represents the opposite polarity from that of L.A. White and the *sui generis* predilection. "Within culturally defined limits—and the limits themselves are subject to progressive redetermination—an individual is a free agent; that is, he or she has *discretion*." p. 52.

[61]And according to L.A. White cultural systems are essentially material systems, "Material systems (which includes cultural systems) . . . p. 15, *The Concept of Cultural Systems* (New York: Columbia University Press, 1975). And "we must understand cultural systems in terms of their respective structures and processes, not in terms of human need purpose or act." p. 16. And cultural systems are in turn determined

by the technological base, which L.A. White conceptualizes in terms of material culture. "The technological component is the basic one; upon it social systems and ideologies—and cultural systems as a whole—depend." pp. 17-18.

[62]The query was presented by Walton Hamilton, *The Politics of Industry,* p. 165 and Marc Tool attempts to answer the query with a "normative theory of political economy." The query, "which direction is forward?" appears frequently in Tool's *The Discretionary Economy,* pp. 85, xvi, 9, 19, 81, 86, 106, 167, . . ., etc. The issue is not simply that social scientists in their sciencing use value judgments but that value can be analyzed scientifically as a process of discretion and choice among alternative paths. For an excellent coverage of the literature note Marc Tool *The Discretionary Economy,* passim and in particular footnote 4, p. 278. And also, in this context, as Sir Julian Huxley notes ". . . Teilhard starts from the position that mankind in its totality is a phenomenon to be described and analyzed like any other phenomenon: it and all its manifestations, including human history and human values, are proper objects for scientific inquiry." p. 12, Pierre Teilhard deChardin, *The Phenomenon of Man* (New York: Harper and Row, 1959).

[63]Clarence E. Ayres, *The Theory of Economic Progress* (New York: Schocken Books, 1962), p. 208. Also, note Marc Tool, "A Social Value Theory in Neoinstitutional Economics," *Journal of Economic Issues* 11 (December 1977), pp. 823-846.

[64]Chapter 15, "Value and Its Corollaries" pp. 291-314, constitutes the central chapter of Tool's book, *The Discretionary Economy,* and for specific statements of his instrumental value principle note pp. 293, 297, 298, 336.

[65]John Ruskin, *The Works of John Ruskin* (New York: John Wiley and Sons, 1887), Volume 12, p. 61.

[66]From Ayres, *The Theory of Economic Progress,* ". . . economics must be a science of value." p. 85, "It is the techonogical continuum which is and always has been, the locus of value: and it has this meaning because of its continuity. . . the locus of value . . . may be understood in terms of the logical significance of the instrumental continuum." p. 220.

[67]"The thesis set forth in the persent book is that . . . Human evolution has two components, the biological or organic, and the cultural or superorganic." Theodosius Dobzhansky *Mankind Evolving* (New Haven: Yule University press, 1962), pp. 18-22, and also, *A Book That Shook The World* (Pittsburgh: University of Pittsburgh Press, 1958) "The time is approaching when man will have to take the management of his evolution in his own hands." pp. 27-29. On the point of the "Series of steps as" man achieved the breakthrough from mammalian to psychosocial (culture) organization, note Sir Julian Huxley in *Evolution After Darwin,* Sol Tax, ed., Vol. II, pp. 250-251; after man emerged as "truly man," "Man's evolution is not biological but psychosocial; it operates by the mechanism of cultural tradition. . ." and, "There is a succession

of successful idea-systems instead of a succession of successful bodily organizations." and, Huxley, *Evolution*, pp. 612-613.

[68]The process of human development continues (exponential) and the underlying structure of culture, as material and social technics, is transformed (logistic surges). Therefore continued advance of human development cannot take place without structural transformation (the principle of similitude). In terms of Tool, *The Discretionary Economy*, "The process continues, the structure changes." p. 192, 73-78, 166-167,172-173, 191-192. The choice then to be resolved through a participatory democratic polity is not one of change versus no change of existing structure but the correct choice of a new structure to serve the instrumental function rather that the ceremonial, pp. 166-167.

[69]Dobzhansky,*Mankind Evolving*, p 22.

[70]To L.A. White, science and understanding will not lead to control: "This is not to say, as we have tried to make clear earlier, that man is going to win control over the course of cultural development through a scientific comprehension of its structure and processes, any more than we have won control over the sun or distant galaxcies by coming to a considerable understanding of them." *The Science of Culture*, p. 405. In the context of cultural economics we agree that man's understanding of gravitation will not enable him to alter the law of gravitation. But the issue of altering "natural law" is not the point; in reference to culture evolution and man's destiny the issue becomes can man use such laws or scientific understanding of the world about him to control and plan his future. Or will the laws of culture evolution, as White claims with his *sui generis*, propel culture forward beyond the control of man? Knowing of kinetic energy and the laws of gravitation has enabled man to control the river flow, control floods and generate hydro-electric power. In so doing, man has not altered the laws of science but rather has used them to his advantage. The option of flood control did not exist for paleolithic man but, rather, as culture and science advanced man's capacity and power for flood control and hydro-electric power increased as well. Given universal laws and rules of the cosmos, in that man will not be able to alter them does not mean culture *sui generis* or that man must always submit to such laws as a bound slave but rather that as culture and science advance, that man will use the laws and rules of the cosmos to his advantage. That the sun rises every day is a fact and one which will not be altered by man but from this need one conclude that man will forever be sunburned? Would it be unrealistic to assume that man has the rational power to step into the shade? Or conversely, can man rationally control and use solar radiation to his advantage?

[71]Cf., Richard Chase "Structural-Functional Dynamics in the Analysis of Socio-Economic Systems: Development of the Approach to Understanding the Processes of Systemic Change," *American Journal of Economics and Sociology* 38 (July 1979), pp. 293-305, and "Structural-Functional Dynamics in the Analysis of Socio-Economic Systems: Adaptation of Structural Change Processes to Biological System of

Human Interaction: *American Journal of Economics and Sociology* 39 (January 1980), pp. 49-64. Note also: Sol Tax, ed., *Evolution After Darwin*, 3 Volumes, e.g., "This is, so far as I am aware, the first time that authorities on the evolutionary aspects of the three great branhes of scientific study—the inorganic sciences, the life sciences and the human sciences—have been brought together for mutual criticism and joint discussion." Sir J. Huxley, Vol. III, p. 249. And Sol Tax, ". . . it seems to me that, while the difference in the mechanism of growth are never to be minimized, there is, nevertheless, a larger view in which human society and culture are seen again as part of the natural order and subject to the same laws of evolution as the rest of nature." p. 246, and, "This broader view of man as a part of a single evolutionary system, at least of this planet, comes to us—or at least to me—as we bring together our various branches of knowledge." p. 247.

[72]The broad conceptualization of evolution to include the inorganic, the organic and the superorganic is in a sense a conceptualization of the whole of reality. As Sir Julian Huxley states: ". . . all aspects of reality are subject to evolution, from atoms and stars to fish and flowers, from fish and flowers to human societies and values—indeed that all reality is a single process of evolution. And ours is the first period in which we have acquired sufficient knowledge to beigin to see the outline of this vast process as a whole." in Sol Tax, ed., *Evolution After Darwin* (Chicago: University of Chicago Press, 1960), Vol. III, p. 249. "CHARLES DARWIN. . . rendered evolution inescapable as a fact, comprehensible as a process, all embracing as a concept. . . Thus, in a certain sense, all phenomenal reality is a single process of evolution." Julian S. Huxley, *A Book That Shook the World*, pp. 1, 11. While evolution is usually thought of primarily in the biological sphere the point being made here is that it is conceptually applicable to all of reality. "*Evolution* is definable in general terms as a one-way, irreversible process in time, which during its course generates novelty, diversity and higher levels of organization. It operates in all sectors of the phenomenal universe but it has been most fully described and analyzed in the biological sector." Sol Sax, ed., *Evolution*, Vol. III, p. 107. However weak, there has been a spillover of the usage of the concept of evolution into the social sciences. What an outstanding achievement, combining intellect and integrity in that an elite core of social scientists was able to hold onto the slender thread of social DNA, and maintain intact and with continuity, the evolutionary concept in the social sciences,. We speak here, among others of V. Gordon Childe, Leslie A. White, Thorstein Bunde Veblen and William F. Ogburn. Their efforts enabled the evolutionary concept to survive in the social sciences during periods of unpopularity and duress and currently evolutionary though in the social sciences is gaining in respectability and acceptance. While still not to the point of inundating the social sciences, the resurgence is nonetheless there, though still perhaps the minority view. The record of economists is somewhat worse than that of social scientists in general.

Orthodox economics whether the "new" or the "old" tends to disembody economic analysis from that of the cultural whole, note, Figure XI-7 "The Rubric of Evolution and the Synthesis of Science," a slice is taken out of the integrated pie of the social sciences and economics has been treated as an autonomous and independent field of inquiry. By comparison, *cultural economics* represents an attempt to integrate economics, via our "wheel of economic development" which might also be called the wheel of economic *evolution*, into the whole of the social sciences as a unified body of thought. And then, further, we suggest the combination of such an integrated pie of the social sciences with the physical and biological sciences, in an overall synthesis, in order to promote a better understanding of evolution as a universal phenomenon. Generally speaking, economists have shown little appetite to eat of the forbidden fruit of the tree of evolution, and in so doing, economists have been avoiding the empirically obvious. In their theoretical explanations economists have historically ignored the issue of evolution. Of the relatively few economists who discussed and endorsed the concept of evolution as an integral part of economic analysis, it is the name of Thorstein B. Veblen which dominates. "Veblen, more than any other economist, is responsible for the introduction of evolutionism. . . into American economics." Joseph J. Spengler, "Evolutionism in American Economics, 1800-1946" in Stow Persons, ed., *Evolutionary Thought in America* (New Haven: Yale University Press, 1950), p. 240. To Veblen: "The theory of evolution begun by biologists must be continued by students of culture, and primarily by economists." Wesley C. Mitchell, *What Veblen Taught* (New York: Augustus M. Kelley, 1964), p. xxiii. That as economics should be evolutionary and should embrace the social and cultural as well as the economic, consequently, is hardly a new idea starting with *cultural economics*, our methods and synthesis are perhaps somewhat different, but not the quest. Currently this recognition as well as quest, frequently appears in the literature: "The difficulty consists in the fact that while development is not necessarily a measurable it is always an evolutionary process." S. Herbert Frankel, *The Economic Impact on Under-Developed Societies* (Cambridge: Harvard University Press, 1959), p. 56; "One notes the phrase 'socio-economic evolution,' for by this is meant the modern-day concept 'economic development'. . . It is this idea of socio-economic evolution, as the key to development. . . "Louis M. Hacker, *The Course of American Economic Growth and Development* (New York: John Wiley and Sons, 1970), pp. 162-163; Joseph J. Spengler, "Evolutionism in American Economics, 1800-1946." in Strow Persons, *Evolutionary Thought in America*, while noting that "Evolutionism as such has not played a prominent part in American economic thought since 1930. . ." (period 1930-1946) p. 249, he concludes, "Economics must be somewhat evolutionary in its approach, both because it is concerned with data in flux, and because it must help man to give direction to this flux" p. 254, and further implies that actually the evolutionists have won any way. "Today the direct and indirect effects of evolutionism—Darwinian, Spencerin, historical, and cultural—are so much a part of our economic thought ways that we are no longer aware of their existence. Could ideological triumph be greater?" pp. 264-265.

[73]Normal science in economics has been negligent and has avoided a "systems approach" or what could also be called an holistic, interdisciplinary or gestalt methodology. But in that such a methodology is relevant and in need other social scientists outside of mainstream economics have introduced "systems thinking" to fill the vacuum. On a brief sampling of some of the introductory literature: C. West Churchman, *The Systems Approach* (New York, Dell Publishing, 1968); Nic J.T.A. Kramer and Jacob de Smit *Systems Thinking: Concepts and Notions* (Leiden: Martinus Nijhoff, 1977); F. E. Emery, ed., *Systems Thinking* (New York: Penguin Books, 1969); Ervin Lazlo, *The Systems View of the World* (New York: George Braziller, 1972). A systems approach also appears in anthropology, for example: L. A. White, *The Concept of Cultural Systems* (New York: Columbia University Press, 1975) and Veblen and Ayres (as mainstream institutional economics) have been practicing "system approach" all along.

[74]In our analysis we have drawn the analogy between biological DNA and social DNA. Culture, as man's social DNA provides a code to regulate and control man's social life as biological DNA does for man's biological life. This approach, of viewing culture as man's social heredity (analogous to biological heredity) is quite common in the literature: "In human being the social heredity is called *culture*." R. Linton, *The Study of Man*, p. 78; "Culture is, so to speak, a form of social heredity." L. A. White, *The Science of Culture*, p. 363; and W. F. Ogburn, *Social Change*, "The terms, the superorganic, social heritage, and culture, have been used interchangeably." p. 6. But the question which we raise concerns whether or not the relations between the organic, the superorganic, and also, the inorganic, are simply that of analogy or are there fundamental principles, rules, laws applicable as universals to the whole of evolution? This is not to deny that the inorganic, the organic and superorganic are different phenomena and that the explanation of biological evolution is indeed different from that of culture evolution. But though the forms are different and, therefore, theory and explanation is different are there still nonetheless underlying basic principles, rules or laws which are operable in the three different realms of evolution? For example, the manifestations or forms of biological evolution are noted for their diversity and variety and yet at root they all go back in origin to the same tiny helix and evidently the same basic principles of evolution. We think here of plant and animal, of *Tyrannosarus rex* on the one hand and the paramecium on the other, the giant *Sequoia sempervirens* on the one hand and the algae on the other. And yet are not the principles of evolution the same for all: ". . . the base of life has been found. It is a tiny coil of matter, in structure a spiral staircase. In it lies the masterplan for all that we are and thread of continuity from the beginning of life. Here in an infinitely small bit

of substance are encompassed all the likenesses and differences of the living world, and the uniqueness of the more than two billion people of this globe and of the earth's myriads of animal, plants and micro-organisms. . . . . Nearly all tests that so far have been devised show that the two tiny spirals of matter determine the form and structure of all life, its functioning, its color, its variety, and its continuity." Ruth Moore, *The Coil of Life* (New York: Alfred A. Knopf, 1961), pp. 3, 408. "In all organisms except viruses, genetic and evolutionary 'information' is carried by DNA . . ," Sol Tax, ed., Vol III, p. 107. As with a kaleidoscope, we deal with the same bits of glass, but we give a twist and a shake and the result is a new form or a new configuration. Can we infer that the different forms, such as the inorganic, the organic and the superorganic, do not necessarily preclude the operation of similar laws or principles in different contexts producing different results and forms? Hans Gaffron states, "There is complete unity, if not uniformity, in the mechanisms that support all living things. The forces driving this living mechanism are exactly the ones that drive inanimate events, and the parts are moving according to the same laws. I doubt if the great scientists of the last century expected as much." in Sol Tax, Vol. I, p. 48. And, George Gaylord Simpson, "Some biologists . . . have reservations, but most now agree that the immanent qualities of organisms are exactly the same as those of inorganic systems. The difference is not in those qualities but in the special structures of the organic systems and their incomparably greater complexity. Given a particular system, it follows the same unchanging laws regardless of whether it is organic or inorganic." Sol Tax, Vol. I, p. 118. And Bernhard Rensch; "Specific Laws of Evolution," pp. 101-113, "Summing up, we may assume that the whole evolution of the cosmos, . . . was pre-existing in consequence of the 'eternal' cosmic laws of casuality, parallelism and logic. However, up to now, such an assumption can be only a philosophical working hypothesis." Sol Tax, Vol. I, p. 113. And, Alfred L. Kroeber, "My point is that, although mechanism of culture is quite different, these three modes can also be distinguished in the evolution of culture. . . . In short, all three modes or aspects of evolution are as recognizable in culture as in biology, and all three must ultimately be studied in their interrelations if we are to have a picture of total human evolution." Sol Tax, Vol. III, pp. 224-225. Also what of patterns and structures related to the process of evolution? There is something about a helix that once it captures the imagination the tendency is to see helices everywhere. "The idea was so simple it had to be right. Every helical staircase that I saw that weekend in Oxford made me more confident that other biological structures would also have helical symmetry." James D. Watson, *The Double Helix* (New York: Antheum, 1968), p. 114. Viewing the staircase versus DNA, R. Moore concludes: "One is large and one is infinitessimally small, but both are built upon the same principle." *The Coil of Life*, pp. 278-281. Is our configuration of culture advance as a spiral one of coincidence or is the pattern and configuration relevant in some way to all of evolution? Our culture configuration was represented by a single helix in that, as we have already noted, there is no need to have boy and girl cultures for culture replication and diffusion. This point also led Watson and Crick to look for a double rather than a single helix—"Francis would have to agree. Even though he was a physicist, he knew that important biological objects come in pairs." Watson, pp. 171, 175. Also, it was our conclusion that if the dynamics of culture evolution were explained in the process of circular causation (our wheel of economic development) that such a circle can only move over time as a spiral or helix. How else? It is to be noted that our spiral may be a cylindrical helix indicative of no growth and development, or if accumulation and development (an open wheel of economic development) in the form of a conical helix. That biological DNA is cylindrical is perhaps therefore related to the constancy of the number of genes (for a given specie) whereas new technics, as the genes of culture evolution, may be constant, therefore a cylindrical helix and culture stagnation or the new technics may accumulate in the context of economic development and a conical helix. Is this all mere analogy or are we dealing with universals of form, structure, and process? Also, our spiral resulted from an abstract process of conceptualization, we have tried to present a schematic configuration of a process in order to better understand the process. Economic development is not a thing but represents a conceptualization of a process of reality. While DNA is in actuality, a substance and is by comparison, a thing, and consequently, facilitates the process of conceptualization and understanding it is still doubtful that anyone will ever really "see" DNA. The configuration of Watson and Crick is also therefore of the nature of model building, of an abstraction, theory and conceptualization. In their article, "Molecular Structure of Nucleic Acids," *Nature*, Vol. 171 (April 25, 1953), pp. 737-738, they note as much, for we see not a picture or replica but an abstraction, "This figure is purely diagrammatic." p. 737. However, a precise picture of real thing is not necessary, for it is the configuration and abstraction of DNA as a double helix and the order and nature of its chemical parts and bonds which now enables us to understand and explain more concerning biological reproduction and evolution. We feel that the same might be said concerning our helical configuration of culture evolution. From all this, a question: can we conclude that it is possible to discern and discover universal laws of form, structure and process concerning the design of overall evolution and from this understanding be consequently in a better position to control culture evolution and human destiny?

[75]Opler on Tylor, note Barringer, ed., *Social Change in Developing Areas*, p. 80.

[76]The reference is actually Huxley via Pierre Teilhard de Chardin, *Activation of Energy* (New York: Harcourt Brace Jovanovich, 1970), p. 161. For Huxley by J.S. Huxley, Note, *A Book That Shook the World*, "Theprocess of evolution, as represented by man, is now for the first

time in its long history becoming conscious of itself and its nature. . . . the idea of evolution, which became scientifically respectable a bare century ago, will find its most important application in the central problem of human destiny." of p. 12. In the Introduction to Pierre Teilhard de Chardin, *The Phenomenon of Man* (New York: Harper and Row, 1959), Sir Julian Huxley comments: "I had independenlty expressed something of the same sort by saying that in modern scientific man, evolution was at last becoming conscious of itself—a phrase which I found delighted Pere Teilhard. His formulation, however, is more profound and more seminal. . ." p. 20.

[77]Edward B. Tylor, *Anthropology* (Ann Arbor: The University of Michigan Press, 1960), abridged and with a foreword by L.A. White, p. 16.

Index